A COMPANION TO

CHARLES DICKENS

EDITED BY **DAVID PAROISSIEN**

WILEY-BLACKWELL

A John Wiley & Sons, Ltd., Publication

This paperback edition first published 2011

© 2011 Blackwell Publishing Ltd except for editorial material and
organization © 2011 David Paroissien

Edition history: Blackwell Publishing Ltd (hardback, 2008)

Blackwell Publishing was acquired by John Wiley & Sons in February 2007. Blackwell's
publishing program has been merged with Wiley's global Scientifi c, Technical, and Medical
business to form Wiley-Blackwell.

Registered Office

John Wiley & Sons Ltd, The Atrium, Southern Gate, Chichester, West Sussex,
PO19 8SQ, United Kingdom

Editorial Offices

350 Main Street, Malden, MA 02148-5020, USA
9600 Garsington Road, Oxford, OX4 2DQ, UK
The Atrium, Southern Gate, Chichester, West Sussex, PO19 8SQ, UK

For details of our global editorial offices, for customer services, and for information about how to
apply for permission to reuse the copyright material in this book please see our website at
www.wiley.com/wiley-blackwell.

The right of David Paroissien to be identified as the editor of the editorial material in this work has
been asserted in accordance with the UK Copyright, Designs and Patents Act 1988.

Library of Congress Cataloging-in-Publication Data

A companion to Charles Dickens / edited by David Paroissien.
p. cm. – (Blackwell companions to literature and culture ; 51)
Includes bibliographical references and index.
ISBN: 978-1-4051-3097-4 (hbk alk. paper); ISBN 978-0-470-65794-2 (pbk)
1. Dickens, Charles, 1812-1870–Criticism and interpretation–Handbooks, manuals,
etc.   I. Paroissien, David.
PR4588.C636 2007
8232.8–dc22

2007019690

A catalogue record for this book is available from the British Library.

This book is published in the following electronic formats: ePDFs 978-0-470-69122-9;
Wiley Online Library 978-0-470-69190-8; ePub 978-1-4443-9564-8

Set in 11 on 13pt Garamond 3 by Toppan Best-set Premedia Limited

Contents

Illustrations

Notes on Contributors

Michael Allen lectures and writes on Dickens. He is the author of *Charles Dickens' Childhood* (1988) and *An English Lady in Paris: The Diary of Frances Anne Crewe 1786* (2006).

Malcolm Andrews is Professor of Victorian and Visual Studies in the School of English at the University of Kent. He edits *The Dickensian* and is the author of *Charles Dickens and his Performing Selves: Dickens and the Public Readings* (2006).

Gill Ballinger is Senior Lecturer at the University of the West of England, Bristol, where she teaches nineteenth-century literature. Her publications include articles on Dickens and the edition of a special issue on the Brontës for *Women's Writing*.

Nicola Bradbury lectures in English and American literature at the University of Reading. She has published several books and articles on Dickens and Henry James, and edited the Penguin *Bleak House* (1996).

Brian Cheadle has published essays on Dickens in *Essays in Criticism*, *Dickens Studies Annual*, and various collections of essays, including *The Cambridge Companion to Charles Dickens* (2001). He is currently working on *The Companion to David Copperfield*.

Gareth Cordery is Senior Lecturer in English at the University of Canterbury, Christchurch, New Zealand. He has published work on Dickens, and is writing a biography of Harry Furniss whose 1905 lecture on Dickens and his illustrators he has edited (2005).

Hugh Cunningham is Emeritus Professor of Social History at the University of Kent. His recent books include *The Challenge of Democracy: Britain 1830–1918* (2001) and *Children and Childhood in Western Society since 1500* (2nd edn., 2005).

Valentine Cunningham is Tutor in English Literature and Professor of English Language and Literature at Corpus Christi, Oxford. He specializes in modern literature and literary theory, and has written on subjects including the novel, the Victorians, literature of the 1930s, postmodernism, and history. His most recent book is *Reading after Theory* (2002).

Paul Davis is Professor Emeritus of English at the University of New Mexico. He is the author of *The Lives and Times of Ebenezer Scrooge* (1990), the Penguin *Dickens Companion* (1999), and *Critical Companion to Charles Dickens: A Literary Reference to his Life and Work* (2007).

Philip Davis is Professor of English at the University of Liverpool. His publications include *Memory and Writing: From Wordsworth to Lawrence* (1983), books on Shakespeare and Samuel Johnson, and, most recently, *The Victorians 1830–1880* (2002), volume 8 in the new Oxford English Literary History series.

John M. L. Drew is Senior Lecturer in English at the University of Buckingham. He co-edited (with Michael Slater) volume 4 of the *Dent Uniform Edition of Dickens' Journalism* and is the author of *Dickens the Journalist* (2003) and the director of the University of Buckingham's Dickens Journals Online project.

Monika Fludernik is Professor of English at the University of Freiburg, Germany. She is the author of *The Fictions of Language and the Languages of Fiction* (1993), *Towards a "Natural" Narratology* (1996), *Echoes and Mirrorings: Gabriel Josipovici's Creative Oeuvre* (2000), and *Einführung in die Erzähltheorie* (forthcoming). She has also edited *Hybridity and Postcolonialism* (1998) and *Diaspora and Multiculturalism* (2003).

Stanley Friedman, Associate Professor Emeritus of English at Queens College, City University of New York, has been one of the editors of *Dickens Studies Annual* since 1996 and is the author of articles on Dickens and, most recently, *Dickens's Fiction: Tapestries of Conscience* (2003).

John Gardiner teaches history at Highsted Grammar School, Sittingbourne. He has reviewed books for *Dickens Quarterly*, and is the author of *The Victorians: An Age in Retrospect* (2002).

Michael Hollington currently teaches at the University of Toulouse-Le Mirail. He is the author of *Günter Grass: The Writer in a Pluralist Society* (1980) and *Dickens and the Grotesque* (1984), and editor of the four volumes of *Charles Dickens: Critical Assessments* (1995).

Anne Humpherys is Professor of English at Lehman College and the Graduate Center, City University of New York. She is the author of *Travels into the Poor Man's Country: The Work of Henry Mayhew* (1977) and, with Louis James, editor of the forthcoming *G. W. M. Reynolds and Nineteenth-century Society: Fiction, Politics, and the Press*. She has written articles on Dickens, Tennyson, the nineteenth-century press and popular culture.

Patricia Ingham is a Senior Research Fellow and Reader at St. Anne's College, Oxford. Her recent publications include *Dickens, Women and Language* (1992), *The Language of Gender and Class: Transformations in the Victorian Novel* (2000), and *The Brontës: A Critical Reader* (2003). She is currently General Editor of Oxford's Authors in Context series, to which she has contributed volumes on Hardy (2003) and the Brontës (2006).

Simon J. James is Senior Lecturer in Victorian Literature in the Department of English Studies at Durham University. He is the author of *Unsettled Accounts: Money and Narrative in the Novels of George Gissing* (2003), and of articles on Gissing, Dickens, and H. G. Wells. He has edited four Wells novels for Penguin Classics and Gissing's *Charles Dickens: A Critical Study* (2004).

Juliet John is Reader in Victorian Literature at the University of Liverpool and Director of the Gladstone Centre for Victorian Studies in Wales and Northwest England. Her principal publications include *Dickens's Villains: Melodrama, Character, Popular Culture* (2001), and, as editor, *Charles Dickens's Oliver Twist: A Sourcebook* (2006).

John O. Jordan is Professor of Literature at the University of California, Santa Cruz, and Director of the Dickens Project, a multi-campus research consortium. He is the editor of *The Cambridge Companion to Charles Dickens* (2001).

Leon Litvack is Reader in Victorian Studies at Queen's University, Belfast. He has contributed many articles to *Dickens Quarterly* and *The Dickensian*. His published volumes include *Literatures of the Nineteenth Century: Romanticism to Victorianism* (1996), *Charles Dickens's Dombey and Son: An Annotated Bibliography* (1999), *Ireland in the Nineteenth Century: Regional Identity* (2000), and *Ireland and Europe in the Nineteenth Century* (2006). He is currently preparing the Clarendon edition of *Our Mutual Friend*.

Brigid Lowe is a Research Fellow at Trinity College, Cambridge, and author of *Victorian Fiction and the Insights of Sympathy: An Alternative to the Hermeneutics of Suspicion* (2007).

Natalie McKnight is Chairman of the Humanities Division of Boston University's College of General Studies and Associate Professor of English. Her recent publications include *Idiots, Madmen and Other Prisoners in Dickens* (1993) and *Suffering Mothers in Victorian Novels* (1997).

Jon Mee is Professor of Romanticism Studies at the University of Warwick. He has edited *Barnaby Rudge* for Penguin (2003) and is the author of *Romanticism, Enthusiasm, and Religion: Poetics and the Policing of Culture in the Romantic Period* (2003). He currently holds a Philip J. Leverhulme Major Research Fellowship for a project looking at the idea of conversation and contention in the Romantic period.

Nancy Aycock Metz is Associate Professor and Associate Chair of English at Virginia University Tech. She has written on Dickens, Trollope, and urban culture, and is the author of *The Companion to Martin Chuzzlewit* (2001).

Robert Mighall is the author of *A Geography of Victorian Gothic Fiction: Mapping History's Nightmares* (1999) and former editor of the Penguin Classics series. He now works as a consultant at a branding and design agency in London.

Leslie Mitchell is Emeritus Fellow of University College, Oxford, and author of *Bulwer Lytton: The Rise and Fall of a Victorian Man of Letters* (2003) and *The Whig World: 1760–1837* (2005).

Goldie Morgentaler is Associate Professor of English at the University of Lethbridge. She is the author of *Dickens and Heredity: When Like Begets Like* (2000) and of essays on Victorian literature. Her most recent publication is an essay on the Child ballads that appeared in *Mosaic* (2007). She has also published translations from Yiddish to English. Her translation of Chava Rosenfarb's *Survivors: Seven Short Stories* won the 2006 MLA book award for Yiddish Studies.

David Parker is the author of *Christmas and Charles Dickens* (2005) and of many publications on Dickens and other literary topics. He served as Curator of the Charles Dickens Museum for 21 years, is currently Honorary Research Fellow at Kingston University, and at work on *The Companion to The Pickwick Papers*.

David Paroissien is Emeritus Professor of English at the University of Massachusetts, Amherst, and Professorial Research Fellow at the University of Buckingham. He edits *Dickens Quarterly* and co-edits, with Susan Shatto, the Dickens Companions series. He is the author of *The Companion to Oliver Twist* (1992), *The Companion to Great Expectations* (2000), and has edited *The Mystery of Edwin Drood* for Penguin (2002).

Catherine Peters is the author of *Thackeray's Universe* (1987, revised as *Thackeray: A Writer's Life*, 1999), *The King of Inventors: A Life of Wilkie Collins* (1991), *Charles Dickens* (1998), and *Byron* (2000).

Trey Philpotts is Professor of English at Arkansas Tech University. He serves as the Book Review Editor of *Dickens Quarterly*, is the author of *The Companion to Little Dorrit* (2003), and is at work on *The Companion to Dombey and Son*.

Lyn Pykett is Professor of English and Pro Vice-Chancellor at Aberystwyth University. Her books include *Emily Brontë* (1989), *The Improper Feminine: The Women's Sensation Novel and the New Woman Writing* (1992), *Engendering Fictions: The English Novel in the Early Twentieth Century* (1995), and *Charles Dickens* (2002) and *Wilkie Collins* (2005) for the Oxford Authors in Context series. She is also the editor of *Wilkie Collins: Contemporary Critical Essays* (1998).

Andrew Sanders is Professor of English at Durham University. Among his publications are *The Victorian Historical Novel* (1978), *Charles Dickens: Resurrectionist* (1982), *The Short History of English Literature* (1994), *Dickens and the Spirit of the Age* (1999), and *Charles Dickens* (Authors in Context series, 2003).

Jan-Melissa Schramm is a lawyer, a Fellow of Trinity Hall and a Newton Trust Lecturer in the Faculty of English at the University of Cambridge. She writes primarily on nineteenth-century fiction, and is the author of *Testimony and Advocacy in Victorian Law, Literature and Theology* (2000).

Robert Tracy is Professor Emeritus in English and Celtic Studies at the University of California, Berkeley, and founder-member of the University of California Dickens Project. His most recent publications include a translation of 81 poems by the Russian poet Osip Mandelstam and *The Unappeasable Host: Studies in Irish Identities* (1998).

Preface

On the matter of prefaces, Dickens sided with Henry Fielding. Be honest about what you have provided, Fielding wrote in his "Introduction" to *Tom Jones* (1750). Let customers peruse the "Bill of Fare," and then make their decision. They will either "stay and regale" themselves with "the Entertainment" provided by the host, or they will depart elsewhere. In a variation of these words, Dickens stated a similar principle when he advised Richard Henry Horne on "the expediency of the preface" Horne had sent him. Don't undercut what you have written with an elaborate justification, Dickens urged. Discerning readers understand that an author or editor "makes a weak case when he writes to explain his writing" (*Letters* 6: 636).

The draft preface in question accompanied a volume of "Minor Poems" for which Horne failed to find a publisher. The advice Dickens gave, however, was sound. Provide too much by way of explanation, and a lengthy preface will take a book "by the throat and strangle it." Of this, Dickens was "quite certain – absolutely sure" – in fact. Keep the preface short and let the contents of the volume "rest manfully and calmly" on what the work has to offer. Readers, like diners, will make their choice.

This *Companion* offers a range of focal points posited on the assumption that factual and referential knowledge from many fields will enhance one's engagement with Dickens's works. Dickens was, is, and will remain a hugely entertaining writer. His fiction is readily accessible without expert guidance. One can read him in ignorance of literary theory; one can invoke the theory of one's preference and read with equal pleasure. Feminists will focus on patriarchy and male domination. Adherents of cultural studies will blur boundaries between low and high cultures. Reader-response practitioners will have their way with the text as well. All readings, however, draw on knowledge of some kind, be it social, historical, cultural, literary, linguistic, or legal.

It is the aim of this volume to provide a selection of contexts, arranged in five sections, which readers can choose to explore with profit. To engage Dickens with understanding, one needs to know something of the man, of the literary education he acquired, largely through self-directed reading, and of the age in which he lived and about which he remains perhaps one of the most widely informed observers. His 15 novels speak for themselves. The authors of this group of essays follow the editor's injunction to avoid any single interpretative or theoretical orientation and treat the principal literary, artistic, and thematic issues of each work. What readers – common and professional – have made of his novels forms the focus of the three essays in the closing section.

Contributors provide details of the works they cite. Readers should note, however, that the suggestions for further reading are simply that. The sheer volume of available material makes impossible in a collection of this length a full bibliographical record of pertinent essays, books, and studies in print. For those who wish to look backwards to admirable guides furnished some years ago but still worth consulting, they would do well to start with Ada Nisbet's "Charles Dickens" (1966). In a later volume, Philip Collins followed with another informative and readable chapter on Dickens in *Victorian Fiction* (1978). Other sources deserve mention: studies devoted to material on a single novel (the annotated Garland Dickens Bibliographies), the first of four volumes of annotated bibliographies of Dickens materials undertaken by Duane DeVries (2004), the yearly survey of publications provided by *Dickens Studies Annual*, and the open checklist published in *Dickens Quarterly*.

Each has its merits and its limitations; collectively, they constitute the means of surveying an impressive record of writing, past and current, of materials missed by entering a sought term or title into an electronic database and accepting the result. Internet resources grow in sophistication and effectiveness. Search engines and the availability of digitalized texts augment literary research and will continue to extend their utility. No one method or printed source, however, will suffice, just as surely as the essays in this volume provide no final word on any one of the featured topics. Rather, each offers readers an opportunity to acquaint themselves with topics set before them. The Bill of Fare is plain to read. May "good digestion" wait on appetite, "And health on both!" (*Macbeth* III. iv. 38).

References

Collins, Philip (1978). Charles Dickens. In George H. Ford (Ed.), *Victorian Fiction: A Second Guide to Research* (pp. 34–113). New York: MLA.

DeVries, Duane (2004). *Bibliographies, Catalogues, Collections, and Bibliographical and Textual Studies of Dickens's Works*, vol. 1 of *General Studies of Charles Dickens and his Writings and Collected Editions of his Works: An Annotated Bibliography*. New York: AMS Press.

Nisbet, Ada (1966). Charles Dickens. In Lionel Stevenson (Ed.), *Victorian Fiction: A Guide to Research* (pp. 44–153). Cambridge, MA: Harvard University Press.

Acknowledgments

Collaborative works incur many debts and this volume of essays is no exception. I am most grateful to all the contributors both for the quality of their essays and for their efficient and prompt cooperation. I am equally indebted to people behind the scenes: to Al Bertrand with whom I first discussed the design of this collection, and to Karen Wilson for all her editorial support. I also extend my thanks to Sue Ashton for her speedy and excellent work as copy-editor.

David Paroissien

Abbreviations

Forster | John Forster, *The Life of Charles Dickens* (3 vols., London: Chapman and Hall, 1872–4). New edition, with notes and index by A. J. Hoppé. London: Dent, 1966. References are to book and chapter only.

Journalism | *Dickens' Journalism*, ed. Michael Slater (4 vols., Columbus: Ohio University Press, 1994–2000).

Kaplan | *Charles Dickens' Book of Memoranda: A Photographic and Typographic Facsimile of the Notebook begun in January 1855*, ed. Fred Kaplan (New York: New York Public Library, 1981).

Letters | The Pilgrim Edition of *The Letters of Charles Dickens*, ed. Madeline House, Graham Storey, Kathleen Tillotson, et al. (12 vols., Oxford: Clarendon Press, 1965–2003).

Oxford Dickens | *Oxford Reader's Companion to Dickens*, ed. Paul Schlicke (Oxford: Oxford University Press, 1999).

Speeches | *The Speeches of Charles Dickens*, ed. K. J. Fielding (Oxford: Clarendon Press, 1960).

Part I
Perspectives on the Life

1
A Sketch of the Life

Michael Allen

All life was grist to the writing mill that was Charles Dickens, particularly his own life and especially his childhood. "All these things have worked together to make me what I am," he wrote of one period of his childhood. Born at Portsmouth on February 7, 1812, he left the town at the beginning of January 1815, carrying memories of a military parade and the landlady of the house in which the Dickens family had lodged, later used in the creation of Mrs. Pipchin in *Dombey and Son*. John Dickens, his father, had started as a clerk in the Navy Pay Office at Somerset House in London in 1805, and in June 1809 had married Elizabeth Barrow, the sister of a colleague. The Admiralty moved the clerk to Portsmouth, a major naval dockyard in the forefront of Britain's war against Napoleon, where the young couple set up home in a brand new house at Mile End Terrace. Here their first child, Frances Elizabeth, was born on October 28, 1810, followed 15 months later by a brother, baptized in the local church as Charles John Huffam Dickens, but known to the family throughout his childhood as Charley. John Dickens's domicile arrangements always had an impermanency about them, and the new baby stayed only five months in his birthplace before being carried across town to lodgings in Hawke Street, much closer to the Navy Pay Office; and 18 months later to Wish Street in the adjacent area of Southsea. Here they were joined by a young widowed sister of Mrs. Dickens, Mary Allen, whose name was given to a third child, Alfred Allen Dickens. Unfortunately, Alfred died of water on the brain just six months later.

With the defeat of Napoleon and the end of a war against America, the Admiralty's presence at Portsmouth was reduced, and on January 1, 1815 the Dickens family was moved back to London, probably staying in lodgings in Norfolk Street. Here a fourth child, Letitia, was born. Situated near Oxford Street, they were close to John Dickens's older brother William, who ran a coffee shop there; they were close also to Grosvenor Street in Mayfair, home of the wealthy Crewe family where Charley's grandmother, now 70 years old, served as housekeeper. His grandfather, William Dickens, butler to the Crewes, had died many years before, in 1785. This early contact with London saw Charley through the ages of three and four, leaving him with a memory of a visit to a bazaar in Soho Square, probably with his grandmother, and the purchase of a harlequin's wand.

Off then went the family to the Navy dockyards on the River Medway in Kent, first to Sheerness for about three months and then on to "the birthplace of [Dickens's] fancy" at Rochester and Chatham (Forster bk. 1, ch. 1), two towns so joined at the hip that it was difficult to say where one ended and the other began. John Dickens rented a house at 2 Ordnance Terrace, in an elevated part of Chatham, commanding beautiful views over the river and the surrounding countryside. Three more children were born, Harriet in 1819, Frederick in 1820, and Alfred in 1822, making the house a little crowded with six children, their parents, Aunt Mary, and two servants, 13-year-old Mary Weller and elderly Jane Bonny. Dickens later wrote happy accounts of his time in Chatham, playing with friends, attending school, visiting the theater and pantomime, and going to parties; there were regular walks with his father and with Mary Weller, trips up the Medway on the Navy Pay Yacht, and hours spent reading. Many years later, he recollected that one of the walks with his father took him past a large house at Gad's Hill and his father promised that if he worked hard then he might come to live there.

It was in Chatham that Charley first tried his juvenile hand at creative writing, where he enacted plays in the kitchen, and where he first enjoyed the applause of an audience, standing on a table and singing at the local inn. These were activities that forever echoed through his life. At the end of 1821, Aunt Mary married Thomas Lamert, an army surgeon, and these two soon after moved to Ireland, taking with them the servant Jane Bonny but leaving behind a stepson, James Lamert, who was later to have a profound influence on Dickens's life. The new baby, Alfred, was given the middle name of Lamert, but the family was shocked soon after when news came from Ireland that Aunt Mary had died, aged just 34.

In Chatham, it is unlikely that Charley had any idea that his father had difficulties with money. John Dickens's salary had rocketed from £200 in 1816 to £441 in 1822, but he handled it badly, and in 1819 borrowed £200 on which he failed to make the repayments, causing a family rift with a brother-in-law who had stood surety. There were other debts in Chatham, and in 1822 the family moved to a smaller house at St. Mary's Place on The Brook where they stayed for a year. That same year John Dickens was moved back to London, but Charley was left behind for several months, staying with his schoolmaster, William Giles. He later recollected his own journey to London, a small child of 10:

> Through all the years that have since passed have I ever lost the smell of the damp straw in which I was packed – like game – and forwarded, carriage paid, to the Cross Keys, Wood Street, Cheapside, London? There was no other inside passenger, and I consumed my sandwiches in solitude and dreariness, and it rained hard all the way, and I thought life sloppier than I had expected to find it. (*Journalism* 4: 140)

His parents had taken a small house at Bayham Street in Camden Town, just on the edge of London. Life was quiet here: Charley was disappointed not to be sent to school, especially since his older sister was boarded at the Royal Academy of Music, and he passed his days running errands, looking after the younger children, and cleaning boots. An unnamed orphan from the Chatham workhouse had been brought with them; so too had James Lamert, who built a toy theater for Charles. This stirred his imagination, as did visits into the city: to his godfather Christopher Huffam who supplied ships from his business on the Thames at Limehouse; to his uncle Thomas Barrow who lived above a bookshop in Soho, where books were borrowed and Charley wrote a description of his uncle's barber, father of the artist Turner; and to his grandmother Dickens who gave him a silver watch and probably told him stories, not only fairytales but reminiscences of her own and stories from the pages of history, as she did with the Crewe children. Such reminiscences most likely included the Gordon Riots and the French Revolution, events with which the Crewes were intimately linked and which became the subjects of Dickens's only two "historical" novels. This casual way of life continued for about 15 months, toward the end of which the financial difficulties of the Dickenses caught up with them and necessitated profound change. A revival of their fortunes, they believed, would be found in the establishment of a school, to be run by Charley's mother, and to this end at Christmas 1823 they moved to a rather grand new house in Gower Street North.

With no pupils registering at the school, the scheme collapsed in a matter of weeks and hope turned to despair. James Lamert tried to help by offering paid employment and some business training to 12-year-old Charley. The 6–7 shillings a week were seized upon by his parents, and a nightmare for the boy began at Warren's Blacking, a firm that produced boot blacking from a rat-infested warehouse beside the Thames. References to Warren's and to boot blacking were later scattered throughout his books and the factory was transposed into Murdstone and Grinby's wine-bottling business in *David Copperfield*. Then, only two weeks after Charley's start at Warren's, his father was arrested for debt and confined to the Marshalsea Prison. It was a tearful, demeaning episode that forever left its mark and legacy in the mind, life, and books of Charles Dickens. The Gower Street home had to be given up, their belongings – including books – sold, and the family moved into prison. Charley was first found a room to share with other boys at Little College Street, Camden Town, the home of a family friend, Ellen Roylance, and after a few weeks a room of his own at Lant Street, not far from the prison.

John Dickens's incarceration lasted only three months, during which time his mother died, leaving him the large sum of £450, which later helped toward paying his debts. His financial position was further improved when the Admiralty granted his retirement on the grounds of ill health with an annual pension of £146, supplemented by modest earnings from a new career in journalism as a correspondent for the *British Press*. Upon release, their friend Mrs. Roylance took the family in for a short while, after which a few months were spent at an address in Hampstead before they all finally settled at Johnson Street in Somers Town.

Meanwhile, throughout this post-prison time, Charley continued to work at Warren's, though his place of work was moved from the warehouse to a rather public position in the front window of a shop in Chandos Street in the colorful Covent Garden area. It was not until March 1825 that his father took him away from a situation in which he felt neglected and unhappy, and sent him once more to school. His year at Warren's Blacking, a year he thought would go on forever, was seared onto his young mind. As an adult, the vulnerable or parentless child featured throughout his books: Oliver Twist, Little Nell, Smike, Jo, David Copperfield, Little Dorrit, Pip, and others. The adult Dickens always drew attention to the plight of poor and neglected young people.

For two years, he returned to what the modern observer would recognize as a normal childhood, attending school at the grandly named Wellington House Academy, at the end of which his parents found a position for him as a clerk with solicitors Ellis and Blackmore of Gray's Inn. The work was dull but later supplied material for his pen, and after 18 months he moved on to another solicitor, Charles Molloy of Lincoln's Inn, where he met his lifelong friend and legal adviser, Thomas Mitton. He stayed for three months; then, aged just 17, displayed a great sense of self-confidence and a level of decision-making probably independent of his parents by striking out as a self-employed, shorthand reporter. His earliest commissions were for civil law cases held in Doctors' Commons where he honed the skills of his craft before adding to his repertoire, probably from 1830, reports of proceedings in the House of Commons, writing for the *Mirror of Parliament* and the *True Sun*. Over nearly five years, he established a reputation for speed and accuracy as one of the best in the business, and was eventually taken on to the regular staff of the *Morning Chronicle* (see chapter 11).

It was during these years as a youth and young man that he developed many of the interests, skills, and traits that were to shape and color the rest of his life. He frequently indulged his love of theater, sometimes serious drama like Shakespeare but often music-hall entertainment. It became a passion for him, attending some theater, he later told Forster, almost every night for at least three years. Trained as a singer at the Royal Academy of Music, his sister Fanny also mixed in theatrical circles, introducing her brother to actor John Harley and musician John Hullah. Indeed, such was his love for the stage that he considered he might have a career there – and in a way that eventually turned out to be the case. Perhaps as part of this aspiration, he became a careful observer of people, their mannerisms, and accents, which he learned to imitate, a talent also ascribed to his mother. A colorful, stylish way of dressing was established, sometimes described as "flashy," which was to stay with him throughout his life.

At this time, London became entrenched as part of his consciousness: building on his wanderings as a child at Warren's Blacking, he was now able to walk further, delve deeper, understand better the people and the institutions of this great and growing metropolis. Although he knew it all, his centrifugal point was established in his teens: the office of Ellis and Blackmore where he started was little more than a half-mile from the office of *All the Year Round*, the periodical he edited at his death.

If London was the spinning center of his life, though, his work as a reporter sent him throughout the country, often at as great a speed as coach and horses would permit: to Birmingham and Bristol, Edinburgh and Exeter, Chelmsford and Kettering.

It was also at this time that he first fell seriously in love. Maria Beadnell, a year older than Dickens, was pretty and flirtatious, and in an unkind game she encouraged, rejected, and teased her admirer for about four years. His letters to her that have survived demonstrate the depth of his feelings and the thinness of her response. It would seem there was little enthusiasm for the match from her parents: as a banker, Maria's father must have frowned upon marriage to a young journalist whose father had been imprisoned as an insolvent debtor and still struggled to keep his head above water. Dickens gave up the pursuit soon after his twenty-first birthday but later reflected on the affair by casting Maria as Dora Spenlow in *David Copperfield*. The Beadnells, with their prestigious address in the City of London's Lombard Street, were doubtless unimpressed with the peripatetic nature of Dickens's home life. Between the ages of 17 and 22 he shared seven different addresses with his parents as they moved around the London area to avoid creditors. In addition, he twice rented rooms, once by himself and once with a friend, before finally separating his living arrangements from those of his parents in December 1834, taking rooms at Furnival's Inn and carrying with him his younger brother Fred.

Dickens's parliamentary reporting had appeared before the public a great many times and his reputation as a reporter was high, but this was nothing to the elation he felt when his first piece of creative writing was published in the *Monthly Magazine* in December 1833. He received no payment but was sufficiently pleased to see his work in all the glory of print to contribute a further six pieces over the next 12 months, the first five unsigned but the sixth, which appeared in August 1834, appearing with the pseudonym Boz. In the same month, he first met his future wife, Catherine Hogarth, daughter of the music and drama editor of the *Morning Chronicle*, and was taken on to the permanent staff of that newspaper, with a not insubstantial salary of £273 a year (his grandmother had earned only 8 guineas a year as a housekeeper; a schoolmaster at that time might earn about £35 a year, a governess or curate only £30).

Besides employing him as a reporter, the *Morning Chronicle* also published five "street sketches" before the end of the year, all under the name of Boz, for which the author still received no payment. However, such was the originality shown in the sketches that when a sister paper, the *Evening Chronicle*, began publication in January 1835, edited by George Hogarth, and when Dickens proposed a series of twenty sketches, the proposal was taken up and his salary was increased, during publication of the sketches, from five guineas a week to seven guineas – his first payment as an author. The sketches attracted attention, and when the series in the *Evening Chronicle* drew to a close in September 1835, Dickens found a further outlet through *Bell's Life in London*, which had the added attraction of paying more money. In another major step forward, the publisher John Macrone, whom Dickens had met socially at the home of William Harrison Ainsworth, suggested book publication for the sketches, including illustrations by the popular engraver George Cruikshank. With an initial payment of £100 on offer, Dickens seized the opportunity.

People like Macrone took to Dickens easily, as did his editor Hogarth, so that Dickens became a regular visitor at Hogarth's home in Chelsea. Here he met, fell in love with, and, in May 1835, proposed to Hogarth's eldest daughter, Catherine. Dickens's letters to her from this period, always treasured by Catherine, help chart the progress of their romance, culminating in their marriage at St. Luke's Chelsea on April 2, 1836 (*Letters* 1). That year proved exceptionally busy and successful. In February, the first series of *Sketches by Boz* appeared, and just two days later Chapman and Hall offered Dickens the authorship of *The Pickwick Papers*, to be written and published monthly in 20 episodes – publication started on March 31. In May, in what seemed a good idea at the time, Dickens agreed to write a three-volume novel for Macrone, but so fast did demand for his work move that this was overtaken three months later by a promise to write two three-volume novels for Richard Bentley.

Eleven new sketches and tales appeared through the year, mostly in the *Morning Chronicle*, to which was added a political pamphlet *Sunday under Three Heads*. Maintaining his fascination with the theater, Dickens wrote and had produced *The Strange Gentleman* in September and *The Village Coquettes* in December; both works were also published in book form. In November, he agreed to edit a monthly periodical called *Bentley's Miscellany*, and in December the second series of *Sketches by Boz* appeared. These events, together with the spiraling popularity of *Pickwick*, ensured a growing reputation and a growing income for Dickens, but his promises and his value outstripped his ability to deliver, resulting, eventually, in acrimony with publishers and renegotiation. So that he could better devote time to writing, he resigned from the *Morning Chronicle*. This whirlwind year ended with his introduction to John Forster, author, critic, editor, and literary adviser, who was to become Dickens's lifelong friend, confidant, and eventually biographer.

Dickens had shown energy and commitment as a newspaper reporter, but to these traits of character was now added extensive demand for his output that resulted in an outpouring of creativity. Commentators and public alike recognized and welcomed an original new voice. Monthly sales of *Pickwick* soared, rising from less than 500 in the early months to 40,000 at the end. Only halfway through *Pickwick*, he started to write *Oliver Twist*, published in monthly parts in *Bentley's Miscellany*; completion of *Pickwick* was followed swiftly with commencement of *Nicholas Nickleby*; he then tumbled into *The Old Curiosity Shop* and *Barnaby Rudge*, both presented through the artificial and not wholly successful publishing vehicle called *Master Humphrey's Clock*. Dickens's output was partly driven by the demands of monthly publication, a device not new but brilliantly suited to and exploited by Dickens and adhered to throughout his career. Still he found time to write a burletta called *Is She his Wife?*, two short collections called *Sketches of Young Gentlemen* and *Sketches of Young Couples*, as well as editing the *Memoirs of Joseph Grimaldi* and *The Pic-nic Papers*. This last item comprised miscellaneous pieces by various authors, including Dickens, published for the benefit of the wife and children of John Macrone, publisher of *Sketches by Boz*, Macrone having died suddenly at the age of 28. Here was a man of dynamism, whom Forster captured in a few lines:

> there was that in the face as I first recollect it which no time could change, and which remained implanted on it unalterably to the last. This was the quickness, keenness, and practical power, the eager, restless, energetic outlook on each several feature, that seemed to tell so little of a student or writer of books, and so much of a man of action and business in the world. Light and motion flashed from every part of it. "It was as if made of steel," was said of it . . . It has the life and soul in it of fifty human beings. (Forster bk. 2, ch. 1)

From the beginning, Dickens was popular with the literary world. Comparisons with other writers, and artists, were numerous. He became the soul of Hogarth, the Cruikshank of writers, the Constable of fiction; he was compared with Smollett, Sterne, Fielding, Defoe, Goldsmith, Cervantes, Washington Irving, Victor Hugo, Wordsworth, Carlyle, and Shakespeare. His schoolmaster from Chatham included in a letter to him the epithet "the inimitable Boz," which Dickens took up and repeated. Some reviewers were more cautious:

> The fact is, Mr. Dickens writes too often and too fast; on the principle, we presume, of making hay whilst the sun shines, he seems to have accepted at once all engagements that were offered to him . . . If he persists much longer in this course, it requires no gift of prophecy to foretell his fate – he has risen like a rocket, and he will come down like the stick. (Collins 1971: 62)

The public spoke with their money: monthly sales of *Oliver Twist* rose to 7,500, *Nicholas Nickleby*'s first number sold 50,000, *Master Humphrey's Clock* started at 60,000, dropped off but picked up to 100,000 during the final installments of *The Old Curiosity Shop*; at only 30,000, sales of *Barnaby Rudge* were good but not spectacular. At the end of each run of monthly parts, the completed book would be published, with the advantage of further sales. Such popularity brought other benefits: election to two clubs, the Garrick and the Athenaeum, an invitation to stand as a Member of Parliament, which he declined, dinners given in his honor, the freedom of the city of Edinburgh, and invitations to public speaking: Dickens reveled in such performances, was reported to be an outstanding speaker, and continued them for the rest of his life (*Speeches*).

If his public life was hectic, so too was his private. Having married in April 1836, his first child, Charles junior, was born nine months later in January 1837, followed by Mary in 1838, Kate in 1839, and Walter in 1841; others followed relentlessly: Francis in 1844, Alfred in 1845, Sydney in 1847, Henry in 1849, Dora in 1850, and Edward in 1852. His children pleased him more as youngsters than they did as adults, never quite matching up to his demanding standards and straining his financial resources. So, too, did his parents and his siblings test his patience and his bank balance, particularly his father.

Charles often invited John Dickens to social events: to theaters, dinners, holidays, and parties. He shared Charles's good fortune, and between 1835 and 1839 we have no evidence of money troubles coming between them. Toward the end of that period it is probable that John Dickens's journalistic work dried up, yet still he was swept along by the new style of life his son was living, the new circle of friends, enjoyment of life, the optimism and energy that surrounded Charles, a growing fame that was attaching to him. John Dickens probably felt himself part of it and he continued to spend more money than he had coming in. His mismanagement burst to the surface in March 1839, and seemed to come as a surprise to his son. But Charles acted swiftly and resolved to move his parents to Exeter in Devonshire, as far away as possible from the temptations of London and the people who were owed money. He set up home for them and settled all the debts, estimating his father to have cost him £300–400. John Dickens's stay in Devon lasted three years, but he borrowed and spent money as easily there as in London, driving his son to new heights of exasperation. He started to sell samples of his son's writing and signature. In his quest for money, he tapped a local newspaper editor, Dickens's bank in London, and Dickens's friend Macready. Dickens put a disclaimer in the London newspapers: "certain persons bearing . . . the surname of our client have put into circulation, with the view of more readily obtaining credit, certain acceptances made payable at his private residence . . . Such bills made payable as aforesaid will not be paid" (*Letters* 2: 225). Dickens considered sending his father abroad but relented and went himself, visiting America for the first six months of 1842.

The following October they were all back in London, the Devonshire exile being given up on both sides. Over the following three years, John Dickens continued to behave as badly as ever he had. Perhaps we will never know the full extent of his misdemeanors, since so many of Dickens's letters were later systematically destroyed or cut by his biographer, his relations, and by Dickens himself to hide the behavior of his father. Nevertheless, enough have survived to demonstrate his anger and frustration. In September 1843, for example, he wrote:

> I am amazed and confounded by the audacity of his ingratitude . . . tell him that his letter has disgusted me beyond expression; and that I have no more reference to anything he wants or wishes or threatens or would do or wouldn't do, in taking on myself this new Burden . . . Nothing makes me so wretched, or so unfit for what I have to do, as these things. They are so entirely beyond my own controul, so far out of my reach, such a drag-chain on my life, that for the time they utterly dispirit me, and weigh me down. (*Letters* 3: 576)

From the earliest times it was clear that John Dickens was not the sort of father who could be relied upon to look after the needs of his family. Charles, as the eldest brother and with his earning power, his talents, his connections, and his personality, effectively became the head of the family. He helped his brothers and sisters with education, used his influence to find them work, advised and castigated them; he entertained them, took them on holiday, helped them set up home; and in death helped support their families. Death came early to all but one: two died in childhood; three failed to reach 40, one died at 48. One of his brothers, Fred, married a young girl of 18, against Dickens's advice, separated from her, committed adultery, was sued for separation, refused to pay, gave up his job, fled abroad, and was arrested for debt on his return; he had a spell in prison, drank too much and died at the age of 48. Another brother, Augustus (born 1827), deserted his wife when she went blind only two years after their marriage, later emigrating to America with another woman, where they lived as man and wife. He died in Chicago at the age of 39 and the woman he lived with killed herself a year later. As the effective "head of the family," Dickens had to deal with these and many more family trials while he worked at writing his books. He found time and money for them all but paid heavily with the anxiety they caused.

In 1842 he made his first journey to America, arriving in Boston on January 22 and leaving from New York on June 7. He traveled extensively, going south as far as Richmond, taking in Philadelphia and Washington, D.C.; however, repulsed by the sight of slaves, he cut short plans to continue on to Charleston; he then turned west as far as St. Louis, passing through Pittsburgh and Cincinnati before proceeding north to Canada where he took in Niagara Falls, Toronto, Montreal, and Quebec. The Americans received him enthusiastically but some did not welcome his calls for an agreement on international copyright. His account of the visit, *American Notes*, published five months after his return to Britain, and the insertion of American chapters in his next novel, *Martin Chuzzlewit*, containing, as they did, elements of criticism and caricature, lost him some American friends, but there remained a large audience for his books in America throughout his life, as there still is.

It was the following year, 1843, that Dickens established himself as the world's favorite author of Christmas with the publication of *A Christmas Carol*. Though he had written of Christmas in *Sketches by Boz*, *Pickwick Papers*, and *Master Humphrey's Clock*, it was not until he created the characters of Tiny Tim, Scrooge, and the ghosts of Christmas Past, Present, and Future that he captured the hearts and minds of the nineteenth-century public and of all future generations. It is the most filmed of Dickens's books (Glavin 2003), as well as being produced for stage, radio, and audio-tape/CD. This small book, together with a further four Christmas books published over the succeeding five years, changed the course of Christmas publishing and so linked the festive season with Dickens in the minds of the public that he subsequently felt loath to leave a gap he ought to fill. Consequently, from 1850 to 1867, he produced Christmas stories for the magazines he edited, the popularity of which were reflected in sales toward the end of that time of nearly 300,000.

Throughout his life there was rarely a settled period to Dickens's living arrangements, inflicted on him as a child by the nature of his father's work and the necessity of eluding creditors, but self-inflicted as an adult. The first real home of his own was in 1834 at Furnival's Inn, Holborn, though he changed from one set of chambers to a larger set just prior to his marriage in 1836. The following year, with his prospects rising, he took a three-year lease on a terraced house at 48 Doughty Street, which he exaggeratedly described as a frightfully first-class, family mansion involving awful responsibilities. Here he completed *Pickwick* and *Oliver*, wrote *Nicholas Nickleby* and worked on *Barnaby Rudge*, but tragically it was also here that his much-loved 17-year-old sister-in-law, Mary Hogarth, died suddenly while Dickens held her in his arms; he took a ring from her finger and wore it for the rest of his life and the ring remains with the Dickens family to this day. So too does the house remain, the foremost Dickens museum and the headquarters of the worldwide Dickens Fellowship.

In 1839, the growing family moved to a larger house in Devonshire Terrace near Regents Park where they remained for 12 years. However, it was not a settled tenancy. Following the six months' American disruption in 1842, Dickens uprooted his family in July 1844 and carried them off to live at Genoa, Italy for a year, which he turned to profitable use with the publication of a travel book, *Pictures from Italy*. After a year back at Devonshire Terrace, he took them abroad again, to Switzerland for five months, then on to Paris for three months. Such restlessness reverberated through his life. He argued with Chapman and Hall, his publishers since *Pickwick*, and switched publication to the printers Bradbury and Evans, whom he remained with until 1859 (see chapter 11).

On behalf of his friend Angela Burdett Coutts, he devoted time to the establishment and running of Urania Cottage, a home set up to help rescue women from prostitution. This commitment lasted from 1846 to 1858. In 1845, he became involved in the establishment of the *Daily News*, a morning paper supporting Liberal politics. Printed by Bradbury and Evans, it employed associates from Dickens's past, such as John Forster and George Hogarth, and others whom he remained close to for the rest of his life: W. H. Wills, Douglas Jerrold, and Mark Lemon. Dickens was made editor on the enormous salary of £2,000 a year and his father was put in charge of reporters. Dickens was not suited, though, to the daily grind of newspaper editorship and resigned after less than three weeks in charge.

It was at this time of his life – his mid-thirties – that his passion for theater led him in a new direction. From his childhood, at home and at school, he had sought to stage theatrical productions, continuing with private theatricals at his parents' house in Bentinck Street in 1833 and assisting officers of the garrison at Montreal during his visit in 1842. Besides writing for the theater and being an avid theatergoer, he had also written the stage into the fabric of his novels, particularly so with the Crummles family in *Nicholas Nickleby*. In 1845, having grown in status, confidence, and influence, he was able to gather about him a small company of actors and friends and to stage-manage and act himself in Ben Jonson's *Every Man in his Humour*, performed at the Royalty Theatre, a small establishment in Soho. He reveled in his organization of the actors, of the scenery and props, the costumes and make-up, the theater, and the audience. He became the creator of the event no less than he was the creator of his novels.

Though some of the audience were critical of the production, they had no impact on Dickens and his friends, for whom the process and the participation were sufficient reward. Nevertheless, the company attracted attention and there was always demand to see them. Three months later, a different play was performed at the same venue, but then Dickens's involvement with the *Daily News* and his travels abroad led to a gap of 18 months before interest was renewed, this time with even greater enthusiasm. In 1847, the company traveled to perform at Manchester and Liverpool, the following year expanding to London, Manchester, Liverpool, Birmingham, Edinburgh, and Glasgow. *The Merry Wives of Windsor* was added to their repertoire, and in 1851 a new Bulwer-Lytton comedy, *Not So Bad as We Seem*; each main performance was accompanied by a selection from a clutch of short farces. In one farce Dickens played six different characters, involving rapid costume change – it was all great fun. There was no money in this for Dickens or his company, all income going to good causes.

Important social changes were taking place around Dickens. He it was who booked his company of actors onto trains to carry them to Manchester. *Martin Chuzzlewit* in 1844 seems a celebration of coach and horse travel, but his next novel, *Dombey and Son* in 1848, reflects the age of the expanding railways. Euston Station, just a short walk from his home in Devonshire Terrace, was completed in 1846; the track out of London took away his schoolhouse at Wellington House Academy. The Houses of Parliament, where he had worked as a reporter, were being rebuilt, having burned down in 1834.

Around 1850, Dickens had his photograph taken for the first time, a daguerreotype by Henri Claudet: it shows a clean-shaven, solid, respectable man, well dressed, unsmiling, a man of business; it makes him look tall, though he was only 5 feet 8 inches. There is a solemnity about his face that was to deepen and age him prematurely, perhaps with good reason, all documented in the numerous photographs of him to appear over the next 20 years. In 1848 his beloved sister Fanny died of consumption, aged only 38, a sadness followed by the death of his youngest daughter Dora in 1850 and his father in 1851. A period of introspection developed as he started to write down an account of his life: this he showed to his wife and to Forster but abandoned the project and wove much of the information into his new novel, *David Copperfield*, written in the first person and telling the early life of an author. Seventeen years later, in a preface to *Copperfield*, he wrote "Of all my books, I like this the best." The many links between reality and fiction in *Copperfield* were not made explicit by Dickens and not placed before the public until after his death, in Forster's *Life of Charles Dickens*.

Journalism was one of the cornerstones of Dickens's career, and it was while working on *Copperfield* that he conceived and established, under his editorship, a weekly magazine called *Household Words*. Unlike the short spells he spent with *Bentley's Miscellany*, *Master Humphrey's Clock*, and the *Daily News*, his editorship this time was of long duration, lasting till his death 20 years later, albeit with a change of title to *All the Year Round* in 1859. Ably supported by his sub-editor, W. H. Wills, the running of his magazine was a major part of the routine of Dickens's life throughout the 1850s and 1860s. And just as he had himself been introduced to journalism by his father, who during his career as a correspondent for the *British Press* had encouraged Charles to bring in notices of accidents, fires, and police reports, for which he was paid a penny for each printed line, so too did Dickens pass the fascination on to his own son Charley, who eventually, after his father's death, took over both owner-ship and editorship, which he held until 1888.

Sales, settling down to a regular 100,000 a week with *All the Year Round*, and rising to 300,000 with the Christmas numbers, provided Dickens with a good income. After *Copperfield*, four new novels through the 1850s – *Bleak House, Hard Times, Little Dorrit*, and *A Tale of Two Cities* – also earned him large sums. Re-issue of the earlier titles began in 1847 with the Cheap Edition, and was repeated from 1858 with a more expensive Library Edition. There followed in the 1860s a People's Edition and a Charles Dickens Edition which between them sold more than 880,000 copies before June 1870. Deals were also made with American publishers and with Tauchnitz to publish in European countries. All of this added considerably to Dickens's income.

In 1851 he moved out of the Devonshire Terrace home and into a larger house at nearby Tavistock Square. However, just five years later, there came onto the market the property of his childhood dreams: the house at Gad's Hill near Rochester, at the gates of which he and his father had stopped in admiration and aspired, in a hopeful sort of way, to own. His purchase of Gad's Hill Place was a step back to his childhood: the area that had first aroused his imagination and creativity became a revived source of inspiration. Chatham, Rochester, and the marshes formed the foundations for *Great Expectations*, written 1860–1; Rochester was the Cloisterham of *The Mystery of Edwin Drood*, started in 1869 though never finished; "Dullborough Town," "Chatham Dockyard," and other essays from *The Uncommercial Traveller*, all published through the 1860s, reminisced about the "birthplace of his fancy."

Gad's Hill Place was the first and only house for which Dickens bought the free-hold; Tavistock House was held on a long lease, which he did not sell until 1860, thus maintaining a London and a country home for four years. His homes may have been an outward sign of Dickens's great success as a writer, but these were troubled years for his personal life. In 1857, while acting in *The Frozen Deep* at Manchester, he met and subsequently fell in love with an 18-year-old actress called Ellen Ternan. Besotted all his life by theater and the people who inhabited this morally doubtful world of escapism, at the age of 45 he surrendered his marriage and risked, but managed to hold onto, his family, his career, and his good name. His wife, perhaps not surprisingly after 10 children, did not compare well with the pretty face and well-developed figure of his mistress. Many years later, his daughter Kate said that the actress came like a breath of spring into his hard-working life and enslaved him. She flattered him, which he liked, and for her part she was 18 and proud to be noticed by such a famous man.

Various homes were set up for her in London, Slough, Peckham, and Boulogne, but for fear of public censure there was no question of them openly living together. Indeed, the relationship was hidden not just by Dickens but by the whole Dickens family for 80 years, and it was not until the 1930s that the truth came out, revealed by Dickens's daughter Kate and confirmed by her brother Henry. As a result of the affair, he separated from his wife but sought ruthlessly, and successfully, to suppress the true reason for the split. Divisions occurred within the families: his son Charley went to live with Catherine for a year; his daughter Mamie, on the other hand, never once visited her mother till after Dickens died; Catherine's sister Georgina and the younger children remained with Dickens. His friendships with Baroness Coutts, with Thackeray, Lemon, John Leech, and others were ruptured by the separation. Dickens protected his public popularity and rode out the storm but the strain of his marriage breakdown, of maintaining a secret love affair, and of supporting the troubled lives of his siblings and his children all told in his aging face.

Such stress in his life was exacerbated by a new direction in which he now took his career. Producing and acting in the plays of others had satisfied him for a while, but his obsession with theater took a life-changing turn as he focused his not inconsiderable acting ability on "readings" from his own works. At first he had given such readings to small groups of friends and then to larger audiences for charitable purposes, but from 1858 he began performances for his own financial benefit. "His reading is not only as good as a play," wrote one critic, "but far better than most plays, for it is all in the best style of acting" (Collins 1975: xvii).

Between April 1858 and February 1859 he gave 108 performances, making a profit in the first month alone of £1,025: this compared with average earnings from his literary output of less than £3,000 a year. Starting and finishing in London, he traveled the length and breadth of England, Scotland, and Ireland, attracting large audiences wherever he went. Now the only actor on stage, he held his audiences in thrall and soaked up their spellbound fascination. His letters swell with pride at the receptions he received, and George Dolby, a later manager of the tours, wrote: "setting aside his pecuniary profits, the pleasure he derived from [this career] is not to be told in words" (Dolby 1912: 451). Of Birmingham, Dickens wrote: "My success is very great indeed"; at Sunderland: "I never beheld such a rapturous audience"; at Edinburgh: "I consider the triumph there, by far the greatest I have made. The City was taken by storm, and carried . . . On the last two nights, the crowd was immense, and the turn-away enormous. Everywhere, nothing was to be heard but praises." Scenes anticipated those given to film stars a hundred years later:

> Arthur told you, I suppose, that he had his shirt front and waistcoat torn off, last night. He was perfectly enraptured in consequence. Our men got so knocked about, that he gave them five shillings apiece on the spot. John passed several minutes upside down against a wall, with his head amongst the peoples' boots. (*Letters* 8: 660)

At Belfast, people stopped him in the street:

> the personal affection there, was something overwhelming. I wish you . . . could have seen the people look at me in the street – or heard them ask me, as I hurried to the hotel after reading last night to "do me the honor to shake hands Misther Dickens and God bless you Sir; not ounly for the light you have been to me this night; but for the light you've been in mee house Sir (and God love your face!) this many a year." Every

night, by the bye, since I have been in Ireland, the ladies have beguiled John out of the bouquet from my coat. And yesterday morning, as I had showered the leaves from my geranium in reading Little Dombey, they mounted the platform after I was gone, and picked them all up, as keepsakes. I have never seen men go in to cry so undisguisedly as they did at that reading yesterday afternoon. They made no attempt whatever to hide it, and certainly cried more than the women. (*Letters* 8: 643)

Through the 1860s, Dickens rode the crest of a wave of popularity: thousands flocked to his readings, the various editions of his books sold in huge numbers, and the periodicals he owned and edited were a great success. But the stress of too much work, too much traveling, too many demands on him, too many problems, all put deep lines on his face and a strain on his body. In 1865, returning from Boulogne, accompanied by Ellen Ternan and her mother, the train in which they traveled careered off a bridge at Staplehurst in Kent where workman were repairing the track. Ten people died in the tragedy and Dickens, located in a coach left hanging from the bridge, was badly shaken. The accident weakened him, gave him nightmares, and he seemed to age rapidly after that. Through the 1860s death intruded constantly into his life: his son Walter died in 1863, aged only 22, his mother the same year, his brothers Alfred, Augustus, and Fred, his brother-in-law Henry Austin, his friends Thackeray, Daniel Maclise, and Clarkson Stansfield; it is said that there was a son born to Dickens and Ellen Ternan who died (Tomalin 1991: 143).

In 1864, Dickens began the last novel he was to complete, *Our Mutual Friend*, finishing it the following year. The readings, though, were more profitable than new novels, and in November 1867 he set off for a second visit to America, believing a tour of the theaters there would yield a fortune to him. Despite attacks in the American press accusing him of avarice and of deserting his wife, he was as much in demand there as he was in Britain. He gave 76 readings, attracting a total audience of more than 100,000 and cleared a profit of £19,000. On the downside, he suffered poor health for most of the five months of his trip. Concern for his health, though, did not stop him from embarking on a further tour back in Britain, starting in October 1868. In January of the following year, he introduced into his repertoire the murder of Nancy from *Oliver Twist*, a performance that terrified his audience, shook his fragile body, and left him drained of all energy. In April 1869, he became seriously ill and the remainder of his tour was canceled, having completed 74 performances out of a planned 100. Forced to rest from the readings, his mind turned once more to a new novel, and the writing of *The Mystery of Edwin Drood* was begun six months later, publication of the first number appearing on March 31, 1870. The readings, he decided, had to be given up altogether, but like any good showman he squeezed in 12 farewell performances, treading the London boards from January to March 1870.

Resting more now, he was able to spend some time at Gad's Hill and some private time with Ellen Ternan at their home in Peckham. Until recently, all accounts of the demise of Dickens record his collapse from a stroke at Gad's Hill on June 8, 1870 and his death the following day. Claire Tomalin, though, suggests that there may have been a more intriguing end, which she writes as a postscript to the paperback edition of her book *The Invisible Woman* (1991: 271). Based on the hearsay of somebody who claimed to be present, and passed down by word of mouth, it is suggested that Dickens collapsed not at Gad's Hill but at Peckham from where, to avoid scandal, he was transported the 24 miles back to Rochester. The case is unproven, yet, given the family's subsequent protection of Dickens's reputation, an adjustment of the truth surrounding his death would not be surprising.

Charles Dickens was buried in Westminster Abbey on June 14, 1870. The first beneficiary in his will, receiving £1,000, was Ellen Ternan.

References and Further Reading

Ackroyd, Peter (1990). *Dickens.* London: Sinclair-Stevenson.

Allen, Michael (1988). *Charles Dickens' Childhood.* London: Macmillan.

Collins, Philip (Ed.) (1971). *Dickens: The Critical Heritage.* London: Routledge and Kegan Paul.

— (Ed.) (1975). *Charles Dickens: The Public Readings.* Oxford: Oxford University Press.

Dolby, George (1912). *Charles Dickens as I Knew Him: The Story of the Reading Tours in Great Britain and America (1866–1870).* London: Everettt.

Glavin, John (Ed.) (2003). *Dickens on Screen.* London: Cambridge University Press.

Johnson, Edgar (1953). *Charles Dickens: His Tragedy and Triumph*, 2 vols. London: Gollancz.

Langton, Robert (1891). *The Childhood and Youth of Charles Dickens.* London: Hutchinson.

Slater, Michael (1983). *Dickens and Women.* London: Dent.

Storey, Gladys (1939). *Dickens and Daughter.* London: Muller.

Tomalin, Claire (1991). *The Invisible Woman: The Story of Nelly Ternan and Charles Dickens*, rev. edn. Harmondsworth: Penguin.

Wright, Thomas (1935). *The Life of Charles Dickens.* London: Jenkins.

2
Dickens's Use of the Autobiographical Fragment

Nicola Bradbury

Charles Dickens recorded his childhood experience of working life alone in London in 1824 during the period when his father fell into debt and was imprisoned in the Marshalsea, but he kept the manuscript secret. It survives only in the mediated version of his friend John Forster. Under "Hard Experiences in Boyhood" in *The Life of Charles Dickens* (Forster bk. 1, ch. 2), the biographer includes some 20 pages centered on the "Autobiographical Fragment" given him by Dickens himself "very shortly [after]" March or April 1847. Dickens had not, according to Forster, yet thought of the "idea of *David Copperfield*, which was to take all the world into his confidence," where parts of the fragment would reappear in the text of David's "Personal History," closely echoing Dickens's early struggles. What interests Forster is how openly "what it had so startled me to know, his readers were afterwards told with only such change or addition as for the time might sufficiently disguise himself under cover of his hero."

The biographer quotes directly from Dickens's autobiography, with brief interruptions:

> I lose here for a little while the fragment of direct narrative, but I perfectly recollect that he used to describe . . . There is here another blank, which it is however not difficult to supply from letters and recollections of my own . . . I have heard him say . . . I must not omit what he told me of . . . I can describe in his own words.

With such assistance, Forster sets out to piece together extracts from the novel and the autobiographical fragment as equivalent source documents for Dickens's *Life*, keeping in view both historical fact and biographical interpretation, besides demonstrating even here Dickens's powers as a writer:

> What had already been sent to me, however, and proof-sheets of the novel interlined at the time, enable me now to separate the fact from the fiction; and to supply to the story of the author's childhood those passages, omitted from the book, which, apart from their illustration of the growth of his character, present to us a picture of tragical suffering,

and of tender as well as humorous fancy, unsurpassed in even the wonders of his published writings.

This brief outline of Forster's handling of the fragment points toward the temptation of expanding on his approach – factual, interpretive, and critical – to explore Dickens's own use of his autobiography. There are, however, further demands in establishing the context for this work. First, there is the question of its secrecy. Forster quotes the fragment:

> From that hour until this at which I write, no word of that part of my childhood which I have now gladly brought to a close, has passed my lips to any human being. I have no idea how long it lasted; whether for a year, or much more, or less. From that hour, until this, my father and mother have been stricken dumb upon it. I have never heard the least allusion to it, however far off and remote, from either of them. I have never, until I now impart it to this paper, in any burst of confidence with any one, my own wife not excepted, raised the curtain I then dropped, thank God.

What caused, and what broke, this silence? How does the utterance of the fragment relate to Dickens's use of the same material in his fiction? Where the fiction expands that material, or re-opens its aporia, is it appropriate, or helpful, to return to the autobiography? Or should the fragment, on the contrary, be regarded as a textual stage toward the greater development of recurrent preoccupations in Dickens's published work?

In a letter of November 4, 1846, Dickens challenged Forster: "Shall I leave you my life in MS when I die? There are some things in it that would touch you very much, and that might go on the same shelf with the first volume of Holcroft's" (*Letters* 4: 653 and n.). Not only does this suggest that Dickens had written the fragment before he was provoked to pass it to Forster (who was already expecting to write his biography) – that it really was for some time "suppressed" – but also that Dickens recognized its textual standing within the genre of autobiographical writings. John Harrison Stonehouse noticed long ago that "Holcroft's *Memoirs* . . . exercised a considerable influence on Dickens," identifying a number of close comparisons between both autobiographies and Dickens's fiction, even showing that "David Copperfield's adventure with the too-friendly waiter at Yarmouth, who ate up his dinner, is evidently founded on [a cited] childish experience of Holcroft's" (Stonehouse 1931: 53–7).[1] Does such an appropriation reflect on the status of the autobiographical fragment itself? Did Dickens regard his own text too as offering rich pickings for his novels? Did he actually write it to that end, construct his own "personal history" as he ventriloquizes David Copperfield's? Forster states: "It had all been written, as fact, before he thought of any other use for it." What was that use?

It was "the accident of a question" Forster put to Dickens in 1847 that provoked the revelation of the autobiographical fragment. Did the author remember as a boy seeing the elder Mr. Dilke, a fellow clerk with John Dickens in Somerset House? Yes – but only when visiting a sick uncle.

Upon which I told him that some one else had been intended in the mention made to me, for that the reference implied not merely his being met accidentally, but his having had some juvenile employment in a warehouse near the Strand; at which place Mr. Dilke, being with the elder Dickens one day, had noticed him, and received, in return for the gift of a half-crown, a very low bow. He was silent for several minutes; I felt that I had unintentionally touched a painful place in his memory; and to Mr. Dilke I never spoke of the subject again.

Twice the notion of the accidental attaches to this incident, set against the counter-pulse of "intended" and "unintentionally." Forster accidentally stings Dickens into silence with the story of the non-accidental meeting, while Dilke's intention now becomes for both unspeakable. He is not mentioned again, though a version of this anecdote, with the central vignette – the half-crown and the bow – blacked out, may be the incident that brings both Dickens's "juvenile employment" and the fragment to a close, with a quarrel between his father and his employer: "It was about me. It may have had some backward reference, in part, for anything I know, to my employment at the window." The embarrassing encounter is elided into "some backward" abysm of what "may have" attached to the author.

Occlusion and exposure surround the "painful place" of the autobiographical fragment, and they also animate its dramatic narrative, but they do not dictate the tone. Shame is a dominant emotion, though anger, self-pity, and guilt also bear a part. There is, however, a remarkable absence of fear, from a small boy alone, and instead a curious joy. Together with the intimacy of indignation is a kind of analytical poise, and a pride in the detail and flourish of recall. What the fragment covers is clearly a formative experience for both Dickens and his art. The author explicitly signals in his text certain figures retrieved for his novels, naming Fagin, Mr. Sweedlepipes, Mrs. Pipchin, Bob Sawyer, the Marchioness, the Garland family, and Mr. Pickwick's fellow prisoners. Forster finds whole episodes transposed to *David Copperfield*. Yet the underlying issues at play, and the relationships through which they are expressed, are characteristic of Dickens's work both before and after this. The autobiographical fragment poses questions, therefore, not only about the source of Dickens's material but his treatment too; about how "backward reference" might operate, or be suppressed; and about the sway of "accident" and "intention" throughout his writings.

The autobiographical fragment focuses on the experience of Charles Dickens, though it is framed by his father's misfortunes. John Dickens's career never equaled his aspirations or expenses, and in the early 1820s the family moved to London and from house to house, making shift to live more cheaply. Charles, taken out of school, learned to trade with the pawnbroker. Worse followed, and here the fragment begins. James Lamert, a relative who had lodged with the Dickenses, found Charles a job at his cousin's business, Warren's Blacking Warehouse, on Hungerford Stairs, behind the Strand. For 6 shillings a week, the boy worked from eight till eight, pasting labels on blacking bottles. James Lamert's undertaking to give him lessons during the lunch hour proved unworkable. Dickens came down and out from his "recess," "side by side" with the other "common men and boys, a shabby child," and eventually, after the business relocated, "for the light's sake, near the second window," where their dexterity would draw "quite a little crowd." Here Mr. Dilke must have tipped him, and Charles bowed low; from this situation John Dickens at last set him free.

An employment history provides the skeleton of Dickens's autobiographical fragment, but not its haunting power. What drives the revelations of the document as a confession are two forms of exposure: the social shame of common work and the personal bitterness of familial abandonment and betrayal. What animates it as a personal history is the opportunity that conjunction of exposures creates: a catastrophic, but liberating, initiation into experience as a child alone in the city. It is an intensely egocentric account, class-bound to the point of snobbery, and self-pitying: the parents' misfortunes providing the context for the child's sufferings, and the siblings' stories subordinated to his own. Yet through his naïve protagonist Dickens registers more than mere self-regard. The city and its people are distinctly drawn. Hunger stimulates the portrait of a consumer society, and misery a fascination with other mishaps. Denouncing his own neglect and declaring his achievement, Dickens retrieves from taboo the latent power of his unspeakable past.

The fragment opens with the facts of Warren's premises and the Lamerts' links with the business, recounted in a flat tone, though with an air of suppressed energy created by the repeated, deliberate pairing of terms: "Hungerford-stairs, or market, Strand"; "the original inventor or proprietor"; "deposed and ill-used"; "selling his recipe, and his name"; "this right and title"; "the blacking business and the blacking premises." Into this account breaks a paragraph (opening on a dash) prefaced with the Miltonic lament: "—In an evil hour for me, as I often bitterly thought." When Lamert's proposition to his parents proves tempting, Dickens echoes Adam's (already ironically echoic) reproach to "Eve in evil hour" (*Paradise Lost* 9, l.1067): his innocence Paradise Lost, at the prompting of the woman. This implication – although Dickens says Lamert's offer "was accepted very willingly by my father and mother" – works beneath the surface throughout the fragment to the climactic denunciation with its triple emphasis: "I never afterwards forgot, I never shall forget, I never can forget, that my mother was warm for my being sent back." It is the betrayal of the mother, seduced by worldly considerations, that underpins the pain of the autobiographical fragment.

The depth of the transgression is proportionate to the distinction of the child "so easily cast away . . . a child of singular abilities, quick, eager, delicate, and soon hurt, bodily or mentally." The parents, however, "quite satisfied," could "hardly have been more so, if I had been twenty years of age, distinguished at a grammar school, and going to Cambridge." Thus, within a paragraph, the infant phenomenon is abstracted, first by his qualities, and then through an extraordinary conjectural "life," from his actual circumstances. The Warren's Blacking story, however factual, stands outside that hypothetical Eden. Moving between them seems an act of authorial will. The relationship of Charles Dickens to the record of his early years determines itself as a curiously controlled performance, even where the history is one of vulnerability,

naivety, or of shame. The child is father to the man. The boy's plight can be as fully
detailed as the world he inhabits, with an energy that may be fuelled by grievance
but emerges as "wonderful." His work now reclaims the past, redeems the fall.

The process begins immediately in the textual resurrection of the vanished warehouse itself, tormented into swarming and squeaking, if not speaking, life, taking on
physical dimensions, then rising up:

> It was a crazy, tumble-down old house, abutting of course on the river, and literally
> overrun with rats. Its wainscotted rooms, and its rotten floors and staircase, and the old
> grey rats swarming down in the cellars, and the sound of their squeaking and scuffling
> coming up the stairs at all times, and the dirt and decay of the place, rise up visibly
> before me, as if I were there again.

His job description is itemized in full detail, textually packaged now in writing as
neatly as the original task:

> My work was to cover the pots of paste-blacking; first with a piece of oil-paper, and
> then with a piece of blue paper; to tie them round with a string; and then to clip the
> paper close and neat, all round, until it looked as smart as a pot of ointment from an
> apothecary's shop.

The orderly reproduction here of that process in black ink on paper becomes a kind
of treatment: a salve, if not salvation. The work attains some "pitch of perfection": a
many-layered phrase in this context, with suggestions of blackness, contamination,
and a sudden fall.

While Dickens claims that "No words can express the secret agony of my soul" as
he sank into such occupation, and such company, the fragment is far from melancholic
throughout. There is anguish, "penetrated with the grief and humiliation" of his
abandonment, but it is revisited in "dreams," as in another kind of existence, and one
which overspills the distance of historical record, so that "even now, famous and
caressed and happy, I often forget in my dreams that I have a dear wife and children;
even that I am a man; and wander desolately back to that time of life."

Forster's account of the experience recounted in the autobiographical fragment
moves forward to a letter of 1862 in which Dickens writes still of the "never to be
forgotten misery of that time" that he has "found come back" (*Letters* 10: 98). Within
the fragment, however, the child's suffering is set against quite other qualities: expertise at work; precocious achievements in household management; early observations
on the arts of performance, in theater, and in verse; an interest in stories and in storytelling: all of which belong to a profession not yet foreseen. So the small city boy
provides a consumer's guide to the working lunch, from the mundane – "commonly
a saveloy and a penny loaf; sometimes, a plate of bread and cheese, and a glass of beer"
– to one peculiarly literary indulgence that strangely anticipates its own account –
"like a book" – and concludes with an inverted version of the humiliating half-crown
episode that triggered Dickens's revelations to Forster:

Once, I remember tucking my own bread (which I had brought from home in the morning) under my arm, wrapped up in a piece of paper like a book, and going into the best dining-room in Johnson's alamode beef-house in Clare-court, Drury-lane, and magnificently ordering a small plate of alamode beef to eat with it. What the waiter thought of such a strange little apparition, coming in all alone, I don't know; but I can see him now, staring at me as I ate my dinner, and bringing up the other waiter to look. I gave him a halfpenny, and I wish, now, that he hadn't taken it.

The complex construction of the fragment repeatedly sets patterns of recurrence against such striking reversals. When, wandering like an innocent Cain, the child is "handed over as a lodger" to a "reduced old lady," within the sentence it is she who falls subject to him; for she "unconsciously began to sit for Mrs. Pipchin in *Dombey* when she took me in." Later, the text turns itself inside out with surreal panache as the child conjures up memories related with uncanny immediacy to himself now, as "reverie" gives way to "shock":

in that door there was an oval glass-plate, with COFFEE-ROOM painted on it, addressed towards the street. If I ever find myself in a very different kind of coffee-room now, but where there is such an inscription on glass, and read it backward on the wrong side MOOR-EEFFOC (as I often used to do then, in a dismal reverie), a shock goes through my blood.

Less dramatic, but equally strange, is the inversion of prison and home. The child "cast away" into lodgings is eventually permitted a room nearer his family in the Marshalsea: "and when I took possession of my new abode, I thought it was a Paradise." When he falls ill at work, however, and is taken "home" by his workmate, he enacts an elaborate charade, knocking on an unknown door as "a finishing piece of reality" to conceal his actual destination. Amongst Warren's employees, he is desperate to maintain "some station." He must protect himself from contempt by "skilful" work, but he must do more to mark his distinction: "Though perfectly familiar with them, my conduct and manners were different enough from theirs to place a space between us. They, and the men, always spoke of me as 'the young gentleman'." The danger is of a further fall: "I know that, but for the mercy of God, I might easily have been, for any care that was taken of me, a little robber or a little vagabond." In fact, what the child does, like David Copperfield at school, is "entertain" his colleagues "with the results of some old readings." He also, like David with Peggotty, or in anticipation of Pip to Joe Gargery, elaborates on his experiences to tell the family's maid-of-all-work "quite astonishing fictions," excusing this behavior: "But I hope I believed them myself." The performing arts are not excluded from the blacking warehouse. Within Warren's, "Poll Green's father had the . . . distinction of being a fireman, and was employed at Drury-lane theatre; where another relation of Poll's, I think his little sister, did imps in the pantomime." Dickens's own elder sister Fanny, while he was at work, attended the Royal Academy of Music. He was taken to see her awarded a prize, and suffered anguish, though he asserts: "There was no envy in this."

What emerges from the autobiographical fragment is a knot of history, confession, record, and performance. Equally potent are the psychological currents of anger and pride, utterance struggling with concealment. One such incident, counter-pointing bravado and vulnerability, is transposed into *David Copperfield* (ch. 11) where the boy "went into a public-house . . . and said to the landlord behind the bar, 'What is your best – your *very best* – ale, a glass?'" and the landlord's wife "opening the little half-door and bending down, gave me . . . a kiss that was half admiring and half compassionate, but all womanly and good." Another episode in which the writer achieves distance from a situation replete with elements of shame by adopting a precociously professional stance is a scene that would generate material for *Little Dorrit* (bk. 1, ch. 6). John Dickens, before leaving the Marshalsea, drew up a petition for the prisoners to be found the wherewithal to fund a birthday drink for the king. Charles "got leave of absence, on purpose, and established myself in a corner" to observe the inmates at the ceremony of signing, and he reports with some satisfaction that "Whatever was comical in this scene, and whatever was pathetic, I sincerely believe I perceived in my corner . . . quite as well as I should perceive it now."

Figures of motherliness people the fragment in reproach. Fathers are relatively indulged. Yet the author who "never afterwards forgot . . . never shall . . . never can forget" his parents' parts in this history, prefaced that incantation with a different assertion: "I do not write resentfully or angrily: for I know all these things have worked together to make me what I am."

Critical response to the autobiographical fragment has registered Dickens's proclamation and protest to different degrees, and plotted the importance of the autobiographical fragment to his work accordingly, swerving between the psychoanalysis of traumatic return and the celebration of triumph in its endless productivity. Freud cuts a figure through this criticism, but the procedure may be simplified by the recognition that Freud was a reader of Dickens. The terminology of psychoanalysis which derives from the Freudian tradition follows the novelist's work rather than interrogating it. John Forster is the pre-Freudian commentator who begins to enquire "In what way those strange experiences of his boyhood affected him afterwards," with reference to "the narrative of his life" (bk. 1, ch. 3), and he puts very succinctly Dickens's own reading of it: "Of this he was himself aware, but not to the full extent." How that acute but imperfect analysis operated in Dickens's oeuvre now becomes the question.

Steven Marcus argues that the fragment "figures in some central way in every novel [Dickens] ever wrote; and we cannot understand the creative thrust of his life without taking into account his developing attitudes towards this episode, as we find them successively transmuted in novel after novel" (Marcus 1965: 363). Thus, "Dickens returned to the theme of the father, the son and the prison throughout his career, most prominently in *David Copperfield* and *Little Dorrit*, but also in *Barnaby Rudge, A Tale of Two Cities* and *Great Expectations*" (1965: 43). Marcus identifies the "extreme and ineradicable feeling of humiliation" (1965: 82) generated by the childhood experiences. But "that epoch" also set a pattern which proved vital to his work, as Dickens discovered when wrestling with *Dombey and Son* abroad, without the stimulus of the London streets. Marcus suggests that Dickens "needed these streets and walks because for him writing was mysteriously and irrevocably connected with that epoch in his life when he was literally a solitary wanderer in the city" (1965: 279). For Marcus, that mystery may hark back to an even earlier "primal scene" of witnessing sexual intimacy between the parents, but this can only remain speculation. What that depends on, however, is traceable in Dickens: it is the preoccupation with seeing and being seen.

That obsession drives Dickens's return, as Christopher Hibbert notices, to the tangle of issues opened in the autobiographical fragment. So Hibbert constructs a sentence-paragraph in tribute to:

> The disquieting sense of being watched in this world, of being spied upon and caught out by gleaming eyes, eager eyes, spying eyes, eyes that stare, inquisitive eyes, which constantly and disturbingly appear; and of being choked or suffocated in a stifling room, or lost in a labyrinth of streets, as in *Oliver Twist*; the images of crumbling riverside houses that totter suddenly into ruin as the houses of Tom-All-Alone's do in *Bleak House* and the Clennams' house does in *Little Dorrit*; the desire to escape from the imprisoning city back to the countryside of innocent childhood, as shown in *The Old Curiosity Shop*; the comfort of pretence that soothes the fears of the characters in *Martin Chuzzlewit*; the fascination with dirty, muddled, crowded, fungus-laden interiors; the concern with money; the plots which time and again revolve round a family mystery and the dread of its revelation; and, of course, the difficulties of the relationships between parents and their children which are investigated in novel after novel – all these ideas and symbols and themes, that repeatedly occur in Dickens's writing, can be interpreted in the light of the traumatic experiences and sufferings of these few months of his thirteenth, pre-pubescent year. (Hibbert 1967: 73–4)

Yet, for all such detailed and specific "debts" to the autobiographical fragment in Dickens's fiction, perhaps Hibbert's most intriguing observation is one he adopts from Humphry House: that the most significant aspect of the work lies in its fascination with the past. It is this orientation that pervades Dickens's novels: the backward inflection, seeking understanding amidst origins. Angus Wilson focuses this further. Dickens, he writes, "put almost every associate of these black months into his novels, but most important is his treatment of himself" (Wilson 1970: 58).

For Michael Slater, Dickens transformed "Experience into Art" through fictional representations of figures from his life. The "bad mother" of the autobiographical fragment recurs in "nightmare" versions of the mother-and-son relationship, though she is also "exorcised" to some extent in nurturing figures such as Emma Micawber (Slater 1983: 23). One original may be divided: "Clara Copperfield and Jane Murdstone are, in fact, the light and dark of Dickens's childhood memories of his own mother" (1983: 20). But what is implied by the words "are, in fact"? An encyclopedic grasp of the novels supports Slater's recognition of recurrent character traits and relationships in Dickens, but it cannot fully explain the links between his life and the fragment.

When Slater invokes two texts in this regard – one a remarkable literary allusion from early in Dickens's adult life, the other a difficult late tale – what is most striking is the distance between these references. First, Slater reports that Dickens urged his fiancée Catherine Hogarth to read Samuel Johnson's *Life of Savage*. This he describes as a "story of maternal rejection and cruelty which, in certain details, Dickens surely identified with his own story" (1983: 13). If so, this episode constitutes a fascinating qualification of Dickens's absolute denial in the autobiographical fragment that he had "raised the curtain" on his early experiences to anyone: "my own wife not excepted." Then, Slater notes, in "George Silverman's Explanation" (1868) comes "Dickens's most lurid exploitation since writing *Oliver Twist*, thirty-odd years before, of his own private legend, that undying memory . . . of an exceptionally gifted and sensitive child, fired with glorious ambition, being nearly ruined for life by a mother transformed by poverty" (1983: 23). Both "Savage and Silverman," then, throw light on what "Dickens surely identified," but surely they do so from different angles. The linking of texts and life is highly problematic.

Alexander Welsh picks out from the fragment not echoes but energy, and the phrase "I did my work." He links that business-like attitude and confidence to Dickens's writing career. By the time of writing *David Copperfield*, Dickens, Welsh finds, had learnt "to celebrate his profession as a writer and accommodate his memories to it" (Welsh 1987: 108). Then David Musselwhite subjects the fragment itself to interrogation: it is "a notoriously difficult document to interpret, for there seems . . . to hover around it a peculiarly insinuating air of deceit" (Musselwhite 1987: 153–4). Musselwhite reads the fragment in deliberate retrospection as "the production of a fitting childhood for the man who is to be Dickens the author" (1987: 163), and protests: "What the threnodic descant of the 'Autobiographical Fragment' seeks to drown out is a marvellous clatter of collisions and engagements and feints and purchases between an endlessly mobile and flexible consciousness and an environment that is itself alarmingly alive and volatile" (1987: 162). The distancing of critical analysis from autobiographical sleuthing reaches its furthest extent in Patricia Ingham's rebuttal of Michael Slater's *Dickens and Women* in her own *Dickens, Women, and Language*, with a rejection of "extralinguistic" "sources" for the women of Dickens's novels, which "relocates such figures where they belong: in the text, not in some specious hinterland behind it" (Ingham 1992: 2).

That Dickens incorporated in his fiction material gathered from his personal experience is evident, and he said as much. That he felt conscious of writing as the product of such experiences is demonstrable in his own words: "for I know all these things have worked together to make me what I am." That some of these impressions, incidents, figures, and feelings were secretly written into his autobiographical fragment, and that some material from the fragment was then adopted into the fiction, particularly chapters 11 and 12 of *David Copperfield*, is also plain. Beyond quotation, however, how Dickens used the autobiographical fragment remains problematic. Three factors must be taken into account: first, the emergence of "autobiographical" material in Dickens's novels before either the fragment or *David Copperfield*; secondly, the persistent recurrence of such themes long afterwards, indeed throughout his career; thirdly, the complex treatment of this material, both in the fragment and in the fiction, moving between the "accidental" and the "intended," or what is revealed and what performed. This critical area invites comment yet resists analysis, so that it remains open to discussion, just as for Dickens it remained open to continuing exploitation as the material of his work.

The preoccupations of the autobiographical fragment are anticipated in both the inter-chapters and the central narrative of Dickens's first novel, *The Pickwick Papers*. From Pickwick's ruminations "on the strange mutability of human affairs" (ch. 2) to the narrator's denunciation (ironic in this context) of the attitude of "Many authors [who] entertain, not only a foolish, but a really dishonest objection to acknowledge the sources from whence they derive much valuable information" (ch. 4), authorial motivation and practice is a subject of comment. But the conjunction of embedded narratives with the continuing Pickwickian quest is executed without explication: challenging interpretation. Suddenly, therefore, come glimpses of potential revelation, which exceed their narrative context. So, in relation to the stranger's Spanish Romance, comes this snippet: "'And her father?' inquired the poetic Snodgrass. 'Remorse and misery,' replied the stranger. 'Sudden disappearance – talk of the whole city – search made everywhere – without success'" (ch. 2) – a moment of anguish that goes beyond its immediate story. To this example could be added "The Stroller's Tale" (ch. 3), which "traced his progress downwards, step by step, until at last he reached that excess of destitution from which he never rose again," with its "long course of cruelty and neglect." "The Convict's Return" (ch. 6) shows a 12-year-old son whose "headlong career" is to "bring death to him and shame to her" (his mother), finally accusing his "Father – devil!" "The Old Man's Tale about the Queer Client" (ch. 21) records: "His recollections were few enough, but they were all of one kind: all connected with the poverty and misery of his parents."

Debt and imprisonment, besides parental abandonment, shame, and guilt, permeate *Pickwick*, and they touch the principals as well as lesser characters. Even "The travellers' room at the White Horse Cellar is of course uncomfortable" (ch. 35): "It is divided into boxes, for the solitary confinement of travellers." Most disturbing of all is the memory (featuring the repeated incantation "Pray, remember") of "an iron cage in the wall of the Fleet Prison, within which was posted some man of hungry looks, who, from time to time, rattled a money-box, and exclaimed in a mournful voice, 'Pray, remember the poor debtors; pray, remember the poor debtors'" (ch. 42) – a vignette that seems to combine aspects of John Dickens's experience in the Marshalsea debtors' prison with Charles's own exposure at the window of Warren's, in a painful resurgence of shame. Intriguingly, however, two explicit Pickwickian references, to Mr. Warren (ch. 10) and "Warren's Blackin" (ch. 33) are jocular and apparently casual. There are different levels of engagement with "boyhood" experiences.

Pickwick is remarkable for the conjunction of extremes in the use of autobiographical material between disciplined structural control and reckless surrender to generic exaggeration, whether melodramatic or comic. In Dickens's subsequent novels, the evidence of his continuing preoccupation with "all these things" continues. *Oliver Twist* is the tale of a boy abandoned (in death) by father and mother to the dangers of solitude, starvation, and a potential criminal career. To the gang-master who takes him in, Dickens gave the name of the boy who had helped him learn his trade at Warren's, Bob Fagin. The disingenuous tone of his announcement in the autobiographical fragment: "I took the liberty of using his name, long afterwards, in *Oliver Twist*," defies analysis. Is this revenge? A counter-annexation? Whose "liberty" is at stake?

It is not difficult to chart the lost children of Dickens's novels; the feckless father figures or failing mothers; the threat of destitution, or worse, contamination by crime. Neither his rage at blundering oppression by legal bureaucracy nor the constant trust in sheer hard work abates, from *Pickwick* to *Our Mutual Friend*. Catalogues, however, do not account for the persistence of Dickens's preoccupations. Nor does listing explain either the immediacy or the endless mutations of this material: the inflections of "accident" and "intention," occlusion and exposure, in performance as record. How does Dickens "work" with the materials he claimed "have worked together to make me"?

One place to examine this is in the extraordinary short story "George Silverman's Explanation" among the late works. The title promises resolution but implicitly acknowledges a prior challenge. The tone of the text is remarkably constrained. The sentences are short, determined. There are nine chapters in a work of 27 pages. The first-person narrator moves within the strictures of his format to a conclusion that foregrounds and embraces those limitations: "I pen it for the relief of my own mind, not foreseeing whether or no it will ever have a reader" (ch. 9). The tale is challenging in form and tone. The story, set out to be deduced by a reader rather than imparted by the speaker, begins in disease, death, and dreadful privation, conveyed without comment or affect. When asked bluntly, "Do you know your father and mother are both dead of fever?" the surviving child responds without apparent emotion: "'I don't know what it is to be dead. I supposed it meant that, when the cup rattled against their teeth and the water spilt over them. I am hungry and thirsty.' That was all I had to say about it" (ch. 4). Isolation and abuse lead to his withdrawal into a scholar's life of unutterable humility. George Silverman even scrupulously diverts his loving pupil's affection to one of her peers, but he suffers in consequence both emotionally and professionally. His only relief is in this writing: one where his exculpation from the unjust charge of impropriety remains merely implicit. In an astonishingly provocative textual procedure, the whole tale therefore repeats the obstructions of its opening two chapters – the first seven lines long, and the next ten – which begin identically:

It happened in this wise:
— But, . . .

– where the most expressive element is the wordless break between the lines, accentuated by the gap between the colon and the dash.

"George Silverman's Explanation" may be read as "a version" of Dickens's boyhood history of poverty, parental abandonment, withdrawal, even his emergence as a writer, but to say this much begs more questions than it answers. How could this macabre story express, or even illuminate, his experience? Surely, only elliptically and by implication, as chapter 1 does chapter 2 in the tale: most powerfully in apposition and through restricted utterance: the colon and the dash, rather than surrounding words.

A more complex instance of the "use" of the autobiographical fragment might also be found through identical disruptions of the text held in apposition to each other between the fragment itself and *David Copperfield*. An image, a form of words, a sensation brings the two together, though the narrative context does not. What this "coincidence" reveals is not the gradual opening up of the author's life story, first in autobiography and later in fiction, but rather an inescapable preoccupation with experience itself, sensation and intention, in terms of immediacy and control. Not warehouse-work nor the work of fiction, but the working of the mind is the mystery here.

The passages I have in mind center on the word "shock." It does what it says. A physical force explodes in the text: one that knocks the impetus from the speaker, creating a sense of exposure to some greater power. The text can only circle around, accommodate, this discharge of energy. In the fragment, Dickens writes that "a shock goes through my blood" if he finds himself reading "backward on the wrong side MOOR-EEFFOC (as I often used to do then, in a dismal reverie)." In the novel (ch. 25), after being cornered in his own rooms into offering his unwelcome guest "more coffee," David Copperfield greets the appalling Uriah Heep's presumptuous profession of love for "my Agnes" with "the delirious idea of seizing the red-hot poker out of the fire, and running him through with it." But he continues: "It went from me with a shock, like a ball fired from a rifle." David, like Dickens, links this sensation with a state he does not label "reverie," but discusses at some length in terms that indicate the suspension of immediacy, and a quasi-spectatorial relationship with experience:

> He seemed to swell and grow before my eyes; the room seemed full of the echoes of his voice; and the strange feeling (to which, perhaps, no one is quite a stranger) that all this had occurred before, at some indefinite time, and that I knew what he was going to say next, took possession of me.

The whole incident, with Uriah spending the night in David's room, seems to a post-Freudian reader almost inconceivably naked in its encounter with overt and repressed sexual ambition: an erotically charged evening, conveyed in terms of violent passion. What is interesting, however, in connection with the phrase echoing the autobiographical fragment – "It went from me with a shock" – is not just the phallic symbolism of rifle and red-hot poker, but the transmission of energy, swelling and growing in the present scene, into a déjà vu reverberation of "some indefinite time" which completes David's displacement, his virtual ravishment, not by the upstart Uriah, but rather by his own prior knowledge: "that I knew what he was going to say next, took possession of me."

More than coincidence, disabling and dazzling at once, this uncanny sensation recurs in *Great Expectations*: another first-person novel which itself stands stylistically in apposition both to the fragment and to *David Copperfield*. The whole story here turns on suppressed memories and belated recognitions. There is a Hamlet motif of ghostly haunting, which crops up not on the first occasion of Waldengarver's (the translated Wopsle's) "massive and concrete" (ch. 31) Shakespearean burlesque, but when Pip returns later to take refuge in the theater (ch. 47). Here it is the actor (now playing the part of Enchanter in a pantomime) who is transfixed by his audience, "and he seemed to be turning so many things over in his mind, and to grow so confused" that disruption is signaled through him on Pip's behalf, taking on an unruly life of its own, and disconcertingly out of place. Textual, perceptual, and temporal categories are dislocated by an uncanny apparition, not on stage but in the stalls. What the actor sees is the old enemy, Compeyson, sitting "like a ghost" behind the "unconscious" Pip. The construct of the self, its assumed privacy, supposed autonomy, and integrity, are taken apart and put on display in this unnerving shadow play.

Then in the following chapter the entanglements of the past intrude again as the sight of Molly's hands at Jaggers' table trigger off for Pip another "thought of the inexplicable feeling that had come over [him]" at Satis House. Further:

> I thought how the same feeling had come back when I saw a face looking at me, and a hand waving to me, from a stage-coach window, and how it had come back again and had flashed about me like a Lightning, when I had passed in a carriage – not alone – through a sudden glare of light in a dark street. (ch. 48)

The "link of association" is looped together with Estella's "knitting action" in a series of imaginative "flashes" less literal than symbolic. Through such sequences the text creates its own knot of memories and anticipations. Their effect on Pip is cataclysmic – but not, of course, wholly unforeseen – at the lime kiln (ch. 53) when his candle is "extinguished by some violent shock, and the next thing I comprehended was, that I had been caught in a strong running noose, thrown over my head from behind."

The "shock" of helplessness as the speaker is caught in the "running noose . . . from behind" expresses, not once but repeatedly, through the fragment itself, *Copperfield*, and *Great Expectations*, Dickens's response to the sudden and disturbing interjection of both past and future, memory and anticipation, into the present moment: an experience of unmediated power that challenges his self-possession.

In *Copperfield*, David's professional success, as the writer penning his own history, is less acutely registered than the vivid, challenging experiences of the boy – some of which Dickens also records in the autobiographical fragment – that "have worked together to make me what I am." The adult professional record is notably brief. So chapter 48, "Domestic," recounts with the least conceivable excitement David's first publication and its reception: "I laboured hard at my book, without allowing it to interfere with the punctual discharge of my newspaper duties; and it came out and was very successful." By chapter 58, the writer reports both a second "Story, with a purpose growing, not remotely, out of my experience," that is "very advantageously" published, and then a third piece that is fictional. Only the second work is signaled as autobiographical and even this is "not remotely" acknowledged as the substance of the novel that is before us. The tone of this professional record is stringently impersonal. It is quite unlike the energetic self-invention, variety, and panache of earlier passages such as chapter 13, which is closer in timbre as well as content to the autobiographical fragment. David, in flight from his demeaning work at Murdstone and Grinby's to Aunt Betsey in Dover, puts together in one paragraph three different statements of accounts: financial, narrative, and fictive in the journalistic mode, together with a dramatic encounter that outdoes them all with the hypnotic power of a half-remembered and dreadful fairytale:

> But my standing possessed of only three-halfpence in the world (and I am sure I wonder how *they* came to be left in my pocket on a Saturday night!) troubled me none the less because I went on. I began to picture myself, as a scrap of newspaper intelligence, my being found dead in a day or two, under some hedge; and I trudged on miserably, though as fast as I could, until I happened to pass a little shop, where it was written up that ladies' and gentlemen's wardrobes were bought, and that the best price was given for rags, bones, and kitchen-stuff. The master of this shop was sitting at the door in his shirt-sleeves, smoking; and as there were a great many coats and pairs of trowsers dangling from the low ceiling, and only two feeble candles burning inside to show what they were, I fancied that he looked like a man of a revengeful disposition, who had hung all his enemies, and was enjoying himself.

It is in such interweaving of commonsense with self-ironizing extravagance, both equally, though very differently, satisfactory, that the novel echoes the greatest strengths of Dickens's autobiography. The triumph of his work is actually to assert its own achievement. Demonstrably, what the autobiographical fragment charts is the making of the writer.

NOTE

1   I am grateful to Michael Allen for drawing my
    attention to this reference.

References and Further Reading

Bodenheimer, Rosemarie (2006). Dickens and the writing of a life. In John Bowen and Robert L. Patten (Eds.), *Charles Dickens Studies* (pp. 48–68). Houndmills, Basingstoke: Palgrave Macmillan.

Collins, Philip (1970). *David Copperfield*: "A very complicated interweaving of truth and fiction." *Essays and Studies*, n.s. 23, 71–86.

—— (1984). Dickens's autobiographical fragment and *David Copperfield*. *Cahiers victoriens & edouardiens*, 20, 87–96.

Dever, Carolyn (2006). Psychoanalyzing Dickens. In John Bowen and Robert L. Patten (Eds.), *Charles Dickens Studies* (pp. 216–33). Houndmills, Basingstoke: Palgrave Macmillan.

Hibbert, Christopher (1967). *The Making of Charles Dickens*. London: Chatto and Windus.

Ingham, Patricia (1992). *Dickens, Women and Language*. New York: Harvester Wheatsheaf.

Marcus, Stephen (1965). *Dickens: From Pickwick to Dombey*. London: Chatto and Windus.

Musselwhite, David E. (1987). *Partings Welded Together: Politics and Desire in the Nineteenth-century English Novel*. London: Methuen.

Slater, Michael (1983). *Dickens and Women*. London: Dent.

Stonehouse, John Harrison (1931). *Green Leaves: New Chapters in the Life of Charles Dickens*, rev. edn. London: Piccadilly Fountain Press.

Welsh, Alexander (1987). *From Copyright to Copperfield: The Identity of Dickens*. Cambridge, MA: Harvard University Press.

Wilson, Angus (1970). *The World of Charles Dickens*. London: Martin Secker and Warburg.

3

"Faithfully Yours, Charles Dickens": The Epistolary Art of the Inimitable

David Paroissien

Thomas Carlyle, prolific correspondent himself, has written as memorably as anyone about the appeal and value of letters. Of those sent to him by his wife in 1857, he speaks of "a piercing radiancy of meaning" which her written words evoked in him. Elsewhere, and in a different context, Carlyle characterized letters as "authentic Utterances," electric showers of brilliance, he believed, clearly of value to the biographer. Letters, for Carlyle, hung in the dark abyss of the past, like stars, "almost extinct, yet like a real star," once all luminous "as a burning beacon, every word . . . a live coal in its time" (Sanders et al. 1970: ix, xii). The importance of letters as documents hardly needs stating, so obvious are they as a source of information about the subject's day-to-day life, the play of his or her shifting moods, interests, and consciousness, the private man or woman behind the public figure.

In Dickens's case his correspondence – the magnificently annotated Pilgrim Edition runs to 12 lengthy volumes – serves many besides his numerous biographers. For a writer to whom the bounds between fiction and correspondence are thin, his incessant and unceasing writing stands as a monument to the age he has come to define. Among his correspondents we note aristocrats, prominent political and governmental figures, civil engineers and military men, lawyers, magistrates and prison officers, policemen, men and women representative of Britain's artistic elite, publishers, public servants, newspaper editors, architects, designers, prominent citizens of France (often addressed in their own language), Italian political exiles, leading American statesmen and intellectuals, tradesmen and workmen of many skills, and a wide circle of intimates, both familial and professional. The social range in fact runs from Queen Victoria herself, whom Dickens addressed indirectly through Arthur Helps, Clerk to the Privy Council and the queen's confidential adviser, to young women, seduced and abandoned and forced to sell their bodies in the streets of London.

Inevitably, the subject matter matches the variety of Dickens's correspondents and the interests that energized the century. Brilliant polemical epistles addressed to newspaper readers, arguing against capital punishment and the repulsive practice of hanging felons in public; private expressions of despair at the sullen imbecility into which the country seemed to have fallen during England's military misadventures in the Crimea in 1854; the need for a reasoned response to the expansion of geological and biological knowledge in the face of theological dogmatism; sympathy for the Italians, priest-ridden and long oppressed; the importance of improving the living conditions of the urban poor by providing clean drinking water and decent housing; indignation at recklessness on the part of engine drivers exceeding safe speeds on the country's expanding rail network; the importance of designing train timetables that made sense – these are only some of the issues of the time which he addressed. Unsurprisingly, he was also adept at defending misreadings of his novels by partisan critics. Reprimanded by one Congregational minister who took offense at the representation in *Bleak House* of philanthropists preoccupied with Africa, Dickens tartly defended the position he took in the novel:

> Indeed, I have very grave doubts whether a great commercial country holding communications with all parts of the world, can better christianize the benighted portions of it than by the bestowal of its wealth and energy on the making of good Christians at home and on the utter removal of neglected and untaught childhood from its streets, before it wanders elsewhere.

These were opinions, Dickens added, founded on "some knowledge of facts and some observation," out of which he refused to be scared by "such easily-impressed words as 'Anti-christian' or 'irreligious'" (*Letters* 6: 707). This exchange is typical of the way in which Dickens's letters delineate different aspects of Britain's national life during the nineteenth century.

The Pilgrim editors print some 15,000 surviving letters – only a fraction of those Dickens must have written. That so much material remains extant we have others to thank rather than Dickens. Had he had his way, England's literary treasure hoard would contain fewer riches. Letters, Dickens is reported to have argued, "are but ephemeral" and we ought not, he advised, to pay attention either to praise or words written "in the heat of the moment." He put this case to justify an act of desecration painful to contemplate: the destruction on September 4, 1860 of all the letters he had received before that date. Two of his sons who assisted in this pyrotechnic despoliation were evidently delighted and took the opportunity to roast onions "on the ashes of the great!" "Would to God that every letter I had ever written was on that pile," Dickens commented (Storey 1939: 107).[1]

Being Dickens, he had a high-minded justification for his action. "A year or two ago, shocked by the misuse of the private letters of public men, which I constantly observed, I destroyed a very large and very rare mass of correspondence," he informed Samuel Hole, in December 1864, who had asked Dickens for letters or recollections that he might use for a biography of John Leech. Although Dickens confessed to grave misgivings, he abided by his determination "to keep no letters" by him, "and to consign all such papers to the fire" (*Letters* 10: 465). A few months later, he reiterated the point to W. C. Macready: "now I always destroy every letter I receive – not on absolute business, – and my mind is, so far, at ease" (11: 21–2).

That principled decision is only a portion of a story complicated by other motives. Among them we can distinguish a wish to protect his own privacy, and that of his family and friends. Also missing from the explanation offered to Hole is the imaginative language with which Dickens usually expresses himself, often casually allusive in the employment of one of his favorite literary sources. In an earlier letter to W. H. Wills, his trusted sub-editor, Dickens heightens his description of the occasion with a reference to "The Story of the Fisherman" in *The Arabian Nights*, who is threatened with death by a giant genie when he opens the coffin he has caught. "Yesterday I burnt, in the field at Gad's Hill, the accumulated letters and papers of twenty years . . . They sent up a smoke like the Genie when he got out of the casket on the seashore; and it was an exquisite day when I began, and rained very heavily when I finished, I suspect my correspondence of having overcast the face of the Heavens" (9: 304).

The reasons why letters from Dickens did not suffer the same inflammatory fate are obvious. To receive a letter from him – even a perfunctory request to renew an order for a dozen bottles of sherry – was to take delivery of a gift. From the beginning of his career as a writer, Dickens became an instant celebrity, a distinguished person whose written words deserved preservation as a memento worth keeping in the family for more than one generation.

Several clusters of letters document variants of this practice. Prominent among them is a group of 22 letters directed to William Woodley Frederick de Cerjat, an intelligent, literate, and congenial older gentleman whom Dickens met in Switzerland in 1846. The wonderful letters he received from Dickens, in return for his own "Christmas letters" annually sent to the novelist, earn him a niche in English literary history. Other and more extensive veins of correspondence include archival materials retained as a matter of business: for example, letters to Thomas Mitton, Dickens's solicitor; to Richard Bentley; to Messrs. Chapman and Hall; and to other publishers and individuals in the field of letters. Others were preserved by family members and friends for personal and sentimental reasons, although there were notable exceptions. R. H. Barham's daughter had letters written to her father burnt because she judged them private; H. K. Browne ("Phiz") also lit a fire "to lessen the lumber" he had accumulated over the years, thereby radically diminishing our knowledge of his work as Dickens's principal illustrator (1: xxii). Not surprisingly, no scrap of paper sent to Ellen Ternan survives, although letters were sent to her at times via Wills, Dickens's sub-editor at *All the Year Round*. Maria Beadnell, however, his first love, cherished every missive she received, as did Dickens's wife Catherine. Shortly before she died, she asked her younger daughter to give the letters Dickens wrote to her to the British Museum, so "that the world may know he loved me once" (Storey 1939: 164).

There were many "Unknown Correspondents," almost all of whom were authors of unsolicited scripts, sent by "every conceivable kind of person of whom I have no sort of knowledge, on every possible and impossible subject with which I have nothing to do." Dickens received "hundreds" of such letters every week of his life (*Letters* 7: 702; for the list of Unknown Correspondents, see the Cumulative Index of Correspondents, 12: 774). He answered them dutifully, despite a natural vexation all the more intense in view of his profession. In an elegantly turned excuse for the delayed response to his friend Cerjat, to whom he *did* like writing, he began by saying that the date of his reply would make him "horribly ashamed" of himself, "if I didn't know that *you* know how difficult letter-writing is, to one whose trade it is to write" (9: 246).

Although Dickens owned the 18-volume set of *Elegant Extracts in Prose, Verse, and Epistles* (1812), and was familiar with *The Complete Letter-Writer* (1768), both of which proffered model letters for every occasion, he did not believe that letter-writing could be reduced to easily learned formulas. "I am the *In*completest Letter Writer imaginable," he informed Wilkie Collins on September 30, 1855, punning on the manual's title. In his view, writers who took their cue from model letters offered for every occasion were likely to fail. He preferred the second of two letters written by the young wife of the veteran actor, William Charles Macready, on the death of her stepdaughter because it contained a "truly affecting account of poor Katie's death," written "wholly under emotion" and without the conventional phrases that had marred the first letter – language, Dickens thought, derived from "Elegant Extracts and Speaker." "This last letter . . . has no such drawback" (12: 323–4).

Dickens's doubts about relying on letter-writing manuals reflect an opinion he seems to have formed early on. His own lack of formal education, together with the strenuous efforts he made to counter it, may explain the skepticism expressed in his own correspondence toward representatives of this self-help genre present in his own library. Issues related to epistolary practice also surface in his fiction. Consider the banter that arises between Sam Weller and his father when the son endeavors to write "a walentine." "'Taint in poetry, is it?" ventures Mr. Weller, a form he regards as incapable of genuine expression. Sam's declaration to Mary that she *is* "a nice gal and nothin' but it" meets his father's approval. "Wot I like in that 'ere style of writin' is, that there ain't no callin' names in it, – no Wenuses, nor nothin' o' that kind." But when Sam closes his address with the flat statement: "My dear Mary I will now conclude," Mr. Weller objects that the "pull up" is "rayther a sudden" one. "'Not a bit on it,' said Sam; 'she'll vish there wos more, and that's the great art o' letter writin'"" (*The Pickwick Papers* ch. 33).

The quality of Dickens's own letters rests on his mastery of two important skills: his exuberant spontaneity and linguistic inventiveness and the subtlety with which he fitted the content and style of his letters to different correspondents. That he wrote so many of them, often at the end of a day, feeling "rather addle headed," and facing on occasions "an unusually violent rush of letters," imposing on him "all sorts of other people's botherations" amplifies this achievement (*Letters* 9: 380; 8: 509). Equally impressive is the ease with which he addresses an extraordinary range of men, women, and children in distinctive idioms. Indeed, we might consider the many modes of expression evident in the letters he sent to real people an extension of perhaps his most distinctive gift as a novelist – the skill with which he created so many individu-alized characters each with his or her voice, vocabulary, and mode of speech. What was said by Betty Higden in praise of Sloppy's ability to "do the police in different voices" applies equally to his inventor in his daily correspondence (*Our Mutual Friend* bk. 1, ch. 16).

Take, for instance, the art of the gracious request. In August 1860, Dickens asked a favor of the 7th Earl of Carlisle, who had helped the 1848 Public Health Bill pass through the Commons. Reminding him that he had always been kind to Dickens's brother Alfred when Alfred worked for the General Board of Health, Dickens explains that it was Carlisle's kindness "that emboldens me to write to you." Extending the context, Dickens mentions that he had just returned from his brother's funeral and how Alfred had "left nothing – worse than nothing." In a pattern repeated throughout Dickens's life, it fell to him to provide for relatives with limited or no means – in this instance, two nephews, one aged 11, the other 13. So, continues Dickens, if "any kind of nomination or presentation should ever fall in your way – which seems just possible to me, remembering the honors that surround you . . . will you think of this letter, if you can?" Aware that he risked annoying Carlisle, Dickens closes with a deft attempt to soothe his request: "I will not ask you to forgive me for putting you to the trouble of reading it. Your gentle heart will have done so, before you come to these words" (*Letters* 9: 279).

Elegant petitions made in a professional capacity also distinguish Dickens's corre-spondence. Abreast of developments in many fields, he was well aware of Michael Faraday's role in creating the Royal Institution's famous Friday Evening Discourses, the Christmas lectures for children Faraday had begun in 1825, and his more recent six lectures in 1850 "on some points of domestic philosophy." What better informa-tion, Dickens concluded, to put "on the breakfast-table" of the large class of readers who subscribed to *Household Words* than to reveal the secrets of "a fire, a candle, a lamp, a chimney, a kettle, ashes." Accordingly, he took the liberty of addressing Faraday as if he knew him personally, "trusting that I may venture to assume that you will excuse that freedom." That said, Dickens goes on to ask the discoverer of electromagnetism if he would consent to favor him with "the loan of your notes of those Lectures" so that he, Dickens, with the assistance of "a friend and contributor [to *Household Words*] who has a practical knowledge of chemistry," might make use of them in order to convey to the reading public "some very small installment of the pleasure and interest I have in them." Ever the diplomat willing to offer a graceful retreat, Dickens ends by saying that he was sensible that Faraday may have reasons of his own "for reserving the subject to yourself. In that case, I beg to assure you that I would on no account approach it" (6: 105–6, 110). With an offer like that, how could Faraday refuse?

Equally engaging is the wording of the stream of invitations Dickens issued to friends and prominent figures. The skill with which he personalizes such requests makes them all the more compelling. An invitation to Lieutenant Augustus Tracey, RN, issued on behalf of the whole Dickens family, typifies these overtures:

We were under the impression – which I swear you gave us – that you were going to weigh anchor on Saturday and beat out to Devonshire. As you said last night that you intended lying in the Downs some days yet, I make this signal (on the white Serjeant's behalf), to ask if it be possible that you and your fair wife (who, if I may whisper a word in your ear, looks handsomer every time I see her) . . . can come and dine with us this very next Sunday at 6?

"Say yes, and I'll make you an Admiral," he closes with a flourish (7: 632). The lapse into naval jargon characterizes several of Dickens's letters to Tracey. Here, Dickens refers to a former naval anchorage actually used by sailing ships near the Goodwin Sands and to the practice of dividing a fleet into squadrons by the colors of the Union Jack. On other occasions he uses purely facetious language, a delightful instance of which occurs on April 8, 1848 when Dickens jokes that he and Tracey might be on opposing sides over the forthcoming Chartist demonstration planned for April 10 on Kennington Common. "My Dear Admiral," he began, addressing Tracey in his capacity as the governor of Tothill Fields prison. "Keep your weather eye on that there Lion figure-head o' yourn, o' Monday, for in the case I hoist my pennant aboard o' the Chartist Flagship, I'm damned if I don't pour in a broadside on you (in answer to your'n) and rake you fore and aft, you swab!" Dickens signs off with a cross designated as "his mark," an allusion to the view that illiteracy prevailed among many of the demonstrators (5: 273).

The reclusive and eccentric Hans Christian Andersen lacked sufficient command of English to permit this kind of foolery, but he, too, was susceptible to warmly expressed invitations. "I hope my answer," wrote Dickens, to the letter Andersen had sent expressing an interest in visiting London, "will at once decide you to make your summer visit to us." What more persuasion would a guest want than the following? A pleasant room of his own, with a charming view; the chance to live as quietly and wholesomely at Gad's Hill "as in Copenhagen itself;" the freedom to travel at will to London and pass the night in Tavistock House, which, from its roof to the cellar will be at his disposal. "A servant who is our friend also," Dickens continued, "who lived with us many years and is married, will be taking care of it; and she will take care of you, with all her heart." Understandably won over by this appeal, Andersen made up his mind to visit, but on this occasion, the normally gregarious Dickens miscalculated. The Dane outstayed his welcome. "We are suffering a good deal from Andersen," Dickens confided to Angela Burdett Coutts in the middle of his visit, perhaps on account of his guest's unexpected independence. On an excursion in London he somehow became separated from the family, took a cab by himself, and was driven off to an unfinished street in Clerkenwell, where, according to Dickens, Andersen imagined he had been taken in order to be robbed and murdered. He subsequently arrived back at Tavistock House, "with all his money, his watch, his pocket book, and documents, *in his boots* – and it was a tremendous business to unpack him and get them off" (8: 373). Following his eventual departure, Dickens posted a brief note in the guest-room: "Hans Andersen slept in this room for five weeks – which seemed to the family AGES!" (Storey 1939: 21–2).

The ability to turn a minor incident into something more extended and amusing runs through many of Dickens's letters. Finding an appropriate person to sweep one's chimneys, for example, would normally have been the task of one of several servants. Not at Gad's Hill, however. The novelist who had exposed the evil of employing boys to clean chimneys and the abuse to which youths like Oliver Twist were subject by the likes of Mr. Gamfield took time to emerge from "the raging sea of correspondence" that so frequently engulfed him to write an extended request to the master sweep who had previously taken care of the chimney in Dickens's study. Since that last intervention, Dickens explained, his chimney had developed some peculiar eccentricities: "Smoke has indeed proceeded from the cowl that surmounts it, but it has seemingly been undergoing internal agonies of a most distressing nature, and pours forth disastrous volumes of swarthy vapour into the apartment wherein I habitually labour." Dickens conceded that this phenomenon might be a relief to the chimney, but it was not "altogether convenient" to him. Thus, the mediation of "a confidential sub-sweep" capable of engaging in social intercourse with the chimney, he concluded, might induce the chimney "to disclose the cause of the departure from its normal functions" (*Letters* 10: 370). The real-life sweep known to Dickens must have had a better command of English than the fictional Mr. Gamfield. When the latter chances on the notice advertising the sale of Oliver, he has to spell through the bill twice in order to make out that the five pounds offered for the parish orphan was "just the sum he had been wishing for" in order to pay "certain arrears of rent" (*Oliver Twist* ch. 3).

Corresponding with people from every quarter of society on equal terms represents one of the defining features of Dickens's correspondence, and nowhere is this more fully shown than in letters he sent to children. Surviving examples nicely document the appeal of his novels to the young. Some were literate enough to negotiate the works for themselves; others needed help from an adult. The five-year-old brother of Thomas Hughes, for example, responded to the illustrations of *Nicholas Nickleby* and an oral version of the hero's adventures read by his father with sufficient understanding as to express his reaction to the end of the story. He was upset that Nicholas received no proper rewards and that Squeers and his family remained unpunished. When these reservations were communicated to Dickens, he answered promptly. "Respected Sir," Dickens began with mock gravity. "I have carefully done what you told me in your letter." The little boys were given "some good ale and porter, and some wine" and Nicholas had some roast lamb. Squeers, by contrast, received "one cut on the neck and two on the head, at which he appeared much surprised and began to cry," the cowardly response one would expect from a bully. "Fanny Squeers shall be attended to, depend on it. Your drawing of her is very like, except that I don't think the hair quite curly enough." Dickens closed by congratulating the young artist for getting her nose and legs right. "She is a nasty and disagreeable thing and I know it will make her very cross when she sees it" (*Letters* 1: 466–7).

Equally charming is the reply to Master Francis Waugh, perhaps the youngest person to send Dickens one of the many fan letters he received. "My Dear Young friend," the novelist began, responding on June 30, 1858:

> I am quite ashamed to find that your letter was written to me so long ago as on the eighteenth of this month . . . The truth is, I have been very busy. Otherwise I should have sent you this present autograph, on the very next day after I received your letter. "Better late than never", and here it is.

Dickens improves on this old expression of regret with a bit of fancy reflecting his professional pursuits:

> I don't write as plainly as you do. But printers can read anything, and they have made me lazy about the shape of my letters, and the clearness of my loops, and the roundness of my O's (there's a round one though), and all that. But I am not lazy in anything else, so I hope to retain your good opinion on the whole. (8: 593)

One test of our epistolary literacy — now withered by a dependence on commercial condolence cards — is the ability to commiserate with others on sorrowful occasions. That Dickens wrote so many letters of this variety might prompt the suspicion that he kept in reserve a stock of appropriate epithets and sentiments. Nothing could be further from the truth. Three letters to Mrs. Maria Winter — formerly Maria Beadnell, his first love — each in respect of different misfortunes, demonstrate how attentively and thoughtfully he personalized his responses. Two days after the death of her one-year-old daughter from bronchitis on June 11, 1855, Dickens wrote to say how truly grieved he was to hear of the death of her "darling baby." In a remarkable letter, he offers both consolation and empathy. "The death of infants is a release from so much chance and change — from so many casualties and distresses — and is a thing so beautiful in its serenity and peace — that it should not be a bitterness, even in a mother's heart." That such deaths strike especially deep, he well knew. Quick to align himself with her misery, he spoke from his own recent experience. "A poor little baby of mine, lies in Highgate Cemetery — and I laid her, just as you think of laying yours, in the catacombs there . . . God bless and comfort you! Mrs. Dickens and her sister send their kindest condolences to yourself and Mr. Winter. I add mine with all my heart" (7: 648–9).

In tone perhaps a little less heartfelt yet expressing concern are letters written three years later. On November 3, 1858, Maria's husband, a former mill owner, was declared bankrupt. Ten days later, Dickens wrote to the unfortunate man to assure him of his sympathy in his "trouble." "Pray do not let it cast you down too much. What has happened to you, has happened to many thousands of good and honorable men, and will happen again in like manner, to the end of all things." To Maria on the same day and in a separate missive he wrote less objectively but added two comments heavy with nuance. "I wish to Heaven it were in my power to help Mr. Winter to any new opening in life. But you can hardly imagine how powerless I am in any such case. My own work in life being of that kind that I must always do it with my own unassisted hand and head." This was from the man who on another occasion mentioned that he had never been left anything but relatives who turned to him for help in times of need. Then follows another observation not without a barb, if scholars are correct to assume that Mr. Beadnell had both objected to young Dickens as a prospective son-in-law and played some part in thwarting his pursuit of Maria. "But I really think that your father, who could do much in such a case without drawing at all heavily upon his purse, might be induced to do, what – I may say to you, Maria – is not a great stretch of sentiment to call his duty." Four years later, Mr. Beadnell died leaving £40,000, not a penny of which seems to have been used to relieve his son-in-law from bankruptcy (8: 703–4).

Mrs. Winter heard again from Dickens in response to a "touching account" she sent him of the last moments of her "poor father." Dickens's reply seems to hover between detached observation and the expression of feelings never far below the surface of his emotional life: "Of course I could not be surprised, knowing his great age, by the wearing out of his vitality; but – almost equally of course – it was a shock too." Offsetting this realistic response to the death of an 89-year-old is a reference to intense times gone by. "For all the old Past comes out its grave when I think of him, and the Ghosts of a good many years stand about his memory" (10: 162) – a sentence which carries a wealth of personal associations Maria would surely have recognized.

Dickens's response to the death of the first Mrs. Macready offers another instance of an inward train of thought unexpectedly flooding into a letter. Shortly after her demise on September 18, 1852, he wrote to Forster in metaphorical language intensified by an allusion to Shelley's elegy on the death of Keats. "Ah me! Ah me! This tremendous sickle certainly does cut deep into the surrounding corn, when one's own small blade has ripened. But *this* is all a Dream, may be, and death will wake us," a reference to Shelley's *Adonais*: "He is not dead, he doth not sleep / He has awakened from the dream of life" (6: 764).

Three years later, the death of his friend the Hon. Richard Watson prompted an equally moving response, expressed in plainer language to Georgina Hogarth on December 19, 1855. On visiting Watson's home, Rockingham Castle, for the first time since Watson's death in 1852, Dickens writes of the weight that fell on his spirits and of feeling "inexpressively sad." After retiring early to bed, "monstrously depressed," Dickens felt obliged to read and smoke well past midnight before "I could become myself again." The next day, as Dickens was about to leave, Watson's widow bid him walk up to "the old Gallery upstairs." Initially Dickens declined, but gave way to persuasion and so they went up to survey the furniture "all piled up in a great ghostly heap in the middle." Mrs. Watson then turned her head away and looked out of a window; "and for the life of me," Dickens relates, "I could not decide upon the delicacy or the friendliness of making allusion to her grief. Consequently I turned my head and looked out of another window, until she moved. Then we both came out together, silently and sadly" (7: 766). This occasion so tenderly described must have been one of the few when Dickens found himself at a complete loss for words.

A category of letters impressive for different reasons belongs to Dickens's career as an editor. From his appointment in November 1837 as the editor of Richard Bentley's *Miscellany* to his death in June 1870, Dickens sat more or less continuously in various editorial chairs, the last 20 of those years conducting *Household Words* and *All the Year Round*. His duties generated a massive amount of correspondence, which followed him even when he took his family to France for extended summer holidays. To read through this material is to experience the dedication and discipline Dickens brought to this sector of his public life. Dickens's editorial integrity was often challenged by unsolicited submissions from friends. In most cases, the needs of the journal predominated, although decisions do not appear to have been taken lightly. "I am most reluctantly obliged to decline the paper on the Cornice in the rain, – not because of any want of merit in itself," Dickens wrote to Mrs. Cowden Clarke in 1861. The Clarkes, old friends who had lived in Nice since 1856, had maintained regular contact with Dickens since they met in 1848; and as an established author with literary friends in common, Mrs. Clarke merited respect. Something about her piece, however, failed to capture Dickens's imagination. *All the Year Round*, he explained, has published "so many descriptions of localities, and [has] so many in type which I very slowly use, that I am really afraid to increase their number, at this time." By way of consolation, Dickens assured her that her paper would be "carefully preserved in my Drawer here, until you tell me, at your leisure and opportunity" whether he should send it to her brother's music shop in Soho (9: 375).

Submissions from other friends sometimes fared better, but again not without a struggle on Dickens's part. A short story by Mary Boyle, frequent family guest, actress, and close friend of Dickens with whom he carried on a mild flirtation, appeared in *Household Words* in March 1851. In his acceptance letter, Dickens tells her how he had devoted a couple of hours this evening, "going very carefully" over her paper. It required his attention, he explained, in order to "give it that sort of compactness which a habit of composition, and disciplining of one's thoughts like a regiment, and of studying the art of putting each soldier into his right place, may have gradually taught me to think necessary." Boyle's contribution had clearly needed the delicate exercise "of the pruning knife" and a new title. "I propose to call it *My Mahogany Friend*. The other name is too long, and I think not attractive." If all of this explanation sounded a trifle solemn, Dickens continued, he wanted to let her know that he found many things in it *"very pretty."* At the same time, he also had a duty not to encourage her falsely "to enter on that thorny track [of authorship] where the prizes are so few, and the blanks so many." One detail he seems not to have shared with the author is the full extent of his role. Credit for the story's ten and a half columns was recorded in the *Household Words* office book as a *joint* contribution: "Mary Louisa Boyle & Charles Dickens" (6: 297–8; Lohrli 1973: 74).

Submissions that met Dickens's exacting standards proved a different matter. Generous with tribute where merited, he was quick to pay it. "If you were not the most suspicious of women, always looking for soft sawder in the purest metal of praise, I should call your paper delightful," Dickens wrote to Elizabeth Gaskell after receiving the second of her eight "Cranford" stories, all of which appeared in *Household Words* between 1851 and 1853. The whole, he thought, was "touched in the tenderest and most delicate manner. Being what you are, I confine myself to the observation that I have called it 'A Love-Affair at Cranford,' and sent it off to the Printer" (*Letters* 6: 558).

At times, though, the volume of work took its toll on Dickens's patience. Sandwiched between "an astonishing quantity of proofs," especially when he prepared Christmas numbers for both journals, and "a pretty large correspondence too," he had no time for pieces with "too much about too little," containing "a quantity of words and a mustard seed of matter" (7: 33), vast clouds of verse, prose that was "wandering and confused," the product of one who writes so loosely that the author "really seems sometimes to write in his sleep." Less disparaging with stories that showed promise, Dickens tempered criticism with advice on crucial matters. Consider the instructions he gave on one occasion about how to handle humor. "Not too pettingly and perserveringly," he cautioned Thomas C. Evans, "to urge to the utmost any humorous little extravagance. I think the dog should not open his mouth so very wide in the barking as to show the whole of his internal mechanism, and the same kind of objection strikes me in reference to the spelling of some of the noises made, both by men and beasts" (9: 107).

Dickens was particularly exasperated by casual writers who believed that dipping one's pen in ink constituted the sole preliminary to publication. To an unknown correspondent who had evidently sent in a packet enclosing multiple submissions from several writers, Dickens wrote: "Between ourselves – and not for the information of *their authoresses* [of the enclosed scripts] – they are of that intensely dreary & commonplace description to which not even the experience of this place reconciles my wondering mind." Asking his correspondent if he felt the same astonishment, Dickens continued: "People don't plunge into churches and play the organs without knowing the notes or having the ghost of an ear. Yet fifty people a day will rush into manuscript for these leaves only, who have no earthly qualification but the actual physical art of writing" (6: 146; cf. 7: 27).

Behind Dickens's varied epistolary voices lurks another: that of "The Inimitable." In conferring the epithet upon himself, Dickens seems to have understood two defining features of his fictional voice: the exuberant quality of his prose and his tendency to dwell "purposely . . . upon the romantic side of familiar things." Incidents narrated in two letters provide a useful perspective on this penultimate sentence of the Preface to *Bleak House* published in August 1853. The first is the account of "the sad circumstances of poor Walter's death," sent to Miss Coutts on February 12, 1864. Walter, Dickens's second son, died of chest disease in India on December 31, 1863, shortly before he was to have been sent home on sick leave from his regiment. "I could have wished it had pleased God to let him see his home again," Dickens wrote, "but I think he would have died at the door." This letter continues with a description of

Walter's sudden end, as it was recorded by the medical personnel in attendance on him. It also includes a brief justification of Dickens's decision to keep specific details from Georgina Hogarth and Walter's younger brother, Sydney. He was anxious to do so because both manifested "strong traces" of the same chest disease. After a paragraph in which Dickens thanks Miss Coutts for the "affectionate letter" he had received from her "this morning," he closes with a description of something uncanny and clearly prophetic that happened on the very night Walter died:

> On the last night of the old Year I was acting in charades with all the children. I had made something to carry, as the Goddess of Discord; and it came into my head as it stood against the wall while I was dressing, that it was like the dismal things carried at Funerals. I took a pair of scissors and cut away a quantity of black calico that was upon it, to remove this likeness. But while I was using it, I noticed that its *shadow* on the wall still had that resemblance, though the thing itself had not. And when I went to bed, it was in my bedroom, and still looked so like, that I took it to pieces before I went to sleep. All this would have been exactly the same, if poor Walter had not died that night. And examining my own mind closely, since I received the news, I recall that at Thackeray's funeral [December 29, 1863] I had sat looking at that very object of which I was reminded. See how easily a marvelous story may be made. (10: 356)

A second illustration that seems to owe more to the fictive than to the factual comes from a letter Dickens sent Georgina Hogarth from Italy in 1853. Written "upon the wing," as Dickens termed letters sent home to friends and family, this is one of many describing an incident of the kind that can only happen to Dickens. Even he admitted that it appeared "ridiculous" despite its origin in something anchored firmly in reality. On holiday with friends, Dickens ran into a former acquaintance, William Lowther, currently England's senior diplomat in Naples, and accepted an invitation to dine at Lowther's residence. At the appointed hour, Dickens set out from his hotel "all in state," hiring an opening carriage for the occasion. The driver, however, unable to ascend the steep hill up to the diplomat's house, simply pointed to "the evening star" and said that "Il Signor Larthoor" lives up there.

So Dickens set off on foot: "a mile and a half I should think. I got into the strangest of places, among the wildest Neapolitans – kitchens, washing-places, archways, stables, vineyards – was baited by dogs, answered in profoundly unintelligible Neapolitan, from behind lonely locked doors, in cracked female voices, quaking with fear." In due course, Dickens finally met an old Frenchman with "an umbrella like a faded tropical leaf," despite the fact that no rain had fallen for six weeks, and "a snuff-box in his hand," staring "at nothing at all." In response to Dickens's question whether he knew "Signor Larthoor," the old man asks if the party Dickens sought had "a servant with a wooden leg?"

> "Great Heaven, sir," said I, "how do I know! I should think not, but it is possible." "It is always" said the Frenchman, "possible. Almost all the things of the world are always possible." "Sir," said I – you may imagine my condition and dismal sense of my own

absurdity, by this time – "that is true." He then took an immense pinch of snuff, wiped the dust off his umbrella, led me to an arch commanding a wonderful view of the bay of Naples, and pointed deep into the earth from which I had mounted. "Below there, near the lamp, one finds an Englishman, with a servant with a wooden leg. It is always possible that he is the Signor Loothere."

By now an hour late and in a state of perspiration and misery "not to be described," Dickens resumed his search "without the faintest hope" of finding his host's house. Eventually he discovered "the strangest staircase up a dark corner, with a man in a white-waistcoat (evidently hired) standing at the top of it, fuming." Dickens dashed in at a venture, found it was the place, made "the most of the whole story, and was indescribably popular" (7: 191–2). Challenge Dickens with exaggeration and most likely he would turn to Byron's Don Juan: " 'Tis strange – but true; for truth is always strange; / Stranger than fiction" (*Don Juan* canto 14, 1.101).

Edgar Johnson ranked Dickens's letters above even the best of his contemporaries, but in George Bernard Shaw's view they were limited to the concrete, the sensuous, and the immediate. In their neglect of art, philosophy, and religion, Dickens's correspondence remained "roast beef and pudding letters" (Johnson 1952: 22). If Shaw had had at his disposal the full range of correspondence, documented by the Pilgrim editors, he might have revised his opinion. To range freely among these volumes is to enter a real and fictional world of incomparable wealth and charm, an imaginative universe truly inimitable. Forster's opinion of the letters he received from Dickens in 1842 can surely serve for the entire collection as it now stands. Those particular letters, written amidst the distraction and fatigue of Dickens's first American tour, nevertheless convey an "unwearied unforced vivacity of ever fresh, buoyant, bounding animal spirits" without parallel for the quickness of observation they record, "the irresistible play of humour," and such pathos "as only humourists of this high order possess." Throughout their lifelong intercourse, Forster continues, "it was the same," true of their continuing correspondence and characteristic of their exchanges throughout most of Dickens's career. Dickens's "keenness of discrimination," Forster added, "failed him never excepting here, when it was lost in the limitless extent of his appreciation of all kindly things; and never did he receive what was meant for a benefit that he was not eager to return it a hundredfold. No man more truly generous ever lived" (Forster bk. 3, ch. 5). If the "excellence of every Art" lies in its intensity, to paraphrase Keats, another great letter-writer (December 21, 1817), then epistolary art flourishes on almost every page of this monumental collection. The 12 Pilgrim volumes are a resource without parallel in the history of letters.

NOTE

1   The accuracy of some of the details of this
    account has been recently contested (see Lewis
    2004).

References and Further Reading

Johnson, Edgar (Ed.) (1952). *The Heart of Charles Dickens.* New York: Duell, Sloan, and Pearce.

Lewis, Paul (2004). Burning the evidence. *The Dickensian*, 100, 197–208.

Lohrli, Anne (1973). *Household Words: A Weekly Journal 1850–1859 Conducted by Charles Dickens.* Toronto: University of Toronto Press.

Rollins, Hyder Edward (Ed.) (1958). *The Letters of John Keats*, 2 vols. Cambridge, MA: Harvard University Press.

Sanders, Charles Richard, Fielding, Kenneth J., Campbell, I. M., et al. (Eds.) (1970). *The Collected Letters of Thomas and Jane Welsh Carlyle.* Duke–Edinburgh Edition, vol. 1: *1812–1821.* Durham, NC: Duke University Press.

Storey, Gladys (1939). *Dickens and Daughter.* London: Muller.

4

Three Major Biographies

Catherine Peters

"Whether I shall turn out to be the hero of my own life . . . these pages must show."
Dickens gave David Copperfield, his fictional alter ego, an uncertainty he did not feel
himself. He knew it was inevitable that his biography would be written, and he was
proud of his achievements. But he was also a fiercely private man. There were things
he preferred to conceal, and by the end of his life one very big secret. How was he to
ensure that authenticity was combined with reticence?

Inaccurate, unauthorized biographical accounts appeared as soon as Dickens became
famous, and though he declared later in life that he wanted to be remembered only
by his books, he had already in the 1840s begun to consider taking charge of the
record himself. He started writing an account of his early life, a task he found
extremely painful. His wife, to whom he showed what he had written, urged him not
to publish because of his harsh criticism of his parents, still both alive. An attempt
to write about his early love for Maria Beadnell was so traumatic that he abandoned
the attempt and destroyed the manuscript. But he could not let go of the past. Much
of this material was directly quarried for *David Copperfield* and *Little Dorrit*, and other
early memories were used in his journalism. The blend of imagination and reality,
emotional truth rather than literal fact, that permeates his fiction gave him the creative freedom he needed to deal with it. The problem of controlling the biographical
record as far as he could do so remained. The task was delegated to his friend John
Forster.

Forster's massive *Life of Charles Dickens* held the field for half a century, but it could
not be the end of the story. There were many discoveries and revelations in the first
half of the twentieth century and many more biographies. The completion of the
definitive edition of Dickens's collected *Letters* has brought the total of letters known
to survive to 14,252. The quantity of information about Dickens from these and other
sources is now bewildering in its extent and complexity.

Even when there are no more facts to be discovered, biography needs to be
rewritten for each generation, as attitudes and expectations change. Biographies, like

historical novels and costume dramas, reveal the date at which they were written as much as the era they describe. The needs of readers change, too. Though critical approaches have become more sophisticated, readers now have less first-hand knowledge of Dickens's work. Few people nowadays read his journalism and short stories and even their mental picture of the novels may be gleaned from film and television adaptations. These changes of emphasis can throw new light on the subject, but the cautious reader will approach biography as critically and interpretatively as if it were a primary literary text.

The biographer is also constrained by the need to create a literary object that is the "right" length and has a shape and trajectory that will hold the reader's attention. With Dickens this should be easy, for the life story is as full of incident as a novel. But though, like any writer, he spent long hours at his desk, he did so many other things that it is dangerously easy for a biographer to give the impression that somehow the novels wrote themselves while Dickens was rehearsing his dramatic company, traveling, editing his magazines, or walking his companions off their feet. The biographer needs to keep all these activities in balance and remember that Dickens is primarily of interest to us because he was a writer of major importance.

John Forster's *Life of Charles Dickens* is the work of a personal friend but not that of an uncritical acolyte. Forster was a respected Victorian man of letters, an historian, and one of the first generation of professional biographers. The *Life* is a full-scale biography, rather than merely personal reminiscence. The American academic Edgar Johnson incorporated the many discoveries that had been made about Dickens's private life into *Charles Dickens: His Tragedy and Triumph* (1952), and also gave a fuller and more sympathetic account of Dickens's journalistic and charitable activities than Forster had done. Peter Ackroyd in *Dickens* (1990) has, as in his other books, deliberately blurred the boundaries of fiction, history, and biography. Ackroyd seeks to bring Dickens alive as a character and animate his surroundings, while also providing an accurate account of his life and giving due weight to his writing. Ackroyd's passion for the history of London and encyclopedic knowledge of the city provide a detailed backcloth to many of his scenes. Ackroyd has also written and presented a television series on Dickens, and the influence of television on the printed word is evident in his account, which is full of visual imagery. The 1999 paperback edition of his biography is still in print, the only one of the three that is easily available.

The Invisible Woman: The Story of Nelly Ternan and Charles Dickens (1990) by Claire Tomalin will be referred to more briefly. Though this is not a full-scale biography of Dickens, Tomalin's account of his relationship with the young actress Nelly Ternan tells us much about the last decade of Dickens's life. There have been a number of discoveries since Edgar Johnson's biography was published, and though Ackroyd also makes use of many of them, Tomalin's detective work goes still further. Forster, in conformity with Victorian conventions and Dickens's own wishes, suppresses all mention of Nelly Ternan.

The biographies by Forster, Johnson, and Ackroyd are all important for the study of Dickens, but each is at first sight forbidding in appearance and daunting in length.

Each is illustrated in black and white by reproductions of Victorian photographs and portraits, pictures of Dickens's homes, and illustrations from the original editions of Dickens's novels. In spite of the advances in reproductive techniques, many of the illustrations in Johnson and Ackroyd are as unattractive as those in the 1928 edition of Forster and do little to support the text. A page of small photographs of Dickens's homes in Ackroyd, for example, is not laid out in chronological order, so that there is no sense of any progression from his modest birthplace to the imposing Tavistock House. For the general reader, who does not require a comprehensive biography, a more accessible introduction to Dickens is provided by Angus Wilson's *The World of Charles Dickens* (1970). It is immediately attractive; in addition to the usual illustrations of Dickens and his family, friends, and homes, there are many full-page colored plates cleverly chosen to set Dickens's life and work in context. The main outline of Dickens's life is clearly told in only 300 pages and Wilson's comments on Dickens's personality and his writing, those of a practicing novelist, are often illuminating.

Forster's *Life*, originally published in three separate volumes in 1872, 1873, and 1874, was re-issued in one volume, with valuable notes by J. W. T. Ley, in 1928. This is the edition referred to here. Ley's notes add another layer of interpretation, itself revealing of critical attitudes in the first half of the twentieth century. Edgar Johnson's biography originally appeared in two volumes, but a one-volume abridgement was issued in 1977. Intended for the general reader, this has no bibliography or references. Much background detail has been pared away, and chapters devoted to critical analysis and assessment of individual novels, which intersperse the biographical account in the original edition, have been omitted. Ackroyd's biography is, as a physical object, even more formidable than Forster or Johnson. A single volume of 1,195 pages, its size and weight make it virtually impossible to read without a table or reading-stand.

The question of the amount and type of annotation is handled differently by each biographer. Forster's original annotation was extremely sparse. He gave no references for his sources and included only a few explanatory footnotes. Ley augmented these with a preface and endnotes, which still do not amount to full annotation. Ackroyd's biography is clearly intended for the reader who is passionate about Dickens, rather than the scholar or student. The discursive annotations to each chapter amount to supplementary essays, adding another layer of information and interpretation. However, they frustrate attempts to trace references to their sources since these are referred to only in the most general terms and are not numbered. This is compensated for, to some extent, by Ackroyd's index, which is comprehensive and intelligently compiled, making it easy to navigate his book. Johnson's meticulous and scholarly endnotes will, however, be needed by the student who wishes to pinpoint a particular source, and can be ignored by the general reader. Johnson gives note numbers in the text. Though this has become unfashionable recently, it is extremely helpful.

Forster's *Life of Charles Dickens* resulted from a long friendship which began when the two young men met at the end of 1836. They quickly became intimate and found they had much in common. They were the same age and both began their careers as outsiders who had to struggle for acceptance by the London literary establishment, similarities which created an instant bond. Both were now beginning to make their way in literary London, Forster as a literary journalist who also acted, in an unofficial capacity, as business and literary agent to older writers such as Leigh Hunt and Lamb; Dickens as a sketch writer and budding novelist.

The year 1836 had been a momentous one for Dickens. *Sketches by Boz* was published, the part-publication of *Pickwick Papers* started to appear, and he had left home and married. He was in demand as a writer and in danger of becoming overstretched; he soon realized that Forster's help could be invaluable to him. Forster became his trusted critic: he claimed to have read everything Dickens ever wrote, either in manuscript or at proof stage, and there is evidence from manuscripts and letters that many of his suggestions were adopted before publication.

Forster's cautious approach restrained Dickens; his later acute sense of what his public would stand for was developed through his relationship with Forster, and on the few occasions when he showed a lack of judgment, it was often in defiance of Forster's advice. Forster also acted as go-between in Dickens's dealings with publishers, spending much time, unpaid, on Dickens's business affairs. Ley points out in the notes to his edition of Forster that Dickens was often in the wrong in his many disputes with publishers, and that Forster's account is unduly favorable to Dickens's side of the arguments. However, these disputes were also skirmishes in the long-fought war for the "dignity of literature" with which both men were passionately concerned. This side of their relationship is dealt with fully in Forster, and though it may not enthrall the general reader, it is of great importance to the Dickens record. Forster's *Life* has been called "not merely the biography of a writer, but also the biography of each of his works" (Monod 1966: 372). Forster had trained as a lawyer, and though he never practiced, was considered to have thrown away a brilliant future as an advocate; much of this skill was channeled into his handling of Dickens's affairs. Dickens's agreement of 1841 with Chapman and Hall for *Martin Chuzzlewit*, for example, was drawn up by Forster, and is entirely in Forster's handwriting. Later, though this is not made explicit in the *Life*, Forster acted for Dickens during the separation from his wife.

It was the publication of Forster's *The Life and Adventures of Oliver Goldsmith* in 1848, dedicated to Dickens, that drew from him the first suggestion that Forster might be his biographer. Praising the book as one "conducive to the dignity of literature," Dickens continued: "I desire no better for my fame when my personal dustyness shall be past the controul of my love of order, than such a biographer and such a Critic" (*Letters* 5: 289–90).

Dickens was fortunately never to be aware that the chaotic lack of organization of Forster's *Life of Charles Dickens* is one of its worst failings. It would certainly have offended his obsessional love of order. Dickens might also have groaned over his biographer's stylistic infelicities, and would certainly have disagreed with some of Forster's comments on his activities. In the main, however, Forster's love and admiration and his discretion at awkward points in the story provided a narrative that would have satisfied him.

Dickens's trust in Forster was emphasized in 1847, with the crucial confidence to him of the shameful secret about his childhood, his father's imprisonment for bankruptcy, and his own employment in Warren's Blacking Warehouse. In January 1849, Dickens gave Forster his written account of this period of his life. This autobiographical fragment was Forster's trump card as a biographer. Dickens himself saw these events as a turning point, a trauma that had made him what he was, and Forster accepted and incorporated this interpretation into his account of Dickens's life.

Every subsequent biographer and reader of Dickens is indebted to Forster for his inclusion of this document, in defiance of Victorian prejudices. Wilkie Collins, himself overtly scornful of nineteenth-century respectability and hypocrisy, nevertheless agreed with Catherine Dickens that it should not have been published because of Dickens's criticisms of his mother. There may also have been some personal resentment in Collins's judgment. In 1856, at a time when Collins was Dickens's colleague and collaborator on plays and Christmas numbers of *Household Words*, as well as a close personal friend who had to a certain extent supplanted Forster, Dickens sent him a discreetly expurgated account of his childhood with no hint of the events Dickens found so shameful (*Letters* 8: 130–1). Collins, like all Dickens's other friends, and even his children, never knew the true story until the publication of Forster's biography.

It may surprise us now that as late as 1928 J. W. T. Ley, in his introduction to Forster's biography, believed that "nothing . . . has so grated on its readers as Dickens's references to his mother . . . It has threatened disillusionment to more people than anything else written by or about Dickens" (Forster 1928: xix). The manuscript has since disappeared, along with most of Dickens's letters to Forster and other materials used in the biography, destroyed by Forster's over-zealous literary executor. Without it, the perception of Dickens's personality would have been distorted forever.

Dickens was wary in his personal relationships, finding it difficult to be totally intimate with anyone, so his absolute trust in Forster's discretion and loyalty was remarkable, especially as they were unlike in many ways and often quarreled. After one particularly unpleasant row at Dickens's house, Dickens wrote angrily that there was "no man, alive or dead, who tries his friends as he does" (*Letters* 2: 116). Ackroyd calls the friendship "complicated and ambivalent" (1990: 207). Johnson sees it as more straightforward and the problems due chiefly to Forster's intransigence. The faults were not all on one side, however. Dickens treated Forster's pomposity and self-importance as comic material from the earliest days of their friendship, often rather disagreeably. In letter after letter to other friends, from the 1830s to the end of his life, Dickens satirized Forster's speech, behavior, and pretensions, christening him "the Mogul," mocking him as a prototype of the Victorian respectability that Dickens himself satirized in his writing. It has been suggested (Davies 1983: 174) that the pugnacious Mr. Dowler, in the number of *Pickwick Papers* published three months after their first meeting, was a caricature of Forster. There is no doubt that the character of Podsnap in *Our Mutual Friend* is closely based on Forster's appearance as well as his less-attractive mannerisms and behavior, and that it betrays, as Ackroyd points out, a considerable irritation with the forms of society that Forster was increasingly bound by at the time Dickens felt more and more alienated from them (1990: 944).

It seems inconceivable that Forster did not recognize the parody, yet he singles out the depiction of "vulgar canting Podsnap" for praise in a novel which he otherwise believed "will never rank with his higher efforts" (1928: 743). Perhaps this was a roundabout way of distancing himself from the caricature. He was well aware of Dickens's lampoons of others, and objected to them, particularly disliking the depiction of Leigh Hunt as Skimpole in *Bleak House* and feeling it necessary to excuse Dickens for his portrait of his father as Micawber.

Forster's biography is still indispensable for its first-hand, detailed evidence of Dickens's working life, as well as much personal reminiscence. Both Johnson and Ackroyd depend largely on Forster for their early chapters, though Ackroyd finds "some of it really very dull" (1990: 894). The *Life* was the target of criticism as soon as it appeared and has been attacked ever since. It aroused hostility among Dickens's other friends, who felt it gave a slanted and partial view. Forster's emphasis on the innocence of Dickens's novels "never sullied . . . by a hint of impurity" (1928: 762) was derided by some. His refusal to use the reminiscences, letters, and other materials offered him, his emphasis on his own relationship with Dickens, to the exclusion of his other friendships, was controversial at the time and does still unbalance his account. His defense, that Dickens wrote to him alone with "unexampled candour and truthfulness" (1928: 817), is to a great extent untrue. Nevertheless, Forster's presence in the narrative lends an intimacy and sense of direct access that is perhaps more attractive to a modern reader than it was at the time. When Ackroyd attempts something similar with two personal "conversations" with Dickens, this novelistic device seems artificial compared with the reality of Forster's lived experience.

Forster had a cavalier way with his sources, changing the dates and sometimes the wording of Dickens's letters to him and silently omitting sections from them. This was common nineteenth-century practice. However, it raises doubts about the accuracy of reported conversations with Dickens. Certainly, Forster's emphasis on their total, lifelong intimacy is exaggerated. Forster was undoubtedly possessive of Dickens, and the biography gave him the opportunity to enshrine his version of their relationship in the public consciousness. But that is not to say that he was always, or often, wrong about Dickens's character and personality.

The hostility of some early reviewers reveals the very different climate of opinion at the time Forster was writing. There were objections to Forster's emphasis on Dickens's undistinguished family background and early struggles and their effect on his character, and complaints that Forster had revealed Dickens as not quite a gentleman. Others objected that the portrait was idealized, and that Forster concealed Dickens's faults. In fact, Forster is not uniformly adulatory, and includes comments critical of Dickens's personality and behavior. He is acute about the streak of cruelty that coexisted with Dickens's energy. With someone who did not challenge his primacy, Dickens was the kindest and most generous of men; with Forster, belligerently ready to stand his ground, he could be the opposite. Though Forster does not relate this trait to his own relationship with Dickens, as others did, he perceptively analyzed it as a consequence of Dickens's early traumas, during which he formed "a passionate resolve, even while he was yielding to circumstances, *not to be* what circumstances were conspiring to make him" (1928: 38). Forster perceived that this resolve accounted for a vein of hardness and aggression in Dickens, a relentlessness in his creative drive and a chronic restlessness. This character analysis is broadly endorsed by Ackroyd.

Forster's strategy for dealing with difficult aspects of Dickens's life was to avoid them as much as possible. He is almost silent about Dickens's wife, as his editor Ley points out: "She is never mentioned save by way of mere record . . . not one picture has he given us of the wife and mother in her domestic circle" (Forster 1928: 680). Ley suggests that Forster's influence over Dickens was disproportionate, and that it may have caused some of the problems in the marriage by displacing Catherine Dickens from her rightful position as Dickens's confidante. Certainly, Forster's interest in appealing to Victorian taste by celebrating Dickens as a family man was in awkward conflict with his problems over portraying the marriage, knowing from the beginning that the separation of Dickens from his wife was looming ahead of him as he wrote. His necessary, if distorted, solution was to include the barest possible references to Catherine Dickens, and very few to the Dickens children, so removing much that was of great importance to Dickens.

This may not have been only for reasons of discretion. Throughout the biography, Forster has difficulty in appreciating the centrality of Dickens's emotional and sexual life. Perhaps there was a hint of jealousy in this. Forster's possessiveness about his friends, Dickens in particular, was legendary. Also, though he was highly gregarious, affectionate to his many friends and fond of their children, his emotional life was lived at a lower level of intensity than Dickens's, and Dickens and his other friends were astonished when Forster made a late, childless marriage with a rich widow. He refused to believe the depth of Dickens's first love for Maria Beadnell, and the humiliation he felt at his rejection, dismissing it as puppy love. Dickens complained, in a letter Forster quotes, "I don't quite apprehend what you mean by my over-rating the strength of feeling . . . it excluded every other idea from my mind for four years" (*Letters* 7: 556–7). Though Forster gives, without comment, a reasonably full account of Dickens's grief at the death of his sister-in-law, Mary Hogarth, he provides no hint of his temporary infatuation with Christiana Weller, and does not mention the strange episode with the hysteric Mme. De La Rue, which caused severe problems in the Dickens marriage and has proved a fruitful hunting ground for psychological interpretation by later biographers. Dickens's obsessional passion for Ellen Ternan is inevitably wiped from the record.

The circumstances in which Forster wrote his biography need to be taken into account. After Dickens's sudden death in 1870, Forster had to take on the burden of being his literary executor and the trustee of his will. He was already a sick man – he died in 1876 – and the thought of writing the biography was almost too much for him. "This book hangs over me now like a nightmare" he wrote to Carlyle (Davies 1983: 249). He knew he could not leave the field clear for too long, as others were jumping in with accounts of Dickens's life very soon after his death. He had already struggled, not very successfully, with a life of his friend Walter Savage Landor. Offers of materials for his life of Dickens poured in, overwhelming him. Forster's decision to use only Dickens's letters to him, and materials in the possession of Georgina Hogarth, becomes more forgivable when these circumstances are taken into account.

For the early years, Forster also used first-hand information volunteered by Dickens's schoolfellows, early friends, and family servants. His first volume, which appeared in 1872, is by far the best, an invaluable account of Dickens's life to 1842. Its liveliness comes in part from lavish quotation from *David Copperfield, Sketches by Boz*, and *The Uncommercial Traveller*, as well as the autobiographical fragment. Forster gives less detail about Dickens's ancestry and family background than later biographers. Relying on Dickens's own impressions, Forster portrays the household in the earliest years of the writer's childhood as relatively untroubled. We now know that John Dickens was in financial difficulties throughout his life. Forster's account of the family's desperate financial situation after their move to London, followed by John Dickens's bankruptcy and imprisonment, therefore bursts on the reader as an unexpected catastrophe, lending it more dramatic force than the greater accuracy of later biographers.

Forster's difficulty with organizing a linear account of Dickens's adult life, his multifarious activities and frequent trips abroad, mirrored his problems with Dickens himself. The reader trying to follow as Forster rushes ahead with one part of the story, only to double back in the chronology to fill in another aspect, gets the impression of an elephant lumbering after a greyhound. This is particularly obvious when Dickens was abroad and Forster is relying on his letters for information, but the second and third volumes of the biography suffered also from the pressure on Forster to publish and the lack of input from other sources that he imposed on himself. As the volumes were published singly, public criticisms of each induced him to double back with justifications of his earlier statements, adding to the confusion.

Forster not only refused the testimony of Dickens's other close friends, he did his best to minimize their appearance in his biography. It is noticeable that friends who were dead by the time he was writing, such as Daniel Maclise and Sergeant Talfourd, get warmer notice than those still alive.

He was jealous of Dickens's important friendship with Angela Burdett Coutts, which had its origin even before his own meeting with Dickens. He also felt the time and energy that Dickens expended during the 1850s in helping her with her charitable enterprises, in particular the foundation and running of her home for rehabilitating former prostitutes and women prisoners, took him away from his proper profession. Dickens's relationship with Miss Coutts and his day-to-day involvement in every aspect of Urania Cottage is dismissed in one sentence, and not one of his more than

500 letters to her is referred to. The friendship with Wilkie Collins, Dickens's constant companion and literary collaborator who supplanted Forster to a great extent
during the 1850s and 1860s, is also mentioned as seldom as possible. Forster was
jealous of Collins's easy-going friendship with Dickens, but he may also have feared
that Dickens's reputation would be tarnished by association with the notoriously
loose-living Collins. Consequently, though early theatrical productions by Dickens's
amateur company, in which Forster took part, are described in some detail, later ones,
collaborations between Collins and Dickens, are censured as a waste of time. Forster
was also vehemently against Dickens's reading tours, and gives characteristic
reasons:

> It was a substitution of lower for higher aims; a change to commonplace from more
> elevated pursuits; and it had so much of the character of a public exhibition for money
> as to raise, in the question of respect for his calling as a writer, a question also of respect
> for himself as a gentleman. (1928: 641)

Yet despite all its faults and omissions, Forster's biography did seek to tell the
truth about the essential Dickens as he saw him. He included their disagreements,
and published sections of Dickens's letters defending his own behavior against
Forster's criticisms. By his generous quotations from Dickens's letters, published
writings, and reported conversations, he gave an impression of "the Inimitable," the
originality of Dickens's personality and imagination. There is a noticeable drop in
pace in those sections where the Mogul's narrative style is not lightened by quotation
from Dickens.

Forster acknowledged that Dickens the man and the novelist were all of a piece
but mostly treats them separately, giving no consideration to the effect Dickens's
other activities had on his work, except in the obvious instances when Dickens uses
an actual event or parodies an actual person. He had no time for other critics of
Dickens's novels, savagely attacking a significant article by G. H. Lewes (Forster 1928:
716) and dismissing the views of Hyppolite Taine. He confines his own discussion to
the novels, barely mentioning the later journalism, and shaping Dickens's literary
career as a parabola. In Forster's account, Dickens, tempered in the fire of his early
traumas, rose rapidly to early triumphs, continued throughout his middle period less
spectacularly but still on a rising curve, only to fall back to earth gradually in the
1850s, more rapidly in his final decade, as he dissipated his energies in other
activities.

Forster's judgments on the novels have been dismissed by Edgar Johnson, who
found in them "very little that seems to me either truly incisive or truly profound"
(Johnson et al. 1962: 32). Yet Forster's critical opinions are interesting for what they
reveal of the Victorian climate of opinion, and generally worthy of more attention
than Johnson suggests. Forster liked Dickens's writing best when it was most picaresque, taking its origin from the eighteenth-century novels both men loved. He
sees "humour," using the term in a now obsolete sense, as Dickens's predominant

characteristic. Consequently, he is enthusiastic about *Pickwick Papers, Nicholas Nick-leby,* and *Martin Chuzzlewit,* which he thought one of Dickens's greatest achievements (1928: 723). He writes of *Nickleby* that it established Dickens's mastery of dialogue, "that power of making characters real existences, not by describing them but by letting them describe themselves" (1928: 722). He also admired *David Copperfield,* but his distaste for *Bleak House* – "a book in which some want of all the freshness of his genius first became apparent" (1928: 562) – signals his lack of sympathy with the later novels now valued as Dickens's most profound. Forster admired the construction of the novel, but found it too insistently didactic, and criticized the "disagreeable and sordid" characters as "much too real to be pleasant" (1928: 561). He also undervalued *Little Dorrit,* in common with the reviewers who found in it evidence of Dickens's decline, damning it with the faint praise that the "humour and satire of its finer parts [are] not unworthy of him," while concluding that the novel "made no material addi-tion to his reputation" (1928: 627), a judgment that was completely reversed in the twentieth century.

Edgar Johnson bases his interpretation of Dickens's character and achievement on a tension between his public success and a deep personal dissatisfaction: "[His life's] tragedy grows out of the way in which the powers that enabled him to overcome the obstacles before him contained also the seeds of his unhappiness. Its triumph is that his inward misery stimulated his powers to that culminating achievement of his work" (Johnson 1952: 1. 51). This theme of an outer and inner life, running in parallel but not in harmony, may seem a little too neat to present-day readers. Johnson, writing when Freudian theory dominated biographical interpretation, attributes virtually everything in Dickens's psychological make-up to the events of his childhood and adolescence. Freudian literary theory can still be traced in Ackroyd's speculation that Dickens suffered all his life from "some guilt of an inexplicable kind" (1990: 830), perhaps stemming from an Oedipal conflict with his father for possession of his mother or from a desire to kill his younger siblings, inducing lifelong guilt when the child next to him in age died at six months. Ackroyd acknowledges that there can be no proof for this interpretation.

More fruitfully, Ackroyd also points out the many ways in which Dickens resem-bled his father. There are elements in Dickens's make-up that seem a less florid version of John Dickens's alternations of grandiose over-spending and suicidal despair so elo-quently described in Dickens's own accounts, both in the characters based on him in the novels, most obviously Micawber, and in his often exasperated letters and the autobiographical fragment. Though none of Dickens's biographers says so, it now seems clear that John Dickens suffered from affective disorder, or "manic depression." Recent work on the strongly genetic basis of this illness, with its alternating mood-swings, expansiveness, and extravagance, succeeded by suicidal depression, and its prevalence in creative people (Jamison 1993), suggest an additional reason both for Dickens's manic energy and for his recurrent restless misery. His symptoms differed from his father's – he was not recklessly spendthrift or overtly suicidal – but this condition, added to the effects of early trauma, would account for much in Dickens's behavior. Ackroyd describes his personality as "highly strung and mercurial" (1990: 828), but attributes this to a fear of failure rather than an inborn personality trait.

Edgar Johnson is not an especially stylish writer, and the tone of his book has dated more obviously than Angus Wilson's less-comprehensive study. However, his biography is still useful. His research was thorough, though necessarily limited to the materials available at the time he was writing, especially the inaccurate and incomplete collections of Dickens's letters. Johnson's omissions and errors of fact are mostly insignificant, though his use of the nineteenth-century medical terms employed by Dickens himself is a minor irritant. Johnson shows caution by not attempting to reinterpret symptoms, but this strategy is not very informative. In contrast, Ackroyd persuasively diagnoses medical symptoms in the light of later scientific knowledge.

Johnson's errors of judgment are more serious. Often these arise from a too-complete identification with Dickens, sometimes from reliance on Forster. He misunderstands the relationship between Dickens and Wilkie Collins, for example, underrating Collins and not noting that Dickens appreciated him as a serious craftsman and literary colleague as well as a convivial companion. His assessment of the deteriorating relationship of Dickens and his wife is heavily biased in favor of Dickens to a degree which becomes misogynistic in tone. Here Ackroyd supplies a necessary corrective, and Claire Tomalin's careful analysis of the whole affair, taking into account the point of view of the women involved, goes even further to restore balance. It is a general failing of Johnson's biography that he assumes that Dickens always tells the truth in his letters. He is also more inclined than either Forster or Ackroyd to assume that Dickens's life is evident in his fiction.

In his early chapters, Johnson's reliance on Forster is augmented by details from other sources, and he goes into the family backgrounds of Dickens's parents more thoroughly and accurately. There is some rather obvious scene-setting in the early chapters: Johnson refers to public events that would have had no impact on Dickens's childhood, in contrast to Ackroyd's vivid evocation of the things and places that Dickens actually saw. This tendency disappears as Dickens's world widens out.

In spite of his reliance on Forster when discussing the childhood years, Johnson does attempt to keep more distance from Dickens. Though he uses Dickens's own writings in the early chapters as extensively as Forster, he also adopts wholesale (and without acknowledgment) J. W. T. Ley's note to Forster's account of the blacking warehouse episode, which mounts a defense of Dickens's parents (Forster 1928: 17) and points out the subjectivity of Dickens's account, while not attempting to minimize the effect on him.

In later chapters, Johnson, freed from the constraints Forster imposed on himself, can be open about Dickens's relationship with his parents and siblings, showing how the burden imposed on him by their feckless ways was a constant source of irritation in adulthood. More importantly, he understands the importance to Dickens of his affective life. His relationship with his sister Fanny, his love for Maria Beadnell, his adoration of Mary Hogarth and his grief at her early death are all given due weight. The marriage and Dickens's family life are fully covered, though Johnson's emphases are sometimes questionable. Johnson takes Dickens's testimony on the role of Georgina Hogarth in the upbringing of the children at face value, and dismisses the role of Catherine Dickens in their lives in almost as cavalier a fashion as Dickens himself. He seldom questions Dickens's self-awareness, in contrast to Ackroyd who sees Dickens not exactly as a liar, but as having a fluid concept of the truth: "he actually believed what he wrote as he wrote it" (1990: 811).

Johnson's belief in the truth of Dickens's account of his unhappiness over Maria Beadnell leads him to the conclusion that the attachment had a profound and lasting effect on his life and work as a reinforcement of the earlier "suffering of helplessness and of undeserved humiliation" (1952: 1. 81), affecting both his use of humor to defuse pain and his sympathy with suffering in his work, and the private bitterness that Johnson detects throughout his years of triumph. Ackroyd sees in Dickens's letters to Maria "a genuinely theatrical display of feeling" (1990: 143), and the oxymoron perhaps comes closer than Forster's skepticism or Johnson's belief to elucidating Dickens's emotional state. Johnson also sees cracks in Dickens's marriage from the beginning, believing Dickens's later insistence in a letter, which Forster published in his biography, that there had been problems since the birth of his second child.

Johnson's account of Dickens's tortuous disagreements with his publishers is clear and balanced. In the long dispute with Richard Bentley, he grants that "it is impossible not to sympathize" with the publisher, who had the law on his side. Dickens, however, "had no case [but] he did have a grievance" (1952: 1. 252), the grievance being the author's perennial complaint that he does the work while the publisher makes the profit. Johnson sees Dickens's victory over Bentley as crucial in the final formation of his implacable will: "Never, from the time of his struggle with Bentley, did Dickens surrender in the smallest point to any antagonist" (1952: 1. 253). He also covers the later quarrel with Bradbury and Evans, omitted by Forster because it related to the separation and the controversial publication of Dickens's "Statement" about it.

Edgar Johnson proclaims in his Preface his "constant endeavor . . . to integrate literary interpretation and life interpretation: to make the critical discussion of Dickens's work illumine his personality and the portrayal of his character clarify his literary achievement" (1952: 1. x), a passage omitted in the paperback abridgement of his biography. This "life and works" approach has become problematic in the generation since Johnson's biography was published, and as Johnson's own literary judgments tend to substitute enthusiasm for critical rigor, the abridgement suffers very little from their omission. Johnson's detachable chapters of literary criticism are the sections of his book that have most obviously dated. He is innocent of literary theory, and his method is to take the novels one or two to a chapter in chronological sequence, explain the social and historical background and Dickens's aims and intentions, rapidly sketching in the outlines of plot and characterization and giving a verdict on each. *Barnaby Rudge* is "the least satisfactory of all Dickens's books" (1952: 1. 330); with *Pickwick Papers* "he invented the realist fairy tale" (1. 174). He usefully points out the many resemblances to folk tale and fairy story, but adjectival enthusiasm too often substitutes for critical thought. Johnson loves Dickens's writing, but does not analyze in any depth how Dickens arrives at his effects.

Johnson reads Dickens as driven by his own experiences and observations to create "a critical analysis of modern society and its problems" (1. viii). Ackroyd, while acknowledging Dickens's social purpose, is more interested in the use he made of it as a literary craftsman, citing his often detailed and technical criticisms of the writings of others. "He never was the jovial improviser and story-teller of the Pickwickian tradition; he was a clever and artful writer who always knew exactly what he was doing" (Ackroyd 1990: 465). Where Johnson provides a readable narrative, with some redundancies and repetitions, Ackroyd attempts, with considerably more daring, to approach Dickens at times through an act of impersonation, alternating passages of straightforward narrative with short, often verbless sentences that echo Dickens at his most histrionic. Not every reader will enjoy this method, particularly noticeable in the early chapters where narrative necessarily takes precedence over interpretation. Later in his book, Ackroyd tells an imaginary interlocutor that he was worried about the opening chapters: "family ties and early childhood are the two most boring elements in anyone's life" (1990: 894), a surprising verdict on Dickens's eventful childhood.

Richard Holmes, one of the best contemporary biographers and writers on the art of literary biography, has written of the imperative need first to identify with the subject as closely as possible, and then to step back from that intimacy to achieve distance (Holmes 1985). Ackroyd attempts and largely achieves this. In his opening chapter, he rightly emphasizes how hard it is to recapture the world Dickens was born into; that it looked different, smelled different, sounded different. The theme of difference is present throughout *Dickens*. The apparently omniscient biographer of the 1950s has been replaced by the searcher on an impossible but endlessly fascinating quest. Ackroyd is always scrupulous in reminding the reader of the inconclusive and open-ended nature of biography, proceeding by questions as often as by statements. His writing is also intensely visual. He gives us vignettes of Dickens which remain in the memory: Dickens hunting down a ghost with a double-barreled shotgun; Dickens exulting at being recognized in the street; Dickens, who was obsessional about cleanliness, using his work "as if it were some shower-bath of the spirit" (1990: 712).

Like Dickens himself, Ackroyd is looking always for the lively example, the telling phrase. Describing Dickens's 1842 visit to America, Forster and Johnson record the attacks on him in the American press and, as a separate issue, Dickens's distaste for the American habit of spitting. Ackroyd links the two: Dickens's distaste is "almost as if he believed they were spitting at him" (1990: 355). Forster's account of Dickens's 1842 visit to America assumes his reader's familiarity with *American Notes* and quotes extensively from Dickens's letters. Johnson is more knowledgeable than either Forster or Ackroyd on the American political background and the extent of Dickens's acute observation and occasional misunderstandings. Ackroyd gives his readers more of a sense of the strangeness of America in the 1840s to an English traveler. A comparison of the details that Johnson and Ackroyd select from Dickens's letters from his travels in America and Europe would furnish material for an essay in itself.

The final period of Dickens's life is handled in very different fashion by the three biographers. Forster was in full possession of the facts and determined to conceal them. Johnson was writing before the most recent research into the details of Dickens's relationship with the young actress Nelly Ternan had been published, and though he includes a general outline of the affair, his emphasis is on the failure of Dickens's marriage as a foregone conclusion. Johnson, with a general belief in Dickens's account, calls his behavior at the time of the separation "unhappy and hysterical." He believes that the separation was wholly caused by the gossiping of the Hogarths, as Dickens claimed. Johnson's judgment that Dickens's own behavior had not been "altogether stainless" (1952: 2. 925) is as far as he goes to condemn him.

Ackroyd's interpretation is more complex, and more convincing. He writes:

> part of the reason for his extraordinary, in some ways inexplicable, behaviour . . . [was] that he had lost control of events – a situation almost unique in his life, and one with which he really did not know how to deal . . . in a sense he was reliving his childhood nightmares even as he was in the act of breaking up his own home. (1990: 810–11)

While Ackroyd makes fewer excuses for the way Dickens treated his wife and children at the time of the separation than Johnson, Claire Tomalin's careful detective work gives an even harsher picture. Dickens emerges from it not as the hero of his life but at times more like one of his own unfeeling villains. Tomalin points out that it was not only his wife who suffered. In the year of the separation, his three sons at school in Boulogne, the youngest only eight, were not brought home for Christmas. The school was not Dotheboys Hall, but, like the neglected children of his novels, his young sons were suddenly and bewilderingly marginalized.

Tomalin is also more realistic in her account of Dickens's relationship with Nelly Ternan than previous biographers. Though Ackroyd includes the evidence of revelations published after Johnson's biography had appeared, he then denies their conclusions by striving to convince the reader of his hypothesis that the relationship, which lasted 13 years, was never consummated. The evidence produced by Claire Tomalin points definitively in the other direction. With great skill, she deciphers and interprets the cryptic entries in Dickens's diary for 1867, thought by Ackroyd to be inconclusive. She also tracks Dickens's movements and unexplained disappearances throughout the 1860s and clears up many mysteries. While agreeing with Ackroyd that Dickens betrayed a strong sense of guilt during his last decade, she does not attribute this to some lifelong Freudian guilt complex, but straightforwardly to his feelings about his treatment of Nelly Ternan and the effect it was having on her life. Tomalin also strengthens her case by tracing Nelly Ternan's life after Dickens's death, when her expressed remorse and shame about her relationship with Dickens suggest the obvious interpretation.

Ackroyd, who writes that he felt "obliged to include" literary criticism (1990: 892) is, in spite of his doubts, a good and perceptive critic whose literary judgment is more sophisticated and more original than that of either Johnson or Forster. He knows Dickens's journalism intimately, and makes excellent use of it, showing how the research done by Dickens himself and others for articles in *Household Words* fed directly into the fiction. Less concerned than Johnson to cover every aspect of every novel fully, still less to pass verdicts on them, he seeks instead, in both narrative and criticism "to find in a day, a moment, a passing image or gesture, the very spring and source of [Dickens's] creativity" (1990: xvi). So he notes of *Nicholas Nickleby*, dedicated to the actor Macready, the obvious fact that "everything about it has the feel of the theatre" (1990: 283) but goes on to show how Dickens, with characteristic doubleness, is satirizing the theater even as he celebrates it. In his critique of *Bleak House*, Ackroyd, like every commentator, examines the use of issues of the day, but also, with more originality, traces how one idea or image gives rise to another to create the theme of interconnectedness that is at the heart of the novel. He is aware, for example, as few critics would be, of such obscure facts as a hold in boxing being known as "in Chancery" (1990: 640).

Both in narrative and interpretation, Ackroyd fulfills his aim of portraying the essential strangeness and originality of Dickens's imagination. He gives a clearer picture than Johnson of the split in Dickens's personality, first noted by Forster; the almost Flaubertian chill that accompanied his ebullience, generosity, and compassion. He makes use of the mass of information now available about the facts of Dickens's life, while remaining aware that some things will never be known. One may disagree with some of Ackroyd's interpretations and conclusions, but the reader will have been held by his narrative skill. No doubt there will be many more biographical interpretations of Dickens, but Ackroyd's portrait is, for the moment, a compelling one of a man both unique and yet very much of his time.

REFERENCES AND FURTHER READING

Ackroyd, Peter (1990). *Dickens*. London: Sinclair-Stevenson (paperback edn., London: Vintage, 1999).

Davies, James A. (1983). *John Forster: A Literary Life*. Leicester: Leicester University Press.

Forster, John (1928). *The Life of Charles Dickens*. (J. W. T Ley, Ed.). London: Cecil Palmer.

Holmes, Richard (1985). *Footsteps: Adventures of a Romantic Biographer*. London: Hodder and Stoughton.

Jamison, K. R. (1993) *Touched with Fire: Manic-depressive Illness and the Artistic Temperament*. New York: Free Press.

Johnson, Edgar (1952). *Charles Dickens: His Tragedy and Triumph*, 2 vols. New York: Simon and Schuster (abridged and revised edn., New York: Viking, 1977).

—, Ford, George H., Miller, J. Hillis, et al. (1962). *Dickens Criticism, Past, Present and Future Directions: A Symposium*. Boston: Charles Dickens Reference Center.

Monod, Sylvère (1966). John Forster's "Life of Dickens" and literary criticism. *English Studies Today*, 4th series (pp. 357–73). Rome: Edizioni di Storia e Letteratura.

Tomalin, Claire (1990). *The Invisible Woman: The Story of Nelly Ternan and Charles Dickens*. London: Viking.

Wilson, Angus (1970). *The World of Charles Dickens*. London: Secker and Warburg.

Part II
Literary/Cultural Contexts

5

The Eighteenth-century Legacy

Monika Fludernik

Dickens's familiarity with the eighteenth-century novel, especially with Defoe, Field-ing, Sterne, Smollett, and Goldsmith, has been a commonplace in Dickens criticism for a long time and rests on autobiographical evidence (Forster bk. 1, ch. 1; *David Copperfield* ch. 4):

> My father had left a small collection of books in a little room up-stairs, to which I had access (for it adjoined my own) and which nobody else in our house ever troubled. From that blessed little room, Roderick Random, Peregrine Pickle, Humphrey [*sic*] Clinker, Tom Jones, The Vicar of Wakefield, Don Quixote, Gil Blas, and Robinson Crusoe, came out, a glorious host, to keep me company. They kept alive my fancy, and my hope of something beyond that place and time, – they, and the Arabian Nights and the Tales of the Genii, – and did me no harm; for whatever harm was in some of them was not there for me. *I* knew nothing of it . . . I have been Tom Jones (a child's Tom Jones, a harmless creature) for a week together. I have sustained my own idea of Roderick Random for a month at a stretch, I verily believe . . . This was my only and my constant comfort.

In addition to this allegedly autobiographical summary of Dickens's own reading, obvious affinities between the (especially early) work of Dickens and the texture of much canonical eighteenth-century literature have been noted, already "continually" by Dickens's reviewers (*Oxford Dickens* 413). To pose the question of Dickens's debt to the eighteenth-century novel today, however, requires a new look at this question. In this chapter, the issue of the eighteenth-century legacy in Dickens's work will be discussed from two perspectives. On the one hand, the eighteenth-century novel is no longer what it was taken to be some 20 or 30 years ago. Recent criticism has sig-nificantly rewritten the history of eighteenth-century fiction, revising our image of the major novelists, as well as adding to the canon and increasingly disregarding some formerly central authors. On the other hand, looking at eighteenth-century texts and Dickens from the perspective of the later development of the novel also helps to put some aspects of Dickens's texts into focus which have perhaps received insufficient attention so far.

Despite emphasis on these two perspectives, I do not, however, pretend to champion a radically new vision of Dickens's debt to the eighteenth-century novel, but perhaps hope to provide a more balanced view of Dickens's relation to the eighteenth century, especially by querying the unity of "a" or "the" eighteenth-century novel and by demonstrating that Dickens's models were perhaps more diverse than is generally assumed. Since my theoretical background is in narrative theory, I will also use my expertise in this area to analyze in greater detail where Dickens adapted and developed eighteenth-century techniques of writing and where he departed from the eighteenth-century tradition.

"The" Eighteenth-century Novel: Revisions of the Canon

Traditional histories of eighteenth-century fiction treat the eighteenth century as equivalent to the output of five or six major novelists: Swift, Defoe, Fielding, Richardson, Sterne, and Smollett. Depending on taste and inclination, some critics also add Johnson, Goldsmith, Frances Burney, and Jane Austen. Since Dickens allegedly had been influenced by these very authors (with the exception of Austen), the fact that Dickens was dominated by the writing of the previous century seems a foregone conclusion.

However, recent developments in eighteenth-century studies have significantly revised previous representations of "the" eighteenth-century novel. Although Defoe, Fielding, Sterne, and Richardson continue to be regarded as touchstones of the rise of the novel, Swift and Smollett no longer retain general appreciation. In John Richetti's *Columbia History of the British Novel* (1994), for instance, Swift and Smollett are discussed in one chapter on "The Satirical Tradition in Prose Narrative," whereas Defoe, Fielding, Richardson, and Sterne each get a chapter to themselves. Moreover, there are four additional chapters on amatory fiction (Behn, Manley, Haywood), the sentimental novel, the Gothic novel, and the radical novel of the 1790s, and a chapter each on Burney and Austen. *The Columbia History of the British Novel* reflects the revolution in eighteenth-century studies and literary theory by devoting three chapters to women novelists and the "rise of the woman novelist," as Kristine Straub calls her chapter on Burney. It also canonizes not merely the Gothic novel (which had been semi-canonical but, like Austen, very late in the eighteenth century and therefore beyond the focus of the core eighteenth century from the 1710s to 1770s), but the sentimental novel, also significantly linked to women writers – the first sentimental novel is Sarah Fielding's *David Simple* (1744) – and the political novels of Wollstonecraft, Godwin, Holcroft, Bage, and Opie at the turn of the century. Richetti moreover reflects the extension of the period into the "long eighteenth century" (Baines 2004), which starts with the Restoration and sometimes continues into the early nineteenth century.

Another recent study of eighteenth-century fiction, John Skinner's *Introduction to Eighteenth-century Fiction: Raising the Novel* (2001), likewise displaces some of the former canonical authors and proposes new patterns. Skinner treats only Richardson and Fielding in separate chapters. Defoe is paired with Aphra Behn; Sterne with Smollett; Lennox with Burney; Radcliffe with Godwin; Austen, again, gets a chapter to herself. Current revisions of eighteenth-century literary history, moreover, tend to marginalize the opposition between Richardson and Fielding in terms of the clockwork metaphor (Richardson as the man who "knew how a watch was made" and Fielding as merely reading off the "dial-plate": Boswell 1934: 2. 49). Although Fielding's and Richardson's work are still treated as being very different in tone and purport, the rather derogatory image of Fielding as a "superficial observer" in contrast with Richardson, who supposedly – like God Almighty – knows the workings of the characters' secret clockwork of emotions and motives, has become obsolete. (In fact, Boswell already dissented from Johnson's views, praising Fielding for "cherish[ing] the benevolent and generous affections.") Not only are Fielding and Richardson nowadays contrasted more regularly in terms of gender – Richardson has become an "honorary" female writer (Scheuermann 2002) – readers also seem to find Fielding's satire and humor more appealing than Richardson's excessive morality, emotionality, and ideological outlook.

More importantly, it is actually incorrect to describe Fielding's narrator as only reading off the dial-plate, presenting characters' minds with a broad brush. Fielding's narrator is not *unable* to look into the minds of his characters; often he is simply not interested in doing so since the plot is more important than the characters' consciousness. When Fielding wishes to do so, he allows his narrator extensive insights into the motives (mostly negative) of figures like Blifil or Thwackum.

> Though the violence of his [Lord Fellamar's] passion had made him eagerly embrace the first hint of this design, especially as it came from a relation of the lady, yet when that friend to reflection, a pillow, had placed the action itself in all its natural black colours before his eyes, with all the consequences which must and those which might probably attend it, his resolution began to abate, or rather indeed to go over to the other side; and after a long conflict, which lasted a whole night, between honour and appetite, the former at length prevailed, and he determined to wait on Lady Bellaston, and to relinquish the design. (*Tom Jones* bk. 15, ch. 3)

Compare this with the following passage from *Little Dorrit*:

> What with these ghostly apprehensions and her singular dreams, Mrs. Flintwinch fell that evening into a haunted state of mind, from which it may be long before this present narrative descries any trace of her recovery. In the vagueness and indistinctness of all her new experiences and perceptions, as everything about her was mysterious to herself she began to be mysterious to others: and became as difficult to be made out to anybody's satisfaction as she found the house and everything in it difficult to make out to her own. (bk. 1, ch. 15)

Dickens, in fact, is better at descriptions of perception than the laying out of characters' motives. Nevertheless, George Eliot's derogatory remarks on Dickens's alleged inability to provide "psychological character," to move "from the humorous and external to the emotional and tragic" (quoted in Sanders 1999: 183–4), a criticism in the dial-plate line of argument, fail to do justice to the true virtues of Dickens's character portrayal. Since Dickens's work combines the sentimental (Richardson) and the satirical (Fielding) traditions, the stark dichotomy between dial-plate and clockwork somewhat loses its conceptual relevance.

In this framework, the works that Dickens relied on as models begin to look fairly conservative and decidedly "male." In his formative years, Dickens seems to have been little affected by the work of women writers; his father's gentleman's library apparently included a selection of novels fit mainly for male taste. Widening one's horizon to take in other eighteenth-century texts also helps to foreground the importance of sentimental fiction for Dickens. Dickens's sentimentalism has, of course, been a noted feature of his work and one that especially feminist critics deplore. Noting that the sentimentalist tradition is a forum for many female writers, however, allows one to see Dickens's dependence on sentimental models in a more positive perspective.

It is, moreover, quite important to look at Goldsmith's *The Vicar of Wakefield* (1766) for an evaluation of Dickens's inspirations in the sentimentalist mode. Goldsmith's popular book combines in ideal manner a moralistic (and religious) worldview, an emphasis on the benefits of work, an extensive illustration of the workings of benevolence and sentiment, and a satiric debunking of pride, vainglory, hypocrisy, and sexual license. Although Smollett and Sterne may be the sources for Dickens's eccentric characters ("two pounds of Smollett, three ounces of Sterne," as the *Athenaeum* reviewer of *Pickwick Papers* put it [quoted in Robison 1970: 258]), and Fielding could arguably have influenced Dickens's humor and his predilection for the figure of the good-natured young man (Oliver Twist, Nicholas Nickleby, all the way to Pip), Goldsmith's novel seems even more important as a model since it combines several of the characteristics of Dickens's novelistic oeuvre in comparable proportion. In particular, Goldsmith, like Dickens, steered clear of typical eighteenth-century licentiousness in plot and diction, criticizing the rake figure rather than vicariously involving the reader in the hero's sowing of wild oats. The vicar's slightly ridiculous naivety and lack of commonsense shrewdness prefigures Mr. Pickwick's helplessness, just as his concern for his parishioners and fellow-prisoners reminds one of the benevolence of Dickens's eccentric well-doers like Mr. Pickwick, Mr. Jarndyce, or Mr. Meagles.

Finally, the recent importance of the radical novel helps to remind one of Dickens's debt to Godwin's work, which may have served as a model for Dickens's social criticism and for the Gothic element in Dickens (Dickens was, of course, also influenced by Poe). Godwin may additionally be one of the sources for Dickens's extensive deployment of prison settings and prison metaphors.

In what follows, I would like to provide a description of typical features (a) that Dickens shares with eighteenth-century novels; (b) that Dickens fails to take over from eighteenth-century fiction; and (c) that are new in Dickens.

Inductive Comparisons: Dickens and his Predecessors

As has been pointed out (Turner in *Oxford Dickens*; Small 2004), Dickens's early fiction is frequently cast in the picaresque mode. Dickens's first works developed out of the sketch tradition (Schor 1999: 325); his predilection for rambling plot structures is evident not only in *The Pickwick Papers* but equally in *Nicholas Nickleby* and *Martin Chuzzlewit*. Since Dickens was an avid reader of travelogues (Collins 1963: 146), and travel is a key ingredient of the eighteenth-century picaresque in *Joseph Andrews*, *Tom Jones*, *Peregrine Pickle*, and *Humphry Clinker*, personal taste and literary models both seem to have predisposed Dickens toward episodic narrative.

A second obvious characteristic of Dickens's fiction concerns the prevalence of quirky, eccentric, or splenetic figures. Dickens is famous for Mr. Quilp, Mr. Micawber, Sam Weller, Flora Finching, and Mrs. Gamp, and a host of other memorable whimsical, capricious, freakish, and fantastical characters. These clearly have antecedents in Lawrence Sterne and Tobias Smollett. Sterne's Uncle Toby (*Tristram Shandy*) and Smollett's Commodore Trunnion (*Peregrine Pickle*), moreover, share the typically Dickensian combination of oddity and a good heart. Similarly, some of the most negative characters in both Fielding and Dickens are hypocrites (compare Blifil with Uriah Heep). Real villains and criminals (Quilp, Rigaud, Mlle. Hortense, Heyling, the "queer client" in *Pickwick Papers*) are often grotesques (Quilp) or driven by invincible passion (Mlle. Hortense); they elicit much less disgust than, say, Heep.

Dickens's adoption of the satirical mode so common in eighteenth-century fiction likewise points to his reliance on eighteenth-century models. Like Fielding, Swift, Sterne, and Smollett, Dickens had an observant eye for human weaknesses, foibles, and vanities. However, his satiric portraits are never vitriolic; even Casby in *Little Dorrit*, justly punished for his extortions, remains a person whose sufferings are not entirely repressed in the text, whereas the publican's punishment of the curate in *Peregrine Pickle* is a farce that leaves little sympathy for either of the men:

The audience would have gone over to Mr. Pancks, as one man, woman, and child, but for the long, grey, silken locks, and the broad-brimmed hat . . . Quick as lightning, Mr. Pancks, who, for some moments, had had his right hand in his coat pocket, whipped out a pair of shears, swooped upon the Patriarch behind, and snipped off short the sacred locks that flowed upon his shoulders. In a paroxysm of animosity and rapidity, Mr. Pancks then caught the broad-brimmed hat out of the astounded Patriarch's hand, cut it down into a mere stewpan, and fixed it on the Patriarch's head.

Before the frightful results of this desperate action, Mr. Pancks himself recoiled in consternation. A bare-polled, goggle-eyed, big-headed lumbering personage stood staring at him, not in the least impressive, not in the least venerable, who seemed to have started out of the earth to ask what was become of Casby . . . Mr. Pancks deemed it prudent to use all possible despatch in making off, though he was pursued by nothing but the sound of laughter in Bleeding Heart Yard, rippling through the air and making it ring again. (*Little Dorrit* bk. 2, ch. 32)

The publican started at this intelligence, and under pretence of serving another company in the next room, went out to the barn, and arming himself with a flail, repaired to a lane thro' which the curate was under a necessity of passing in his way home. There he lay in ambush, with fell intent; and when the supposed author of his shame arrived, greeted him in the dark with such a salutation, as forced him to stagger backward three paces at least. If the second application had taken effect, in all probability that spot would have been the boundary of the parson's mortal peregrination; but, luckily for him, his antagonist was not expert in the management of his weapon, which, by a twist of the thong that connected the legs, instead of pitching upon the head of the astonished curate, descended in an oblique direction on his own pate, with such a swing, that the skull actually rung like an apothecary's mortar, and ten thousand lights seemed to dance before his eyes. (*Peregrine Pickle* ch. 32)

The eighteenth-century type of practical joking, on the other hand, does not figure in Dickens's work at all (Small 2004): as with eighteenth-century standards of sexual license, Dickens regarded these as in very bad taste. Compare, for instance, Peregrine's excesses in collaboration with Cadwallader with Dickens's disapproving presentation of Mr. Pickwick's kidnapping and exposure to rotten eggs in the pound (ch. 19).

One aspect of the eighteenth-century novel that Dickens developed in his social criticism is the eighteenth-century satire on governmental and bureaucratic inefficiency. Whereas Fielding and Godwin concentrated on the farcical or tragic failure of justice by focusing on juries and judges (the imprisonment of Captain Booth at the instance of Justice Thrasher: Fielding, *Amelia* bk. 1, ch. 2; see also *Pickwick Papers* ch. 25), and Smollett ridiculed the scams of "the Great Man" and his financial advisers in *Peregrine Pickle* (ch. 97), Dickens in his mature writing focused on the Court of Chancery (*Bleak House*), the Circumlocution Office (*Little Dorrit*), or on social snobbery (the Lammles in *Our Mutual Friend* as Dickens's version of "How to Live on Nothing a Year"). Smollett's portrait of election campaigns in *Peregrine Pickle* is developed even further in George Eliot's *Felix Holt* (1866) or in Trollope's *Can You Forgive Her?* (1864) and *The Way We Live Now* (1875), but these realistic and politically savvy analyses no longer share the humor and whimsicality of Dickens's predecessors. Dickens also branched out into scathing social criticism when the plight of human subjects was at issue as in his criticism of the Poor Laws in *Oliver Twist*, of the slums in *Bleak House* or of working conditions and strikes in *Hard Times*. Yet it is again institutions and their inefficient and/or hypocritical representatives that receive the brunt of the verbal attack. (This is especially noteworthy in *Hard Times*, where Bounderby rather than capitalist exploitation figures as the villain.)

Another prominent feature of Dickens's work that he shares with eighteenth-century models is his celebration of the human heart and of a sentimental attitude toward the victims of society. As Boswell already remarked in criticism of Johnson's denigration of Fielding: "He who is as good as Fielding would make him, is an amiable member of society, and may be led on . . . to a higher state of ethical perfection" (Boswell 1934: 2. 49). Benevolence is a characteristic of Dickens's most likeable characters, even when these people are also satirized for their whimsicality and foibles: Mr. Dick (*David Copperfield*) and Mr. Meagles (*Little Dorrit*) are both ultimately harmless fools with a good heart (and a fair share of self-interest). Likewise, Dickens's heroes all have sympathy for their fellow sufferers and are generous in helping others: Nicholas Nickleby, David Copperfield, and Oliver Twist share these characteristics, and Pip and Martin Chuzzlewit learn to acquire them.

The benevolent heart derives not from Fielding exclusively: it merely strikes one as prominent in Fielding because of his otherwise satirical presentation of humanity. Smollett's heroes likewise demonstrate generosity and soundness of affection (despite the occasional lapses into anger, practical joking, and sexual predatoriness), and Goldsmith and the sentimental tradition generally are, of course, steeped in benevolence and feature generous and warm-hearted heroes. Dickens can therefore be argued to have continued a tradition that predominated in eighteenth-century fiction. However, Dickens's use of sentiment emphasizes Christian virtue and active sympathy more thoroughly than is typical of the eighteenth-century sentimental novel. Sentiment in and by itself is no longer considered morally improving, and Dickens's satiric portraits of excessive sentiment must not be ignored (*Oxford Dickens* 513).

As I noted earlier, Dickens also shares a number of thematic concerns with eighteenth-century texts. Foremost among these one can mention the prison. Prison settings were common in eighteenth-century fiction. A short list of canonical texts including a prison setting would feature *Moll Flanders*, *Tom Jones*, *Amelia*, *Clarissa*, *Peregrine Pickle*, *Humphry Clinker*, *Caleb Williams*, *The Vicar of Wakefield*, *The Sentimental Journey*, and *Maria*, not to mention all the Gothic and radical novels. Dickens transformed the Newgate novel of the 1830s when writing *Oliver Twist* (Schor 1999: 328–9), but – unlike most of his contemporaries, who rarely used a prison setting (some of the exceptions are George Eliot in *Adam Bede* and *Felix Holt* and Reade's *'Tis Never too Late to Mend*) – Dickens kept returning to the debtors' prison and other (sometimes metaphorical) carceral settings throughout his career: Mr. Pickwick, Fagin, Magwitch, Mr. Dorrit, Arthur Clennam, Sydney Carton, and Barnaby Rudge all experience prison from the inside.

Clearly, Dickens had a personal reason for this obsession with carcerality, but the prison also haunted him as an aspect of his social concerns (cf. his prison journalism: Collins 1963: 148), and it seems to have been a familiar scenario from Dickens's reading. In fact, Dickens's prisons are based on the eighteenth-century model: predominantly debtors' prisons, they were no longer in existence when Dickens wrote his novels. But after *Pickwick Papers*, Dickens significantly modified the eighteenth-century tradition of writings about prisons. No longer is the prison mainly a site of sentimentality that is meant to provoke the reader's tears; no longer does it justly confine criminals under less than human conditions. Nor did Dickens produce a revival of the Newgate novel and its glorification of criminals (*Oxford Dickens* 414). Already in *Oliver Twist*, the prison acquires a nightmarish quality, one that resembles but does not actually reproduce the characteristics of the Gothic novel. Dickens knew too much about prisons to continue with the sentimentalized models used in *Sketches by Boz*. He utilized traditional modes of writing about imprisonment to probe the psychological terrors of the inmate and to analyze the stultifying and demoralizing atmosphere of incarceration. Despite Dickens's public pronouncements on pampered convicts ("Pet Prisoners" and *David Copperfield* ch. 61), Dickens had a keen sense of the cruelties of solitary confinement (*American Notes* ch. 7) and an even more uncanny understanding of the warping of prisoners' minds under continued captivity (see *Little Dorrit*).

A final thematic concern that Dickens shares with the eighteenth-century novel is his treatment of women. As has often been noted, Dickens's women are either angels of the house, who display a cloyingly sentimental vision of womanhood, or they are shrews and (sometimes lovable) monsters (Kucich 1994). The second category has received most attention: Miss Havisham and Mrs. Joe Gargery in *Great Expectations* and Miss Wade and Mrs. Clennam in *Little Dorrit* are great studies in pathology and demonstrate Dickens's uncanny grasp of human psychology. On the other hand, his heroines, Little Nell, Little Dorrit, even Agnes and Lucie Manette (*The Old Curiosity Shop*, *Little Dorrit*, *David Copperfield*, and *A Tale of Two Cities*) have proved disappointing to the twenty-first-century reader, although some critics have managed to rehabilitate Dickens's women characters, arguing "that characters sometimes regarded as insipidly feminine, like Esther Summerson and Little Dorrit, are psychologically more subtle than they may at first appear" (*Oxford Dickens* 132). In particular, Dickens suggests a complex underlying psychology for his women, whose external blandness belies their subtle mental makeup. With the help of Freud, repressions and unacknowledged desires emerge from between the lines, as can be seen in the figure of Esther Summerson.

A comparison with the eighteenth-century novel shows that here, too, Dickens may have relied on proven models, though clearly not on Defoe, Richardson, or Wollstonecraft. Fielding's Sophia and Amelia, and Smollett's Emilia (*Peregrine Pickle*), despite some interim sauciness and initiative, clearly cannot compete with the vivacity and interest of the picaresque hero. Even the sentimental novel does not usually grant much agency or intelligence to the virtue-in-distress figure (in contrast to the Gothic novel). It is significant that Dickens only read Austen late in life, if at all (*Oxford Dickens* 414); her oeuvre would have been a model of intelligent womanhood to emulate. Since Dickens had to eliminate all explicit sexual references from the description of his positive women, these became even less attractive than their models already were in the eighteenth-century canon. However, the responsibility for Dickens's unsatisfactory depiction of (good) women must not be entirely laid at the door of the eighteenth-century novel. Victorian idealizations of womanhood in the mode of Coventry Patmore and the influence of the fairytale and the theatrical melodrama equally have a share in this story.

Besides the eighteenth-century *novel*, one other major inspiration for Dickens was the work of William Hogarth, whom he greatly admired and whose prints both thematically and stylistically (the satirical mode, the grotesqueness of his figures) resemble Dickens's early writing (see chapter 7).

Dickens vs the Eighteenth-century Novel

In this section I will look at those features of eighteenth-century fiction which do not show up in Dickens's work, and then consider Dickens's innovations, those aspects of his writing in which he departed from tradition and became genuinely creative.

Most prominently, of course, one here needs to note Dickens's typically Victorian rejection of sexual license and sexual innuendo, a staple of much eighteenth-century literature. In the wake of the sentimental novel, including Richardson's *Sir Charles Grandison*, Dickens avoided sexual licentiousness and banned the rake as a hero from his fiction. Steerforth in *David Copperfield* is perhaps the only such figure in Dickens's work, and he is presented as a fascinating tempter who ultimately leaves us with a taste of disgust at his cruelty to Emily. This definite hiatus can be connected with the middle-class status of Dickens's dramatis personae and his distrust of the gentry and aristocracy – in contradistinction to the works of Fielding and Smollett, in which landed interest and the life of a gentleman still functioned as social ideals.

As Small (2004) notes, the quirkiness of Dickens's characters in the early books may be a compensation for the lack of erotic (and even pornographic) interest which is so striking in much eighteenth-century fiction. Clearly, this avoidance of explicit reference to sexuality rewrites not only the picaresque tradition but also modifies the eighteenth-century sentimental novel in significant ways. Perhaps the prevalent impression of Dickens's sentimentality as regards women characters (a prudishness and emotionality observable also in Gaskell and Trollope to some extent) is due less to an excess of sentiment than to the absence of an implicit erotic subtext. *Pamela* belongs with the sentimental tradition, but it is full of titillating scenes; likewise, in Burney's *Evelina* sentimentalism and a frank treatment of (female) sexuality work for a robust view of society.

In addition to this lack of innuendo and explicit sexual reference, Dickens's prudery moreover emerges from the avoiding of typically eighteenth-century wit. Not only does Dickens eschew the paradoxes and repartee tradition current on the seventeenth-century and eighteenth-century stage, he introduces a tradition of benevolent humor and shrewd verbal dexterity (Sam Weller) in comparison with which typical eighteenth-century wit smacks of arrogance and class elitism.

As already noted, Dickens's novels generally provide a "male" view on life: he does not follow Richardson and the Gothic and sentimental traditions (or even Defoe) in writing female *Bildungsromane*; Esther is the only female, first-person narrator in his oeuvre, and (for some) a problematic one at that. This choice may also link to the fact that decency and propriety in women do not allow for authorship – just imagine the impossibility of rebellious Jane Eyre as a Dickens heroine and narrator!

Dickens did not imitate Fielding's urbane narrator with his aura of classical education, knowingness, teasing of the narratee, and indulgence in metanarrative games. Dickens's humor, unlike Fielding's, does not derive from tongue-in-cheek metafictional commentary. In fact, Dickens – developing the narrative discourse of Scott and the rural novel of Edgeworth (Collins 1963: 146) – moves into the creation of a new type of novel writing that resembles George Eliot's realism but also transcends it by means of fantasy, imaginative distortion, and fairytale-like grotesquerie.

Finally, Dickens also avoided the derogatory presentation of the lower classes which proliferates in the eighteenth-century picaresque novel (Small 2004: 23–4). Dickens, on the contrary, acquired great familiarity with the working classes (Kucich 1994: 383); his fictional servants and the poor were loyal friends, factotums (Sam Weller), or objects of pity (the Marchioness).

Among Dickens's innovations, one can observe some thematic departures, changes in plotting, moral and social aspects that modify eighteenth-century models, and aspects of Dickens's language. First and foremost, Dickens moves from mere satire into social criticism. This move may have been initiated by Dickens's journalism and the interest he developed in social issues apparent in such pieces as "A Visit to Newgate." Whereas Godwin, Wollstonecraft, and the Romantics in general were agitated about the tyranny of the old regime, the feudal bases of English society, and patriarchy, Dickens focuses on the working classes and their miseries, and he was not alone in this, as the example of Elizabeth Gaskell shows.

Dickens's delineation of social injustice and the predicament of the poor, however, is not so much notable in and by itself as in its conjunction with Dickens's linguistic heightening of these issues by means of symbolism and metaphor. Especially from *Hard Times* onward, Dickens tailored his rhetorical strategies in such a manner that each novel was underpinned by a network of metaphoric reasoning which frequently merged into one overall symbol (the prison in *Little Dorrit*). In fact, Dickens's use of metaphor is a feature noteworthy in and by itself as is his use of parody and pastiche. None of Dickens's contemporaries – most of whom were resolutely "realistic" (Gaskell, Eliot, Trollope) and/or satirical (Thackeray, Trollope) – employs metaphor as frequently and as centrally in their work as does Dickens, though color symbolism and irony are prevalent in their texts. The density of metaphors in Dickens is especially noteworthy, as is the complexity of his imagery. For instance, in *Great Expectations*, prison metaphors are used to describe Pip's guilty conscience (the bread he hides for the convict on the marshes; his assumption that the soldiers have arrived to arrest him for theft of the pie) and his general situation (guilty of being a burden to his sister; feeling like a convict when he is apprenticed to Joe). Later, when Wemmick takes Pip on a tour of Newgate, he describes the clients of Jaggers as flowers to be cut off in full bloom (i.e., executed). This flower imagery links with Miss Havisham's wasted garden and the wasteland of the marshes in the opening chapters (complete with a gibbet). Metaphors such as these provide for a network of associations that adds considerably to the meanings of the novel. On the other hand, Dickens's imagery serves not only to complicate and diversify his presentation but also tends to distort, simplify, or render grotesque, to defamiliarize the story world. Dickens's metaphors are not merely rhetorical but underline the fantastic quality of his writing.

Dickens's works, moreover, differ from the eighteenth-century novel in being considerably more tightly plotted than most of his eighteenth-century models. This is an aspect relating to Dickens's development: his early fiction was still beholden to the picaresque tradition of episodic narrative. However, already in *Oliver Twist*, the detective subtext makes for a much more tailored plot. In fact, Dickens manages to combine the leisurely concatenation of different plot strands and humoristic scenes typical of eighteenth-century fiction with the carefully woven themes, incidents, and characters necessary for the resolution of mystery which is so typical of his late novels like *Bleak House* or *Our Mutual Friend* and, presumably, *The Mystery of Edwin Drood*.

Dickens's innovations, moreover, prompt him to broaden the social range from which he drew his characters. Whereas most eighteenth-century novels focus on heroes or heroines from the gentry (*Pamela* and the radical novel are notable exceptions), Dickens's personnel cover a very wide range indeed and also centrally include the downtrodden, the poor, the insane, the mad. The development in Dickens is especially striking in his move from Sam Weller in *Pickwick Papers* – in many respects a latter-day Humphry Clinker – to the depiction of Carker in *Dombey* or Mrs. Rouncewell in *Bleak House*. Although the loyal servant of the eighteenth-century novel is a typical flat character figure, Dickens's application of stereotypical quirks to all levels of society makes an important step within the comic tradition in English fiction toward a less stigmatized presentation of the comic other. (In the regional novel, Scott already moved in this direction, as in the figure of Caleb in *The Bride of Lammermoor*.) Yet, as Kucich points out, Dickens's Sams and Nubbleses provide "the lower-class carnival backdrop" to the "middle-class seriousness, reserve, and self-control" of his protagonists (Kucich 1994: 386).

Dickens additionally introduces new topics to the novel hitherto untreated by his predecessors. The two most important of these are the themes of childhood and the theme of nostalgia and memory. In fact, one might argue for a link to the sentimental tradition and particularly to the Wordsworthian type of Romanticism. Yet Dickens's *Bildungsromane* (*Martin Chuzzlewit, Nicholas Nickleby, David Copperfield, Great Expectations*) and his (child-like) protagonists Little Dorrit, Little Nell, Pip, Florence Dombey, or Paul Dombey betray a consciousness of childhood as a unique period in a person's life, one which is beset with terrors, wonder, and a magic vision of life. To take childhood away from them is presented as a crime. No eighteenth-century models exist for these waif-like children and their frail existence as victims of cruelty and neglect, poverty and pedagogic terrorizing. Many of his adult characters (Skimpole, Micawber, Maggy in *Little Dorrit*) are children at heart, children who have not grown up. A good example of Dickens's ingenuity in describing children's perception of the world is little David's view of Miss Murdstone:

> When she paid the coachman she took her money out of a hard steel purse, and she kept the purse in a very jail of a bag which hung upon her arm by heavy chains, and shut up like a bite. I had never, at that time, seen such a metallic lady altogether as Miss Murdstone was. (*David Copperfield* ch. 4)

An emphasis on pastoral nostalgia and a romantic vision of the countryside as re-creative, as the idyllic opposite of grimy London, are also features of much Dickens. These display a post-Romantic impulse but have no immediate models in previous fiction, though the poetry of Goldsmith and Gray's "Elegy Written in a Country Churchyard" (1751) come closest to the pastoral nostalgia of *The Old Curiosity Shop* or the Meagles' garden home (*Little Dorrit*), or Mr. Pickwick's rambles in the English countryside:

> A delightful walk it was: for it was a pleasant afternoon in June, and their way lay through a deep and shady wood, cooled by the light wind which gently rustled the thick foliage, and enlivened by the songs of the birds that perched upon the boughs. The ivy and the moss crept in thick clusters over the old trees, and the soft green turf overspread the ground like a silken mat. (*Pickwick Papers* ch. 11)

One final feature of Dickens's novels that is innovative and as deeply "Victorian" as his nostalgia for childhood and the countryside is his emphasis on domesticity (see also Kucich 1994: 392–3). Dickens's angel-in-the-house ideology does not have many precedents in eighteenth-century fiction (Amelia comes to mind), perhaps because most eighteenth-century heroines are from the gentry and have servants to perform the necessary household duties. Dickens's clearly middle-class focus on women's domestic qualifications is even more strikingly supplemented by his depiction of the home as an alternative quasi-pastoral setting, a refuge from the miseries of (city) life. Although houses and homes are ambivalent sites – think of the prison-like homes of Mrs. Clennam or Lady Dedlock – ideal domestic spaces abound in Dickens's novels. They are linked to happiness, love, and security, to food, jollity, and community. Dickens's celebration of Christmas draws attention to the appeal of home and hearth: "Christmas was close at hand, in all his bluff and hearty honesty; it was the season of hospitality, merriment, and open-heartedness" (*Pickwick Papers* ch. 28). Less than ideal homes are also abundant – the house of Mr. Merdle, in which he feels unwanted; David's home after the Murdstones have moved in – but there is always the contrast to the loss of that womb-like innocence and coziness which is symbolized by the contrastive settings of real homes.

Dickens and the Genre of the Novel

This takes me to a final point: the question of how to place Dickens in the context of the development of the novel. So far we have focused on the relationship of his novels to the eighteenth century: in what respects they continue eighteenth-century traditions; where they clearly initiate new developments; and in what way they turn away from eighteenth-century attitudes and formal concerns. I will conclude with a brief comment on the extent to which Dickens's work constitutes a major turning point for the development of the novel form.

One way of considering the significance of Dickens in this respect is to compare his narrators with those of other Victorian novelists. Dickens is much less concerned with history and philosophy than with an imaginative portrait of society and with the individuality of his characters. Although clearly influenced by Sir Walter Scott's narrative practice, he nevertheless did not write historical novels (with two exceptions, whose difference to Scott is manifest). Dickens's brand of realism seems to put into practice the leading rule of George Eliot's *Adam Bede*, where in chapter 17 Eliot's narrator says that the novel should present one's ugly, badly dressed neighbors as they are and persuade the reader to love them. This is precisely what Dickens manages to do, particularly because of his lack of social snobbery. He presents to us a menagerie of odd characters who are both lovable and fantastic, yet their closeness to recognizable types demonstrates that they are only exaggerated versions of warped humanity in real life.

By abstaining from the didactic moralism of George Eliot, the caustic satire of Thackeray, and the romantic passion of the Brontës, Dickens molds a type of realism that embraces Gothic and fantastic elements and prepares the way for the developments beyond realism at the turn of the century. By not even pretending to narrowly imitate reality, Dickens manages to avoid the trap of an overly mimetic realist theory. He therefore does not need to indulge in metanarrative and metafictional stances such as those employed by Thackeray and by Trollope, whose brand of realism nevertheless shares significant features with Dickens in their satiric insights into human foibles or their (less prominent) use of metaphor and metonymy, for instance. Whereas Thackeray closely follows the patterns of Fielding and Austen in his novel of manners, Dickens's satire concentrates not on manners but on emotions, experiences, and the exuberance of human life in all its fantastic, seamy, and cheerful aspects.

Dickens's experiments in narrative tone, most memorably in the opening paragraphs of *Bleak House*, *Little Dorrit*, or *A Tale of Two Cities*, moreover point to a resurrection of Fielding's Olympian narrator, but with a difference. This knowing narrator is not an urbane gentleman but a chronicler of the malaises of the century, a narrator whose individuality lies in his experimental use of language – metaphoric, sweeping across the cityscape and social horizon of Victorian society but doing so by providing a uniquely imaginative vision of it. For all its affinity with contemporary Victorian novels, Dickens's oeuvre provides an important stepping stone toward the *fin-de-siècle* novel. Dickens's novels are both a synthesis of earlier modes of writing and an anticipation of what was to emerge at the end of the century, while the work of his contemporaries more immediately served as a foil to such new developments. Perhaps it was precisely Dickens's eighteenth-century legacy that allowed him to transcend the more narrowly mimetic concepts of his colleagues and prepared the way for the extensive narrative experiments of Kipling, Conrad, or Wilde.

Anticipations of Modernism can be observed in two areas of Dickens's oeuvre: his aestheticization of the city[1] and his uncanny grasp of the subconscious. Despite the nostalgia for rural England in Dickens's work, and despite the extensive depiction of poverty, grime, and despair in London, Dickens's oeuvre also moves toward a new aesthetics of the city, one in which walking the city and appreciating its bustle, its inhabitants, its variety of neighborhoods becomes a major aspect of the texts. Here Dickens moves beyond eighteenth-century depictions of London as a setting of corruption and licentiousness (masquerades and so on) to concentrate on the city as a home with its landmarks, streets, and public institutions. This is not to deny Kucich's (1994) insightful comments on Dickens's symbolization of the city as "general moral chaos": "His metaphors for the urban landscape – fog, mud, dirt, pestilence – suggest a systematic, animated evil, as if the city's growth had taken on a destructive, all-consuming life of its own" (1994: 396). Balancing this image of London as an ogre of Gothic or fairytale provenance, the inns, bustling thoroughfares, clubs, theaters, and the Thames display London as a carnival of vivacity, grief, hypocrisy, industry, honor, villainy, and general exuberance. As Andrew Sanders puts it, "Dickens was essentially 'modern' . . . because he responded so distinctively to the leading traits of the increasingly transformed, democratized, industrialized, and urbanized society which was, and remains, 'modern'" (1999: 186).

The second proto-Modernist aspect of Dickens's work, his uncanny rendering of fantastic and traumatic psychological experience, was of course first popularized by Edmund Wilson in 1940 in "Dickens: The Two Scrooges", yet its pervasiveness already in the early Dickens has perhaps not received sufficient attention. Thus, to take *Pickwick Papers* as an example, this novel contains a large number of phantasmal passages that prefigure the better-known scenarios in *David Copperfield* or *The Mystery of Edwin Drood*: for instance, there is the chair turning into an old gentleman in "The Bagman's Tale" (ch. 14); more traumatic still is the nightmare of Heyling in "The Queer Client's Tale":

> There was another vessel before them, toiling and labouring in the howling storm: her canvas fluttering in ribbons from the mast, and her deck thronged with figures who were lashed to the sides, over which huge waves every instant burst, sweeping away some devoted creatures into the foaming sea. Onward they bore, amidst the roaring mass of water, with a speed and force which nothing could resist; and striking the stern of the foremost vessel, crushed her, beneath their keel. From the huge whirlpool which the sinking wreck occasioned, arose a shriek so loud and shrill – the death-cry of a hundred drowning creatures, blended into one fierce yell – that it rung far above the war-cry of the elements, and echoed, and re-echoed till it seemed to pierce air, sky, and ocean. But what was that – that old grey-head that rose above the water's surface, and with looks of agony, and screams for aid, buffeted with the waves! One look, and he had sprung from the vessel's side, and with vigorous strokes was swimming towards it. He reached it; he was close upon it. They were *his* features. The old man saw him coming, and vainly strove to elude his grasp. But he clasped him tight, and dragged him beneath the water. Down, down with him, fifty fathoms down; his struggles grew fainter and fainter, until they wholly ceased. He was dead; he had killed him, and had kept his oath. (ch. 21)

Even more stirring is the truly frightening description of the clown's death in which a fantastic and grotesque visual impression is laced with horror, disgust, and sympathy:

> His bloated body and shrunken legs – their deformity enhanced a hundred fold by the fantastic dress – the glassy eyes, contrasting fearfully with the thick white paint with which the face was besmeared; the grotesquely ornamented head, trembling with paralysis, and the long, skinny hands, rubbed with white chalk – all gave him a hideous and unnatural appearance, of which no description could convey an adequate idea, and which, to this day, I shudder to think of. His voice was hollow and tremulous. (*Pickwick Papers* ch. 3)

Dickens here not only moves significantly beyond the framework of the sentimental and Gothic novel but also enters the realms of Hugo, Dostoevsky, and Kafka.

Anticipations of Modernism can even be noted in the humorous passages, as in the staccato discourse of Jingle, which looks suspiciously as if it might have served as a model for one of the interior monologues in Joyce's *Ulysses*:

> "Ah! fine place," said the stranger, "glorious pile – frowning walls – tottering arches – dark nooks – crumbling staircases – Old cathedral too – earthy smell – pilgrims' feet worn away the old steps – little Saxon doors – confessionals like money-takers' boxes at theatres – queer customers those monks – Popes, and Lord Treasurers, and all sorts of old fellows, with great red faces, and broken noses, turning up every day – buff jerkins too – matchlocks – Sarcophagus – fine place – old legends too – strange stories: capital"; and the stranger continued to soliloquise until they reached the Bull Inn, the High Street, where the coach stopped. (*Pickwick Papers* ch. 2)

Jingle's associative move from one commonplace to another at first seems to be mere quirkiness, but it acquires more sinister overtones as the perfidy of Jingle emerges in the tale.

Dickens's oeuvre more than that of his contemporaries gestures toward the heterogeneity, bathos (for example, in "Prufrock"), and limited perspective of literary Modernism, ironically so since the Modernists failed to appreciate their affinity with his writing. Perhaps it was precisely those features of Dickens that appeared most obsolete, most linked to eighteenth-century models, that – with the hindsight of 150 years – now emerge as truly progressive: Dickens's refusal to subordinate himself to rationality and control; his invocation of the uncanny, the subconscious drives, the repressed; his juxtaposition of tragedy and comedy, of didactic, satiric, and emotional catharsis; the insertion of tales within the tale to present multiple perspectives and views. At the beginning of the twenty-first century, Dickens, to adapt the title of Jan Kott's study of Shakespeare, truly seems to be "our contemporary" and to have three faces: an Augustan, a Victorian, and a Modernist mask. And like the three grotesque monkeys, covering ears, eyes, and mouth in the traditional image, the three faces of Dickens cannot perhaps all be appreciated simultaneously.

NOTE

1 I was alerted to this aspect of Dickens's fiction
by Paul K. Goetsch, who also responded helpfully to the first draft of this chapter.

REFERENCES AND FURTHER READING

Allott, M. (1959). *Novelists on the Novel*. New York:
Columbia University Press.

Baines, P. (2004). *The Long Eighteenth Century*.
Oxford: Oxford University Press.

Boswell, J. (1934). *Boswell's Life of Johnson*, 4 vols.
Oxford: Clarendon Press.

Bradbury, N. (2001). Dickens and the form
of the novel. In J. O. Jordan (Ed.), *The
Cambridge Companion to Charles Dickens* (pp.
152–66). Cambridge: Cambridge University
Press.

Collins, P. (1963). Dickens's reading. *The Dickensian*, 59, 136–51.

Dickens, C. (1850). Pet prisoners. *Household Words*,
April 25.

Flint, K. (1986). *Dickens*. Brighton: Harvester
Press.

Hibbert, C. (1967). *The Making of Charles Dickens*.
London: Longmans.

House, H. (1941). *The Dickens World*. Oxford:
Oxford University Press.

Kucich, J. (1994). Dickens. In J. Richetti (Ed.),
The Columbia History of the British Novel (pp.
381–406). New York: Columbia University
Press.

Langbauer, L. (1990). Streetwalkers and homebod-
ies: Dickens's romantic women. In *Women and
Romance: The Consolations of Gender in the English
Novel* (pp. 127–87). Ithaca, NY: Cornell
University Press.

Marcus, S. (1965). *Dickens: From Pickwick to Dombey*.
London: Chatto and Windus.

Richetti, J. (Ed.) (1994). *The Columbia History of
the British Novel*. New York: Columbia University Press.

— (Ed.) (1996). *The Cambridge Companion to the
Eighteenth Century Novel*. Cambridge: Cambridge
University Press.

Robison, R. (1970). Dickens and the sentimental
tradition: *Mr. Pickwick* and *My Uncle Toby*.
University of Toronto Quarterly, 39, 258–73.

Sanders, A. (1999). *Dickens and the Spirit of the Age*.
Oxford: Clarendon Press.

Scheuermann, M. (2002). Visions and revisions:
the feminist rewriting of the eighteenth-century
novel. In K. L. Cope and R. Ahrens (Eds.),
*Talking Forward, Talking Back: Critical Dialogues
with the Enlightenment* (pp. 281–317). New
York: AMS.

Schilling, B. N. (1965). *The Comic Spirit: Boccaccio
to Thomas Mann*. Detroit: Wayne State University Press.

Schor, H. (1999). Fiction. In H. F. Tucker (Ed.),
A Companion to Victorian Literature and Culture
(pp. 323–38). Oxford: Blackwell.

Skinner, J. (2001). *An Introduction to Eighteenth-
century Fiction: Raising the Novel*. Basingstoke:
Palgrave.

Small, H. (2004). The debt to society: Dickens,
Fielding, and the genealogy of independence. In
F. O'Gorman and K. Turner (Eds.), *The Victori-
ans and the Eighteenth Century: Reassessing the
Tradition* (pp. 14–40). Aldershot: Ashgate.

Stone, H. (1963). Dark corners of the mind:
Dickens' childhood reading. *Horn Book Magazine*, 39, 306–21.

Wilson, E. (1941). Dickens: the two Scrooges. In
*The Wound and The Bow: Seven Studies in Litera-
ture* (pp. 1–93). London: Methuen (original
work published 1940).

6

Dickens and the Gothic

Robert Mighall

Defining the Gothic

One of the most perceptive views on Gothic literature comes from one of its most famous detractors. When Jane Austen deflates Catherine Morland's Gothic imaginings in *Northanger Abbey* (1818) she establishes the ground rules of the fiction at that time:

> Charming as were all Mrs. Radcliffe's works, and charming even as were the works of all her imitators, it was not in them perhaps that human nature, at least in the midland counties of England, was to be looked for. Of the Alps and Pyrenees, with their pine forests and their vices, they might give a faithful delineation; and Italy, Switzerland, and the South of France, might be as fruitful in horrors as they were there represented . . . But in the central part of England there was surely some security for the existence even of a wife not beloved, in the laws of the land, and the manners of the age . . . Among the Alps and Pyrenees, perhaps there were no mixed characters. There, such as were not spotless as an angel, might have the dispositions of a fiend. But in England it was not so. (ch. 10)

Austen appears to accept the Gothic's geographical and generic segregations. With hindsight, we might see this as the moment when the novelist of contemporary manners, the delineator of complex, "mixed" characters, sounded the death-knell of romance, and heralded the triumph of realism. For, by 1818, the Gothic romance (initiated by Horace Walpole and perfected by Mrs. Radcliffe) was pretty much on its last legs. Appearing two years later, Charles Robert Maturin's *Melmoth the Wanderer* (1820) is generally regarded as the original Gothic's swansong.

Disappearing from mainstream fiction at this time, the Gothic reappeared with Robert Louis Stevenson's *Strange Case of Dr. Jekyll and Mr. Hyde* (1886), and the clutch of *fin-de-siècle* horrors that followed. With *Jekyll and Hyde*, Oscar Wilde's *The Picture of Dorian Gray* (1890), Bram Stoker's *Dracula* (1897), and the fantasies of Arthur

Machen, preternatural phenomena, monstrous vices, and lurid horrors returned with a vengeance, but were no longer segregated along the lines upon which Austen insisted. This "new" Gothic was set in the London of the present day, and self-consciously disrupted the very certainties the earlier form had relied upon. The Gothic had changed; and no small part of this transformation is down to Dickens, whose works stand to refute the notion that the Gothic went away. For in terms of innovation and influence (not to mention the mere volume of content that can be characterized as "Gothic"), no writer has a greater claim to importance in the history of the Gothic during its supposed sabbatical than Dickens. This chapter examines the way in which Dickens explored and innovated within the Gothic literary mode, and assesses the lasting influence this had on how we have come to see and create Gothic fictions, and on how we understand the times and places he represented and made his own.

The Gothic is obsessed with the historical past and how this affects the present.[1] In the original Gothic, this tended to involve historical distancing, with novels typically set in earlier centuries (any time between the thirteenth and the sixteenth centuries), or in countries where religion or politics marked them out (to the Protestant mind) as time-bound or regressive. As Sir Walter Scott put it, when describing the essentials of the Gothic, Mrs. Radcliffe had "uniformly selected the south of Europe for her place of action . . . where feudal tyranny and Catholic superstition still *continue to hold their sway* over the slave and bigot . . . [For] these circumstances are skilfully selected, to give probability to events which could not, without great violation of truth, be represented as having taken place in England" (Scott 1825: 243). This emphasis on anachronism, on forms of chronological disparity or conflict, is essential to understanding the Gothic. For it plays a defining role in its development and diversification in the nineteenth century and beyond. It is what allows the Gothic still to function even when the historical and geographical distancing of the early mode was rejected as it was in Victorian versions. It is his anachronism that qualifies the 500-year-old Count Dracula as an exemplary Gothic figure, and it is out-of-timeness that demarcates a domicile as "Gothic," whether it is set in contemporary London, New Orleans, or a "place in Lincolnshire." An emphasis on anachronism, on unwelcome vestiges from the past, is one of the most consistent properties that encourage us to consider Dickens as a Gothic writer.

Dickens's Early "Streaky" Gothic

From his earliest works, Dickens displayed an awareness of, and an apparent fondness for, aspects of Gothic literary convention. The recurrence of ghostly, grotesque, or fearful happenings in the interpolated tales in *The Pickwick Papers* suggests that making his readers' flesh creep as well as their bellies laugh was part of the young writer's understanding of his role as an entertainer. A famous passage from *Oliver Twist* provides a useful metaphor for understanding Dickens's early art in this respect. Having put poor Oliver in a heightened state of peril and misery, the narrator observes how:

"It is the custom on the stage in all good, murderous melodramas, to present the tragic and the comic scenes in as regular alternation as the layers of red and white in a side of streaky, well-cured bacon" (ch. 7). This rather homely metaphor to justify Dickens's self-conscious manipulation of conventions also neatly encapsulates the way Gothic elements appear in his early fiction. The melodramatic stage maintained a strong connection with the Gothic throughout the nineteenth century, providing a refuge for many of the stock figures and plots that largely disappeared from more polite fictional fare. Dickens's analogy also recalls John Ruskin's outrage at the way in which Dickens slaughtered Little Nell "like a lamb for the market" (Page 2000: xi) in a novel which perhaps best demonstrates the "streaky bacon" effect of Dickens's early comic adaptation of Gothic fictional elements.

The Old Curiosity Shop betrays a number of Gothic characteristics. Like many a Gothic novel from *The Castle of Otranto* (1764) to *Dracula* (1897), the narrative is mediated through an editorial frame, in this case Master Humphrey's compendium of grotesque tales and curiosities. The eponymous setting, as well as the principal persecution plot, suggest Dickens's conscious intention to explore a number of Gothic conventions. This is hinted at in his Preface to the Cheap Edition of 1848, which states that his intention was to "surround the lonely figure of the child with grotesque and wild, but not impossible companions, and to gather about her innocent face and pure intentions, associates as strange and uncongenial as the grim objects that are about her bed." In so doing, Dickens transplants a self-consciously "Gothic" *mis en scène* into near contemporary London. Its "old and curious" relics of "monkish cloisters" (ch. 1) could almost be seen as the spoils of this officially abandoned novelistic convention, sold as a job lot at the break up of the Radcliffe estate. They provide an appropriate stage set to enact a version of the Gothic persecution narrative best exemplified by Radcliffe's *Mysteries of Udolpho* (1795). Dickens's novel appears to follow what Victor Sage has identified as the "paradigm of the horror-plot: the journey from the capital to the provinces" (Sage 1988: 8), with Nell and her Grandfather fleeing London and the villainous clutches of Quilp.

However, the plot's apparent adherence to this pattern is far from conventional. In abandoning the Old Curiosity Shop to wander through the villages and industrial regions of Britain, Nell leaves a version of the Gothic castle (traditionally the setting for imprisonment in remote settings) to enter a wider world of experience, and one which even affords a fleeting glimpse of possible freedom. The paradigm is partly in reverse. For, despite its grotesqueness, Nell felt none of the incongruity Dickens or Master Humphrey insists upon, feeling safe and at home in the Curiosity Shop until it is appropriated by Quilp. Significantly, when Nell's earthly wanderings come to an end, it is in an equally Gothic simulacrum of her former home. Gothic setting and plotting are at variance in the novel.

Quilp's actions do, in part, conform to those prescribed for the Gothic villain. Like Radcliffe's Montoni before him, and Le Fanu's Uncle Silas after, he is in part motivated by a desire to get his hands on a prime Gothic property that should rightfully fall to the heroine. And yet, having secured ownership of the Old Curiosity Shop, which should have provided a setting as appropriate for such a "monster" as it was deemed incongruous for Nell, he loses interest in it, and takes up residence in his squalid riverside slum. If Gothic dramatis personae are either "spotless as an angel" or have "the dispositions of a fiend," then the Nell–Quilp conflict appears to fit this pattern. Dwarfish, apelike, and brutal, Quilp provides a prototype for one of the most famous Gothic monsters, Stevenson's "hardly human" Mr. Hyde. And yet, unlike Hyde, and unlike all his Gothic antecedents, Quilp is also delightfully and self-consciously comic. He spends almost as much time laughing at his own antics as he does menacing others with his machinations or grimaces. Amusement at another's discomfort or misery appears to be an end in itself for Quilp: "With these hasty words, Daniel Quilp withdrew into a dismantled skittle-ground behind the public-house, and, throwing himself upon the ground, actually screamed and rolled about in the most uncontrollable delight" (ch. 21). If Quilp is a devil, he is, like Fagin, a merry one. His villainy is of effect more than deed, and has little directly malign effect on Nell after it has impelled her initial flight.

If unmixed characters denote Gothic fiction, then *The Old Curiosity Shop* ultimately fails to qualify. As the narrative demonstrates, you do not need a "fiend" like Quilp or a grotesque setting to enact persecutions on innocents. The world Nell encounters is full of exploitative opportunistic people, and where everyone and everything appears to have its price. Indeed, the most terrifying and characteristically "Gothic" passage in the text describes the robbery perpetrated by the man Nell loves as her natural protector. Her Grandfather, transformed by his addiction to gambling, assumes a shape arguably more terrifying that the comic diablerie of Quilp:

> The terror she had lately felt was nothing compared with that which now oppressed her. No strange robber, no treacherous host conniving at the plunder of his guests, or stealing to their beds to kill them in their sleep . . . could have awakened in her bosom half the dread which the recognition of her silent visitor inspired. The grey-haired old man gliding like a ghost into her room and acting the thief while he supposed her fast asleep, then bearing off his prize and hanging over it with the ghastly exultation she had witnessed, was worse . . . than anything her wildest fancy could have suggested. (ch. 31)

The superlatives used to enforce the moral and sentimental conflict at the heart of Nell's discovery almost deliberately strive to compete with the Gothic standards Dickens's own "wild fancy" had suggested in Quilp. Comic and Gothic, sentimental and cynical, Dickens's fictional storehouse of curiosities appears to delight in overturning conventions.

Arguing with the Past

The Gothic against the grain of Dickens's early fiction is further illustrated in the next narrative to fall out of Master Humphrey's clock, *Barnaby Rudge. Barnaby Rudge* is an intriguing hybrid of styles, genres, and influences. It explores elements of the historical novel as perfected by Scott, the Newgate novel Dickens was determined to distance himself from, and the mode that the other two genres were themselves heavily influenced by, Gothic fiction.[2] Rudge senior is clearly cast in the classic Gothic mold, but without the comic characteristics that made Fagin or Quilp difficult to take seriously in the role. Regularly referred to as "spectre," or "phantom," this "wanderer upon the earth" (ch. 17) could trace a lineage back to Radcliffe's villainous monk, Schedoni (*The Italian*, 1797) or to Maturin's self-tormented outcast, Melmoth:

> I, that in the form of man live the life of a hunted beast; that in the body am a spirit, a ghost upon the earth, a thing from which all creatures shrink, save those curst beings of another world, who will not leave me; – I am, in my desperation of this night, past all fear but that of the hell in which I exist from day to day. (*Melmoth* ch. 17)

And yet, unlike his Gothic ancestors, Rudge rarely takes center stage, his principal crimes pre-date the events of the narrative which they haunt, and his presence is as spectral and shadowy as these metaphors suggest.

Dickens's most unconventional use of the Gothic, however, appears in his treatment of Catholic characters in a novel that is about, but does not subscribe to, anti-Catholic bigotry. Received Gothic wisdom decreed that intolerance and bigotry were representative Catholic traits, a consequence of the ideological fetters that supposedly bound Catholics to the past. In Dickens's novel these attributes define those who staunchly defend the good old British way. As John Bowen (2003: xx) observes:

> Dickens is deeply sympathetic to the victimized Catholics of the story: Geoffrey Haredale is consummately virtuous, and it is his enemy, the sinister Protestant conspirator Sir John Chester, who has the classically "Jesuitical" qualities of deceit and guile. The Protestant Association is brutal and bigoted, and it is Dennis the public hangman who describes his job as "sound, Protestant, constitutional, English work."

The fervent Protestants, and those that make a fetish of the "Constitution," are bound by, because obsessed with, the past, filling the air "with whispers of a confederacy among the Popish powers to degrade and enslave England, establish an inquisition in London, and turn the pens of Smithfield market into stakes and cauldrons . . . and by-gone bugbears which had lain quietly in their graves for centuries, were raised again to haunt the ignorant and credulous" (ch. 37). The 'prentice knights provide a comic-Gothic example of this mindset, resisting "all change, except such change as would restore those old English customs, by which they would stand or fall. [Thus] illustrating the wisdom of going backward, by reference to that sagacious fish, the crab, and the not infrequent practice of mule and donkey" (ch. 8). With the (comic) Gothic solemnity of their ceremonies, and "crablike" adherence to the past, the knights neatly exemplify the anachronistic principle that is the object of Gothic representation. But Dickens employs this emphasis to satirize the very foundations of English identity that had once anchored Gothic meanings and fictions. In *Barnaby Rudge*, intolerance, violence, superstition, and oppression – the supposed vices of

Gothic ages and (time-bound) Catholic cultures – are exemplified by those who fervently subscribe to the very sectarian chauvinism that originally informed Gothic fictional history. Gothic historical allegory is thus used against itself, decoupling and re-aligning moral and ideological determinants to depict the cataclysmic consequences of intolerance and hatred, whatever its agenda.

Arguing with the Past in the Present: Dickens's Reformist Gothic

Humphry House once pointed out an apparent paradox in Dickens's view of the past, observing how: "It is curious that he, who was so scornful of the moral abuses of the times in which he lived, should have almost universally condemned the times before him. There is no trace of idealizing the past" (House 1960: 34). This is illustrated by the famous false book-backs that Dickens commissioned in 1851 to adorn his study, including "The Wisdom of our Ancestors: I. Ignorance. II Superstition. III. The Block. IV. The Stake. V. The Rack. VI. Dirt. VII. Disease" (House 1960: 35). However, by exploring Dickens's use of Gothic conventions, principally his emphasis on malign legacy and the survival of specific anachronistic vestiges, the apparent paradox identified by House is resolved. For Dickens laid the responsibility for many of the current abuses he anathematized as originating in the past, finding the Gothic useful both as a rhetorical structure and metaphorical repertoire to serve his progressive and reformist agenda.

Michael Hollington has identified a reformist impulse informing Dickens's project for a "new Gothic" in his earliest writings. As he suggests, Boz's remark in "Criminal Courts" that the prison reformer Mrs. Fry "certainly ought to have written more romances than Mrs. Radcliffe," implies that Dickens was establishing a new object and function for Gothic representation (Hollington 1999: 160). He was using the conventions of the mode to figure and denounce the horrors and abuses found on the immediate doorstep. To a large extent, *Oliver Twist* does just that, transplanting the Radcliffian fictional scenario to within a noose-length of Newgate prison. The Preface to the 1841 edition suggests that this was a conscious strategy on Dickens's part, rejecting the picturesque landscapes and fancy dress of the Gothic and Newgate schools of fiction, for the "cold, wet shelterless midnight streets of London; the foul and frowsy dens, where vice is closely packed and lacks the room to turn; the haunts of hunger and disease." Not just a Gothic *in* the modern city, but *of* it, evoking horror as an agent for awareness of the necessity of urban reform.[3]

But if *Oliver Twist* mapped out a new space for (reformist) Gothic representation, *Bleak House* went even further, undermining any assured divisions between the lawless and the lawful by depicting the law itself, and the institutions and values that support it, at the very heart of a dark, foggy labyrinth. Dickens's most all-embracing social critique is also his most consummate and sustained Gothic performance. The Gothic provides a rich metaphorical, thematic, and atmospheric repertoire to depict a haunted British society and anathematize its abuses. This is partly achieved rhetorically through its numerous, near-obsessive references to "ghosts," "phantoms," "vampires," and "witches," culminating in the *Walpurgisnacht* of Krook's spontaneous combustion. Indeed, references to "ghost" or "ghostly" number more than half those to "lawyer" in a book that is about the legal system (46 ghosts to 82 lawyers). Such imagery supports Dickens's intention to dwell on "the romantic side of familiar things" in his novel. He defamiliarizes what is accepted by rendering it fantastic and sinister, with his principal target being that great Gothic institution, the High Court of Chancery, "most pestilent of sinners" (ch. 1).

Chancery is the master metaphor in his novel, wielding a malign significance and influence by borrowing attributes of various Gothic conventions. The Court, with its sovereign Lord Chancellor, assumes the dimensions of a vast feudal castle, whose dominion holds sway over scores of hapless vassals. Having:

> its decaying houses and its blighted lands in every shire . . . its worn-out lunatic in every madhouse, and its dead in every churchyard . . . [it] so exhausts finances, patience, courage, hope; so overthrows the brain and breaks the heart; that there is not an honourable man among its practitioners who would not give . . . the warning, "Suffer any wrong that can be done you, rather than come here!" (*Bleak House* ch. 1)

Its victims act like deluded, doomed, or even damned courtiers. By pursuing wills (records of legacy), they lose their own wills (agency). Miss Flite's description of the malign influence of Mace and Seal could be taken from the opening pages of a typical vampire tale, where a frightened villager warns against visiting "the castle." These supposed symbols of equity and justice: "Draw people on, my dear. Draw peace out of them. Sense out of them. Good looks out of them. Good qualities out of them. I have felt them drawing my rest away in the night. Cold glittering devils!" (ch. 35). This analogy is made more explicit through the figure of Vholes, whom both Esther and Ada liken to a vampire. Richard taking lodgings in this parasite's chambers confirms his final surrender to the power that transforms and destroys him. The detail of his mouth being full of blood at the moment when the infamous case collapses completes the inference that a diabolical force has claimed another victim.

This process is described by Tom Jarndyce shortly before he puts an end to his sufferings: "it's being ground to bits in a slow mill; it's being roasted at a slow fire; it's being stung to death by single bees; it's being drowned by drops; it's going mad by grains" (ch. 5). Chancery thus resembles that consummate Gothic icon, the Inquisition, as imagined in the pages of Charles Maturin or Edgar Allan Poe. This is reinforced by the "mingled dread and veneration" with which Guster, Snagsby's servant, holds the law stationers "as a store house of the awful implements of the great torture of the law: a place not to be entered after the gas is turned off" (ch. 10). This suggestion implies that the contemporary legal process is analogous to those symbols of ancient brutality and unreason, the Block, the Stake, and the Rack, that characterized "The Wisdom of our Ancestors." Chancery is indeed, like the Inquisitors imagined by Gothic fiction, implacable in its heartless indifference to suffering, and sinister in the tortuous "mysteries" only its initiates can understand.

The ancestral curse is perhaps the most persistent trope of Gothic fiction, providing a potent vehicle for the past to haunt the present. From *The Castle of Otranto* to *The House of the Seven Gables* (1851), hapless victims have labored under burdens of inheritance that blight their own destinies. Unwelcome legacies of disorder, wrong-doing, or oppression, curses are the warp and weft of the Gothic as it developed in the nineteenth century. An ancestral curse is a key driver of narrative in *A Tale of Two Cities*. The curse of the Evrémondes is visited upon Darnay, imperiling the happiness of the aristocrat who has renounced the very principles of legacy and genealogy that the curse entails, along with his "hated" name. *Bleak House* also has its curses: in the legend associated with the Ghost's Walk, and, of course, in Jarndyce and Jarndyce. As John Jarndyce implores Richard Carstone: "for the love of God, don't found a hope or expectation on the family curse! Whatever you do this side the grave, never give one lingering glance towards the horrible phantom that has haunted us so many years" (ch. 24). Whilst this could be passed over as a mere figure of speech, lending rhetorical weight to stigmatize the *idée fixe* of the "wig-ridden" John Jarndyce, his use of the central trope of Gothic narrative is appropriate. For it points to the broader concept of malign legacy that provides a central focus for Dickens's indignant satire. The third-person narrator thus describes the curse of Chancery's prize case:

> Innumerable children have been born into the cause; innumerable young people have married into it; innumerable old people have died out of it. Scores of persons have deliriously found themselves made parties in Jarndyce and Jarndyce, without knowing how or why; whole families have inherited legendary hatreds with the suit . . . [and so] Jarndyce and Jarndyce still drags its dreary length before the Court, perennially hopeless. (ch. 1)

What makes this particular curse all the more unjust and terrifying is that, unlike the curses of Otranto, the Evrémondes, or the Ghost's Walk, this curse was initiated by no worse crime than the folly of someone once entering the "labyrinth" of Chancery. If, like *The Castle of Otranto*, Dickens's text illustrates how the "sins of the fathers will be visited upon the children to the third and fourth generation," then these fathers must be the patrician institutions of governance, and their sins the customs, precedents, and attitudes that prevent true justice and true progress in the land.

The curse of Jarndyce and Jarndyce (as a metonym for the abuses of Chancery), no less than that associated with the Ghost's Walk, can trace its origins to Chesney Wold, and the "world of Fashion" it represents. For "Sir Leicester has no objections to an interminable Chancery suit. It is a slow, expensive, British, constitutional kind of thing" (ch. 2). That word again – "constitutional" – occurring whenever a sacred principle of ancient wrong-headedness and obsolescence is invoked to justify a current abuse or folly. The "world of Fashion," with Chesney Wold at its epicenter:

> is not so unlike the Court of Chancery . . . Both . . . are things of precedent and usage; over-sleeping Rip Van Winkles, who have played at strange games through a deal of

thundery weather . . . But the evil of it is, that it is a world wrapped in too much jeweller's cotton and fine wool, and cannot hear the rushing of larger worlds, and cannot see them as they circle round the sun. It is a deadened world, and its growth is sometimes unhealthy for want of air. (ch. 2)

In short, it is anachronistic, removed from the "rushing" world of the nineteenth century, as it spins forever down the ringing grooves of change. But, as Dickens suggests, the real evil is that this obsolescent order, whilst remote from the spirit and reality of the age, is still in charge. Its Coodles, Doodles, and Noodles play at their strange games in the very corridors of power.

Dickens's reference to the "unhealthiness" of the aristocratic world is significant, as it provides a strand that binds his Gothic and his reformist objectives tightly together. Disease becomes a Gothic agent in *Bleak House*. It is not just the local church at Chesney Wold that is moldy with "a general smell and taste as of the ancient Dedlocks in their graves" (ch. 2); for this taint seeps into the whole constitution. It mingles with the miasmic properties of the crowded city graveyard where "Nemo" is buried: "here, they lower our dear brother down a foot or two: here sow him in corruption, to be raised in corruption: an avenging ghost at many a sick-bedside: a shameful testimony to future ages, how civilization and barbarism walked this boastful island together" (ch. 11). Dickens, special correspondent to posterity, self-consciously fastens on a glaring anomaly between the official spirit of the age and a shameful vestige of barbarism. His use of a ghostly metaphor to characterize this vestige and its consequences neatly sums up his reformist Gothic practice. The ancient Dedlocks retain a ghostly grip on a morbid or even moribund social order, imagined as a tainting smell, which finds its embodiment in miasmic pestilence. In other words, the Wisdom or deference to Ancestors continues to breed both Dirt and Disease. This, as Dickens's portentous description of Tom-all-Alone's suggests, carries its own nemesis:

Much mighty speech-making there has been, both in and out of Parliament, concerning Tom . . . [who] will be reclaimed according to somebody's theory and nobody's practice . . . But he has his revenge. Even the winds are his messengers, and they serve him in these hours of darkness. There is not a drop of Tom's corrupted blood but propagates infection and contagion somewhere. It shall pollute, this very night, the choice stream (in which chemists on analysis would find the genuine nobility) of a Norman house, and his Grace shall not be able to say Nay to the infamous alliance. There is not an atom of Tom's slime, not a cubic inch of any pestilential gas in which he lives, not one obscenity or degradation about him, not an ignorance, not a wickedness, not a brutality of his committing, but shall work its retribution through every order of society up to the proudest of the proud and to the highest of the high. Verily, what with tainting, plundering, and spoiling, Tom has his revenge. (ch. 46)

Blood as symbol of nobility and blood as carrier of disease thus conjoin through the conceit of contagion. The taint of the ancient Dedlocks finds both its agent and nemesis in the slum cultures that its anachronistic influence nurtures. Ghosts of antiquity and spirits of pestilence create a literal Gothic "atmosphere," which haunts Britain "through every order of society." Fog everywhere.

Castles and Prisons of the Mind: Dickens's Domestic Gothic

Bleak House imagines a Gothic that involves all parts of modern society, dispensing entirely with the geographical, historical, or class-based exclusions and distancing that had formerly been essential for representation. Bleak House is neither a slum nor a castle, but an ordinary bourgeois household, threatened by but eventually purged of the curses, phantoms, and burdens of malevolent legacy that hung over it. In *Little Dorrit* and *Great Expectations* Dickens would go even further in probing ordinary life for Gothic meaning, using the theme of malign legacy to show how dark memories can taint the very springs of bourgeois identity. Like *Bleak House, Little Dorrit* deals with the burdens of the past. But whilst the ancestral "curse" of Jarndyce and Jarndyce is enacted through the public mechanism and public arena of the law court, the legacies of *Little Dorrit* take effect in the private realms of domestic grievance and individual memory.

The House of Clennam is a house of secrets and bad memories; it groans, creaks, and eventually collapses under their weight. By depicting its fall, Dickens moves the Gothic scene into the world of business, showing a family bank haunted by guilty secrets and memories that refuse to be buried. Like the "unhealthy" world of Chesney Wold, and like all Gothic edifices from Otranto to the Bates Motel, the House of Clennam is an anachronism:

> our House has done less and less for some years past, and our dealings have been pro-gressively on the decline . . . the track we have kept is not the track of the time; and we have been left far behind . . . Even this old house in which we speak . . . is an instance of what I say . . . it is a mere anomaly and incongruity here, out of date and out of purpose. (bk. 1, ch. 4)

But this essential component of anachronistic incongruity is not used to depict an institution like Chancery or a social sore like Tom's. Dickens has shifted the scene of haunting into the realms of domesticity and small business, from the public to the private. Memory is now the principal vehicle for hauntings.

Little Dorrit shows how memory can be a much stronger prison than the ones con-structed by the state, and how lives can be blighted by the burdens it entails on future generations. By brooding on Arthur's father's infidelity, Mrs. Clennam confines herself within a self-imposed prison of her own resentment. The narrator draws a general lesson from her condition:

> To stop the 'clock of busy existence, at the hour when we were personally sequestered from it; to suppose mankind stricken motionless, when we were brought to a stand-still;

to be unable to measure the changes beyond our view, by any larger standard than the shrunken one of our own uniform and contracted existence; is the infirmity of many invalids, and the mental unhealthiness of almost all recluses. (bk. 1, ch. 29)

The stopped clock, the confined scope, the unhealthiness that characterized the "over-sleeping" world of "Fashion" in *Bleak House,* are here located in an individual, but one whose isolation from the rushing world still perpetuates further wrongs. Mrs. Clennam's imprisonment derives from her refusal to forget. And, true to Gothic pattern, this burden is in part a generational legacy. It is a form of "curse," albeit in a suitably scaled down form. Both Mrs. Clennam and Arthur's father were brought up under similar regimes of "wholesome repression, punishment and fear," joined in a loveless marriage because of similarly "severe" upbringings. This laid the foundations for Mr. Clennam's transgression, which, in turn, sanctions his wife's perpetuation of "severe restraint" in Arthur: "I devoted myself to reclaim the otherwise predestined and lost boy . . . to bring him up in fear and trembling, and in a life of practical contrition for the sins that were heavy on his head before his entrance into this condemned world" (bk. 2, ch. 30). It is this pattern of ancestral repetition and legacy that Arthur attempts to break by renouncing his share in the family business, and by attempting to resolve and make reparation for the crimes and memories that hang heavy over the House of Clennam.

The humiliating mental collapse of William Dorrit further demonstrates how memory can act as a burden, proving a much stronger prison than the one that confined him throughout most of his adult life. He carries it around with him, unable to accept his freedom and seeing everywhere mocking references to his former state. Significantly, the final stage of his mental collapse is referred to as "castle building," constructing an edifice of ambition that, like the Castle of Otranto, collapses under the burdens of the past. The "curse" of memory in this case resides entirely within the individual and his own imaginings. There is not the broader dimension of generational legacy or ancestral repetition that blighted the Clennam family (although Fanny and Tip suggest that Dorrit has sown his own harvest in the next generation). As such, *Little Dorrit* suggests a scaling down of focus for Gothic dramatization. The castles William Dorrit builds, and the prisons he is unable to escape from, are of his own imagining. The sphere of haunting is now confined to the mind: a development that would be explored much more fully in *Great Expectations*. Dickens's second major experiment in first-person narrative combines the Gothic with the *Bildungsroman* to lay bare the very foundations of bourgeois identity.

Great Expectations, Greater Fears

In Miss Havisham, Dickens develops further the theme of self-incarceration. Female imprisonment has been a stock device of Gothic fiction, from *The Mysteries of Udolpho* to *The Woman in White* (1860). In these treatments, women are victims of male scheming or cruelty. In *Little Dorrit* and *Great Expectations*, ill treatment by males results in incarceration that is self-imposed. In Miss Havisham's case, this imprisonment is peculiarly self-conscious and systematic, as is the way she transfers her resentment to an innocent recipient in the form of Estella. However, unlike Mrs. Clennam, there is no ancestral pattern to which her behavior conforms. Her resentment originates from her early adulthood, rather than her own up-bringing in fulfillment of ancestral antecedent or malign legacy. Her being jilted by Compeyson creates what we would now call the "trauma" upon which she fixates, and which she then bequeaths to Estella. Thus the scale and scope of Gothic legacy is here restricted to one generation, and is caused by agents who are still living for most of the narrative.

The restricted scope of Gothic enactment, as well as the entirely behavioral means of its perpetuation, are reinforced by the decidedly self-conscious and even theatrical way in which Miss Havisham turns her trauma into Gothic spectacle. Her self-incarceration is accompanied by a studied self-Gothicization, and stage-management of effect. The Gothic status of an environment traditionally accrues slowly over time. For it is usually a function of time moving on and leaving it behind: "a mere anomaly and incongruity here, out of date and out of purpose" to quote Arthur Clennam again. Satis House, however, is Gothicized instantaneously and according to Miss Havisham's fiat. The clocks are stopped, the wedding feast is left on the table, the wedding dress remains on her back. Similarly, Gothic figures tend to acquire their quirks and idiosyncrasies, which render them also "out of date and out of purpose," over time and usually unconsciously. Dracula retreats to his castle, emerging 400 years later a terrifying atavism; Roderick Usher retreats into obsession; Uncle Silas succumbs to laudanum and scheming. These figures gradually *become* objects of Gothic representation, but Miss Havisham is both subject and object of the Gothic spectacle she enacts, acutely aware of its effect on her audience. "There, there! I know nothing about times" (ch. 12), she is quick to assert to Pip, protesting too much in her urgency to maintain her performance: " 'Dear Miss Havisham,' said Miss Sarah Pocket. 'How well you look!' 'I do not,' returned Miss Havisham. 'I am yellow skin and bone' " (ch. 11). Parading around and around her parlor, haunting its corridors by night, Miss Havisham is her own Gothic folly. Pip's first impression of her sets the tone:

> Once, I had been taken to see some ghastly waxwork at the Fair, representing I know not what impossible personage lying in state. Once, I had been taken to one of our old marsh churches to see a skeleton in the ashes of a rich dress that had been dug out of a vault under the church pavement. Now, waxwork and skeleton seemed to have dark eyes that moved and looked at me. (ch. 8)

Miss Havisham appears to fashion herself on that most famous of Gothic spectacles, the waxwork effigy of a corpse Emily discovers in the Castle of Udolpho. This icon of Popish deception is reproduced in the shape of Miss Havisham, and elicits a suitable response from Pip: "I should have cried out, if I could." A "sham" perhaps at first, but in time she becomes what she sets out to be, and her demise is in high Gothic style – hoist by her own Gothic petard.

But whilst Miss Havisham's Gothic self-creation is effected within her own lifetime and without ancestral antecedents, she extends her project to the formation of Estella, the (behavioral) legatee of her resentment. She even refers to her project as a "curse." As she tells Pip on the occasion of her birthday: "'When the ruin is complete,' said she, with a ghastly look, 'and when they lay me dead, in my bride's dress on the bride's table, – which shall be done, and which will be the finished curse upon him, – so much the better if it is done on this day!'" (ch. 11). Estella's "monstrous" creation plays a role in this curse.

The Frankensteinian sub-texts and echoes have been very usefully identified in Dickens's novel, with Chris Baldick (1987) exploring the role of monstrous creation. Estella, made "stock and stone" by her schooling in artful heartlessness, turns on her creator, a "monster" of ingratitude: "I am what you have made me. Take all the praise, take all the blame" (ch. 38). Estella is made in Miss Havisham's emotional image, a cultural creation, spawned out of a brooding sense of wrong. Pip is another educational project. As Baldick puts it, he is "worked upon first by Miss Havisham, as a plaything, and then reconstructed by Magwitch as a gentleman" (Baldick 1987: 119). This new perspective troubles his own review of the events of his life. His whole narrative is refracted through a distorting lens of guilty memory and imagining, lending it a distinctly nightmarish tenor. Indeed, nightmare is a recurrent theme. From the fitful night anticipating his theft and adventure on the marshes, to the night he spends at Satis House and sees Miss Havisham haunting its corridors, to his feverish imaginings when he comes close to death, Pip scarcely records a peaceful night's sleep.

Nightmare, however, is not confined to the hours of darkness, for Pip is fearful throughout his narrative. The Gothic aspects of the text take their coloring from and are largely enacted within the theater of his troubled memory. The opening scenes on the marshes set the tone in this respect, so brilliantly captured in David Lean's film adaptation of 1946. As Magwitch departs: "he looked in my young eyes as if he were eluding the hands of the dead people, stretching up cautiously out of their graves, to get a twist upon his ankle and pull him in"; or, as he approaches the gibbet, Pip imagines "he were the pirate come to life, and come down, and going back to hook himself up again. It gave me a terrible turn when I thought so" (ch. 1). But whilst graves claiming the living or corpses returning to life are potent images of Gothic representation, symbolizing the dead hand of the past, they are not entirely appropriate symbols in this particular novel. For ancestors are not to blame here. The ghosts in this novel are all living. Thus when Pip meets Magwitch again in adult life, and learns the horrible truth about his expectations, he doubts:

> if a ghost could have been more terrible to me, up in those lonely rooms in the long evenings and long nights, with the wind and the rain always rushing by. A ghost could not have been taken and hanged on my account, and the consideration that he could be, and the dread that he would be, were no small addition to my horrors. (ch. 40)

It is not the dead that drag him back into their past, but the living, into his own.

If Pip is haunted, it is by his own past – by guilt, and by moral failure. And if he is a monster, then he is constructed entirely out of cultural parts, clothes, tastes, and educational accomplishments. Not the cosmos, nor ancestry, nor politics can be blamed for the burdens both Estella and Pip carry around with them. The Gothic has begun to loosen its external moorings to geography, ideology, or politics. Satis House is but a Gothic stage set, the real terrors take place in the guilty and troubled recollections of a constructed bourgeois "experiment." Legacies, burdens, hauntings are within the mind and confined to one lifetime. The domain that Freud would come to claim as his own is here laid out by Dickens's Gothic imaginings.

Dickens's own Gothic Legacy

Dickens helped to change the face of Gothic fiction. He is also largely responsible for Gothicizing our view of Victorian England, and specifically London. In his hands, the Gothic moved from the remote and exotic to the familiar worlds of everyday existence. From fictions where plausibility was premised on their being distanced in time and space, horrors were now found in the very heart of the modern metropolis. Dickens's Gothic dispenses with the disavowals and distancing of romance, demarcating a new Gothic terrain, where crumbling, ancient tenements preserving criminal memories exist cheek-by-jowl with, and yet are removed from, the law-bound modern metropolis. In *Bleak House*, the labyrinth is extended to embrace all of Britain, mired in the fog and inertia of a political order deadlocked by deference to "The Wisdom of our Ancestors." That novel's extraordinary opening transforms London in our imaginations, contributing to a version of the capital that will ever invite the epithet "Dickensian." "Fog everywhere . . . Gas looming through the fog in divers places in the streets . . . Most of the shops lighted two hours before their time – as the gas seems to know, for it has a haggard and unwilling look" (ch. 1).

Perhaps Oscar Wilde, never a fan of Dickens, got it wrong when he suggested in "The Decay of Lying" (1889) that Turner and the Impressionists "invented" the fogs of London. Dickens, perhaps, has a greater or more lasting claim to our seeing London in this way. For when the term "Dickensian London" is used, it often evokes a Gothic vision – of swirling fogs, cobbled labyrinthine streets, with menace or mystery stalking their ways. *Oliver Twist* and *Bleak House* mapped out the cityscape through which Stevenson's Mr. Hyde, and his avatar Jack the Ripper, would permanently stalk in our imaginations. The London of Sherlock Holmes, of David Lean's *Elephant Man* (1980), of Peter Ackroyd and Iain Sinclair is first of all Dickens's London. He made the capital Gothic.

From the public to the domestic, from the geographical to the psychological, Dickens also contributed to a scaling down of the scope and emphasis of Gothic representation. He made Gothic ordinary, and therefore arguably more disturbing. In *Dombey and Son*, *Little Dorrit*, and *Great Expectations* the world of bourgeois existence is rendered Gothic. London town houses, and the secret breasts and pockets of individuals, become the repositories of guilty secrets and mysteries. The sensation novels of Wilkie Collins and Mary Elizabeth Braddon were called at the time the "Dickensian" School. And rightly so, for their suburban Gothic narratives, which discarded, in Henry James's words, the "terrors of Udolpho" for "those most mysterious of mysteries, the mysteries that are at our own doors" (quoted in Taylor 1998: xiv), were following Dickens's example.

It is a truism of Gothic criticism that its significance is "psychological," and that the authentic sphere of its enactments is the "dreamscape" of unconscious meaning. Using Freud as the master key to Gothic meaning, critics have projected twentieth-century models back onto eighteenth- and nineteenth-century texts, imagining a universal pattern which these fictions conform to and confirm. But psychology does have its due (albeit without the need for Freudian back-projection), for in *Little Dorrit* and *Great Expectations*, and in the midnight "spectres" of John Jasper's opium reveries, or the "demons" he carves "out of his own heart" (Paroissien 2002: 312), the mind does become the legitimate domain for Gothic representation. What we witness in the nineteenth century is a scaling down of Gothic focus. From landscapes to mindscapes, the Gothic found and came to rest in a new domain. This transformation can be traced through the Dickensian canon.

NOTES

1 For a much fuller discussion of this defining attitude throughout the development of Gothic fiction, see Mighall (1999); or, more succinctly, Baldick (1993: xi–xxiii).

2 On Dickens's debt to Scott, see Ian Duncan (1992) and John Bowen (2000, 2003). The best study of the Newgate novel is still Hollingsworth (1963).

3 For a full discussion of Dickens's urban Gothic landscape, see Mighall (1999: ch. 2).

REFERENCES AND FURTHER READING

Baldick, Chris (1987). *In Frankenstein's Shadow: Myth, Monstrosity and Nineteenth-century Writing.* Oxford: Clarendon Press.

— (Ed.) (1992). *The Oxford Book of Gothic Tales.* Oxford: Oxford University Press.

Bowen, John (2000). *The Other Dickens: Pickwick to Chuzzlewit.* Oxford: Oxford University Press.

— (Ed.) (2003) *Barnaby Rudge.* London: Penguin.

Duncan, Ian (1992). *Modern Romance and Transformations of the Novel: The Gothic, Scott, Dickens.* Cambridge: Cambridge University Press.

Hollingsworth, Keith (1963). *The Newgate Novel 1830–1847: Bulwer, Ainsworth, Dickens, and Thackeray.* Detroit: Wayne State University Press.

Hollington, Michael (1999). Boz's Gothic gargoyles. *Dickens Quarterly*, 16, 160–76.

House, Humphry (1960). *The Dickens World.* London: Oxford University Press (original work published 1941).

Mighall, Robert (1999). *A Geography of Victorian Gothic Fiction: Mapping History's Nightmares.* Oxford: Oxford University Press.

Page, Norman (Ed.) (2000) Introduction. *The Old Curiosity Shop.* London: Penguin.

Paroissien, David (Ed.) (2002) *The Mystery of Edwin Drood.* London: Penguin.

Sage, Victor (1988). *Horror Fiction in the Protestant Tradition.* Basingstoke: Macmillan.

Scott, Walter (1825). Mrs Radcliffe. In *Lives of the Novelists*, vol. 1. Paris: A. and W. Galighani.

Taylor, Jenny Bourne (Ed.) (1998). *Lady Audley's Secret.* Penguin: Harmondsworth.

7

Illustrations

Malcolm Andrews

Dickens was the most intensely visual of Victorian writers and yet his novels, more than any by his contemporaries, have come to seem incomplete without their original illustrations. Several questions arise from this apparent contradiction. I shall address three of them in particular in this chapter: how well served was Dickens by his illustrators, Cruikshank and Phiz particularly; what are the functions of illustration; and does Dickens need illustrating? As to the last question, we seem to have become conditioned into thinking that those original illustrations are inseparable from the verbal text, and much ingenuity has been exercised in analysis of their iconography with the implicit or explicit aim of justifying their integral presence in Dickens's books. This chapter offers a dissenting view.

It might be helpful at the outset briefly to take stock of the particular graphic traditions to which Dickens's principal illustrators were heirs. This is ground already covered in considerable detail elsewhere, and the reader who wishes to explore it more extensively and in greater depth is recommended to the work of, among others, John Harvey (1970), Jane Rabb Cohen (1980), and Martin Meisel (1983). I am going to focus on the issue of caricature and on some of the tensions between narrative and tableau, which book illustrations traditionally generate.

Early Dickens drew heavily on traditions of graphic satire both for his narrative structures and for his characterization. He was a lifelong admirer of William Hogarth, and his Gad's Hill home contained 48 prints by the artist. Hogarth was his great ideological model, as uncompromising social realist, moral propagandist, and satirist, "with a power and depth of thought which belonged to few men before him," as he wrote in his 1841 Preface to *Oliver Twist*. Dickens saw himself as the literary successor to the great artist in his own candid, unromanticized portrayal of "the very dregs of life" in *Oliver Twist*.

The affinities between Dickens and Hogarth were recognized early in Dickens's career. Sydney Smith in 1837 remarked of *Sketches by Boz* that "the Soul of Hogarth has migrated into the Body of Mr. Dickens" (Smith 1837: 5). T. H. Lister in 1838 wrote:

What was in painting, such very nearly is Mr. Dickens in prose fiction. The same turn of mind – the same species of power displays itself strongly in each. Like Hogarth he takes a keen and practical view of life – is an able satirist – very successful in depicting the ludicrous side of human nature, and rendering its follies more apparent by humorous exaggeration – peculiarly skilful in his management of details, throwing in circumstances which serve not only to complete the picture before us, but to suggest indirectly antecedent events which cannot be brought before our eyes. Hogarth's cobweb over the poor-box, and the plan for paying off the national debt, hanging from the pocket of a prisoner in the Fleet, are strokes of satire very similar to some in the writings of Mr. Dickens. (Lister 1838: 76)

R. H. Horne in 1844 developed an extended comparison between the two. He argued that they were "in their true element" and at their best "when dealing with characters full of unscrupulous life, of genial humour, or of depravities and follies; or with characters of tragic force and heart-felt pathos" (Horne 1844: 94); that they both had a predilection for the lower classes of society; that both used principal characters not so much to concentrate attention on them as to function as "centres of attraction" to introduce numerous other characters which "circle them continually with a buzzing world of outward vitality" (1844: 95); and that both had an inclination for what Charles Lamb called "the dumb rhetoric of the scenery", for animating furniture and houses.

Cruikshank, regarded as the "modern Hogarth," was the obvious choice for illustrator, both for the "Every-day Life and Every-day People" portrayed by Boz in his *Sketches* and for *Oliver Twist*. Cruikshank was familiar not only with Hogarth but the whole tradition of graphic satire, the work of Rowlandson (especially admiring his tinted drawings), and Gillray, acclaiming the latter as "the prince of caricaturists" (Patten 1992: 83).

In insisting on his own realism in *Oliver Twist*, Dickens does not comment on Hogarth's zest for caricature – that aspect would not help his case. And yet caricature is one issue that complicated the affinities between Dickens and Hogarth, made Cruikshank and Boz ideal collaborators for a short while, and then later bedeviled Dickens's more ambitious mature work. Social realism does not necessarily entail pictorial naturalism, and both Dickens and Hogarth, and Dickens's illustrators, are caught up in the complexities of this relationship. What *is* caricature? Thackeray pin-pointed what he felt to be Dickens's deviation from true realism in the depiction of Nancy, in the course of an essay published the year before Dickens's Preface: indeed, Dickens may well have been responding to this criticism in his Preface. Thackeray is reporting on his attending a public hanging. Dickens is coupled with Cruikshank and the case against them is made carefully; the passage needs quoting at some length:

There were a considerable number of girls, too, of the same age; one that Cruikshank and Boz might have taken as a study for Nancy. The girl was a young thief's mistress evidently; if attacked, ready to reply without a particle of modesty; could give as good ribaldry as she got; made no secret (and there were several inquiries) as to her profession and means of livelihood. But with all this, there was something good about the girl; a sort of devil-may-care candour and simplicity that one could not fail to see. Her answers to some of the coarse questions put to her, were very ready and good-humoured. She had a friend with her of the same age and class, of whom she seemed to be very fond, and who looked up to her for protection. Both of these women had beautiful eyes. Devil-may-care's were extraordinarily bright and blue, an admirably fair complexion, and a large red mouth full of white teeth. *Au reste*, ugly, stunted, thick-limbed, and by no means a beauty. Her friend could not be more than fifteen. They were not in rags, but had greasy cotton shawls, and old, faded, rag-shop bonnets. I was curious to look at them, having, in late fashionable novels, read many accounts of such personages. Bah! what figments these novelists tell us! Boz, who knows life well, knows that his Miss Nancy is the most unreal fantastical personage possible; no more like a thief's mistress than one of Gesner's shepherdesses resembles a real country wench. He dare not tell the truth concerning such young ladies. They have, no doubt, virtues like other human creatures; nay, their position engenders virtues that are not called into exercise among other women. But on these an honest painter has no right to dwell; not being able to paint the whole portrait, he has no right to present one or two favourable points as characterizing the whole; and therefore, in fact, had better leave the picture alone altogether. (Thackeray 1840: 45–6)

Caricature is the selective amplification of specific features, moral or physical, and represents personality as dominated by those features. Its synechdochic manipulation of character distorts by both commission (deliberate exaggeration) and omission (deliberate neglect of elements that would compromise the narrowed focus). It needs to upset the dynamic balance of the heterogeneous elements that go to make up human personality, and in doing so simplifies identity and flattens character, and this can result in reductively grotesque forms as well as reductive idealization. Charlotte Brontë, for example, thought Esther's narrative in *Bleak House* "weak and twaddling," and that in Esther herself "an amiable nature is caricatured, not faithfully rendered" (Brontë 1852: 4). Thackeray's carefully balanced picture – "the whole portrait" – of these two prostitutes emphasizes the mixed composition of characteristics that makes them both attractive and repulsive, physically and morally. It is from this point of view that he challenges Dickens's creations on the grounds that Dickens has been too selective in his portrait of Nancy: the girl's virtues dominate her character and distort her into a caricature of pious remorse and womanly tenderness. Nancy's first appearance, with her friend Bet, is actually not dissimilar to Thackeray's description of the two girls at the hanging:

They wore a good deal of hair: not very neatly turned up behind; and were rather untidy about the shoes and stockings. They were not exactly pretty, perhaps; but they had a great deal of colour in their faces; and looked quite stout and hearty. Being remarkably free and agreeable in their manners, Oliver thought them very nice girls indeed. As there is no doubt they were. (*Oliver Twist* ch. 9)

Oliver asking for More

Figure 7.1   George Cruikshank, *Oliver Twist*.

Oliver plucks up a Spirit

Figure 7.2   George Cruikshank, *Oliver Twist*.

Dickens is ironically using Oliver's naïve viewpoint here, probably so as to avoid too explicit an introduction to the girls' appearance and profession. Stout, hearty, and disheveled – these are the guidelines for the illustrator, and this is the figure that Cruikshank renders in the few illustrations to feature Nancy. Dickens might argue that, as Nancy changes, these virtues (remorse and womanly tenderness) do indeed represent the core of the girl, her essence, and they have come to dominate her life. But how are the caricaturist illustrators to respond to these problems? Cruikshank, in following Dickens's story in *Oliver Twist*, sometimes moved from one caricature mode to another in depicting characters who undergo development. In the famous illustration of Oliver asking for more food (figure 7.1), the hero is depicted as indistinguishable from the other boys, broken-spirited, emaciated, head craning up. He and the others, rendered in Expressionist manner, resemble hungry baby birds, all mouths and plaintive eyes. But when Oliver's spirit is roused, and in his impassioned loyalty he fells Claypole for insulting his mother, Cruikshank not only depicts him in heroic posture but also performs cosmetic surgery on him (figure 7.2). Oliver's features have been grecianized. The lank, dark hair of the earlier portrait has been crisped and gilded, and the profile given classical nobility with the nose now continuing the line of the forehead. Both versions caricature the subject in externalizing the psychological transformation.

These two plates and the relationship between them have drawn much discussion, and not surprisingly, since they raise fundamental questions about the purpose and value of book illustration, as well as more specific questions about Dickens's relationship with his illustrator. Let us take the second of those questions first. Dickens does not comment on these two plates in the surviving correspondence between him and Cruikshank, beyond telling his publisher that for the first scene he thought he had "hit on a capital notion for myself, and one which will bring Cruikshank out" (*Letters* 1: 224). However, Cruikshank did have something to say about their initial collaboration on the story. In a letter to *The Times* (December 30, 1871) he claimed that he and Dickens had disagreed about the appearance of Oliver:

> Mr. Dickens wanted rather a queer kind of chap, and although this was contrary to my original idea, I complied with his request, feeling that it would not be right to dictate too much to the writer of the story, and then appeared "Oliver Asking for More" . . . I earnestly begged of him to let me make Oliver a nice pretty little boy, and if we so represented him, the public – and particularly the ladies – would be sure to take a greater interest in him, and the work would then be a certain success. Mr. Dickens agreed to that request, and I need not add here that my prophecy was fulfilled: and if any one will take the trouble to look at my representations of "Oliver", they will see that the appearance of the boy is altered after the first two illustrations. (Kitton 1899: 21)

Cruikshank's claims here and elsewhere to have originated much of *Oliver Twist*'s characterization and storyline (see, for example, Patten 1996: 56) remain largely uncorroborated. It is interesting, incidentally, that in that letter to *The Times* Dickens is reported as envisaging Oliver as "rather a queer kind of chap." If those were

Dickens's own words, they closely resemble the way he used to talk about his own childhood self, "a very odd little child" (*Letters* 8: 51), and the "queer small boy" (his former self) encountered in his Uncommercial Traveller essay "Travelling Abroad" – all of which suggests a degree of identification with his hero. However, there is no such description of Oliver in the text. Cruikshank's account certainly helps to explain the change in Oliver's appearance evident in the plates shown in figures 7.1 and 7.2, though subsequent portraits of Oliver never quite restore the classical nobility of that third plate (figure 7.2), nor make him conspicuously "pretty."

Oliver Twist is in some respects an allegory, as Dickens hinted in his 1841 Preface: "I wished to shew, in little Oliver, the principle of Good surviving through every adverse circumstance, and triumphing at last." In this mode of fiction the illustrator has a license to mark moral change in the language of physical alterations (how else could it be done?), even though such change seems to flout realist consistency. Here is Dickens amused by the sight of some moralistic prints in the window of a bookshop in "Dullborough," where Goodness and Evil are depicted in the transformation of a Dustman and Sailor from tipsy layabouts to virtuous citizens:

> When they were leaning (they were intimate friends) against a post, drunk and reckless, with surpassingly bad hats on, and their hair over their foreheads, they were rather picturesque, and looked as if they might be agreeable men if they would not be beasts. But when they had got over their bad propensities, and when, as a consequence, their heads had swelled alarmingly, their hair had got so curly that it lifted their blown-out cheeks up, their coat-cuffs were so long that they never could do any work, and their eyes were so wide open that they never could do any sleep, they presented a spectacle calculated to plunge a timid nature into the depths of Infamy. (*Journalism* 4: 146)

This is what has happened to Oliver as his righteous indignation acts like a dose of steroids and he seems to burst out of his meager clothing, his head impressively enlarged and his hair thick with curls. Something of the same process happens to Fagin, but in reverse. The "merry old gentleman" of the first scenes in which he appears becomes "the hideous old man . . . like some loathsome reptile, engendered in the slime and darkness through which he moved" (ch. 19). The same process happens to Sikes, who looks increasingly simian in the illustrations as the story moves toward its end. The bestialized Fagin is finally represented by Cruikshank in the condemned cell as a scrawny bird of prey, with his claw hands up to his beak nose (figure 7.3). It is a wonderful image, as is the plate of Sikes on the roof, "The Last Chance." It is worth noting, though, that the bestialization of both villains is counterpointed in the text when the narrator briefly discloses their mental anguish and underlines their humanity in their last days and hours (Fagin at his trial and Sikes in flight tormented by his deed).

These are touches disappointingly beyond the reach of the illustrator, who simply confirms them as caricatured evil, and concentrates on the cruder counterpointing of good and evil as the story reaches its end. Thus the wholly opposite fortunes of the story's villain and hero are focused in the comparison between the "Condemned Cell" plate and the last plate, "Rose Maylie and Oliver" (figure 7.4). The hunched animal

Fagin in the Condemned Cell

Figure 7.3   George Cruikshank, *Oliver Twist*.

Rose Maylie and Oliver

Figure 7.4　George Cruikshank, *Oliver Twist*.

posture of Fagin is contrasted with the upright statuesque young Oliver; and the contrast is paradoxically accentuated by a degree of parallelism in the two designs. The configuration of the two rooms has similarities. In each case, we view a right-hand corner, a high-set window (with harsh cross-barring on the one and delicate diamond lattice on the other), a bench against the wall, an inscription on the right-hand wall (the Sheriff's order for execution on the one and the memorial to Oliver's mother on the other). Light from outside falls on the dread notice and rims the dark figure of the condemned man. In the church picture, the light seems to come from inside and bathes Oliver in its glow.

Parallels of this kind occur also near the start of the story, in the two plates "Oliver Asking for More" (figure 7.1) and "Oliver Introduced to the Respectable Old Gentleman [Fagin]." In each one, Oliver is seen standing in supplicant posture before his adult provider. The spoon and plate in his hands in the first are replaced by stick and hat in the second. Immediately behind him in each is a group of boys, all hungry eyes and mouths in the first and all plump-faced and pipe-smoking in the second. The adult providers are contrasted: the workhouse master is fat and outraged, Fagin is shriveled and genial.

This system of structural parallelism and thematic contrast is something that Cruikshank continued to rely on, in, for example, his sequence of prints warning of the evils of drink, *The Bottle* (1847). Cruikshank drew this scheme of parallels from Hogarth's Progress pictures. The first, second, and fourth plates of *Industry and Idleness* (1747), for example, show the Industrious Apprentice on the right, bathing in the approval of his adjacent master or in the pious adoration of his master's daughter, soon to be his wife. It is as though that corner becomes reserved for Virtue and Beauty and the other side for Vice and Ugliness. This kind of schematic patterning worked well for Cruikshank not only in his own "Progress," *The Bottle*, but also for his collaboration with Dickens. *Oliver Twist* was a kind of Progress novel: indeed, it was subtitled *A Parish Boy's Progress*, in allusion to Bunyan's *Pilgrim's Progress* and Hogarth's Progress sequences. It is no wonder the early collaboration with Cruikshank was so successful. Their artistic relationship was symbiotic, and recognized as such. The *Spectator* in 1836 acclaimed Boz as "the Cruikshank of writers."

Hogarth was also highly influential on Dickens in formal terms. His Progress paintings and their wide dissemination as prints provided Dickens with models for constructing a narrative as a sequence of significant scenes, especially in cautionary fables. One early example can be seen in "Meditations in Monmouth Street." In this sketch, Boz puts an imaginary inhabitant into a second-hand suit of boy's clothes and fancies he can trace the growth and development of that boy, stage by stage through other sets of second-hand clothes, into a delinquent man and eventually into a hardened criminal. The sequence is strongly visualized as if a succession of scenes were literally being paraded before Boz: "We knew at once, as anybody would, who glanced at that broad-skirted green coat, with the large metal buttons . . . We saw the bare and miserable room . . . crowded with his wife and children, pale, hungry and emaciated; the man . . . staggering to the tap-room" (*Sketches by Boz* 100–1). The tableau-esque format of the narrative, the attention to telling small details, and the over-arching didactic agenda all derive from Hogarth and from Hogarth's descendants in that graphic tradition. The same technique is detectable in *Oliver Twist*.

Cruikshank's illustrations depicted *Oliver Twist*'s action in shallow spaces, with dramatic chiaroscuro, and to that degree matches Dickens's theatrical mode in *Oliver Twist*. Most of the scenes happen in small rooms like low-budget stage sets. The characters, singly or in groups, press forward with urgency and energy. When we turn to Phiz's illustrations to *Pickwick Papers* we are, of course, in different country. For one thing, much of what is illustrated *is* countryside. Spaces open wide, and fade away into the distance. Characters are rather more recessed in the picture space; they have more room to move. They do not bear down on the reader as they do so often in Cruikshank. The wonderfully concentrated, grotesque vitality of Cruikshank is diffused as Phiz finesses scenic details that absorb much of the energy drawn from the characters themselves. Phiz followed a steep learning curve in *Pickwick*. John Harvey (1970) has demonstrated clearly how, when Phiz had to redraw the early plates for *Pickwick* (as the originals for the part-issue were too worn to use for the volume edition), he transformed the scenes. The stiff poses of the figures in the originals became relaxed and more diverse and more expressive in attitude. Spatial proportion was better defined, and more fully and more eloquently detailed.

This development of greater anecdotal depth and dramatic energy can be seen in the two versions of the plate "Mrs. Bardell Faints in Mr. Pickwick's Arms" (a focus for interesting discussions and conflicting evaluations by John Harvey [1970], Michael Steig [1978], and James Kinsley [1986]). In the first version (figure 7.5), the figures are arranged in a frieze, absolutely parallel to the picture plane, as are the open door and the back wall of Mr. Pickwick's room. The characters lack volume and animation. In fact, they look like little cut-outs for a toy theater, mounted on a single batten and slid in from stage left. The room is fairly featureless. The great blank space of the mirror is surmounted by a picture of dull, sketchy landscape. On top of the bookcase behind the door is a bust of what is probably a philosopher and (according to Steig) a stuffed owl, two shadowy items presumably to signify Mr. Pickwick's philosophical inclinations. ⁴

The revised plate (figure 7.6) dispenses with these and introduces much more commotion in the main scene. A larger Mrs. Bardell collapses more realistically against Pickwick, who braces his leg to receive the weight of his "lovely burden," only to have it kicked by a bigger and more ebullient Master Bardell. The door is angled out, the better to suggest that it has just been opened, and the tall middle character is caught in mid-stride as he enters. The group of clubmen is broken up: they tilt in different directions to express their astonishment, and the one on the far right breaks the straight ground-line. The recession in the room is better managed, and some pertinent detail is introduced. The blank of the mirror is interrupted by a clock with the figure of Father Time, and the framed picture replaces the empty landscape with a drama depicting Cupid aiming his bow at a languorous woman, as a comic take on

Figure 7.5   Phiz, "Mrs. Bardell Faints in Mr. Pickwick's Arms," etching for first edition of *Pickwick Papers*.

the action below. Thus the setting and the human event collaborate more energetically.

How does it relate to the text at this point? This raises important issues of focus and selection, of the kind well exemplified by Edward Hodnett in his discussion of the famous scene of Don Quixote and the windmills:

> The decision to illustrate that passage is only the beginning. There are roughly four moments to choose from in order to illustrate it: (a) Don Quixote and Sancho Panza

Figure 7.6 Phiz, "Mrs. Bardell Faints in Mr. Pickwick's Arms," new etching for second edition of *Pickwick Papers*.

disagreeing about whether they are looking at giants or windmills at a distance in the mist; (b) Don Quixote with spear leveled riding toward the windmills; (c) the moment of impact; and (d) the moment after. But each of these moments can be subdivided. The fourth choice can show Don Quixote whirled aloft on a sail, deposited on the ground in disarray, or being put back together by Sancho Panza. Then the artist has to decide at what distance the action takes place. (Hodnett 1982: 7–8)

The Election at Eatanswill

Figure 7.7   Phiz, The Pickwick Papers.

Mr. Bob Sawyer's Mode of Travelling

Figure 7.8   Phiz, *The Pickwick Papers*.

Phiz in the fainting scene, as in so many other illustrations, confronts the same problems. What he designs here looks like the freezing of one particular moment in the narrative, but in fact he has compressed a sequence of incidents into one image: first, the sudden entry into the room of the clubmen and Master Bardell; second, the paralyzed moment when everyone is staring at everyone else; third, Master Bardell's assault on Mr. Pickwick. The revised plate gives the impression of the clubmen walking in to discover Master Bardell hard at work kicking Mr. Pickwick. The first version, for all its stiffness, is probably the more accurate snapshot of a single moment in the text, the third one described above.

Phiz is now well into his stride. In fact, there had been rapid development in his work in the months following the fainting scene. He was managing boisterous crowds with gusto and skill, especially given the confined picture space in which he had to work. The very next illustration, "The Election at Eatanswill" (figure 7.7), establishes a pattern in the relationship between the stately, would-be detached Pickwick and the unruly world he is commissioned to observe and report on. Robert Patten (1969) has pointed out how, in the illustrations to Part VII, Pickwick is shown relatively isolated from either the community, as in "Mr. Pickwick in the Pound," where he is fenced off from the jeering villagers, or officialdom, as in "Mr. Pickwick and Sam in the Attorney's Office," where the smirking clerks look down on Pickwick, "the supposed trifler with female hearts," as he waits in humiliation for his appointment with Mr. Fogg. In each case, baffled dignity is thrown into strong relief by the environing riotous or wily populace.

It is the story of the novel itself, and Phiz tunes into it from Eatanswill onward as this motif is enacted in illustrations across the whole book. In the Eatanswill plate (figure 7.7), Pickwick and the civic dignitaries are literally elevated above the mob, and their stiff upright poses, accentuated by their top hats, are counterpointed by the swirling, brawling human chaos below. It looks like a cartoon representation of the British class system. In a later plate, "Mr. Bob Sawyer's Mode of Travelling" (figure 7.8), Pickwick is boxed in again, inside the carriage, his dignity affronted by his traveling companion's conspicuously boozy nonchalance, which forms a disreputable spectacle for the coachload they are about to pass (seen above Pickwick's head) and the Irish family of beggars swarming round the carriage itself, their shapes almost assimilated to the clouds of dust stirred up by the carriage.

The plate could serve almost as an emblem-picture figuring the novel's theme. The relationship captured between Pickwick and the crowds gives visual form to Bakhtin's concept of carnival and the bodily element in grotesque realism, which is "something universal, representing all the people":

> As such it is opposed to severance from the material and bodily roots of the world . . . [it] is contained not in the biological individual, not in the bourgeois ego, but in the people, a people who are continually growing and renewed . . . The leading themes of these images of bodily life are fertility, growth, and a brimming-over abundance . . . The people's laughter which characterized all the forms of popular realism from immemorial

times was linked with the bodily lower stratum. Laughter degrades and materializes. (Bakhtin 1984: 19–20)

This schema is caught by Phiz in plate after plate: the monolithic "bourgeois ego" of Pickwick, standing on his dignity, isolated from and harried by "the people" with their laughter and "brimming-over abundance" of vitality. Once caught, he could repeat the confrontational theme with endless variations throughout *Pickwick*.

The 1840s saw Phiz developing some of his best work, and joining a group of other illustrators for various new publishing projects by Dickens. *Master Humphrey's Clock* (1840–1) had woodcut illustrations incorporated into the pages of text and carried work by George Cattermole, Samuel Williams, and Daniel Maclise. The five Christmas books, beginning with *A Christmas Carol* (1843), were illustrated by John Leech, Maclise, Richard Doyle, Clarkson Stanfield, Edward Landseer, John Tenniel, and Marcus Stone. *Pictures from Italy* (1846) had four engravings by Samuel Palmer. But it was Phiz, and Phiz only, who illustrated the twenty-number novels of the 1840s, *Martin Chuzzlewit*, *Dombey and Son*, and *David Copperfield*. Thereafter, he illustrated just three more of the monthly-number novels: *Bleak House*, *Little Dorrit*, and *A Tale of Two Cities*.

The *Pickwick* plate just discussed (Bob Sawyer traveling, figure 7.8), its functioning both microcosmically as an illustration of a particular moment in the novel and macrocosmically as a kind of allegory of the novel's master-motif, represents Phiz the book-illustrator at his best. It also prompts questions about the strategic role of book illustration, especially its dual agenda: should illustration be sharply localized or more broadly summative, or some hybrid of the two? The issue arises in interesting ways in *Dombey and Son*.

In the monthly wrapper design for *Dombey and Son* (figure 7.9), Phiz was presumably charged with giving a broad outline of the rise and fall of the House of Dombey. In the event, Dickens was pleased: "I think the cover very good: perhaps with a little too much in it, but that is an ungrateful objection" (*Letters* 4: 620). Phiz has depicted a wheel-of-fortune chronicle, moving clockwise from the dawn of mercantile prosperity up the left side as people scramble toward the throne of Dombey triumphant, with scenes from the firm's office on the left and on the right Dombey MP and Dombey's wedding; then we follow down via the fragile house of cards to scenes of shipwreck and crippled old age as Dombey and *Daughter* are reconciled. This is narrative, promising a lively, developing history of Dombey and his fortunes, a reconfiguration in circular form of the Progress. Dickens referred to Phiz's wrapper designs as "shadowing out [the story's] drift and bearing (*Letters* 4: 648–9), and commended the work as a kind of model for what he called the "general illustration" he required for one of his Christmas books.

Phiz had to come up with his wrapper design before the story was written. But his frontispiece was done once the novel had finished its run. This time he produced a more concentrated allegorical picture (figure 7.10), and it represents a rather different novel. The wrapper design was predominantly about the public world of Dombey

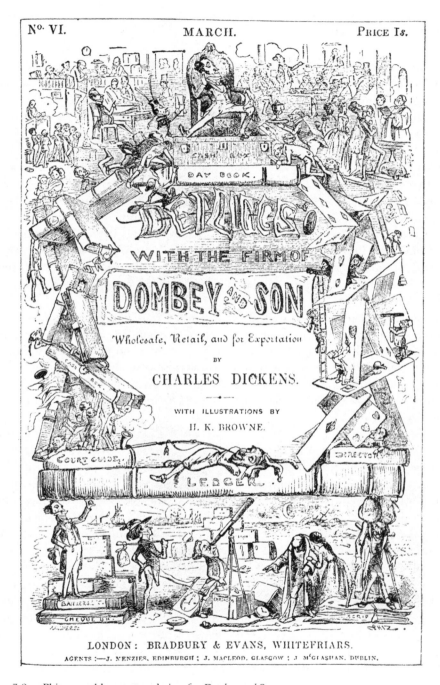

Figure 7.9   Phiz, monthly wrapper design for *Dombey and Son*.

Figure 7.10   Phiz, frontispiece to *Dombey and Son*.

and his business, patriarchy and plutocracy, and linearly mapped. The frontispiece accentuates the other story, the feminine narrative, curvaceous rhythms, the language of the waves and of Florence's dissolving in tears, a world teeming with children seeming to pay tribute to the two central children, Paul and Florence. Instead of circling up to images of Dombey's supreme commercial, material power, this picture rises to heavenly radiance. Avenging angels and demon figures on either side lower over the doomed figures of corruption, Carker and Mrs. Skewton. The wrapper mapped the story that was planned; the frontispiece distilled the story that was written.

The question presses out at us from these reflections: what is an illustrator supposed to do? Is his (or her) primary job to intervene in the reading experience with a freeze-frame moment in the passing story, a still from the movie? Or should he (or she) try to encapsulate within his (or her) single vignette hints of the larger thematic design to which this brief moment relates? Book illustrations are "Bursts of lateral development in a progressive movement," as Martin Meisel put it in his excellent discussion of these issues in *Realizations* (1983: 56). They are browsing pastures, rest areas on the narrative journey. They may have direct service value in relation to the text in, for example, amplifying information or giving sharp visual focus to character, but they can absorb the reader in other ways – and powerfully so. It can take some time to wander around Phiz's "sets," whether exterior or interior, absorbing the details and the general ambience. The illusion of the fictional world is reinforced, as the mind's-eye construction from the text of a scene, a room, a figure, is supplemented by the actual eye's spectacle of the picture of that room and figure. Illustrations can thus tuck you more tightly and deeply into the world of the novel, and increase the competition for your attention between its own world and the real world.

Testimony to the power of illustration to do just this comes from the recollections of the poet Norman Nicholson. He is recalling his childhood (he was born in 1914) and his early reading of Dickens – in this case *Dombey and Son* – and was particularly struck by the plate "Paul and Mrs. Pipchin" (figure 7.11):

> [It] shows old Mrs. Pipchin, in her widow's weeds, sitting beside little Paul Dombey, and staring into the fire. I had never seen widow's weeds, of course, but everything else in that illustration, drawn in the 1840s, was as familiar to me eighty years later, as the flags of my own back yard. The little, high, wooden chair, with rails like the rungs of a ladder, is the chair I sat in at meal-times when I was Paul Dombey's age. The fireplace itself, the bars across the grate, the kettle on the coals, the bellows hanging at the side, the brass shovel on the curb, the mirrored over-mantel, the mat, the table swathed in plush, the aspidistra on the wall-bracket – all these I had seen many times in my own house, or Grandpa Sobey's, or Grandma Nicholson's or Uncle Jim's. On a winter tea-time, before the gas was lit, the fitful firelight populated the room with fantasies as weird as any in Dickens. I would pick up my book sometimes and try to read by the glow of the coals, and the world I entered seemed not far removed from the world I had left. It was no more than walking from one room to another. (Nicholson 1975: 144–5)

Figure 7.11 Phiz, *Dombey and Son*, "Paul and Mrs. Pipchin."

slimy piles, now hiding it in mud or long rank grass, now dragging it heavily over rough stones and gravel, now feigning to yield it to its own element, and in the same action luring it away, until, tired of the ugly plaything, it flung it on a swamp—a dismal place where pirates had swung in chains, through many a wintry night—and left it there to bleach.

And there it lay, alone. The sky was red with flame, and the water that bore it there, had been tinged with the sullen light as it flowed along. The place, the deserted carcase had left so recently, a living man, was now a blazing ruin. There was something of the glare upon its face. The hair, stirred by the damp breeze, played in a kind of mockery of death—such a mockery as the dead man himself would have revelled in when alive—about its head, and its dress fluttered idly in the night wind.

CHAPTER THE SIXTY EIGHTH.

LIGHTED rooms, bright fires, cheerful faces, the music of glad voices, words of love and welcome, warm hearts, and tears of happiness what a change is this! But it is to such delights that Kit is hastening. They are awaiting him, he knows. He fears he will die of joy before he gets among them.

They have prepared him for this, all day. He is not to be carried off to-morrow with the rest, they tell him first. By degrees they let him know that doubts have arisen, that inquiries are to be made, and perhaps he may be pardoned after all. At last, the evening being come, they bring him to a

Figure 7.12   Phiz, *The Old Curiosity Shop*, "Death of Quilp."

CHIRP THE FIRST. **11**

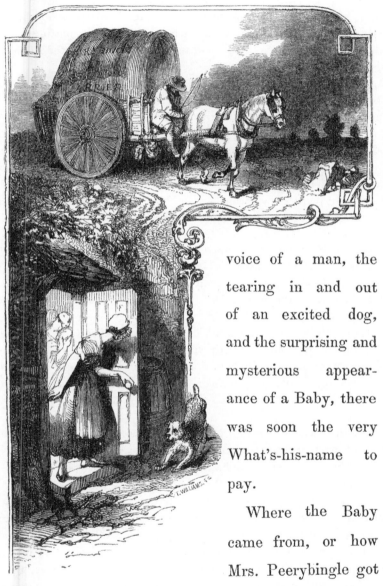

voice of a man, the tearing in and out of an excited dog, and the surprising and mysterious appearance of a Baby, there was soon the very What's-his-name to pay.

Where the Baby came from, or how Mrs. Peerybingle got hold of it in that flash of time, *I* don't know. But a live Baby there was, in Mrs. Peerybingle's arms ; and

Figure 7.13 Stanfield, *The Cricket on the Hearth.*

This degree of closeness between Dickens's imaginary world and the real world of the reader has largely passed away. The furnishings that Nicholson describes as part of his life have now passed into museums, where they lie in period-room reconstructions. The pictures, like the old furniture they contain, are similarly period pieces, with a period charm, but Dickens, though very much of his time, has amazingly transcended his period. Dickens in modern dress is not unimaginable; the pictures date him more than he deserves.

Let us return to the tensions between text and illustration. The issue depends a lot on their physical relationship, the positioning of the illustrations, and here Dickens made a number of interesting experiments. The 1840s saw Phiz joining a group of other illustrators for a variety of new publishing projects by Dickens. *Master Humphrey's Clock* (1840–1), as already noted, inserted woodcut illustrations into the pages of the text, not as separate plates, and carried work by George Cattermole, Samuel Williams, and Daniel Maclise. The Christmas books tried other combinations and positioning of pictures by various artists. Here are two examples, the sensational page 187 from *The Old Curiosity Shop* in *Master Humphrey's Clock* (figure 7.12) and a page from *The Cricket on the Hearth* (figure 7.13).

How does the Phiz woodcut work? The picture functions as a dark paragraph in the text, to borrow Martin Meisel's (1983) evocative description, and its positioning precisely here has great impact on the reading experience. It is intimately part of the rhetoric of the novel. The text at the top revels in the lurid details of Quilp's corpse battered and flung onto a desolate spot out on the Estuary marshes: death, chill, and darkness. The text immediately below the picture pulls us abruptly away to life, warmth, and light with "Lighted rooms, bright fires, cheerful faces, the music of glad voices." The page as a whole, the composite of text and illustration, spectacularly epitomizes the design of the novel as articulated in chapter 53: "Everything in our lives, whether of good or evil, affects us most by contrast."

Sometimes, then, as in this instance, the text sandwiches a vignette. At other times, the picture coils itself around the text, as in Stanfield's wood engraving for *The Cricket on the Hearth*. The words here are subordinated to the picture, assuming the status of a straggling narrative caption. Both these combinations of text and picture are intimate alliances, and are helped to be so not only because of their positioning but also because of their format. The Quilp woodcut is a vignette. The *Cricket* engraving is part-vignette and part-framed: it is decoratively bordered off at the top but not below; Dot Peerybingle opens her door to a dog and the unscrolling text. The vignette's porous borders, and its being composed of black marks on a white page, give it a kind of organic affinity with printed text. The reader's movement from text to picture has no barrier to cross, such as might be constituted by a frame or by color-printing or by some other feature that would more clearly territorialize the difference between the image and the text.

The usual format for the novels was a ration of two plates for each monthly number. The editions of Dickens that we read today usually aim to position the illustrations close to the text they illustrate, as happened when the novels finished their monthly run and were published in volume form. However, the illustrations for the monthly numbers were separated from the text and stood between the advertisements and the opening chapter of that number, rather like frontispieces. So when one says that Dickens's novels were illustrated, it can give a slightly misleading impression as far as the original publication was concerned. The illustrations were *there*, but they did not intercept the reading process, as illustrations customarily do: rather they could be referred to, as one might refer to an endnote for fuller elaboration of something in the text, and that would entail a voluntary interruption of the reading experience.

These may seem finicky discriminations, but consider some of the implications from one particular example of interruption, Phiz's famous dark plate, "Tom-all-Alone's," for *Bleak House* Number 14. In the first single-volume edition of the novel, the illustration stood as the recto facing a page with the last few paragraphs of chapter 45 and the opening paragraph of chapter 46 (figure 7.14). Chapter 45 is Esther's narrative. She comes to the alarming realization that Richard is ill and, while waiting for the coach to take her away, asks Woodcourt if he could help Richard sometimes with his companionship while he is in London. Woodcourt agrees to do so, with a warmth that says more about his feelings for Esther than for Richard; and as Esther is driven away she struggles with her own feelings for Woodcourt. The illustration, as one turned over to this page of the text, would have been a spectacular distraction, bearing no relationship to this part of the story, tugging attention away from the narrative and yet seeming to bear down upon it.

This kind of inappropriate intrusiveness is one problem involved in integrated illustration. But I want to stay with this example in order to identify another, more serious problem to do with the appropriateness or otherwise of illustrations to Dickens. The start of chapter 46 immediately engages the plate, with its brooding evocation of Tom-all-Alone's by night:

Darkness rests upon Tom-all-Alone's. Dilating and dilating since the sun went down last night, it has gradually swelled until it fills every void in the place. For a time there were some dungeon lights burning, as the lamp of Life burns in Tom-all-Alone's, heavily, heavily, in the nauseous air, and winking – as that lamp, too, winks in Tom-all-Alone's – at many horrible things. But they are blotted out. The moon has eyed Tom with a dull cold stare, as admitting some puny emulation of herself in his desert region unfit for life and blasted by volcanic fires; but she has passed on, and is gone. The blackest nightmare in the infernal stables grazes on Tom-all-Alone's, and Tom is fast asleep.

This is powerful writing, agile and muscular in its descriptive movement, sonorous in tone, edging into surrealism, heaving with animism. The darkness, like the fog at the novel's opening, becomes an almost palpable agent, "dilating," "swelling"; light

TOM-ALL-ALONE'S.

Figure 7.14   Phiz, *Bleak House.*

burns "heavily" and winks at the horrors of this god-forsaken slum. The moon, personified, takes a casual, passing interest in the place, like everyone else. How is all this embodied or implied in Phiz's image? Clearly, it can't be. The sinister life of natural forces at work in night-time Tom-all-Alone's is not there at all. This is a carefully drawn slum court, with rickety houses on crutches, heaps of garbage, derelict businesses, the graveyard at the end. Just above the foreground porches on each side are the mirror-flaps leaning out at 45-degree angles, straining pathetically to catch any light from the sky and reflect it back through the windows into the houses. Everything is observed with care, and designed to illustrate the miserable condition of this quarter. And it worked, certainly for some: "What a sermon that little drawing preaches," remarked Beatrix Potter of this plate (Cohen 1980: 110). But compared with Dickens's description, it is lifeless.

We accept that he and Phiz are working in different media, that Phiz has all the problems facing any adapter of Dickens (and illustrations are a form of adaptation, just as stage or movie versions), but here Phiz simply doesn't belong to the same idiom in which Dickens is working. This opening description is preparing for the statement two paragraphs further on of the great theme of the book: "[Tom] has his revenge . . . not a drop of Tom's corrupted blood but propagates infection and contagion somewhere. It shall pollute . . . the choice stream . . . of a Norman house . . . not an atom of Tom's slime . . . but shall work its retribution, through every order of society, up to . . . the highest of the high" (ch. 46). Just like the creeping, drooping, pinching fog, so the "dilating" darkness, the "heavily" burning light, Tom's blood and slime, all take on a malignant life, they become the virulent agents of revenge on those who have forsaken their responsibilities.

This kind of thing cannot be adequately illustrated, and yet it is one of the principal modes in which Dickens is now working: it is what is distinctively powerful about his writing in *Bleak House*. Was there any longer any point in illustrating only those elements that lent themselves to illustration of the kind in which Phiz specialized, such as the lively plate of Richard and Vholes, showing Richard haggard with exasperation and the office littered with supportive allegorical detail? The question is not new, of course, and most verdicts have gone against Phiz in his work for Dickens from *Bleak House* onward.

Not every novel in those last two decades of Dickens's life was illustrated in its original publishing format. Those run initially only in weekly installments in Dickens's journals, *Hard Times* and *Great Expectations*, had no pictures, either in their original serial form or in their first volume editions. Does anyone seriously regret the lack of illustration in these books? If not, what does that say about the value of illustration in his other books? Dickens's choice of Marcus Stone and Luke Fildes to illustrate his last two novels was a reflection of his realization that the Cruikshank–Phiz idiom was out of fashion and that their mode of caricature was inappropriate to his fiction of the 1860s. He was in favor of a more naturalistic, low-key style. This is clear from his comments in 1867 on Sol Eytinge's illustrations to the American edition of *Our Mutual Friend*: "They are remarkable for a most agreeable absence of exaggeration . . . and a general modesty and propriety which I greatly like" (*Letters* 11: 349). The reaction against the caricature style of Phiz and Cruikshank in the 1860s is reflected in Dickens's own histrionic illustrations of his characters as performed in his public readings. These surprised many who had come to view Dickens as an inveterate caricaturist:

> The great value of Dickens's readings was the proof they afforded that his leading characters were not caricatures. His illustrators, especially Cruikshank, made them often appear to be caricatures, by exaggerating their external oddities of feature or eccentricities of costume, rather than by seeking to represent their internal life; and the reader became accustomed to turn to the rough picture of the person as though the author's deep humorous conception of the character was embodied in the artist's hasty and superficial sketch . . . – when [the audience] saw him visibly transform himself into Scrooge or Squeers . . . [these] characters then seemed, not only all alive, but full of individual life; and, however odd, eccentric, unpleasing, or strange, they always appeared to be natural, always appeared to be personal natures rooted in human nature. (Whipple 1912: 2. 328–9)

So Dickens himself unwittingly (perhaps deliberately?) contributes to the discrediting of his illustrators.

Harry Furniss, himself one of the most elegant and witty book illustrators, remarked that "When we mentally recall Boz's characters it is through Phiz's etchings that we see them" (Cordery 2005: 54), a view similar to R. H. Horne's observation 60 years earlier: "That Mr. Dickens often caricatures, has been said by many people; but if they examined their own minds they would be very likely to find that this opinion chiefly originated, and was supported by certain undoubted caricatures among the illustrations" (Horne 1844: 96). Dickens in his Readings could begin to repair the damage done to him by his illustrators, and on the platform he proved to be a more resourceful and subtler illustrator than any of them.

Even the best of Dickens's artists reduced his art. They distilled it to caricature and tableau; they developed a greater density of allegorical detail as an attempt to match the fullness, richness, and vitality of Dickens's scenes, but still fell short; and they made his human beings into small toy figures. Furniss thought that "Dickens's pen was worth a thousand pencils, and if ever a writer could dispense with an artist to illustrate his works, that author was Charles Dickens" (Cordery 2005: 54). That is something that each reader of Dickens will decide for himself or herself. Of course, it is difficult to think of Dickens's books and characters without many of those drawings. They have the effect not only of reinforcing the caricature mode but more generally of preserving Dickens in a particular period. For some that is part of their – and Dickens's – charm; for others, Dickens under a bell-jar is a melancholy spectacle. "I cannot help thinking," said Furniss, knowing he was risking heresy, "that it would have been better for Boz today, had Phiz never existed" (Cordery 2005: 54). We see Dickens better without the illustrations.

REFERENCES AND FURTHER READING

Bakhtin, M. M. (1984). *Rabelais and his World*. (H. Iswolsky, Trans.). Bloomington, IN: Indiana University Press.

Brontë, Charlotte (1852). Letter to George Smith. In Jeremy Tambling (Ed.), *Bleak House: New Casebook* (p. 4). Houndmills: Macmillan, 1998.

Cohen, Jane Rabb (1980). *Charles Dickens and his Original Illustrators*. Columbus, OH: Ohio State University Press.

Cordery, Gareth (2005). *An Edwardian's View of Dickens and his Illustrators: Harry Furniss's "A Sketch of Boz."* Greensboro, North Carolina: ELT Press.

Harvey, John (1970). *Victorian Novelists and their Illustrators*. London: Sidgwick and Jackson.

Hodnett, Edward (1982). *Image and Text: Studies in the Illustration of English Literature*. Aldershot: Scolar Press.

Horne, R. H. (1844). Charles Dickens. In Michael Hollington (Ed.), *Charles Dickens: Critical Assessments*, vol. 1 (pp. 94–101). Mountfield, East Sussex: Helm Information, 1995.

Kinsley, James (Ed.) (1986) *The Pickwick Papers*. Oxford: Clarendon Press.

Kitton, F. G. (1899). *Dickens and his Illustrators*. London: George Redway.

Lister, T. H. (1838). [Review of Dickens's early works]. *Edinburgh Review*, 68, 75–97.

Meisel, Martin (1983). *Realizations: Narrative, Pictorial, and Theatrical Arts in Nineteenth-century England*. Princeton, NJ: Princeton University Press.

Nicholson, Norman (1975). *Wednesday Early Closing*. London: Faber and Faber.

Patten, Robert L. (1969). Boz, Phiz, and Pickwick in the Pound. *English Literary History*, 36, 575–91.

— (1992). *George Cruikshank's Life, Times, and Art*, vol. 1. London: Lutterworth Press.

— (1996). *George Cruikshank's Life, Times, and Art*. Vol 2. London: Lutterworth Press.

Smith, Sydney (1837) Letter of September 1837. In Philip Collins (Ed.), *Charles Dickens: The Critical Heritage* (p. 5). London: Routledge, 1971.

Steig, Michael (1978). *Dickens and Phiz*. Bloomington, IN: Indiana University Press.

Thackeray, W. M. (1840). Going to see a man hanged. In Philip Collins (Ed.), *Charles Dickens: The Critical Heritage* (pp. 45–6). London: Routledge, 1971.

Whipple, Edwin P. (1912). *Charles Dickens: The Man and his Work*, 2 vols. Boston: Houghton Mifflin.

8

The Language of Dickens

Patricia Ingham

Dickens's mastery of language is unique amongst nineteenth-century novelists in its inventiveness and multilayered density which makes him in effect the James Joyce of the Victorian period. He deploys every available linguistic resource from word-making to literary allusion. Though Dickens is sometimes thought of as an untaught genius, his linguistic choices are rarely without earlier literary models, which he often develops beyond recognition.

Name-making

Dickens's powers are already evident not only in his narration and dialogue but in the initial process of christening his characters. Familiarity with John Bunyan's *The Pilgrim's Progress* had shown him the practice of using transparently allegorical names to indicate character or disposition: figures such as Christian, the pilgrim; Mercy, the kind neighbor; the giant Despair, slain by Great-heart. Dickens gives similarly obvious names to individuals like Smallweed and Dedlock in *Bleak House* to suggest their natures, but this is not all. More often, he draws on his vast knowledge of vocabulary and uses the native speaker's silently acquired knowledge of *phonotactics*, the rules or patterns governing the combination of sounds in a given language, to refine such allegorical usage. He creates names which by association of sound and meaning hint at the significance of his characters.

His attention to such name-making is well illustrated in his notes, which show him, for instance, considering alternatives for his eponymous hero, such as *Chuzzlewig, Chubblewig, Chuzzlebog, Sweezleden, Chuzzletoe, Sweezleback*, and *Sweezlewag*, before settling for Chuzzlewit. The choice provides a name analogous to *halfwit* plus the element *chuzzle* – reminiscent of "puzzle" – to suggest a somewhat obtuse or confused individual in need of enlightenment, as Martin undoubtedly is. Mrs. Clennam's psychosomatic paralysis in *Little Dorrit* is hinted at by a first syllable containing most of the verb *to clench* with the addition of a plausible suffix derived from the frequent name-ending *ham*. Bella Wilfer in *Our Mutual Friend* is both beautiful and willful, while Carker in *Dombey and Son* derives his name from the verb *to cark* (to trouble or harass), which is his typical behavior. Crook was a common term for "trickery," which Dickens made seem less didactic by giving it a new spelling as the name of the disreputable rag-and-bottle merchant Krook in *Bleak House*. Murdstone, Copperfield's brutal stepfather, is perhaps half murderer, half heart-of-stone. Or perhaps, like Merdle, the crooked financier in *Little Dorrit*, he takes the first part of his name from the then current usage as a swear-word of French *merde* (excrement).

Dickens also excels at tossing off strings of names for characters seen as generic and indistinguishable from one another. *Boodle* and *noodle* were already current in the sense of "idiot" when he cloned Foodle, Coodle, Noodle, Koodle, Loodle, Moodle, Poodle, and Quoodle for the interchangeable politicians who flourish alongside the Dedlocks. Similarly, the lawyers who haunt the Court of Chancery, the clones Mizzle, Chizzle, and Drizzle, and by implication a string of others up to Zizzle, draw their names from the verb *mizzle* (to fiddle or confuse) or from an alternative form of *chisel* (to cheat). By contrast, Jo All-alone has only a single name which is the shortest possible in English, given to a character generally seen as not quite human.

The Listening Narrator

Once satisfactorily named, characters in Dickens's fiction are described by what John Forster called their "outward and visible oddities" (Forster bk. 7, ch. 2), but this needs to be modified to "visible and audible oddities" since the narrators not only look but listen and notice features of speech which they read off as a form of body language. These include aspects of voice quality, enunciation, sentence structure, vocabulary, and other more nebulous effects. If these were comprehensively recorded, they would indicate the speaker's *idiolects*: those features of a speaker's utterance that enable a skilled listener to recognize the identity of their interlocutor or at least their age or gender or class. With a full account, an expert can identify an individual as surely as a forensic scientist can from a fingerprint. But Dickens is not aiming at such an account, though – as will be shown later – he attempts the outline of an idiolect for a few of his eccentric creations such as Mrs. Gamp and Captain Cuttle.

Generally, the narrator makes local inferences about their dispositions or temporary moods from the ways in which characters speak. Barney, Sikes's Jewish accomplice in *Oliver Twist*, utters his words which "whether they came from the heart or not, made their way through the nose" (ch. 15). The innocent inventor Doyce in *Little Dorrit*, with a name related to *douce* (quiet, sober, steady), speaks "in that quiet deliberate manner, and in that undertone, which is often observable in mechanics who consider and adjust with great nicety. It belonged to him like his suppleness of thumb" (bk. 1, ch. 10). By contrast, in the same novel, the villainous Flintwinch speaks "with a twist, as if his words had come out of him in his own wry shape" (bk. 1, ch. 15).

More nebulously, Micawber has a way of speaking with "a certain indescribable air of doing something genteel" (*David Copperfield* ch. 11); Steerforth's wily servant Littimer makes "no use of superlatives" but sticks to a "cool calm medium always" (ch. 21). Dombey, reluctant when discussing the introduction of his future bride Edith to Carker, is observed "making as if he swallowed something a little too large for his throat" (*Dombey and Son* ch. 26). Edith herself, loathing Dombey's attentiveness, reveals her feelings, as the narrator hears it, by answering questions "with a strange reluctance; and with that remarkable air of opposition to herself, already noticed" (ch. 21). As is obvious from these examples, narratorial inferences are often fortified by analogies and some of these are particularly telling. Podsnap patronizingly asks an unfortunate foreigner "How Do You Like London?," uttering the words "as if he were administering something in the nature of a powder or potion to a deaf child" (*Our Mutual Friend* bk. 1, ch. 11). The jealous Headstone, responding to Lizzie Hexam's acceptance of lessons from someone other than himself, is heard "grinding his words slowly out, as though they came from a rusty mill" (bk. 2.1, ch. 1). Mrs. Clennam, bent on ignoring the fact that Amy Dorrit lives in a debtors' prison, speaks the words " 'wherever she lives' as if she were reading them off from separate bits of metal that she took up one by one" (*Little Dorrit* bk. 1, ch. 15).

Local Varieties of Speech

But the listening narrator hears more than these idiosyncratic ways of speaking: he also registers the forms of speech that indicate the areas and class that the speakers belong to. In doing so, he is following well-established literary models that already existed, noticeably in the late eighteenth-century dramatic farces that he read in Mrs. Inchbald's collection. There, non-standard speech was used for Londoners, Irish and Scottish individuals, as well as those from the north of the country. From Sam Weller (*Pickwick Papers*) onward, the commonest dialect speakers are Cockneys, though Dickens goes on to use northern forms briefly in *Nicholas Nickleby* and more extensively in *Hard Times*, as well as East Anglian speech for the Peggottys in *David Copperfield*.

None of these representations is realistic in linguistic terms: they work on the assumption that once distinctive pronunciations have been indicated, they can be assumed to recur when appropriate. So standard forms occur alongside non-standard ones. In part, with some writers, this is to ensure that unfamiliar forms do not impede understanding: when Emily Brontë aimed at verisimilitude for the speech of the Yorkshire servant, Joseph, in *Wuthering Heights*, Charlotte later had to tone down the spellings in the interests of intelligibility.

By the time Dickens wrote his novels, there were already stylized markers of dialect in use. For instance, certain spellings indicating non-standard forms were already familiar. For Cockney speech, there were *v* for *w*, *w* for *v*, and loss of the initial aspirate *h-*. Spellings like *hoonger* (hunger) and *loove* (love) indicated the usual north-country pronunciation.[1] For the Peggottys' East Anglian dialect in *David Copperfield*, Dickens deployed forms like *bahd* (bird), *fust* (first), and *arks* (asks).

Other features of the varieties of language are items of lexis/vocabulary such as thieves' slang which laces through *Oliver Twist* as through the Newgate novels, as well as being found by Dickens in a contemporary glossary of "Flash language." They include items like *crack* (burgle), *crib* (house), *nab* (arrest), *swag* (loot), *conkey* (informer), and *fogle* (handkerchief). Dickens avoids another flash term, *oliver* (moon) to keep it for his hero who represents, as he says in his Introduction to the third edition, "the principle of Good surviving through every adverse circumstance and triumphing at last" (Horne 2003: 457). The choice of name is illuminated by an item in the *Glossary* Dickens used: "Oliver is in town: a phrase signifying that nights are moonlit, and consequently unfavourable to depredation."

As for syntax (the structuring of phrases or sentences), all dialect speakers in Dickens's novels show poor control: sentences lose their thread; *and* is frequently used as a link instead of a range of words like *but* or *if* or *though*; and repeated negatives are used for emphasis instead of canceling each other out logically. Indeed, all these practices imply a failure in logic which, along with non-standard forms like *draw'd*, *know'd*, *a-going*, *which* for *who*, and others, suggests to the standard speaker a social and intellectual inferior.

By the late eighteenth century, not only were such usages common in Dickens's favorite farces but also in fictionalized accounts of "low life" in London; in the performances of the admired theatrical comedian and mimic, Charles Mathews; and in semi-comic crime-reporting in the *Morning Chronicle* for which Dickens wrote at one time. These all used (stylized) Cockney which for historical reasons was perceived as the most "deviant" from Standard English, which came to be called Received Pronunciation. This reputation derived from the fact that the latter developed from an upper-class and literate variety of London-based speech in the sixteenth century. Consequently, the proximity of lower-class or Cockney English caused it to be seen as a deviation. Throughout the eighteenth century, there were many comments like that of John Walker in his popular *Critical Pronouncing Dictionary and Expositor of the English Language* (1791): "The vulgar pronunciation of London, though not half so erroneous as Scotland, Ireland, or any of the provinces, is, to a person of correct taste, a thousand times more offensive and disgusting" (xiv). Dickens's first use of Cockney language for Sam Weller is followed by many others. Like Mathews, Weller is a sharp stand-up comedian, but when it comes to serious issues, such as a love affair, his comic status undermines any effect of real emotion.

Simple models from the farces and the other sources mentioned are what Dickens uses for his lower-class Londoners, but for other dialect speakers he drew on would-be scholarly sources. For *Hard Times*, he consulted John Collier's *Tim Bobbin, A View of the Lancashire Dialect with Glossary* (1846). Similarly, for the Peggotty family's speech in *David Copperfield*, he used Edward Moor's *Suffolk Words and Phrases* (1823) as well as Robert Forby's *Vocabulary of East Anglia* (1830). In both of these novels, Dickens wants to represent the dialect speakers as morally admirable and is evidently aware of the potential usefulness of a newly developing attitude to regional speech fostered by antiquarians such as William Gaskell and Moor. The latter wrote of his return to Suffolk after a long absence that he was "much struck on my return by our provincialisms . . . I was agreeably surprised to find so many still current; and that so many were the words of Shakespeare" (v–vi). Dialect words not found in standard usage were now vetted by such people for ancient origins and could then be seen as valuable antiques. Forby wrote: "No where, indeed, is 'the well of English undefiled' to be found; but everywhere some streamlets flow down from the fountain head retaining their original purity and flavour" (1830: 19).

It can be inferred from this that Dickens was aware of this romantic view of dialect vocabulary (later taken by Hardy) in representing Ham and Mr. Peggotty at their stoical best after Emily's seduction. But such a view is not compatible with the idea of vulgarity that adheres to the other features of their language, such as non-standard grammar and syntax. Dickens attempts to deal with the problem by the device of showing the young Copperfield charmed by the quaintness of Suffolk words. When Mr. Peggotty speaks of him and Emily as "two young mavishes," Copperfield comments "I knew this meant in our local dialect, like two young thrushes and received it as a compliment" (ch. 3). But when the Peggottys erupt into the middle-class world David inhabits, they appear as the repetitive and guffawing buffoons of the farces. Steerforth's comment that Peggotty is "a thorough-built boatman" evokes a clownish reaction: "So 'tis, sir, so 'tis, sir . . . you're right, young gen'lm'n: Mas'r Davy, bor, gen'lm'n's right. A thorough-built boatman! Hor, hor! That's what he is, too!" (ch. 7).

In his later work, the same kind of problem occurs when Dickens wishes to represent lower-class characters as morally admirable. Such individuals are usually Londoners who use what Walker called "offensive and disgusting" forms of speech. The most significant case is that of Lizzie Hexam (*Our Mutual Friend*), a working-class woman whose father makes a living robbing corpses dragged from the Thames. Naturally she might be expected to speak in a language associated with a lack of intelligence and refinement, and with no understanding of higher values. Lizzie's role in the novel is to show an integrity and selflessness that contrasts with a self-seeking materialistic middle class represented by Wrayburn, Lightwood, the Veneerings, Bella Wilfer, and others. Further, Lizzie is to have her virtue rewarded by an upwardly mobile marriage to her failed seducer, Wrayburn.

The problem for Dickens is to dissociate her from the vulgarity implied by Cockney speech, and he evidently tries to do this. From the start he gives her none of the markers of substandard pronunciation used by her father, and replaces them with colloquial expressions such as *the like of that*, *revenge-like*, *a drop of brandy*, *in atremble*, *abed*, *afire*, *a-looking*. She uses these in short simple and clear sentences, sometimes with the colloquial use of the historic past tense: "Sometimes it rains, and we creep under a boat or the likes of that . . . up comes father, and takes us home" (bk. 1, ch. 3). Later, Dickens carefully introduces a tutorial arrangement made by Wrayburn to instruct Lizzie and enable her, as her brother puts it, to "pass muster" and not be taken as "an ignorant person." Evidently this works since Lizzie later rejects a similar offer of teaching from the lunatic Headstone. She now uses no colloquialisms but instead chooses abstract words, while her now lengthy sentences are perfectly controlled:

> I cannot doubt . . . that your visit is well meant. You have been so good a friend to Charley that I have no right to doubt it. I have nothing to tell Charley, but that I accepted the help to which he so much objects before he made any plans for me; and certainly before I knew of any. It was considerately and delicately offered, and there were reasons that had weight with me which should be as dear to Charley as to me. (bk. 2, ch. 11)

Nonetheless, this middle-class speech occurs in a situation where Wrayburn's friends are verbally weighing in the balance "whether a young man of very fair family, good appearance, and some talent makes a fool or a wise man of himself in marrying a female water-man turned factory girl" (bk. 4, ch. 17). In this context, Lizzie's ability to "pass muster" by speaking like any middle-class woman suggests that Dickens is unable to accept her as Wrayburn's bride without it.

Strikingly, Dickens did not endow his working-class hero in *Hard Times* with the standard language he bestowed belatedly on his working-class heroine. Stephen Blackpool speaks throughout with pronunciations Dickens clearly tried hard to make authentic, but Blackpool, like Lizzie, is supposed to be an ideal figure, resisting the temptation of anarchic trade unionists, deferential to his employers, trusting to those about him. He too represents working-class integrity, opposed to exploitative employers, and in this role he confronts Bounderby verbally as John Barton confronts an employer in Gaskell's *Mary Barton* (Ingham 1986). In this situation, controlled language might come to the rescue as it does for Barton but Blackpool's plea to Bounderby serves only to create the impression of a dim, confused mind:

> Look how you considers of us, an writes of us, an talks of us, and goes up wi' yor deputations to Secretaries o' State 'bout us, and how yo are awlus right, and how we are awlus wrong, and never had'n no reason in us sin ever we were born. Look how this ha' growen, sir, and growen bigger an' bigger, broader an' broader, harder an' harder, fro year to year . . . Who can look on't, sir, and fairly tell a man 'tis not a muddle? (bk. 2, ch. 11)

Quite what grows bigger, broader, and harder is unclear; the final limp question carries no punch; and the now recurrent mantra " 'Tis aw a muddle" seems to describe Blackpool's own state of mind.

It is only when Dickens is not directly addressing class divisions in contemporary society that he is free to exploit the deviant associations of non-standard speech for his own purposes by deploying his linguistic ingenuity to full effect. He does this in two forms of speech in *Martin Chuzzlewit*: that of Mrs. Gamp and that of the Americans whom Chuzzlewit encounters.

Fantasy Language

Mrs. Gamp is the extreme example in the novel of a satire on a solipsistic character who creates a world and a language to suit her fantasies. In 1882, Mowbray Morris had already recognized that she is able to carry off her opaque remarks such as "Gamp is my name, and Gamp my nater" (*Martin Chuzzlewit* ch. 26) as meaningful. Morris cites her comment on the departing ship which she refers to as the "Ankworks package" (Antwerp Packet) and confuses Jonah and the whale in the biblical story (ch. 40). We understand, Morris says, because we are already familiar with Mrs. Gamp's "marvellous phraseology, her quaint illustrations, her irrelevant turns of thought" (Morris 1882: 607).

The language Morris refers to is built on the basis of her excessively frequent use of substandard markers, such as *nater* (nature), *pint* (point), *chimley* (chimney), *feller* (fellow), *kep* (kept). Only Jo the crossing-sweeper (*Bleak House*) and Rogue Riderhood (*Our Mutual Friend*) match this frequency.[2] Added to these are idiosyncratic forms like *reconsize* (reconcile), *guardian* (garden), *proticipate* (anticipate), and *owldacious* (audacious), which are peculiar to her. But most distinctive of all is her use of two unusual sounds: that found medially in Standard English *pleasure*, which she uses as a frequent pronunciation for *s*, and that found initially in *judge*. These are indicated by the various spellings *g*, *dg*, or *j*. For some of the words in which they occur, there are rare examples in contemporary sources of some such forms in London speech. But there are no instances for such forms as *brickbage* (brickbat), *parapidge* (parapet), *topjy-turjey* (topsy-turvy), and, as the novel progresses, the number of strange forms increases.

The narrator stresses the authoritative effect of what Mrs. Gamp says and her confidence is unqualified: she is described as delivering "her inauguration address"; uttering "an oration"; "apostrophising" the ship; and speaking "prophetically" of Mercy "going like a lamb to the sacrifige." Her speech appeals to biblical authority in the form of distorted allusions which seem oracular rather than erroneous: she claims that "Rich folks may ride on camels, but it ain't so easy for 'em to see out of a needle's eye" (ch. 25). And she quotes Betsey Prig as having alleged of some offense that "lambs could not forgive . . . nor worms forget" (ch. 49), a statement that hints by its form at a biblical source.

Accompanying all these markers is the confused organization of Mrs. Gamp's sentences, for chaotic syntax is the norm of her speech. She can even confuse her report of an exchange with her imaginary friend Mrs. Harris: "I says to Mrs. Harris when she say to me, 'Years and our trials, Mrs. Gamp, sets marks upon us all' — 'say not the words, Mrs. Harris, if you and me is to continual friends'" (ch. 25). The figure of Mrs. Harris is the pivot around which Mrs. Gamp's utterances resolve. Her language is fantastic and it mirrors a fantasy world. She is necessarily the only speaker of her peculiar tongue, though other people, convinced of its authenticity, try to explain her to her listeners. There is an underlying assumption here that as she bends form and syntax, so she can also bend meaning to prevent opposition from others. As an article written in 1861 points out: "By means of that invaluable ally [Mrs. Harris] Mrs. Gamp is able to mix up a fictitious dialogue with her own monologue; and thus we have something dramatic to give life and point to her oration" (Collins 1971: 197). Mrs. Harris is supposed to speak only gospel truth, and always supports Mrs. Gamp's view of her drunken and malicious self as competent, compassionate, and reliable. It is when Betsey Prig announces that there is no such person as Mrs. Harris that the Gamp world crumbles. After this, when Jonas asks her to nurse Chuffey, her eloquence is lost. She can speak only in a "quavering croak," and the narrator comments: "It was extraordinary how much effort it cost Mrs. Gamp to pronounce the name she was so commonly ready with" (ch. 51). When her imaginary world collapses, she meets her comeuppance and is ultimately silenced.

American English as Newspeak

It is also in *Martin Chuzzlewit* that Dickens is able to convert the connotations of non-standard English to a more widespread satirical use in his handling of American speech. He was not the first to record a visit to America in print and he had read several of his predecessors: Harriet Martineau's *Society in America* (1837) and her *Retrospect of Western Travel* (1838), Frederick Marryat's *A Diary in America* (1839), and James S. Buckingham's *America: The Northern and Free States* (1841). These all touched on the subject of differences in how Americans spoke, and Charles Mathews staged comic impersonations of a "Yankee," a Kentuckian, and an American Irishman.

Like Martin Chuzzlewit's, Dickens's trip to America was a journey from illusion to disillusion as what he encountered changed his attitude. At first, he was flattered by his popularity but the attention became troublesome, while American pushiness and the common practice of spitting in public by all classes offended his sense of proper manners. More seriously, the piracy of his books and the copyright question, as well as slavery, increasingly became issues. Growing weariness and disappointment led him, like Mathews, to see Americans, with a single exception, as generic clones of different categories but coarse and hypocritical, with social and moral pretensions. The medium that Dickens chooses for his satire on America is one that Orwell was later to use with Newspeak in *Nineteen Eighty Four*: language itself. The complications that affect Dickens's treatment of non-standard English speakers disappear once he is able to use the connotations of linguistic deviance to figure its moral equivalence. This is what he does with the speech of all Americans bar one, deploying non-standard forms of grammar already described such as *draw'd*, *know'd*, *you was*, *didn't ought to*, *ain't*, and others. To these were added spellings of lexical items found in his representations of Cockney speech: *bile* (boil), *bust* (burst), *feller* (fellow), and many more.

Two simple devices increase this sense of a debased language. The first is the omission of syllables, as in *cap'n*, *p'raps*, *sing'ler*, *gen'ral*. The other is the effective tactic of indicating by a hyphen a change of stress from that in British usage and a consequent change in pronunciation. Sometimes it represents a stress on the first syllable as in *do-minion, re-tard, po-ssession, con-sider;* at other times it indicates a stress on the second syllable instead of the first, as in *ac-tive* and *Eu-rope*. Notice is also taken of supposed semantic "errors": *fix* meaning almost anything from "to treat medically" to "to open a bottle of wine"; *smart* for "clever"; *guess* or *calculate* for "think," and many others.

To represent the ubiquitous nature of Americans' hypocrisy, Dickens illustrates their use of rhetorical and pretentious language. This includes a preference for elaborate vocabulary, such as *disputate* for "dispute," *opinionate* for "opine," and *slantingdicularly* for "indirectly." Equally important is the use of florid metaphor, needless repetition, and lengthy, rambling sentences. These are combined, for instance, in the speech of General Choke, who is involved in the Eden scam into which he intends to draw Martin. The context is a chapter in which England and America are explicitly compared, typically by describing those who cloak concerns with money, self-advancement, and status beneath a façade of patriotism. After some gratuitous jeering at Queen Victoria, Choke addresses Martin:

> I thank you, sir, in the name of the Watertoast Sympathisers . . . and I thank you, sir, in the name of the star-spangled banner of the Great United States, for your eloquent and categorical exposition . . . if, sir, in such a place, and at such a time, I might venture to con-clude with a sentiment – glancing – however slantin'dicularly – at the subject in hand, I would say, sir, May the British Lion have his talons eradicated by the noble bill of the American Eagle, and be taught to play upon the Irish Harp and the Scotch Fiddle that music which is breathed in every empty shell that lies upon the shores of green Co-lumbia! (ch. 21)

By this time it is clear that the "deviance" of American speech in the novel is used to indicate more than a lack of social refinement: it is revealed as the symbol of a deviant nation illogically hostile to the "mother" country, a nation as self-deluding and corrupt as Pecksniff.

Literary Allusion: The Bible and *The Book of Common Prayer*

Dickens was a voracious reader, and in his autobiographical fragment he lists some of the works he read: *Roderick Random, Peregrine Pickle, Humphry Clinker, Tom Jones, The Vicar of Wakefield, Don Quixote, Gil Blas, The Arabian Nights,* and *Tales of the Genii.* These evidently came to hand, but so also did the essential sacred books of any literate household of the time: the Bible, *The Book of Common Prayer*, and John Bunyan's *The Pilgrim's Progress.* As a young man, longing to be an actor, he became familiar with most of Shakespeare's plays in performance, while his many echoes of them in his novels also reveal a familiarity with their written form. Less frequent sources range from then recent poets like Byron to popular songs and street ballads.

As a result of his reading, there is in Dickens's writing a wealth of what would now be called intertextuality. This is a feature of other Victorian novels but none shows the inventiveness of his literary allusions. It is often assumed that authors' references to existing canonical texts are a way for them to claim canonical status for their own works. It is not so with Dickens, though critics intent on showing what Valerie Gager calls "a deeper significance than mere verbal embellishment" (1996: 10) argue for broad parallels of a thematic kind. *The Old Curiosity Shop* and *Dombey and Son* are said to be thematically related to *King Lear*, and *Great Expectations* to *Hamlet*. Such interpretations and many others are no more than a version of the "claim to authority" theory, implying vaguely that Dickens's novels draw power, grandeur, and status from earlier texts.

When, however, thematic parallels to religious texts are claimed, there is, as will be shown, substance in the interpretation.[3] The obvious reason for this is that, while the New Testament and *The Book of Common Prayer* present a simple and coherent morality – "Love thy neighbor" – readily built into even a multiplot novel, the same is not true of Shakespeare's plays which offer ambiguous perspectives not transformable into an overarching theme. Thus, clear thematic connections with other texts are only to be found between three of Dickens's novels and the familiar religious works, and they vary in effectiveness when built into the structure of the thinly plotted *Old Curiosity Shop*, the more elaborate *Hard Times*, and the complexity of *Bleak House*.

It is easy to read the story of Nell and her grandfather as an update of *The Pilgrim's Progress* since it centers on their journey from the horrors of their present life to a better and happier place. Or, as the subtitle of Bunyan's story puts it, to flee "from this world to that which is to come": they find a happier place and move to a better world by dying. *The Pilgrim's Progress* is said to be well known to Nell, and she identifies herself and her companion with its central figure: "I feel as if we were both Christian, and laid down on this grass all the cares and troubles we brought with us" (ch. 15). The external dangers the original Christian encounters, such as the Slough of Despond, are translated into the old man's addiction to gambling which he succumbs to in the course of their journey. Parallels are also drawn with the kind or vicious individuals that Christian encounters and these stand out in the simple plot structure. The thematic connection with the earlier didactic text is evident, but whether the intertextuality works to make an effective case for human life as a simplistic pilgrimage is unclear. Indeed, the novel seems to have been read and applauded as a suitably sentimental presentation of a virtuous child's death.

A more effective use of religious sources is found in *Hard Times*, even though its plot is overtly structured around a simple text from Galatians: "whatsoever a man soweth, that shall he also reap" (6: 7). Moreover, the narrative takes the form of a classic sermon divided into biblical quotation, developed at length into an exemplum or illustrative story, and a final admonitory address to the congregation/readers, repeating the moral of the story. The exemplum takes up most of the novel and has three sections, spelling out the metaphor in the initial quotation: *Sowing, Reaping, Garnering*. It is underpinned throughout by references to the Bible and *The Book of Common Prayer* so that the story updates as it expands the metaphor, translating it into the terms of an industrial society which values not virtue but profit.

In the characters of the Utilitarian and political economist Gradgrind and the entrepreneur Bounderby, *Hard Times* figures the world entirely as a marketplace where "the relations between master and man were all fact . . . and what you couldn't state in figures, or show to be purchaseable in the cheapest market and saleable in the dearest, was not, and never should be, world without end, Amen" (bk. 1, ch. 5). The victims of such a society are the innocents Sissy Jupe and Stephen Blackpool who believe that the "first principle of political economy" is to be found in the echo of Matthew (7: 12): "Therefore all things whatsoever ye would that men should do to you, do ye even so to them." So the masters and their victims sow very different seeds, and what each side harvests validates the biblical assertion that "Ye shall know them by their fruits." Those who plant thorns and thistles, as Gradgrind and Bounderby do, will reap a bitter harvest; those like Sissy and Blackpool who plant good seed will harvest the "grapes" and "figs" of salvation (Matthew 7: 16).

The prediction is borne out by the narrative: Gradgrind rears a thieving son and a would-be adulterous daughter; Bounderby is humiliated, loses his wife, and dies ignominiously in the street. Though Stephen dies, he does so as a martyr with religious imagery around his death, suggesting eternal rewards. Sissy's stoicism and kindness bring her more material forms of grapes and figs in the shape of a happy marriage. With the final garnering, all that remains for the narrator/preacher to do is to draw the lesson from the exemplum for his readers/congregation that "the Good Samaritan was a Bad Economist" (bk. 2, ch. 12) and to admonish them: "Dear reader! It rests with you and me, whether, in our two fields of action, similar things shall be or not" (bk. 3, ch. 9).

But the most complex treatment of thematic reference to New Testament morality, with its admonition to love your neighbor and the enforcing threat of damnation for not doing so, occurs in *Bleak House*. These ideas are not superimposed as in *Hard Times* but are intimately related to central themes and to the form of the novel itself. For instance, the so-called omniscient narrator presents a panoramic view, implying vast scale and an eschatological dimension. Here it is not individuals who, in biblical terms, sow and reap, but a whole society that fails in diverse ways.

Also, the very form of such a multi-plotted novel itself raises the question of what connection there can be between all these disparate people, ranging from the Dedlocks to the inhabitants of Tom-all-Alone's (ch. 16). As things stand, Jarndyce points out, they are linked "by unreason and injustice from beginning to end" (ch. 60). The narrative reveals the many ways in which it is true that this is how the better-off treat the poor. Like Dives, the rich man in the biblical story, who sees "a great gulf" between himself and the beggar Lazarus, they are unaware of any connection (Luke 16: 26; *Bleak House* ch. 16). In due course, it emerges that they have missed a crucial physical connection as fever spreads from Jo to Charley the maid, to Esther and possibly beyond Boodle to Zoodle and the Dedlocks. The significance of this is reinforced by conflating the comment on hypocrites in Matthew (6: 16) – "Verily I say unto you, They have their reward" – with Romans (12: 19) – "Vengeance is mine; I will repay, saith the Lord" – and writing "Verily . . . Tom has his revenge" (*Bleak House* ch. 46).

Throughout the novel, an ominous warning is figured in the real continuing Chancery suit from which rich and poor "expect a judgement" (ch. 3) or a real Day of Judgment. This (latter) biblical phrase occurs four (out of five) times in the Bible to threaten damnation to sinners. The expectation in the narrative of a legal judgment images the Judgment Day of Doomsday paintings, and its outcome is predicted by the deaths of corrupt characters: Krook, Tulkinghorn, Lady Dedlock, and Richard Carstone. Just as the fever represents retribution on a grand scale, these deaths themselves become a metaphor for the contamination seeping from the paupers' burial ground to which Nemo is consigned. Of his body it is said: "sow him in corruption, to be raised in corruption" (ch. 11). This narratorial comment at his funeral parodies the fate of the Just in Corinthians: "So also is the resurrection of the dead. It is sown in corruption; it is raised in incorruption" (1 Cor. 15: 42). Here the parable of sowing and reaping recurs as a subtext, and so too does the idea of a bitter harvest for the oppressors, as Jarndyce reminds the wealthy that they cannot gather "grapes from thorns, or figs from thistles" (ch. 60; Matthew 7: 16).

Serious contrasts between biblical allusions and a local context are infrequent in Dickens's novels but can be powerful: the story of Cain who murders his brother Abel (Genesis 4: 8) is pointedly used in this way in two instances. There is an ironic discrepancy between Carker's unthinking reference to the minor delinquent, Rob the Grinder, as a "young Cain" and his recent abuse and cutting rejection of his own brother (*Dombey and Son* ch. 22). In another context, it is the narrator who comments bitterly on Jonas Chuzzlewit's behavior as he sets out to murder Montague Tigg: "When he looked back, across his shoulder, was it to see if his quick footsteps still fell dry upon the dusty pavement, or were already moist and clogged with the red mire that stained the naked feet of Cain?" (*Martin Chuzzlewit* ch. 47).

Shakespeare

Dickens draws as comprehensively on Shakespeare's plays as on the religious texts already discussed, alluding in particular to the tragedies, *Hamlet*, *Macbeth*, and *King Lear*, in that order. Less frequently he refers to *Othello*, though he wrote, directed, and acted in a musical burlesque *O'Tello*. As the form of the latter indicates, the earnest approach to religious texts is not matched here. Instead, the plays become a common language, presumed to be shared with readers, which Dickens can put into the mouths of narrators and characters to create linguistic fireworks whose effectiveness depends on the ability of the readership to make a comparison between the original and the new context.

Such comparisons seldom reveal a match between the earlier and the present texts, though occasional instances occur. Lady Macbeth's fear that her husband is "too full o' the milk of human kindness" (*Macbeth* I. v. 13) is fittingly used to describe Mr. Varden (*Barnaby Rudge* ch. 80) and ironically to underline the absence of compassion in Mrs. Pipchin (*Dombey and Son* ch. 8), Pecksniff (*Martin Chuzzlewit* ch. 3), and Casby (*Little Dorrit* bk. 2, ch. 32). Ralph Nickleby, planning to use his niece as bait for his decadent friends, finds that his attempt to say "God bless you" to her sticks in his throat as "Amen" sticks in Macbeth's (*Nicholas Nickleby* ch. 19; *Macbeth* II. ii. 30–2). The seducer Steerforth dismisses his guilty feelings as Macbeth does his fear of Banquo's ghost: "Why, so; being gone, I am a man again" (*David Copperfield* ch. 22; *Macbeth* III. iv. 107–8). Similarly, Lear's description of himself as "a very foolish fond old man" (*King Lear* IV. vii. 60) is echoed by the apt description of Nell's weak grandfather as a "harmless fond old man" (*Old Curiosity Shop* ch. 29). Equally appropriate is Jenny Wren's ironic allusion to her "troublesome child" of a father as "sharper than a serpent's tooth, if he wasn't as dull as ditch-water" (*Our Mutual Friend* bk. 3, ch. 10), mimicking Lear's condemnation of his "thankless child" Goneril as "sharper than a serpent's tooth" (I. iv. 288–9).

For the most part, however, intertextuality works as it does in T. S. Eliot, not by confirming expectations but by overthrowing them to create pyrotechnic effects of contrast. This tactic is carried to extremes in an invocation of *Hamlet* which even includes a chapter-length parodic performance of the grim tragedy in *Great Expectations*. The deficiencies of the event are vivaciously detailed: the overdressed and over-buxom queen; the ghost's graveyard cough; the too-recognizable boy in multiple roles; and the feeble posturing of Waldengarver (né Wopsle) as the hero (ch. 31). To the accompaniment of verbatim accounts of abusive heckling and the helpless laughter of Pip and Herbert Pocket, the play acquires farcical status.

The narrators in other novels make equally derisive use of the play to satirize even minor characters. The gloomily portentous Mrs. Henry Spiker, with her "black velvet dress" and "great black velvet hat," is described repeatedly as "Hamlet's aunt" since she looks like his "near relation" (*David Copperfield* ch. 25). The nurse, Mrs. Wickam, self-pitying and pessimistic, conducts herself in the sickroom like "a female grave-digger" before retiring to her "funeral baked meats" (*Dombey and Son* ch. 58; *Hamlet* I. ii. 180). Traddles's spikey hair is reminiscent of "a fretful porcupine" (*David Copperfield* ch. 41) to which the ghost in *Hamlet* compares the effect of his story upon the hearer (*Hamlet* I. v. 20).

Characters who allude to *Hamlet* to bolster their social or intellectual status are themselves the object of satire from the narrator as they misappropriate Shakespeare's words. These range from Mr. Micawber to Montague Tigg: the former makes pompous reference to "the philosophic Dane" (*David Copperfield* ch. 52) merely to introduce his trite observation that "worse remains behind" (*Hamlet* III. iv. 179) in relation to Uriah Heep's conduct. Montague Tigg, by contrast, parodies Hamlet's reference to what lies beyond suicide as the "undiscover'd country, from whose bourn no traveller returns" (*Hamlet* III. i. 79–80) as "that what's-his-name from which no thingumbob comes back" (*Martin Chuzzlewit* ch. 4). Later, bidding for cash, he even mangles Hamlet's mad rant to Laertes over Ophelia's grave:

> What is the reason that you use me thus?
> I lov'd you ever. But it is no matter.
> Let Hercules himself do what he may,
> The cat will mew, and dog will have his day.
> (*Hamlet* V. i. 283–6)

This ironic acceptance of fate is translated in Tigg's mouth into a comically flat-footed form: "Well never mind! Moralise as we will, the world goes on. As Hamlet says, Hercules may lay about him with his club in every possible direction, but he can't prevent the cats from making a most intolerable row on the roofs of the houses, or the dogs from being shot in the hot weather if they run about the streets unmuzzled" (ch. 4). The grotesqueness involved in such thwarting of expectations led Michael Slater to argue that Dickens "really seems to have found Hamlet an irresistibly comic character" who "excited derisive laughter from Dickens" (quoted in Gager 1996: 10).

There are many straightforward uses of phrases from *Macbeth* in the novels and several by Micawber, but occasionally Dickens is prepared to allow even his narrator to evoke surprisingly comic effects by allusions to the bloody tragedy at its height. The defiant order "Hang out our banners on the outward walls" (*Macbeth* V. v. 1), which Macbeth gives before his last hopeless battle, is used to describe the view from Miss Tox's back window in *Dombey and Son* where "the most domestic and confidential garments of coachmen and their wives and families, usually hung like Macbeth's banners on the outward walls" (ch. 7). Another linguistic firework is exploded by the unexpected reference to Macbeth's guilty hallucination – "Methought I heard a voice cry 'Sleep no more'; / 'Macbeth does murder sleep'" (II. ii. 35–6) – in *Bleak House*. It is no murderer who acts here but Snagsby's epileptic servant Guster whose snoring "murders sleep" by "going . . . out of one fit into twenty" (ch. 11).

The only instance in which Dickens plays on a single Shakespearean drama is in *Dombey and Son* and, unlike the thematic uses of religious texts, these repeated allusions are linked to a single character, Mrs. Skewton, a withered septuagenarian, mother and pimp of Dombey's second wife. For uniquely here *she* believes herself a Cleopatra and is mockingly referred to in this style by those around her: by Dombey and Bagstock as well as by the narrator. The contrast with the original beauty with whom she identifies (after a portrait of her in youthful beauty called "Cleopatra") could not be greater. In the tragedy *Antony and Cleopatra*, Enobarbus famously describes the queen as she lies in her barge:

> The barge she sat in, like a burnish'd throne,
> Burn'd on the water. The poop was beaten gold:
> Purple the sails, and so perfumed that
> The winds were love-sick with them . . .
> For her own person
> It beggar'd all description . . .
> O'erpicturing that Venus where we see
> The fancy out-work nature.
> (II. ii. 195–205)

Mrs. Skewton plays up to this image, despite her "forlornly faded manner" and "wrinkled face," which the sun makes "more haggard and dismal" (ch. 21) for the paint upon it, by reclining in her "wheeled chair" (or bath-chair), using it as *her* barge. As she baits Dombey with her beautiful but indifferent daughter Edith, her puppet-master Bagstock fosters her delusion by such comments as "Cleopatra commands" (ch. 21) as he kisses her hand. The narrator also colludes in the satire by referring to her, as her lover Antony does to Cleopatra, as the "Serpent of old Nile" (*Antony and Cleopatra* I. v. 25) in a headline added in 1867 (ch. 37). The savage derision persists through other running titles Dickens added in 1867: "Cleopatra keeps up Appearances" (ch. 30), "Cleopatra going down-hill" (ch. 40) and "Cleopatra's Obsequies" (ch. 41). In this last chapter, the satire is still unsparing as she lies on her death-bed, "ugly and haggard," "crooked and shrunk up," "painted and patched," "a dumb old woman." Even her death is a black comedy as "with a girlish laugh, and the skeleton of her Cleopatra manner," she "rises in her bed" and dies deluded. With the help of a Shakespearean tragedy, Dickens creates one of his cruelest satires.

The features of Dickens's writing already discussed are striking evidence of his dazzling linguistic inventiveness, but recent studies have also demonstrated that his use of the mechanisms of language, its infrastructure, are also masterful. New statistical work on his collocation, the habitual co-occurrence of lexical items, reveals "unique creative collocations used only by Dickens in the body of eighteenth- and nineteenth-century literature" (Hori 2004: 205). Similarly, it can be shown that he deploys features like negation, tense, and deixis to powerful thematic effect. In *Little Dorrit*, the use of repeated negation in relation to that "Nobody," Arthur Clennam, "releases underlying contradictions in the construction of gender and social class" (Ingham 2000: 144–64). In *Bleak House*, the contrast between Esther's time-bound, past-tense narrative and the first-person narrator's true-at-all-times, present-tense version mimics significantly the overarching relationship between Esther and those around her, especially Jarndyce (Ingham 2000: 93–115). There appears to be no aspect of the English language that Dickens is not able to exploit in unique ways.

NOTES

1   For details of Dickens's spellings of non-standard English, see Gerson (1967).

2   This information is based on Glenn (1979).

3   A full account of Dickens's use of the Bible is given in Larson (1985).

REFERENCES AND FURTHER READING

Collins, Philip (Ed.) (1971) *Dickens: The Critical Heritage*. London: Routledge and Kegan Paul.

Cook, Dutton (1883). Charles Dickens as a dramatic critic. *Longmans Magazine*, 2, 29–42.

Forby, Robert (1830). *Vocabulary of East Anglia*. London: J. B. Nichols and Son.

Fowler, Roger (1989). Polyphony in *Hard Times*. In Ronald Carter and Paul Simpson (Eds.),

Language, Discourse and Literature: An Introductory Reader in Discourse Stylistics (pp. 77–94). London: Unwin Hyman.

Gager, Valerie L. (1996). *Shakespeare and Dickens: The Dynamics of Influence*. Cambridge: Cambridge University Press.

Gerson, Stanley (1967) *Sound and Symbol in the Dialogue of the Works of Charles Dickens*. Stockholm Studies in English, vol. 19. Stockholm: Almquist and Wiksell.

Glenn, R. B. (1979) Linguistic class indicators in the speech of Dickens's characters. Unpublished thesis, University of Michigan (Universal Microfilm International).

Harbage, Alfred (1976). Shakespeare and early Dickens. In G. B. Evans (Ed.), *Shakespeare: Aspects of Influence* (pp. 109–34). Cambridge, MA: Harvard University Press.

Hori, Mashiro (2004). *Dickens' Style: A Collocational Analysis*. Basingstoke: Palgrave Macmillan.

Horne, Philip (Ed.) (2003). *Oliver Twist*. London: Penguin.

Ingham, Patricia (1986). Dialect as "realism": *Hard Times* and the industrial novel. *Review of English Studies*, 37, 518–27.

— (2000). *Invisible Writing and the Victorian Novel:*

Readings in Language and Ideology. Manchester: Manchester University Press.

Larson, Janet L. (1985) *Dickens and the Broken Scripture*. Athens, Georgia: University of Georgia Press.

Lodge, David (1988). *Language of Fiction*. London: Routledge and Kegan Paul.

Moor, Edward (1823). *Suffolk Words and Phrases*. Woodbridge: R. Hunter.

Morris, Mowbray (1882). Charles Dickens. In Philip Collins (Ed.), *Dickens: The Critical Heritage* (pp. 599–611). London: Routledge and Kegan Paul, 1971.

Page, Norman (1988). *Speech in the English Novel*. Basingstoke: Macmillan.

Paroissien, David (1984). What's in a name? Some speculations about Fagin. *The Dickensian*, 80, 41–5.

Quirk, Randolph (1959). *Charles Dickens and Appropriate Language*. Durham: Durham University Press.

Sorensen, Knud (1985). *Charles Dickens: Linguistic Innovator*. Aarhus: Arkona.

Walker, John (1791). *Critical Pronouncing Dictionary and Expositor of the English Language*, reprint. Menston: Scolar Press, 1968.

9

The Novels and Popular Culture

Juliet John

"People mutht be amuthed" (*Hard Times* bk. 1, ch. 6) is the memorable mantra not only of the lisping circus-master, Mr. Sleary, but of Dickens himself. As Paul Schlicke observes in *Dickens and Popular Entertainment*, "Central to his role as an artist, integral with his social convictions, rooted in his deepest values . . . popular entertainment reaches to the core of Dickens's life and work" (1985: 4). Many of the popular entertainments Dickens enjoyed, deployed, and represented in his works were "distinct from elitist culture which demanded education, wealth and social position"; entertainments like the circus, stage melodrama, and pantomime, to offer just a few examples, were "broad-based" in appeal, "inexpensive and widely available" (Schlicke 1985: 4). What was different about Dickens, however, and shocked some of his contemporaries, was that he insisted that his novels, and the popular entertainments they foregrounded, be taken seriously. He was not content to be regarded as a lowbrow author, arguing consistently for the cultural worth of the novel as a genre and envisaging the novel as a porous form imbibing popular cultural influences yet appealing to all sections of the populace. The kind of popular forms that Dickens valued, therefore, including at that time the novel, he did not view as merely entertainment. He regarded popular entertainment as culture, not simply popular culture; in so doing, Dickens destabilized the familiar idea of a binary opposition between high and low culture and subverted established cultural hierarchies.

A measure of the intensity with which Dickens held his belief that popular art forms were crucial to the cultural life of the nation is the number of essays Dickens wrote on the subject. In general, Dickens was notoriously and willfully quiet on his own art and artistry, believing that an artist's work should speak for itself. In refusing to explain the origin of a passage from *Oliver Twist* to G. H. Lewes, for example, he commented rather impertinently: "if readers cannot detect the point of a passage without having their attention called to it by the writer, I would much rather they lost it and looked out for something else" (*Letters* 1: 404). The exception to this is his writings on popular culture, which are numerous and vociferous. Dickens's belief in cultural inclusivity was held with uncharacteristic consistency. In fact, one might go so far as to say that a belief in "popular" culture is Dickens's most firmly held political view. Apart from certain key passages in *Oliver Twist* (the 1841 Preface and the opening passage of chapter 17), however, his feelings on popular culture are vented mainly in his journalistic writings.

Perhaps the best known of these is "The Amusements of the People," a two-part essay published in *Household Words* (March 30, 1850; April 13, 1850). This essay contains one of Dickens's clearest statements of his belief in, and vision of, popular culture; it is also a lucid articulation of his vision of "dramatic entertainment" as the most effective instrument of cultural cohesion and somehow the natural imaginative outlet of the "common people." "It is probable," he begins, "that nothing will ever root out from among the common people an innate love they have for dramatic entertainment in some form or other. It would be a very doubtful benefit to society, we think, if it could be rooted out." Dickens's belief in "dramatic entertainment" as ideally a crucial site of communal imaginative experience goes some way toward explaining his lifelong passion for the theater, his early desire to be an actor, and, later in his career, the high-profile, one-man public readings of his novels that he performed throughout Britain and America. For Dickens, "dramatic entertainment" has the socially cohesive potential to counter the forces of fragmentation at work in industrialized Britain. "The lower we go," he writes in "The Amusements of the People," "the more natural it is that the best-relished provision for this [imagination] should be found in dramatic entertainments; as at once the most obvious, the least troublesome, and the most real, of all the escapes out of the literal world" (*Journalism* 2: 181).

Dickens's sense of a need for escape from "the literal world" is informed by his awareness of the industrial context. Like Marx, he was concerned that for the working classes, the hard, monotonous life of industrial labor involved the dehumanization of people who were expected to behave like cogs in a machine. In the "Preliminary Word" to *Household Words*, an editorial manifesto published on March 30, 1850, he verbalizes the healing, communal function of imagination in the industrial world that he was to dramatize in *Hard Times* just a few years later:

> In the bosoms of the young and old, of the well-to-do and of the poor, we would tenderly cherish that light of Fancy which is inherent in the human breast . . . to teach the hardest workers at this whirling wheel of toil, that their lot is not necessarily a moody, brutal fact, excluded from the sympathies and graces of imagination. (*Journalism* 2: 177)

His belief in drama as a populist form, and the dramatic as a culturally inclusive artistic mode, is borne out by Dickens's own theatrical and externalized novelistic style and by the outwardly orientated style of so many of the popular cultural modes informing Dickens's works (not only melodrama and pantomime, but Newgate fiction, the Penny Dreadfuls, and the sensation novel). Dickens understood that the illiterate and semi-literate who spent long hours isolated in monotonous factory labor wanted to escape in an imaginary communal experience. We first meet Joe Whelks, Dickens's imaginative working-class archetype, in "The Amusements of the People." Joe, who reappears in essays contributed to *All the Year Round* by other writers, we are told, is:

> not much of a reader, has no great store of books, no very commodious room to read in, no very decided inclination to read, and no power at all of presenting vividly before his mind's eye what he reads about. But put Joe in the gallery of the Victoria Theatre . . . tell him a story . . . by the help of live men and women dressed up, confiding to him their innermost secrets, in voices audible half a mile off; and Joe will unravel a story through all its entanglements, and sit there as long after midnight as you have anything left to show him. (*Journalism* 2: 181)

The urge Dickens describes a decade later in "Two Views of a Cheap Theatre" as "the natural inborn desire of the mass of mankind to recreate themselves and be amused," however, is not best satiated by shoddy cultural fare, but by pleasurable entertainments with an educational and moral drive (*Journalism* 4: 61). In his 1866 series of articles for *All the Year Round* on the state of popular culture imbibed by Mr. Whelks, Andrew Halliday, expressing opinions Dickens endorsed, concluded that he "deserves better things of those who, in catering for his amusements, thrive upon him remarkably well" (*All the Year Round* 16: 35). Dickens wanted caviar for the masses.

Dickens's beliefs in popular culture as a vehicle of education and in the feelings as the seat of the educational process, expressed so uncompromisingly in *Hard Times*, made him fiercely critical of much of the educational provision for the working classes. He distrusted Polytechnic Institutions, for example, which to Dickens symbolized a Utilitarian view of education and a mechanized view of humanity. Adult education institutions, though well meaning, could in his view be informed by intellectual snobbery and anti-theatrical prejudice. In "Dullborough Town," finding that no mechanics belong to the Dullborough Mechanics' Institution, the narrator concludes: "I fancied I detected a shyness in admitting that human nature when at leisure has any desire whatever to be relieved and diverted; and a furtive sliding in of any poor make-weight piece of amusement, shamefacedly and edgewise." Dickens despises what he calls in the same article, "the masking of entertainment, and pretending it was something else – as people mask bedsteads when they are obliged to have them in sitting-rooms, and make believe that they are bookcases" (*Journalism* 4: 144–5). He also fought a fierce battle in print against the Sabbatarians, who believed in the sacred nature of Sundays and consequent restrictions on popular amusements on the one day of the week that workers and their families should have leisure time. A vociferous lobby upheld the church, religious meetings, or Polytechnic lectures as morally superior creations to the theater, for example (Schlicke 1985: 191–225).

Dickens's defense of intelligent popular entertainments for working people was not, however, part of any radical reformist agenda, at least not in any straightforward way. His ideal of "popular" culture was of a culture that included high and low alike, rather than a culture that gave voice to exclusively working-class concerns. He desired a culture of the many rather than a counter-culture of the proletariat, and was careful to avoid supporting aggressively working-class movements like Chartism. He explains the rationale and "main object" behind *Household Words* as a wish "to be the comrade and friend of many thousands of people" irrespective of sex, age, or condition, and to bring "the greater and the lesser in degree" together, promoting "a better acquaintance and a kinder understanding" between them (*Journalism* 2: 177). Dickens repeats this agenda after a reading of *A Christmas Carol* in 1855, affirming on that occasion that it was his earnest aim and desire "to do right" by his readers. Doing so, he explained how he wanted to leave "our imaginative and popular literature more closely associated than I found it," promising to be "faithful, – to my death – in the principles that have won your approval" (*Speeches* 209).

Schlicke argues that Dickens is "basically conservative about entertainment," his commitment to popular amusements arising from fears about the erosion of communal and familial values that he associates with the past (1985: 19). Although nostalgia for the past and concern about the fragmentation of a society fueled by an industrial economy are indeed prominent in Dickens's social vision of popular culture, it is also true that, in cultural terms, Dickens's insistence on the value of popular amusements, and their desirable prominence in the legitimate and literary cultural life of the nation, has consistently been seen as subversive of the cultural status quo. *Oliver Twist*, for example, came under sustained attack in *Fraser's Magazine*. William Makepeace Thackeray, the literary reviewer at the time, disparaged the work in 1839 as a Newgate novel, a genre Thackeray and others believed glamorized low-life criminals and so brought serious literature into disrepute. We could hug rogues like Bill Sikes and Fagin in private, Thackeray conceded. "In public, it is, however, quite wrong to avow such likings, and to be seen in such company" ([Thackeray] 1839: 408).

Dickens's 1841 Preface to *Oliver Twist* rebuts the assumption by Thackeray and other critics that the lower classes infect culture. "I saw no reason, when I wrote this book," Dickens responded confrontationally, "why the very dregs of life, so long as their speech did not offend the ear, should not serve the purpose of a moral, at least as well as its froth and cream." Indeed, as part of Dickens's ethical and political purpose was to embrace all levels of society in fiction and attract an equally broad audience, the inclusion of low life was principled and not simply subservient to a larger moral message. Dickens makes this point clearly and uses the opportunity the Preface presented to distance himself altogether from his opponents. He omits any reference to the word "Newgate," with the exception of a disingenuous reference to *Paul Clifford* (1830) as Bulwer Lytton's "admirable and most powerful novel," and offers a new, distinguished literary genealogy for novels based on crime. Such precedents can easily be found in "the noblest range of English literature," which included Defoe, Fielding, Smollett, Richardson, and Hogarth. "I find the same reproach levelled against them every one, each in his turn, by the insects of the hour, who raised their little hum, and died, and were forgotten."

The buzz raised by Thackeray and others has proved more persistent than Dickens forecast, breeding a confusion among critics that lasted well into the twentieth century. One consequence has been the tendency to underestimate the complexity and indeed ambiguity of Dickens's attitudes to popular culture. F. R. Leavis in 1948, for example, could grant Dickens his ability to "entertain" but at the same time excluded him from his "Great Tradition" on account of an apparent lack of seriousness. Robert Garis's *The Dickens Theatre* takes some corrective steps by arguing that readers must be willing to cooperate with Dickens's "theatrical mode" (1965: 40). But neither Garis nor Leavis in his later re-evaluation (Leavis and Leavis 1970) gets far beyond negative assessments of popular culture as something antithetical to cultural health and progress. Typically, Leavis and those who shared his assumptions failed to appreciate how Dickens uses, analyses, and transforms popular cultural modes in complex and ambiguous ways.

Dickens's treatment of "low life" in *Oliver Twist* illustrates this point. Far from exploiting criminal matter for its sensational effect, the novel reveals a sustained seriousness. This is most apparent in its self-reflexive critique of the attractions and dangers of Newgate fiction and in Dickens's consciousness of the controversial nature of his chosen materials. The character of Fagin, for example, a compound of stage, literary, and anti-Semitic archetypes, also plays the role of "generalised Newgate novelist" (Tracy 1988: 20). He is conscious from the outset that fiction, drama, and comic entertainment have the power to corrupt. For instance, in chapter 9, he "directs" a dramatic representation of pick-pocketing, an inverted morality play performed by the Artful Dodger and Charley Bates, which Oliver perceives as "a very curious and uncommon game." In chapter 18, he again directs the scenes as the Dodger and Charley Bates use the capitalist vocabulary of self-help and "pantomimic representation" to persuade Oliver of the greatness of the life of the thief. When these attempts fail, Fagin tells Oliver comic tales, oral narratives about crime that make Oliver laugh "heartily . . . in spite of his better feelings." They are the sugar to make the poison go down, and Fagin is conscious of what we can call, literally, the arts of corruption (ch. 18). His intended masterstroke is to leave Oliver a volume that bears no accidental similarity to *The Newgate Calendar*, a popular collection of criminal biographies, whose prototype was first published in 1728. Fortunately and improbably, the book does not have the desired effect:

> It was a history of the lives and trials of great criminals; and the pages were soiled and thumbed with use. Here, he read of dreadful crimes that made the blood run cold . . . The terrible descriptions were so real and vivid, that the sallow pages seemed to turn red with gore . . . In a paroxysm of fear, the boy closed the book, and thrust it from him. Then, falling upon his knees, he prayed Heaven to spare him from such deeds . . . (ch. 20)

The success that Fagin has had in persuading the Dodger and Bates of the "greatness" of crime is everywhere evident, even in the Dodger's doodling; the Artful amuses himself "by sketching a ground-plan of Newgate on the table with the piece of chalk" (ch. 25). But perhaps the most striking illustration of Fagin's manipulation of the myth of romantic criminality comes when the Dodger is captured by the police. Bates is so distraught that his friend has been caught for stealing a snuff-box and not for something glamorous like robbing an old gentleman of his "walables" that he comes very close to realizing that fame is rarely the lot of juvenile delinquents. What upsets him most is that the Dodger will not feature in *The Newgate Calendar*. Fagin persuades Charley, however, that newspaper reports of the criminal trials will make the Dodger's name, acting out the court-room scene so brilliantly that Charley eventually sees his friend's capture as "a game! a regular game!" (ch. 43).

Throughout *Oliver Twist*, Dickens both utilizes and analyses not only Newgate narratives, but also the variety of specifically *popular* cultural forms through which such myths are disseminated. A morality play, a "pantomimic representation," oral narrative, comic tales, sketches, acting, and newspaper reports are all invoked by Fagin and his boys in their attempts to corrupt Oliver. The text makes clear the power of popular cultural modes, many of which do not demand literacy in order to be appreciated. It is significant, for example, that Oliver's encounter with the book Fagin gives him proves the least successful. When faced with the written word, Oliver takes the soiled and grubby pages as a warning of their power and resolutely resists the message Fagin hoped they would convey. When indoctrination is disguised as pleasure, or entertainment, by contrast, Dickens shows Oliver as far more susceptible. Dickens attempts to harness this pleasure, and the power that attends it, to a constructive moral and social vision.

Dickens is thus not simply an apologist for popular culture; he is also a cultural critic. Cultural theory has taught us to be wary of the view that because an author demonstrates popular cultural influences, he or she promotes the interests of the populace. Indeed, the notion of "appropriation" – that established cultural voices highjack less respectable modes for their own purposes – has become so popular in critical circles that it is often assumed that when popular cultural forms are deployed outside their place of origin, then the act of redeployment must involve "appropriation." In other words, authors like Dickens must be exploiting and silencing the influences they incorporate; they must be up to no good. In the case of Dickens, any generalized statement about the effect of his cultural borrowings must be a simplification. Too much depends on the specific popular cultural form and the specific novel. Dickens clearly has reservations about the Newgate novel, as *Oliver Twist* and its 1841 Preface make plain. But it is also clear that Dickens understands and values the imaginative power of the Newgate novel, and exploits that power, whilst attempting to embed it within a moral framework. A similar relationship exists between Dickens and the Penny Dreadfuls, cheap sensationalist accounts of criminality and the macabre, popular from the 1830s, initially with the working classes and, illicitly, with many of the younger middle classes.

If Dickens borrowed from popular modes like the Newgate novel and the Penny Dreadful, it is also true that popular writers borrowed (or, as Dickens would have seen it, stole) from Dickens. In 1836, for example, the popular radical and Penny Dreadful writer G. W. M. Reynolds had some success with *Pickwick Abroad, Or The Tour in France*, believed to be one of the best plagiarisms of Dickens. Similarly, his more widely known novel, *The Mysteries of the Court of London* (1849–56), like *Oliver Twist*, featured the London underworld, and utilized slang, humor, and recognizable street stereotypes. The free-for-all that in some ways characterized the early modern cultural marketplace is evidenced by the fact that Reynolds himself was widely plagiarized.

Like Dickens, Reynolds was influenced by and influenced popular stage melodrama, and both authors were prey to loose copyright laws, which meant that their works were extracted in newspapers and plagiarized in print, as well as pirated for the stage. Cultural influence in the 1830s was thus not as controlled in some respects as it is today, now that copyright laws clearly identify the "owners" of cultural products and a global culture industry, presided over by Hollywood and American multinational companies, prevails. Dickens's society was fast becoming commercial, however. Bulwer Lytton made this point in 1847 when he wrote in "A Word to the Public": "The essential characteristic of this age and land is *publicity*" (Lytton 1847: 314). Cheaper access to print and increasing literacy meant that the days when an educated elite or "clerisy" dictated to the rest were over. Both Reynolds and Dickens were caught up in the energized, chaotic, cultural traffic of "the first age of mass culture," which had some similarities to the excited confusion of this first age of Internet access (Brake et al. 2000: 7).

The idea of appropriation is less helpful perhaps than the model of a circular and endlessly circulating relationship between Dickens's works and the popular modes that informed them, as illustrated by his relationship with stage melodrama. Melodrama was the most popular kind of drama in the nineteenth century, a century when more people went to the theater than in any other. Originally designed for those who could not read, melodrama was particularly popular with lower-class and artisan audiences, who dominated the theaters in the first half of the nineteenth century. Imported from France at the time of the French Revolution, melodrama offered Dickens an inclusive, populist, even anti-intellectual aesthetics.

The backbone of melodrama is a battle between good and evil, "a world of absolutes where virtue and vice coexist in pure whiteness and pure blackness" (Booth 1965: 14). It fulfills the infamous definition of fiction supplied in 1895 by Oscar Wilde's Miss Prism: "The good ended happily, and the bad unhappily. That is what Fiction means" (*The Importance of Being Earnest*, Act II). In melodrama, all is externalized. Character, for example, is normally "transparent." Good people look good and bad people look bad (and usually ugly). As a genre that was originally non-verbal, even mature verbal melodrama places no particular premium on language. Dialogue is functional and characters communicate as much through physiognomy, gesture, and the body as they do through language. Melodrama is, finally, an intensely emotional genre, in which a passion felt is a passion expressed. Dickens makes clear the similarity between melodrama and opera in "The Amusements of the People."

Discussing the "conventional passion" common to melodrama and "the Italian Opera," he concludes: "So do extremes meet; and so there is some hopeful congeniality between what will excite MR. WHELKS, and what will rouse a Duchess" (*Journalism* 2: 201).

The emotional, moral, and populist tendencies of melodrama all appealed to Dickens. His attendance at, and enjoyment of, melodrama were lifelong. One of Dickens's school friends claimed that he and his playmates at the Wellington Academy "mounted small theatres, and got up very gorgeous scenery to illustrate *The Miller and his Men* and *Cherry and Fair Star*." According to John Forster, "Dickens's after-taste for theatricals might have had its origin in these affairs" (Forster bk. 1, ch. 3). Dickens was introduced early to Shakespearean protagonists, Macbeth and Richard III, in melodramatic versions of Shakespeare at the Little Theatre Royal in Rochester.

> It was within those walls that I had learnt, as from a page of English history, how that wicked King [Richard III] slept in war-time on a sofa much too short for him, and how fearfully his conscience troubled his boots . . . Many wondrous secrets of Nature had I come to the knowledge of in that sanctuary: of which not the least terrific were, that the witches in Macbeth bore an awful resemblance to the Thanes and other proper inhabitants of Scotland; and that the good King Duncan couldn't rest in his grave, but was constantly coming out of it and calling himself somebody else. (*Journalism* 4: 143)

Affectionate humor characterizes many of Dickens's journalistic and novelistic writings on melodrama. In "Greenwich Fair" from *Sketches by Boz*, for instance, the villain, or wrongful heir:

> comes in to two bars of quick music (technically called "a hurry"), and goes on in the most shocking manner, throwing the young lady about as if she was nobody, and calling the rightful heir "At-recreant — ar-wretch!" in a very loud voice, which answers the double purpose of *displaying his passion*, and preventing the sound being deadened by the sawdust. (*Journalism* 1: 117, emphasis added)

In *Nicholas Nickleby*, Dickens classically exposes melodrama's representation of passion in his depiction of the Crummles' savage in the rehearsal for *The Indian Savage and the Maiden*:

> the savage, becoming ferocious, made a slide towards the maiden . . . after a little more ferocity and chasing of the maiden into corners, he began to relent, and stroked his face several times with his right thumb and four fingers, thereby intimating that he was struck with admiration of the maiden's beauty. Acting upon the impulse of this passion, he (the savage) began to hit himself severe thumps in the chest, and to exhibit other indications of being desperately in love, which being rather a prosy proceeding, was very likely the cause of the maiden's falling asleep. (ch. 23)

In *Great Expectations*, likewise, Mr. Wopsle's rendering of Collins's *Ode on the Passions*, particularly his representation of Revenge – "throwing his blood-stain'd sword in thunder down, and taking the War denouncing trumpet with a withering look" – is "venerated" by the young Pip, but mocked by the older narrator. In later life, Pip "fell into the society of the Passions, and compared them with Collins and Wopsle, rather to the disadvantage of both gentlemen" (ch. 7).

From the examples above, it would be easy to argue that Dickens is patronizing about melodrama and does not take it seriously. However, a more accurate reading would maintain that, even though Dickens can be patronizing about aspects of the form, he also takes it extremely seriously. In chapter 17 of *Oliver Twist*, for example, a long passage, unique in Dickens's works, argues for popular stage melodrama as indelibly linked with the novel. "It is the custom of the stage: in all good, murderous melodramas: to present the tragic and comic scenes, in regular alternation," the narrator proposes. Such changes, he continues, between misfortune and comedy, between danger and comfort, and the high and the low, "appear absurd": "but they are not so unnatural as they would seem at first sight." Their justification, in fact, reflects the "transitions" which occur "in real life" "from well-spread boards to death-beds, and from mourning weeds to holiday garments." Moreover, "such sudden shiftings of the scene, and rapid changes of time and place" have two additional sanctions. They have been approved by books in "long usage" and by many who consider them "as the great art of authorship: an author's skill in his craft being, by such critics, chiefly estimated with the relation to the dilemmas in which he leaves his characters at the end of every chapter" (ch. 17).

Though Dickens's use of melodramatic models becomes less obvious as his career progresses, he nonetheless remains true to the "streaky bacon" model of the novel, using "sudden shiftings" of scene, "violent transitions," and "abrupt impulses of passion or feeling" throughout. He remains dependent on externalized, stereotypical characters and representations of emotion – exactly the kinds of conventionalized formulations, in fact, that he mocks in some of his writings. Dickens's perspective on melodrama is a little like Pip's perspective on his narrative: at the same time immersed in and sincerely committed to his vision *and* aware of the limitations of the vision and a commitment to it. He was conscious of melodrama's potential relevance to the primal emotional, moral, and political life of its culturally diverse audience. He recognized that, far from being a laughable departure from reality, melodrama at its most ambitious could comprise what Peter Brooks calls "the expressionism of the moral imagination," as well as a salve or antidote for the alienating forces of modernity (Brooks 1976: 55). At the same time, however, Dickens was aware that melodrama does not always realize its potential, the stylized nature of melodramatic aesthetics turning readers from "actors" to "spectators."

If Dickens's novels often promote melodramatic (transparent, externally focused) models of identity at the same time as revealing their fictional, idealized underpinnings, however, they also use melodramatic models to expose the limitations of the internalized, intellectualized modes of representing character that became dominant in the classic realist novel. In *Great Expectations*, for example, Mr. Wopsle's melodramatic rendering of Hamlet's "To Be or Not to Be" soliloquy is an instrument as well as an object of mockery. Dickens's point is as much about the alien nature of Hamlet's introspective angst to an artisan audience as it is about Wopsle's bad acting. Dickens's comic master-stroke is to make an audience weaned on melodrama and with little leisure for angst answer back, thus revealing the absurdity of certain psychological renderings of identity to those who are outside rather than inside the world of abstract speculation:

> Whenever that undecided Prince had to ask whether 'twas nobler in the mind to suffer, some roared yes, and some no, and some inclining to both opinions said "toss up for it;" and quite a Debating Society arose. When he asked what should such fellows as he do crawling between earth and heaven, he was encouraged by loud cries of "Hear! Hear!" (ch. 12)

In Dickens's novels therefore, melodrama is naturalized, problematized, and used to interrogate the psychologized models of identity of high cultural status in the period.

True to the circular and circulating relationship between Dickens and the popular cultural modes he deployed, his works were recycled by the Wopsles of his day who ensured that the relationship between Dickens and stage melodrama was not simply one of upward cultural appropriation. Although there were some good-quality adaptations of Dickens's works, Dickens disliked and disapproved of many of them. George Almar's version of *Oliver Twist* (November 19, 1838), for example, was one of several that appeared before the serialized novel had run its course. It was the most successful of the contemporary stage adaptations, but Dickens disliked it so much that when he saw it at the Surrey Theatre, "he laid himself down upon the floor in a corner of the box and never rose from it until the drop-scene fell" (Forster bk. 2, ch. 4). In *Nicholas Nickleby*, Dickens uses Nicholas as a mouthpiece for an attack on one of the most well-known hack adapters of his work, W. T. Moncrieff, whose *Nicholas Nickleby and Poor Smike or The Victim of the Yorkshire School* was produced at the Strand Theatre on May 20, 1839. Nicholas tells "a literary gentleman" (hack adapter) to whom he is speaking that whereas Shakespeare:

> brought within the magic circle of his genius, traditions peculiarly adapted for his purpose, and turned familiar things into constellations which should enlighten the world for ages . . . you take the uncompleted books of living authors, fresh from their hands, wet from the press, cut, hack, and carve them to the powers and capacities of your actors . . . all this without his permission, and against his will; and then, to crown the whole proceeding, publish in some mean pamphlet, an unmeaning farrago of garbled extracts from his work, to which you put your name as author, with the honourable description annexed, of having perpetrated a hundred other outrages of the same description. Now, show me the distinction between such pilfering as this, and picking a man's pocket in the street. (ch. 48)

Dickens had a very modern sense that his authorship of novels entitled him to financial reward when they were reworked elsewhere, and the issue of plagiarism was to anger him throughout his lifetime. During his 1842 trip to America, in particular, he made himself unpopular by attacking America for not signing an international copyright agreement, and for pirating his works. Dickens's sense of cultural ownership in many ways militated against the idea of him as an idealist desiring the greatest access to culture for the greatest number. On the other hand, when we read in his letters from his second trip to the States over two decades later – "They are doing Crickets, Oliver Twists, and all sorts of versions of me" and "Nothing is being played here scarcely that is not founded on my books" – we understand the scale of the problem that irked him so much (*Letters* 11: 521, 527).

His plan to promote a stage adaptation in the United States of the 1867 Christmas story "No Thoroughfare," which was published both in *All the Year Round* and in *Every Saturday* in Boston, failed because "They are pirating the bill as well as the play here" (*Letters* 11: 572). The plan reminds us not only of the degree to which Dickens's works were exploited, but also of Dickens's continued desire to make a direct impact on the popular stage of the day. "No Thoroughfare" did run successfully at London's Adelphi Theatre from Boxing Day 1867 for 200 performances, and at the Olympic Theatre in November 1876. Dickens also wrote a different version in French called "L'abime," first produced at the Vaudeville in Paris on June 2, 1868. The play, like other stage melodramas Dickens wrote, lacks the sophistication, range, and subtlety of his novels. Yet despite his limited talent as a playwright, Dickens wrote and acted for the stage from his childhood until his death.

Two possible explanations account for this. He held a justified belief in his own potential as an actor, and might have been "successful on the boards," he notes, had not "a terrible bad cold and an inflammation of the face" kept him from a stage audition he arranged when he was young. He also admitted to a second motive: that his thoughts about the stage were closely tied to those of making some money. Work as a shorthand reporter, he told Forster in a letter reminiscing about his early days, "though not a very *bad*" living, was not "a very good" one, a fact which, combined with the uncertainty of the work, made him think of the theater "in quite a business-like way" (*Letters* 4: 245).

Dickens's mention of money as the stimulus for his interest in the stage sits oddly with the more high-minded statements he made during his career about his belief in, and vision for, the stage. Indeed, in one description of the experience of acting in *The Frozen Deep* (1856), the melodrama written by Collins and revised by Dickens, Dickens suggests that acting is the ultimate art:

> As to the Play itself; when it is made as good as my care can make it, I derive a strange feeling out of it, like writing a book in company. A satisfaction of a most singular kind, which has no exact parallel in my life. A something that I suppose to belong to a Labourer in Art, alone, and which has to me a conviction of its being actual Truth without its pain, that I never could adequately state if I were to try never so hard. (*Letters* 8: 256)

The idea of acting as "writing a book in company," as "actual Truth without its pain," goes some way to explaining Dickens's controversial decision, against the advice of Forster and to the detriment of his health, to embark on the grueling reading tours of his novels from 1858 onward. The paid readings proved highly successful and contributed substantially to Dickens's income. But they were not solely profit oriented. Dickens had a deep-rooted belief in "that particular relation (personally affectionate and like no other man's)" between himself and "the public" (Forster bk. 8, ch. 2). The public readings were thus integral to both Dickens's need for a live audience (like other famous people after him, to make him feel valued and real) and his populism, his perception that readers needed him and his works. In Schlicke's phrase, the readings were a sign of his "abiding commitment" to the public (1985: 6).

Yet the paid readings were indubitably a means of making money, and the motivation for the reading tours captures the fusion of commercial acumen and idealism that characterized Dickens's career from his early aspirations to be an actor onward. Whereas Dickens's first public readings in 1853 were "charity" readings, given in aid of an adult education institution in Birmingham, by the time he toured America in 1867–8, money and profit dominate his correspondence, seeming to overshadow at times his interest in America itself. Staggeringly, for example, he tells Forster: "It is as well that the money has flowed in hitherto so fast, for I have a misgiving that the great excitement about the President's impeachment will damage our receipts" (*Letters* 12: 59). The raising of ticket prices when space is at a premium brings no remark from him other than: "A charming audience, no dissatisfaction whatever at the raised prices . . . £300 in it" (*Letters* 12: 38). This kind of acceptance of market forces sits awkwardly with the "earnest desire" he expresses in a letter of December 14, 1867 "to render the tickets for my Readings as widely and easily accessible as possible" (*Letters* 11: 510). He is moreover reluctant to appear in public when he is not paid: "the less I am shown – for nothing – the better for the Readings!" (*Letters* 11: 483). He regularly uses the discourse of business, in one letter even writing about "anticipating and glutting 'the market'" (*Letters* 12: 8). Most striking are the images Dickens creates of himself literally (or perhaps materially) staring at his money: there is "such an immense untidy heap of paper money on the table that it looks like a family wash" (*Letters* 11: 508). The images almost remind us of Fagin surveying his hoard of stolen treasures except for the fact that Dickens seems to experience an uncanny alienation from his money rather than a joyous absorption: "The manager is always going about with an immense bundle that looks like a sofa-cushion, but is in reality paper-money, and it had risen to the proportions of a sofa on the morning he left for Philadelphia" (*Letters* 12: 5).

Taken out of context, this obsession with money seems to suggest a man who sold out on an original belief in ethical populism for financial gain, and, in the words of George Gissing, "died in the endeavour to increase (not for himself) an already ample fortune" (1903: "Autumn" XXII). But the idea that Dickens had turned his back on his previous principles would be simplistic and inaccurate. Dickens's money-mindedness on the American reading tour can be partly explained by perceived need (his complex personal life meant that he had many dependants and establishments to support). It can also be seen as retaliation against a nation that he felt had violated his privacy on his first trip to the States, and also his financial rights as an author. In 1867–8, the deliberate professionalization of his appearances in public, or the deliberate splitting of his identity into public and private compartments, suggests that Dickens learned lessons on the first tour about the adverse effects on himself of too much uncontrolled public exposure. If America would not pay for his works, he seemed to say, it would have to pay to see him.

The violation of his privacy on the first trip in 1842 was indeed staggering in its proportions. Dickens must have been the first global media star, and he experienced the price of fame in a mass culture when his initial accessibility in the States was rewarded by barbers selling locks of his hair for profit, to give just one example, leaving Dickens paranoid about having his hair cut (*Letters* 3: 149). To try to restrict public appearances to those made in a professional capacity may have seemed like a wise precaution. His commercialism was also an acceptance that the future of popular culture may be closer to the American, commercial model he had disliked so intensely on his first visit and which had no doubt influenced the paternalistic, communal ideals of his journals. Dickens combined a nostalgic yearning for a bygone paternalistic culture with an understanding that if authorship was to be relevant in an age of mass culture, authors had to acknowledge the mass market and seek to influence it.

Modern cultural theorists have seen a tension between the goals of commercial culture and those of a genuinely "popular" culture consonant with the values and interests of the populace. At the dawn of "the first age of mass culture," Dickens did not see this tension as inevitable. As he announced in a speech in Boston, "I would rather have the affectionate regard of my fellow men, than I would have heaps and mines of gold. But the two things do not seem to me incompatible" (*Speeches* 21). It may be, of course, that the "affectionate regard" with which the public viewed Dickens was not in fact in their interests, and there is a complex debate to be had about Dickens's place in the global mass market and the growth of modern cultural imperialism. Dickens's awareness of literature as a business, for example, was not new to him in his later years. He had always been addicted to "working the copyrights" of his works (*Letters* 4: 121); that is, promoting the reproduction of his works for maximum profit. He was highly aware of himself as a brand, promoting the image of Dickens from his first fame onward. He ruthlessly "managed" public knowledge of his life – most famously in the case of Ellen Ternan (see chapter 1) – in order to maintain the familiar image of "Dickens." He was a journalist as well as a novelist, and in founding two journals of his own, he was also an entrepreneur. His Christmas stories alone, especially *A Christmas Carol*, have been enormously successful in commercial terms and have shaped perceptions and celebrations of Christmas among the public at large since their first publication (Parker 2002).

Dickens's combination of idealism and commercialism, tradition and modernity, is evident not only in his impact but in his popular cultural influences. Paul Schlicke's

Dickens and Popular Entertainment focuses on Dickens's belief in the traditional forms of entertainment that were disappearing: as well as those touched upon here, he includes fairs, pantomime, Punch and Judy and waxworks (both featured in *The Old Curiosity Shop*), to name just a few. In addition to these inherited pastimes, however, Dickens was also fascinated by more sensationalist cultural pursuits which may not all have been new in themselves but whose increasing cultural prominence demonstrates the growing prurience that has characterized the modern mass culture of the lowest common denominator. Like other Victorians, for example, he was intrigued by the spectacle of dead bodies and visited the tourist attraction that the Paris Morgue became; he was interested in criminal trials and criticized some newspaper reporting of them, while writing on them himself; he disapproved of public hangings, but was clearly fascinated by them, as *Barnaby Rudge* makes clear.

While Dickens, like the sensation- and detective-fiction writers of his time, was intrigued by the urge to violence and sensation which has become so influential in modern mass culture, he was also intrigued by the technical advances of the time. He made the most of train travel, and, as Grahame Smith (2003) among others has documented, he was fascinated by those technologies that eventually gave rise to film: photography, magic lanterns, phantasmagorias, dioramas, and panoramas. Indeed, Smith argues convincingly that Dickens, the man who saw his novels as "moving pictures," dreamt or imaginatively foresaw cinema, a point made earlier by Sergei Eisenstein, who famously cited Dickens as the prime parent of film, claiming: "our cinema is not without an ancestry and a pedigree, a past and traditions, or a rich cultural heritage from earlier epochs" (Eisenstein 1942: 212).

Dickens is arguably the only author to have aimed to have a huge impact on global mass culture and to have consistently done so without jeopardizing, despite Leavis's efforts, his central place as an object of study in the academy. The reasons for his unrivaled success at straddling academic and popular culture are many: his belief in popular culture, his semi-educated, urban upbringing, the visual qualities of his writing, his historical position at the dawn of a democratic age and in the midst of industrialism. Then there is his literary genius, his business acumen, his self-promotion, his work ethic, and his ability to hold both radical and conservative values simultaneously. Does Dickens continue to appeal because he offers solace in the disorientating environment of modernity or because of his inherent modernity, which informs his writings and the Dickens industry he started? Studying Dickens's fiction in fact shows the limitations of such oppositional thinking, but also highlights the way in which such oppositions have become integral to the modern cultural imaginary. In 1939, George Orwell cited Dickens to demonstrate that in England "there does exist a certain cultural unity": "It is difficult otherwise to explain," he argued, "why he could be both read by working people (a thing which has happened to no other novelist of this stature) and buried in Westminster Abbey" (Orwell 1968: 459–60). What Orwell does not stress is that Dickens's uniqueness problematizes more than proves the existence of the kind of cultural unity Dickens so desired.

REFERENCES AND FURTHER READING

Booth, M. R. (1965). *English Melodrama*. London: Jenkins.

Brake, L., Bell, B., and Finkelstein, D. (Eds.) (2000). Introduction. In *Nineteenth-century Media and the Construction of Identities* (pp. 1–7). Basingstoke: Palgrave Macmillan.

Brooks, P. (1976). *The Melodramatic Imagination: Balzac, Henry James, Melodrama and the Mode of Excess*. New Haven, CT: Yale University Press.

Eisenstein, S. (1942). Dickens, Griffith and ourselves. In R. Taylor and W. Powell (Eds.), *Selected Works*, vol. 3 (pp. 193–238). London: British Film Institute.

Garis, R. (1965). *The Dickens Theatre: A Reassessment of the Novels*. Oxford: Clarendon Press.

Gissing, G. (1903). *The Private Papers of Henry Ryecroft*. London: Westminster.

Halliday, A. (1866). Mr. Whelks in the East. *All the Year Round*, 16, 31–35.

Leavis, F. R. (1948). *The Great Tradition*. London: Chatto and Windus.

— and Leavis, Q. D. (1970). *Dickens the Novelist*. London: Chatto and Windus.

Lytton, B. (1847). A word to the public. In J. John (Ed.), *Cult Criminals: The Newgate Novels*, vol. 3 (pp. 297–334). London: Routledge.

Orwell, G. (1968). Charles Dickens. In S. Orwell and I. Angus (Eds.), *Collected Essays, Journalism and Letters*, vol. 1: 1920–1940 (pp. 413–60). London: Secker and Warburg.

Parker, D. (2002). Dickens and the American Christmas. *Dickens Quarterly*, 19, 160–9.

Schlicke, P. (1985). *Dickens and Popular Entertainment*. London: Allen and Unwin.

Smith, G. (2003). *Dickens and the Dream of Cinema*. Manchester: Manchester University Press.

[Thackerary, W. M.] (1839). Horae Catnachianae. *Fraser's Magazine*, 19, 407–24.

Tracy, R. (1988). "The old story" and inside stories: modish fiction and fictional modes in *Oliver Twist*. *Dickens Studies Annual*, 17, 1–33.

Part III
English History Contexts

10

Dickens as a Reformer

Hugh Cunningham

Both in his lifetime and afterwards, Dickens had a reputation as a reformer. Many have credited him with creating the climate of opinion that facilitated the reforms in education, public health, and criminal law that helped to make Britain a safer and less strife-ridden society. He was also well known as a critic of existing structures of power, puncturing the pomposity and self-delusion of politicians and other office-holders. And yet, examined closely, and case by case, it becomes less and less easy to see him straightforwardly as a reformer. There were others with a claim to the title of reformer who had much clearer diagnoses for and solutions to British ills than did Dickens. Dickens stood on shifting and uncomfortable ground amongst such reformers, his responses to situations often seeming to attract the label of "conservative" as much as "radical." This does not mean that he did not attack abuses in his society, nor that his reputation as a reformer was undeserved; rather, his responses to particular issues were shaped by his abiding concern for decency and humanity, and not by any coherent doctrine of the proper role of the state.

Britain during Dickens's lifetime was undergoing changes unprecedented in speed and scope. Brought up in the age of the stagecoach, Dickens lived as an adult in the age of the railway, the telegraph, and the steam vessel. Economic historians are now often cautious about describing what was happening in the late eighteenth and first half of the nineteenth centuries as an "industrial revolution," but, even though annual growth rates in the economy may not have been as dramatic as once thought, no one at the time was in doubt about the transformation that the economy and society were undergoing. The changes were most dramatic in the growth of towns, particularly the cotton towns of the industrial north, but fully evident to Dickens in the city he knew so well, London; it grew from over one million inhabitants in the year of his birth to over three million by the time he died. By mid-century, over half of the British population lived in towns. Many doubted whether an urban civilization, so dependent on industry, could survive. Sir Robert Peel, prime minister for much of the 1840s, when the fate of Britain seemed to be in the balance, wondered whether it might have been better for Britain to have remained a fundamentally agrarian society.

Three men had a reputation that lasted long after their deaths for their understanding of, and contribution to, these dramatic changes. Adam Smith, through his *The Wealth of Nations* (1776), had become the oracle for those who believed that government should withdraw as far as possible from any interference with the economy. If everyone worked for his own advantage, Smith's famous "invisible hand" would ensure that this worked for the public good. There were things that governments had to do because they could not be left in the hands of individuals: they included the defense of the country, the provision of a coinage, and a system of law-making and enforcement; perhaps also some means of relieving the worst poverty. But beyond that, interference in the economy would be harmful. The "political economists," as the followers of Smith were known, were a powerful influence in Dickens's lifetime. Their stock negative to any suggestion of government interference in the economy was rarely challenged.

Thomas Malthus's fame came from his argument at the turn of the eighteenth and nineteenth centuries that population growth had a natural tendency to exceed food supply. Britain's population was growing at a rate that, if Malthus was correct, presaged disaster. Malthus's own remedy for what would otherwise be a reduction of population through starvation or war was self-control on the part of parents. He gained the reputation of being a killjoy, a gloomy pessimist always looking to a disaster ahead. Dickens instinctively set himself against the doctrines associated with Smith and Malthus. In *Hard Times*, Thomas Gradgrind's youngest children were called Adam Smith and Malthus, and Dickens amused himself by imagining a book called *Malthus's Nursery Rhymes*. Thomas Gradgrind himself was the embodiment of Utilitarianism, a body of thought stemming from the work of Jeremy Bentham. At one level, Dickens had no problem with a philosophy that judged human actions, and the actions of government, by the extent to which they contributed to the greatest happiness of the greatest number. In practice, the Utilitarians, whose leading members occupied key positions in journalism, the civil service, and government, tended to put as much emphasis on humans' wish to avoid pain as on their search for pleasure.

Dickens was to cooperate closely with some Utilitarians, particularly over health reform, but he was by instinct opposed to the philosophies and policies associated with Smith, Malthus, and Bentham, the three interlinked and powerful influences on government in his day. He could not but acknowledge their power, and he did not offer any radical critique of their understanding of society. Rather, he saw them as dry, desiccated, and inhuman. Traveling to Preston in 1854 to see for himself what was happening in the midst of a lockout, he fell into conversation with a man he thought of as "Mr. Snapper." Snapper was a firm advocate of political economy and could see no good in the strikers, no harm in the masters: "I retorted on Mr. Snapper, that Political Economy was a great and useful science in its own way and its own place, but that I did not transplant my definition of it from the Common Prayer Book, and make it a great king above all gods." Refusing to engage in discussions of capital and labor, Dickens, desperately seeking a *modus vivendi* between warring factions, stated his belief:

> that into the relations between employers and employed, as into all the relations of this life, there must enter something of feeling and sentiment; something of mutual explanation, forbearance, and consideration; something which is not to be found in Mr. McCulloch's dictionary, and is not exactly stateable in figures; otherwise those relations are wrong and rotten at the core and will never bear sound fruit. (*Journalism* 3: 198–9)

Yet, confusingly for us, Smith, Malthus, and Bentham could all be, and were, heralded as reformers. Their aim was radically to reform the system of government as it existed in the early nineteenth century. Dickens's distancing of himself from them meant that he was in some danger of being seen as a conservative, wedded to old and traditional ways of doing things. This, as we shall see, was by and large not the case, but it points to the difficulty of placing Dickens within the range of reform in the nineteenth century.

There were other critics of early nineteenth-century government besides Smith, Malthus, and Bentham. On Dickens's left were radicals for whom a simple term described Britain's government: it was "Old Corruption." The phrase was used most tellingly by the journalist and campaigner, William Cobbett. Cobbett and others argued that a government whose civil servants were recruited by patronage, and whose support in the House of Commons depended on the purchase of votes in elections from the small minority of men who formed the electorate, was in essence a system to enable those in government to become rich without any regard for the poor. If Cobbett, like Dickens later, attacked government mainly through words, many of his followers took to the streets in protest. Their most famous moment came in 1819 when they marched to St. Peter's Fields in Manchester in the cause of reform. Soldiers were sent out to control them, and killed 11 of the protesters.

"Peterloo," as it became known in mockery of the victory over Napoleon at Waterloo four years previously, resonated in radical circles for years afterwards. To radicals, it signaled the government's willingness to stop at nothing in its attempts to protect its own privileged position. But to conservatives, street protests all too easily summoned up memories of the French Revolution, which cast a pall over reforming endeavor for half a century. Fear of the mob was deep rooted in respectable British society, and Dickens feared it as much as anyone else. He never aligned himself with those reformers or radicals who were willing to pit numbers, out on the streets, against government. He had no sympathy for Chartism, which from 1838 to 1848 was the most organized attempt in his lifetime to bring about a more democratic system of government. In *Barnaby Rudge*, written in the midst of the Chartist decade, he did not hold back in his critique of mob action.

Dickens's dislike of Chartism had its roots in a cast of thinking that emerged in his writings in the late 1830s and early 1840s. Civilization, Dickens thought, was a fragile construction dependent on human beings restraining some of their natural impulses, not least their aggression. Dickens had no time at all for those who believed that a human being was born good. To the contrary, the civilizing process that made people participants in society was what prevented anarchy. If in their childhood and youth they failed to undergo this process, they posed a danger to society. "Mawkish sentimentality" was quite out of place in dealing with them. It was the first duty of government to protect citizens against lawbreakers. Dickens favored strong prison discipline for those who broke the law; he was a great admirer of the police, and particularly of detectives, and generally supported the institutions of law and order (Magnet 2004).

A move to reform government can be dated back to the later eighteenth century. It took the form in large part of "retrenchment," a word much used in the nineteenth century to refer to a reduction in the expense of government. The movement had considerable success. Government expenditure almost halved between its peak in 1811–15 and 1831–5. This was primarily due to a reduction in the expense of the armed forces after victory at Waterloo, but there was also a cut in the number of civil servants and their cost. Sinecures, salaried jobs with few if any duties attached to them, had all but disappeared by 1830. Radicals continued to rail against "Old Corruption," but in many ways by the 1830s the state had cleaned up its act. It had also, under the influence of Adam Smith, and in the name of freeing up the economy, cut many of its powers, for example, to control prices and wages, or to insist that those who wished to enter a skill or craft serve a seven-year apprenticeship.

If the period from the 1830s onward comes to seem one of growing government intervention, the years before that were ones of less intervention. Those who attacked "Old Corruption" were much less happy about this tendency than they were about the reduction of sinecures. In a free economy, the one-quarter of a million people dependent for their livelihoods on handloom weaving were without any protection from government when power-loom weaving spread in the 1820s and 1830s. The handloom weavers instinctively turned to government for protection, and the government, now equally instinctively, rejected their claims. "Political economy," the doctrine of Adam Smith, triumphed over the "moral economy," a belief that government had a duty to protect those who were in need through events beyond their control.

The pace of reform stepped up with the election in 1830 of a Whig government. From the 1780s, the Tories, or the Conservatives as they came to be called in the 1830s, had dominated government. The Whigs came to power with a reputation not only as reformers of government itself, something shared with the Tories, but also of the processes by which governments came to be formed, of the electoral system. Dickens, a shorthand parliamentary reporter for the *Mirror of Parliament* in 1831–2, was a first-hand observer of the exciting events leading up to the passage of the First Reform Act in the summer of 1832 and of the ensuing general election. It was a time when many thought the country on the verge of revolution. The reform itself was much less far-reaching than many had hoped: in England and Wales the percentage of the adult male population entitled to vote increased from 13 percent to 18 percent;

82 percent of adult males and all females remained without the vote. Elections, as Dickens portrayed them at Eatanswill in *The Pickwick Papers*, remained violent occasions. The Reform Act was not democracy, though it may have opened the door to it.

The reforms of the Whig government included the abolition of slavery in British possessions (1833), the first effective Factory Act (1833), the first government grants in support of elementary schooling (1833), the criminal justice system, at last reserving hanging almost exclusively for murder, and municipal government (1835). All of these were issues that Dickens would engage with. But the reform that most concerned him was the reform of the Poor Law achieved in the Poor Law Amendment Act of 1834. The Poor Law dated back to the late sixteenth century. In England and Wales, it held each of the 15,000 parishes responsible for making provision for the poor. By the end of the seventeenth century, parishes were raising a rate from their wealthier inhabitants to meet the costs involved. At the end of the eighteenth century, at a time of acute hardship, some parishes began to distribute relief on the basis of the level of wages and the number of children a family had to support. This, it came to be felt, was a signal to employers that they could keep wages down, and an encouragement to the poor to breed recklessly (Malthus's response can be imagined). The poor rates began to rise inexorably, and that was one strong incentive for reform.

The Whig government set up a Royal Commission to report on the Poor Laws and to recommend reforms. Edwin Chadwick, Bentham's disciple, was the most important influence on it. He and other Utilitarians believed that the poor needed the threat of pain if they were to emerge from the demoralization that seemed to be engulfing them. There was no recognition that the problem, particularly in southern rural areas, might be overpopulation and unemployment. The solution that the Utilitarians advocated was the workhouse test and less eligibility. What this meant was that those who applied for relief would have to accept that they might be placed in a workhouse, and the workhouses themselves would provide a standard of living and comfort lower than that of the lowest paid day laborer. In short, there was to be every incentive to avoid applying for relief. On top of this, the Utilitarians, with their desire for efficiency, wanted to take away from each individual parish the right to determine its own poor law policy. Parishes were to be grouped into unions, and all would be subject to inspection by a central authority.

The Poor Law Amendment Act was passed in 1834. Its implementation was strongly resisted, especially in the north of England. The workhouses became known as Bastilles after the symbol of royalist misrule in France. Many working-class radicals saw the new Act as removing a right to relief that was rooted in history. Chartism grew directly out of this opposition to the New Poor Law, as it came to be called. In practice, the new Act was less radical than it appeared in anticipation. Poor Law unions rightly understood that it was economic madness to build enough workhouse places for conditions in a bad winter at an unfavorable point in the economic cycle, leaving beds empty at other times. They continued to do as they had always done, to give most relief "outdoors": that is to say, they did not enforce the workhouse test,

but allowed the poor to receive relief while staying in their own homes. In 1844, 84
percent of those in receipt of poor relief received it outdoors. Those who did end up
in the workhouse were not "able-bodied paupers," perfectly capable of doing a day's
work, but the old, the young, and the ill; in 1859, only 16 percent of those in poor
law institutions were able-bodied adults; 42 percent were non-able-bodied adults, and
38 percent were children. Dickens knew this well. In 1850, in "A Walk in a Workhouse," he described what he found:

> Groves of babies in arms; groves of mothers and other sick women in bed; groves of
> lunatics; jungles of men in stone-paved downstairs day-rooms, waiting for their dinners;
> longer and longer groves of old people, in upstairs infirmary wards, wearing out life,
> God knows how – this was the scenery through which the walk lay, for two hours.
> (*Journalism* 2: 238–9)

Dickens was working for the *Morning Chronicle* during the debates on the reform
of the Poor Law. Its editor, John Black, was a supporter of the reforms, and Dickens
recalled "How often used Black and I to quarrel about the effect of the poor-law bill!"
(quoted in Schlicke 1975: 152). For Dickens, the Act was an embodiment of the worst
elements in the Smith/Malthus/Bentham axis of opinion. But in truth he was no lover
of the Old Poor Law either. Oliver Twist was born under the Old Poor Law, and is
presented to us in chapter 2 under the New. Both lack humanity, and it is to humanity that Dickens appeals in his critique. The workhouse test is ridiculed for establishing a rule "that all poor people should have the alternative . . . of being starved by a
gradual process in the house [workhouse], or by a quick one out of it" (ch. 2). The
costs of outdoor relief can be cut easily enough. "The great principle of out-of-doors
relief," Mr. Bumble explains, "is, to give the paupers exactly what they don't want;
and then they get tired of coming" (ch. 23). Money can be saved, too, by wherever
possible transferring paupers to another parish, a task devolving on Bumble when he
accompanies two dying paupers to London: "we find it would come two pounds
cheaper to move 'em than to bury 'em" (ch. 17).

The treatment of the Poor Law in *Oliver Twist* was not a root-and-branch attack on
a new piece of legislation. It reflected, rather, an instinctive Dickensian response to
the inhumanity that can all too easily infect those, like Bumble, invested with authority, and to the narrowness of thinking of those who devise and make policy. Dickens
aligned himself with those who were the victims of these policies, and the thinking
that went with them, whether a child like Oliver or an old man like Nandy in *Little
Dorrit*. Nandy was a "poor little reedy piping old gentleman, like a worn-out bird;
who had been in what he called the music-binding business, and met with great
misfortunes, and who had seldom been able to make his way, or to see it or to pay
it, or to do anything at all with it but find it no thoroughfare." He is "shut up . . . in
a grove of two score and nineteen more old men, every one of whom smells of all the
others." The lack of sympathy for him is expressed through Fanny, Little Dorrit's
sister, who, meeting Little Dorrit accompanying Nandy on his way to meet her father,

is outraged that she should be "'coming along the open streets, in the broad light of day, with a Pauper!' (firing off the last word as if it were a ball from an air-gun)". A pauper was anyone in receipt of poor relief. To the Fannys of the world that signaled a total lack of respectability and self-esteem. Little Dorrit, by contrast, "very gently" asks "Does it disgrace anybody . . . to take care of this poor old man?" (*Little Dorrit* bk. 1, ch. 31).

At much the same time, in 1856, Dickens wrote an impassioned account for *Household Words* of a scene outside Whitechapel workhouse. On a wet, dark, November night, he came across "five bundles of rags," women who had been refused access to the casual ward because it was full. He gave a shilling to each of them, and in his reflections summed up his attitude to Utilitarianism and political economy:

> I know that the unreasonable disciples of a reasonable school, demented disciples who push arithmetic and political economy beyond all bounds of sense (not to speak of such a weakness as humanity), and hold them to be all-sufficient for every case, can easily prove that such things ought to be, and that no man has any business to mind them. Without disparaging those indispensable sciences in their sanity, I utterly renounce and abominate them in their insanity; and I address people with a respect for the spirit of the New Testament, who do mind such things, and who think them infamous in our streets. (*Journalism* 3: 351)

It was easy enough to attack the inhumanity of the Poor Law, less so to propose any alternative to it. Dickens did support one reform, the equalization of the poor rates, though it was not to be achieved until 1894, long after his death. The issue was brought home to him in 1860 when a police court magistrate criticized the state of affairs in Wapping workhouse for female paupers. Dickens went to see for himself. He found the building in desperate need of upgrading, but the care at least adequate, the matron efficient. But he could not doubt that these wards should not exist: "no person of common decency and humanity can see them and doubt it." The problem for Wapping was that it was a poor parish, with many paupers. It was unfair, Dickens and others argued, that Wapping's inhabitants should have to pay much higher rates than the richer parishes to the west of London: equalization of the rates was the answer (*Journalism* 3: 41–51).

The political economists, rigorous with regard to the economy itself, acknowledged that in the social sphere there were some necessary exceptions to their general rule that the state should avoid interference in individuals' enterprise in money-making activities. One of those exceptions was the use of child labor. The state had always maintained legal oversight of children who were apprenticed out by their parishes. This became a larger and more politicized issue when urban parishes began to supply cotton manufacturers in remote, water-powered mills with pauper apprentices – often by the cartload. A law to regulate this had been passed in 1802, ten years before Dickens's birth, and further laws reached the statute book subsequently when pauper apprentices began to be replaced by what was called "free labor" in cotton mills. This essentially meant a contract between employer and parent. The political economists recognized that a child needed protection in this kind of labor market, and in 1833 the first effective act to restrict child labor was passed.

Dickens visited Lancashire factories in 1838. What he saw "disgusted and astonished me beyond all measure. I mean to strike the heaviest blow in my power for these unfortunate creatures" (*Letters* 1: 483–4). Curiously, this never really happened, even in *Hard Times*. In the early 1840s, the work of children underground in mines and in trades and manufactures began to be highlighted. Dickens was appalled by what he read (*Letters* 3: 459–61). He was due to write on the topic for the *Edinburgh Review*, but failed to produce copy. He did, however, support Ashley's efforts to prohibit child and female labor in mines. He wrote an impassioned letter to the *Morning Chronicle* (October 20, 1842), attacking the House of Lords for the amendments he feared they were about to make to the bill. As was often the case, while unremitting in his criticism of the Lords, he sought some middle ground:

> In these times, when so wide a gulf has opened between the rich and the poor, which, instead of narrowing, as all good men would have it, grows broader daily; it is most important that all ranks and degrees of people should understand whose hands are stretched out to separate these two great divisions of society each of whom, for its strength and happiness, and the future existence of this country, as a great and powerful nation, is dependent on the other. (*Letters* 3: 278–85; *Journalism* 2: 44–51)

Dickens also, in the mid-1850s, published a number of articles in *Household Words* on industrial accidents, blaming mill-owners and magistrates who lent over backwards to understand their situation.

Dickens was certainly alive to the issues posed by child labor in the new work situation of the industrial revolution, but it is striking that none of his child heroes or victims was directly involved in such work. He landed his "Sledge hammer" blow on behalf of poor children at work in *A Christmas Carol*. Two children, Ignorance and Want, symbolize Christmas Present (*Letters* 3: 461). Both pose dangers, but Ignorance more than Want. Dickens seems to have been more concerned about the lack of education for children than about the work that they had to do. He returned again and again to the dangers of ignorance. In "A December Vision" in 1850:

> I saw a Minister of State, sitting in his Closet; and round about him, rising from the country which he governed, up to the Eternal Heavens, was a low dull howl of Ignorance. It was a wild, inexplicable mutter, confused, but full of threatening, and it made all hearers' hearts to quake within them. But, few heard. In the single city [London] where this Minister of State was seated, I saw Thirty Thousand children, hunted, flogged, imprisoned, but not taught . . . (*Journalism* 2: 307)

The government, in the person of the Minister of State, should have been providing the schooling.

In the early nineteenth century there were voices questioning whether it was desirable to offer any kind of schooling to the mass of the working class: their lot was to work, and education would only make them restless. By the time Dickens had come through his own varied experience of schooling, the consensus was that every child should have some kind of schooling. In 1833, the Factory Act insisted on some schooling for child workers, and in the same year the government gave a small grant in support of schooling. The questions, then, when Dickens was a young adult, were not whether there should be schooling, but how much, of what kind, and who should supply it.

The future of schooling for the working classes in the 1830s and 1840s seemed to lie with two organizations that were the recipients of the government's grants: the National Society for Promoting the Education of the Poor in the Principles of the Church of England, and the nonconformist British and Foreign Schools Society. Besides the schools that they ran, there was a wide range of privately supported schools, some of them dame schools like the one Dickens himself had attended. The issues that confronted all those concerned about schooling in England in Dickens's adulthood fundamentally centered on these two forms of provision and possible alternatives to them. The first of these, and the one that absorbed most attention and energy, was the religious issue. Should taxpayers' money be used to support schools that were so closely tied to particular denominations? Or more precisely, since the National Society had many more schools than the British and Foreign Schools Society, should taxpayers disproportionately support the established Church of England to which many nonconformists were bitterly opposed? Any schemes for state funding invariably ran into trouble because of this sectarian issue. Dickens's attitude was a plague on both your houses. Schooling should be Christian but undenominational.

The second issue centered on the content of the school syllabus and the tone of the school. The private schools flourished because they gave parents some control over times of attendance, modes of punishment, and syllabus. They offered training in skills such as reading and writing. The schools run by the two societies with government support had wider ambitions: they wanted schools to provide training in behavior and in cast of mind. Because they received government grants, these schools were subject to government inspection, providing some control over quality. Key voices in the educational world increasingly wanted to see this kind of school superseding the private schools.

Dickens was not directly involved with this issue, nor with the national bodies that in the 1860s were campaigning for state-supported schooling for all children. The Education Act of 1870, passed in the year of his death, made provision for the establishment of school boards in areas where so-called voluntary schools (i.e. denominational schools) were unable to offer enough school places. Dickens would probably have offered some support for such a solution, but his preference, and he was not alone in this, would have been to start from scratch, freed from the incubus of denominational rivalry from the past. On the general issue of state intervention in education, he offered nothing beyond a reiteration that the state had a responsibility to make provision.

Dickens's contribution to the education debates was not really at all on the role of the state: it was on the way in which the ethos of a school and the quality of teaching could make or mar a child. We are confronted with innumerable educational establishments, many of them ghastly, some of them good, that leave us in no doubt about the kinds of schooling he liked and disliked. The bad teachers range from the brutal, like Wackford Squeers, to those, like Mr. M'Choakumchild, who concentrate on the inculcation of facts (and political economy). M'Choakumchild was a product of the new system of training teachers associated with Dickens's former ally, James Kay-Shuttleworth. Bright children at elementary schools became pupil-teachers, and then went to training college. M'Choakumchild had been "lately turned out at the same time, in the same factory, on the same principles, like so many pianoforte legs" as 140 other schoolmasters. His subjects had included "orthography, etymology, syntax, and prosody." "If he had only learnt a little less, how infinitely better he might have taught much more!" (*Hard Times* bk. 1, ch. 2). But M'Choakumchild is a relatively harmless figure compared to Bradley Headstone, the "highly certificated stipendiary schoolmaster" in *Our Mutual Friend* whose personal failings, his short temper, his selfishness, his conceit, are seen to stem from his rise to apparent respectability through the pupil-teacher system. If the pupil-teachers were the advance guard of mass popular education, Dickens seemed peculiarly disenchanted with them.

Dickens saw education as a vital ingredient in the fight against crime. The Ragged Schools seemed to offer some hope and received much support from Dickens from 1843 onward. The schools as Dickens encountered them were the work of the London City Mission. They were set up, as he explained in a letter to the *Daily News* in 1846, to provide rudimentary instruction to "the most miserable and neglected outcasts in London . . . to commence their recognition as immortal human creatures, before the Gaol Chaplain becomes their only schoolmaster" (quoted in *Oxford Dickens* 84–5). Dickens pleaded, unsuccessfully, for government funding for the schools. Visiting a dormitory attached to a Ragged School in 1852, he wrote:

> I do not hesitate to say — why should I, for I know it to be true! — that an annual sum of money, contemptible in amount as compared with any charges upon any list, freely granted in behalf of these Schools, and shackled with no preposterous Red Tape conditions, would relieve the prisons, diminish county rates, clear loads of shame and guilt out of our streets, recruit the army and navy, waft to new countries, Fleets full of useful labor, for which their inhabitants would be thankful and beholden to us. (*Journalism* 3: 57)

It was not to happen.

Increasingly, Dickens came to think that reform should be concentrated on something even more fundamental than education, the housing and sanitation of the poor. Strong in the sanitary cause since the 1830s, Dickens told the Metropolitan Sanitary

Association in 1851 that his experience since then "has strengthened me in the conviction that Searching Sanitary Reform must precede all other social remedies, and that even Education and Religion can do nothing where they are most needed, until the way is paved for their ministrations by Cleanliness and Decency" (*Speeches* 129). Dickens's active engagement in the campaign for what in this period came to be called "public health" owed something to family connections: his brother-in-law, Henry Austin, a civil engineer, was one of the founders of the Health of Towns Association, and, for example, sent him a report on intramural burials and the health hazards they posed, causing Dickens to dream of "put[r]efaction generally" (*Letters* 6: 47). Dickens also had close ties with another ardent sanitary reformer, Thomas Southwood Smith. But the constant descriptions of insanitary environments, from *Sketches by Boz* onward, perhaps most famously in the account of Jacob's Island in *Oliver Twist*, suggest that Dickens himself had always been alert to the issue. "In all my writings," he wrote in a Preface to *Martin Chuzzlewit* in 1849, "I hope I have taken every possible opportunity of showing the want of sanitary improvements in the neglected dwellings of the poor" (*Speeches* 104).

What prompted a renewed level of engagement with the issue in mid-century were two factors: first, cholera, which had struck Britain in 1832 and returned in 1848; although its exact cause was not at this time known, it was widely thought to be linked to a bad environment. And, secondly, the politics of public health. Edwin Chadwick, in nearly all respects at one with Dickens on this issue, had in 1842 produced a celebrated report on public health, but political action was slow to follow. Eventually, in 1848 a Board of Health was set up with powers to act where mortality rates were especially high. But London was omitted from its scope. Dickens was determined to do all he could to push London toward sanitary reform, cholera making action all the more necessary.

In January 1849, cholera claimed the lives of 150 pauper children at an institution in Tooting run by Bartholomew Drouet. Drouet had ignored the precautionary measures recommended by the Board of Health, and then rejected advice to remove uninfected children. Dickens was outraged and fired off four highly critical articles (*Journalism* 3, especially "The Paradise at Tooting," 147–56). He met head on the arguments of those who opposed reform on the grounds that it involved centralization, or doing away with the powers of local vestries. "Centralization," said Dickens, was "a combination of active business habits, sound medical knowledge, and a zealous sympathy with the sufferings of the people" (*Speeches* 130). Mr. Podsnap in *Our Mutual Friend*, saying "Centralization. No. Never with my consent. Not English" (bk. 1, ch. 11) was not the voice of Dickens.

Dickens returned to the public health issue many times in *Household Words* and *All the Year Round*, arguing in 1854 that the middle and working classes should unite to insist that central government discharge its "first obligation" which was to secure "to the people Homes, instead of polluted dens." "A Board of Health," he went on, "can do much, but not near enough. Funds are wanted, and great powers are wanted; powers to over-ride little interests for the general good; powers to coerce the ignorant, obstinate, and slothful, and to punish all who, by any infraction of necessary laws, imperil the public health" (*Journalism* 3: 228). This was powerfully put. Dickens, who, as we shall see, had many reservations about the powers of government, on this issue was forthright: funds should be provided and government should have the powers to do what was necessary.

Dickens's views about government and politicians were formed when he was a parliamentary reporter on the *Morning Chronicle* in the early 1830s. What he saw there – self-importance, long speeches and little action, maneuvering for power – remained with him for the rest of his life. He was instinctively on the side of the reformers and against the Tories or Conservatives, but, in truth, came to have little time for either. In 1869, he summarized his political creed: "My faith in the people governing is, on the whole, infinitesimal; my faith in The People governed, is, on the whole, illimitable" (*Speeches* 407). Dickens focused much of his anger on the unelected House of Lords. Discussing the Mines and Collieries Bill of 1842, he wrote that:

> All measures which have for their object the improvement of the popular condition, or the elevation of the popular character, are very troublesome children to their fathers in the House of Lords. They cost a world of trouble in the bringing up; and are, for the most part, strangled by the Herods of the Peerage, in their cradles. (*Journalism* 2: 47)

Dickens correctly discerned that aristocratic control of government remained a dominant feature despite reform acts. Changes of government did not amount to much. In *Bleak House*, Lord Boodle tells Sir Leicester Dedlock that "supposing the present government to be overthrown, the limited choice of the Crown, in the formation of a new ministry, would lie between Lord Coodle and Sir Thomas Doodle, supposing it to be impossible for the Duke of Foodle to act with Goodle" (*Bleak House* ch. 12). In short, it did not really matter who was in power.

This was largely the case because changes of government did nothing to change the machinery of government, or what was coming to be called the civil service. *Little Dorrit*, written in the 1850s, is set in a period 30 years earlier, before the First Reform Act, and at a time when the machinery of government was still being cleaned up. The Circumlocution Office, "the most important Department under Government," was controlled by the Tite Barnacle branch of the Barnacle family, and was devoted to the art of not doing things. Things had changed by the early 1850s, but not that much. In 1853, in their famous *Report on the Organization of the Civil Service*, Sir Stafford Northcote and Sir Charles Trevelyan described how "Those whose abilities do not warrant an expectation that they will succeed in the open professions . . . and those whom indolence of temperament or physical infirmity unfit for active exertions, are placed in the Civil Service, where they may obtain an honourable livelihood with no labour and little risk" (Briggs 1955: 85). They recommended opening up entry to the civil service to competitive examination, but it was slow to take effect (Hoppen 1998: 110–12). A report such as this fed into Dickens's lifelong hatred of "red tape," and his concern about it reached fever pitch because of the conduct of government during the Crimean War (see chapter 15).

In 1854, the British and French, in a rare alliance, went to war with Russia. Some control over the declining Ottoman empire was crucial to the maintenance of British routes to India, the jewel in the crown of empire. Dickens, in tune with the weight of public opinion, was a firm supporter of the war and full of "burning desires to cut the Emperor of Russia's throat" (*Letters* 7: 454). But he also, like many others, came to think that the efforts of Britain's valiant soldiers were being seriously hampered by the incompetence and bumbling of the senior command and the inefficiency of the support services. In the winter of 1854–5, far more soldiers died from sickness than were killed by Russian arms. Dickens was both angry and alarmed. In April 1855, he wrote to his friend A. H. Layard that he found smoldering discontent "extremely like the general mind of France before the breaking out of the first Revolution" in 1789 (*Letters* 7: 587).

Between April and August 1855, Dickens attacked government incompetence in *Household Words*. Dickens only rarely joined reform organizations, so it is a sign of how exercised he was about what was happening – or not happening – that he should join the Administrative Reform Association. On June 27, he addressed a meeting of the Association, declaring it to be "the first political meeting I have ever attended." Again, he expressed his fear of revolution, new "discord piled on the heaving basis of ignorance, poverty and crime, which is always below us," and called for "the awakening of the people, the outspeaking of the people, the uniting of the people in all patriotism and loyalty to effect a great peaceful constitutional change in the administration of their own affairs." He had, he said, "the smallest amount of faith in the House of Commons at present existing" where "personal altercations . . . are always of immeasurably greater interest . . . than the health, the taxation, the education, of a whole people." And he gave pointed expression to what was a commonplace of the day among reformers:

> The great, broad, true case that our public progress is far behind our private progress, and that we are not more remarkable for our private wisdom and success in matters of business than we are for our public folly and failure, I take to be as clearly established as the existence of the sun, moon, and stars. (*Speeches* 200–6)

A month after this, Dickens began writing *Little Dorrit*. It included a chapter "Containing the Whole Science of Government," and the attack on the Circumlocution Office. But this turned out to be the legacy of his feverish anxiety about reform in the first half of 1855, rather than a means of maintaining and furthering the struggle. The Administrative Reform Association withered away, the moment of danger and of the possibility of reform faded, and with it Dickens's public profile on reform. The first half of the 1850s was his moment in the public eye, the time when he was prominent both in sanitation reform and in the Administrative Reform Association.

Dickens shared with many radicals in Britain a deep suspicion of the state and of office-holders. Look at the state, many said, and ask what it does: it gets Britain engaged in numerous wars, it subjects people to the indignities of the Poor Law, it taxes knowledge, it, until 1846, gives a privileged financial position to aristocratic farmers, and so on. And who makes up the state? Aristocrats and their hangers-on. In the 1830s and 1840s, a new kind of state official loomed large, personified by Edwin Chadwick, ruthlessly efficient and myopically logical. Symbolically, Chadwick, Britain's "Prussian Minister" as he was called, was hounded from office by people who were no more enamored of this kind of state than they were of the bumbling inefficiency and nepotism of the old. If you took this critical attitude to the state, you were left with a problem: industrializing and urbanizing Britain faced problems of government that no one could deny. The statistics of mortality and ill health, so laboriously collected by the agents of the state, indicated the scale of the problem. What should be done?

Philanthropy was one answer, and Dickens engaged fully in it. No one in Dickens's lifetime could imagine the development of a welfare state that would give people rights to support and help, without loss of civil status. Philanthropy was the accepted alternative, and Dickens was unstinting in his involvement in a range of philanthropic projects. They had in common an ambition to offer relief to people in need and to spare them from the taint of pauperization. Urania Cottage, the home for homeless women that he set up and ran with Angela Burdett-Coutts, was his most sustained and time-consuming work of philanthropy, keeping him occupied for a full decade. This was preventive work, aiming to keep women out of prison or the workhouse, and assisting their emigration to Australia. He supported many other causes; for example, the Hospital for Sick Children at Great Ormond Street. Opened in 1852, it struggled in its early years, receiving a boost from Dickens's appeal on its behalf in 1858, "in the sacred names of Pity and Compassion" (*Speeches* 246–53). Dickens also gave much attention to trying to get housing schemes for the working classes off the ground.

But Dickens could also be fiercely critical of the spirit and practice of much philanthropy. He had no time for such as Mrs. Pardiggle in *Bleak House* who thought that "the only one infallible course was her course of pouncing upon the poor, and applying benevolence to them like a strait-waistcoat" (ch. 30). There had to be a better way of doing things than rival philanthropists peddling their different wares. Dickens found it in the many public institutions for the care of the sick and poor in Boston, and held them up as an ideal against what he found in Britain.

In our own country, where it has not, until within these later days, been a very popular fashion with governments to display any extraordinary regard for the great mass of the people or to recognise their existence as improvable creatures, private charities, unexampled in the history of the earth, have arisen, to do an incalculable amount of good among the destitute and afflicted. But the government of the country, having neither act nor part in them, is not in the receipt of any portion of the gratitude they inspire; and, offering very little shelter or relief beyond that which is to be found in the workhouse and the jail, has come, not unnaturally, to be looked upon by the poor rather as a stern master, quick to correct and punish, than a kind protector, merciful and vigilant in their hour of need. (*American Notes* ch. 3)

Here Dickens sets out his ideal of the relationship between government and people. It sat uneasily with his analysis of Britain. We may summarize the ingredients of this as follows: a fear that "the heaving basis of ignorance, poverty and crime" might ignite with some random element to produce a French-type revolution; an acceptance of capitalism, together with a belief that "capital and labour are not opposed, but are mutually dependent and mutually supporting" (*Speeches* 153); an acknowledgment that a consequence of capitalism was that, as he put it in 1850, "great contrasts of rank, great contrasts of wealth, and great contrasts of comfort must, as every man of sense was aware exist among all civilized communities" (*Speeches* 106); a wish wherever possible to bridge these contrasts by human contact between rich and poor, employer and employee; a realization that some human beings needed care in an institution, and a concern to make such institutions as humane and decent as possible, preferably, as in Boston, as public rather than private facilities; a belief that government must take leadership and responsibility in the delivery of some public services, especially sanitation and education.

As to forms of government, he was ambivalent and uncertain. Democratic by principle, he was much less happy with it in practice. Occasionally, he had a good word for a political leader. He enjoyed the friendship of Lord John Russell, a key figure in the reform debates of 1831–2, and later prime minister. He came to admire Sir Robert Peel, who, although a Tory, seemed to govern in the 1840s in the interests of the country as a whole, not least through the repeal of the Corn Laws in 1846. But he never lost his impatience with the red tape of government, nor with the talking shop that was parliament. Against them, and in opposition to political economy, he posed humanity, decency, and a frequent appeal to the values of the New Testament.

REFERENCES AND FURTHER READING

Briggs, Asa (1955). *Victorian People*. Harmondsworth: Penguin.

Collins, Philip (1962). *Dickens and Crime*. London: Macmillan.

— (1963). *Dickens and Education*. London: Macmillan.

Cunningham, Hugh (2001). *The Challenge of Democracy: Britain 1832–1918*. Harlow: Longman.

Goodlad, Lauren M. E. (2003). *Victorian Literature and the Victorian State: Character and Government in a Liberal Society*. Baltimore, MD: Johns Hopkins University Press.

Hoppen, K. Theodore (1998). *The Mid-Victorian Generation 1846–1886*. Oxford: Oxford University Press.

Magnet, Myron (2004). *Dickens and the Social Order*. Wilmington, DE: ISI Books.

Paroissien, David (2004). Ideology, pedagogy, and demonology: the case against industrialized education in Dickens's fiction. *Dickens Studies Annual*, 34, 259–82.

Pope, Norris (1978). *Dickens and Charity*. London: Macmillan.

Schlicke, Paul (1975). Bumble and the Poor Law satire of *Oliver Twist*. *The Dickensian*, 71, 149–56.

11

Dickens's Evolution as a Journalist

John M. L. Drew

In November 1836, Dickens resigned as a reporter for the *Morning Chronicle*. By doing so, he explained, he was "quitting a most arduous and thankless profession, as other prospects" dawned upon him (*Letters* 1: 197). On one hand, we might read this decision as Dickens's growing sense that his future as a writer lay in fiction rather than in journalism. With *Sketches by Boz*, first series, behind him and *The Pickwick Papers* well under way, he had reason to feel confident of his development as a novelist. At the same time, we need to recognize the move for what it was: the exchange of one kind of specialized stress for another. While giving up parliamentary reporting for the editorship of *Bentley's Miscellany*, a new monthly magazine, he would remain intimately bound with journalism and periodical publications for the rest of his life. It was therefore no mere rhetorical flourish over 30 years later when he described to a packed audience of American journalists his "grateful remembrance of a calling that was once my own" and of his "loyal sympathy towards a brotherhood which, in the spirit, I have never quitted" (*Speeches* 379).

At the point where fiction and journalism intersect it should be stressed that no definitive break between the two exists. Neither in the spirit nor in the flesh did Dickens ever quit the profession of journalism. The contours of his career and the characteristic poise of his writing may be said, indeed, to derive from a grounding in the graphic technique and the timely, topical dimension of periodical writing, against which the priorities of the imaginative artist continually pull and stretch. For this reason, his career as a working journalist needs to be carefully mapped and its evolutionary nature emphasized. Like that of the professional author, the social status of the journalist was a volatile property during the four decades of Dickens's writing life, never entirely free from Grub Street associations and class prejudice. However, in standing firm by his assertion of the "dignity of literature," Dickens helped lift the writer's profession to increased upward mobility throughout this period (*Letters* 5: ix; Chittick 1988: 154–6). Three main, overlapping phases can be distinguished in his own rise from obscurity to press celebrity, in which he functions as a newspaper reporter and sketch-writer, then as a reviewer and commentator, and finally as an editor, essayist, and, eventually, magazine proprietor.

Newspaper Reporter and Sketch-writer, 1831–1836

Dickens's introduction to the craft of reporting came early in life. At 16, and shortly before leaving employment as a lawyer's clerk in the firm of Ellis and Blackmore in 1829, he acquired a copy of Thomas Gurney's popular shorthand treatise, *Brachygraphy* (1750). Mastery of its contents, combined with an introduction to the trade Dickens had acquired previously with the *British Press* between March 1825 and October 1826, provided his passport to parliamentary reporting. Samuel Carter Hall, a reporter on this London morning paper, recalled how now and then "there came to the office a smart, intelligent, active lad, who brought what was then called . . . 'penny-a-line stuff'; that is to say, notices of accidents, fires, police reports, such as escaped the more regular reporters, for which a penny a printed line was paid" (Hall 1883: 1. 111). This was the young Dickens, aged 13 or 14, newly entered as a pupil at Wellington House Academy and released from Warren's Blacking warehouse. Although none of his submissions can be identified with certainty, the following little notice from the paper is a likely candidate: "Yesterday, a gentleman of the name of Gilham, resident near Brentwood, was thrown from his horse and killed on the spot, not far from his residence. We are sorry to hear he has left a widow and a very numerous family" (October 18, 1826, 3c).

Until the advent first of Taylor's and then of Pitman's less cumbrous methods of stenography in the late 1830s, Gurney's *Brachygraphy* was still the approach most commonly used by parliamentary reporters, at a time when the speed and accuracy of their transcripts of debates could make or break a newspaper, and when public attention was transfixed by political rhetoric and its media representation during the long build-up to the Parliamentary Reform Act of 1832. Under the eye of his maternal uncle, the lawyer-turned-journalist John Henry Barrow, Dickens learned and practiced the complex combinations of points, circles, lines, and curves that make up the code. Although his abilities (particularly in writing out in longhand from his own notes) remained imperfect, he found paid work as a freelance shorthand writer at Doctors' Commons, a series of London law courts dealing in naval and ecclesiastical affairs.

But having fully tamed "the savage stenographic mystery," as he described the ordeal in *David Copperfield* (ch. 38) by early 1831, Dickens joined the permanent staff of his uncle's new venture, the *Mirror of Parliament*, a voluminous periodical dedicated to publishing unofficial transcripts of the debates in both Houses of Parliament. While the writers working on T. C. Hansard's better-known but also unofficial *Parliamentary Debates* worked outside the House at second-hand, collating various newspaper accounts of speeches into definitive copy, Barrow's men were actually sent into the Gallery, alongside the newspaper reporters. Engaged under this superior arrangement, they were able to produce verbatim reports of more or less everything. During the passage of the Reform Act itself, between March and August 1832, Dickens was also on the reporting staff of the *True Sun*, a radical evening paper, though the exact scope of his work for it is uncertain.

For at least four sessions (1831–4), Dickens worked to transcribe the lengthy and often scarcely audible speeches from the cramped public galleries of the old House of Commons (St. Stephen's Chapel) and the old House of Lords (Westminster Hall). It was exhausting and high-pressure work, at which he came to excel. According to fellow-reporter and friend Thomas Beard, Dickens's command of Gurney's system was by now nothing short of "perfect"; "there never *was* such a reporter," Beard noted. The journalist Charles Mackay, sub-editor of the *Morning Chronicle* during Dickens's later employment there, came to the same conclusion. His young colleague, Mackay observed, was "universally considered the rapidest and most accurate shorthand reporter in the gallery" (Kent 1881: 363, 371).

While Dickens was making what he called his "great splash in the gallery" (Forster bk. 1, ch. 4), the most eminent and grandiloquent politicians of the day were debating parliamentary reform, Catholic emancipation, the abolition of slave labor in the colonies, the future of the East India Company, amendments to England's Poor Law, reductions in the taxes on newspapers, Sunday observance, and dozens of other legislative proposals destined to alter British society at the start of the Victorian era. In the process of transcribing such debates, first in shorthand, and then in longhand for the compositors, Dickens absorbed a great deal of information, forming opinions about politicians and the parliamentary process that were to stay with him for life. He was paid an average of 15 guineas a week for the privilege, but only when parliament was in session (in 1833, a mere 142 days), which helps explain why he developed a sideline in more imaginative freelance work. This included writing "puff" (advertising) verses in praise of Warren's Blacking for the newspapers (Drew 2005: viii–x), and contributing short stories on comic suburban themes to the *Monthly Magazine*. In the autumn of 1834, he accepted a post as a staff reporter on the *Morning Chronicle* for the smaller, but regular, salary of 5 guineas a week.

For the next two and a half years, Dickens was a hardworking servant of the paper, fully identified with its fortunes. Looking back on his commitment, he later described how on "many occasions at a sacrifice of health, rest, and personal comfort, I have again and again, on important expresses in my zeal for the interests of the paper, done what was always before considered impossible, and what in all probability will never be accomplished again" (*Letters* 1: 196).

The *Chronicle*'s veteran editor, John Black, seems to have known how to exploit Dickens's talents. Besides covering public events throughout England, he was given two other assignments. In October 1834, he started to supply theatrical reviews. At the same time, he also contributed five "Street Sketches" to the *Chronicle*, a sequence that led to a second series, "Sketches of London Life," in the paper's new tri-weekly offshoot, the *Evening Chronicle*. These 20 sketches were all reprinted in the main paper before the year's end. In recognition of this extra work and its popularity with readers, 2 guineas a week were added to Dickens's salary.

In all that has been identified of Dickens's early work for these papers, a new journalistic voice emerges: rhetorically gymnastic, genial in tone, precise in its recording of detail and dialogue, but merciless in its ridicule of sham and imposture. Dickens's brief as a reporter and sketch-writer did not usually require him to produce detailed analyses of public affairs, and when permitted to trespass onto political topics, in such papers as "The Story without a Beginning" (December 18, 1834), he always did so in a humorous and satirical vein (*Journalism* 2: 10–13). Nevertheless, when subsequently invited by John Macrone to collect in a single volume the sketches, papers, and tales previously published under the pseudonym of "Boz," Dickens sought recognition as a master of pathos and powerful sentiment. The sketches specially written for *Sketches by Boz* (first series, February 1836), such as "A Visit to Newgate," "The Black Veil," and "The Drunkard's Daughter," are somber pieces. Heavy in melodrama, violence, and sorrow, they anticipate the tales of Edgar Allen Poe or the historical romances of Harrison Ainsworth, except for the social conscience also manifest in the writing.[1]

As a literary figure then, the Dickens of 1836 was still unavoidably somebody "connected with the newspapers" (*Letters* 4: 460). The name was, above all, a journalistic by-line; and it was the name "Boz" that Richard Bentley sought to acquire when he appointed Dickens as the editor of his new monthly *Miscellany* in November 1836, prompting the latter's resignation from the staff of the *Chronicle*. It is customary to say that Dickens's experiences as a parliamentary reporter inspired him with a contempt for parliament and party politics that lasted the rest of his life, but his position in the Gallery had gifted him two invaluable things: a vantage point from which to overview, with literal superiority, the conduct of public affairs, and a style (if not a wardrobe of styles) for his representation in politicized prose of London's "Every-Day Life, and Every-Day People" (the subtitle of *Sketches by Boz*).

Reviewer and Commentator, 1837–1849

Due to the nature of Bentley's venture and his controlling temperament, Dickens's opportunities for shaping and directing the *Miscellany* as its editor were, in fact, far more limited than he expected. In his farewell "Familiar Epistle" to readers on resigning from the post after only two years at the helm, Dickens lamented in February 1839 that it had "always been literally 'Bentley's' Miscellany and never mine" (*Journalism* 1: 554). Bentley had promised the public a comic feast, and a "neutral page" free from party political wrangling. The 26 monthly numbers edited by "Boz" certainly contained plenty of uncontroversial matter: travel narratives from around the world; biographical sketches; papers on actors, acting, and the theater; lyric poetry; short stories and serial fiction. Sales were high, earning Dickens a bonus for exceeding 6,000 copies on several occasions, and topping 7,500 midway through his editorship (*Letters* 1: 402n.; Patten 1977: 77).

Yet, from the outset, the idea of neutral fun was one that Dickens provocatively failed to embody in his own contributions to the *Miscellany*, which included installments of a satirical new serial, entitled "Oliver Twist; or, The Parish Boy's Progress." The role that he had established for "Boz" as the chronicler of everyday people, whose lives were approached ironically through the languages of public reporting, led him straight back into a kind of sketch-writing, which, as it comically invoked parliamentary proceedings, topics of current national debate, and newspaper journalese, was hardly apolitical. Most notable were its attacks on aspects of the government's Poor Law Amendment Act of 1834 and the worst features of the old regime (Schlicke 1975). Friends complained to Bentley of a "Radicalish tone" about *Oliver Twist*, and the same could be said of such skits as "The Public Life of Mr. Tulrumble," "The Pantomime of Life," and the two "Mudfog Association" reports (disparaging satires on the proceedings of the British Association for the Advancement of Science). Gradually, however, as Kathryn Chittick observes, Bentley's ambition to push "commodities, not opinions," of which serial fiction was the most profitable, "elbowed out the traditional notion of a monthly periodical as a flexible commentator on contemporary affairs" (1990: 113). Dickens, too, felt elbowed out by the interference of the man he nicknamed "the Burlington Street Brigand" (*Letters* 1: 619).

Thereafter, Dickens proceeded, on the one hand, to enhance, as he saw it, the literary value of his serial fiction by imitating in *Master Humphrey's Clock* the machinery and sentimental mannerisms of the well-known eighteenth-century periodical essayists, and, on the other, to progress to a more serious kind of journalistic work, through his connection with the *Examiner* newspaper. This fivepenny Sunday weekly, which Leigh Hunt had founded and edited until 1821, still occupied a distinguished niche in the London press of the 1840s. With John Forster as sub-editor from 1836 and then editor from 1847 to 1855, Dickens was invited to commentate on or review a wide range of topics and publications. But with a Liberal government in office, led by Lord John Russell (one of the few ministers Dickens admired), he steered clear of the most obviously political issues of the day. On Europe in turmoil, Irish insurrection, the success of the "Ten Hours" movement to restrict factory shifts, and the failure of Chartism, Dickens was silent. Instead, he focused on matters such as legal and sanitary reform and trimmed his naturally exuberant and facetious style to the *Examiner*'s requirements.

The result was a total of over 40 articles. Many of these are lengthy and display a serious commitment to social reform, in line with the established ethos of the paper. Others reveal perhaps surprising areas of interest and expertise on the part of the author. In a series of three carefully researched articles, Dickens analyses Sir Walter Scott's relationship with his publishers, and presents a strong case for the dignity of literature (*Journalism* 2: 32–9; Matz 1914: 75–89). Opinions on art and drama are discussed within a clear aesthetic and ethical framework, when Dickens reviews the virtues of Macready's acting, the engravings of George Cruikshank in aid of the Temperance movement, or the dainty caricatures of John Leech (*Journalism* 2: 55, 102, and 142ff.). The existence of ghosts and the status of ghost stories are considered in a skeptical review of Catherine Crowe's *The Night Side of Nature*. The folly of foreign philanthropy and colonial intervention in Africa at the expense of social legislation at home are questioned in a provocative review of a firsthand account of the disastrous Niger Expedition of 1841 (2: 108ff.).

Opinions on recent discoveries in the fields of biology, geology, astronomy, and chemistry are delivered in a review of a recent scientific publication that suggests that "Dickens appears to have been a God-fearing evolutionist" almost "a dozen years before *The Origin of Species*" (*Journalism* 2: 129ff.; Fielding and Lai 1977: 10). The notorious case of one Monsieur Drouet, accused of criminally neglecting the children living in his "Infant Pauper Asylum," is investigated and followed through the courts in a series of four cogently argued articles (*Journalism* 2: 149–56; Matz 1914: 146–51). Numerous reports, based as much on factual material (government statistics, commissioner's reports, and recent court cases) as on fanciful personal observation, deal with the spirit and application of the law, crime, punishment, and the influence of education and environment on all three. In researching and writing these accomplished papers, scholars conclude, Dickens "learned to be a journalist rather than a reporter" (Brice and Fielding 1981: 1).

Newspaper and Magazine Editor and Owner, 1846, 1850–70

Dickens was never more than a freelance contributor to the *Examiner*, but throughout the 1840s he aspired to a greater role in the presentation of social issues and their mediation between the public and government leaders. *American Notes* (1842), for example, shows a remarkable seriousness of purpose and a strict, journalistic preoccupation with attempting to capture *all* impressions of a scene, whether flattering to his hosts or no. Shortly after his return from the United States in June 1842, he expressed an interest in reviving the recently defunct *Courier* newspaper, telling Lady Holland that the "notion of this newspaper was bred in me by my old training – I was as well acquainted with the management of one, some years ago, as an Engineer is, with the Steam engine." Dickens also believed that the subjects most newspaper editors ignored were "exactly the questions which interest the people, and concern their business and bosoms most" (*Letters* 3: 265–6). Other letters of this period show him seriously considering the prospect of becoming a police magistrate, or applying for "some Commissionership, or Inspectorship," in order to turn his "social knowledge to practical account" (*Letters* 4: 566–7).

It is in this context of frustrated philanthropy searching for a practical outlet that his decision to accept the editorship of the *Daily News* in 1846 should be viewed. Although he later described his resolve as a "brief mistake" ("The Reader's Passport," *Pictures from Italy*), Dickens wholeheartedly entered the project, filled with the desire to found a new nationwide morning paper in the Liberal interest. His role, as the subsequently discovered Deed of Co-partnership indicates, was that of "*first* Editor of the said paper" (emphasis added). In other words, Dickens wanted to get the paper launched, a task that he certainly accomplished even though he remained as editor for a mere 19 days (Tillotson 1982). As the paper's sales and fortunes fluctuated through its first few weeks of life, recriminations and accusations of incompetence abounded, some of which appear to gainsay Dickens's presumption of familiarity with newspaper management. "[N]obody could be a worse editor than Dickens" declared Forster (Forster bk. 5, ch. 1), voicing an opinion shared by others. According to W. J. Fox, the paper's leader writer, Dickens ultimately "broke down in the mechanical business" of the paper, while J. T. Danson, the financial journalist, faulted him for his ignorance of political economy (Garnet 1910: 282; Macready 1912: 2. 231; Fielding 1972). Having the reputation as the best reporter in London was one thing; possessing the management and business skills capable of running a daily newspaper was another matter.[2]

These negative views overlook two considerations. The first concerns the more personal aspects of Dickens's performance. Energetic and characteristically "hands-on" in approach, he directed affairs with theatrical panache, and was never afraid of practical work. The Saturday before the launch (January 17, 1846), he supervised the composition and printing of an entire dummy issue of the new paper, printed with the brand new fonts specially cast for the *Daily News* by Thorowgood and Besley. Ever master of the personal touch, he also composed at least one spoof article especially for the dummy number, as well as a version for family and friends of the first of eight installments of his Italian travel narrative, later completed as *Pictures from Italy* (Drew 2003: 78). After the appearance of mistakes in the first real edition of the paper, including in the City data, Dickens himself "sat at the Stone" (the slab on which pages of type were imposed) and made up the second issue "with my own hands" (*Letters* 4: 479).

The second matter relates to the burden on the editor exerted by a daily newspaper. If the relentless pressure on Dickens exposed his lack of administrative experience, the more relaxed pace of weekly editorial duties proved one he could master. Within less than five years of revealing himself at the *Daily News*, according to William Howard Russell as "not a good Editor" (Atkins 1911), he had founded two weekly magazines, which he was to edit and "Conduct" for the remainder of his life. Appearing first as *Household Words* (1850–9) and then as *All the Year Round* (1859–70), these two journals show Dickens as an inspired editor, one who, in the words of Lord Northcliffe, stands out as "the greatest magazine editor either of his own, or any other age" (quoted in Maurice 1909: 111). The history of these two successful and durable examples of popular journalism should be read as the natural development of Dickens's early training as a reporter and sketcher of metropolitan life, and his later experience as a reviewer and commentator.

Dickens's "Preliminary Word" in the first issue of *Household Words* strikes the keynote of his career as a crusading journalist. "We aspire," he writes, in language that fuses personal allegory with metaphors drawn from fairytales and adventures:

> to live in the Household affections, and to be numbered among the Household thoughts, of our readers . . . No mere utilitarian spirit, no iron bending of the mind to grim realities, will give a harsh tone to our Household Words . . . To show to all, that in all

familiar things, even in those which are repellent on the surface, there is Romance enough, if we will find it out . . . is one main object of our Household Words . . . [T]o wering chimneys . . . spirting out fire and smoke upon the prospect . . . have their thousand and one tales, no less than the genii of the East, and these, in all their wild, grotesque, and fanciful aspects, we design to tell . . . Thus, we begin our career! The adventurer in the old fairy story, climbing towards the summit of a steep eminence on which the object of his search was stationed, was surrounded by a roar of voices, crying to him, from the stones in the way, to turn back. All the voices *we* hear, cry Go on! With a fresh heart, a light step, and a hopeful courage, we begin the journey. (March 30, 1850)

The resemblance of this manifesto – as much an outline of an aesthetic as a rallying cry – to the better-known "romantic side of familiar things" statement in the Preface to *Bleak House* has been frequently noted. But two further points need stressing. First, that the policy Dickens announces in the magazine offers a much fuller and richer articulation of his aims than the single sentence about literary objectives in the 1853 Preface to *Bleak House*. Secondly, that the convergence of views expressed in both documents is as eloquent of the journalistic subtext of Dickens's fiction as it is of the pioneering and imaginative approach to narrative method encouraged in his journals (see *Letters* 6: 790–1).

The first number was indicative of the range and quality of writing that was to characterize *Household Words* for the next nine years and raise it above the so-called "Saturday trash" purveyed in cheaper magazines (cited in Kellett 1934: 2. 66). After the "Preliminary Word" by Dickens, came the first episode of "Lizzie Leigh," Mrs. Gaskell's three-part Manchester tale of a fallen woman and her family; then a well-researched and imaginatively presented article about mail-sorting technology by Wills and Dickens ("Valentine's Day at the Post-Office"); a dramatic blank verse "parable" on religious presumption by Leigh Hunt ("Abraham and the Fire-Worshipper"); and a translation by George Hogarth of a supernatural "Incident in the Life of Mademoiselle Clairon." These were followed by a poetic apostrophe to "The Wayside Well" by the young Irish poet William Allingham, an article compiled by Dickens and Caroline Chisholm encouraging working-class emigration to Australia through the provision of no-interest loans ("A Bundle of Emigrants' Letters"), and, finally, a pair of makeweight items reprinted from other sources (the only occasion *Household Words* made use of "selected" material). It was not so much the variety of offerings to a mass readership that characterized *Household Words* as the polish with which non-fictional pieces combined field research with imaginative coloring. These characteristics are particularly striking in the many composite articles co-authored by Dickens and his core staff (W. H. Wills, Henry Morley, R. H. Horne, and others), which often take as their subject some arcane industrial or administrative process, and explain in magical and mythological terms how it achieves its beneficial results. "Discovery of a Treasure near Cheapside," about a visit to Brown and Wingrove's Smelting Works, is typical of this innovative subgenre of investigative journalism (Stone 1968: 2. 443–54).

From the outset, the magazine was a runaway success. Sales of the first number exceeded 100,000 before the weekly circulation settled down to an estimated average of 38,000. This figure in turn was augmented by sales of monthly parts at 11d and sales of bound six-monthly volumes at 5s 6d. Further gains resulted from the publication of the monthly *Household Words Narrative* and, once a year, the hugely popular *Extra Christmas Numbers* (1850–8), which brought sales to over 80,000. Although these figures fell below those of popular penny weeklies (compare *The Family Herald*, which, according to one estimate, sold 300,000 copies per week), *Household Words* was aimed at a more discerning and affluent class of reader, and capitalized to return a healthy profit at these circulation levels.

Today, the magazine's format and general appearance seem unremarkable, even pedestrian. Sold at 2d, the weekly issue was printed in two columns from a single large sheet of cheap paper ("quad crown duodecimo") folded to make a 24-page booklet, whose contents offered readers six to ten items of new material: articles, poems, short stories, and the occasional serialized novel, a total of about 22,000 words. However, as Lorna Huett has shown, *Household Words* was "an oddity" in the mid-century magazine market: the result of some "daring and noteworthy" decisions on Dickens's part that combined "publishing practices from both ends of the marketplace" (Huett 2005: 68, 76). On the one hand, the magazine's Spartan appearance, paper quality, and size aligned it with the mass-circulation "penny bloods" and morally instructive penny journals like *Chambers's Journal* and *The Family Herald*, allowing it to encroach successfully upon the upper-end of this huge working-class market. On the other, its higher price, availability as a monthly reissue and in a handsome bi-annual volume, its lack of advertisements and illustrations, and the combined originality and quality of its contents – all published under the header "Conducted by Charles Dickens" – meant that *Household Words* also "outwardly resembled the highbrow reviews" and was "welcomed into the drawing rooms of the middle classes, and into the reading rooms of . . . reputable institutions" (Huett 2005: 79, 70).

After 15 issues, Dickens was reporting that, although an expensive venture, *Household Words* was taking "a great and steady stand" and "no doubt already yield[ing] a good round profit" (*Letters* 6: 131). In addition to the editor's salary, after one year of operating he received a personal profit-share of over £850 pounds, which rose to a high of more than £1,100 in the third year. For the remainder of Dickens's life, profits from *Household Words* and then *All the Year Round* augmented the income he derived from the serialization and republication of his novels in various editions. In this way, he realized a long-held ambition to supplement his earnings from fiction with a steady salary from journalism. But Dickens identified himself rather too closely with his designated role of "Conductor" of *Household Words* when he felt that the magazine's publishers, Bradbury and Evans, had failed to take his side in the aftermath of his acrimonious separation from Catherine Dickens. In 1858, he moved swiftly to dissolve the partnership agreement between himself and the publishers, close down the journal, and found another – of which he would be the controlling proprietor and publisher.

Although identical to its predecessor in appearance, *All the Year Round* was, in fact, rather different – most notably in the much greater emphasis placed on fiction. Pride of place in each number went to the current installment of a long-running serial, while shorter-run serials and short stories appeared additionally in most numbers. Dickens drew the line, however, at running more than two serials simultaneously. The public, he explained to Sheridan Le Fanu, "have a natural tendency, having more than two serial stories to bear in mind at once, to jumble them all together, and do justice to none of them" (*Letters* 12: 443). He himself inaugurated the sequence of long serials with *A Tale of Two Cities* (April–November 1859), and later successfully countered falling sales by serializing *Great Expectations* (December 1860–August 1861).

In terms of simple journalistic output, Dickens contributed far fewer articles to *All the Year Round* than he had to *Household Words*. But despite the imbalance – 51 papers in the later journal as opposed to 168 in its predecessor, including collaborations – consensus prevails, in the words of Grahame Smith, that *All the Year Round* represents "the summit of [Dickens's] journalistic career" and "the climax" of his work as a periodical essayist (Smith 1995: 80, 82). This is mainly on account of the papers collected under the title *The Uncommercial Traveller* (1861; first complete edition, 1898) which, as well as testifying, in design, research, and execution to Dickens's consummate skill as a journalist, contain some of his finest writing, in any genre. Readers anticipating the polysyllabic facetiousness and rhetorical spin typical of much Dickensian satire will encounter instead a chastened and self-ironic narrator not dissimilar to the Pip of *Great Expectations*. "I travel for the great house of Human Interest Brothers," the Uncommercial Traveller explains on introducing himself to readers, "and have rather a large connexion in the fancy goods way." A thoughtful man of "no-business," marginalized and sidelined by the railroad of Victorian progress, the narrator wanders here and there, "now about the City streets: now about the country bye-roads." Constantly on the move, he sees "many little things, and some great things, which, because they interest me, I think may interest others" (*Journalism* 4: 43).

Looking over the achievement of Dickens's journals, and his own contributions to them, one is struck both by their astonishing stylistic versatility (anticipating modernism in their use of the free indirect and stream-of-consciousness techniques) and by their continued commitment to understanding the political not as a set of theoretical abstractions or the result of historical minutiae, but in terms of how communities of people caught up in a dilemma actually behave (Stone 1959; Childers 2006). Innovative forms of reporting often work to reduce emphasis on the subjective, controlling self and invite middle-class readers to adopt otherwise alien perspectives – as in the paradigmatic "On Strike" (*Journalism* 4: 196–210) – but when Dickens encounters hollowness and hypocrisy rather than solidarity, as he does in the antics of the various coalition governments of the 1850s, he gleefully fulfils his promise to give familiar things an "Arabian Nights" makeover. A trio of papers beginning with "The Thousand and One Humbugs" and followed by "The Story of Scarli Tapa and the Forty Thieves" and "The Story of the Talkative Barber" lets loose Dickens's satirical genius on a series of national institutions, absurdly dressed up as "Howsa Kummauns,"

"Mistaspeeka," "Scarli Tapa," the lovely "Reefawm," and the manipulative "Talkative Barber" (Prime Minister Palmerston). As principal storyteller, Dickens replaces Scheherezade with "Hansardadade," perhaps a reference to his own beginnings as a parliamentary reporter (Matz 1914: 516–36).

In these, as in the other articles that he commissioned, sub-edited, and discussed with the journals' several hundred contributors, Dickens was aiming, as David Pascoe observes, "for nothing less than an absolute engagement with the processes of the world around him: the way it was run, its goings-on, its falling into decay and final ends" (Pasco 1997: xvi). As an editor, at times ruthless with submissions written in slack prose, Dickens worked tirelessly to get the best out of his contributors. If his journals display at times some disappointingly paternalistic, patriarchal, and overly patriotic assumptions – as in their handling of colonial topics, the "Woman Question," or aspects of Roman Catholic worship – they show as often a curiosity, open-mindedness, and democratic commitment eloquent of the best of Victorian liberalism (Schor 1992: pt. 2; Drew 2003: 125–28).

While readers of Dickens's fiction might find it hard to overturn G. M. Young's verdict that in "all Dickens's work" he seems "equally ready to denounce on the grounds of humanity all who left things alone, and on the grounds of liberty all who tried to make them better," close readers of Dickens's non-fiction are likely to agree with Humphry House that Young's criticism "is hardly true at all of the occasional journalism" (House 1942: 201n.). Whether he is anatomizing the London streets as "Boz," or strolling forth in his "Uncommercial Traveller" guise, Dickens's self-elected appointment as "people's witness" demanded, as a matter of honor, a balance and restraint that is often lacking in his storytelling narrators. Nevertheless, few will fail to discover in much of Dickens's periodical and newspaper journalism the same capacity to move readers to anger, to laughter, or to sorrow, or the same linguistic artistry that characterizes his novels. "There has never been a greater novelist than Dickens," stated one newspaper columnist in the year 2000, confirming a status quo reached earlier in the century, before enviously advancing the new critical orthodoxy for the twenty-first century: "it seems entirely unfair that he should so unarguably, so effortlessly, have acquired the mantle of the greatest journalist along the way" (Hensher 2000: 41).

Notes

1 In 1850, Dickens sought to distance himself from the "imperfections" of *Sketches by Boz* through extensive cuts, rewriting, and changes in substance and style. Paul Schlicke's forthcoming Clarendon edition restores this former dimension, a task made easier, Schlicke notes, on account of the congruence between Dickens's reporting "and his imaginative writing –

the foundation in fact, the sharpness of observation, the raciness of style – which is fundamental to the kind of writer which Dickens was."

2 The five public letters arguing against capital punishment and his paper on crime and education show Dickens's aptitude as a journalist, which is where his real strength lay.

REFERENCES AND FURTHER READING

Atkins, John B. (1911). *Life of Sir William Howard Russell*. London: John Murray.

Brice, A. W. and Fielding, K. J. (1981). A new article by Dickens: "Demoralisation and Total Abstinence." *Dickens Studies Annual*, 9, 1–19.

Childers, Joseph W. (2006). Politicized Dickens: the journalism of the 1850s. In John Bowen and Robert L. Patten (Eds.), *Palgrave Advances in Charles Dickens Studies* (pp. 198–215). Basingstoke: Palgrave.

Chittick, Kathryn (1988). Dickens and parliamentary reporting in the 1830s. *Victorian Periodicals Review*, 21, 151–60.

— (1990). *Dickens and the 1830s*. Cambridge: Cambridge University Press.

Drew, John M. L. (2003). *Dickens the Journalist*. Basingstoke: Palgrave.

— (2005). *"The Pride of Mankind": Puff Verses for Warren's Blacking with Contributions Attributed to Charles Dickens*. Oswestry: Hedge Sparrow Press.

Fielding, K. J. (1972). Dickens as J. T. Danson knew him. *The Dickensian*, 68, 151–61.

— and Shu-Fang Lai (1997). Dickens, science, and *The Poetry of Science. The Dickensian*, 93, 5–10.

Garnett, R. (1910). *The Life of W. J. Fox*. London: John Lane.

Hall, Samuel Carter (1883). *Retrospect of a Long Life, from 1815 to 1883*, 2 vols. London: Richard Bentley and Son.

Hensher, Philip (2000). A genius at his best and worst: review of *The Uncommercial Traveller and Other Papers, 1859–70*, vol. 4: *Journalism. The Spectator*, December 9, 40–1.

House, Humphry (1942). *The Dickens World*. London: Oxford University Press.

Huett, Lorna (2005). Among the unknown public: *Household Words, All the Year Round* and the mass-market weekly periodical in the mid-nineteenth century. *Victorian Periodicals Review*, 38, 61–82.

Kellett, E. E. (1934). The press. In G. M. Young (Ed.), *Early Victorian England, 1830–1865*, vol. 2 (pp. 1–97). Oxford: Oxford University Press.

Kent, Charles (1881). Charles Dickens as a journalist. *Time*, 361–74.

Macready, W. C. (1912). *The Diaries of William Charles Macready, 1833–1851*, 2 vols. New York: G. P. Putnam.

Matz. B. W. (1914). *Miscellaneous Papers*. London: Chapman and Hall.

Maurice, Arthur Bartlett (1909). Dickens as an editor. *Bookman*, 30, 111–14.

Pascoe, David (1997). *Charles Dickens: Selected Journalism*. Harmondsworth: Penguin.

Patten, Robert L. (1977). *Charles Dickens and his Publishers*. Oxford: Clarendon Press.

Schlicke, Paul (1975). Bumble and the Poor Law satire of *Oliver Twist. The Dickensian*, 71, 149–56.

— (forthcoming). *Sketches by Boz*. Oxford: Clarendon Press.

Schor, Hilary (1992). *Scheherezade in the Marketplace: Elizabeth Gaskell and the Victorian Novel*. New York: Oxford University Press.

Smith, Grahame (1995). *Charles Dickens: A Literary Life*. Basingstoke: Macmillan.

Stone, Harry (1959). Dickens and interior monologue. *Philological Quarterly*, 38, 52–65.

— (1968). *Charles Dickens' Uncollected Writings from Household Words, 1850–59*, 2 vols. Bloomington, IN: Indiana University Press.

Tillotson, Kathleen (1982). New light on Dickens and *The Daily News. The Dickensian*, 78, 89–92.

12
Dickens and Gender

Natalie McKnight

Critical Context

Dickens has suffered a good deal of negative press about his stereotypical portrayals of angelic young women – such as Kate Nickleby, Rose Maylie, Ruth Pinch, Florence Dombey, Agnes Wickfield, Esther Summerson, and Amy Dorrit – and earnest young gentlemen – such as Nicholas Nickleby, Martin Chuzzlewit, David Copperfield, and Pip. Edgar Johnson in *Charles Dickens: His Tragedy and Triumph* discusses how critics have thought of Dickens's characters as "mere caricatures," with E. M. Forster pronouncing them "flat" (Johnson 1952: 2. 1138). Michael Slater in *Dickens and Women* (1983) notes the same tendency and offers a compelling defense of Dickens's women (1983: 244–76). John C. Ward summarized the negative criticism of Dickens's female figures when he wrote: "it is commonplace to observe that Dickens's view of women is sentimental, sexist, patriarchal and derogatory" (1983: 37). But Dickens criticism over the past 25 years has increasingly emphasized ways in which Dickens was far more prone to bend and blend stereotypical gender roles than many had previously thought. I use the term "gender" here to refer to the differentiated behavioral characteristics expected of males and females, the "representation of biological sexuality . . . sexual difference, and . . . sexual relations" that is "social, not natural" (Poovey 1988: 2). Even Dickens's most stereotypically angelic women offer far more complex explorations of gender than might be supposed at first glance.

Slater's *Dickens and Women* presents one of the earliest and most comprehensive defenses of Dickens's characterization of women. He explores Dickens's relation to his mother and his sister as crucial influences on his treatment of female characters, and he suggests a three-part development in these portrayals: an early stage during which Dickens drew on the sentimentalized woman common in popular literature, the theater, and conduct books; a second stage in mid-career, characterized by more psychologically realistic women, who emerged in response to Dickens's resolve to improve his art; and the third and final stage of the last four novels, in which Dickens shifts "away from women themselves and on to men as lovers of women, especially as lovers of women they cannot have" (Slater 1983: 297).

Diane Sadoff in *Monsters of Affection: Dickens, Eliot and Brontë* (1992) uses Freud's theory of "primal fantasies" (a child witnessing parental sex, a child's seduction by a father, and/or a child fearing castration by a father) to analyze the psychological complexities of Dickens's gender portrayals. Sadoff further explores the pattern of identifying with the father – and resisting identification with the father – as part of the protagonist's search for his or her own identity (1992: 11–17). In Sadoff's hands, traditional gender roles yield highly complex, ambiguous family dynamics. Patricia Ingham, in *Dickens, Women and Language* (1992), presents a different defense of Dickens's characterizations of women, demonstrating how they present a "subversion of the gender roles that underpin familial identities" (1992: 126). Ingham examines the relationship between Florence Dombey and her father in *Dombey and Son*, and between Esther and Jarndyce and Esther and Ada in *Bleak House*, as particularly disturbing portrayals of the interference between gender norms and familial roles (1992: 126). Ingham notes Dickens's tendency to remove biological mothers from the narratives or to portray them as "monsters of selfishness," partly because of his animosity toward his own mother, which will be discussed further below; nurturing females tend not to be biological mothers in Dickens's fiction (1992: 119; see also McKnight 1997: 37–56).

In *Charles Dickens and the Image of Woman* (1993), David Holbrook relies on psychoanalytic mothering theory to trace patterns in Dickens's relations to women and their effect on his characterizations. Holbrook argues that Dickens's frustrations with his mother for wanting to send him back to the blacking factory when he was a child probably disturbed him as deeply as it did because it emphasized "earlier weaknesses in the relationship" (1993: 28–9). Like Diane Sadoff, Holbrook attributes Dickens's hostilities toward women in his fiction to Freudian "primal fantasies," and he argues that Dickens acted out this fantasy in his dramatic readings of the murder of Nancy from *Oliver Twist*, performances that many critics have suggested hastened his death (Holbrook 1993: 166).

In the past 20 years, critics examining Dickens's attitudes toward gender have increasingly emphasized new historical approaches, which means that they use Victorian periodicals, conduct books, parliamentary papers and investigations, census information, and other historical materials to reconstruct the context that influenced and was influenced by fictional portrayals. In *Dickens and the Politics of Family* (1997), Catherine Waters explores how "the worship of the family" in Victorian culture emphasized the separation of the spheres of men's and women's worlds: men belonged to the world of work, women to the domestic world, and the home was to be a haven for men from the heartless realities of work. But Dickens blurs the boundaries between work and family by shaping the Victorian domestic ideal through his professional life, his writings. The blurred boundary between the two spheres led to many ironies for Dickens: Waters particularly examines the irony of Dickens being a Dean of Domesticity when his own home life fell into such public disarray with the separation from his wife Catherine and the rumors of his affairs with his sister-in-law Georgina and the young actress Ellen Ternan (see chapter 1).

Waters points out that Dickens's fictional treatments of domesticity and gender roles are seldom straightforward, and therefore perhaps not as at odds with his own domestic troubles as one might initially think. For instance, in *Great Expectations*, Joe and Mrs. Joe embody inversions of the usual domestic roles, with Joe being the kind, nurturing one and Mrs. Joe the stern inflictor of discipline and corporal punishment. Waters notes a similar gender inversion in Mr. and Mrs. Wilfer in *Our Mutual Friend*, and a subversion of the usual ideals of femininity and domesticity in "the deadly knitting of the patriotic women" in *A Tale of Two Cities* (Waters 1997: 35, 128, 178). Fagin in *Oliver Twist* complicates gender roles by displaying both paternal and maternal traits.

In *Nobody's Angels: Middle-class Women and Domestic Ideology in Victorian Culture* (1995), Elizabeth Langland similarly complicates the idea of the strict separation of men's and women's spheres, and argues that "a Victorian wife, the presiding hearth angel of Victorian social myth, actually performed a more significant and extensive economic and political function than is usually perceived" since she managed the money earned by the husband while advancing the couple's social status (1995: 8). Langland questions prevailing notions of the passive, subservient Victorian woman, and argues that the dissonance between the female gender norms and the actual realities of middle-class Victorian women influenced the growing women's movement of the second half of the century.

Lyn Pykett in *Charles Dickens* (2002) offers a fine survey of recent criticism on Dickens and gender, and notes that in Dickens's novels gender expectations are always tied to class. David Copperfield's concept of masculinity or Pip's in *Great Expectations* reflects the expectations of the class they aspire to. Pykett, like Waters, emphasizes the effect of the separation of men's and women's spheres on Dickens's depictions of gender and sees this separation as the basic structural principle of *Dombey and Son*, which she argues is "organized around a series of gendered polarities . . . [such as] private/public; domestic/commercial; nature/culture; organic/mechanical." Dickens drives home these polarities to underscore "the faultlines of mid-Victorian constructions of gender, and particularly of the 'separate spheres' ideology" (Pykett 2002: 104). In another recent new historical analysis, *Gender and Madness in the Novels of Charles Dickens* (2004), Marianne Camus argues that Dickens's fascination with mad characters allowed him to bend gender expectations without overtly challenging Victorian gender norms. Dickens's mad women seem more fully human, for instance, than his sane female figures (2004: 2).

The increased appreciation of Dickens's complex gender portrayals parallels an increase in socio-historical studies of nineteenth-century gender norms within and beyond the literary tradition. Several studies have contributed to the understanding of Dickens's gender portrayals in different ways. Gilbert and Gubar's *The Madwoman in the Attic* (1984) situates key Victorian novels by women within a patriarchal literary and social context, while Elaine Showalter traces the interconnections between limiting gender expectations for women and the high rate of women institutionalized for insanity (1985: 52–5). *Desire and Domestic Fiction* by Nancy Armstrong (1987) explores the role of the domestic novel as a disciplinary mechanism in shaping gender norms. Mary Poovey's *Uneven Developments* (1988) demonstrates how "the oppositional, gendered organization of social relations at mid-century" critically shaped all aspects of Victorian culture, including its economic and legal structures and its imperial mission (1988: 199, 2). *Rewriting the Victorians: Theory, History, and the Politics of Gender*, edited by Linda M. Shires (1992), presents a range of articles examining the social construction of gender roles in Victorian texts from conduct books through medical treatises and semi-fictional memoirs to novels. And works such as *Family Fortunes: Men and Women of the English Middle Class, 1780–1850*, edited by Leonore Davidoff and Catherine Hall (1987), and Elizabeth Langland's *Nobody's Angels*, discussed above, examine the intersection of expectations of gender and family roles.

While gender studies in the 1970s and 1980s concentrated primarily on the social construction of female gender norms, works in the past 15 years have been focusing increasingly on masculinity. These studies have revealed that Victorian men suffered from limiting gender norms in many cases as much as women, and that the construction of gender expectations for men served the needs of an industrial, capitalist society as much as did gender norms for females. The competitive and increasingly fast-paced nature of the industrial economy required men to suppress their emotions and render themselves almost as machine-like as the mechanisms of industry around them. Only in the safety of the home could the man become fully human again, so the separation between home and work underscored a separation between heart and head as well as female and male. Wemmick in *Great Expectations* offers a perfect example of the rigid separation of these dichotomies, acting like an automaton at work, with his mouth compressed into the shape of a postbox slot, but at home behaving in the most affectionate, domestic, and imaginative way as he takes care of his aged father in the mock-gothic castle he has built.

Eve Kosofsky Sedgwick's *Between Men* (1985) is often cited as a pivotal literary study of masculinity. Sedgwick suggests that Dickens in *Our Mutual Friend* replaces homosexual patterns (implied in the relation between Eugene Wrayburn and Mortimer Lightwood) with more socially acceptable heterosexual and homophobic behaviors, such as those in Eugene's and Bradley Headstone's relationships with Lizzie Hexam (Sedgwick 1985: 177). More recent studies have emphasized men's domestic roles and the ways in which gender expectations for males changed after mid-century. For instance, the collection of essays that comprise *Manful Assertions: Masculinities in Britain since* 1800 explores the "divergent, often competing and above all *changing* forms" of masculinity in the nineteenth century (Roper and Tosh 1991: 1). In particular, the editors stress the triumph of the "Imperial Man" as the ideal of masculinity with "the emphasis on face-to-face authority [and] the celebration of the will," character traits that would help to fuel the imperialist project (1991: 17).

John Tosh in *A Man's Place: Masculinity and the Middle-class Home in Victorian England* (1998) traces changes in expectations of fathers in Victorian England, noting that, in the eighteenth century, advice books for parents had been written primarily for men, but by the mid-nineteenth century they were written primarily for women. He goes on to say that the affectionate father of the early Victorian period gave way to the more distant father of the mid and late Victorian periods, possibly due to pressures caused by the growing divide between work and home. Herbert Sussman in *Victorian Masculinities: Manhood and Masculine Poetics in Early Victorian Literature and Art* (1995) asserts that middle-class Victorians defined masculinity as "success within the male sphere, the new arena of commerce and technology in which sexual energy is transmuted into constructive labor" (1995: 4). These studies, and others, reveal that while the gender expectations of women and men were sharply divided throughout the nineteenth century, they were also changing under the pressures of economic, technological, and social developments. Dickens captured the divisions between male and female constructions of gender, as well as the continuing changes in both those constructions.

Social/Historical Context

While the survey above demonstrates that critics have come to appreciate the richness of Dickens's portrayals of gender, along with the complex web of social influences affecting Victorian attitudes toward gender in general, the out-dated criticism of Dickens's stereotypical young women and young men had *some* basis in fact. One cannot ignore, in particular, the preponderance of young and angelic female figures I listed at the beginning. Moreover, their presence in his fiction is hardly surprising given prevailing models of womanly behavior as they appeared in conduct books and other forms of popular reading. Works such as Sarah Lewis's *Woman's Mission* (1840) and Sarah Ellis's *Women of England* (1843), *Wives of England* (1843), and *Mothers of England* (1844) stipulated that women should always be self-sacrificing, subservient, dutiful, meek – in short, angelic. Lewis, in fact, refers to women as the "guardian angels of man's infancy" who have a "mission" which is "the implanting of that heavenly germ to which God must indeed give the increase, but for the early culture of which they are answerable" (1840: 30). This role falls to women because men are too consumed with the world of work. Lewis regrets that fathers cannot play a more vital role in childrearing, but she does not seem to feel that much can be done about the situation. The spheres of men and women had become more distinct by the early Victorian period than they had been previously, and to women had fallen the role of keeper of the flame of heart, hearth, and spirituality. Sarah Ellis concurs with Lewis's assessment of a woman's role. The woman must be the one to "cultivate the mind – the immortal nature of her child" (1844: 15). Isabella Beeton, in her famous and often-reprinted book *Mrs. Beeton's Household Management* (1859–60), strays from her emphasis on the quotidian details of housekeeping to assert that the moral training of youth is a solemn duty of mothers, a duty that no one else can accomplish more successfully (Beeton 1949: 1621, 1624).

Conduct books for women required angelic behavior from women in general, not just mothers. As Sarah Ellis asserts in her comments about the social duties of women and their domestic habits, a good woman must:

> lay aside all her natural caprice, her love of self-indulgence, her vanity, her indolence – in short, her very *self* – and assuming a new nature, which nothing less than watchfulness and prayer can enable her constantly to maintain, to spend her mental and moral capabilities in devising means for promoting the happiness of others, while her own derives a remote and secondary existence from theirs. (1843b: 15)

Basically, a woman should not have a "self" apart from her role as servant to others. Yet Ellis also warns that women should not be drudges, nor should they sacrifice more than they are willing to give cheerfully. This advice does not really undercut her overarching emphasis on self-abnegation; instead, it adds to her message the increased burden of being a drudge without appearing to be one, and forcing oneself to be cheerful about sacrifices that might very well inspire resentment.

Coventry Patmore's *The Angel in the House* has often been cited as a literary crystallization of Victorian expectations of women. In the second section, "The Wife's Tragedy," Patmore summarizes the sadly divergent roles of men and women:

> Man must be pleased; but him to please
> Is woman's pleasure; down the gulf
> Of his condoled necessities
> She casts her best, she flings herself:
> How often flings for naught! And yokes
> Her heart to an icicle or whim,
> Whose each impatient word provokes
> Another, not from her, but him;
> While she, too gentle even to force
> His penitence by kind replies,
> Waits by, expecting his remorse,
> With pardon in her pitying eyes.
> And if he at last, by shame oppress'd,
> A comfortable word confers,
> She leans and weeps against his breast,
> And seems to think the sin was hers.
> (sect. 2, ll. 1–16)

The woman's role, Patmore makes clear, is to be ever-patient, ever-meek, ever-loving; men, however, have little expected of them in terms of human relations, it would seem, except to work, return home after work, be an emotional icicle, and throw out a kind word now and then. Patmore does not suggest that the husband in the above scene is loving but incapable of showing it – he simply does not love, as the following lines indicate: "And if, ah woe, she loves alone, / Through passionate duty love flames higher, / As grass grows taller round a stone" (sect. 2, ll. 22–4). An icicle and a stone

– these are the images Patmore uses for the man, while the woman must not only be fully, feelingly human, she must be more than human – an angel.

Victorian laws would have made female meekness and resignation a necessity. Married women had no rights to their own property: anything they owned became the sole property of their husbands once they were married; this law remained in effect throughout Dickens's life and was only changed between 1870 and 1882 through several acts of parliament. Women had few legal rights even to their own children: before 1839 women who were separated from their husbands were typically not granted custody of their children; in 1839, they were given the right to care for children under seven. It took 34 more years before women were permitted to raise children of 16 and under (Altick 1973: 58). Divorce was close to impossible during much of this period, except by an act of parliament, which would only be available to those with means to pursue it. In 1857, the Matrimonial Causes Act relaxed divorce regulations, allowing divorce to be handled in law courts instead of parliament, but still divorce was prohibitively expensive and the rules favored men; for instance, a woman's adultery was considered sufficient grounds for divorce but a man's was not.

It is hardly surprising that the extreme expectations of Victorian women might lead to reactionary characterizations in literature. Gilbert and Gubar in *The Madwoman in the Attic* discuss the connection in literature between angels and monsters (1984: 28). Assertive women are often portrayed as monsters in Victorian fiction precisely because assertiveness is a male trait and therefore seems unnatural when adopted by a female who is supposed to be angelic. An exception would be a woman's assertiveness in response to threats to her chastity, such as Kate Nickleby's firmness in dealing with the lecherous Sir Mulberry Hawk in *Nicholas Nickleby* (ch. 27). At other times, Kate embodies the passive, selfless traits of the Angel in the House, while the assertive Mrs. Squeers plays the monster (and the garrulous Mrs. Nickleby a comic monster).

The gender expectations for women thus far described related primarily to middle- and upper-class women who had the luxury of not working. Lower-class women who had to make their own livings or supplement the family income would fall outside the realm of these norms since the norms evolved in part from the separation of men's and women's spheres of influence. With men relegated to the world of work, and women more removed from it than they had been for the previous two centuries, women could place greater emphasis on the importance of the domestic front, and in fact needed to do so to affirm a sense of identity. As Richard Altick points out in *Victorian People and Ideas* (1973), women had not traditionally been so separated from work; they took active roles in family businesses in the seventeenth and eighteenth centuries. But when work was removed from the home during the industrial revolution and rendered increasingly complicated and competitive, women were no longer seen as fit for such activities. Lower-class women, however, had no choice. Households could not dispense with their wages and so women remained part of the workforce.

Elsewhere, the subservient behavior of women predominated, ironically reinforced by the powerful sovereign of a great empire. As a devoted wife, mother of nine children, and traditionalist concerning women's roles, Queen Victoria elevated the Angel in the House to the Angel in the Country (Langland 1995). Sarah Ellis refers to Victoria as an ideal for all English women (1843b: 20), and dedicated *The Wives of England* to "Her Majesty the Queen, In whose exalted station the social virtues of domestic life present the brightest example to her countrywomen, and the surest presage of her empire's glory." Yet this "ideal" woman often failed to meet in her personal life the norms established by Ellis and others. The queen hated pregnancy, loathed young babies, and seemed barely to tolerate the sex act – and far from keeping such sentiments to herself, voiced her complaints bluntly to her daughters. She told her daughter Vicky in a letter dated March 9, 1859 that it was "dreadful what we have to go through and men ought to have an adoration for one, and indeed to do everything to make up, for what after all they alone are the cause of! I must say it is a bad arrangement" (Fulford 1964: 165). In a particularly un-angelic mode, Victoria wrote: "I hated the thought of having children and have no adoration for very little babies" (Fulford 1964: 167). Pregnancy had ruined her first years of marriage, she felt, so later when her daughters and granddaughters would tell her of their pregnancies, she referred to the information as "horrid news" (quoted in St. Aubyn 1992: 161).

Private sentiments like these point to other ways in which the queen's behavior contradicted the image of the Angel in the House, revealing hitherto unexpected openings for change in women's gender expectations. Committed to her domestic role as wife and mother, she nevertheless presided over the most influential nation in the world at the time. As Langland observes, the queen helped create "a new feminine ideal that endorsed active public management behind a façade of private retirement" (1995: 63). Certainly, her success helped fuel women's rights movements that emerged in the second half of the century, even though she had no patience for them and referred to them as a "mad wicked folly" (quoted in Altick 1973: 58). Women's rights advocates had been growing in numbers throughout the century, influenced by Mary Wollstonecraft's *A Vindication of the Rights of Woman* (1792, reissued 1840) and John Stuart Mills's *The Subjection of Women* (1869). As interest increased during the following decades, the movement eventually gave rise to the "new woman" of the 1880s and 1890s, a gender image that replaced the passive Angel in the House with an active, independent, sports-playing, bicycle-riding female who sought legal and civic equality. Since Dickens died in 1870, he only witnessed the beginnings of these major changes, yet they still affected his final female protagonists, with the willful Bella Wilfer and the "female waterman, turned factory girl" Lizzie Hexam in *Our Mutual Friend*, and the independent-minded Rosa Bud in *The Mystery of Edwin Drood*.

Gender Trends in Dickens's Life and Work

Dickens's relationships with women in his own life constitute another source contributing to their portrayal in his fiction. Naturally, his mother had the deepest and most pervasive effect on his female characters, influencing both his depictions of monstrous mothers as well as angels. Psychoanalysts would argue that the angel/monster dichotomy seen not only in Victorian literature but also in folklore and fairytales evolves from children's inability to deal with their anger toward their mothers and the darker aspects of their mothers' behaviors, so they repress the negative feelings which then take shape in images of witches or demons. The preponderance of docile, sweet young girls and destructive, dangerous older women in Dickens's work reflects both the limiting gender expectations for women described above and some very unsettled feelings about his own mother.

Dickens certainly had reason to be angry with Elizabeth Dickens. As he wrote in his abandoned autobiography, it was his mother who wanted him to continue working at Warren's Blacking warehouse when he was 12, even after his father had been released from the Marshalsea debtors' prison and his financial circumstances had improved with a legacy and retirement pension from the Admiralty. "I never afterwards forgot, I never shall forget, I never can forget, that my mother was warm for my being sent back" (Forster bk. 1, ch. 2). As Michael Slater has argued, Elizabeth Dickens's indifference to her son's misery in his demeaning job would have been particularly painful to the young boy as she had been the first one to stir his intellectual curiosity and rouse in him a sense of his own potential (Slater 1983: 10). Finding his prospects for a better life buried at such a young age, while his sister Fanny was allowed to pursue her studies at the Royal Academy of Music, Dickens suffered terribly.

Dickens's frustrations with his mother continued into adulthood. She embarrassed him with her requests for money and her tendency to dress inappropriately. He wrote to his former girlfriend Maria Beadnell Winter that his mother, 65 at the time, "has a strong objection to being considered in the least old, and usually appears here on Christmas Day in a juvenile cap which takes an immense time in the putting on" (*Letters* 7: 534). Five years later, he reported to another correspondent that she took to dressing "in sables like a female Hamlet" which gave her appearance "a ghastly absurdity" (*Letters* 9: 287). Even at the end of her life, when she was deteriorating mentally and physically, Elizabeth Dickens would rally herself to borrow money from him: "the instant she saw me," Dickens recounted to Georgina Hogarth, "she plucked up a spirit and asked me for 'a pound'" (*Letters* 9: 342). Dickens no doubt found his mother's performances particularly embarrassing as he was keen on getting as far away as possible from his family's early financial misfortunes in order to establish himself as a gentleman.

Dickens's relationship with his mother was mirrored in other relationships he had with women. When in 1855 he received a letter from Maria Beadnell Winter, who had encouraged then rejected his advances when they were young, he felt all the excitement and torment of that early infatuation renewed. But when he actually met her, and found her to be silly, fat, and garrulous, his boyish spirits were crushed. She seemed monstrous to him, a "grotesque revival" of her former self, in the words of Arthur Clennam similarly disenchanted on coming face to face with Flora Finching, the woman he had ardently loved in his youth (*Little Dorrit* bk. 1, ch. 13).

Dickens blamed his wife Catherine for similar shortcomings: he felt he betrayed him by not maintaining the image of the slight, young girl that was his romantic ideal. In his eyes, she had allowed herself to become slow, dull, and fat after 10 children, and he also felt that she never gave the children sufficient attention. In a letter to his manager, Arthur Smith, explaining his separation from Catherine (a letter that eventually appeared in the *New York Tribune*) Dickens wrote: "the peculiarity of [Catherine's] character has thrown all the children on someone else" (*Letters* 8: 740). He added that Catherine's sister, Georgina, had to make up for Catherine's deficiencies. Yet the reports of their children suggest a different picture. Their daughter Kate, for instance, claimed that "there was nothing wrong with my mother . . . she was a sweet, kind peace-loving woman, a lady – a lady born" (Storey 1971: 22–3). But Dickens was quick to see his mother's betrayal repeated in the behavior of other women, and he was also quick to find excuses for his relationship with the young actress Ellen Ternan, who better fitted his image of the feminine ideal.

In his fiction Dickens repeats the pattern of female betrayal in monstrous mothers and mother-figures who are punished for their sins; he also repeats the pattern of young, delicate females who reflect his own female ideal as well as the ideal promulgated by mainstream Victorian culture. His young male protagonists tend to reflect his own aspirations to gentlemanliness while exhibiting basic qualities of honor and good character. Father-figures in Dickens's fiction often demonstrate more idiosyncratic behaviors, such as the colorful Captain Cuttle or the endearing but perennially insolvent Micawber, based in part on Dickens's father. Fathers, in Dickens's fiction, are allowed to be more aberrant and even erring while still being appealing and relatively free of narrative hostility or punishment.

Dickens's young women characters are the ones most open to the charge of "stereotypes" because they so consistently reflect the gender expectations of young Victorian women. Rose Maylie in *Oliver Twist*, Kate Nickleby in *Nicholas Nickleby*, Little Nell in *The Old Curiosity* Shop, Mary Graham and Ruth Pinch in *Martin Chuzzlewit*, Florence Dombey in *Dombey and Son*, Agnes Wickfield in *David Copperfield*, Esther Summerson in *Bleak House*, and Amy Dorrit in *Little Dorrit* all share the docile, dutiful, and devoted characteristics of the Angel in the House ideal, while also exhibiting good housekeeping skills. This is the young woman who Dickens had hoped his own wife would be and who his sister-in-law Georgina seemed more able to emulate. As the survey of criticism above suggests, critics have increasingly come to appreciate that these characters, while undoubtedly reflecting mainstream gender norms, also reveal contradictory and even dangerous patterns in these norms. Little Nell's self-sacrificing devotedness to her grandfather, for instance, hastens her own death. Florence Dombey's meekness renders her more alienating and irritating to her father. Esther Summerson's self-denial would have kept her from marrying the man she loves, if her fiancé Jarndyce had not been similarly inclined to self-denial. Little Dorrit's selfless labors enable the rest of her family to sink deeper into selfishness and denial. So, while Dickens uses the stereotypical image of the Angel in the House, he almost always does so in a way that reflects the fault-lines in the image.

Many of Dickens's females fall far outside the Angel in the House image. Dickens's resentment of his own mother shapes his portrayals of monstrous mothers who seem to be the inversion of the maternal ideals established by Sarah Ellis, Sarah Lewis, Isabella Beeton, and others. Mrs. Skewton in *Dombey and Son* and Miss Havisham in *Great Expectations* reflect aspects of Elizabeth Dickens that her son found disturbing. Like Dickens's mother, Mrs. Skewton has a tendency to dress in juvenile clothes and absurd accoutrements, such as "diamonds, short sleeves, rouge, curls, teeth, and other juvenility" (ch. 37). Miss Havisham goes to more horrific lengths in her refusal to abandon the clothes of her youth since she continues to wear the wedding dress she had donned on the day she was jilted. Both women also enact Elizabeth Dickens's chief sin against her son: they use their children to advance their own selfish aims. Mrs. Skewton basically serves as a pander, selling her daughter Edith off to the highest bidder, while Miss Havisham raises Estella for the sole purpose of seeking revenge on men. Dickens punishes both women with protracted, disfiguring, and painful deaths, Mrs. Skewton dying of a series of strokes that turn her into a "horrible doll" (ch. 37) and Miss Havisham dying slowly of burns she suffers when her wedding dress catches fire (ch. 49). While Dickens seems to vent some hostilities toward his mother in these portrayals, he also punishes these women for their refusal to abide by the Victorian norms of motherhood. Yet the plights of both women also reveal the dangers of such norms; if middle- and upper-class women are to see marriage and domesticity as the ultimate goals of their existence, is it any wonder that a woman might go to excessive and embarrassing lengths to place her daughter in a good marriage, or lose her mind when jilted on her wedding day?

Dickens punishes other negative mother-figures in his novels. In *Great Expectations*, Pip's sister and surrogate mother Mrs. Joe regularly beats him with the Tickler but gets beaten into paralysis and muteness herself by Orlick. Miss Barbary in *Bleak House* is similarly punished for her emotional abuse of Esther by a stroke that paralyzes and silences her. In *Nicholas Nickleby*, Mrs. Nickleby offers another fictionalization of Dickens's mother, with her garrulousness and pretensions to youthfulness, and her obliviousness to her daughter Kate's misery in trying to fend off Sir Mulberry Hawk. While she does not suffer a terrible stroke, beating, or burning as punishment, she suffers a narrative silencing by the end of the novel, with her loquacious monologues reined in.

Dickens does offer positive mother-figures in the guise of Betsy Trotwood in *David Copperfield*, Mrs. Boffin in *Our Mutual Friend*, and Mrs. Lirriper in "Mrs. Lirriper's Lodgings," but none of these is a biological mother. Mrs. Micawber is a kindly biological mother but ineffective. Biological fathers and surrogate fathers fare somewhat better, perhaps because expectations of their performance were more realistic, so that they did not disappoint quite as often or as deeply. Pickwick and Tony Weller in *The Pickwick Papers*, Newman Noggs in *Nicholas Nickleby*, Daniel Peggotty and Mr. Dick in *David Copperfield*, Jarndyce in *Bleak House*, Meagles in *Little Dorrit*, Magwitch, the Aged P, and Joe in *Great Expectations*, and Boffin and Wilfer in *Our Mutual Friend* all offer portraits of faulty but nevertheless lovable father figures who nurture and remain loved in spite of their weaknesses. Mother figures are never granted as much leniency.

It is easy to overemphasize Dickens's reliance on Victorian gender stereotypes, but to do so is to miss the richness of his fictional characterizations. Does Dickens rely on gender stereotypes? Certainly. Does he reveal the contradictions and dangerous tensions in these stereotypes? Absolutely. Does he transcend the gender stereotypes? Almost always.

REFERENCES AND FURTHER READING

Altick, Richard D. (1973). *Victorian People and Ideas*. New York: W. W. Norton.

Armstrong, Nancy (1987). *Desire and Domestic Fiction: A Political History of the Novel*. New York: Oxford University Press.

Beeton, Isabella (1949). *Mrs. Beeton's Household Management*. London: Ward, Lock and Co. (original work published 1859).

Camus, Marianne (2004). *Gender and Madness in the Novels of Charles Dickens*. Lewiston, NY: Edwin Mellen Press.

Davidoff, Leonore and Hall, Catherine (Eds.) (1987). *Family Fortunes: Men and Women of the English Middle Class, 1780–1850*. Chicago: University of Chicago Press.

Ellis, Sarah (1843a). *The Wives of England: Their Relative Duties, Domestic Influence and Social Obligations*. New York: J. and H. G. Langley.

— (1843b). *The Women of England: Their Social Duties and Domestic Habits*. New York: J. and H. G. Langley.

— (1844). *The Mothers of England: Their Influence and Responsibility*. New York: D. Appleton and Co.

Fulford, Roger (Ed.) (1964). *Dearest Child: Letters between Queen Victoria and the Princess Royal 1858–61*. New York: Holt, Rinehart and Winston.

Gilbert, Sandra and Gubar, Susan (1984). *The Madwoman in the Attic: The Woman Writer and the Nineteenth-century Literary Imagination*. New Haven, CT: Yale University Press.

Holbrook, David (1993). *Charles Dickens and the Image of Woman*. New York: New York University Press.

Ingham, Patricia (1992). *Dickens, Women and Language*. Toronto: University of Toronto Press.

Johnson, Edgar (1952). *Charles Dickens: His Tragedy and Triumph*, 2 vols. New York: Simon and Schuster.

Langland, Elizabeth (1995). *Nobody's Angels: Middle-class Women and Domestic Ideology in Victorian Culture*. Ithaca, NY: Cornell University Press.

Lewis, Sarah (1840). *Woman's Mission*. Boston: William Crosby.

McKnight, Natalie (1997). *Suffering Mothers in Mid-Victorian Novels*. New York: St. Martin's Press.

Poovey, Mary (1988). *Uneven Developments: The Ideological Work of Gender in Mid-Victorian England*. Chicago: University of Chicago Press.

Pykett, Lyn (2002). *Charles Dickens*. New York: Palgrave.

Roper, Michael and Tosh, John (Eds.) (1991). *Manful Assertions: Masculinities in Britain since 1800*. New York: Routledge.

Sadoff, Diane (1992). *Monsters of Affection: Dickens, Eliot and Brontë on Fatherhood*. Baltimore, MD: Johns Hopkins University Press.

St. Aubyn, Giles (1992). *Queen Victoria*. New York: Athenaeum.

Sedgwick, Eve Kosofsky (1985). *Between Men: English Literature and Male Homosocial Desire*. New York: Columbia University Press.

Shires, Linda M. (Ed.) (1992). *Rewriting the Victorians: Theory, History, and the Politics of Gender*. New York: Routledge.

Showalter, Elaine (1985). *The Female Malady: Women, Madness, and English Culture 1830–1980*. New York: Pantheon.

Slater, Michael (1983). *Dickens and Women*. Stanford, CA: Stanford University Press.

Storey, Gladys (1971). *Dickens and Daughter*. New York: Haskell House (original work published 1939).

Sussman, Herbert (1995). *Victorian Masculinities: Manhood and Masculine Poetics in Early Victorian Literature and Art*. Cambridge: Cambridge University Press.

Tosh, John (1998). *A Man's Place: Masculinity and the Middle-class Home in Victorian England*. New Haven, CT: Yale University Press.

Ward, John C. (1983). *Dickens Studies Newsletter*, 14, 37–42.

Waters, Catherine (1997). *Dickens and the Politics of Family*. Cambridge: Cambridge University Press.

Zangen, Britta (2004). *Our Daughters Must Be Wives: Marriageable Young Women in the Novels of Dickens, Eliot, and Hardy*. New York: Peter Lang.

13

Dickens and Technology

Trey Philpotts

More than 50 years before Dickens's birth in 1812, Britain experienced the first stages of a technological revolution. Even a highly abbreviated list of some of the major inventions during his lifetime is impressive: among them we might note the steam printing press, the iron steamboat, the passenger railway, the electric telegraph, and photography. This was, as Carlyle pronounced in 1829, "the Age of Machinery, in every outward and inward sense of that word" (1967: 23). With the advent of the steam engine, power became a freestanding quantity: it no longer depended on humans or animals, and was no longer limited by weather conditions. The steam engine placed a premium on rationalized and regularized modes of behavior and necessitated the building of large factories, which encouraged monopolies and the concentration of wealth. The need for better engines, in turn, required improvements in machine crafts, including the invention of the boring machine and the boring cylinder, and the standardization of parts (Mumford 1963: 160–1; Landes 1969: 41).

Although "the very notion of 'technology' as an agent of change scarcely existed" in the late eighteenth century, the transformative potential of the machine became evident as the nineteenth century advanced, betokening, in the major magazines of the day, "an unprecedented release of human energy in science, politics, and everyday life" (Marx 1973: 149, 191). Steam power made life easier, improved living standards, and made possible both the steamboat and the railway. Yet it is also true that steam power spread slowly, most of it concentrated in the textile industry until 1870, and that most mid-century factories remained small and most trades technologically primitive (Hoppen 1998: 38).

The pre-eminent embodiment of steam power was the railway and, beginning in 1830, the introduction of both passenger and freight services on a regular schedule. Within two decades, 6,000 miles of tracks had been laid, carrying 80 million passengers a year. By 1862, the existing track had increased to almost 10,000 miles and the passenger total to 170 million (Perkin 1971: 104, 114). The railway demanded an elaborate system of support: a network of iron tracks, organized movements of passengers and goods, and a vast number of employees, about 275,000 by 1873 (Marx 1997; Hoppen 1998: 291). The railway enhanced the demand for raw materials such as pig iron and bricks; sped up travel and made it more affordable; encouraged trips to the coast, which led to the growth of seaside towns; influenced "engineering techniques, business organization, management methods, and the provision of an expanded range of professional services"; and uprooted towns and changed the face of the countryside. It also brought together people, mixing women with men, rich with poor (Hoppen 1998: 290; Keep 2002: 140).

In the view of contemporary observers such as Henry Booth, the treasurer of the Liverpool and Manchester Railway, "perhaps the most striking result produced by the completion of this Railway, is the sudden and marvellous change which has been effected in our ideas of space and time." "Man has become a bird," Sydney Smith observed. "[H]e can fly quicker and longer than a Solan goose . . . Everything is near, everything is immediate – time, distance and delay are abolished" (quoted in Perkin 1971: 92, 104). It is this tendency of the railway to annihilate space and time, a favorite phrase of the day,[1] that made it "a sort of synonym for ultra-modernity in the 1840s" (Hobsbawm 1969: 111). If, as Sydney Smith pointed out, railways made distant destinations seem "near" and "immediate," railways also cut off passengers from their surroundings: trains moved rapidly through an artificial environment of cuttings and tunnels, which blocked the travelers' line of vision, and on railway viaducts that rose high above the landscape.

Such momentous changes inevitably left their impress on Dickens's writing. Although he never seems to have used the word *technology*,[2] it is clear that, by the 1850s at least, he had begun to conceive of individual inventions in the aggregate, as collectively embodying a certain progressive ethos. It is this progressivism that led Ruskin to proclaim Dickens "a pure modernist – a leader of the steam-whistle party *par excellence*" (*Works* 37: 7), though this characterization requires qualification.

It is certainly true that, in his more optimistic moments, Dickens expressed the view that Western civilization was progressive. These times, he wrote in 1849, "are marked beyond all others by rapidity of change, and by the condensation of centuries into years in respect of great advances" (*Journalism* 2: 174). In 1851, Charles Knight, writing in *Household Words*, proclaimed the steamboat, the railway, and the printing machine to be "the three powers which are more and more lessening the inequalities of condition, of locality, of laws, amongst the great family of mankind" ("The May Palace" 3: 124). In "The Great Exhibition and the Little One," written with R. H. Horne, Dickens insisted that "we are moving in a right direction towards some superior condition of society – politically, morally, intellectually, and religiously" (*Household Words* 3: 356). This "greatest and grandest" fact received expression in the original "scheme and List of subjects" for *Household Words*, which indicated that the journal's focus was to be "the extraordinary condition, social, *non*-political & moral of the present day to be brought out by comparison with the past." This "extraordinary condition" consisted of a "looking forward or *progress*" (quoted in Collins 1970: 44–5). Dickens was especially aggrieved by those sentimentalists who romanticized the past:

"If ever I destroy myself," he wrote to Douglas Jerrold on May 3, 1843, "it will be in the bitterness of hearing those infernal and damnably good old times, extolled" (*Letters* 3: 481). A year later in Italy, Dickens elaborated on the point:

> there are hundreds of parrots who will declaim to you in speech and print by the hour together, on the degeneracy of the times in which a Railroad is building across the Water to Venice! Instead of going down upon their knees, the drivellers, and thanking Heaven that they live in a time when Iron makes Roads instead of Prison Bars, and engines for driving screws into the skulls of innocent men. Before God! – I could almost turn bloody-minded, and shoot the Parrots of our Island, with as little compunction as Robinson Crusoe shot the parrots in his! (*Letters* 4: 220)

To underscore his dislike of such "parrots," he lined his library with a set of dummy books called "The Wisdom of the Ancestors," which had such derisive titles as "The Block," "The Stake," "Ignorance," and "Superstition."

Although Dickens considered the correlation between technological progress and social advance to be largely self-evident, he occasionally furnished details. In "The Great Exhibition and the Little One," he and Horne claimed that technological progress was vital to a world economy and to the health of the British people. "Our machinery and workshops," he predicted, would produce the manufactured goods that could be sold in foreign markets for food, which would help England meet the dietary needs of its growing population (*Household Words* 3: 357). Charles Knight, contributing earlier to *Household Words*, had expanded on these sentiments:

> If Rome sends her costly mosaics for the halls of princes [in the Great Exhibition of 1851], Cornwall shows her serpentine and porphyry for the cheap adornment of our common English hearths . . . [H]ere are also the ribbons of Coventry, the shawls of Paisley, the calicoes of Manchester, the broadcloths of Leeds. They are for the comfort and the decent ornament of the humblest in the land. ("The May Palace" 3: 123)

Dickens also believed that machinery, and the new technology that enhanced productivity, could improve the life of the worker. In "On an Amateur Beat" (February 27, 1869), he expressed the hope that new forms of machinery would eliminate the threat of white lead poisoning, itself the product of modern factory life (*Journalism* 4: 386). In "Plate Glass" (February 1, 1851), Dickens and W. H. Wills proclaimed the blast furnace, and its attendants, "the agents of civilization . . . making a light in England that shall not be quenched by all the monkish dreamers in the world!" (Stone 1986: 1. 211). In stark contrast to the glass factory is the home silk-weaving industry in Spitalfields, which rejects such simple improvements as the fly shuttle and refuses to turn "aside from the old ways," though these changes might improve the workers' health ("Spitalfields," April 5, 1851, *Household Words* 3: 28). Dickens and Wills juxtapose the master silk weaver of Spitalfields, immured in his cramped home, lacking mechanical improvements, with the speeded-up world of modern technology that exists just outside his window: "The arches of the railroad span the house; the wires

of the electric telegraph stretch over the confined scene of his daily life; the engines
fly past him on their errands, and outstrip the birds; and what can the man of prejudice
and usage hope for, but to be overthrown and flung into oblivion!" (*Household Words*
3: 28). This weaver of plain silks and velvets would be better off, Dickens makes clear,
in a large provincial factory with more sophisticated machinery.

Despite this progressivism, Dickens's brand of modernism was hardly "pure," as
Ruskin would have it. Although he himself occasionally indulged in rhetorical
excesses, as in "The Great Exhibition and the Little One," Dickens expressed skepticism about the more zealously chauvinistic rhetoric that exaggerated the case for
Britain's material advancement, and he was often careful to hedge his own language.
In "An Old Stage-Coaching House," for instance, he explains that he has been asked
to sign a petition requesting that a railway branch be extended to what had once been
a "great-stage coaching town" but which had been "killed" and "buried" by "the
ruthless railways" (*Journalism* 4: 270). "To the best of my belief," Dickens writes, "I
bound myself to the modest statement that universal traffic, happiness, prosperity,
and civilisation, together with unbounded national triumph in competition with the
foreigner, would infallibly flow from the Branch" (*Journalism* 4: 277). The irony is
obvious: this "modest" statement makes exaggerated claims that the railway branch
would "infallibly" lead to "universal traffic, happiness, prosperity, and civilisation"
together with an "unbounded" growth in foreign trade. Dickens here accedes to the
general proposition – railways were good for England – but bristles at the inflated
rhetoric, vague formulations, and the smug complacency, though in the end he does
sign the railway petition to extend the railway branch, despite his reservations about
the language.

This kind of ambivalence is also apparent in the many articles on the railway in
Household Words and *All the Year Round*. Although Dickens's correspondents frequently praise the railway for its beneficial impact on society, some worry that railway
construction has displaced large populations of the urban poor, and others complain
that railway companies have neglected to take responsibility for railway accidents and
have done a poor job of ensuring the safety of the public. Still other writers describe
the dangers of railway speculation and provide vivid accounts of the fraudulent practices that have bankrupted gullible investors. In several instances, it is not the "bright,
clean, and new" face of railway construction that receives emphasis, but rather the
ruin, desertion, and waste that accompanies failed speculations (for example, "Railway
Nightmares," November 13, 1858, *Household Words* 18: 505–8). As a material invention, the railway is described in almost wholly favorable terms. As an embodiment of
laissez-faire practices, the irresponsible trading in shares, and the maladministration
of large corporations, it is frequently derided (Mengel 1989: 3).

Dickens's ambivalence about the facile equation of technological innovation with
"unbounded national triumph" is most evident in his mixed feelings about the Great
Exhibition of the Works and Industry of All Nations, the massive display of technological prowess that opened in Hyde Park on May 1, 1851. He himself had served as
Vice-President of the Society of Arts from 1850 to 1851, during the period that it

was planning the Exhibition (though his letters suggest that he was more preoccupied with the Guild of Art and Literature), and he helped raise money for the Great Exhibition Fund (contributing £5 himself). He also served, briefly, on the Central Committee of the Working Classes for the Great Exhibition, which was supposed to encourage working-class participation in the great event, though he moved to dissolve the Committee when he realized it lacked the support of the Royal Commission that had organized the Exhibition. Although his personal involvement was limited, he expressed hope that the "industrial excitement" surrounding the Great Exhibition might prove a salutary substitute for the social unrest of the 1840s, and that "the political rights of nations may be more easily and permanently attained by works of peace, by studious observation, and by steady persevering resolution, than by any number of *émeutes*" (*Household Words* 3: 357).

But Dickens's enthusiasm for the Exhibition was short-lived. Although he was impressed with the design of the building, the iron and glass structure that *Punch* dubbed the Crystal Palace (*Speeches* 134), and with the representative value of the display – its association between technology and progress – he expressed considerable irritation about the Exhibition itself, which struck him as oversold and muddled. He complained of the huge crowds and was exasperated with the self-congratulatory tone that accompanied its aggressive promotion, going so far as to posit a very different type of Exhibition, one that would put on display England's "sins and negligences" (*Journalism* 2: 313). He also felt overwhelmed by the incomprehensible size and scale of the display: "I don't say 'there's nothing in it' – there's too much. I have only been twice. So many things bewildered me" (*Letters* 6: 428–9). When the Crystal Palace finally closed in October 1851, Dickens confessed to being "fervently thankful" (*Letters* 6: 542).

Dickens's distaste for the Great Exhibition, and its oversold promotion of England's social and political progress, seemed to receive confirmation three years later, during the winter of 1854–5, the first months of the Crimean War. Correspondents for several British newspapers reported that the soldiers laying siege to Sebastopol were dying because they were relying on antiquated equipment and ordnance that failed to meet the standards of the French and even of the "barbaric" Russians. The problem was not with the technology itself – potentially useful inventions supposedly existed in abundance – but with the bureaucratic red tape and managerial ineptitude that hindered its implementation (see chapter 15). It was widely reported, for instance, that the Board of Ordnance had been slow to adopt a special gas stove that could heat cakes of candle material and had failed to replace the standard issue Minié rifle, which was slow to fire and prone to foul, with the American-made Sharpe's breech-loading rifle, which could be fired 14 times a minute (instead of the Minié's two or three).

A special concern was that British inventors, who had been frustrated by repeated delays at home, would be driven to other countries, and that these countries would reap the benefits. The *North British Review*, writing about the Paris Exhibition of 1855, which attracted more than five million visitors, wondered whether "the mechanical and other useful arts which have so long been the pride of England . . . are now in danger of passing into other hands" (*North British Review* 24: 130). The appearance of Daniel Doyce in *Little Dorrit* resonates with this fear. It is Doyce, we are told, who "had an offer to go to Lyons, which he had accepted; and from Lyons had been engaged to go to Germany, and in Germany had had an offer to go to St. Petersburg, and there had done very well indeed" (bk. 1, ch. 16). Dickens's confidence that Britain was inexorably moving forward had given way, by 1855, to a much darker view. As he explained in *Little Dorrit*, the English bureaucracy had displayed "its fixed determination to be miles upon miles, and years upon years, behind the rest of us," while pig-headedly persisting "in the use of things long superseded, even after the better things were well known and generally taken up" (bk. 1, ch. 10).

Whatever his reservations about the chauvinistic rhetoric that exaggerated England's social and political progress, especially in light of its failure to make use of new inventions in the Crimea, it is certainly true that technological innovation, and the corporate and political interests that sustained such innovation, proved to be of immense practical importance to Dickens. Developments in printing and publishing – the invention of the steam press (first widely used in the 1840s), the use of cloth bindings, and the development of the stereotyping process, along with the use of new machines to make paper, and cheaper ingredients – made books and periodicals much more affordable, and thus more available to a wider audience. The steam ship made it possible to publish his works, almost at the same time, in both the United States and Great Britain (Patten 2006: 19). It was these sorts of advances that "contributed to the professionalization of the writer" and helped make Dickens a household name (Kucich 2002: 132; also see Altick 1957: 277–78). In 1859, Dickens used the major railway terminals and London stations, along with railway carriages, to announce the publication of his new journal, *All the Year Round* (Drew 2003: 141).

Dickens benefited from the expansion of the railway in other ways as well. Trains made it possible for him to travel back and forth between London and his home at Gad's Hill, "only an hour and a quarter from London by the Railway" (*Letters* 8: 51). And because Gad's Hill was on the Dover line, he could easily take the "Mail Train" to Dover, and a steam packet across the Channel to France, whenever he needed rest, and perhaps when he needed to be with Ellen Ternan, and still return "fresh as a Daisy" (*Letters* 10: 445). But rail travel eventually took its toll. By the 1850s, Dickens began to complain more frequently about the weariness of long train trips, and of being "used up" (*Letters* 8: 69). "I seem to have been doing nothing all my life, but riding in railway carriages and reading," he wrote to Georgina Hogarth on September 12, 1858 (*Letters* 8: 658), lamenting eight months later that "a long railway ride is a serious trial to an aching body" (*Letters* 9: 59).

In September 1862, having just learned of the disappointing sales of his Christmas story, "Somebody's Luggage," he wondered "how many people among those purchasers have any idea of the number of hours of steamboat, railway train, dusty French walk, and looking out of window, boiled down in 'His Boots?'" (*Letters* 10: 181). This passage makes clear how railway and steamboat travel had become an integral part of

Dickens's imaginative experience, every bit as valuable as walking or quiet contemplation by a window. The railway is "always a wonderfully suggestive place to me when I am alone," he confided parenthetically to a correspondent (*Letters* 6: 65). As Humphry House has observed, it is this close "physical experience" of the railway that informs Dickens's "emotions" about trains (1942: 145).

At no time did the "physical experience" of the railway leave a more indelible impression than on June 9, 1865. On this day, at about 3 p.m., Dickens, Ellen Ternan, and her mother were traveling on board a tidal express from Folkestone when it hit some loosened plates just east of Staplehurst Station, Kent, sending eight first-class carriages into the stream below. In all, ten people were killed and 14 badly injured in the accident (*Letters* 11: 49, 54, 83; 12: 704). Eight months after the wreck, Dickens remained "not quite right within"; three years later, he still suffered "in any sort of conveyance" from "a vague sense of dread" that would momentarily come over him and that he had "no power to check" (*Letters* 11: 314, 12: 161).

For Dickens, the Staplehurst accident also laid bare a larger problem: the unrestrained and chaotic expansion of an "enormous Railway No-System," as he phrased it, that had "grown up without guidance" and that seemed impervious to parliamentary influence ("no Minister dare touch it," he declared; *Letters* 11: 68). This "No-System" represented an abnegation of responsibility, a return of the "Nobody's Fault" mentality of the mid-1850s: there was "a muddle of railways in all directions possible and impossible, with no general public scheme, no general public supervision, enormous waste of money, no fixable responsibility, [and] no accountability but under Lord Campbell's Act" (*Letters* 11: 116), the Act of 1846 that rendered companies financially liable only when their neglect led to the death of passengers (*Letters* 11: 66n.; Pope 2001: 449–50).

For all of the practical importance to Dickens of technological innovations, it is also true that they play a relatively small part in his fiction. Predictably, the novels set in the eighteenth century – *Barnaby Rudge* and *A Tale of Two Cities* – rarely or never mention modern technology. In many of the other novels that do, the references are scattered and generally minor, and they are rarely integrated in any meaningful way into the fictional world, and mostly then to indicate time and location. Again, this is not surprising since novels like *David Copperfield*, *The Old Curiosity Shop*, and *Great Expectations* take place in Dickens's childhood or his youth, when steam technology was in its infancy, and before the advent of the rail transport system. In only a few novels does technology play a functional role – *Dombey and Son*, *Hard Times*, and *Little Dorrit* – but even here the importance of technology can be overstated. For all the critical ink spilled on the railway in *Dombey*, descriptions of rail transport take up a very small portion of the overall length of the novel, between four-and-a-half and eight-and-a-half pages, with significant railway content appearing in only four chapters (Carter 2001: 75).

The only modern technological devices to show up consistently in Dickens are the railway, the steam engine, the steam ship, and gas lighting. Otherwise, there are scattered references to assorted other forms of modern technology, some of which do not seem very modern or very technological by today's standards – the helium balloon, for instance – and others of which were either superseded or developed in drastically different forms, such as the air-gun, electrifying machine, or the diving-bell. Other forms of technological prowess in the early to mid-nineteenth century, such as construction in iron, which *would* have impressed contemporaries, are largely invisible as technology to the modern reader. Who today would think of Southwark Bridge as it existed in the 1820s as technologically sophisticated? Yet Little Dorrit's Iron Bridge, which was completed in 1819, included three cast-iron arches, the center one spanning 240 feet, which was the largest cast-iron arch erected in Britain at the time.

In Dickens's earliest work, the essays collected as *Sketches by Boz*, the steam engine serves mainly as background for the scenes of character and comedy. It is vaguely disruptive, and attracts some mildly satiric interest, but otherwise retains little hold on his imagination. In "The Steam Excursion" (October 1834), for example, the steamboat creates comical disturbances that suggest its newness and unfamiliarity: it is noisy and steamy and the engine causes everything on board to vibrate, magnifying the shaking motion, and thus the seasickness, brought on by the wind and rain. But the smoke and noise, each of which he mentions exactly once, are only minor annoyances without further significance.

In *The Pickwick Papers*, Dickens uses technological allusions to expand the metaphoric range of the English language, often to great comic effect. Much of the comedy derives from the discrepancy between Sam's comfortable cockney and the new-fangled and idiosyncratic nature of the inventions. Generally in *The Pickwick Papers*, steam functions as a convenient intensifier, most commonly to denote rapid speed. To encourage someone to talk faster, Bob Sawyer tells the person to "put a little more steam on" (ch. 48). And Alfred Jingle expects that his married years will "*run* on – they'll fly on – bolt – mizzle – steam-engine – thousand-horse power" (ch. 10). Such innovations vaguely figure modernity as a small number of somewhat bewildering mechanical innovations, but there is little to suggest their overall transformative potential. They have speeded up life, and perhaps made it slightly more puzzling or convenient, but they are essentially marginal, their marginality underscored by the infrequency with which they enter what is still primarily a world of coaches and hostelries, of slow travel and personal relations.

Dickens's first extended fictional description of railway travel appears in *Master Humphrey's Clock* (1840–1). As he will do throughout his career, he chooses an ignorant or naïve working-class character – in this case, Sam Weller's stagecoach-driving father – to voice his concerns. In the view of Mr. Weller, the train is:

> alvays comin' to a place, ven you come to one at all, the wery picter o' the last, vith the same p'leesemen standin' about, the same blessed old bell a ringin', the same unfort'nate people standin' behind the bars, a waitin' to be let in; and everythin' the same except the name, vich is wrote up in the same sized letters as the last name, and vith the same colours'. ("Further Particulars of Master Humphrey's Visitor")

"Everything the same except the name" – this comic formulation captures precisely the abstract sense of geographical space associated with the railway. This is a closed space of interchangeable places and people, of rationalized points and lines (Schivelbusch 1986: 53). What has been lost is the traveler's intimate experience of the surrounding landscape. In its place is the impersonal railway system itself, which has turned the passenger into a commodity.

One of the more dispiriting admissions in "Dullborough Town" (June 30, 1860) – a fictionalized version of Chatham, Strood, and Rochester – is Dickens's realization that he has given over control of himself to an organizational structure. The personal relations, and system of family ownership, that underwrote stagecoach travel have been replaced by corporate abstractions, the mysterious names and numbers on the side of the locomotive: "The coach that had carried me away, was melodiously called Timpson's Blue-Eyed Maid, and belonged to Timpson . . . the locomotive engine that had brought me back was called severely No. 97, and belonged to S. E. R., and was spitting ashes and hot-water over the blighted ground" (*Journalism* 4: 140). Even the "playing field" of Dickens's youth, and all the richly personal experiences associated with it, has been given over to an abstraction embodied in iron, what Dickens in 1851 in "Railway Strikes" called a "vast system of skilful combination, and a vast expenditure of wealth" (*Journalism* 2: 317).

If the railway has effectively reduced travel to a rationalized and corporate system, it has acted on its passengers in a similar way: it has abstracted them from the surrounding landscape, eliminating most of the human interaction that had characterized the cumbersome stagecoach experience. They might well think, as Dickens puts it in "Railway Dreaming," "I am coming from somewhere, and going somewhere else" (*Journalism* 3: 370). Or, as he writes of an express train in "A Lazy Tour of Two Idle Apprentices": "It was like all other expresses, as every express is and must be" (*Journalism* 3: 423). Such abstraction can encourage avoidance or misperception. In *Hard Times*, Mr. Bounderby, who lives in the countryside 15 miles from Coketown, returns home "by a railway striding on many arches over a wild country, undermined by deserted coal-shafts, and spotted at night by fires and black shapes of stationary engines at pits' mouths" (bk. 2, ch. 7). The railway line that rises above the undermined ground is a perfect example of this abstraction from context, an abstraction with dire consequences: it makes impossible the discovery of Stephen Blackpool, lying in one of those deserted coal-shafts. In a similar way, it is "the travellers by express train" who see the illuminated factories as "Fairy palaces," a sort of naïve vision only possible from a distance, and only on the fly. Wolfgang Schivelbusch has theorized that the rapid speed of railway travel undermined the sensitivity of the traveler both by transforming everything outside the moving train into a fragment, and by greatly increasing the number of fragments – the visual impressions – that the traveler had to assimilate (1986: 58, 189). As Murray Baumgarten has suggested, it is this panoramic vision that constitutes the essence of Dombey's railway trip in chapter 20: "For Dombey, the smells and sounds as well as the synaesthetic perceptions that were part of stagecoach travel had disappeared: for him, all reality is abstract, as it is for train travellers. The dreamlike experience of train travel . . . turns Dombey in upon himself" (1990: 76).

This process of abstraction is complicated and, as it relates to the railway system, works in antithetical ways. In Dombey's case, this turning inward forces him to reflect on his dead son. But in other instances a more positive effect prevails: it can free one from responsibility, encouraging dreaming and stimulating the imagination. As Dickens observed with pleasure in "Out of Town" (September 29, 1855), he had become "an irresponsible agent, made over in trust to the South-Eastern Company" (*Journalism* 3: 327). In "A Flight" (August 30, 1851) and "Railway Dreaming" (May 10, 1856), he takes pleasure in the release from responsibility and from the haste and hurry outside the train. For Dickens, everything that presses from the outside "is all one to me in this drowsy corner"; "I have but to sit here thinking as idly as I please"; "I am not accountable to anybody for the idleness of my thoughts" (*Journalism* 3: 28, 370). In this case, technology, as embodied in the railway, has little to do with engagement, and everything to do with "flight," a word used paradoxically here to describe Dickens's sensation of speed, the train moving like a bird, but also the sense of disengagement and irresponsibility, the train making possible a flight from reality.

If the train trip to France relieves Dickens of responsibility, it also frees him from the usual experience of space and time, and even from the usual grammatical considerations. The speed of the train, it turns out, outpaces grammatical expression itself: "Here we are – no, I mean there we were" and "The streaks [of daylight] become continuous . . . became I mean." In a similar manner, by the time a concrete object is rendered in words, the concrete object has already vanished, the present having given way, instantaneously, to the past: "The distant shipping in the Thames is gone"; "The little streets of new brick and red tile . . . have been fired off in a volley"; "There we were at Croydon." Finally, verbs are elided altogether, rendered moot by the speed of the train: "Whizz! Dust-heaps, market-gardens, and waste grounds, Rattle! New Cross Station. Shock! . . . Bur-r-r-r! The tunnel" (*Journalism* 3: 28–9). In the end, sound effects do the best job of capturing the flight of time and space. What exists outside of the train – the people and objects at "a scenic sort of station" – are rendered in fragments: "Houses, uniforms, beards, moustaches, some sabots, plenty of neat women, and a few old-visaged children" (*Journalism* 3: 33). That this is ultimately a movement toward abstraction is captured by Dickens's phrasing at key points – "Something snorts for me, something shrieks for me, something proclaims to everything else that it had better keep out of my way" (*Journalism* 3: 28). It is this abstraction from context that frees Dickens's imagination to wonder "lazily" (*Journalism* 3: 35).

In this particular incarnation – an express train to Paris – and as experienced by a "dreamy" Dickens, technology is effectively freed of its associations with the competitive bustle of modern industrial capitalism. It thus prefigures the prejudice "against the spirit of commercialism, especially in its more aggressive, assertive forms," which Malcolm Andrews sees as characteristic of the sketches Dickens wrote for *All the Year Round* under the name of the Uncommercial Traveller between 1860 and 1869 (1994:

44). Thus, the railway had the potential both to imprison and to liberate. It drove Dickens from place to place, confirming him in his role, and it freed him to imagine other possibilities. The railway represented, on the one hand, a regularized and geometric system, and, on the other, a mysterious and otherworldly force akin to flying. It deadened travelers to the sensory pleasures of natural experience, and it liberated them to dream. The railway was both a business and a marvelous idea.

As we have already seen, Dickens and his writers frequently invest such innovations with a spirituality and soul that transcend commonplace materiality. "The mightier inventions of this age are not, to our thinking, all material," Dickens explains to readers of *Household Words* on March 30, 1850, "but have a kind of souls in their stupendous bodies." He intended the journal to stimulate the railway and steamboat traveler to develop "new associations with the Power that bears him onward," for "The swart giants, Slaves of the Lamp of Knowledge, have their thousand and one tales, no less than the Genii of the East" ("A Preliminary Word"; *Journalism* 2: 177–8). To the charge that he was living in a "material age," and thus an "irreligious" one, Dickens countered, "has electricity become more material in the mind of any sane, or moderately insane [*laughter*] man, woman, or child, because of the discovery that in the good providence of God it was made available for the service and use of man to an immeasurably greater extent than for his destruction?" (*Speeches* 404). Particularly magical was the ability of technology to transform objects: "How to get a pennyworth of beauty out of old bones and bits of skin, is a problem which the French gelatine-makers have solved very prettily" (George Dodd, "Penny Wisdom," October 16, 1852, *Household Words* 6: 99). "And who shall say," a writer in 1862 in *All the Year Round* asks rhetorically, "that this age of machinery and steel is without its appeal to the imagination and to our sense of the beautiful?" ("Small-Beer Chronicles" 7: 585).

This sense that technology has its own special beauty and "esthetic compensations" stems, in part, from new insights into the fluid nature of material reality itself, for it is during the nineteenth century, as Lewis Mumford has explained, that "solid matter" changed to "flowing energy" (1963: 199, 217). But this emphasis on the magic of technology serves as a consoling counterweight to the very different qualities that Dickens also associated with the machine, namely its fundamental deadness and reliance on repeated motions (Ostry 2001). In *Hard Times*, he observes that "The smoke-serpents were indifferent" to the human drama being played out in Coketown: "the melancholy mad elephants, like the Hard Fact men, abated nothing of their set routine, whatever happened. Day and night again, day and night again. The monotony was unbroken" (bk. 3, ch. 5). In fact, Dickens frequently equates the steam engine – not with anything magical or transcendent – but with its opposite: dreary utility and superficial notions of "improvement." In *The Old Curiosity Shop*, Miss Monflathers, the school mistress who is both a snob and a bully, reprimands Nell for enjoying Jarley's waxworks: " 'how naughty it is of you', resumed Miss Monflathers, 'to be a wax-work child, when you might have the proud consciousness of . . . improving your mind by the constant contemplation of a steam engine' " (ch. 31).

This contrast between Jarley's waxworks, suggesting the importance of imagination and fancy to the well-being of a young child, and "the constant contemplation of a steam engine," with its nose-to-the-grindstone emphasis on factual knowledge, will be elaborated at length in *Hard Times*, 13 years later. And, again, it is the metaphoric use of the steam engine that expresses the problem. M'Choakumchild, we learn, along with "some one hundred and forty other schoolmasters had been lately turned at the same time, in the same factory, on the same principles, like so many pianoforte legs" (bk. 1, ch. 2). This is a reference to the recently mechanized furniture trade, and the steam engine which would "turn" a piece of wood, enabling the mass production of pillars, posts, legs, and much else. Dickens is suggesting, of course, that a narrowly utilitarian education produces an inferior product, just as the turning machine produces items of standard design and poor quality (Simpson 1997: 49). Appropriately, Thomas Gradgrind, the utilitarian patron of the school, is represented as a technological man: "He seemed a galvanizing apparatus, too, charged with a grim mechanical substitute for the tender young imaginations that were to be stormed away" (bk. 1, ch. 2). This mechanistic way of thinking also infects life in the mills. Just as the educational "factory" produces "pianoforte legs" en masse – educational leaders with the same limited outlook – so the industrial factory mass produces "Hands," factory operatives who are treated as parts of a soulless machine. Accordingly, Dickens's description of Coketown closely recalls Mr. Weller's characterization of the railway system, a system that had so abstracted human relations: "All the public inscriptions in the town were painted alike, in severe characters of black and white. The jail might have been the infirmary, the infirmary might have been the jail, the town-hall might have been either, or both, or anything else, for anything that appeared to the contrary in the graces of their construction" (bk. 1, ch. 5).

In such a world, man and machine threaten to draw perilously close together: Stephen, standing in the street outside his factory, immediately after work, has "the old sensation upon him which the stoppage of the machinery always produced – the sensation of its having worked and stopped in his own head" (bk. 1, ch. 10). But, for all the harm it does him, Stephen is finally different from his machine. "A special contrast," Dickens insists, obtains between the "quiet, watchful, and steady" Stephen and "the crashing, smashing, tearing piece of mechanism at which he laboured." He then adds, in a direct address to the reader: "Never fear, good people of an anxious turn of mind, that Art [artifice, or the machine] will consign [Human] Nature to oblivion. Set anywhere, side by side the work of God and the work of man; and the former, even though it be a troop of Hands of very small account, will gain in dignity from the comparison" (bk. 1, ch. 11). This "special contrast" was probably inspired by the strikers in Preston, whom Dickens had visited on January 28, 1854, a few days after he began to write *Hard Times*: "Perhaps the world could not afford a more remarkable contrast than between the deliberate collected manner of these men proceeding with their business, and the clash and hurry of the engines among which their lives are past" ("On Strike," February 11, 1854, *Household Words* 8: 553–9; *Journalism* 3: 207).

Elsewhere, though, the boundary between men and machines is less sharply defined, despite Dickens's adjuration to "Never fear." This is perhaps most evident in Dickens's description of a "great manufacturing town" in *The Old Curiosity Shop*, a description based on Dickens's 1838 visit to Birmingham and Wolverhampton, part of the industrialized region in the West Midlands known as the Black Country, the greatest iron-producing district in Britain.[3] As characterized by Dickens, the Black Country is an industrialized hell, driven by machines that dominate everything around them: "Men, women, children, wan in their looks and ragged in attire, tended the engines, fed their tributary fires . . . Then, came more of the wrathful monsters, whose like they almost seemed to be in their wildness and their untamed air" (ch. 45). The inanimate and animate become one here. The engines are like "tortured creatures," the tortured creatures like the engines, figured as "the wrathful monsters." The machines suffer agonies and so do the people. Throughout the passage, there is a sense of profound disturbance bordering on madness.

This confusion between the animate and inanimate, rendered here as hellish phantasmagoria, frequently manifests itself in Dickens on a psychological level. In *Martin Chuzzlewit*, for instance, the steam packets are said to reproduce their passengers' "fretting and chafing": "They all appeared to be perspiring and bothering themselves, exactly as the passengers did; they never left off fretting and chafing" (ch. 40). Here, personification explicitly links the representation of a technological innovation – a steam ship – with the representation of the mind. Modern technology figures the condition of restlessness and unease associated with modernity and industrial capitalism, the kind of haste and hurry that Dickens had briefly escaped on the express train to Paris in "A Flight." Similarly, in "An Unsettled Neighbourhood" (November 11, 1854): "The trucks that clatter with such luggage, full trot, up and down the [railway] platform, tear into our spirits, and hurry us, and we can't be easy" (*Journalism* 3: 247). In extreme forms, this sense of psychological disturbance might take the form of complete mental collapse, as seems to be the case in Dickens's late short story, "The Signalman," which reflects contemporary concerns about "railway nerves" brought on by "the pressure of always having to send the correct signal" (Cooke 2005: 101).

At other times, the machine threatens to impinge on, or take precedence over, human physiology. In *Martin Chuzzlewit*, Sairy Gamp complains that "Them confugion steamers" have the tendency to induce premature labor, a common concern at the time, which "has done more to throw us [midwives] out of our reg'lar work" (ch. 40).[4] Most movingly, in "Spitalfields," Dickens and W. H. Wills observe that looms have displaced a weaver's children from "the best accommodation," condemning them to a life of unrelenting, mechanized noise: "They bestride the room, and pitilessly squeeze the children . . . into corners. The children sleep at night between the legs of the monsters, who deafen their first cries with their whirr and rattle, and who roar the same tune to them when they die" (*Household Words* 3: 28).

On other occasions, steam technology evokes the opposite response. Frequently, it figures a sort of useful and directed energy applied toward socially productive ends. In *The Old Curiosity Shop*, for example, Sally Brass is said to have continued "scratching on with a noisy pen, scoring down the figures with evident delight, and working like a steam-engine" (ch. 33). And Mr. Boffin, in *Our Mutual Friend*, proudly compliments his wife on her intelligence, on two different occasions: "What a thinking steam-ingein this old lady is! And she don't know how she does it. Neither does the ingein!" (bk. 1, ch. 9); "And she is a steam-ingein at it [at thinking] . . . when she once begins. It mayn't be so easy to start her; but once started, she's a ingein'" (bk. 2, ch. 10).

Most substantially, steam technology, as embodied in railway construction, has tremendous transformative potential, most notably in *Dombey and Son*. As character-ized in chapters 6 and 15, the railway changes Staggs's Garden, a seedy backwater suburb of London, with its "little row of houses, with squalid patches of ground before them," into a bustling and thriving community: with "palaces" and warehouses crammed "with rich goods and costly merchandise" and "wholesome comforts and conveniences." The emphasis is on new prosperity and activity, a healthy circulation of people and goods that produces a "fermentation . . . always in action." The progress of the railway has been inexorable, and appears here as a good thing. The unsettled quality of Staggs's Garden – its incompletion, confusion, and unintelligibility, with "its bridges that led nowhere; thoroughfares that were wholly impassable, Babel towers of chimneys," all of which had seemed so ominous – turns out to have been a necessary precondition for a total transformation. For the railway has "vanquished" without doing obvious harm. Instead of displacing the master chimney-sweep, who had expected the railway to fail, it has only made him more prosperous.[5] It has also provided new employment to Mr. Toodles, a new house for his family, and relative prosperity, while rendering ridiculous the sentimental pastoralism of the residents of Staggs's Garden and their confidence that their "sacred grove" would outlive "any such ridiculous inventions."[6] The trains, in Dickens's representation, are "tame dragons" that glide "into the allotted corners grooved out to the inch for their recep-tion . . . as if they were dilating with the secret knowledge of great powers yet unsus-pected in them, and strong purposes not yet achieved."

As should be obvious by now, in different contexts Dickens represents the steam engine in contradictory ways. Though the steam engines in Doyce's foundry in *Little Dorrit* comically threaten "to grind the business to dust and tear the factory to pieces," they are represented in a generally positive manner. They generate noises that "blend into the busy hum" and are accorded an exuberant life that graces the men who work them: "The patient figures at work were swarthy with the filings of iron and steel that danced on every bench and bubbled up through every chink in the planking . . . The whole had at once a fanciful and practical air in Clennam's eyes" (bk. 1, ch. 23). These are "patient" men, clearly comfortable with the job and their employer, who work in concord with the machine, without hurry or the slightest trace of discontent. In contrast, in *Hard Times*, the novel that immediately precedes *Little Dorrit*, the steam engine is represented as an implacable and very dangerous monster that spews oil and heat and that is quite good at "chopping people up" (bk. 2, ch. 1), including Rachael's sister in the manuscript version ("Wi' her child arm tore off").

In other words, Dickens is using a technological device, in this case the steam engine, to manipulate the readers' responses. If an employer is to be validated, as is the case with Daniel Doyce, then the machine produces iron and steel filings that bubble and dance; if the employer is to be condemned, as is the case with the factory owners in Coketown, then the machine chops people up. What matters is less the machine *per se* than the business model that informs its use. The factory operatives in *Hard Times* are plagued by instrumental ways of thinking; they are "Hands" subservient to the demands of large-scale industrial processes whose utilitarian ethos they cannot fathom. The workers in Doyce's foundry, producing the kind of uniform machine parts that facilitated the technological revolution, work for an entirely different type of business organization, one that embodies personal responsibility and trust, a type of privately owned business that was largely outmoded by the time of the novel's publication, the mid-1850s, the years of limited liability reform and what Dickens saw as a drift toward irresponsibility and indifference.

The elusiveness of the machine as signifier is evident in other ways as well. At several points, Dickens shows how the human mind – its worries and concerns – can color any account of the machine. In *Dombey and Son*, for instance, the locomotive figures as "a type of the triumphant monster, Death." But this figuration, we learn, is a projection of the depressed ego of Mr. Dombey, not of anything inherent in the train itself. Dickens explains that Dombey "carried monotony with him, through the rushing landscape, and hurried headlong, not through a rich and varied country, but a wilderness of blighted plans and gnawing jealousies" (ch. 20). Similarly, when Dombey draws a correspondence between the railway and the "ruinous and dreary" landscape of the industrialized Midlands, this too is a projection, as Dickens takes pains to point out: "the monster who has brought him there has let the light of day in on these things: not made or caused them." The railway, in other words, does not exploit or destroy but opens up and reveals. It is not "a type of the triumphant monster, Death," after all, despite the emphatic repetition of the phrase that would suggest otherwise.

In Dickens's Christmas story "Barbox Brothers," a similar reversal occurs, and again it hinges on the state of mind of the two major protagonists. Here, we meet "a downcast, taciturn man" named Jackson, who sees the railway as a symbol of his misspent and pointless life. Accordingly, he invests Mugby Junction with death-haunted imagery: "Mysterious goods trains, covered with palls and gliding on like vast weird funerals, conveying themselves guiltily away from the presence of the few lighted lamps" (ch. 1). In the course of the story, however, we learn that there is a different perspective on the trains, and on life more generally, which is clearly the "correct" one. Phoebe, a 30-year-old schoolteacher with a physical disability, has a "happy disposition" derived from her father who looks "always on the bright side, and the good side" of things. For Phoebe, the railway celebrates the pleasures of activity and engagement: "And those threads of railway, with their puffs of smoke and steam changing places so fast make it so lively for me . . . I think of the number of people who *can* go where they wish, on their business, or their pleasure" (ch. 3).

Typically, Dickens desires to have it both ways: to acknowledge the dark side of industrialization and technological innovation, but also to promote a more positive outlook, one that accords with his general optimism and personal buoyancy. As an imaginative artist, he was less concerned with methodical consistency than with exploring the look and feel of things, and rendering them in both a terrifying and an exhilarating way. His imaginative engagements with the technological world, in other words, reflect the same ambivalences and contradictions that mark the rest of his fiction, and that make him such an endlessly fascinating writer.

NOTES

1 According to Leo Marx, "No stock phrase in the entire lexicon of progress appears more often than the 'annihilation of space and time', borrowed from one of Pope's relatively obscure poems ('Ye Gods! Annihilate but space and time, / And make two lovers happy')" (1973: 194).

2 The term was first coined in the 1820s.

3 The technological revolution of the first half of the nineteenth century depended on iron: trains ran on wrought-iron rails, steam ships' hulls and boilers were made of wrought-iron plates, as were the newly constructed iron bridges (Rolt 1974: 123).

4 A tragically prophetic allusion in the case of Catherine Dickens, who miscarried "in the railway carriage" en route to Glasgow in December 1847 (*Letters* 5: 221).

5 In a speech on June 5, 1867, Dickens makes fun of the prediction that "the railway system . . . would infallibly throw half the nation out of employment." In fact, he explained, "it has called into existence a specially and directly employed population of upwards of 200,000 persons" (*Speeches* 362).

6 His job as a stoker is not without its costs, however. As he tells, Miss Tox, he likes his trade "pretty well," though " 'The ashes sometimes gets in here,' touching his chest, 'and makes a man speak as gruff as at the present time. But it *is* ashes, Mum, not crustiness'" (ch. 2).

REFERENCES AND FURTHER READING

Altick, Richard Daniel (1957). *The English Common Reader: A Social History of the Mass Reading Public, 1800–1900*. Chicago: University of Chicago Press.

Andrews, Malcolm (1994). *Dickens and the Grown-up Child*. Iowa City: University of Iowa Press.

Baumgarten, Murray (1990). Railway/reading/time: *Dombey and Son* and the industrial world. *Dickens Studies Annual*, 19, 65–89.

Carlyle, Thomas (1967). Signs of the times. In George Levine (Ed.), *The Emergence of Victorian Consciousness: The Spirit of the Age* (pp. 19–38). New York: The Free Press (original work published 1829).

Carter, Ian (2001). *Railways and Culture in Britain: The Epitome of Modernity*. Manchester: Manchester University Press.

Collins, Philip (1970). W. H. Wills' plans for *Household Words*. *Victorian Periodicals Newsletter*, 8, 33–46.

Cooke, Simon (2005). Anxious travelers: a contextual reading of "The Signalman." *Dickens Quarterly*, 22, 101–8.

Drew, John M. L. (2003). *Dickens the Journalist*. Basingstoke: Palgrave Macmillan.

Hobsbawm, E. J. (1969). *Industry and Empire*. Harmondsworth: Penguin.

Hoppen, Theodore K. (1998). *The New Oxford History of England: The Mid-Victorian Generation 1846–1886*. Oxford: Clarendon Press.

House, Humphry (1942). *The Dickens World*, 2nd edn. London: Oxford University Press.

Keep, Christopher (2002). Technology and information: accelerating developments. In Patrick

Brantlinger and William B. Thesing (Eds.), *A Companion to the Victorian Novel* (pp. 137–54). Oxford: Blackwell.

Kucich, John (2002). Scientific ascendancy. In Patrick Brantlinger and William B. Thesing (Eds.), *A Companion to the Victorian Novel* (pp. 119–36). Oxford: Blackwell.

Landes, David (1969). *The Unbound Prometheus: Technological Change and Industrial Development in Western Europe from 1750 to the Present*. Cambridge: Cambridge University Press.

Marx, Leo (1973). *The Machine in the Garden: Technology and the Pastoral Ideal in America*. London: Oxford University Press (original work published 1964).

— (1997). Technology: the emergence of a hazardous concept. *Social Research*, 64, 965–88 (Academic Search Elite, June 3, 2005, http://web.ebscohost.com).

Mengel, Ewald (Ed.) (1989). *The Railway through Dickens's World: Texts from Household Words and All the Year Round*. Frankfurt am Main: Verlag Peter Lang.

Mumford, Lewis (1963). *Technics and Civilization*. New York: Harcourt, Brace (original work published 1934).

Ostry, Elaine (2001). "Social wonders": fancy, science, and technology in Dickens's periodicals. *Victorian Periodicals Review*, 34, 54–78.

Patten, Robert (2006). Publishing in parts. In John Bowen and Robert L. Patten (Eds.), *Palgrave Advances in Dickens Studies* (pp. 11–47). New York: Palgrave Macmillan.

Perkin, Harold (1971). *The Age of the Railway*. Newton Abbot, Devon: David and Charles.

Pope, Norris (2001). Dickens's "The Signalman" and information problems in the railway age. *Technology and Culture*, 42, 436–52.

Rolt, L. T. C. (1974). *Victorian Engineering*. Harmondsworth: Penguin.

Ruskin, John (1903–12). *The Works of John Ruskin*, 39 vols. (E. T. Cook and Alexander Wedderburn, Eds.). London: G. Allen.

Schivelbusch, Wolfgang (1986). *The Railway Journey: The Industrialization of Time and Space in the Nineteenth Century*. Berkeley, CA: University of California Press (originally published 1977).

Simpson, Margaret (1997). *The Companion to "Hard Times."* Robertsbridge: Helm Information.

Stone, Harry (Ed.) (1986). *The Uncollected Writings of Charles Dickens: Household Words 1850–1859*, 2 vols. London: Penguin.

14

Dickens and America (1842)

Nancy Aycock Metz

America changed Dickens in ways he could not have predicted or necessarily desired when he first contemplated his 1842 transatlantic journey. These changes did not simply befall him as a result of external events – overwhelming and memorable as these events undoubtedly were. Dickens's own readiness for change made a critical difference. His published correspondence in the years just prior to the American journey offers ample evidence of a dawning realization on Dickens's part that the time was ripe – and the New World the perfect catalyst – for a fundamental re-creation of himself as a professional author. In the face of class-based ignorance and poverty at home, America offered him the chance to glimpse firsthand the healthy, living embodiment of the republican principles he had come to espouse. In the face of cheap imitators in the teeming literary marketplace, America beckoned as a subject worthy of the modern age, offering Dickens the opportunity to separate himself from the rabble of cheap serialists and emerge as a social analyst and populist man of letters.

From the moment Dickens began to think of the trip as likely and imminent, it was connected in his mind to his recent negotiations with Chapman and Hall, suspending serial publication so that he could become for a year a free man. In practical terms, such an arrangement made the American trip possible by providing Dickens with time, leisure, and an income (£150 per month for a year while not working, £200 for each monthly part, and a substantial share of the profits when he resumed writing; Forster bk. 2, ch. 12). The Chapman and Hall negotiations and the plans for visiting the United States both took place in the context of Dickens's larger re-evaluation of his role as a novelist: an evaluation that involved him in his first sustained interrogation of the value and purposes of fiction and the conditions that made it possible for him to thrive as an artist. Dickens's rise had been meteoric, his literary labors unremitting and prolific. At the point of focus between the negotiation of the contract and the departure for America, he found himself preoccupied, really for the first time, with the arc of his own career – a source both of profound anxiety and of bold ambition.

As Dickens's thinking about the American trip evolved, it became more and more apparent that, in a variety of ways, the New World answered Dickens's need to make *himself* anew. Not only did it offer the opportunity to reverse an increasingly unfavorable supply/demand relationship for his intellectual labors, it promised him a connection he genuinely craved with a transatlantic readership he envisioned from his desk at Devonshire Terrace. Dickens also desired to develop his friendship with Washington Irving whose works he had loved from childhood, and who had recently written to "express the delight he felt in reading the story of Little Nell" (Wilkins 1912: 117). He sought in the company of Irving and other distinguished American writers a likeminded and deeply humanitarian appreciation for the higher ideals of literature far removed from the values of those purveyors of "trash and rot" with whom his name had been habitually coupled of late (*Letters* 2: 365).

Most importantly, Dickens's American journey would help him to consolidate his emerging role as a fearless and forward-thinking social critic by providing a "bully pulpit" for his increasingly radical political views. In the process, he would boldly enter the lucrative and influential conversation about America dominated by Frances Trollope, Harriet Martineau, and others. Although only 30 years old at the time, Dickens had every reason to be confident in his readiness for such a task: his powers of keen observation were by common consent unrivaled; he possessed a broad knowledge of social welfare issues and firsthand experience inspecting public institutions; and, most importantly, he could claim a complete freedom from the Tory prejudices distorting so many previous accounts.

At the time he first thought seriously about making his own trip to America, Dickens seemed to be already occupying a middle distance, estranged from the conservative politics that held sway in his own country – and from the palpable effects of this class-based economic system – and, in equal measure, drawn to the theoretical principles of democracy. As a novelist, he embraced more and more overtly the perspective of the poor, the outcast, and the prisoner. He wrote to Forster on September 11, 1841, as he was finishing writing *Barnaby Rudge*: "I have just burnt into Newgate, and am going in the next number to tear the prisoners out by the hair of their heads" (*Letters* 2: 377). A week later, he had "let all the prisoners out of Newgate, burnt down Lord Mansfield's, and played the very devil" (*Letters* 2: 385).

Set against this passionate identification with the oppressed was Dickens's reputation, then just emerging, as an analyst skilled in abstracting from local instances the systemic flaws in society's fabric (Meckier 1990: 79). To make this move with finesse – both to *be* the prisoner and to *understand* incarceration as a politically constructed system – was to distance himself once and for all from the literary rabble. In the years before Dickens's American trip, he followed politics closely and even briefly considered standing for parliament himself. He was especially engaged in the horrific findings of the Children's Employment Commission and made "solemn pledges to write about [mining] children in the *Edinburgh Review*" (*Letters* 2: 317; see chapter 10). So many books about America had foundered on a superficial reading of quirks and oddities; he intended to look deeply into the democratic social system with a view to gleaning from it perspectives relevant to the great social issues of the day. He had every reason to believe that his fundamental radicalism would empower him to see what others had overlooked – and in the process allow him to extend and consolidate his reputation as a keen and incisive social thinker.

But even during this period of self-professed "radicalism," Dickens also embraced a contrary set of values quite at odds with democratic beliefs in the primary right of an individual to do as he likes. Dickens highly valued the rule of law, viewing any form of street protest, for example, as a dangerous form of mob rule – a faint shadow (perhaps even a portent) of destructive revolutionary anarchy (Magnet 1985: 140–5). Moreover, his work as a novelist in the years just prior to the American trip engaged him in probing analyses of the role of civilization in moderating and channeling the aggression he believed to be inborn in human beings. In Dickens's view, the rules and customs of ordered society freed individuals from the prison of self, giving them a richer, deeper life as contributing members of an interdependent whole. In *Nicholas Nickleby* (1838–9) and again in *Barnaby Rudge* (1841), Dickens explored the cost in human suffering, and ultimately in the very health and viability of the social fabric when a reliance on rational self-interest was made the first principle of human relationships. Thus, if Dickens entered passionately and imaginatively into the burning of Newgate, he also and simultaneously recoiled in horror from the resulting anarchy (Magnet 1985: 5, 101–17).

Well before he sat down to his first American boarding-house meal, Dickens had given careful thought to the role of forms, ceremonies, and conventions in the healthy functioning of civilized society. His radicalism was less a belief in individual rights *per se*, still less a leveling egalitarianism. Democracy was as yet a theory to him. But he did correctly anticipate that the lived experience of democratic society in America would somehow help him go "to the root of things," deepening his insights as a social observer and reformer in a world where injustice and suffering were pervasive and change was rapid and inevitable. Throughout his career, Dickens continued to negotiate these conflicting sides of his social philosophy but never in so concentrated or fruitful a way as in the four and a half months he spent in the New World. At first, however, the trip unfolded in a rush – as a series of discrete experiences, whose connections and larger implications only gradually became clear.

On January 22, 1841 Dickens landed at Boston and received his first impressions of the New World in a "beautiful" sunlit city of "handsome" public buildings and "elegant" private homes, a city whose proximity to Harvard University made it the acknowledged center of "intellectual refinement and superiority" (*American Notes* [hereafter *AN*] ch. 3). The relatively long time he spent here and in surrounding New England towns brought him into contact with writers, publishers, painters, intellectuals, lawyers, and forward-thinking abolitionists and reformers. It gave him an opportunity to tour the institutions of South Boston, which he declared "as nearly perfect, as the most considerate wisdom, benevolence, and humanity, can make them," and the Merrimack Mills in Lowell, as stark a contrast to the factories of England as "between the Good and Evil, the living light and deepest shadow" (*AN* chs. 3, 4).

New York, which he visited next, was busier, dirtier, and more commercial than Boston, and it was the headquarters of the most powerful organs of the scurrilous penny press. It was in New York that Dickens's enthusiasm for the New World first soured. When the city attempted to rival Boston's welcome with a grand subscription gala for 3,000 at the Park Theater and then to reprise the whole affair at half-price, Dickens's initial euphoria at the extravagant adulation gave way to unease and then resentment. A sore throat prevented him from attending the second Boz Ball. Meanwhile, confined to his hotel for several days, he had time to absorb the newspapers' unflattering representations (*Letters* 3: x). According to the press, he had allowed himself to become the property of handlers who had converted what should have been "an act of courtesy to a private gentleman into a raree-show" (quoted in *Letters* 3: 66). Worse, he was accused of vulgarity in using celebratory occasions to press for international copyright reform, an action that marked him, some said, as "shop rank."

Published slanders of this kind made Dickens more and more conscious of his celebrity as a form of entrapment; he felt silenced and shouted down. Tocqueville had written in lines Dickens would later paraphrase as his own: "I know no country in which, speaking generally, there is less independence of mind and true freedom of discussion than in America" (Tocqueville 1969: 1. 254–6). With respect to the copyright issue, Dickens felt the justice of Tocqueville's earlier observation in quite a personal way, nourishing an anger that ultimately led him to exaggerate his role as the sole spokesman for an unpopular cause. On Friday, February 18, at a dinner presided over by Washington Irving, Dickens announced his intention to accept no more public engagements. In the meantime, his visits to the State Hospital for Insane Paupers on Blackwell's Island ("a lounging, listless, madhouse air, which was very painful"), the Bellevue Almshouse ("badly ventilated, and badly lighted"), and the notorious Tombs Prison showed him a darker side to American institutions (*AN* ch. 6).

The impressions created in New York were confirmed and deepened in Philadelphia, where a newspaper notice published without his consent brought 500 people to the United States Hotel to shake Dickens's hand (*Letters* 3: 75, n.1). While in Philadelphia, Dickens spent most of a day interviewing prisoners at the Eastern Penitentiary, a "model" prison conducted on the "solitary system." According to his hosts, Dickens expressed no reservations at the time; afterwards, he wrote to David Colden that, though the sight of the prisoners was "inexpressibly painful," the system "seems, from all one can learn, to do good: and now and then to effect that reclamation which gives joy in heaven" (*Letters* 3: 124, n.5, 110). In retrospect, however, Dickens came to associate the prison, and others built on the same model, with the spirit of reform gone badly wrong.

From Philadelphia, Dickens traveled south to Baltimore and Washington where he met President John Tyler, visited the Senate and the House of Representatives, and witnessed firsthand debates in Congress about a postmaster "charged with malpractises" (*Letters* 3: 119). He was impressed by Henry Clay ("one of the most agreeable and fascinating men I ever saw") and John Quincy Adams ("very accomplished and perfectly 'game'"), but he observed that in the legislature, spitting, factionalism, and bad speaking carry the day and "the strife of politics [is] so fierce and brutal" that principled leaders are apt to abandon the fray to ruffians and tricksters (*Letters* 3: 117; *AN* ch. 8).

The furthest south Dickens traveled on the east coast leg of his journey was Fredericksburg. By then he had abandoned his original attention, confided to Lady Holland just before his departure for America, to "go into the slave districts . . . to ascertain by personal inspection the condition of the poor slaves" (*Letters* 2: 447). Beyond some chance encounters with slaves in the streets and as domestics in hotels, he engaged in no "inspection" more probing than the choreographed tour of a Richmond tobacco factory arranged by his hosts, where he was treated to the sight of "happy slaves singing at their work" (quoted in Wilkins 1912: 178). In the end, Dickens resolved to register his disapproval of slavery passively by turning his back on it and receiving "no mark of public respect" in slave districts (*Letters* 3: 90).

Retracing his steps through Baltimore and then traveling north to Harrisburg, Dickens began the long western portion of his tour on March 25, visiting Pittsburgh, Cincinnati, and Louisville, passing within sight of Cairo ("a slimy monster hideous to behold"), and arriving in St. Louis on April 10 (*AN* ch. 12). The obligatory side trip to an American prairie proved a disappointment. During most of this time, his experiences of America were filtered through the often primitive traveling conditions aboard railroads, canal-boats, and steamboats. Brief stays in the larger cities were taken up with official sightseeing and the inevitable public receptions hosted by minor dignitaries, with the occasional unscripted glimpse into local culture, such as the Temperance Festival that passed under his hotel window in Cincinnati.

On April 14, Dickens left St. Louis, heading east and north back through Louisville and Cincinnati on a route that would take him to Columbus, Sandusky, Cleveland, Erie, and Buffalo and then across to Niagara Falls, Toronto, Montreal, and Quebec. The roughest portion of the journey, the route from Columbus to Sandusky, involved a 15-hour trek over jolting, corduroy roads through fierce thunderstorms to a rough log-house, where – with doors flapping insanely in the wind – Dickens feared that he would be robbed of his £250 in gold (*Letters* 3: 206). Dickens crossed over into Canada on April 26, enjoying a month in surroundings more familiar and congenial to English sensibilities while he immersed himself in elaborate preparations for an amateur production of "A Roland for an Oliver." On May 31, he re-entered the United States, taking up residency again at the Carlton House Hotel in New York City on June 2. He enjoyed a brief tour of the Hudson River Valley, blessedly free of levees and official obligations, before departing New York for home on June 6.

Excluding the month he spent in Canada, Dickens spent only about three and a half months in America, a superficial jaunt compared to the year or more of residency on which previous travelers like Mrs. Trollope and Harriet Martineau had based their accounts. In the main, he followed a well-worn path, checking off the sights which former travelers "on their more leisurely visits . . . had [seen] before him – the Lowell Mills, the Perkins Institution, the Eastern Penitentiary, a Shaker colony . . . like them he went on the Mississippi, to a prairie and inevitably to Niagara Falls" (*Letters* 3: ix). Dickens's celebrity status meant that these visits, carried out as they were under the confining sponsorship of the various welcoming committees who escorted him on his sightseeing tours, often greatly restricted his opportunity to penetrate beneath the surface and acquire an original viewpoint. As he famously complained to Forster:

> I can do nothing that I want to do, go nowhere where I want to go, and see nothing that I want to see. If I turn into the street, I am followed by a multitude. If I stay at home, the house becomes, with callers, like a fair. If I visit a public institution, with only friend, the directors come down incontinently, waylay me in the yard, and address me in a long speech. (*Letters* 3: 87)

Moreover, Dickens's journey was so compressed – his time was so short and his 4,000-mile journey so sprawling – that much of his time was spent simply in transit from place to place (McCarthy 1999: 73).

Inevitably, these conditions skewed and simplified Dickens's understanding of the varieties and contradictions within American culture. He saw less of settled society and a narrower range of social classes and backgrounds than he might have experienced had he spent less time with the East Coast gentry or on the road with the "small businessmen, the sharpers, predators and self-promoters" he later vividly immortalized in *Chuzzlewit* (McCarthy 1999: 73). In the same way, although Dickens clearly saw and lamented what was *absent* in American cities (old graves, crooked streets, traces of a long human history marked out in irregular stones and architectural fragments), he failed to glimpse in any very specific way what was substantial, complex, and evolving in the American metropolis-in-the-making. No one captured more vividly than Dickens the sometimes surreal sights of this urban world in process: dwelling houses on wheels, city streets leading nowhere, the bright, flimsy façades of American structures threatening to fall inward like packs of cards. But, to Dickens, such sights were merely evidence of a chronic national failure to follow through – of grand intentions built on insubstantial foundations, of unseemly boasting, and a morally compromised ethic of investment and development. When he returned to America in 1868, Dickens bore eloquent witness to "changes in the rise of vast new cities, changes in the growth of older cities almost out of recognition," but from the vantage point of 1842, he could not make the imaginative leap necessary to glimpse the specific futures shadowed forth in these rough beginnings (*Martin Chuzzlewit/AN* Postscript).

Nevertheless, for Dickens, the great question of America was always, in its largest sense, the question of the future, and to a very great extent his hopes and fears for the future rested on the outcomes of the grand republican experiment across the water. He was particularly interested in the provision that democratic society made for those at the margins – for the poor, the disabled, the criminal, and the mad. Not only were Dickens's deep humanitarian sympathies engaged by the needs of the outcast and disadvantaged, but also, as we have seen, the conservative strain in him recognized the threat of violence and revolution posed by social pathologies left to fester in the body politic. Since Americans were reputedly in the vanguard of institutional reform, most British travelers to America spent time walking the halls of the more famous prisons and schools, chatting with wardens and directors, and interviewing inmates. But no one gave proportionately so much attention to this facet of American society or pursued the subject through so many examples and variations as Dickens did.

In the first month of his journey alone, he visited over a dozen such institutions. As the grueling journey wore on, he complained about being "forced on by my poverty of time," but thought nothing of devoting an entire day to Philadelphia's Eastern Penitentiary and then following up the visit by touring another solitary confinement prison in Pittsburgh (*Letters* 3: 114). Jeremy Tambling has remarked that Dickens visited "each and every institution he could in what reads like a form of repetition, and with a confidence, almost colonial about his power to judge them" (2001: 26). The structure of *American Notes* reflects this emphasis. Most readers expected a typical traveler's critique of American society; what they found instead was a series of essays in which observations on American society and manners were interwoven with extended narratives built around these amateur tours of inspection (Drew 1996: 82).

In the beginning, it seemed that Dickens would give the "fair report" on American institutions earnestly solicited by his American hosts (Wilkins 1912: 97). A note of relief is discernible in his letter to Forster written just two weeks into his American journey: "how much I have, even now, in store . . . the American poor, the American factories, the institutions of all kinds – I have a book, already (*Letters* 3: 50). Dickens admired the "good order, cleanliness, and comfort" he found in the Boston institutions (*AN* ch. 3). Here, as in the Lowell mills, he was pleased to see that girls dressed neatly and attractively and that the proprietors encouraged modest ornamentation, thereby cultivating self-respect and individuality. Here there were provisions for wholesome entertainment and opportunities to participate in communal life. Even in the State Hospital for the Insane, where the occupants might justly be considered dangerous, Dickens found the same pervasive spirit: an atmosphere of trust and politeness, an invitation to participate in harmonious social life by means of conversation, weekly dances, and musical concerts. For those who had forfeited trust, such as the inmates in the House of Reformation for Juvenile Offenders, the system allowed for gradual restoration and reclamation based on demonstrated behaviors.

Dickens applauded the assumptions behind these practices. If institutions drew their populations from the ranks of the poor, neglected, and outcast, then relying on short commons, harsh restraints, and punishments to subdue and control them could only make things worse. By cultivating the full humanity of each individual and, most importantly, by appealing to all as "members of the great human family," the institutions of South Boston seemed to recognize as reclaimable elements of society previously seen as merely "evil-disposed and wicked" (*AN* ch. 3). The old system bred a dangerous solidarity in "demoralization and corruption"; the new could "snatch [the fallen] from destruction, and restore him to society a penitent and useful member," an alternative Dickens found infinitely preferable "with reference to every consideration of humanity and social policy" (*AN* ch. 3). To be sure, Dickens took pains to dissociate himself from "the sickly feeling which makes every canting lie or maudlin speech of a notorious criminal a subject of . . . general sympathy"; he wanted a jail to look like a jail and convicts to perform the kind of work everywhere recognizable as prison labor (*AN* ch. 3). But he also believed that "the strong Heart" ruled more wisely than the "strong . . . Hand," "however, afflicted, indigent, or fallen" the citizen might be (*AN* ch. 3).

Citizenship was, in many ways, the crucial issue for Dickens. If the test of an effective institution was its ability to develop human potential, making the outcast a contributing member of society, the test of a society was the care it took of its most vulnerable citizens. In England, a wide range of religious and philanthropic societies, each with its own creeds and agendas, ministered to the needs of those who required such care. Some of these operated on "those enlightened principles of conciliation and kindness" Dickens so admired in the South Boston institutions; others employed harsher methods in less wholesome facilities (*AN* ch. 3). As Dickens's tour continued, he would discover significant variations in the quality of American institutions as well. But with respect to the single most important principle of social policy, America, Dickens felt, had much to teach England:

> It is a great and pleasant feature of . . . institutions in America, that they are either supported by the State . . . or (in the event of their not needing its helping hand) that they act in concert with it, and are emphatically the people's . . . a Public Charity is immeasurably better than a Private Foundation, no matter how munificently the latter may be endowed. (*AN* ch. 3)

In making this claim in the context of the 1840s, Dickens did not need to remind his readers of the possible consequences when governments fail "to display any extraordinary regard for the great mass of the people" (*AN* ch. 3). Would it not be better for society as a whole, he argued, if the "destitute and afflicted" felt gratitude for their government as "a kind protector, merciful and vigilant in their hour of need" rather than resenting the "stern master, quick to correct and punish" (*AN* ch. 3). What Dickens was advocating was a model of state responsibility based broadly on New Testament ideals of compassion and stewardship. Even after his feelings about America began to sour, he returned to this theme, remarking to Forster in language echoing the Book of Common Prayer, that in America "The State is a parent to its people; has a parental care and watch over all poor children, women labouring of child, sick persons, and captives" (*Letters* 3: 135).

This last category, however, proved problematic, and Dickens's experience at Philadelphia's Eastern Penitentiary put his thinking about all these issues to the test. Here was an institution supported by the state whose every feature was designed to promote the reclamation of the criminal and his restoration to productive life. "Beautifully – exquisitely – kept, and thoroughly well managed" by an administration about whose "excellent motives . . . there can be no kind of question," the prison had been warmly praised by Harriet Martineau and other English visitors (*Letters* 3: 111, 110, n. 4; *AN* ch. 7). In its clean design, orderly functioning, and humane attention to the physical and spiritual needs of prisoners, the Eastern Penitentiary answered the call by reformers for improvements in the filthy, noisy, overcrowded prisons of an earlier era, where women and children were heaped together with the most hardened malefactors in de facto schools for crime (Paroissien forthcoming).

Two influences converged in the design of the Eastern Penitentiary. Quakers, who were among the most vocal and active critics of the old abuses, envisioned a system that encouraged reflection and penitence. They believed that only in solitude and silence, with all distractions and temptations rigorously stripped away, could the criminal hear the call of conscience, come face to face with the full implications of his or her wrongdoing, and open him- or herself up to the transformative teachings of religion. Thus while the eyes of prison officials and pastoral counselors must be steadily fixed on the individual prisoner in order to enforce his or her isolation from all external influences, the prisoner's own eyes were to be directed ever inward. Bentham's idea of the panopticon provided the perfect architectural model for this theory. Prisoners led hooded to their cells in one of the seven long wings radiating from a central hub could be kept in a confinement so absolute, they might never even be aware of their own location in the prison, much less the whereabouts of other prisoners. With anecdotal evidence bearing strong testimony to the conversions effected by this treatment, Americans were quick to adopt the basic design elsewhere. In doing so, they pioneered a system of penal reform widely believed to be both salutary and progressive, an example to England and indeed to the rest of Europe (Paroissien forthcoming).

The evidence suggests that Dickens initially struggled to find the system exemplary. Not only had he heard favorable reports about the penitentiary from a variety of reputable sources, he genuinely liked the "extremely kind and benevolent" inspectors who invited him to tour the facility without constraint or concealment (*Letters* 3: 124). But by the time he came to write *American Notes*, his disapproval had become adamant and unqualified: "The system here, is rigid, strict, and hopeless solitary confinement. I believe it, in its effects, to be cruel and wrong" (*AN* ch. 7).

In the end, the lingering images of the prisoners he interviewed, "written, beyond all power of erasure, in my brain," outweighed for Dickens all the authorities and case studies that could be cited in support of the solitary system (*Letters* 3: 124). He saw in the typical prisoner's uncontrollable trembling and averted gaze not an awakened and repentant spirit but a crushed and lifeless one. Many had acquired the blank look of the blind; others had become quite literally deaf. He wrote in *American Notes*, "I hold this slow and daily tampering with the mysteries of the brain, to be immeasurably worse than any torture of the body" (*AN* ch. 7). Dickens believed that those who eventually emerged from this legally sanctioned entombment suffered a marked diminution of their humanity, re-entering society as "morally unhealthy and diseased" (*AN* ch. 7). That such cruelty was conducted out of the range of public scrutiny, leaving no scars and provoking no outcry, only deepened his sense of responsibility: "therefore I the more denounce it, as a secret punishment which slumbering humanity is not roused up to stay" (*AN* ch. 7).

But in denouncing the solitary system, Dickens by no means embraced a sentimental view of the prisoners themselves. Indeed, one of his chief objections to the system was that it cultivated the rankest hypocrisy and cant. Deprived of all other stimuli and dependent on their keepers for their only forms of human contact, the prisoners were easily shaped to say what well-meaning prison officials wanted to hear. When a bold burglar regaled him with a long, "racy" account of his exploits, "narrated with . . . infinite relish," Dickens had good reason to doubt the man's concluding statement "that he blessed the day on which he came into that prison, and that he never would commit another robbery as long as he lived" (*AN* ch. 7). Dickens carefully differentiated among the prisoners he interviewed. Some were capable of penitence and reform, he believed; others clearly were not. Indeed, the notion that human nature could be restored to its original state of innocence by isolating the criminal from all negative environmental influences struck him as naïve in the extreme. In the first place, Dickens believed aggression to be intrinsically and forever present in human nature (Magnet 1985: 27). In the second, he considered the crude laboratory conditions of the prison a poor match for the infinite complexity of the human mind operating on a world of multiplying possibilities and temptations. Although Dickens never says so explicitly, his tour of the Eastern Penitentiary reveals a sharp philosophical difference between his emerging outlook and the philosophy of even those American institutions he praised most highly. Dickens did not believe that all criminals *could* be reclaimed. Granting that many were led to wrongdoing through the usual routes of poverty and abuse, others were simply made differently. The true criminal intellect, as Dickens was later to write of John Jasper, was "a horrible wonder apart" (Paroissien forthcoming; *The Mystery of Edwin Drood* ch. 20).

Dickens's extensive, thorough, and probing tours of American institutions distinguish his journey to America from those of other travelers who gave the subject more passing and superficial attention. Afterwards, he continued to work through the issues raised by these encounters; their influence on his thinking was diffuse and long lasting. The spirit of South Boston – and in particular its potent mix of "conciliation and kindness" with hard-headed pragmatism – is discernible in many of Dickens's reform efforts in the 1840s and 1850s: his involvement in the Ragged School movement, Urania Cottage, and the Great Ormond Street Hospital for Sick Children, to name only a few examples (Paroissien 1985: 180). In his journalism and fiction as well, Dickens continued to advocate vigorously for the destitute and afflicted and to raise before his readers the specter of the avenging anarchy that would follow in the wake of criminal negligence and indifference. The allegorical figures of Ignorance and Want in *A Christmas Carol*, which Dickens wrote immediately after his American trip, are the first in a long succession of such admonitory characters and scenes. Jerome Meckier writes: "Dickens became the only major Victorian debunker of America whom the loss of an alternative vision did not deter from later stepping up his attacks on his own country" (1990: 21). In the meantime, Dickens's fiction probed ever more deeply the consequences of solitary imprisonment on the functioning of the human psyche; both Dr. Manette and Mrs. Clennam owe something to the prisoners of the Eastern Penitentiary. Dickens's imaginative projections into the anxiety-ridden and hallucinatory states of these prisoners, moreover, tapped into a deep fascination which he continued to explore throughout his career and which emerges most memorably in his last, unfinished novel. *The Mystery of Edwin Drood* begins in the mind of John Jasper under the influence of opium, and was to have ended, according to Forster, in the condemned cell.

In these ways, Dickens's intense scrutiny of American institutions played an important role in developing both his art and his professional identity as a public-spirited man of letters. It also helped him to connect the separate strands of his American experiences and make sense of the whole. Insofar as American society resembled the institutions of South Boston, Dickens saw grounds for hope in its example to the world. But increasingly, as his journey wore on, America itself came to seem "like some vast Solitary Prison," denying "participation in a fertile communal life" and thus producing "stunted, undeveloped selves, whose individuality never blooms" (Magnet 1985: 187). A "melancholy air of business" so consumed the Americans Dickens met on the latter part of his travels, he remarked, that "at every new town I came to, I seemed to meet the very same people whom I had left behind me, at the last" (Magnet 1985: 187; *AN* ch. 18).

Dickens's experiences confirmed him in his belief that unbridled individualism, so far from developing a healthy sense of self, actually reduced individuals to their primitive wants and aggressions. He believed himself to be personally the victim of these unmoderated impulses in the crude attempts by the press to profit from his celebrity status and pirate his books. Dickens's visit to Washington, D.C. convinced him that America was a country where special interests and narrow factionalism in politics obliterated any possibility of working effectively for the common good. As for the principle of rational self-interest, Dickens utterly repudiated it, both as a rationale for individual behavior and as a principle of government. It was not in the interest of slave-holders to abuse their slaves, he pointed out; nevertheless, the newspapers bore daily witness to hideous beatings and injuries. On board steamboats, where diners abandoned all social graces to compete greedily for food, in remote frontier towns where lawlessness reigned supreme, Dickens became ever more convinced that America needed more rather than less communal life and that release from the prison of solitary individualism was the first step toward whole and healthy development (Magnet 1985: 188–9). If he could not completely share the optimism of the South Boston reformers, he nevertheless recognized a duty to act vigorously in the present as if such optimism were truly justified – to use his art and his influence to bring the "afflicted, indigent, or fallen" within the network of relationships composing "the great human family" (*AN* ch. 3).

In this way, Dickens did gradually distinguish himself from cheap imitators in the literary marketplace, and although he did not find in America what he initially expected to find, he came back – without doubt – a changed man. His experience of America in 1842 was but one influence on the direction his career began now to take, but it was a powerful one, both "instructive and constructive of his art" (Welsh 1987: 12). Although his journey had lasted little more than a brief season, it would be the work of a lifetime to consider and reconsider what he had seen – to put the resulting questions, contradictions, and insights to the test in his fiction and in his life.

References and Further Reading

Drew, John M. L. (1996). *Voyages extraordinaires*: Dickens's "Travelling Essays" and *The Uncommercial Traveller*, I. *Dickens Quarterly*, 13, 76–96.

McCarthy, Patrick (1999). Truth in *American Notes*. In Anny Sadrin (Ed.), *Dickens, Europe and the New Worlds* (pp. 67–76). New York: St. Martin's Press.

Magnet, Myron (1985). *Dickens and the Social Order*. Philadelphia: University of Pennsylvania Press.

Meckier, Jerome (1990). *Innocent Abroad: Charles Dickens's American Engagements*. Lexington, KY: University of Kentucky Press.

Paroissien, David (Ed.) (1985). *Selected Letters of Charles Dickens*. London: Macmillan.

— (forthcoming). Victims or vermin? Contradictions in Dickens's penal philosophy. In Jan Alber and Frank Lauterbach (Eds.), *Masters of the Prison Pen: Imprisonment as Discursive Correlative of Victorian Culture*. Toronto: Toronto University Press.

Payne, Edward F. (1927). *Dickens's Days in Boston*. New York: Houghton Mifflin.

Putnam, George W. (1870). *Four Months with Charles Dickens during his First Visit to America (in 1842)*. Boston: Fields, Osgood.

Slater, Michael (Ed.) (1979). *Dickens on America and the Americans*. Austin: University of Texas Press.

Stone, Harry (1957). Dickens' use of his American experiences in *Martin Chuzzlewit*. *Proceedings of the Modern Language Association*, 72, 464–78.

Tambling, Jeremy (2001). *Lost in the American City: Dickens, James, and Kafka*. New York: Palgrave.

Tocqueville, Alexis de (1969). *Democracy in America*. (George Lawrence, Trans.). New York: Doubleday (original work published 1835).

Welsh, Alexander (1987). *From Copyright to Copperfield: The Identity of Dickens*. Cambridge, MA: Harvard University Press.

Wilkins, W. Glyde (1912). *Charles Dickens in America*. New York: Scribner's.

15

Dickens and Government Ineptitude Abroad, 1854–1865

Leslie Mitchell

In the 1850s and 1860s, few people would have challenged the idea that Great Britain was a superpower, perhaps *the* superpower. Its economic and industrial progress provided a model for the rest of the world to follow, and it governed an empire on which the sun famously never set. Both considerations drew the country into contact with other countries and other cultures, often controversially. Every decision by a British government in foreign or colonial affairs carried wide implications. Every entanglement abroad forced the British into introspection, as they examined themselves and their beliefs against the competing claims of other cultures. In these debates, unanimity would be hard to find. For some, British actions overseas demonstrated all that was best in the breed. For others, like Charles Dickens, terrible mistakes were repeatedly made that glaringly exposed the deficiencies of all British government.

Without doubt, the most contentious debate concerned the Crimean War of October 1854 to March 1856. As with some recent conflicts, the war divided the nation from the beginning. Its objectives were unclear, and its justification was dubious. Once under way, it seemed to be conducted with an incompetence that was almost willful. Some 22,000 soldiers died, but only 4,600 on the battlefield (Philpotts 2003: 500). Disease and malnutrition were the greatest enemies. In nursing and journalism, Florence Nightingale and William Russell established national reputations in reporting the consequences of mismanagement. Two Commissions of Enquiry merely concluded that no one in particular was to blame. Great questions remained unanswered.

Initially, Dickens supported the war. The autocratic system in Russia represented for him the antithesis of everything liberal. Tsar Nicholas I had recently suppressed a nationalist uprising in Hungary with a shocking savagery. Russia's ambition to dominate the Turkish empire and the eastern Mediterranean had to be resisted. Proposing a toast to "the Allied Armies of England and France" at a dinner in December 1854, Dickens observed that:

if ever there were a time when the true spirits of the two countries were really fighting in the cause of human advancement and freedom . . . if ever there were a time when noble hearts were deserving well of mankind by exposing themselves to the obedient bayonets of a rash and barbarian tyrant, it is now, when the faithful children of England and France are fighting so bravely in the Crimea. (*Speeches* 170)

In private, he expressed "a burning desire to cut the Emperor of Russia's throat" (*Letters* 7: 454). On a visit to France at the beginning of the war, it was both "astonishing" and "irritating" to witness the pacifist sentiments of the French (*Letters* 7: 430). By contrast, Dickens declared himself a patriot, ready "to illuminate the whole house" at the news of a Russian defeat. The faintest rumor of victory was enough to turn him into "a mere driveller – a moonstruck, babbling, staring, credulous, imbecile, greedy, grasping, wooden-headed, addle-brained, wool-gathering, dreary, vacant, obstinate Civilian" (*Letters* 7: 437–8).

The courage and forbearance of British troops were beyond praise. Operating under the command of incompetent officers and corrupt civil servants, they nevertheless displayed unimaginable fortitude. In his own terms, Dickens did what he could to alleviate their condition. He asked his publisher to send the troops "a complete set of my Cheap Edition" (*Letters* 7: 475). More practically, he persuaded Angela Burdett Coutts to pay for and dispatch a new drying machine to the hospital at Scutari. Its arrival in the Crimea was, in his view, "the only solitary 'administrative' thing connected with the War, that has been a success" (*Letters* 7: 672). Throughout the war, the loyalty of Dickens to the common soldier never wavered.

Very quickly, however, the honorable purpose of checking Russia's ambitions had to give way to other priorities. For Dickens, the war quickly exposed a terrible malaise at the heart of British government. The importance of the adventure in the Crimea was actually less to do with foreign affairs than with its disclosure of gangrene in British politics. In discussing the war, the focus of Dickens is directed to dissecting disease in London, not on the shores of the Black Sea. In his view, the illness had three clearly established symptoms.

First, the Great Reform Bill of 1832 had been an aristocratic confidence trick. True, the electorate had been increased from 14 to 18 percent of adult males, but such a change had left the exclusive nature of public life untouched. Patronage structures remained intact; birth rather than merit or ability was the essential qualification for holding office; powerful families squeezed relations and clients into jobs, with little or no concern for the national interest. As a consequence, the civil service was both incompetent and self-seeking, and members of both Houses of Parliament saw their involvement in politics as nothing more than a way of protecting vested interests. Jobbery was everywhere and corruption had become a system of government of which British soldiers were the victims. For Dickens, something had gone terribly wrong and someone was to blame.

In *Household Words*, he repeatedly tried to alert his readers to the scale of the problem:

> The humble opinion of the present age, is, that no privileged class should have an inheritance in the administration of the public affairs, and that a system which fails to enlist in the service of the country, the greatest fitness and merit that the country produces, must have in it something inherently wrong . . . Yet, to the governing class in the main, the sentiment is altogether so novel and extraordinary, that we may observe it to be received as an incomprehensible and incredible thing. I have been seriously asking myself, whose fault is this? (*Journalism* 3: 300)

The journal's pages are full of elaborate, and not so elaborate, satire that sought to make the same point, namely that government was a synonym for aristocratic jobbery. In "Cheap Patriotism" (*Household Words*, June 9, 1855), for example, Dickens described a department of state. There was a head clerk called Mr. Tapenham, who "did all the usual things. I wasted as much writing paper as I possibly could. I set up all my younger brothers with public penknives. I took to modelling in sealing-wax." His colleagues included a Mr. Killymollybore, the barely literate nephew of an Irish peer, and Percival Fitz-Legionite, who took his quarter's salary "for the sake of having something to do." For part of the day, the office devoted all its energies to playing "at hockey with the coals" (*Journalism* 3: 305–6). Such sallies were intended to be comic and disquieting in equal measure.

The second, sure symptom of disease was what Dickens called "Red Tapism." Nothing vital could be expected of an official world recruited by cronyism. No initiatives could be expected, no new projects supported. For people of little or no talent the safest and most comfortable way was to do nothing. New ideas were to be smothered in red tape and byzantine procedures. His concern about "Red Tapism," one of the major themes of *Little Dorrit*, was prefigured in "A Poor Man's Tale of a Patent," which appeared in *Household Words* (2: 73–5) in October 1850, and in "Red Tape" (2: 481–4) of February 1851:

> Your public functionary who delights in Red Tape – the purpose of whose existence is to tie up public questions, great and small, in an abundance of this official article – to make the neatest possible parcels of them, ticket them, and carefully put them away on a top shelf out of human reach – is the peculiar curse and nuisance of England . . . Your Red Tapist is everywhere. (Pascoe 1997: 420)

Disasters in the Crimea demonstrated the baleful effects of allowing incompetent men to reduce all government to obstruction and delay. The unforgiving description of the Circumlocution Office in *Little Dorrit* was intended to pour light onto a very contemporary problem, and its impact was everything that Dickens could have wished. Circumlocution and the Office where its arts were practiced entered the language as a metaphor for bad government. In 1858, Anthony Trollope took up the image in his own novel set in Whitehall called *The Three Clerks* (ch. 1). Calls for a reform of the civil service, not least those culminating in the Northcote–Trevelyan proposals of 1853, had been getting louder ever since the early 1850s. Dickens was able to give these demands images and metaphors that materially enhanced the campaign.

The third, and perhaps the most virulent, symptom of diseased government was a refusal to accept the principle of responsibility or accountability. Government by incompetents was bound to involve mistakes and gross mismanagement. Yet no one seemingly was to blame. Two major enquiries identified bad luck in the Crimea and faulty intelligence, but failed to pin the blame on any individual. The miseries of this war were quite literally nobody's fault. Significantly, the original title of *Little Dorrit* was to have been *Nobody's Fault* (Forster bk. 8, ch. 1; Philpotts 2003: 517). Dickens was simply infuriated by a complacency that covered up corruption. Men had died in the Crimea because transports and equipment had been defective, hospital provision inadequate, and military leadership unprofessional (*Speeches* 187). It just had to be someone's fault.

The men of government disclaimed all responsibility for their actions. No one paid a price. True, Lord Aberdeen's government was forced to resign, but then the same men returned to office under Palmerston, "the emptiest imposter" (*Letters* 8: 177). In apportioning blame, the name of "Nobody" was mentioned again and again. Desperately, Dickens demanded the name of "Somebody":

> The power of Nobody is becoming so enormous in England, and he alone is responsible for so many proceedings, both in the way of commission and omission; he has so much to answer for, and is so constantly called to account; that a few remarks upon him may not be ill-timed. The hand which this surprising person had in the late war is amazing to consider. It was he who left the tents behind, who left the baggage behind, who chose the worst possible ground for encampments, who provided no means of transport, who killed the horses . . . who decimated the British army . . .
>   . . . for the sake of Everybody, give me Somebody! I raise my voice in the wilderness for Somebody. My heart, as the ballad says, is sore for Somebody . . . Come, responsible Somebody; accountable Blockhead, come! (*Journalism* 3: 392–3, 396)

The Crimean War may have been just in its inception, but the disasters it visited on British soldiers changed the agenda of politics at home. Dickens saw the war no longer as an aspect of foreign policy but as creating new priorities in domestic government.

Anger propelled Dickens into campaigning mood. For the whole period of the war, he was anxious to join any movement for administrative reform, and a leader in such a cause was not hard to find. Sir Austen Henry Layard, the distinguished archaeologist and now Liberal MP for Aylesbury, had visited the Crimea and had been appalled by what he had found. In December 1854, he opened a parliamentary campaign designed to expose incompetence. He frankly told the Commons that "if any private establishment were to attempt to carry on business as Ministers have attempted to carry on this war, it would be bankrupt in a week" (*Hansard* 136: 194). Over the next six months, he moved motion after motion in a battle that culminated in June 1855 with a proposal to recruit to all public offices by competitive examination: "we want an examination which will really test the fitness of one man above that of others who may apply for the office," he argued (*Hansard* 138: 2074). Unfortunately, the impact of Layard's words was dulled by his tendency to muddle facts and to indulge in intemperate language, which Dickens deplored (*Letters* 7: 617).

Even so, Layard became an heroic figure for Dickens. In his opinion, the Member for Aylesbury was "the most useful man in the house . . . If I can exercise any influence with him, I hope it will be to keep him cooler and steadier. No man can move me on such a matter, beyond what I have made up my mind is right" (*Letters* 7: 619–20). He offered Layard the pages of *Household Words* as a means of spreading his message, and mobilized friends in the journalistic world, such as Mark Lemon and Douglas Jerrold, to take a similar line. As he told Layard himself, "If you see any new loophole, cranny, needle's-eye, through which I can present your case in Household Words, I do most earnestly entreat you, as your staunch friend and admirer – you *can* have no truer – to indicate it to me at any time or season, and to count upon my being Damascus Steel to the core" (*Letters* 7: 582).

On May 5, Layard formed the Administrative Reform Association, and Dickens became an early member. He was happy to explain his motives to a friend:

> I have enrolled myself a member of the Administrative Reform Association because I believe it to be impossible for England long to hold her place in the world, or long to be at rest within itself, unless the present system of mismanaging the public affairs, and mis-spending the public money, be altogether changed . . . [and] because the steady union of great numbers of earnest men is essential to the result. (*Speeches* 198–9)

On June 27, he addressed a large meeting of the Association. It was, he claimed, "the first political meeting" he had ever attended.

The speech he gave on this occasion was blunt and hard-hitting. He announced that he had "the smallest amount of faith" in the House of Commons as then constituted, and that he could not understand why, "many years after a Reform Bill," everything was "so little changed." Parliament commanded no respect, busying itself only with "drowsy twaddle, unmeaning routine or the absurdest worn-out conventionalities." It was deaf to demands for reform and apparently blind to the obvious corruption in everything it did. Voices outside parliament had to be mobilized. The closed world of Westminster had to be shaken by a noise so terrible that inaction became an impossibility. Dickens asked that the subscription for membership of the Association be lowered, so that working men could join. Even those too poor to enjoy the franchise should be invited to speak (*Speeches* 198–206).

Words such as these were highly controversial. In 1848, Europe had been challenged by revolution after revolution. Socialistic ideas became part of the political dialogue. To invoke those outside the political nation to agitation was desperate and frightening for many. In fact, Layard's motion for substantial change had been defeated in the Commons on June 18 by 359 to 40 votes. Within a year, the Association itself disintegrated. But if the country at large could not be moved, the attention of Dickens had been permanently caught. In July 1855, he began writing *Little Dorrit*, which, seen as a tract for the times, kept the issue of administrative reform fully in the public eye. For Dickens, the writing of this particular novel was a necessary cathartic experience. As he told a friend, "I have been blowing off a little of the indignant steam, which would otherwise blow me up" (*Letters* 7: 716).

Two memorable creations in the novel forcefully highlight the administrative incompetence that had ended in the slaughter in the Crimea. The first was the Circumlocution Office, the quintessential government department, which spent its days in "form-filling, corresponding, minuting, memorandum-making, signing, counter-signing, counter-counter-signing, referring backwards and forwards, and referring sideways, crosswise, and zig-zag" (*Little Dorrit* bk. 2, ch. 8). Its aim in life seemed to be to produce enough red tape "to stretch, in graceful festoons, from Hyde Park Corner to the General Post Office." Acting out the motto "How Not To Do It," the Office supervised all other departments, ensuring their competence only in inaction and obstruction. Even if another Gunpowder Plot had been discovered, no remedial action could have been taken until "a family-vault-full of ungrammatical correspondence" had been written by the Office. Innovation and improvement were, of course, out of the question (bk. 1, ch. 10). The unfortunate Daniel Doyce had little or no chance of registering his patent. Inertia and ignorance had become the supreme virtues in government.

The second image conjured up was that of the very specialized creatures who inhabited this world, and who gorged themselves on its profits. The Barnacles and the Stiltstalkings were caricatures of those aristocratic families which had transformed government into nothing but patronage and clientelism. These people lived lives that were completely cut off from those of their countrymen; "the question was all about . . . Tom, Dick or Harry Barnacle or Stiltstalking, because there was nobody else but mob" (bk. 1, ch. 26). They joyfully intermarried to create a social exclusivity that was impenetrable. At the head of the clan was Lord Decimus Tite Barnacle, a thinly disguised satire on Palmerston, who opposed all action on the grounds that it would "damp the independent self-reliance" of the people (bk. 1, ch. 34). Below him, Mr. Tite Barnacle and Mr. William Barnacle lorded it at the Circumlocution Office, where they neutered all reform proposals by insisting either that there was no precedent or that change would be precipitate: "Precedent and Precipitate were, under all circumstances, the well-matched pair of battle-horses of the able Circumlocutionist" (bk. 1, ch. 34). Below them were shoals of "hungry and adhesive" Barnacles who faithfully followed the same principles.

Dickens was unrepentant about the bitterness in his creations. He frankly told his readers to look for contemporary reference: "If I might offer any apology for so exaggerated a fiction as the Barnacles and the Circumlocution Office, I would seek it in the common experience of an Englishman, without presuming to mention the unimportant fact of my having done that violence to good manners, in the days of the Russian War, and a Court of Enquiry at Chelsea" (*Little Dorrit*, Preface). Readers of *Little Dorrit* were explicitly invited to see the incompetence and corruption portrayed in the book as a commentary on government in their own time.

After all, the evidence was all around them. Poverty, illiteracy, and disease ran unchecked, as government did nothing on the excuse that its priorities had to be elsewhere. In October 1854, Dickens reminded readers of *Household Words* that ten thousand people had died of cholera in London while the Commons talked only of the funding of a religious community in Maynooth and a crisis in Abyssinia (*Journalism* 3: 227). Similarly, he warned Angela Burdett Coutts that foreign adventures would always be used as excuses to ignore the English poor: "It is more than ever necessary to keep their need of social Reforms before them [the people] at this time, for I clearly see that the War will be made an Administration excuse for all sorts of shortcomings, and that nothing will have been done when the cholera comes again" (*Letters*: 7: 444). In this respect, the Crimean War was a confidence trick. It was a device to label all protest and complaint unpatriotic. Inevitably, "every miserable Red Tapist flourishes the war over the head of every protester against his humbug" (*Letters* 7: 495). It was heart-rending to see war being used to silence criticism of the very incompetence that had brought it about.

Worse still, this tactic of smothering everything in patriotism seemed to work. The English, even the poorest, were too easily distracted from their own just claims on their governors. Dickens saw, "with something like despair," how "the old cannon smoke and blood-mist obscure the wrongs and sufferings of the people at home." It was "as if the world had been pushed back, five hundred years" (*Letters* 7: 454). Nor was this a new experience for him. He had noted in *The Pickwick Papers* that the inhabitants of Muggleton had presented parliaments with 1,420 petitions against slavery abroad and an equal number against any interference with the enormities of the factory system at home (Nayder 2002: 113). Only campaigners for total abstinence seemed to notice the English poor, and Dickens loathed both their moralizing and their determination to add to the miseries of poverty by chaining it in sobriety (*Journalism* 2: 161). No more poignant image of concern for foreign wrongs overlaying injustice at home can be found than in the pages of *Bleak House*. Jo, the impoverished crossing-sweeper, sits on the steps of the Society for the Propagation of the Gospel in Foreign Parts, excluded from its charity because "he is not a genuine, foreign-grown savage" (Chennells and Jacobson 2000: 163–4). Dickens confirmed himself "sick and sour to think of such things at this age of the world" (*Letters* 7: 571).

So the governing elite ignored the English poor and used the excuse of war to cover this neglect. Their irresponsibility was magnified by the attention they gave to the grievances of black and brown peoples in the empire. Joyfully embracing the notion of "the Noble Savage," they lavished praise and assistance on Asians and Africans while denying both to their fellow countrymen. Dickens had no time for such misplaced sentimentality. For him, a savage represented something closer to savagery than nobility. In 1843, Ojibway Indians were exhibited in London, to be followed by Bushmen in 1847 and Zulus in 1853. Crowds flocked to admire their songs, dances, and handicrafts. London society gushed over their primitive nobility, but Dickens begged to differ. In an article entitled "The Noble Savage" printed in *Household Words*

(8: 337–9) in June 1853, he could not have been blunter: "To come to the point at once, I beg to say that I have not the least belief in the Noble Savage. I consider him a prodigious nuisance, and an enormous superstition . . . I call him a savage, and I call a savage a something highly desirable to be civilised off the face of the earth" (*Journalism* 3: 143). The Ojibways only indulged in squatting and spitting, the Bushmen were filthy, and the Zulus "diabolical." It may be no coincidence that one of the most villainous characters in Dickens's novels, Daniel Quilp, was likened to "an African chief squatting on matting" (David 1995: 60).

None of this justified slavery or other violence against indigenous peoples in Dickens's mind. Rather, he simply wanted to criticize the sentimentality with which they were described and the preference given to them over the English poor. Dickens thought it was absurd to pretend that they were basically Englishmen with a different-colored skin. Of course, a black man should be free, but "the melancholy absurdity" of making former slaves voters at present glares out of "every roll of their eyes, chuckle in their mouths, and bump in their heads" (*Letters* 12: 27). Dickens detested missionaries and those who supported them like Mrs. Jellyby in *Bleak House*, who was at the same time capable of weeping over the plight of the inhabitants of Nigeria while remaining oblivious to the poverty that surrounded her at home. For Dickens, this was mere "platform-sympathy with the black" (*Letters* 12: 115), and an insult to the English poor.

The home of this meretricious sentimentality stood in the Strand. Exeter Hall was the forum for all kinds of do-gooding from the Temperance and Anti-Slavery Societies to the YMCA. Its lecturers traveled the land, peddling what Thomas Carlyle called "rose-pink sentimentalism" (Semmel 1962: 19). No fad, from vegetarianism to Bloomerism, was too silly for consideration. In one of the *Sketches by Boz*, entitled "The Ladies Societies," Dickens had practiced a satirical contempt for missionaries:

> The application was successful, the meeting was held; the orator (an Irishman) came. He talked of green isles – other shores – vast Atlantic – bosom of the deep – Christian charity – blood and extermination – mercy in hearts – arms in hands – altars and homes – household gods. He wiped his eyes, blew his nose, and he quoted Latin. The effect was tremendous – the Latin was a decided hit. Nobody knew exactly what it was about, but everybody knew it must be affecting, because even the orator was overcome. (*Journalism* 1: 40).

After 1850, the attack on Exeter Hall and its minions is remorseless. In "Whole Hogs" of August 1851 (*Household Words* 3: 505–7; *Journalism* 3: 21), an account is given of a "Grand Teetotal Demonstration" at the Hall, which was addressed by the "Rev. Jabez Fireworks." Two years later, "Frauds or Fairies" (*Journalism* 3: 167–74) attacked the priggishness that underlay so much of its activities. The essay illustrates Dickens's earlier axiom laid down in "The Niger Expedition": "as a very good general rule of social and political guidance, that whatever Exeter Hall champions, is the thing by no means to be done" (*Journalism* 2: 110).

Under sustained attack, Exeter Hall became a metaphor for everything hypocritical. Wilkie Collins blackened a villain's character in *Hide and Seek* by associating him with its activities (ch. 8). The nonsense pouring out of the Strand could only be the product of hypocrisy or ignorance. Either could lead to the preferring of black and brown people to the English poor. Before the Indian Mutiny in 1857, Dickens was happy to make a distinction between African "savagery" and Indian "culture," but, after that date, such distinctions were lost and only slowly regained (Moore 2004: ch. 6). For him, adventures abroad were designed to bedazzle those in England with legitimate claims on government. He responded to crises abroad from a very insular perspective.

In 1857, Indian troops mutinied across much of northern and central India. Massacres of Europeans, particularly the violation and murder of women and children, badly affected the psychology and values of the imperial power. Dickens followed these events closely, relying once again on the reporting of William Russell, whose journalism he likened to "the most scholarly productions of the most deliberate historians" (*Speeches* 245). Witnessing such atrocities must have been "morally and physically burning" (*Letters* 8: 600). On the basis of evidence such as this, Dickens reacted to the Mutiny by following arguments that had been in gestation for some time.

First, as in the Crimea, there could be nothing but praise for the British common soldier. Once again, they had shown "a Christian resignation under the shadow of death, only to be equaled by the modesty, gentleness, and the perfect and profound self-command always attendant on their great bravery" (*Speeches* 239). Just as heroic had been the courage displayed at Lucknow, Cawnpore, and Delhi. So moved was Dickens by tales of astonishing fortitude that he determined to honor it in print. He began to canvass ideas for a story in homage to "the bravery of our ladies in India." The context should be "circumstances, in which a few English people – gentlemen, ladies and children – and a few English soldiers, would find themselves alone in a strange wild place and liable to hostile attack" (*Letters* 8: 469). The result was "The Island of Silver Shore," written jointly with Wilkie Collins and published in *Household Words* in December 1857. In this tale, a party of English people is betrayed by a treacherous black man into the hands of Caribbean pirates drawn from many different nations, including English convicts. Authority figures prove unable to deal with the crisis, and leadership devolves upon a common soldier and a remarkable woman. The story therefore picks up and expands ideas which had been elements in Dickens's thinking for some time.

Secondly, the Mutiny had cruelly exposed once again the incompetence of British government, which was naturally reflected in the military high command. British troops died under the command of officers who owed their positions to birth and patronage rather than merit (*Letters* 8: 503). Even more startling was the fact that the Mutiny had been provoked by the British authorities affronting Hindu and Muslim sensibilities. Ignorance of the people they governed seemed to be considered a virtue among officials. Angrily Dickens asked:

Why did they know nothing of the Hindoo character? Why? Do you ask why? Because it was the system to know nothing of anything; and to believe that England, while doing nothing, was doing everything. There are Thousands of Asses now – and Asses in power: which is the worst of it – who will hold this faith – if one can dignify such idiocy by the name – until they have done for all of us. (*Letters* 8: 472–3)

This argument was vital for Dickens. Using it, he could bring the Crimean War and the Mutiny into line. Misery abroad was the consequence of mismanagement at home.

Lastly, the Indian disaster forced Dickens's views on race into sharp focus. There would be no ambiguity here. In spite of the lumbering ignorance of British government, Dickens still judged it to be "immeasurably superior to any Asiatic rule" (*Speeches* 247). The Indian princes, so often fêted in London as the most civilized of their kind, were like "dogs – low, treacherous, murderous, tigerous villains" (*Letters* 8: 472–3). In a notorious letter addressed to Miss Burdett Coutts on 4 October 1857, he observed that, if he were in charge of India:

The first thing I would do to strike that Oriental race with amazement (not in the least regarding them as if they lived in the Strand, London, or at Camden Town), should be to proclaim to them, in their language, that I considered my holding that appointment by the leave of God, to mean that I should do my utmost to exterminate the Race upon whom the stain of late cruelties rested. (*Letters* 8: 459)

Admittedly, these words were written in response to hearing of massacres, but the contempt that Dickens had always felt for notions of "the noble Savage" had been of long standing, and was now totally confirmed.

Over time, Dickens tempered his language but never changed his views. In October 1865, a disturbance at Morant Bay in Jamaica led Governor Eyre to hang 364 black residents. The incident provoked a major confrontation in England within the intellectual and parliamentary worlds. A "Jamaica Committee" was formed, involving among others John Stuart Mill, Thomas Hughes, and John Bright, which was determined to prosecute Governor Eyre for a gross misuse of authority. A comparable committee was formed in Eyre's defense. Among Eyre's supporters were numbered Carlyle, Charles Kingsley, John Ruskin, and Alfred, Lord Tennyson.[1] In parliamentary debates and review articles, there was a vigorous debate about the proper relationship between an imperial power and its subject races.

For Dickens, the Morant Bay affair never had the importance of either the Crimean War or the Indian Mutiny. He lent his name to the committee defending Eyre and sent a subscription, but he did nothing more. Only one letter survives in which the business is discussed. It is, however, an important letter, rehearsing as it does most of the major themes in his thinking on British policy overseas:

The Jamaica insurrection is another hopeful piece of business. That platform-sympathy with the black – or the native, or the devil – afar off, and that platform indifference to our own countrymen at enormous odds in the midst of bloodshed and savagery, makes me stark wild . . . So we are badgered about New Zealanders and Hottentots, as if they were identical with men in clean shirts at Camberwell, and were bound by pen and ink accordingly. So Exeter Hall holds us in mortal submission.

Once again, ignorance on the part of the governors matched violence among the governed. Eyre had to be defended from "a knot of nigger philanthropists," but the Jamaica incident profoundly underlined the extent to which England was "ill-governed" (*Letters* 11: 115–16).

As Dickens contemplated British policy abroad between 1854 and 1865, detailed criticism gave way to two great fears. His language became frankly apocalyptic. First, parliament now deserved nothing but contempt. Lords and Commons had become Houses of Incurables. Everything was fatally and "fearfully adulterated" with inaction and corruption (*Speeches* 223). The result was that parliament and the English people were moving further and further apart. Mutual incomprehension created ever greater distance between them. "The popular spirit" was "so entirely separated from the Parliament and Government" that it would be "the death of England" (*Letters* 7: 523). Blunder after blunder led "every man in England [to] feel something of the contempt for the House of Commons that I have" (*Journalism* 2: 221). The greed displayed by the aristocratic classes, and their willful refusal to consider further reform, had "put *their* class in opposition to the country – not the country which puts itself in opposition to them" (*Speeches* 203 n.1).

Secondly, Dickens could only dread the outcome of this polarization. For the moment, a divorce between parliament and people had only resulted in a strange, ominous apathy in the latter. But Dickens was clear that, outside Westminster, there was "that other Public," which, sooner or later, would make just demands (*Journalism* 3: 270). Writing between the great revolutions of 1848 and the Paris Commune of 1871, it was not unreasonable to be fearful. Layard freely likened the condition of England in the 1850s to that of France in 1788 (*Hansard* 136: 1522). Dickens did the same. The national mood, in 1855, was so "extremely like the general mind of France before the breaking out of the first Revolution" that the merest accident could produce "such a Devil of a conflagration as has never been beheld since" (*Letters* 7: 587–8).[2]

Dickens took no comfort, therefore, from the fact that the English had refused the option of revolution in 1848, or from the loyalty of common soldiers to their officers, however incompetent. Such obedience was born of apathy, not affection. Sooner or later, accumulated resentment would break out, and be all the more terrible for being so long contained. As he confessed to a friend: "I become particularly uneasy when I find the Public so apathetic to the inefficiency of the Government. It is a new and unhealthy symptom – the kind of unnatural lull that precedes an earthquake – and I mistrust there being something sullen working among the people, which we don't at all understand" (*Letters* 7: 511). Common soldiers in the Crimea, the English poor, and subject races in India and Jamaica were all in a sense victims of a blistering gangrene at the heart of government. It is easy to describe mid-Victorian England in terms of industrial progress, invention, and the optimism that built the Crystal Palace. This was a view that Dickens could not share.

Notes

1 For details of the crisis, see Semmel (1962). For the case against Eyre, see *Hansard* 181 (February 20, 1866): 920.

2 Dickens developed this point later in *A Tale of Two Cities*, a novel that deliberately links events in France with their counterparts in London.

References and Further Reading

Anderson, B. (1988). *Imagined Communities*. London: Verso.

Brantlinger, P. (1988). *Rule of Darkness: British Literature and Imperialism, 1830–1914*. Ithaca, NY: Cornell University Press.

Chakravarty, G. (2005). *The Indian Mutiny and the British Imagination*. Cambridge: Cambridge University Press.

Chennells, A. and Jacobson, W. (2000). *Dickens and the Children of the Empire*. Basingstoke: Palgrave.

David, D. (1995). *Rule Britannia: Women, Empire and Victorian Writing*. Ithaca, NY: Cornell University Press.

Hansard (1855/1866) *Hansard's Parliamentary Debates*, 3rd series, vols. 136, 138, 181. London: Cornilius Black.

Lohrli, A. (1973). *Household Words*. Toronto: University of Toronto Press.

Moore, G. (2004). *Dickens and Empire: Discoveries of Class, Race and Colonialism in the Works of Charles Dickens*. Aldershot: Ashgate.

Nayder, L. (2002). *Unequal Partners*. Ithaca, NY: Cornell University Press.

Pascoe, D. (Ed.) (1997). *Charles Dickens: Selected Journalism 1850–1870*. London: Penguin.

Philpotts, T. (2003). *The Companion to "Little Dorrit"*. Mountfield: Helm Information.

Poovey, M. (1995). *Making a Social Body: British Cultural Formation, 1830–1864*. Chicago: University of Chicago Press.

Said, E. (1993). *Culture and Imperialism*. London: Chatto and Windus.

Semmel, B. (1962). *Jamaican Blood and Victorian Conscience: The Governor Eyre Controversy*. Westport, CT: Greenwood Press.

Young, R. J. C. (1995). *Colonial Desire: Hybridity in Theory, Culture and Race*. London: Routledge.

16

Dickens and the Uses of History

John Gardiner

Charles Dickens's reputation as an historian has not always been happy. The charge, made by writers like Georg Lukács, is quickly and forcefully leveled: Dickens often takes a cavalier approach to the past, using it merely as a convenient backdrop for purely fictional concerns. In the process, historical generalizations can be so sweeping as to induce giddiness, personal biases so unfair as to dispirit the open-minded reader.

The heart of the problem here is what we expect history to "do" or "be." Yet those who are uncomfortable with Dickens's "use" of the past can themselves be cavalier about historical context. For while it is valid to judge Dickens by the standards of today, it is arguably more instructive still to consider him in the context of the practice of his own day. "Professional" history as we understand it – objective, based on detailed evidence, practiced by experts festooned with academic qualifications – simply did not exist for most of the nineteenth century. By the time of Dickens's death, academic history – History with a capital "H" as it were – was considered a "new" subject, and could not be studied at Oxford or Cambridge until the 1870s.

This is not, of course, to suggest that the Victorians were ignorant of the past. Far from it. At the threshold of modernity, facing the massive disruption of industrialization and urbanization, the impact of evolutionary theory, the blights of disease, high mortality, and social injustice, and, just as Dickens's life was drawing to a close, the first fears about national and racial decline, they turned to history for consolation and inspiration. Heirs to the romantic revolution, they developed an acute awareness of private as well as public history.

Dickens, with his interest in generational history and keen sense of the self's private past, was no exception. Although he made no claims to originality or authority as an historical commentator, his "uses" of history, and his adaptation of various models of historical writing to suit his novelistic purpose, make, I would argue, for a powerful and still too easily underrated intellectual achievement. This chapter considers historical dimensions in three of Dickens's works: *A Child's History of England*, and the novels *Barnaby Rudge* and *A Tale of Two Cities*.

A Child's History of England

The least known of these three works is *A Child's History of England*, published between January 1851 and December 1853 in *Household Words*. Why the neglect? Perhaps it is because Dickens is thought of as a novelist; like his journalism and travel writing, still largely unfamiliar to the general reader, this foray into historical writing might seem somehow "out of character." Perhaps people are skeptical about reading a book "for" children. But perhaps most important is its reputation as a "trouble" work, not especially popular during Dickens's lifetime, and afterwards attracting a thin but steady trickle of dismissals and apologias.

What readers expect from *A Child's History of England* will to a large extent determine their attitude to it. By the standards of modern overviews of English history, including books for children, it has to be said that the work is weak. Its preoccupation with monarchs is restrictive; its impatient close at 1688 is desultory and unsatisfactory for those interested in later history; its lack of dates or clear exposition of dynastic lines is confusing; its biases are politically incorrect; and its bloodthirstiness is vaguely pornographic. (Nor will it do, I think, to defend the work as being "only" for children – a condescending and evasive solution.)

Dickens was not, as we have noted, a recognizably modern, professional historian; neither, perhaps more significantly, was he an experienced historical writer. Accordingly, he may have drawn heavily upon a number of already published sources for *A Child's History of England*, such as Thomas Keightley's *History of England* (1837–9) and Charles Knight's *The Pictorial History of England* (1837–40), "Charles Knight" being a collective pseudonym for a number of authors. Both of these works were in Dickens's library, and carried his annotations. He might have consulted popular children's textbooks like *Mrs. Markham's History of England* by Elizabeth Penrose (1823) and *Little Arthur's History of Britain* by Maria Callcott (1835). And scholars agree that Dickens was probably influenced by David Hume's *History of Great Britain* (1754–61) and the type of history exemplified by Thomas Babington Macaulay in his *History of England* (1849–61; the first two volumes Dickens would have had opportunity to read before undertaking his child's history).

From Keightley he might have picked up a strong anti-papal stance. Not that he need much encouragement to be suspicious of Roman Catholicism. Dickens's comment to Douglas Jerrold in May 1843, when he was first thinking about writing a history book for his six-year-old son Charley, is often quoted: "For I don't know what I should do, if he were to get hold of any conservative or High church notions; and the best way of guarding against any such horrible result, is, I take it, to wring the parrots' necks in his very cradle" (*Letters* 3: 482). There was a delay of nearly eight years before Dickens began working on *A Child's History of England*; part of the renewed impetus at the end of 1850 may have been the "Papal Aggression" scare, when the Pope ("so indefatigable in getting the world into trouble" [ch. 27]) moved to reinstate a Roman Catholic hierarchy in Britain. (Dickens made vitriolic comment on the subject in "A

Crisis in the Affairs of Mr. John Bull" in *Household Words*, November 23, 1850, two months before the same magazine began running the child's history.)

Dickens's anti-Catholicism is tangible in running asides ("the pride and cunning of the Pope and all his men" [ch. 20]), in his black-and-white view of the Reformation ("set the people free from their slavery to the priests" [ch. 28]), and in effectively ending the work in 1688 with the Glorious Revolution, when "the Protestant religion was established in England" (ch. 36). As prejudices go, it is not necessarily worse than others in the work (racism and anti-Irishness, for example, or wholesale dynastic dismissal of the Stuarts as "a public nuisance altogether" [ch. 37]), but it is characteristic of Dickens's bumptious mid-Victorian voice. A number of topical references seem to be made: in praising the United States for being "honourably remarkable for protecting its subjects, wherever they may travel" (ch. 37), Dickens may be alluding to Lord Palmerston's decision in 1850 to send the Royal Navy to protect the interests of an individual claiming British citizenship in Greece.

Patriotism, jingoism, and a Christian God (rather given, in a twist of Dickensian violence, to Old Testament smiting) are very much part of *A Child's History of England*. These are qualities with which many in mid-Victorian Britain would have identified. One of these was Thomas Babington Macaulay, the Whig MP and historian of whom Lord Melbourne once commented: "I wish I was as cocksure of anything as Tom Macaulay is of everything." Macaulay is the man generally credited as being the epitome of the Whig version of history. Originating from the mid-seventeenth century, when parliamentary lawyers drew up the case against Charles I, and taking account of such subsequent landmarks as the Glorious Revolution and the 1832 Reform Act, this emphasized the continuity of parliamentary development and the individual's freedom from tyranny. It was reflected in optimistic, forwards-moving linear narratives, and, with its eye always on the sunny uplands of the present, ransacked the past to bolster and flatter contemporary interests.

It is not hard to see how this confidently judgmental approach to history would have appealed to Dickens. Although he claimed that *A Child's History of England* embodied a defense of "The People," his approach to what we would now call social and economic history is thin, and his attitude to ordinary people ambivalent: this is almost entirely a briskly forwards-moving story of kings, queens, and famous events, with sideways digressions only to paint vignettes of individual (and almost invariably famous) figures. Macaulay worked a celebrated slice of social history into his *History of England*, describing the country in 1685, but he was focused on the light shone by the political and religious settlement of 1688–9, and had little time for the dark obscurities of the past.

So too, in many ways, Dickens. Hume's *History of Great Britain* may have provided an outline structure and basic materials for Dickens, beginning with the Druids and ending with the Glorious Revolution, as does *A Child's History of England*; yet Hume's predilection toward nuance and cautious skepticism, supporting civil liberties while avoiding an explicitly party-political approach to the past, was felt to be fussy and uncommitted by Victorians of Macaulay's ilk. (And perhaps of Dickens's: his sweeping dismissal of the Stuarts reads almost as a robust response to Hume's thoughtful defense of a family line all too easily caricatured.)

Progress was the thing for Macaulay and Dickens, and we know much about Dickens's impatience with old practices. Often cited are the titles of the false book-backs in his study in the 1850s: "The Wisdom of our Ancestors" comprising volumes on "Ignorance," "Superstition," "The Block," "The Stake," "The Rack," "Dirt," and "Disease." In *A Child's History of England* his condescension toward the past, and those who would idealize it, comes out in recurrent use of the word "improve" in early chapters, in dry qualifications ("King Stephen was, for the time in which he lived, a humane and moderate man" [ch. 11]) and in more developed set-pieces, such as the savagely exhilarating satire on Charles II as the "Merry Monarch" (ch. 35):

> Let me try to give you a general idea of some of the merry things that were done, in the merry days when this merry gentleman sat upon his merry throne, in merry England . . . Ten [people who had supported Charles I's execution] were merrily executed . . . These executions were so extremely merry, that every horrible circumstance which Cromwell had abandoned was revived with appalling cruelty. The hearts of the sufferers were torn out of their living bodies; their bowels were burned before their faces; the executioner cut jokes to the next victim, as he rubbed his filthy hands together, that were reeking with the blood of the last; and the heads of the dead were drawn on sledges with the living to the place of suffering.

The approving reference to Oliver Cromwell (a "great genius" who ruled England "wisely" [ch. 34]), probably reinforced, incidentally, by the bicentennial craze for all things Cromwellian, reminds us of how few famous individuals emerge favorably from Dickens's pages. He is remarkably hostile to most English rulers, finding them time and again to be cruel, duplicitous, and self-serving. (The epitaph on Henry VIII – "a blot of blood and grease upon the History of England" [ch. 28] – is unusual only in its extremity.) Alfred alone emerges with much credit, again perhaps echoing how Victorian historians traced the origins of English political liberty to Saxon times. (Dickens being Dickens, he tempers his enthusiasm with comments on Saxon back-wardness: "greedy eaters and great drinkers . . . their feasts were often of a noisy and drunken kind" [ch. 3].)

Other figures to emerge creditably include the Black Prince, given romantic treat-ment, and the rebels Simon de Montfort and Wat Tyler. Dickens himself thought *A Child's History of England* iconoclastic, and indeed, even across the safe span of five centuries, his comment that, in comparison with Richard II, Tyler easily emerges "the truer and more respectable man of the two" (ch. 19) is striking. (Dickens the loyal patriot will have the last say in the work, however, with the flourish "God save the Queen!") If Tyler is a champion of the people, then de Montfort is seen, as he tended to be seen by Victorians, as a martyr to the parliamentary ideal.

So long as there was a worthy cause behind uprisings in the past – and that gener-ally meant curbing abuses of royal power – Dickens's anxiety about anarchy could be kept at bay. Yet the mob does appear at various points in *A Child's History of England*, with the anti-Jewish riots under Richard I (ch. 13) described in terms strongly reminiscent of the riot scenes in *Barnaby Rudge*:

> the crowd rushed through the narrow streets of [London], slaughtering all the Jews they met; and when they could find no more out of doors (on account of their having fled to their houses, and fastened themselves in), they ran madly about, breaking open all the houses where the Jews lived, rushing in and stabbing or spearing them, sometimes even flinging old people and children out of window into blazing fires they had lighted up below.

Dickens's treatment of Jews in *A Child's History of England* provides valuable reading for anybody uncomfortable with his portrayal of Fagin. It is not an engagement with Jewish history or culture in its own terms, or in any depth, but more a recurrent motif for how innocent people can be victimized by the mob or by political oppression, as with the Jews' expulsion from England (ch. 16). (Dickens's capacity for empathizing with victimhood is strikingly revealed, too, given his anti-Catholicism, in his dismissal of claims that Catholics started the Great Fire of London as "a malicious and stupid untruth" [ch. 35].)

Mention of this imaginative strength brings us to some of the other positive and resonant qualities in the work. Since G. K. Chesterton, there has been a tradition of viewing *A Child's History of England* not as a scholarly work but as one with close correspondences to the often theatrical presentation of history in *Barnaby Rudge* and *A Tale of Two Cities*. This makes good, if obvious, sense. What complicates this theatrical or novelistic reading of the work – or perhaps more accurately lends credence to it – is Dickens's inconsistencies and reversals of feeling. Occasionally, his imagination is fired by a particular event, or by individuals in suddenly reduced circumstances. Such sympathy is extended, for example, to Charles I as he makes his preparations to die (ch. 33); once the oppressor becomes the condemned, Dickens's portrayal is far more inward and human. He was clearly fascinated, too, by Perkin Warbeck (ch. 26), pretender to Henry VII's throne. The story of the *doppelgänger* who claimed to be one of the princes in the Tower exercises Dickens's novelistic imagination, haunted as it was by doubles, at some length. (Far more, it might be added, than the exploits of Christopher Columbus, hastily shuffled off in the space of a mere sentence at the end of the chapter.)

Ultimately, though, *A Child's History of England* does not present Dickens at anywhere near the top of his form. To defend it in the light of what it tells us about Dickens, and its echoes and pre-echoes of various novelistic devices, is, at heart, an exercise in damage limitation. History – "straight" history – was not really his medium. The relative lack of control over "characters" and "plot" did not suit his creative identity, which has repetitive recourse to the merely bloody. (There are some nice asides – "Hung high or hung low, however, hanging is much the same to the person hung" [ch. 26] – but how lacking is *A Child's History of England* in Dickens's usual humor.)

Nor, arguably, did he get the most out of his linear model. Partly this is because, while a believer in progress, Dickens was less certain that the mid-Victorian present represented the apogee of political and social development. A defender of the parliamentary ideal, Dickens had little time for most contemporary politicians and their hot air, and shortly after completing *A Child's History of England* would launch a series of scathing attacks on the government's direction of the Crimean War (see chapter 15). Equally, the work's comments on racial "backwardness" ("The Indians of North America, – a very inferior people to the Saxons, though – do the same [name people after animals] to this day" [ch. 2]), though by implication reserving top slot for the mid-Victorian English male, suggest anxieties about human evolution which contemporaries like Darwin were just then mapping out.

The linear model may also have been less congenial to Dickens because of the nature of his mental processes. His was a mind that seemingly worked in roundabout ways, responding more readily to the power of unexpected developments, repetition, and the hold of past over present – all aspects of storytelling (whether "real" history or imagined) not best served by linearity. And it is the non-linear approach, tellingly enough, that is explored with growing power and sophistication in Dickens's historical fiction.

Barnaby Rudge

Dickens's two historical novels occupy an overlapping timespan: in the case of *Barnaby Rudge* (excluding the final summary chapter), 1775 to 1780, and in *A Tale of Two Cities*, 1775 to 1794. The impact of the French Revolution (discussed below) helps partly to explain his interest in this period, but the setting of both novels at this time suggests something beyond coincidence. *Barnaby Rudge* has for its main historical prop the Gordon Riots of June 1780. This uprising, in which a mob rampaged through London for eight days attacking private homes and public property (including – the climax of Dickens's depiction – Newgate prison), was brought about by resistance to government measures to improve the rights of Catholics. The Protestant Association, led by Lord George Gordon, was the mere catalyst; for violent and criminal elements took over, and the riots have been identified by historians as an expression of wider political, social, and economic unrest in the late eighteenth century.

In 1841, when Dickens was writing *Barnaby Rudge*, much of this unrest was in a sense unfinished business. Two key pieces of legislation had been passed since 1780: Catholic Emancipation in 1829, allowing Catholics to hold public office and be MPs, and the Reform Act in 1832, extending the vote to only about a fifth of men in England and Wales, but signaling, nevertheless, the government's ability to adjust the electoral map. Both are seen in hindsight as important measures. Both were seen at the time, at least by certain parties, as failures. Catholic Emancipation alienated many people, leading to a wave of petitions and the rekindling of ancient hostility. The Reform Act disappointed hopes that extended back at least to 1780, with the

American Revolution an inspiring backdrop for reformers and the French Revolution still to come.

Not enough men had the vote, reformers felt, identifying the vote as the means by which social and economic deprivation might be addressed. Britain in the 1840s, the "Hungry Forties" as they became known, was still in a state of painful adjustment to industrial and urban life, with recurrent trade depressions, widespread poverty, dangerous working conditions, and almost non-existent public health measures in cities. *Barnaby Rudge* needs to be seen in the context of a number of protests against these conditions: the movement against the New Poor Law, of which Dickens was part; the agitation against the Corn Laws; the trade unionism of the 1830s (reflected in the novel's 'Prentice Knights); and incidents such as the attempted assassination of Queen Victoria by a supposed madman in June 1840.

What Dickens and his contemporaries would have found the most troubling symptom of social unrest, however, was Chartism. Formed in 1838, the Chartist movement had at its core the radical notion of votes for all men. What was "radical" about this was the way that it flew in the face of established political practice. It was, after all, the profound conviction of the political and social elite that not all men were fit for the vote. What of the poorly educated or weak-minded (such as Dickens's Barnaby) who had no sense of politics? What of those with no material stake in the nation who might take their responsibilities less seriously? What of the immoral? What of the fanatics who might want to go further and overthrow government altogether?

Chartism operated largely through the presentation of "monster" petitions to parliament (the last, in 1848, claimed by supporters to contain over 5 million signatures). But there were more violent elements within the movement, and the rising of November 1839 in Newport, Wales, in which 20 Chartists were killed following a shoot-out with government troops, must almost certainly have fed into Dickens's sense of mob violence in *Barnaby Rudge*.

It is ultimately a little too difficult to tell. We know that Dickens drew on a number of published accounts such as the *Narrative of the Late Riots* (1780) by William Vincent (really Thomas Holcroft), *Historical Memoirs of My Own Time* (1815) by Nathaniel Wraxall, and *The Life of General Gordon* (1795) by Robert Watson, all of which played up the Gordon Riots as a political plot against the government, feasibly even an attempted revolution. These he supplemented with the anti-revolutionary musings of Edmund Burke, eyewitness accounts from Hester Thrale, Frederick Reynolds, and Samuel Romilly, and a trawl for picturesque detail through contemporary newspapers and the *Annual Register* for 1780. This is a fairly impressive array of sources. Yet, rumblings of social and economic discontent aside, the mob in *Barnaby Rudge* has no set of coherent objectives. How could it, when Dickens is so intent on dissolving all identities save those of his principal characters (none of whom is a purely political radical) in a vortex of collective violence? (Rudge Senior, indeed, even talks of hiding himself away in the mob: "my only hope of safety lay in joining them" [ch. 62], a gesture that resonates even more paradoxically when we know how many rioters were killed and how many were condemned to death – 62 in the first instance – after their arrest.)

Concerning the contemporary resonances that the Gordon Riots may have had for Dickens, a very complicated attitude is perhaps best put concisely: for all Dickens's sympathy with the downtrodden poor, and for all his anger with government neglect, he believed in changing things by peaceful constitutional means, and was fearful of the potential for anarchy unleashed by the mob. That fear was shared by many in Dickens's day, partly because, in an age of greater social stratification, there was often less middle- and upper-class sense of (and hence less sympathy for) the reality of working-class existence. Something unknown became something threatening and inferior; something threatening and inferior became, *en masse*, something easily given to the destructive and brutish.

Dickens the middle-class conservative speaks out in the portrayal of mob violence in *Barnaby Rudge*: amidst the inferno, the fate of sparrows (ch. 64) and canaries ("the poor little creatures screamed, it was said, like infants" [ch. 66]) signals the wrongness of what is going on in a novel that has a bird as one of its most agreeable characters. The mob, "composed for the most part of the very scum and refuse of London" (ch. 49) is frequently described as a living sea (thereby anticipating *A Tale of Two Cities*); as a "mad monster" (ch. 49); as an agent of "moral plague" (ch. 53); and as demons (ch. 55): "The more the fire crackled and raged, the wilder and more cruel the men grew; as though moving in that element they became fiends, and changed their earthly nature for the qualities that give delight in hell." As in *A Child's History of England*, Dickens puts aside his anti-Catholicism to sympathize with the victims of the mob (ch. 61): Dickens was never one to side with tyrants or bullies. (The Oxford Movement had just begun to gain serious notoriety around the time that *Barnaby Rudge* was written; one wonders whether Dickens's sympathy would have been quite so generous had the novel been written, say, five years later.)

Yet Dickens is always so hard to pin down. While clearly unsympathetic to the 'Prentice Knights and the fetish they make of "the Constitution" (ch. 8), echoing Dickens's real-life ambivalence toward trade unions, about the mob proper he is less clear cut. An instinctive feel for the anarchic and the violent complicates his attitude, so that outer manner and inner compulsion pull in different directions. In terms of historical accuracy, Dickens is diligent (the account of rioters drinking burning spirits [ch. 68], for example, is based on fact); and the stance of horrified disapproval is impeccably middle-class Victorian. But the disapproval – or more exactly the horror – is anything but sober in itself; rather, it has a visceral abandon and grim joy in the shape-shifting and normality-dissolving chaos, the stream of molten lead from a roof that dissolves one young rioter's head "like wax" (ch. 55) being only one of a series of gruesomely indelible effects.

The portrayal of Hugh, too, suggests the contradictory nature of Dickens's attitude to the rioters. Hugh is both user of the mob and someone who is used by it, initially mistaking the Protestant Association cry of "No Popery!" for "No Property!" (ch. 38) and not caring about the error so long as he is taken on to pursue his violent nature, but at the close of the novel he makes the "savage prophet" speech about the lot of victims in society (ch. 77). Like the mob, he has a physical presence that is both threatening and, perhaps because threatening, alluring (a point reinforced by several of Hablot Knight Browne's original illustrations). Dickens refers to him as being "like a handsome satyr," and has Sir John Chester call him a "centaur" (chs 15, 23, 75). These references are hardly coincidental: just as the Pan-like (Pan-ic) Hugh emerges through the trees to induce panic in Dolly (ch. 21) – a scene charged with sexual danger – so might the animalism of the mob of which he becomes part have carried for Dickens-the-respectable-Victorian a frisson of inner excitement.

With Barnaby himself, the case is slightly different. His "blindness of the intellect" (ch. 45) makes him a political innocent who is corrupted by the mob. The French revolutionary mob may, it has been argued, have formed part of the idea behind Frankenstein's monster. Dickens appears to have known *Frankenstein* (there is an allusion to it in *Great Expectations*), and it is tempting to see him playing in *Barnaby Rudge* with ideas from that earlier work. In particular, the confrontation between Stagg and Mrs. Rudge (chs. 45–6) reads like a dark mirror-image of the scene in Shelley's novel where the monster meets the blind man in his cottage. This confrontation sends Barnaby and his mother back to London, where they are caught up in the early stages of Gordon's agitation. Both monsters are ejected from a private haven: Dickens's equally innocent "monster" into the hands of a far more pernicious monster and onto the stage of public history.

Indeed, the relationship of private to public history in *Barnaby Rudge* is a key element in Dickens's handling of the past. The writings of Sir Walter Scott, especially the *Waverley* novels, were an important influence on Dickens's conception of the historical novel. Scott's exploration of the relationship between private individuals and the public world is echoed in both Dickens's historical novels. So, too, is Scott's interest in generational dynamics and how past events can shape and impinge on present-day reality. Other literary influences may have included the conventions of Gothic fiction (the novel has its fair complement of ruins, shadows, and ghosts), as well as Tobias Smollett, Oliver Goldsmith, and Henry Fielding (an early interweaver of "real" history with fiction), and Thomas Carlyle, whose "Chartism" (1839) would have supplied Dickens with a more apocalyptic view of mob unrest.

Scott set *Waverley* (1814) 60 years in the past. This is a precedent Dickens followed in both *Barnaby Rudge* and *A Tale of Two Cities*, each of which was written at about that remove of history. To a limited degree – Dickens not sharing Scott's interest in the precise delineation of political and social change – this allowed him to trace the origins of certain modern trends. Sixty years is also, however, a resonant period of time for human beings: roughly a lifetime for a healthy, middle-class Victorian, or three generations' worth. Dickens, always so sensitive to family and generational history, set many of his novels not in the present but a generation or two back, which makes the two historical novels under discussion less of an anomaly. So we should not rush to assume that Dickens used the platform of the historical novel to impart a particular "theory" about the late eighteenth century.

His attitude to that period is, in fact, less flatly condescending than some have suggested. (The opening paragraph of *A Tale of Two Cities* – really a joke against distorted historical characterization – repays careful reading for those who think otherwise.) It does admittedly, though, tend more toward the condescending than not. In *Barnaby Rudge*, the "profound obstinacy and slowness of apprehension" of John Willet, lapped up by his Maypole cronies, may hint at the torpidity of life in "olden times" (ch. 1). More troublingly, Sir John Chester, that "smooth man of the world" as Haredale puts it (ch. 12), embodies, in his calculating hypocrisy and effete rationality, easily exaggerated aspects of the Enlightenment that Dickens and other Victorians loathed. The attack on Chester, sustained in oleaginous prose throughout *Barnaby Rudge*, is even more vitriolic than the attack on the aristocrats in *A Tale of Two Cities*.

If Dickens has any theory at all about the recent past, it may be, as Patrick Brantlinger (2001) has argued, that it is the patriarchal generation's duty to rule responsibly. What links the first half of *Barnaby Rudge* (where, famously, no "real" historical events occur) with the second half is the theme of paternalism. The mob violence is a kind of psychic reaction thrown up by the consequences of corrupt leadership and flawed fathers, whether it is in the neglected state of London (ch. 16), the ineffectual Lord Mayor (ch. 61), Barnaby's being driven into the mob by the "ghost" of his father (ch. 48), or in the revelation that Hugh is Sir John Chester's bastard son (ch. 75). Chester is also an unloving father to Edward, which reminds us of other examples of paternal or avuncular misrule: the overbearing John Willet and the overprotective Geoffrey Haredale. Only Gabriel Varden emerges as an exemplary father-figure in *Barnaby Rudge*, this status established at an early point by the "coherent and sensible advice" he offers in the quarrel between Joe Willet and his father (ch. 3). It is not therefore surprising that Varden serves as a center of moral gravity against the rioters. His stout resistance to them, if nothing else, signals where Dickens's conscious sympathies lay (ch. 63).

Perhaps this helps to explain why *Barnaby Rudge* does not, for all the relative carefulness of Dickens's research, give us an especially sharp insight into the political history of the late eighteenth century. One of its wry little jokes – and again, it has good historical basis – is that Lord George Gordon is mentally unsound, a figure more of pathos than anything else. His meeting with Barnaby (ch. 57) shows more than a little correspondence between the characters of the two men. (The real villain of the riots is, of course, Gashford, the equivalent on the novel's "historical" stage to Sir John Chester on its "imaginary" stage. Dickens based Gashford on Robert Watson, whose elderly body he may actually have viewed in 1838.) Gordon's hollowness, a hollowness that Dickens perhaps exaggerates, is echoed by the dangerous incoherence of the mob.

Dickens is not primarily interested in *Barnaby Rudge* in political or social history as we might recognize it today. Yet he does explore how individuals' private pasts can affect the present, and be illuminated against the backdrop of those events that make up the record of public history. What we see in *Barnaby Rudge* is Dickens beginning to master a non-linear approach to history, an approach that sees tensions in the first half of the novel echoed and then resolved by tensions in the second half: two great overlapping cycles of private and public history. This non-linearity, and this fascination with how private and public histories overlap, is something he would explore even more richly in *A Tale of Two Cities*.

A Tale of Two Cities

Eighteen years separate *Barnaby Rudge* from *A Tale of Two Cities*, published in 1859. Much had changed in that time. The "Hungry Forties" had been weathered, and, while social injustice was rife and wealth far from evenly spread, the Great Exhibition of 1851 had confidently declared Britain's arrival as the "workshop of the world." The political arrangement of 1832 had not been significantly altered, but Chartism had died out, its last flurry coinciding (peacefully) with revolutions across Europe in 1848. For the peace and prosperity that Britain had achieved, for the relative social harmony and adjustment to industrial life, historians have seen fit to describe the 1850s and 1860s as something separate from the troubled 1840s – this is the mid-Victorian period, high noon, the age of equipoise.

Whether contemporaries would have agreed with such epithets is, of course, a moot point. Dickens, never one to rest on his laurels, still less to be satisfied with a political and social elite that did the same, would almost certainly not. Significantly, *A Tale of Two Cities* is dedicated to Lord John Russell, the Whig statesman who had been so important in pushing through the 1832 Reform Act, and who had sponsored an unsuccessful reform bill as recently as 1854. Opponents of the bill had deployed all the usual arguments: that 1832 had gone quite far enough (some would say too far); that the best interests of the nation would not be served by giving the vote to men without sufficient material interest or social accountability; that tinkering with the constitution was a slippery slope that could lead to disaster. And the disaster of disasters, the nightmare that would have had politicians clammily waking in the early hours, was a British repetition of the French Revolution.

It is difficult to exaggerate the impact of the French Revolution on mid-Victorian political sensibilities, not least because, though 60 years off by the 1850s, it was still in what might be called imaginative currency, just as World War II is still (just) in imaginative currency today. As we have seen, the Victorians prided themselves on being the heirs of the Glorious Revolution of 1688, a revolution that was glorious, they would have reminded us, on grounds of it being not only constitutional and Protestant but bloodless. In works like *Reflections on the Revolution in France* (1790) by Edmund Burke, a view of British political development was propounded in which the emphasis was firmly placed on organic evolution. Evolution not revolution; continuity not disruption; harmony not bloodshed.

Many of these priorities were shared by Dickens, good Victorian that he was, and, as we have seen, a man deeply troubled by the violent mentality of the mob. But the point about Dickens's lack of social complacency holds true; and his view of what oppression can drive people to, coming as it does near the end of *A Tale of Two Cities*, might almost have been addressed to those politicians who had thrown out Russell's reform bill only a few years before (bk. 3, ch. 15): "Crush humanity out of shape once more, under similar hammers, and it will twist itself into the same tortured forms. Sow the same seed of rapacious licence and oppression over again, and it will surely yield the same fruit according to its kind."

These images of sowing and reaping, pregnant perhaps with an allusion to the Grim Reaper, echo the Burkean notion of the nation-state as an organic entity, and even more the world of the work that was Dickens's greatest model for *A Tale of Two Cities*, Thomas Carlyle's *History of the French Revolution* (1837). A great deal has been written about Carlyle's influence on Dickens, and about how, responding to a request for research materials from Dickens, Carlyle sent two cartloads of books from the London Library round to Dickens's home. The story goes that Dickens started wading through these but soon realized that Carlyle had synthesized them so brilliantly that he was content to return to that "wonderful book" as his main source.

The story can be a little misleading. It is worth noting that *A Tale of Two Cities* is based on a far wider range of material than once believed. Dickens appears to have consulted, for example, the *Annual Register* for 1774 through to 1776; Louis-Sébastien Mercier's contemporary accounts of Parisian street life, prison conditions, and aristocratic salons (one of Dickens's more fantastic-seeming conceits, the four servants helping the Monseigneur to his cup of hot chocolate [bk. 2, ch. 7], is based on fact); Rousseau; Dumas; Arthur Young's accounts of traveling through pre-revolutionary France; trial accounts (Darnay's trial [bk. 2, chs 2–3] possibly being based on that of Francis Henry de la Motte in 1781); and prison memoirs from those who had been incarcerated in the Bastille like Henri Masers de Latude and Simon-Nicolas-Henri Linguet.

This is impressive testimony to Dickens's determination to make *A Tale of Two Cities* rooted in something like concrete fact. In the Preface he talks about any references being "truly made, on the faith of the most trustworthy witnesses." Still, we should not, I think, take this as indication of Dickens suddenly developing acute sensitivity to historical objectivity, partly because he admitted in the same Preface that his novel was intended only as an addition to "the popular and picturesque means of understanding that terrible time," and, more importantly, because truth, for Dickens, really meant dramatic and emotional truth. Facts were to be respected, but it was the significance of these facts for human beings that counted for so much more.

It was Carlyle's view of history that Dickens most readily assimilated in pondering the significance of all this evidence. Thomas Carlyle, a friend of Dickens from the 1840s, had an essentially apocalyptic view of history. He disliked modernity, and, though not a religious man in the conventional sense, his writing is imbued with quasi-mysticism. Behind all his humans, buffeted around as if in an Old Testament story, lie the arcane workings of agents like Time and Eternity. For Carlyle, history did not follow a progressive linear course, but moved in large cycles with the kind of elasticity that gave the present access to both the past and the future. Carlyle's distrust of man-made social theory, his vision of the French Revolution as a tragic cleansing of a corrupt old order (tragic because the violence came to consume the revolutionaries too), and his readiness to collapse past, present, and future – all these appealed to Dickens's imagination, in itself no stranger to the apocalyptic.

Many of Carlyle's key themes, for example the fall of the Bastille and the Terror, are replicated in *A Tale of Two Cities*. So is some of Carlyle's grandly rhetorical style. Carlyle writes, for instance, about the emotional "noise" of men driven by instinct. This noise, he comments, is "the greatest a man encounters, among the sounds and shadows which make up this World of Time. He who can resist that, has his footing somewhere *beyond* Time." In Dickens's work, too, there is reference to the "powerful enchanter, Time," when again, perhaps significantly, Carton talks about heaven as an escape from the exigencies of time (bk. 3, ch. 15). Such correspondences can be over-drawn, and indeed there are significant differences between the approaches of Carlyle and Dickens, not least in Dickens's gentler Christian optimism and in his more tren-chant belief in the power of the individual to withstand what time (or, more grandly, Time) can do to us.

A Tale of Two Cities is a novel just as much about private as public history, and about the connections between the two. Here we find history not necessarily being driven by individuals (famous revolutionary leaders, Danton, Robespierre, and so on, are noticeably absent), but history being lived and influenced by individuals. Indi-vidual influence was important to Dickens; and that, perhaps, helps to explain why *A Tale of Two Cities* has a small cast of closely interrelated principal characters. What is being articulated is a view of history attuned to a moral understanding of how individuals might relate to one another. (Put this way, the revolutionary mob, treated as an inhuman "living sea" [bk. 2, ch. 21], is largely an abhorrent irrelevance; it is really individuals' power to send others to the guillotine that provides emotional grip in Book 3.)

In earlier novels, Dickens had already explored how individuals' pasts, usually unhappy or compromising ones, can catch up with their present and endanger their future. That elastic sense of time is developed even further in *A Tale of Two Cities*. Across this tautly structured work, Dickens stretches two carefully interwoven histori-cal strands. One is the public and "real" history of the French Revolution, a history with which many of Dickens's original readers would have been well acquainted. Like them, we know what is coming; and, even more than the succession of actual events, it is the placing of a series of ominous symbols that delineates the unfolding tragedy.

These symbols resonate like musical motifs, and are either pre-echoes of the future or grim echoes of a past that has already stumbled to disaster. They include the (semi-biblical) analogy of wine or water with blood (bk. 1, ch. 5; bk. 2, ch. 9; bk. 3, ch. 2); knitting, the notorious pastime of women around the guillotine (bk. 1, ch. 6; bk. 2, ch. 7; bk. 2, chs. 15–16; bk. 3, chs. 14–15); and footsteps, perhaps most explicitly, but also most hauntingly, measuring the tread of time (bk. 2, ch. 6; bk. 2, ch. 21; bk. 3, ch. 7). Before the revolution, for example, Doctor Manette, Lucie, and Darnay sit at home in London, in a place described as "a wonderful corner for echoes," awaiting the pathetic fallacy of a thunderstorm. Lucie reflects: "I have sometimes sat alone here of an evening, listening, until I have made the echoes out to be the echoes of all the footsteps that are coming by-and-by into our lives" (bk. 2, ch. 6).

The other strand stretched across *A Tale of Two Cities* is the private history of Dickens's imagined characters. In as far as we know that parts of the novel have striking resonances with Dickens's own personal life in the late 1850s, above all his love for Ellen Ternan, this is not to be overlooked. Perhaps more importantly, though, it does not make sense to separate the public from the private (or the real from the imaginary) in Dickens's view of history, because he saw the past as a backdrop against which to project and develop a moral view of the world in which the private histories of people help to determine the impact they have on public history. That is how "real" life is experienced, and how "real" history is made. Dickens understood and portrayed that in *A Tale of Two Cities* even more powerfully than in *Barnaby Rudge*.

So encumbered with memory and trauma is *A Tale of Two Cities* that it has a peculiar mood, again making elastic our sense of time, by which the possibility of death-in-life is repeatedly put forward. Doctor Manette is "recalled to life" (the title of Book 1); Darnay, on acquittal from his trial as a spy, has the same epithet attached (bk. 1, ch. 3), but again, on being imprisoned in Paris, thinks to himself "Now I am left, as if I were dead" (bk. 3, ch. 1); Carton proclaims "I am like one who died young" (bk. 2, ch. 13); and arguably the most surreal passage in the novel is when young Jerry Cruncher (the son of a "Resurrection man") imagines himself being chased down the street by a living coffin (bk. 2, ch. 14).

All of this Dickens connects, with mounting explicitness of biblical reference ("I am the Resurrection and the Life"), to the idea of love as a force of resurrection. Despite the inward prison of memory, both the traumatized Doctor Manette and melancholic Carton allow themselves to be saved by love, and, in doing so, make it possible for Darnay, Lucie, and their daughter to be saved. (Carton's prison is consistently darker than Manette's, and he is effectively a living corpse until emotional resurrection by bodily sacrifice at the last.) By contrast, Madame Defarge, the harpy-like figure who represents the spirit of revolutionary vengeance, allows the prison of her own unhappy memories to corrupt her feelings. She is the link to the more public and literal theater of death-in-life that is Paris during the Terror, the guillotine's status as the outcome of the death of love signaled by the grim comment on it replacing the Cross and becoming "the sign of the regeneration of the human race" (bk. 3, ch. 4).

Public history, Dickens seems to be saying in *A Tale of Two Cities*, is made by individuals with private histories; and however sympathetic we may be to the suffering that shapes those private histories, we should remember that public history can go tragically wrong if people allow themselves to be consumed by bitterness. There is a choice. The sins of forefathers (Darnay's story shows) do not have to be visited on the living; we can try not to yield to memories and impulses that will incarcerate us in ill-feeling or inhumanity.

On that note, it may be worth pointing out that in *A Tale of Two Cities*, this most temporally sensitive of works, Dickens's interest in doubles is turned to fascinating account as a comment on contingency. A sense of contingency, of how things might have turned out otherwise, is not always to be expected from Victorian historical writing, especially that of the Whig variety. It would be idle to suggest that Dickens was in any way attempting to add nuance to his depiction of the past, as much as anything because his primary consideration would understandably, and rightly, have been novelistic.

And yet it is interesting how Carton and Darnay, the look-alikes who between them bear the load of autobiographical identification for Dickens, follow trajectories that are at times like negative images of one another, yet, under the pressure of public events at the end of the novel, come to cross physically and then complement one another: Darnay for the second time recalled to physical life with his escape from Paris, Carton recalled to emotional life with his bodily sacrifice. Dickens sentimentally reassures us that Carton is remembered by Darnay and his wife, and has a boy named after him; but it is the earlier comment about Lucie's children (one, significantly, a dead boy) having "a strange sympathy with him – an instinctive delicacy of pity" (bk. 2, ch. 21), recognizing him as their father-that-might-have-been, which lingers more in the memory; that, and the terse little comment as Darnay writes his valedictory letters in prison in Paris (bk. 3, ch. 13): "He never thought of Carton. His mind was so full of the others, that he never once thought of him."

It is here that Dickens sketches in both a ghostly alternative to the tale he recounts, and shows that eighteenth-century people were as much vulnerable to the inscrutability of others' minds, and to the unknowability of the future, as those in any age. By projecting these insights backwards, and humanizing what he found there through the story of individual characters, he provided Victorian readers with a consoling vision of the past. It is a vision which still has its consolations.

REFERENCES AND FURTHER READING

Bowler, P. J. (1989). *The Invention of Progress: The Victorians and the Past.* Oxford: Oxford University Press.

Brantlinger, P. (2001). Did Dickens have a philosophy of history? The case of *Barnaby Rudge*. *Dickens Studies Annual*, 30, 59–74.

Glancy, R. (1993). *A Tale of Two Cities: An Annotated Bibliography.* New York: Garland.

Rice, T. J. (1987). *Barnaby Rudge: An Annotated Bibliography.* New York: Garland.

Sanders, A. (1978). *The Victorian Historical Novel, 1840–1880.* London: Macmillan.

— (2002). *The Companion to A Tale of Two Cities.* Mountfield: Helm Information.

17

Dickens and Christianity

Valentine Cunningham

Dickens is, of course, a Christian writer. A very English, Protestant, and Anglican-inflected one. He is steeped, as most Victorian writers were, in the knowledge, the words, the stories, the rhetoric, the practices of the national religion, but to a quite outstanding degree. His parents, worldly theater-lovers, notoriously did not go much to church, but he, it would seem, could hardly stay away. Wherever he was, in London, in Europe, in America, he was drawn to Christian assemblies. Sermon-tasting was what he did a lot of on Sundays.

He was baptized conventionally into the Church of England, and, like his beloved sister Fanny, was sent regularly to church. Church of England on Sunday morning, chapel on Sunday evening. Whichever female it was who scrubbed him up and dragged him off on a Sunday evening to some Chatham chapel to "sit under" the powerful preaching of the Rev. Boanerges Boiler – a servant maybe, but nobody knows – the recollection in "City of London Churches" has the ring and vehemence of personal experience about it, for all the Dickensian conventions of its satirical thrusts – being "steamed like a potato in the unventilated breath" of the Boiler and his congregation, and so forth (*Journalism* 4: 108). On weekdays, the young Dickens attended the school in Chatham run by the local Baptist minister, William Giles. It was Giles who gave Dickens his nickname "The Inimitable." Dickens habitually sent him his novels ("To the Reverend William Giles from his old and affectionate pupil, Charles Dickens"). Sister Fanny and her husband Henry Burnett were converted evangelically through the preaching of a Manchester Congregationalist, James Griffin, and gave up their secular musical career to take charge of the music at Griffin's Rusholme Road Congregationalist chapel. Dickens kept in close touch with them. The "poor mis-shapen" boy mourned in the important Christmas piece "What Christmas is, as We Grow Older" (*Household Words*, Extra Number for Christmas, 1851) is the Burnett's crippled son, Dickens's cherished nephew and said to be a model for Paul Dombey, who died in 1849 not long after his mother.

By one means or another, the biblical ideas, words, phrases, and episodes got ingrained early, and stuck. As did words and phrases from the Anglican Book of

Common Prayer, especially from the great rites-of-passage services for marriage and burial. Biblical and Prayer Book tropes inform and form Dickens's imagination, his plots, his moral and social perspectives and judgments. Dickens's narratives are greatly held, like his people, in a literal and imaginative landscape charged with the flavor and force of a strongly Christianized *imaginaire*. Churches and chapels and what they stand for and offer are an inescapable part of the Dickensian topography, his mapping of the self as well as of town and country. The cathedral is always there, rooted in the landscape, the townscape, a simulacrum for every mood, melancholy or cheerful – whether dusty and rotting as at the beginning of *The Mystery of Edwin Drood* (ch. 3) or "surpassingly beautiful" in "brilliant morning sunshine" as at the end (ch. 23) of that unfinished text (in almost the last words Dickens ever wrote). "Halloa! Here's a church!" says Wemmick to Pip, as they walk toward Camberwell Green, and "There was nothing very surprising in that," Pip thinks. And there is not; there is always an ecclesiastical edifice of some sort on a Dickens perambulation.

But still Pip is "rather surprised" when Wemmick says "Let's go in!" and even more as Wemmick finds white gloves in his pocket and Miss Skiffins waiting to be married (*Great Expectations* ch. 55). But Pip should not be. This is what churches are there for in the Dickens world. This is how good people end up in Dickens. It is what Christian England is about; it is how Christian English people – the majority in Dickens, for all the many unchurched people he takes in, and his many Jews, and occasional Indian or Chinese – should behave.

Admittedly, even Dickens's good Christian people don't spend as much time in church on Sundays as their author seems to have. They are practical endorsers of Dickens's hostility to the Sabbatarians who would compel the citizenry into church and chapel by keeping shops and parks and tea-gardens and beer-houses and theaters closed on Sundays.[1] Dickens emphasizes the absenteeism. The "perplexing" mystery about the churches and chapels of Coketown's "eighteen religious persuasions" is "Who belonged to the eighteen denominations? Because, whoever did, the laboring people did not" (*Hard Times* bk. 1, ch. 5). The sound of one of the many bells of the City of London churches gets more and more despondent in Arthur Clennam's annoyed ears as its importuning fails to elicit custom: at ten minutes to the hour "it became aware that the congregation would be scanty, and slowly hammered out in low spirits, they *won't* come, they *won't* come, they *won't* come! At the five minutes, it abandoned hope, and shook every house in the neighbourhood for three hundred seconds, with one dismal swing per second, as a groan of despair" (*Little Dorrit* bk. 1, ch. 3).

The keynote of the City churches that Dickens spent so many Sundays visiting in 1860 (*Journalism* 4: 110) is thin and eccentric congregations, dust, "rot and mildew": the smell of decay and dead Londoners makes a "snuff" that gets up everyone's nose ("we cough and sneeze dead citizens"). These are places of the missing, much like the City churchyards in "The City of the Absent" – places of the dead, as magnetizing as the Morgue Dickens cannot stay away from in Paris ("dragged by invisible force," *Journalism* 4: 88). Perennially melancholy and elegiac, Dickens feels "the attraction of repulsion" – the gothic strain of rotting tombstones, illegible memorials, effaced traces, all the pull of late-romantic ruin. Here is a piety that is affecting without being threatening: a scene of slow ruination which consoles him as it consoles Little Nell, reading the Bible all alone in the quiet of a decrepit village church, surrounded by moldering graves. She finds there a sanctuary of "calm delight" because of what the quiet eloquence of traditional, memorializing, Christian ruin can teach a sad and lonely heart by way of "deep and thoughtful feelings" (*The Old Curiosity Shop* ch. 52).

It is no accident that Nell is finding rest for her weary soul in an old-fashioned English church and churchyard. It is a traditional and Protestant place, as Nell's repeated recourse to the quiet pages of the Bible indicates, a kind of visible Broad Churchiness for the commonality of all decent English people, far from the specializing evangelical and Calvinist hot-gospellings of Dissent, the ragings and howlings of Stiggins and Chadband, Melchisidech Howler and Boanerges Boiler and their kind, as well as from the melodramatics of London's Anglo-Catholics, religious theater put on by overdressed priests playing out "their little play" for the benefit of adoring "young ladies" (*Journalism* 4: 115). Anglo-Catholics are sorry, homegrown imitators of the splendid Roman Catholic churches and ceremonials Dickens deplored in *Pictures from Italy*: "sprawling effigies of maudlin monks, and the veriest rash and tinsel ever seen" in Genoa (p. 49); the "impertinent frippery" and flashy theatrical tawdriness of St. Peter's in Rome ("like a splendid bonbon," p. 119).[2] The gentling spirit of what Dickens advocates as true Christianity is what grants calming, healing respite to Little Nell, the religion of the gentle Jesus of Dickens's very personalized reading of the New Testament. The religion he spelled out for his children in the narrative eventually published as *The Life of Our Lord*.

"No one ever lived, who was so good, so kind, so gentle, and so sorry for all people who did wrong, or were in any way ill or miserable, as he was" (*Life of Our Lord*, p. 11). Jesus was especially sorry for the poor. He chose his disciples

> from among Poor Men, in order that the Poor might know – always after that; in all years to come – that Heaven was made for them as well as for the rich, and that God makes no difference between those who wear good clothes and those who go barefoot and in rags. The most miserable, the most ugly, deformed, wretched creatures that live, will be bright Angels in Heaven if they are good here on earth. Never forget this, when you are grown up. Never be proud or unkind, my dears, to any poor man, woman, or child. If they are bad, think that they would have been better, if they had had kind friends, and good homes, and had been better taught. So, always try to make them better by kind persuading words; and always try to teach them and relieve them if you can. And when people speak ill of the Poor and Miserable, think how Jesus Christ went among them and taught them, and thought them worthy of his care. And always pity them yourselves, and think as well of them as you can. (pp. 27–8)

Goodness is to imitate this Jesus of good human fellowship and neighborliness, especially toward the poor, and to do so without fuss or loud demonstration.

REMEMBER! – It is christianity TO DO GOOD always – even to those who do evil to us. It is christianity to love our neighbour as ourself, and to do to all men as we would have them Do to us. It is christianity to be gentle, merciful, and forgiving, and to keep those qualities quiet in our own hearts, and never to make a boast of them or of our prayers or of our love of God, but always to shew that we love Him by humbly trying to do right in everything. If we do this, and remember the life and lessons of Our Lord Jesus Christ, and try to act up to them, we may confidently hope that God will forgive us our sins and mistakes, and enable us to live and die in Peace. (pp. 124–7)

It is impossible to think of a Dickens plot, a Dickens fabulation, that is not arranged on this Christianized model of best behavior, best ethicity, and what is thought of as the best kind of learning curve, or *Bildung*, for his fiction's characters. As he explained to the Reverend David Macrae, who had complained in 1861 that there were no good Christians in the novels to balance the many religious hypocrites:

> With a deep sense of my great responsibility always upon me when I exercise my art, one of my most constant and most earnest endeavours has been to exhibit in all my good people some faint reflections of the teachings of our great Master, and unostentatiously to lead the reader up to those teachings as the great source of all moral goodness. All my strongest illustrations are derived from the New Testament: all my social abuses are shown as departures from its spirit; all my good people are humble, charitable, faithful, and forgiving. Over and over again, I claim them in express words as disciples of the founder of our religion; but I must admit that to a man (or woman) they all arise and wash their faces, and do not appear unto men to fast. (*Letters* 9: 556)

(So Dickens's good people are not what Jesus thought of as hypocrites in Matthew 6: 16–18, showing off their piety by going scruffy and unwashed.) The claim to a New Testament position is strong – and repeated by Dickens at every opportunity – but this is, of course, New Testament Lite, a theology that is ethically generous but also rather vague at crucial places. Jesus (this is *The Life of Our Lord* again) "was always merciful and tender. And because he did such Good, and taught people how to love God and how to hope to go to Heaven after death, he was called Our Saviour" (p. 34). So much for centuries of soteriological debate! This is a gospel of the broadest and most liberal of Broad Church sorts. It amounts to what came to be called the Social Gospel, a Christianity putting social good works before credal content and demand.

There is nothing in Dickens's affirmations of faith that the broadest of Victorian churchmen, in an age of intense dilution of creed and erasure of faith in the tighter strictures of dogma, could object to. It is no accident that Dickens's talk of doing to others as you would they do to you should find its echo in the Do As You Would Be Done By lessons of the Reverend Charles Kingsley's popular piece of high Victorian religious dilutedness, *The Water Babies* (1863). There is nothing here either that Dickens's friend and biographer, the Unitarian John Foster, or Dickens's friend and collaborator, the good poor-minded but theology-thin, Unitarian novelist Mrs. Gaskell, would not agree with.

It is symptomatic that Dickens started attending Thomas Madge's Essex Street Unitarian chapel on his return from America in October 1842, and a month later took out a family pew at Edward Tagart's Little Portland Street Unitarian chapel. Unitarianism was a usual resort for Victorian Christians in retreat from credal fullness. Dickens had been impressed in North America by the Unitarian Dr. Channing's opposition to slavery, and was attracted to the ministry of the cultured and socially concerned Tagart by the memorial sermon he preached for Channing. Dickens was, he told C. C. Felton, so disgusted with the rise of Anglo-Catholicism within the Anglican Church – religion for backward-looking medievalizers and Pre-Raphaelite painters – that he had "carried into effect an old idea of mine and joined the Unitarians, who *would* do something for human improvement, if they could; and who practise Charity and Toleration" (*Letters* 3: 455–6). His Unitarian leanings became well known. Robert Browning thought it hypocritical of Dickens as "an enlightened Unitarian" to have his children baptized into the Church of England (Cunningham 1975: 194).

Manifestly, Dickens's Jesus was a highly sentimentalized version of the Christian's Master. For all his stress on Christianity's real-world effects, on the practical embodiment of faith, especially among the poor, as the only test for professing Christians, he shied way from the unetherealized Holy Family of Millais' painting *Christ in the House of His Parents* (1849–50), a scene of hateful slum-dwellers, a realistic embodiment far too far:

> In the foreground of that carpenter's shop is a hideous, wry-necked, blubbering, red-headed boy, in a bed-gown; who appears to have received a poke in the hand, from another boy with whom he has been playing in an adjacent gutter, and to be holding it up for the contemplation of a kneeling woman, so horrible in her ugliness, that (supposing it were possible for any human creature to exist for a moment with that dislocated throat) she would stand out from the rest of the company as a Monster, in the vilest cabaret in France, or the lowest gin-shop in England . . . Wherever it is possible to express ugliness of feature, limb, or attitude, you have it expressed. Such men as the carpenters might be undressed in any hospital where dirty drunkards, in a high state of varicose veins, are received. Their very toes have walked out of Saint Giles's.

This is not the way to represent "the most solemn passage which our minds can ever approach," "to render reverence and homage to the faith in which we live and die!" (*Journalism* 2: 245).

Nor, you might think, is this jeering the way to describe the future savior of the poor with a proleptic nail wound in the palm of his hand. But Dickens is quite unable to tolerate Millais' attempt at a body-realistic envisioning of incarnation. It is too hard-edged for this softener of the Jesus story. He prefers something wetter, especially at the Christianized ends he keeps arranging for his people and his plots. G. K. Chesterton – a thoroughly unsentimental Roman Catholic – thought the "softening of the heart" that Mr. Dombey is made to undergo at the end of his novel (the Dickensian version of Christian conversion which Dombey shares with so many other originally hard-hearted men, Scrooge, Gradgrind, Redlaw, and so on) "seems to bear too close a resemblance to softening of the brain" (Washington 1995: 564). It is certainly a dedicated softening of the fiction.

For tears at the end, the ending in tears – tears of the characters, tear-inducements for readers – are the repeated outward signs of the Christ spirit – and, of course, of the favored and much-repeated Dickensian Christmas spirit, "*Carol* philosophy" – in action. It is thus that the old dying sinners – the likes of crooked Magwitch, hard-hearted Miss Havisham, and the fallen Alice Marwood in *Dombey and Son* – get to repent, more or less like the dying thief on the cross (an effect spoiled rather in the case of Magwitch by Pip's turning the repentant publican's word in Jesus's parable, "God be merciful to me a sinner," into the curiously offensive "O Lord, be merciful to him a sinner!" [*Great Expectations* ch. 56]). It is by being bathed in tears – theirs and ours – that the sanctification of Dickens's mass of dying innocents is affirmed. Little Nell, of course. And little Johnny in *Our Mutual Friend*, learning that all the sick children in the charity ward are his "brothers and sisters," brought "together there" by God, bequeathing his toys to "the mite with the broken leg" in the next bed (bk. 2, ch. 9). And Jo, the homeless, illiterate crossing-sweeper (*Bleak House* ch. 47), thinking of down-and-out Captain Hawdon who "wos wery good" to him, coached by the good Dr. Woodcourt, friend of the poor, in a few scraps of the Lord's Prayer. And "old-fashioned" little Paul Dombey, forever wondering what the waves are saying, and dying in "the old, old fashion" of the Dickensian sick child, carried off along the river of death, heading for the heavenly river of life, in a welter of tears, remembering his working-class wet-nurse Richards, his hands clasped together as if in prayer around the neck of his beloved sister Florence, kindly recommending Walter to his father, touching his father's heart in a proleptic anticipation of the old man's later softening of heart which will finally unite all these mourners in a wash of Christianized togetherness (ch. 16). And Stephen Blackpool, in *Hard Times*, victim of the unfair marriage laws and conventions that Dickens so deplored,[3] cast out by harsh trade unionists, sacked by judgmental boss Bounderby, wrongly charged with the rich Gradgrind brat's crime, dying, physically broken, at the bottom of the Old Hell mine shaft in starlight that reminds him of the Star of Bethlehem, the original light of Christmas that led the magi to Jesus. "I thowt it were the star as guided to Our Saviour's home. I awmust think it be the very star" (bk. 3, ch. 6).

That is the light at the apogee of Dickens's Christmas celebrations, the light on his own Christmas trees, the light of his Christmas Tree philosophy, the tree around which the perennial images of his Christmas Christianity cluster – as he harks on them in the wonderful remembering autobiographical celebration "A Christmas Tree" (*Household Words*, December 21, 1850): pictures from the life of gentle Jesus, raising a dead girl and a widow's son from the dead, forgiving his killers from the cross. In an arresting take on traditional theology of the cross, the Christmas tree is blended into the "Tree" on which Christ died, and its blessing invoked on all: "In every cheerful image and suggestion that the season brings, may the bright star that rested above the poor roof, be the star of all the Christian world." Dickens prays he may turn a "child's heart . . . a child's trustfulness and confidence" toward the Jesus of the Christmas Tree. And in an astonishing though not too surprising move, the Tree then speaks a version of Jesus's eucharistic words at the Last Supper about remembering him in the sacrament of the bread and wine, "Do this in remembrance of me": "This, in commemoration of the law of love and kindness, mercy and compassion. This, in remembrance of Me!" (Pascoe 1997: 16). You celebrate Christmas then, as if by divine command; the annual festival is a sacrament. As if all the eating and drinking which are at the necessary heart of the Dickensian Christmas – to deny which, as Scrooge would, is to deny the Christmas message itself – were now the realest, only guaranteeable, and certainly very relishable embodiment of the real presence of Christ in the world. Dickens works hard to give Christmas tuck – and tucking in at Christmas – the feel of the sacred, and of sacred obligation. But though he impresses on us that gormandizing has its good, it cannot ever feel that good. This is a sacramentalism reeking of worldliness, even childishness: a sentimentalism certainly rooted in easy gusts of (gustatory) nostalgias for Christmas feasts long gone by.

One can sympathize with George Orwell's vexation over Dickens's sentimentalized vision of social change through "a change of spirit rather than a change of structure" – the "change of heart" being "*the* alibi of people who do not wish to endanger the *status quo*." But even Orwell grudgingly comes around to accept that "'If men would behave decently the world would be decent' is not such a platitude as it sounds" (Orwell 1970: 468–9). And the intensity with which Dickens promotes the change of heart does indeed keep a sense of mere platitude at bay. The kept-up message of the tearful ending, that the only way to social change is through individual Christlikeness in the matter of charity, fellow feeling, goodness toward others at the personal level and on the individual occasion, and that only through practical acts of fellow feeling might heaven come down to earth, like Christ at Christmas, certainly has its force.

As when Pip brings food to Magwitch. At Christmastide, naturally – or spiritually. So it is a little Christmas feast, a sort of sacramental offering, for a poor starving man – cheese and meat, mincemeat, pork pie, brandy. Though he has been terrified into stealing the food, Pip pities Magwitch's "desolation." "I am glad you enjoy it" (ch. 3). The sexton Wopsle, very loud-voiced in church, one of those noisy Christians Dickens thinks of as hypocrites, preaches Pip a nasty-minded sermon at the Christmas Day table about gratitude in orphans. Joe, though, shares Pip's pity for the hunted man, refusing to condemn the convict when he confesses to theft of the pie, to get Pip out of trouble. "God knows you're welcome to it . . . We don't know yet what you have done, but we wouldn't have you starved to death for it, poor miserable fellow-creatur. – Would us, Pip?" And Pip hears again the curious click in Magwitch's throat (ch. 5). Magwitch is moved by genuine Christian charity; the softening of this self-confessed murdering hard-man has begun. And Dickens expects us to be moved too, to feel the regenerative force of the presented, active fellow feeling of good

Christian people, living out the good life of Jesus. It is the fellow-feeling test. Wopsle and Pumblechook and the rest fail this test. Pip will nearly fail his re-sit when Magwitch returns from Down Under, but he passes it in the end.

It is a test that the institutions and institutional practitioners of Christian England in Dickens's book and books – the law, parliament, education, Church and chapel, industry, trade unions, the class system, the charity system, all the definers of who is an insider, who an outsider, who is a transgressor, especially a sexual transgressor, and who not – keep failing. The list has a loud coercive ring. Here are Michel Foucault's subordinating, surveying, and punishing authorities all collaboratingly in place in Dickens's fiction long before Foucault arrived to brand them as an oppressive collective: the look-alikes and act-alikes of Coketown ("The jail might have been the infirmary, the infirmary might have been the jail, the town-hall might have been either or both" [*Hard Times* bk. 1, ch. 5]). And the louder these deniers of fellow feeling invoke the name of Christ, the further, it seems, from Dickens's sense of true Christianity they are. It is only heavily ironic that the Service for the Burial of the Dead in the Established Church of England's Book of Common Prayer should talk of "our dear brother (or sister) here departed" in the case of a Captain Hawdon: "our dear brother here departed" taken to:

> a hemmed-in churchyard, pestiferous and obscene, whence malignant diseases are communicated to the bodies of our dear brothers and sisters who have not departed; while our dear brothers and sisters who hang about official back-stairs – would to Heaven *they* had departed! – are very complacent and agreeable. Into a beastly scrap of ground which a Turk would reject as a savage abomination, and a Caffre would shudder at, they bring our dear brother here departed, to receive Christian burial.
>
> . . . here they lower our dear brother down a foot or two: here, sow him in corruption, to be raised in corruption: an avenging ghost at many a sick-bedside: a shameful testimony to future ages, how civilisation and barbarism walked this boastful island together. (*Bleak House* ch. 11)

An island boastful of its Christian character. It is a grave indictment that Hawdon is sown in corruption, but not, as St. Paul put it in the words of 1 Corinthians 15: 42, which are read in the burial service, to be raised "in incorruption." An impertinent mockery of true Christian burial. And practiced widely in Dickens's view.

The whole charity system enshrines the blasphemy. In *Oliver Twist*, the clergyman turns up late for the pauper woman's interment in yet another indecently overcrowded grave, "putting on his surplice as he came along" and walking off "having read as much of the burial service as could be compressed into four minutes" (ch. 5). What distinguishes the Rev. Milvey of *Our Mutual Friend* as a good cleric – and one of the very few good clergymen in Dickens – is his giving old Betty Higden the benefit of a full burial service, claiming and accepting her fully as a sister. She has been a very simple-minded Christian, believing vaguely in "the Power and the Glory," but as practicable in her charity as could be, minding orphans for the parish, giving them a loving home very different from the workhouse, on the run at her end from the

workhouse and the harsh doings of the Poor Law, her burial fee sewn into her clothing, dying at the foot of a tree that both she and Dickens take as a version of Christ's
cross. "It brought to her mind the foot of the Cross, and she committed herself to
Him who died upon it." The poor-woman Good Samaritan Lizzie Hexam found her,
brought her brandy, lifted up her dead body "as high as Heaven," took the body into
the Jewish-owned factory where she works. Here is real Christianity, not least from
those Jews, matched, for once, by a clergyman.

"WE GIVE THEE HEARTY THANKS FOR THAT IT HATH PLEASED THEE TO DELIVER THIS
OUR SISTER OUT OF THE MISERIES OF THIS SINFUL WORLD." So read the Reverend Frank
Milvey in a not untroubled voice, for his heart misgave him that all was not quite right
between us and our sister – or say our sister in law – Poor Law – and that we sometimes
read these words in an awful manner, over our Sister and our Brother too. (*Our Mutual
Friend* bk. 3, ch. 9)

Even Milvey's wife is wobbly on how far the human connection extends. She is worried
about the charitable Jews Lizzie works for. Won't they try to convert her? The Rev.
Frank should "talk to her." But he knows their true kindness in fellow feeling and
quiet, unproselytizing goodness. "There are plenty of talkers about," and Lizzie "will
soon find one."

Dickens's novels are full of such talkers. They are united in professedly do-good
societies, churchy subsets of church, parodic versions of Dissent's "gathered churches,"
and the focus of Dickens's great dyspepsia against the numerous evangelical societies
for improving the nation's moral life by imposing on it the cramps of teetotalism and
Sabbatarianism. These are fellowships that undo true human fellowship as Dickens
conceives it, disserving rather than serving the social good. As, for instance, the
Wilberforcian Society for the Suppression of Vice to which spoilsport, methodistical
Nicodemus Dumps belongs in "The Bloomsbury Christening" (in *Sketches by Boz*). Or
hard-drinking Stiggins's Brick Lane Branch of the United Grand Junction Ebenezer
Temperance Association (*The Pickwick Papers* ch. 33). Or the Indigent Orphans'
Friends' Benevolent Institution (*Journalism* 1: 162). Or the bitchy, bigoted, rivalrous
parish groups mocked in "The Ladies Societies" (*Journalism* 1: 36): "the ladies' soup
distribution society, the ladies' coal distribution society . . . the ladies' blanket
distribution society . . . the ladies' child's examination society . . . the ladies'
childbed-linen monthly loan society," and especially the ladies' Bible and Prayer Book
distribution society, in league with the Dissenters' Missionary Society. And then there
is the Society for the Propagation of the Gospel in Foreign Parts, in whose grand
doorway Jo the crossing-sweeper kips for the night (*Bleak House* ch. 16).

Jo "admires the size of the edifice, and wonders what it is all about. He has no
idea, poor wretch, of the spiritual destitution of a coral reef in the Pacific, or what it
costs to look up the precious souls among the cocoa-nuts and bread-fruit." Dickens
hated evangelical missions of every kind, but especially foreign ones, the large Victorian missionary effort. London's Exeter Hall, where the evangelicals' mammoth annual
May Missionary Meetings were held, became Dickensian shorthand for any grouping

of the Christian hypocrites, as he saw them, followers of "the Honorable Member For Whitened Sepulchres," the reforming parliamentarian, Anthony Ashley Cooper (Lord Shaftesbury), tireless enemy of the working-man's Sunday recreation (*Journalism* 2: 255). Overseas missions are all a case of "telescopic philanthropy," blind to home need. They are a main instance for Dickens of the Christians' failure to understand how the Gospel, true Christian charity, should work.

It is absurd – an absurdity Dickens delights in – that Stiggins's women followers collect for the "society for providing the infant Negroes in the West Indies with flannel waist-coats and moral pocket-handkerchiefs" (which "combine amusement with instruction"), but it is no joke that they are "wastin' all their time and labour in making clothes for copper-coloured people as don't want 'em, and taking no notice of flesh-coloured Christians as do" (*The Pickwick Papers* ch. 27). Just so, *Bleak House*'s telescopic philanthropist herself, Mrs. Jellyby, is preoccupied with the immense correspondence for her African project – education and coffee-cultivation in nonsensical "Borrioboola-Gha, on the left bank of the Niger" (ch. 4) – and the novel's Anglo-Catholic Mrs. Pardiggle, pre-eminent among England's female subscription raisers, is devoted to the faraway Tockahoopo Indians (ch. 8), all to the neglect of Jo's kind, so close at hand. Mrs. Jellyby's philanthropic telescope and Mrs. Pardiggle's prominent spectacles are useless for spotting home needs.

> Jo . . . is not one of Mrs. Pardiggle's Tockahoopo Indians; he is not one of Mrs. Jellyby's lambs, being wholly unconnected with Borrioboola-Gha; he is not softened by distance and unfamiliarity; he is not a genuine foreign-grown savage; he is the ordinary home-made article. Dirty, ugly, disagreeable to all the senses, in body a common creature of the common streets, only in soul a heathen. Homely filth begrimes him, homely parasites devour him, homely sores are in him, homely rags are on him: native ignorance, the growth of English soil and climate, sinks his immortal nature lower than the beasts that perish. Stand forth Jo, in uncompromising colours! From the sole of thy foot to the crown of thy head, there is nothing interesting about thee. (ch. 47)

The would-be good Christian ladies of England are accused of limiting charitable interest to the exotically distant other, the attractively *unheimlich* overseas, the uncannily not-at-home ones. For Dickens, charity begins at home, or exists nowhere. His mission is on behalf of the *heimelig* waif and stray.[4]

A loud signal of the badness of the Jellyby–Pardiggle brand of Christian goodness is precisely the mess they make of their homes, their housekeeping, their home-life. The little Jellybys dine off uncooked meat and potatoes out of the coal-scuttle (nothing Christmassy or sacramental about their meals). Caddy Jellyby is close to tears at being enslaved as secretary to the Africa correspondent ("I wish Africa was dead!"). The little ones litter the floor, tumble down the stairs, get their heads stuck between the area railings (ch. 4). The little Pardiggles have to load the good causes with their pocket money. Five-year-old Alfred "has voluntarily enrolled himself in the Infant Bonds of Joy, and is pledged never, through life, to use tobacco in any form" (ch. 8).[5]

It is no surprise, when in chapter 8 Mrs. Pardiggle lifts her gaze from the Tocka-hoopo Indians for a while to take in the drunken brickmaker's impoverished family, that her home-front charity — pressing invitations to church, words against dirt and gin, an insultingly babyish tract ("Mr. Jarndyce said he doubted if Robinson Crusoe could have read it, though he had no other on his desolate island") — is remorseless and punitive. Mrs. Pardiggle "pulled out a good book, as if it were a constable's staff, and took the whole family into custody. I mean into religious custody, of course; but she really did it as if she were an inexorable moral Policeman carrying them all off to a station-house." Ada and Esther "both felt painfully sensible that between us and these people there was an iron barrier, which could not be removed by our new friend." She leaves without noticing the sick baby in her bashed-up mother's lap, which dies there and then. Ada and Esther try to comfort the stricken mother: "we whispered to her what Our Saviour said of children." Another bashed-about woman comes in to condole with the mother. Esther recognizes something divine in the ensuing scene of humble caring. "What the poor are to the poor is little known, excepting to them-selves and GOD." Esther sees a halo around the dead baby's head. This is one more of Dickens's eloquently Christianized child death-beds. Esther has covered the little corpse with her handkerchief. It is a plain one, not one of those moral ones sporting texts and religious pictures, but in Dickens's view plainly signifies the real morality of a simple young woman's Christ-like fellow feeling. (And not least among its sig-nificant child-care work is that it will eventually guide Esther back to her long-lost mother Lady Dedlock.)

What especially condemns Mrs. Jellyby and Mrs. Pardiggle is the way children suffer at the expense of their religiosity. For at the core of Dickens's Christian human-ism is a child. What the consequences are for children is his greatest test for the ethicity of people and society, and, of course, for professing Christians and Christian groups. In *The Life of Our Lord* Dickens paraphrases and glosses Jesus's reply in Luke 9 to the disciples' question about who was greatest:

> Jesus called a little child to him, and took him in his arms, and stood him among them, and answered, "a child like this. I say unto you that none but those who are as humble as little children shall enter into Heaven. Whosoever shall receive one such little child in my name receiveth me. But whosoever hurts one of them, it were better for him he had a millstone tied about his neck, and were drowned in the depths of the sea. The angels are all children." Our Saviour loved the child, and loved all children. Yes, and all the world. (p. 55)

Be kind and loving to a child and you are on Jesus's side. And the little-child treat-ment test which differentiates Ada and Esther from Mrs. Jellyby and Mrs. Pardiggle is the one Dickens universally applies. Benefactors such as Brownlow, the Cheerybles, and Jarndyce shine especially in the benefit they bring the young. Any protector of a child — Betty Higden, Joe Gargery, Walter Gay, Peggotty, Little Nell's old guardian, Tiny Tim Cratchitt's family, Will Fern and Trotty in *The Chimes*, and so on and on — is on the side of the Dickens angels. Dickens works his devoted ethical revisionism — making us think better than society customarily does of moral outsiders — by getting them to show a saving kindness to little ones — as in Hawdon's goodness to Jo, Magwitch's bank-rolling of Pip, the prostitute Nancy's care for Oliver, the anonymous prostitute's concern for the young-looking Little Dorrit out with simple Maggie on the night-time London street in that extraordinary encounter in *Little Dorrit* (bk. 1, ch. 14): " 'Poor thing!' said the woman. 'Have you no feeling that you keep her out in the cruel streets at such a time as this?' " (It is a kindness to the child whose moral marking is confusingly enjoyed by Fagin in his short-lived role of surrogate to Oliver Twist.) On the other hand, neglect, or be malevolent and cruel to a child, and you reveal yourself as utterly un-Christ-like, however strong your Christian pretensions. Which is, notably, the case with so many of Dickens's keenest professing religionists: Mrs. Clennam, the Chadbands, the Murdstones, Esther Summerson's aunt, the Boanerges Boiler-like preacher in Kit Nubbles's mother's Little Bethel who makes little Jacob cry with terror (*The Old Curiosity Shop* ch. 41). The pietistic Christianity of such *mal-faisants* is particularly harsh on children. The Little Bethel pastor would characteristically deny his flock the sort of worldly pleasure to be got at Astley's theater (with oysters afterwards) — those circus joys that Gradgrind and Bounderby so hate in *Hard Times*. These Christians specially suppress the delights of children. In giving young Arthur and Pip, David and Esther and Kit a self and a mind of their own, Dickens is speaking up for these repressed ones of evangelical child-rearing regimens, giving a voice to the likes of that weirdly silent little girl Dickens notices in one of the City churches, dressed up to look like an adult, with a "currant jelly" birthmark on her chin, sipping from a green bottle, but otherwise motionless, standing "on the seat of the large pew, closely fitted into the corner, like a rain-water pipe" (*Journalism* 4: 114).

Children need play-time, time and space for pastoral release, a weekly sabbatical in fact, a sort of Christmas once a week, not least on Sundays. Not Sundays *As Sabbath Bills Would Make It*, Sunday on the Sabbatarians', on Mrs. Clennam's, model, but Sunday as Dickens's "mild, majestic" Jesus would have it, inaugurating "the authority of the Christian dispensation over the letter of the Jewish Law" by plucking ears of corn for the enjoyment of poor men on the Sabbath, uttering the "One Christian sentence . . . all sufficient with us, on the theological part of this subject, 'The Sabbath was made for man, and not man for the Sabbath'" (Mark 2: 27; *Journalism* 2: 251). As he listens to the City churches' bells, Arthur Clennam remembers his own early Sundays:

> There was the dreary Sunday of his childhood, when he sat with his hands before him, scared out of his senses by a horrible tract which commenced business with the poor child by asking him in its title, why he was going to Perdition? — a piece of curiosity that he really in a frock and drawers was not in a condition to satisfy — and which, for the further attraction of his infant mind, had a parenthesis in every other line with some such hiccupping reference as 2 Ep. Thess. c. ii, v. 6 & 7. There was the sleepy Sunday

of his boyhood, when, like a military deserter, he was marched to chapel by a picquet of teachers three times a day, morally handcuffed to another boy; and when he would willingly have bartered two meals of indigestible sermon for another ounce or two of inferior mutton at his scanty dinner in the flesh. There was the interminable Sunday of his nonage; when his mother, stern of face and unrelenting of heart, would sit all day behind a bible – bound, like her own construction of it, in the hardest, barest, and straitest boards, with one dinted ornament on the cover like the drag of a chain, and a wrathful sprinkling of red upon the edges of the leaves – as if it, of all books! were a fortification against sweetness of temper, natural affection, and gentle intercourse. There was the resentful Sunday of a little later, when he sat glowering and glooming through the tardy length of the day, with a sullen sense of injury in his heart, and no more real knowledge of the beneficent history of the New Testament, than if he had been bred among idolaters. There was a legion of Sundays, all days of unserviceable bitterness and mortification, slowly passing before him. (*Little Dorrit* bk. 1, ch. 3)

It follows naturally in Dickens's reckoning that Nicodemus Dumps of "The Blooms-bury Christening," supporter of the Society for the Suppression of Vice – "for the pleasure of putting a stop to any harmless amusements" – should have "adored King Herod for his massacre of the innocents; and if he hated one thing more than another, it was a child" (*Journalism* 1: 448).

Such evangelicals confine and curtail children because they believe that their souls need saving from the wrath of God against the descendants of fallen Adam and Eve and that early discipline will set children on the strait and narrow path to that salvation. It is a theology Dickens abhors. The idea that children are born sinful does not square with his notion of the child-approving Jesus. The "gloomy theology of the Murdstones made all children out to be a swarm of little vipers (though there *was* a child once set in the midst of the Disciples" (*David Copperfield* ch. 4). There is no original sin in Dickens's theology. He is keen to advertise certain characters as evil, Fagin and Monks it might be in *Oliver Twist*, or Carker in *Dombey and Son*, or Orlick in *Great Expectations*, but he has no theological rationale of evil. His people resent being labeled original sinners. Tony Weller, for instance, does not want the Method-istical "Shepherd" calling him a "miserable sinner" and a "wessel of wrath" (*The Pickwick Papers* ch. 22). Kit Nubbles won't have baby Jacob brought up "to call itself a young sinner (bless its heart) and a child of the devil (which is calling its dead father names)" (*The Old Curiosity Shop* ch. 22). Dickens would rather the Bible-puncher at the Hoxton Theatre Sunday service (he who "soundingly slapped" his Bible at "frequent intervals," "like a slow lot at a sale") had addressed his audience as "fellow-creatures" rather than as "fellow-sinners" (*Journalism* 4: 59–60).

If Dickensian children die they go straight to heaven, there to star as angels, like Paul Dombey or Little Nell – one more "angel added to the Host of Heaven" as the kindly schoolmaster advises Nell (ch. 54). Dickens cannot conceive of a God who might want to punish a sinner for his sin. There is certainly no hellish future in his theology. Those threatening, hiccupping verses from 2 Thessalonians that so irked the young Arthur Clennam are about "the mystery of iniquity" at work in some awkward customer whom the Lord is going to "take out of the way," and, in the following verse, "consume with the spirit of his mouth, and . . . destroy with the brightness of his coming." Which is by no means Dickens's idea of the Lord. Dickens is, of course, greatly thrilled by apocalyptic fire and brimstone in the here and now. He greatly enjoys "looking down, for a moment, into the Hell of boiling fire" up Mount Vesuvius, breathing the sulfur, getting "blackened, and singed, and scorched, and hot, and giddy" (*Pictures from Italy*, p. 175). He likes narrating the "last day" blazes of the riots in *Barnaby Rudge* (ch. 68), and arranging Krook's spontaneous combustion in *Bleak House* and Miss Havisham's fiery end in *Great Expectations*, and raising the terrible French Revolutionary fires in *A Tale of Two Cities* (bk. 2, ch. 23). The socially transgressive might expect to meet their end in some such revolutionary conflagration of the kind Dickens (and his friend Carlyle) fear might be coming Britain's way. But eternal punishment for sinners in the fires of Hell is not on Dickens's agenda. He is some kind of universalist. The Christian tradition's Hell exists only in the mind of that "fierce-eyed, spare old woman" Dickens spots in "City of London Churches" walking up Aldersgate Street of a Sunday morning "to some chapel where she comforts herself with brimstone doctrine, I warrant" – a type of all the harsh, sin-obsessed women treating Dickens's little ones so badly: Jane Murdstone, jingling her little steel fetters of a bracelet and relishing the phrase "miserable sinners" in church; Esther's aunt loading her charge not just with the "common sinfulness and wrath" of all the fallen human race but with the extra degradation of having been born out of wedlock (*Journalism* 4: 109; *David Copperfield* ch. 4; *Bleak House* ch. 3).

What Dickens finds amiss with these child-abusing, sin-and-judgment obsessives is that they are stuck fast in the Old Testament, are imperceptive about the New Testament's rewritings of the Old, the Christian dispensation's abolition of Judaic law. "I was stern with him," says Mrs. Clennam of her son Arthur, "knowing that the transgressions of the parents are visited on their offspring, and that there was an angry mark upon him at his birth." This is Old Testament doctrine – God repeatedly said to "visit the iniquities of the fathers upon the children" (as in Exodus 20: 5). Mrs. Clennam has been "an instrument of severity against sin," justifying her crooked cheating over the will with reference to "the old [Old Testament] days," "when the innocent perished with the guilty, a thousand to one[.] When the wrath of the hater of the unrighteous was not slaked even in blood, and yet found favour." Little Dorrit retorts in the voice of Dickens with the theology of "later and better days": "Be guided, only by the healer of the sick, the raiser of the dead, the friend of all who were afflicted and forlorn, the patient Master who shed tears of compassion for our infirmities . . . There is no vengeance and infliction of suffering in His life, I am sure" (*Little Dorrit* bk. 2, ch. 31).

But Mrs. Clennam reads, as it were, another Bible than Dickens's and Little Dorrit's, preferring an Old Testament culture of vengeance for the transgressor. "Forgive us our debts as we forgive our debtors, was a prayer too poor in spirit for her. Smite thou our debtors, Lord, wither them, crush them; do Thou as I would do, and Thou shalt have my worship: this was the impious tower of stone she built up to scale heaven" (bk. 1, ch. 5). She is as blasphemous as the builders of the Tower of Babel in the Book of Genesis, doomed to a confusion of tongues. Her theology is, in Dickens's view, babelic nonsense. She might as well be talking gibberish like Mrs. Jellyby with Borrioboola-Gha on her tongue. It is a nonsense aided by biblical commentators of a certain stripe. Mrs. Clennam actually waves a volume of one such at her son, who has offended her by talking of making reparations to anyone done down by the family business.

> "In the days of old, Arthur, treated of in this Commentary, there were pious men, beloved of the Lord, who would have cursed their sons for less than this: who would have sent them forth, and sent whole nations forth, if such had supported them, to be avoided of God and man, and perish, down to the baby at the breast." (bk. 1, ch. 5)

"[P]ray daily," urges Esther's aunt, "that the sins of others be not visited upon your head, according to what is written." According to what is written. Like all of her child-offending sort, she is a literalist, but – as biblical literalists often are – an inconsistent one. Such Christians are not, according to Dickens, taking the New Testament literally enough, not hearing its claim to have rewritten the Old Testament's legalisms and judgmentalisms, and certainly not listening to the gentle Jesus of the Gospels.

Dickens makes no bones about being himself a selective reader of the Bible, an extremely patchy literalist. He cheerfully absorbed contemporary critical ideas about the construction of the Old Testament text, its outdated science, its unreliable history, its archaic theology modified later through what was called "progressive revelation" – at least as such skepticisms got publicized in the great public furor over Benjamin Jowett and company's *Essays and Reviews* (1860) and the attempts to demote Bishop Colenso of Natal as a heretic. Dickens was on Colenso's side in the matter of his *Critical Examination of the Pentateuch* (1862–3) and presumably too of his universalist commentary on the Book of Romans (1861). The Pentateuch – "books of an immense age and of (at the best) doubtful origin" – cannot be relied on. Quarreling over "the letter of obscure parts of the Old Testament which itself has been the subject of accommodation, adaptation, varying interpretation without end" puts the "Master of the New Testament" "out of sight." Dickens thought Colenso was in the grand Protestant tradition of using "private judgement" when it came to reading the Bible, the tradition set in train by Wickliffe and Luther, as described admiringly in *A Child's History of England* (ch. 27; see *Letters* 10: 252–4, 443–5). The example of Colenso egged on, so to say, Dickens's own sense of the importance of a private reading of the Bible, one focused on the New Testament, and on his own, particular, privatized, selective New Testament. "I exhort my dear children" – this is his last word on the subject, in his Last Will and Testament – "humbly to try to guide themselves by the teaching of the New Testament in its broad spirit, and to put no faith in any man's narrow construction of its letter here and there" (Forster "Appendix").

Dickens is, of course, narrowing the Bible, but in aid of its "broad spirit," which makes his own selectivity seem all right. It is other people's narrowings, working against his sense of the broad spirit, that he objects to: people who "have tried to tear to narrow shreds" the "broad benevolence and goodness" of the Christ of Christmas (as he puts it at the end of his Christmas polemic, "What Christmas is, as We Grow Older," *Household Words*, Extra Number for Christmas, 1851, pp. 1–3). The evangelical literalist others of his fiction (the appropriate label *fundamentalist* had not yet been coined) are presented as woefully bad, stupid expositors of the Word. Brother Gimblett and Brother Hawkyard, the deplored preachers of "George Silverman's Explanation" (1868), are simply deficient "expounders." Silverman sees through their interpretative practice; he is not so weak, we are told, as "to consider these narrow creatures, interpreters of the Divine majesty and wisdom."

This is Dickens's common charge against his evangelical and, especially, Dissenting preachers and would-be Bible expounders. They are men, and women, in the old admired Protestant line of private readers of the Bible, but too stupid – and, as it is commonly put of the freelance Dissenters, too uneducated, too unschooled, being self-appointed ministers off the street – to get their readings right. Like Chadband, the grisly doyen of all Dickens's freelance Dissenting pastors. Jo the crossing-sweeper is never going to be swept up savingly into Chadband's heap of useless, pseudo-Old Testament biblicisms, "a Gentile and a Heathen . . . devoid of flocks and herds," and all that – a farrago of emptily floating signifiers if ever there was one. And Jo's complete ignorance of the New Testament is never going to be improved by Chadband's way with the sacred text. Chadband blots out any light from the simple Gospel story from the completely bored and yawning boy.

> Though it may be, Jo, that there is a history so interesting and affecting even to minds as near the brutes as thine, recording deeds done on this earth for common men, that if the Chadbands, removing their own persons from the light, would but show it thee in simple reverence, would but leave it unimproved, would but regard it as being eloquent enough without their modest aid – it might hold thee awake, and thou might learn from it yet! (*Bleak House* ch. 25)

Exemplary opposites of Chadband are hard to find in the Dickens world. The Welsh clergyman celebrated at the beginning of *The Uncommercial Traveller* stands out in his rarity. He has devoted himself to the dead of a foundered Australian ship, burying them with love, writing hundreds of letters to their relatives. He does not go in for sermons "improving" the biblical text. Nor need he, for everything about him is eloquent of the Dickensian New Testament, of the Christ of the Dickensian Christmas (he is the man Dickens must meet "In the Christmas season of the year").

> So cheerful of spirit and guiltless of affectation, as true practical Christianity ever is! I read more of the New Testament in the fresh frank face going up the village beside me, in five minutes, than I have read in anathematising discourses . . . in all my life. I heard

more of the Sacred Book in the cordial voice that had nothing to say about its owner, than in all the would-be celestial pairs of bellows that have ever blown conceit at me. (*Journalism* 4: 32)

He is, this walking exemplum of the good Word of God, notably the producer and receiver of good text, surrounded by a "shipwreck of papers" from the grateful bereaved, Jewish as well as Christian, epistles steeped in biblical words and the ordinary poetry of the Christian church (letters quoting "Abide with Me" and "When Peace like a river"): a heap of words and a litter of papers markedly at odds with Chadband's vexing long-windedness or Mrs. Jellyby's piles of missionary correspondence.

What is at issue hereabouts is nothing less than a war: biblical hermeneutics, a conflict of interpretations, a contest over the meanings and the possible enactments, the performative, of Scripture. Eugene Wrayburn (*Our Mutual Friend* bk. 3, ch. 10) is "charmed" by the "very word, Reading, in its critical use" ("An actress's Reading of a chambermaid . . . a singer's Reading of a song, a marine painter's Reading of the sea," and so forth). Dickens is preoccupied with contemporary Christianity's reading of the Bible. Whose reading, whose commentary, whose expositions, and so whose idea of the righteous life, is to prevail? Whose Sunday? Whose pulpit? Which Protestants? For Dickens the novelist is also Dickens the Protestant Bible reader, the Bible hermeneute, a Bible teacher and preacher, wrestling with rival interpreters and expounders of the Big Book, rival teachers and preachers of righteousness.

Defending the Christian purposes of his fictions to the Reverend Macrae, Dickens singled out his Christmas books, a genre he claims to have invented: "absolutely impossible, I think, to be separated from the exemplification of the Christian virtues and inculcation of the Christian precepts." They do this by being sermons on biblical texts. "In every one of those books there is an express text preached on, and the text is always taken from the lips of Christ" (*Letters* 9: 556–7).

Sermons on New Testament texts, expanded illustrations of New Testament texts in action, the five Christmas books certainly are, though only one of them is based precisely on words from Jesus's lips. *A Christmas Carol* has one of the Cratchitt children pointedly reading Matthew 18: 2, strictly words about Jesus rather than from him: "And He took a child, and set him in the midst of them" ("Where had Scrooge heard those words?"). *The Chimes*, which forcefully replays several biblical passages, including the prisoner Fern accusing Victorian Christians of not imitating Ruth in Ruth 1: 16 ("thy people are Not my people; Nor thy God my God!"), makes most, perhaps, of an incident in the life of Christ when the fallen woman Lilian thinks of Jesus letting the prostitute Mary Magdalene wash his feet with her tears and dry them with her hair (Luke 7: 38) as the good Meg forgives and accepts her: "His blessing on you dearest love. Kiss me once more! He suffered her to sit beside His feet, and dry them with her hair. O Meg what Mercy and Compassion!" In *The Cricket on the Hearth* the apparent text is John 9: 19, the words of a blind man Jesus healed, again not the words of Jesus himself ("one thing I know, that, whereas I was blind, now I see"), appropriated by blind Bertha, happy to have her eyes opened at last to the love of her father in shielding her from truths about their poverty. The good Heathfield in *The Battle of Life* has "learned and proved" in ministering to the sick and poor "the truth of his old faith," namely "how often men still entertain angels, unawares, as in the olden time" – as explained, not in the Gospels, but in Hebrews 13: 2, in a passage about letting "brotherly love continue" by entertaining strangers and thus letting angels into your home. Only in *The Haunted Man* are actual words of Christ in play – when old Redlaw is redemptively softened, getting his memory back through the salvific love of Molly, "which was the memory of Christ upon the cross, and of all the good who perished in His cause," and turning into the Jesus of Matthew 19: 13–14 ("Suffer little children, and forbid them not, to come unto me: for of such is the kingdom of heaven. And he laid his hands on them") as he claims and blesses the anonymous, illiterate, savage street-boy (a very severe case of Jo the crossing-sweeper):

> Then, as Christmas is a time in which, of all times in the year, the memory of every remediable sorrow, wrong, and trouble in the world around us, should be active with us, not less than our own experiences, for all good, he laid his hand upon the boy, and silently calling Him to witness who laid His hand on children in old time, rebuking, in the majesty of His prophetic knowledge, those who kept them from him, vowed to protect him, teach him, and reclaim him. (*The Haunted Man* ch. 3)

But whether based literally on the words of Jesus or not, these sermonic fictions for Christmas reach into the heart of Dickens's gospel for the poor and the outsider. Their Bible-textual range embraces, indeed bounds, the repeated Dickensian repertoire of biblicisms which fire his social and ethical, and thus his Christian, message. Their biblical path is Dickens's well-trodden one. Here is his, admittedly narrow, biblical focus, clear and close up and in action, in the matter of the child and the magdalen, the practice of brotherhood and sisterhood in the "entertaining" of the strange, the outcast and downcast, the poor, the criminal, the despised human other. "Of such is the Kingdom of Heaven" declares the running-title at the head of the page in Chapman and Hall's one-volume edition of *Dombey and Son* as Paul dies (ch. 16). It is Dickens's point about all his little ones. Every Christmas, Dickens thought, angelic little ones return from heaven to be entertained unawares by the living children around the Christmas fire.

This, according to "What Christmas is, as We Grow Older," is "Entertaining angels unawares as the Patriarchs did," an essence of practical Christmas and Christian entertaining, shutting out no one, forgiving even your enemy – letting Magwitch, as it were, share your Christmas fare. Which is clearly, as Dickens would have it, an encapsulation of what the really good Dickens people do, namely ministering to Christ as they feed and water and clothe the hungry and thirsty and naked, visit the sick and care for the prisoner. "Inasmuch," said Jesus, "as ye have done it unto one of the least of these my brethren, ye have done it unto me" (Matthew 25: 34ff). Which is the Gospel passage hovering over prisoner Fern's outcry in *The Chimes* against the shunning gentlefolks, and the protracted diatribe by the Phantom in *The Haunted Man* against peoples, countries, religions which would let the boy of the streets "pass" unassisted. People who would, in other Gospel words, "pass by on the other side," ignoring the man, in Jesus's parable, "who fell among thieves," was robbed and beaten up: that is, refusing to be a Good Samaritan, he who bound the victim's wounds, and paid "two pence" for his lodging at an inn (Luke 10: 30–7).

There is a huge shortage of Good Samaritans among Dickens's professing Christians. We are shown Mr. Gradgrind writing out his proofs "that the Good Samaritan was a Bad Economist" (bk. 2, ch. 12). From first to last in his fiction, it is Dickens's commonest charge against parish charity, the workhouse system, that it is not the Good Samaritan it thinks it is being. Beadle Bumble, Charity's hatchet-man and notoriously bad feeder of the hungry ("long grace . . . short commons"), ironically sports "the Good Samaritan healing the sick and bruised man" on his buttons, a gift for his so-called good works from the parish whose seal bears the same image (*Oliver Twist* ch. 4). Old Mr. Plornish of *Little Dorrit* has had to retire to the workhouse, "which was appointed by law to be the Good Samaritan of his district (without the twopence, which was bad political economy)" (bk. 1, ch. 31). Old Betty Higden was in flight precisely from this Not-Good Samaritan: "That night she took refuge from the Samaritan in his latest accredited form, under a farmer's rick; and if – worth thinking of, perhaps, my fellow-Christians – the Samaritan had in the lonely night, 'passed by on the other side,' she would have most devoutly thanked High Heaven for her escape from him" (*Our Mutual Friend* bk. 3, ch. 8).

Passing by on the other side, what the uncaring priest and Levite did in the parable, is not "doing it" as unto Christ. It is not doing as you would be done by, either, that proverbial adaptation of Matthew 7: 12 ("Therefore all things whatsoever ye would that men should do to you, do ye even so to them: for this is the law and the prophets"), the "golden rule" which the as-yet worldly lawyer Snitchey in *The Battle of Life* says most people adapt as "Do, or you'll be done brown" ("Part the First"). That is not the forgiving Christmas spirit that outcast magdalens are owed – as in the Bible read by the good, forgiving Harriet to Alice Marwood at the end of *Dombey and Son*:

> [She] read the eternal book for all the weary and the heavy-laden; for all the wretched, fallen, and neglected of this earth – read the blessed history, in which the blind lame palsied beggar, the criminal, the woman stained with shame, the shunned of all our dainty clay, has each a portion, that no human pride, indifference, or sophistry, through all the ages that this world shall last, can take away, or by the thousandth atom of a grain reduce – read the ministry of Him who, through the round of human life, and all its hopes and griefs, from birth to death, from infancy to age, had sweet compassion for, and interest in, its every scene and stage, its every suffering and sorrow. (ch. 58)

(Alice dies "murmuring the sacred name that had been read to her.") Such redemptive textual understandings are not ones that Dickens's Old Testament Christians can bear.

Like Miss Barbary, Lady Dedlock's evangelical sister, who tries to cancel out Esther's reading from John 8 about the woman taken in adultery – "how our Saviour stooped down," writing with his finger in the dust, when they brought the sinful woman to him. "So when they continued asking him, he lifted up himself, and said unto them, He that is without sin among you, let him first cast a stone at her!" Miss Barbary's response is a kind of curse; she cries out, "in an awful voice," from quite another part of the book, "Watch ye therefore! . . . Lest coming suddenly he find you sleeping. And what I say unto you, I say unto all, Watch!" She prefers the minatory Jesus of Mark 13: 35–7. She falls into a frowning coma, and dies with "no word of blessing and forgiveness," not even for the child of her sister the sinner (*Bleak House* ch. 3).

To embrace and not reject the magdalen is to raise the fallen – to effect a kind of resurrection. Sharing in Christ's resurrection morally like that is of the Christmas essence according to "What Christmas is, as We Grow Older." In that account of Christmas Day, Dickens's sister-in-law, Mary Hogarth, is said to return, "recalled to life" for the festivity. "Recalled to life": it is the theme of *A Tale of Two Cities*, with its no-good pastiche "Resurrection Man" Jerry Cruncher, on the one hand, and, on the other, the good resurrectionist Sidney Carton, saving his rival's life in a version of Christ's substitutionary death on the Cross and rising to newness of moral life in the process. Mary Hogarth's resurrection recalls for Dickens Jesus recalling the dead daughter of Jairus to life in the Gospel (Mark 5: 35–43). That girl, though, as Dickens points out, was raised from the dead only "to die again." Mary Hogarth, "more blest, has heard the same voice, saying unto her, 'Arise for ever!'" Her everlasting resurrection is, Dickens believes, reaffirmed as it is repeated every Christmastide. This is resurrection as remembering, as memorial – all one with how Dickens believes Christ and his meaning should be recalled, and are recalled, "in the season of immortal hope, and on the birthday of immortal mercy." And they are recalled in Dickens's own repeated resurrections of the Bible stories and texts he is so fond of.

At the end of his account of the Sunday night preachings at the Britannia Theatre, Hoxton, Dickens coaches the Sunday preachers whose effort, at least, to reach the non-churchgoer he rather approves. Imitate the New Testament model for preaching, he advises. Retell New Testament history, "the most beautiful and affecting history conceivable by man." The illiterate cannot read the book; "the young and ignorant" will not read it because they are put off by the book's printed layout in verses; so nothing remains but to just "set forth the history in narrative." And to narrate what? The answer is – resurrection stories: the raising of the widow's son (Luke 7: 14), of Jairus's daughter, of Lazarus the brother of Mary and Martha (John 11). (Dickens had forgotten, perhaps, how the story of the raising of Lazarus upset the young David Copperfield.) The resurrectionist Christ should be the story's focus, the

> figure at the door when the brother of the two sisters was dead, and one of the two ran to the mourner, crying "The Master is come, and calleth for thee" . . . Let the preacher who will thoroughly forget himself and remember no individuality but one, and no eloquence but one, stand up before four thousand men and women at the Britannia

Theatre any Sunday night, recounting that narrative to them as fellow creatures, and he shall see a sight. (*Journalism* 4: 61–2)

The preacher as Resurrection Man, giving new life to certain old Bible narratives, re-narrating the Bible as a set of resurrection narratives, doing sermon as narrative and narrative as sermon: this is, we can well believe, Dickens's vision of himself, as the only effective Christian preacher for his time. And one effective because, being the intense picker and chooser he is, in order to get at the "broad spirit" of the New Testament, he is willing to take liberties with the Bible story in aid of narrative and imaginative force. That silent, mourning figure of Jesus at the door, for instance, is all Dickens's own invention. He is an actively intervening appropriator of the Gospels he so admires.

NOTES

1 Dickens's anti-Sabbatarianism was, like his hostility to teetotalism and vegetarianism, one of his most sustained crusades. He hated any extremist ("whole hog"), pious constrictions of the pleasures of the ordinary person. See Timothy Sparks [pseud.], *Sunday Under Three Heads: As It Is, As Sabbath Bills Would Make It, As It Might Be Made* (1836), and in *Household Words*: "The Sunday Screw" (June 22, 1850), "Whole Hogs" (August 23, 1851), "Frauds on Fairies" (October 1, 1853), "The Great Baby" (August 4, 1855), and "The Murdered Person" (October 11, 1856).

2 Dickens hates the fancy dress of the Anglo-Catholic "dandy boys" ("A Crisis in the Affairs of Mr. John Bull," *Household Words*, November 23, 1850), the "sanctimonious" waistcoats, cassocks, and aprons arriving from Rome which are scooped rudely into Dickens's jeering at the fashion for women's "bloomers" coming in from the USA: "Sucking Pigs," *Household Words* (November 8, 1851).

3 See his fierce polemic in "The Murdered Person," *Household Words* (October 11, 1856), p. 290.

4 The *unheimlich*: *heimelig* (the uncanny/not-at-home: the at-home/not strange) opposition from Sigmund Freud, "Das Unheimliche" (1919), an opposition frequently travestied by literary theorists into the actually non-existent *unheimlich*: *heimlich* opposition. The word *heimlich* as the opposite of *unheimlich* is not known in Freud, or German, a position obscured in James Strachey's (standard) English translation, which omits some of Freud's etymological detail (Freud 1985).

5 He toddled out of Dickens's polemic against the absurdity of children signing the anti-alcohol pledge in the Juvenile Temperance Bands of Hope and the Infantine Brigade of Regenerators of Mankind: "Whole Hogs," *Household Words* (August 23, 1851), p. 505.

REFERENCES AND FURTHER READING

Cunningham, Valentine (1975). *Everywhere Spoken Against: Dissent in the Victorian Novel*. Oxford: Clarendon Press.

Dickens, Charles (1934). *The Life of Our Lord, Written Expressly for his Children by Charles Dickens*. London: Associated Newspapers.

— (1998). *Pictures from Italy*. London, Penguin (original work published 1846).

Freud, Sigmund (1985) The "uncanny". In Albert Dickson (Ed.), *Art and Literature*. Pelican Freud Library, vol. 14 (pp. 335–76). Harmondsworth: Penguin.

Jay, Elisabeth (1979). *The Religion of the Heart: Anglicanism and the Nineteenth Century Novel.* Oxford: Clarendon Press.

Kent, William (1930). *Dickens and Religion.* London: Watts and Co.

Orwell, George (1970). Charles Dickens. In *The Collected Essays, Journalism and Letters of George Orwell*, vol. I (Sonia Orwell and Ian Angus, Eds.) (pp. 468–9). Harmondsworth: Penguin (original work published 1939).

Pascoe, David (Ed.) (1979). *Charles Dickens Selected Journalism 1850–1870.* London: Penguin.

Pope, Norris (1978). *Dickens and Charity.* London: Macmillan.

Reed, John R. (1975). *Victorian Conventions.* Athens: Ohio University Press.

Walder, Dennis (1981). *Dickens and Religion.* London: George Allen and Unwin.

— (1985). Dickens and the Rev. David Macrae. *The Dickensian*, 81, 45–51.

Washington, Peter (Ed.) (1995). G. K. Chesterton, Appendix: Introduction to the Original Everyman Edition (pp. 559–69). *The Old Curiosity Shop.* London: David Campbell (original work published 1907).

Wolff, Robert Lee (1977). *Gains and Losses: Novels of Faith and Doubt in Victorian England.* New York: Garland.

18

Dickens and the Law

Jan-Melissa Schramm

Charles Dickens's sketches and novels tell us much about the engagement of law and the community at a time when legal process was changing fast. Dickens himself seems to have sensed the pace of reform: in the 1847 Preface to the Cheap Edition of *The Pickwick Papers* (1836), he notes (with considerable satisfaction) that, although

> the license of Counsel, and the degree to which Juries are ingeniously bewildered, are yet susceptible of moderation . . . legal reforms have pared the claws of Messrs Dodson and Fogg; a spirit of self-respect, mutual forbearance, education, and co-operation, for such good ends, has diffused itself among their clerks . . . the laws relating to imprisonment for debt are altered; and the Fleet Prison is pulled down!

By the mid-Victorian period, many institutions and procedures remained in need of reform: the demise of the Court of Chancery (the target of Dickens's most excoriating criticism in *Bleak House*) as a separate jurisdiction in 1873–5 was roughly coterminous with Dickens's own death in 1870. Legal historians nevertheless suggest that the course of change in the first half of the nineteenth century was largely ameliorative.

Yet Dickens was not an historian of legal development as manifest in either institutional or conceptual terms. On many occasions, it suited his purposes as a satirist to reproduce a portrait of the law in all its unreformed excesses; on many occasions, he chose to denigrate and disparage the law in order to define for the mid-Victorian generation the heuristic power of fiction. So, too, his role as a dramatist required that he evoke the terror of procedures that were passing from regular usage – the brutality of the scaffold, and the clumsiness of detective processes based only upon superstition and rumor. Dickens documents for us many of these changes, yet he also retains an abiding interest in the primitive, atavistic superstitions that clustered around the sign of the scaffold.

In this way, we cannot necessarily look to Dickens's work for an unbiased portrait of nineteenth-century legal process: instead, his fiction is deeply committed to the binary model of Victorian intellectualism which places fact in competition with fancy, science in disagreement with the powers of the imagination, and law at war with the discourses of sentiment and sensibility. The representation of the law in Dickens's novels tells us more about his philosophy of fiction than it does about the statutes of the time, but it is no less powerful and engaging for that.

Nineteenth-century Legal Reforms

To understand the legal environment in which Dickens moved, we must first address the nature of nineteenth-century legal change. Criminal trial procedure in Tudor and Stuart times had been largely non-adversarial, with judges playing an important part in the interrogation of witnesses, and counsel (where present) largely passive as a consequence; on the whole, these features still characterized trial procedure at the beginning of the nineteenth century. Those accused of felony (the most serious criminal offenses) were denied legal assistance: there was an assumption that the truth of an allegation would be revealed most effectively by a vigorous oral contest between undefended amateurs.[1] As a consequence, trials rarely lasted more than 30 minutes, and there was little protection or assistance given to the prisoner who was poorly educated, injured, or ill. There was virtually no appellate procedure, and those convicted of capital offenses were usually executed within three days of the verdict being handed down. The notorious Bloody Code prescribed death as the penalty for approximately two hundred crimes, primarily against property (although this sanction was not always implemented as a consequence of appeals to the Crown for clemency).

However, by the middle of the nineteenth century, prosecution counsel appear more regularly, and those defendants who could afford it were in turn permitted legal representation. Consequently, the criminal trial adopted a more professional format, with the presentation of ordered arguments, and the rules of evidence assumed a less inchoate form: the accused's right to test the quality of the evidence offered by the prosecution, and indeed the presumption of his or her innocence on which proceedings were predicated, were now accepted as a matter of course.

There was still no appellate procedure, but the Bloody Code had been largely dismantled: by 1842, prisoners only went to the scaffold for a handful of offenses, the most prominent of which was murder. Michel Foucault sees this as part of a pan-European movement away from the inscription of punishment upon the body of a malefactor toward an insistence that forensic process and then rehabilitative incarceration would first identify and then reform an offender (Foucault 1977: ch. 1). The spectacle of the trial gradually replaced that of the scaffold in the popular cultural imagination, and the character of the lawyer began to assume a particular significance as a self-reflexive figure of the author in works of narrative fiction.

Dickens's Experience of the Law

Critics have differed in their assessment of the quality and extent of Dickens's legal knowledge. In his famous, if somewhat reductive, appraisal of Dickens's writing entitled "The License of Modern Novelists," Fitzjames Stephen dismissed his legal learning in rather incisive terms; unlike the accomplishments of Sir Walter Scott, who was both "a lawyer and an antiquarian," Dickens's superficial knowledge of the law was that "of an attorney's clerk" (Stephen 1857: 128). Subsequent critics have been more generous in their appraisal of Dickens's grasp of legal material: William Holdsworth assures us that "we get in his books that account of the human side of the rules of law and their working, which is essential to the legal historian" (1929: 7). Phillip Collins, in his authoritative study *Dickens and Crime*, adopts Holdsworth's approach as his precedent, deploying a broader definition of "law" in order to include the activities of men like Dickens – reporters, copywriters, and so on – who worked at the margins of the legal profession (Collins 1962: ch. 1).

Dickens began his foray into the legal world when he took employment as a clerk in the office of Ellis and Blackmore in May 1827. That he found this occupation less than compelling may be inferred from Quilp's ironic description of Dick Swiveller's fate as clerk to Mr. Brass and his sister Sally in *The Old Curiosity Shop*: "With Miss Sally . . . and the beautiful fictions of the law, his days will pass like minutes. Those charming creations of the poet, John Doe and Richard Roe, when they first dawn upon him, will open a new world for the enlargement of his mind and the improvement of his heart" (ch. 33).

Of course, Dickens is only too conscious that the utilitarian vocabularies of the law will permit no such expansion of the sympathies: as Mr. Micawber is compelled to confess, to "a man possessed of the higher imaginative powers, the objection to legal studies is the amount of detail which they involve. Even in our professional correspondence . . . the mind is still not at liberty to soar to any exalted form of expression. Still, it is a great pursuit. A great pursuit!" (*David Copperfield* ch. 39). To Dickens's mature judgment, the greatness of the legal profession is the worst form of self-promotion: it is a hollow social gentility which he mocks remorselessly throughout his fictional corpus. But whatever Dickens's initial assessment of his vocation, his family's straitened circumstances required him to remain within the profession, and although his service with Ellis and Blackmore was brief, sometime after November 1828 he moved to the firm of Charles Molloy in Lincoln's Inn. He subsequently joined the staff of the *Mirror of Parliament* in 1831, a move which afforded him access to some of the first Reform Bill debates (see chapter 10). In the following year, he commenced freelance work in the Court of Doctors' Commons.

Dickens gives us a vivid picture of this now defunct legal forum in *David Copperfield*. As Steerforth explains to the eponymous protagonist:

> "It's a place that has an ancient monopoly in suits about people's wills and people's marriages, and disputes among ships and boats . . . You shall go there one day, and find

them blundering through half the nautical terms in Young's Dictionary, apropos of the 'Nancy' having run down the 'Sarah Jane', or Mr. Peggotty and the Yarmouth boatmen having put off in a gale of wind with an anchor and cable to the 'Nelson' Indiaman in distress; and you shall go there another day, and find them deep in the evidence, pro and con, respecting a clergyman who has misbehaved himself; and you shall find the judge in the nautical case, the advocate in the clergyman case, or contrariwise. They are like actors: now a man's a judge, and now he is not a judge: now he's one thing, now he's another; now he's something else, change and change about; but it's always a very pleasant, profitable little affair of private theatricals, presented to an uncommonly select audience." (ch. 23)

Dickens here pillories legal business as essentially both self-generating and trivial (although time-consuming and expensive, all themes he returns to throughout his work). Articled to Mr. Spenlow, David finds that the evidence in his first case "was just twice the length of *Robinson Crusoe*" (ch. 26) – a comment perhaps on its fictionality as well as its interminable extent. The theatricality of the law also troubles him – the actors "change and change about"; they do not assume consistent roles and are thus more likely perhaps to produce the rhetoric untethered to ethically identifiable purposes which Dickens most feared. Mr. Spenlow tells David that the work of the proctors in Doctors' Commons "was the genteelest profession in the world, and must on no account be confounded with the profession of a solicitor: being quite another sort of thing, infinitely more exclusive, less mechanical and more profitable" (ch. 26). Holdsworth (1929) provides us with a careful picture of the different categories of legal practitioner at the time Dickens was writing: many of these distinctions are of little significance to the literary critic, but it is noteworthy that solicitors (and indeed their equivalent, attorneys) were perceived by Mr. Spenlow as "an inferior race of men, universally looked down upon by all proctors of any pretensions" (ch. 26) – we can think here of the ambivalence with which the likes of Jaggers, Tulkinghorn, and Vholes were regarded by the wider community.

Matters dealt with by the civil law (contracts and wills, for example) were not to hold Dickens's attention for long. They all feature in his fiction, but it was increasingly the criminal law that preoccupied him after he became a reporter for the *Morning Chronicle* in August 1834. There are exceptions to this generalization – one of the cases he reported for that paper was the notorious adultery trial *Norton* v. *Melbourne* (1836), which may well have served as an evidentiary template for the parodic farce of *Bardell* v. *Pickwick* – but Dickens's interest in the human drama of transgression, as well as the epistemological drama of proof and inference, soon led him to the prisons and the condemned cells. Dickens was becoming interested in the power of place to generate story, and this was increasingly to bring him into conflict with the utilitarian and prescriptive lexicons of the law which he saw as institutionally blind to human suffering and indeed human feeling. Newgate, Tyburn, the old Inns of Court – all were "strange old places" of passionate drama capable of stimulating embryonic narrative:

"How many vain pleaders for mercy, do you think have turned away heart-sick from the lawyer's office, to find a resting-place in the Thames, or a refuge in the gaol? They are no ordinary houses, those. There is not a panel in the old wainscoting, but what, if it were endowed with the powers of speech and memory, could start from the wall, and tell its tale of horror – the romance of life, sir, the romance of life! Commonplace as they may seem now, I tell you they are strange old places, and I would rather hear many a legend with a terrific sounding name, than the true history of one old set of chambers." (*Pickwick Papers* ch. 21)

It suits Dickens's agenda for the moral aggrandizement of fiction to argue that the law is inattentive to the "romance of life," and this is a critique that he sustains throughout his fiction; the disparagement of forensic technique creates the space for fiction to lay claim to the discovery and perhaps creation of sentimental, affective truths which more fully account for the complexities of the human condition. He allows the young David to lament that the proctors in the Court of Doctors' Commons would care little for the musical enchantments of Dora which had captured his own imagination: "I despised them, to a man! Frozen-out old gardeners in the flower-beds of the heart, I took a personal offence against them all. The Bench was nothing to me but an insensible blunderer. The Bar had no more tenderness or poetry in it, than the bar of a public-house" (*David Copperfield* ch. 23).

As he comments with such penetrating insight in *The Pickwick Papers*, the "body" is simply an example of callous legal shorthand – "it is the lawyer's term for the restless whirling mass of cares and anxieties, affections, hopes and griefs, that make up the living man" (ch. 44). Time and time again, Dickens's protagonists contemplate the void between literary and legal language, the latter tainted by both relentless empiricism and prison-vapors. After every case, Jaggers must "wash . . . his clients off, as if he were a surgeon or a dentist" (ch. 26); Wemmick must separate fully his affectionate, if idiosyncratic, private life from that of his professional calling; and Pip must wipe the grime of Newgate from his garments and exhale its air from his lungs before he meets Estella. For Dickens, the language of the law contaminates the heart.

Early Sketches

The composition of Dickens's earliest sketches coincides with important debates within the legal profession about the extension of full legal representation to those accused of felony. In two of his most striking contributions to *Sketches by Boz* (1836), namely "Criminal Courts" and "A Visit to Newgate," we see that Dickens shares with the Bar an interest in the psychology of the criminal mind: on the other hand, Dickens simultaneously repudiated the professionalization of the discourse of guilt and regretted the displacement of first-person narratives of responsibility by the slippery rhetoric of legal actors. A decade of agitation concerning the ethics of legal rhetoric culminated in the enactment of the Prisoners' Counsel Act in 1836, which permitted a barrister to address the jury on behalf of a felon for the first time (similar rights had been extended to those accused of treason in 1695; those accused of misdemeanors had always been entitled to such assistance).

This confirmation of a fully adversarial format for the pursuit of justice and truth was perceived by some as a much-needed corrective of the advantages enjoyed by prosecution counsel (who featured more regularly in criminal cases at the Old Bailey toward the end of the eighteenth century), but was seen by others as an embarrassing and potentially scandalous acceptance of the role played by persuasion rather than knowledge in fact-finding forums.[2] The difficulty arose from a procedural requirement implemented from 1837 onward that if a prisoner should choose to employ counsel, he or she was no longer permitted to address the jury on his or her own behalf. Stripped of its right to hear the voice of the accused in answer to any charges made against them, the court could now be potentially misled or deceived by the speech of a barrister who lacked any immediate access to the "true" facts of the case. In other words, legal professionals did not supplement the voice of the accused: they replaced it. Thus the possibility of sham defenses – attempts to secure acquittals based upon technicalities rather than substance – presented a new problem for the Victorian court.

From the very beginning of his career, Dickens seems to have been greatly troubled by the power of rhetorical force seemingly divorced from a clearly defined and person-ally held ethical objective; once barristers were empowered by act of parliament to work on behalf of those whom the community might consider guilty, they became vulnerable to accusations of greed and amorality. Dickens's attitude to the profession is evident from the start of his career in fiction as he embarks upon a lifetime's offen-sive against the deployment of rhetoric untethered to ethics. Although the case of *Bardell* v. *Pickwick* is a civil case for breach of promise of marriage, Dickens's concise, humorous representations of Dodson and Fogg provide an excoriating attack upon the perceived amorality of the profession. Dodson's pre-trial advice to Pickwick is a gem of adversarial bluster:

> "We, sir, we, are guided entirely by the statement of our client. That statement, sir, may be true, or it may be false; it may be credible, or it may be incredible; but, if it be true, and if it be credible, I do not hesitate to say, sir, that our grounds of action, sir, are strong, and not to be shaken. You may be an unfortunate man, sir, or you may be a designing one; but if I were called upon, as a juryman upon my oath, sir, to express an opinion of your conduct, sir, I do not hesitate to assert that I should have but one opinion about it." (*Pickwick Papers* ch. 20)

But Dickens reserves much of his ironic antagonism for the figure of their counsel, Serjeant Buzfuz, a caricature allegedly based upon the figure of the prominent barrister Charles Phillips, who was called to the Irish Bar in 1812 and was practicing at the Old Bailey by 1821:[3]

Serjeant Buzfuz began by saying, that never, in the whole course of his professional experience – never, from the very first moment of his applying himself to the study and practice of the law – had he approached a case with feelings of such deep emotion, or with such a heavy sense of the responsibility imposed upon him – a responsibility, he would say, which he could never have supported, were he not buoyed up and sustained by a conviction so strong, that it amounted to positive certainty that the cause of truth and justice, or, in other words, the cause of his much-injured and most oppressed client, must prevail with the high-minded and intelligent dozen of men whom he now saw in that box before him. (*Pickwick Papers* ch. 33)

Dickens implies that this bombastic, hyberbolic address lacks specificity and moral groundedness, but it nevertheless produces a "visible effect" upon the jury, with several members "beginning to take voluminous notes with the utmost eagerness" (*Pickwick Papers* ch. 33). As a consequence of this hollow oratory, Pickwick could lose his assets or perhaps his liberty (although the conventions of the comic genre will dictate that the outcome is ultimately favorable); in a criminal trial, however, the stakes were higher – the accused could pay with his life for the irresponsible words of the prosecuting counsel.

In the 1840s, during an impassioned public debate regarding the license of counsel in criminal cases, Dickens exchanged bitter words with Charles Phillips in the press, and Phillips may well again have afforded the template for the address of the Attorney-General at Darnay's trial for treason in *A Tale of Two Cities*:

Mr. Attorney-General had to inform the jury that the prisoner before them, though young in years, was old in the treasonable practices which claimed the forfeit of his life. That this correspondence with the public enemy was not a correspondence of today, or of yesterday, or even of last year, or of the year before . . . That the proof would go back five years, and would show the prisoner already engaged in those pernicious missions, within a few weeks before the date of the very first action fought between the British troops and the Americans. That, for these reasons, the jury being a loyal jury (as he knew they were), and being a responsible jury (as they knew they were), must positively find the prisoner guilty, and make an end of him whether they liked it or not. That they never could lay their heads upon their pillows; that they never could tolerate the idea of their wives laying their heads upon their pillows; that they could never endure the notion of their children laying their heads upon their pillows; in short, that there never more could be, for them or theirs, any laying of heads upon pillows at all, unless the prisoner's head was taken off. That head Mr. Attorney-General concluded by demanding of them, in the name of everything he could think of with a round turn in it, and on the faith of his solemn asseveration that he already considered the prisoner as good as dead and gone. (bk. 2, ch. 3)

The rhetorical climax is absurd, yet a man may die as a consequence. Literary portraits of criminal trial procedure offer an opportunity for fiction to redeem the innocent: only Dickens the author can represent Darnay's substantive worthiness and draw attention to the miscarriage of justice that the Attorney-General had sought. This discursive competition – which discipline can most fully account for the causes and motives of transgression? Which discipline can most fully reveal the truth of character? – was thus heightened in criminal matters by the power of the state to silence the speaking subject, and Dickens often dwelt suggestively upon the plight of the prisoner condemned to death: "Imagine what have been the feelings of the men whom that fearful pew [in the prison chapel] has enclosed, and of whom, between the gallows and the knife, no mortal remnant may now remain!" ("A Visit to Newgate," 1836).

Dickens dramatizes several "last nights alive" with fascination (notably those of Fagin and Rudge), and he allows the reader to contemplate the dissection of the youthful Darnay in *A Tale of Two Cities* with a shameful pleasure that is of course tantalizingly deferred after his acquittal on the charge of treason:

> The sort of interest with which this man was stared and breathed at was not a sort that elevated humanity. Had he stood in peril of a less horrible sentence – had there been a chance of any one of its savage details being spared – by just so much would he have lost in his fascination. The form that was to be doomed to be so shamefully mangled was the sight; the immortal creature that was to be so butchered and torn asunder, yielded the sensation. Whatever gloss the various spectators put upon the interest, according to their several arts and powers of self-deceit, the interest was, at the root of it, ogreish. (bk. 2, ch. 2)

Dickens could not escape the conclusion that whilst barristers may have been the culturally preferred narrators of transgression, they did not hold a monopoly of interest in all things criminal: authors and readers were also transfixed by accounts of horrific crime, and this left him open to allegations of complicity in the discursive and narratological defense of violence that characterized popular culture in the 1830s and, particularly, the 1840s.[4]

The Newgate Novel Controversy

The implementation of the Prisoners' Counsel Act, which allowed barristers to address the jury on behalf of those charged with felony, coincided in literary terms with the early stages of the so-called "Newgate Novel" controversy. The formulation of speech on behalf of a felon was a question of ethics as well as etiquette, and it was being addressed by the Bar at the same time that novelists such as Edward Bulwer-Lytton, William Harrison Ainsworth, William Makepeace Thackeray, and the young Dickens were arguing about the ethical implications of the representation of criminality in fiction. Both groups sought to justify the legitimacy of their own practices by promulgating the binary model favored by satirists, deliberately misrepresenting the activities of their opponents. Debate was bitter, and the crux of the dispute was the relationship between words and criminal action: if a defense lawyer worked for the "manumission of murderers" (in Anthony Trollope's memorable phrase) and allowed a criminal to escape punishment, he would be free to murder again; if an author described criminal motives and intention in too sympathetic terms, then more people might be incited to embark upon a life of crime. This was the allegation made against works such as Bulwer-Lytton's *Paul Clifford* and *Eugene Aram*, and Ainsworth's *Jack Sheppard*.

A compelling example of both these charges can be found in the case of François Courvoisier, who was accused of murdering his master, Lord William Russell, in June 1840. Retained as his defense counsel, Charles Phillips seems to have lied in his client's cause – a rather liberal interpretation of the license of counsel in criminal cases which elicited two stern letters from Dickens in the *Morning Chronicle*. Whilst conceding the importance of an independent Bar, and "recognis[ing] the right of any counsel to take a brief from any man, however great his crime, and keeping within due bounds, to do his best to save him," Dickens denied that legal representation could impart "the right to defeat the ends of truth and justice by wantonly scattering aspersions upon other people."[5] Courvoisier was convicted, and in his final confession he registered the influence of Ainsworth's *Jack Sheppard* upon his decision to commit the crime – an admission that made authorial criticism of the Bar seem a little more self-interested. Dickens was clearly conscious of such a potential charge himself as the author of *Oliver Twist*, with its portrait of both a sympathetic prostitute, Nancy, and her vicious killing. Yet he seeks to avert any association with Newgate traditions by asserting that the responsibility lies with the reader to interpret his words wisely and well (a strategy reminiscent of Daniel Defoe's Preface to the equally notorious *Moll Flanders*).

Oliver, like Tom Jones, seems destined to be hanged, after an apparent descent into a life of crime is encouraged by an older relation who would profit from the youngster's demise (although Dickens's reinterpretation of Fielding's narrative paradigm requires that the hero remain unfeasibly innocent – he lacks any criminal capacity as a consequence of his inability to stay awake at the scene of any crime). Fagin does his best to contaminate Oliver with an involvement in criminal activity, and the method he chooses first is an exposure to the *Newgate Calendar*, a gory tome of scandalous crimes and punishments first published in 1773:

[Oliver] turned over the leaves carelessly at first; but, lighting upon a passage which attracted his attention, he soon became intent upon the volume. It was a history of the lives and trials of great criminals; and the pages were soiled and thumbed with use. Here, he read of dreadful crimes that made the blood run cold; of secret murders that had been committed by the lonely wayside; of bodies hidden from the eye of man in deep pits and wells: which would not keep them down, deep as they were, but had yielded them up at last, after many years, and so maddened the murderers with the sight, that in their horror they had confessed their guilt, and yelled for the gibbet to end their agony. Here, too, he read of men who, lying in their beds at dead of night, had been tempted (so they said) and led on, by their own bad thoughts, to such dreadful bloodshed as it made the flesh creep, and the limbs quail, to think of. The terrible descriptions were so real and vivid, that the sallow pages seemed to turn red with gore; and the words upon them, to be sounded in his ears, as if they were whispered, in hollow murmurs, by the spirits of the dead. (ch. 20)

Patrick Brantlinger (1998) sees in this "rhetoric of toxicity" a wider cultural anxiety about the transmissibility of criminal conduct in the mid-nineteenth century. Although the mechanism by which secrets are revealed was changing by the time Dickens wrote *Bleak House* – from providential intervention to surveillance and detection by trained professionals – this anxiety of transmission appears in his fiction in a variety of forms, such as the gaol fever feared by the Bench at the Old Bailey in *A Tale of Two Cities*, the elemental disturbances of *Barnaby Rudge*, and the unsanitary state of Tom-all-Alone's, the property tied up in Chancery proceedings, which breeds cholera and pestilence.

Dickens was also fascinated by the threateningly plastic criminal morphology evidenced by the likes of Quilp. As he notes in *Hard Times*, "When the Devil goeth about like a roaring lion, he goeth about in a shape by which few but hunters and savages are attracted" (bk. 2, ch. 8) – in other words, the most successful disguise of evil is that which allows it to enter surreptitiously into the heart of the bourgeois family unit in the form of association with the superficially respectable man. Barristers seemed to afford evil a socially acceptable disguise, but, as Brantlinger accurately points out, there are ways in which *Oliver Twist* and its genre become not just an indictment of the "rhetoric of toxicity" but also an example of it, with its own scenes of "dreadful bloodshed" in the vividly realized murder of Nancy at the hand of Sikes: crime novels invariably involve the re-enactment of violent crime and the concomitant release of transgressive energies as well as subsequent acts of detection and punishment which re-establish order and control (Brantlinger 1998: ch. 6).

Perhaps given his sense of the slipperiness of guilt when masked by professional rhetoric, it is unsurprising that Dickens requires his innocent figures to be transparently so. Suspicious of the legal profession's belief that all are guilty, Pickwick tells Serjeant Snubbin that:

> "I distinctly wish you to understand . . . that I am innocent of the falsehood laid to my charge; and although I am very well aware of the inestimable value of your assistance, sir, I must beg to add, that unless you sincerely believe this, I would rather be deprived of the aid of your talents than have the advantage of them." (*Pickwick Papers* ch. 30)

Throughout Dickens's fictional corpus, we see a fear of the effects of rhetoric produced solely for profit. Lawyers are at fault here, but so too are professional orators in other walks of public life, such as Mr. Slackbridge in his address to the workers' meetings in *Hard Times*: as the plain-speaking Stephen says, " 'Tis this Delegate's trade for t' speak . . . an' he's paid for 't, and he knows his work" (bk. 2, ch. 4). Trooper George states the case for the rejection of legal representation in *Bleak House* when he is wrongly accused of the murder of Tulkinghorn:

> "I should have got a lawyer, and he would have said (as I have often read in the newspapers), 'my client says nothing, my client reserves his defence – my client this, that and t'other'. Well, 'tis not the custom of that breed to go straight, according to my

opinion, or to think that other men do. Say, I am innocent, and I get a lawyer. He would be as likely to believe me guilty as not; perhaps more. What would he do, whether or not? Act as if I was; – shut my mouth up, tell me not to commit myself, keep circumstances back, chop the evidence small, quibble, and get me off perhaps! . . . I would rather be hanged in my own way . . . What I say is, I must come off clear and full or not at all. Therefore when I hear stated against me what is true, I say it's true; and when they tell me, 'whatever you say will be used,' I tell them I don't mind that: I mean it to be used. If they can't make me innocent out of the whole truth, they are not likely to do it out of anything less, or anything else. And if they are, it's worth nothing to me." (ch. 52)

Dickens was fascinated by the figure of the man wrongfully accused: Pickwick, Stephen, and George all fall under suspicion when circumstances conspire to suggest their guilt. The difficulties of establishing one's innocence clearly continued to preoccupy Dickens. In his last, unfinished work, *The Mystery of Edwin Drood*, Jasper observes of Neville Landless with sinister intent that "Circumstances may accumulate so strongly even against an innocent man, that, directed, sharpened, and pointed, they may slay him" (ch. 19). Rachel hopes that Stephen will "come back of his own accord to clear himself, and put all those that have injured his character, and he not here for its defence, to shame" (bk. 3, ch. 4), but as in the case of George and Mr. Pickwick, careful fictional advocacy is required to prove his inherent worthiness.

As an advocate, Dickens works carefully to unpick suspicious circumstances and establish sound alibis (the importance of the latter in the law of the time is indicated by Sam Weller's father's insistence that Pickwick will not win his case without an alibi; *Pickwick Papers* ch. 32). In both his fiction and a number of his non-fictional pieces (most notably "The Demeanour of Murderers," *Household Words* [June 14, 1856], a response to the trial of the notorious poisoner, William Palmer in 1856), Dickens continues to suggest that the courts – confused by oratory for hire and the application of pedantic rules of evidence – lack the necessary skills to read character properly and make the appropriate findings of fact. "Nature never writes a bad hand," Dickens asserts: "her writing, as it may be read in the human countenance, is invariably legible, if we come at all trained to the reading of it" ("The Demeanour of Murderers"). He believed that authors possessed those skills whereas lawyers did not. He seems to have preferred not to acknowledge that self-evident innocence would leave little room for the entertaining inventions of authors of fiction, or, indeed, that he too could have been accused of writing for hire and profit.

Dickens and the Scaffold

To be falsely accused of murder in the mid-Victorian period was to stand in deadly peril of the scaffold. In *Barnaby Rudge*, Dennis tells us that the hangman's employment was "sound, Protestant, constitutional, English work" (ch. 37), the "peculiar pet and panacea" (ch. 74) of every English parliament. (Dennis is nevertheless hanged

for his part in the Gordon Riots, whereas Collins [1962: 221] tells us that his historical counterpart was in fact pardoned because of his intrinsic utility in the preservation
of social order.) Dickens attended a number of public executions in the course of his
career – most notably those of Courvoisier in 1840 and Frederick and Maria Manning
in 1849. Courvoisier's execution was the subject of Thackeray's powerful piece "On
Going to See a Man Hanged," which appeared in *Fraser's Magazine* in August 1840.
Both men experienced a profound revulsion at the spectacle, and in 1846 Dickens
wrote five letters to the *Daily News* calling for the abolition of capital punishment.
Despite the "wickedness of [Courvoisier's] defence" (aided and abetted by the allegedly deceitful lawyer Charles Phillips), Dickens nevertheless argued that execution
was no deterrent to crime: that it in fact hardened society's sensibilities; that it fascinated and impelled toward it those in whom criminal proclivities were already discernible. By 1849, however, Dickens's attitude had changed. In two letters written
to *The Times* after the execution of the Mannings, he calls only for the abolition of
public executions.[6] Instead, he argued, such punishments should be carried out within
the privacy of prison walls, an amendment to penal process which was effected
in 1868.

Dickens and the Court of Chancery

The 1840s were a seminal period for Dickens's engagement with, and understanding
of, the civil law as well as the criminal system. Preoccupied with the exploitation of
his work as a consequence of piracy overseas, Dickens brought five actions in Chancery
in 1844 to restrain breaches of copyright. His financially unsuccessful attempts to
protect his own work left Dickens outraged:

> My feeling . . . is the feeling common, I suppose, to three fourths of the reflecting part
> of the community in our happiest of all possible countries; and that is, that it is better
> to suffer a great wrong than to have recourse to the much greater wrong of the law. I
> shall not easily forget the expense, and anxiety, and horrible injustice of the *Carol* case,
> wherein, in asserting the plainest right on earth, I was really treated as if I was the
> robber, instead of the robbed . . . And I know of nothing that *could* come, even of a
> successful action, which would be worth the mental trouble and disturbance it would
> cost. (*Letters* 4: 650–1)

A similarly energetic indignation characterizes *Bleak House*. Like the Circumlocution Office, which thwarts effective government in *Little Dorrit*, Chancery:

> gives to monied might the means abundantly of wearying out the right; which so
> exhausts finances, patience, courage, hope; so overthrows the brain and breaks the heart;
> that there is not an honourable man among its practitioners who would not give – who
> does not often give – the warning "Suffer any wrong that can be done you, rather than
> come here!" (ch. 1)

The Court of Chancery "has its decaying houses and its blighted lands in every shire . . . its worn-out lunatic in every madhouse, and its dead in every church-yard," yet although the case of *Jarndyce* v. *Jarndyce* "has been a death to many . . . it is a joke in the profession" (ch. 1). Lawyers in training have "been in the habit of fleshing their legal wit upon it" (ch. 1): it is "a monument of Chancery practice . . . in which . . . every difficulty, every contingency, every masterly fiction, every form of procedure known in that court, is represented over and over again" (ch. 3). Sir Leicester Dedlock labels it "a slow, expensive, British, constitutional kind of thing" (ch. 2) – the label closely resembles that which Dennis affords the scaffold in *Barnaby Rudge*. As Mr. Jarndyce explains, "The Lawyers have twisted it into such a state of bedevilment that the original merits of the case have long disappeared from the face of the earth. It's about a will, and the trusts under a Will – or it was, once. It's about nothing but costs now. All the rest, by some extraordinary means, has melted away" (ch. 8). Richard and Ada's inheritance is solely that "of a protracted misery" (ch. 5), and the listless Richard, unsettled by the suit, "before [he] quite knew the difference between a suit at law and a suit of clothes" (ch. 23) is left prey to the parasitic Vholes whose self-interested generation of legal work ("The one great principle of the English law is, to make business for itself"; ch. 39) epitomizes the conservativism that prevents the implementation of reform.

Critics remain unsure whether or not Dickens's portrait of this destructive legal lethargy is in fact an accurate representation of Chancery process in the 1850s. Writing in the *Edinburgh Review* in 1857, Fitzjames Stephen argued that Dickens had willfully portrayed abuses which no longer existed in an attempt to bring the law into disrepute. Holdsworth suggests that the figure of the Chancellor in *Jarndyce* v. *Jarndyce* may be based upon Lord Lyndhurst, and that the state of Chancery practice in the novel could be evidenced by "the witnesses who gave evidence before the Chancery Commission, which reported in 1826"; consequently, the action of the novel may take place as early as 1827 (Holdsworth 1929: 79–81). Although Dickens states in the Preface that he seeks to represent Chancery practice "with substantial . . . tru[th]," he seems to ignore the significant reforms of the 1830s and 1840s (which impacted favorably upon such matters as the length of Chancery suits) in an attempt to allow the law's excesses to act as the foil to his philosophy of fiction – an aesthetic manifesto based upon the affective truths uncovered and practiced by Esther. It is Esther who voices the repugnance in which all men of feeling must hold the law:

> To see everything going on so smoothly, and to think of the roughness of the suitors' lives and deaths; to see all that full dress and ceremony, and to think of the waste, and want, and beggared misery it represented; to consider that, while the sickness of hope deferred was raging in so many hearts, this polite show went calmly on from day to day, and year to year, in such good order and composure; to behold the Lord Chancellor, and the whole array of practitioners under him, looking at one another and the spectators, as if nobody had ever heard that all over England the name in which they were assembled was a bitter jest; was held in universal horror, contempt and indignation; was known for something so flagrant and bad, that little short of a miracle could bring anything

good out of it to any one: This was so curious and self-contradictory to me, who had no experience of it, that it was at first incredible, and I could not comprehend it. (ch. 24)

That Dickens chooses Tulkinghorn to bear the burden of narrative guilt – and, indeed, to participate in the activity of narration by the compilation of the evidence that will disgrace Lady Dedlock – confirms the discomfort which the author of fiction feels at the industry of the legal profession (see Weisberg 1992: ch. 4). Their rhetorical skills are similar, but Dickens wants the reader to believe that these talents are deployed for radically distinct purposes. Tulkinghorn "wears his usual expressionless mask – if it be a mask – and carries family secrets in every limb of his body, and every crease of his dress" (ch. 12). He is no more motivated by anger or hostility than Jaggers is animated by self-interest – both are inscrutable. Once Tulkinghorn has identified the nature of Lady Dedlock's indiscretion, he holds the secret in trust for Sir Leicester and the credit of the baronetcy: "it is part of Mr. Tulkinghorn's policy and mastery to have no political opinions: indeed, no opinions" (ch. 40). His misogyny is institutional, a product of the rise of the professions in the nineteenth century which invariably exposed the female body (and the language of sensibility, sentiment, and passion) to the rational scientific gaze of the male clinician or lawyer (see Thomas 1999: chs. 1 and 6). Tulkinghorn's demise affords Lady Dedlock no reprieve; instead, it provides the opportunity for the introduction of Inspector Bucket as the investigative agent who drives the narrative forward to its resolution and Lady Dedlock to her death. Dickens admired the work of the Detective Force, established in 1842 (12 years after the professionalization of the police force itself), but its arts are often indistinguishable from those of the criminals whose activities it sought to police. Only the author's sanction can differentiate the work performed in the narrative by Bucket from that performed by the eloquent, educated Tulkinghorn whose rhetorical facility marks him out as the author's scapegoat for the transgressions countenanced by the text.

Dickens's Use of the Law in his Fiction

Dickens was not the first to use the law as an organizational principle in his narrative fiction: Fielding, Richardson, and Godwin were amongst those who offered examples of how such epistemological marriages might be undertaken. But his innovation lies in the way in which he allows legal procedure to shape his choices of narrative form, whilst simultaneously suggesting the powerlessness of the law truly to uncover the truths of human character. He mines the lexicon of the law for its richly comic and metaphoric possibilities: Miss Flite awaits the Day of Judgment – "I have discovered that the sixth seal mentioned in the Revelations is the Great Seal [of Chancery]. It has been open a long time. Pray accept my blessing" (ch. 3) – whilst Mr. Guppy "models his conversation on forensic principles" and "manifests an enquiring mind in matters of evidence" in his relentless interrogation of "witnesses" like Jo (ch. 19). In *A Tale of Two Cities*, Dickens incorporates into his account of Darnay's trial the staccato shorthand of answers given in cross-examination in a successful attempt to undermine the credibility of witnesses for the prosecution. The case against Darnay is thus shown to be poorly conceived.

> Had [Barsad] ever been a spy himself? No, he scorned the base insinuation. What did he live upon? His property. Where was his property? He didn't precisely remember where it was. What was it? No business of anybody's. Had he inherited it? Yes, he had. From whom? Distant relation. Very distant? Rather. Ever been in prison? Certainly not. Never in a debtors' prison? Didn't see what that had to do with it. Never in a debtors' prison? – Come, once again. Never? Yes. How many times? Two or three times. Not five or six? Perhaps . . . Expect to get anything by this evidence? No. Not in regular government pay and employment to lay traps? Oh dear no. (bk. 2, ch. 3)

Whilst often humorous in tone, Dickens's imaginative appropriations of legal process serve a darkly satirical purpose. The language of the law is callous to the core. Richard Carstone's acquisition of a "litigious character" as a consequence of his immersion in *Jarndyce* v. *Jarndyce* – "the uncertainties and delays of the Chancery suit had imparted to his nature something of the careless spirit of a gamester, who felt that he was part of a great gaming system" (ch. 17) – suggests an incisive pun on the chance-riddled procedures of Chancery, which places the Court in opposition to the providential qualities of fairness, benevolence, and justice promulgated by Mr. Jarndyce himself. In a particularly uncomfortable juxtaposition of humor and tragedy, the Chancellor forgets whom the wards in Chancery are to be placed with, and counsel must intervene to remind him:

> "I will see them and satisfy myself as to the expediency of making the order for them to reside with their uncle."
>   Mr Tangle on his legs again.
>   "Begludship's pardon – dead."
>   "With their," Chancellor looking through his double eye-glass at the papers on his desk, "grandfather."
>   "Begludship's pardon – victim of rash action – brains." (ch. 1)

The Jarndyce family has been devastated by the emotional and financial impact of the case; they have succumbed to ill health and self-harm. There is no more concise and economic indictment in Dickens's writing of the damage that the factual, utilitarian language of the law can inflict upon the heart. Dickens claims for literature the power to restore and rehabilitate these fractured family inheritances: evidence is lost, the case dissolves in costs, but a new Bleak House is established at the point of narrative closure. Dickens's attacks on the law impart a legitimacy to his quest to claim for fiction the power to account more fully and truthfully for the human condition.

NOTES

1 On criminal trial procedure in the period, see Douglas Hay, "Property, Authority and the Criminal Law" in Hay et al. (1975: 17–63) and Langbein (2003: ch. 1).

2 On the implementation of the Prisoners' Counsel Act (1836), see Cairns (1998) and Langbein (2003). For the impact of this legislation on narrative form, see Schramm (2000: ch. 3).

3 See Dickens, *Letters* (2: 86–7), and Schramm (2004: 290–5).

4 See, for example, "Murder-mania," *Chambers's Edinburgh Journal* n.s. 12 (1849): 209–11.

5 The two letters are dated [?June 21, 1840] and June 26, 1840. They are signed "Manlius" and they are attributed to Dickens by the editors on evidence of considerable strength (*Letters* 2: 86–9, 90–1).

6 The letters to the *Daily News* are dated February 23 and 28, then March 9, 13, and 16, 1846. For their texts, see Paroissien (1985: 213–48). The letters to *The Times* are dated November 14 and 19, 1849. They are discussed at length in Collins (1962: ch. 10).

REFERENCES AND FURTHER READING

Bender, John (1987). *Imagining the Penitentiary: Fiction and the Architecture of Mind in Eighteenth-century England*. Chicago: University of Chicago Press.

Brantlinger, Patrick (1998). *The Reading Lesson: The Threat of Mass Literacy in Nineteenth-century British Fiction*. Bloomington, IN: Indiana University Press.

Cairns, David (1998). *Advocacy and the Making of the Adversarial Criminal Trial 1800–1865*. Oxford: Oxford University Press.

Clark, Cumberland (1919). *Talfourd and Dickens*. London: Chiswick.

Collins, Phillip (1962). *Dickens and Crime*. Basingstoke: Macmillan.

Dolin, Kieran (1999). *Fiction and the Law: Legal Discourse in Victorian and Modernist Literature*. Cambridge: Cambridge University Press.

Foucault, Michel (1977). *Discipline and Punish: The Birth of the Prison*. London: Allen Lane.

Gatrell, V. A. C. (1994). *The Hanging Tree: Execution and the English People 1770–1868*. Oxford: Oxford University Press.

Grossman, Jonathan (2002). *The Art of Alibi: English Law Courts and the Novel*. Baltimore, MD: Johns Hopkins University Press.

Hay, Douglas, Linebaugh, Peter, Rule, John G., et al. (Eds.) (1975). *Albion's Fatal Tree: Crime and Society in Eighteenth-century England*. London: Allen Lane.

Holdsworth, William (1929). *Charles Dickens as a Legal Historian*. New Haven, CT: Yale University Press.

Hollingsworth, Keith (1963). *The Newgate Novel 1830–1847: Bulwer, Ainsworth, Dickens, and Thackeray*. Detroit: Wayne State University Press.

Langbein, John (2003). *The Origins of Adversary Criminal Trial*. Oxford: Oxford University Press.

Paroissien, David (Ed.) (1985). *Selected Letters of Charles Dickens*. Basingstoke: Macmillan.

Pettitt, Clare (2004). *Patent Inventions: Intellectual Property and the Victorian Novel*. Oxford: Oxford University Press.

Rodensky, Lisa (2003). *The Crime in Mind: Criminal Responsibility and the Victorian Novel*. Oxford: Oxford University Press.

Schramm, Jan-Melissa (2000). *Testimony and Advocacy in Victorian Law, Literature and Theology*. Cambridge: Cambridge University Press.

— (2004). "The anatomy of a barrister's tongue": rhetoric, satire, and the Victorian Bar in England. *Victorian Literature and Culture*, 32, 285–303.

Stephen, Fitzjames (1857). The license of modern novelists. *Edinburgh Review*, 106, 124–56.

Thackeray, William Makepeace (1840). On going to see a man hanged. *Fraser's Magazine*, 22, 150–8.

Thomas, Ronald (1999). *Detective Fiction and the Rise of Forensic Science*. Cambridge: Cambridge University Press.

Ward, Ian (1995). *Law and Literature: Possibilities and Perspectives*. Cambridge: Cambridge University Press.

Weisberg, Richard (1984). *The Failure of the Word: The Protagonist as Lawyer in Modern Fiction*. New Haven, CT: Yale University Press.

— (1992). *Poethics: And Other Strategies of Law and Literature*. New York: Columbia University Press.

Welsh, Alexander (1987). *From Copyright to Copperfield: The Identity of Dickens*. Cambridge, MA: Harvard University Press.

— (1992). *Strong Representations: Narrative and Circumstantial Evidence in England*. Baltimore, MD: Johns Hopkins University Press.

Part IV
The Fiction

19

The Pickwick Papers

David Parker

On February 16, 1836, Dickens accepted a proposal from Chapman and Hall to provide copy for a book "illustrative of manners and life in the Country to be published monthly" (*Letters* 1: 648). The publishers turned to Dickens when they failed to engage other writers to supply 28 pages of text to accompany four woodcuts designed by Robert Seymour, whose original idea it had been to supply a series of engravings depicting Cockney sporting life. The first number was published on March 31, 1836 at 1 shilling, after which quick adjustments were made when Seymour committed suicide on April 20, to be replaced initially by R. W. Buss and then by Hablot Browne, who illustrated the fourth number. The publishers agreed to increase Dickens's salary (from £14 a month to 20 guineas) in return for more copy (32 printed pages), and the serial took off, running for 20 monthly numbers (missing June 1837) until November 1837, when the novel also appeared in one volume.

The Pickwick Papers was launched thanks to a proposal from an illustrator. In February 1836, publishers Chapman and Hall invited Dickens to write only "a monthly something," to link etchings by Robert Seymour depicting members of a "Nimrod Club." They were to "go out shooting, fishing, and so forth, and [get] themselves into difficulties through their want of dexterity." Dickens put a counter-proposal. He wanted to write about "a freer range of English scenes and people," and urged that the plates should arise from the text, rather than the other way round. "My views being deferred to," he later recalled, "I thought of Mr. Pickwick, and wrote the first number."

The scheme scarcely seemed promising, however. Friends – probably Harrison Ainsworth and Edward Bulwer-Lytton – warned him against such a "low, cheap form of publication" (Preface to the Cheap Edition, 1847). In the early nineteenth century, fiction in parts could be published at a fraction of the cost of a three-volume novel, and usually targeted readers at the bottom of the market. Writers concentrated upon producing sensational numbers, at the expense of overall coherence. Raffish and disjointed, Pierce Egan's *Life in London* (1820–1) is perhaps the most durable example before 1836. Illustrations, by George and Robert Cruikshank, were as much an attraction as Egan's text (Tillotson 1954: 24–32). Seymour would have been mindful of this.

The first part of *Pickwick* was published at the end of March 1836, but to begin with, aware of the reputation of serial fiction, Dickens did not venture to call it a novel. Sales climbed steeply after the introduction of Sam Weller in the fourth part. It was not until November, however, that Dickens showed signs of revaluing the book's status. "If I were to live a hundred years, and write three novels in each," he told the publishers, "I should never be so proud of any of them, as I am of Pickwick" (*Letters* 1: 189). Even so, as late as August 1837, speaking of his plan to publish *Barnaby Rudge* in the conventional three volumes, he allowed himself to think of that as his "first Novel" — no matter that *Pickwick* was by then a publishing phenomenon only three months from completion (*Letters* 1: 165, 283).

Thanks to a melancholy event soon after the book was launched, Dickens obtained undisputed control of the project, and the opportunity to mold it as he chose. On April 20, 1836, in the grip of depression, Seymour committed suicide. Yet traces of his plan lingered, Dickens's protestations notwithstanding. A contrasting Gothic font highlights the "Sporting Transactions" of the Pickwick Club in Seymour's design for the wrapper of the parts. Sportsmen and sporting equipment adorn it. Only Mr. Winkle professes devotion to sport in the first chapter of the book, but Seymour's illustration for it features fishing tackle, a gun, a billiards triangle, a bulldog, and the skull and antlers of a stag. Most of his illustrations draw attention to activities likely to intimidate the city-bred, unused to outdoor pursuits — and the text follows suit.

The process of finding a replacement for Seymour is equally revealing. R. W. Buss was the first candidate tried. Two of his plates were printed. "The Cricket Match" has a sporting subject; "The Arbour Scene" does not, but it does feature Mr. Tupman, wounded as a result of Pickwickian sporting ineptitude. Buss was replaced in turn by Hablot Knight Browne. "Phiz," as he would soon be calling himself, was to remain Dickens's principal illustrator for 24 years. Some of his plates for *Pickwick* preserve the spirit of Seymour's plan. "Mr. Pickwick Slides," for instance, depicts a timid venture into winter sports. Most, though, scarcely conform to anything Seymour had in mind. Yet evidence suggests that Phiz was selected because he was qualified to succeed Seymour. The young William Makepeace Thackeray was still seeking work as an illustrator in 1836. A dozen years later he inadvertently revealed why his application for the position might have been rejected. "I have not the slightest idea how to draw a horse, a dog, or a sporting scene of any sort," he confessed (Welcome 1982: 135). Phiz, on the other hand, was probably best known for a prize-winning etching illustrating William Cowper's "John Gilpin." His discomfited linen-draper, astride a runaway horse, strikingly resembles images he was to make of Mr. Pickwick.

These lingering traces of Seymour's proposals suggest that his and Dickens's intentions tallied more closely than we are wont to allow. In later years, Seymour's widow strove to exaggerate her husband's role in the launching of *Pickwick*. In response, Dickens strove to belittle it. The truth is that Seymour's plan triggered something in Dickens's own sensibility. He resisted the notion of a "Nimrod Club": "the idea was not novel," he remarked (Preface to the Cheap Edition, 1847). But he did not reject it so much as sublimate it.

Thanks to wealth created by the industrial revolution, the urban middle classes were acquiring power at the expense of the gentry. The Reform Act of 1832 had enfranchised more prosperous members of the middle classes. Middle-class experimentation with country sports had become an emblem of this shift of power. Stringent game laws had for centuries effectively barred almost anyone but landowners from enjoying the pleasures of the chase. The more draconian acts, however, had been repealed in 1827 and 1831. *The Sporting Magazine*, launched in 1792, featured writing by "Nimrod," pen-name of Charles James Apperley, who celebrated the adventures and misadventures of fox-hunting gentlemen. But from 1831, *The Sporting Magazine* was challenged by a *New Sporting Magazine*. Its editor, R. S. Surtees, created a new sporting icon – Jorrocks, a fox-hunting grocer endowed with the passion, skill, and courage of his gentlemanly predecessors, but not with their elegance of deportment and discourse.

Others chose to represent members of the urban middle classes dabbling disastrously in country pursuits. As early as 1782, Cowper had achieved success with his comic poem "John Gilpin." It tells the story of a "linen-draper bold" on a family excursion, whose borrowed horse runs away with him. Thomas Hood's poem, *Epping Hunt* (1829), is about the misadventures of a city grocer on a stag hunt. A genre took shape, centered upon the mishaps of Cockney sportsmen. *Cockney*, it should be understood, meant no more than "town-bred" in the early nineteenth century. Its use was not restricted to working-class inhabitants of east London.

A graphic genre developed in parallel. Thomas Rowlandson had introduced an element of caricature into the sporting paintings and prints popular in the eighteenth century. As the nineteenth century began, James Gillray published his first etchings of Cockney sportsmen. George Cruikshank, who was to illustrate Dickens's first book, *Sketches by Boz*, provided plates for *Epping Hunt*. Phiz illustrated an edition of "John Gilpin." Seymour had followed the fashion with his comic plates for Richard Penn's *Maxims and Hints for an Angler* (1833).

In a crude way, the genre addressed something that mattered to Dickens. Like many of the *Sketches by Boz*, its subject matter is social mobility. But in *Pickwick* he tries something he had attempted in none of the sketches, something no one had attempted in tales of Cockney sportsmen. He strove to reconcile social mobility with the getting of wisdom. He created a fable about new prosperity and opportunity leading, not just to self-exposure, but to self-discovery. The Pickwickians make fools of themselves in all sorts of unaccustomed activities, not just in country pursuits. The book seized the public's imagination, not least because Dickens saw beyond the emblematic significance of country sports, and represented the middle-class demand for a place in the sun more squarely.

As he became more conscious of his craft later in his career, Dickens made more and more of his decisiveness and initiative in the launching of *Pickwick*. But in 1836, instinct seems to have been his guide. He used the term *novel* or avoided it, as the mood took him. He adapted as much as he rejected of Seymour's proposal. But from the outset the book began to take the shape of a novel. Wherever the idea came from, whatever the mode of publication, however episodic the book, whether he acknowl-edged it or not, he was going to write a story which develops about characters who change.

Contemporary readers of the novel certainly sensed that there were developments to be followed, and eagerly awaited the next issue. John Forster tells a story of a cler-gyman "administering ghostly consolation to a sick person," afterwards overhearing the man say: "Well, thank God, *Pickwick* will be out in ten days any way!" (Forster bk. 2, ch. 1). *Pickwick* in fact transformed the reputation of serialized fiction, made it a vehicle for carefully crafted novels, and enlarged its audience. Many a reader unable to afford a guinea and a half for a three-volume novel could find a shilling for a monthly part. Readers still poorer – plus people unable to read – clubbed together, bought parts, and circulated them, or listened to them being read aloud (*Oxford Dickens* 514–19).

Seymour's plan for a "Nimrod Club" inspired Dickens to develop something better because social mobility was so important to him. He was content to write about middle-class characters being humiliated, but literary fashion could not obliterate what ascent within the middle classes meant to him, what the threat to that ascent had meant, posed by Warren's Blacking warehouse and the Marshalsea Prison. At Warren's, Dickens had felt his "early hopes of growing up to be a learned and distin-guished man" crushed (Forster bk. 1, ch. 2). Mr. Pickwick's insistence that he is a learned and distinguished man is the same anxiety, viewed through the prism of comedy. For all that he insists too loudly, and cannot match his pretensions, we do not sneer. We rejoice both in his silliness and in his cultural heroism.

He is different from Cowper's John Gilpin and Hood's John Huggins. All three are middle class, and yearn to demonstrate mastery in activities they have not been bred to. But the callings of John Gilpin and John Huggins are foregrounded. John Gilpin is eager to serve his customers. John Huggins's business week is described. Mr. Pickwick, in contrast, is retired. His former business activities are unidentified and barely alluded to. The middle-class status of the Pickwickians is indicated chiefly in oblique hints, such as the scarcely patrician names of club members – Smiggers, Blotton – and the suburban settings of Mr. Pickwick's early researches – "Hornsey, Highgate, Brixton, and Camberwell" (ch. 1).

The pretensions of Cowper's hero, and of Hood's, are modest. John Gilpin wants only to ride a horse to Edmonton and back; John Huggins only to ride in a stag hunt. Mr. Pickwick, in contrast, demands acclaim as a sage. In doing so, he is as ill advised as any Cockney sportsman, but readers find themselves more than a little complicit. The Cockney sportsman genre is postulated upon social stability and unquestioned hierarchy. Readers are invited to take pleasure in the spectacle of Cockneys learning not to have ideas above their station. No such pleasure is offered by *Pickwick*.

Mr. Pickwick's pretensions owe something to a model Dickens heeded, quite dis-tinct from the Cockney sportsman model. It showed him how to organize his book around the misadventures of a central character, how to use preposterous objectives to make that character funny, and how to develop that character. Contemporary reviews recognized that *Pickwick* was in the tradition launched by *Don Quixote* (Johnson 1952: 1. 155). Like Cervantes, Dickens conceived a hero whose follies, far from exciting readers' scorn, endear him to them. Like Cervantes, Dickens pillories those who humiliate the hero, more than he does the hero himself. For Don Quixote's infatuation with knight-errantry, Dickens substitutes Mr. Pickwick's infatuation with learning and learned speculation of a kind rarely open to men of his background. He sets himself up as a sage, and expects due deference. Similarly deluded, his nearest friends grant it. Early in the novel, however, there are hints that Mr. Pickwick needs to listen more to his heart, less to his head.

The first chapter of *Pickwick* gives an account of a club meeting, and details the pretensions of the central figures: Mr. Tupman's amorous inclinations, Mr. Snodgrass's poetic ambitions, and Mr. Winkle's sporting interests. Each seeks to excel in a pursuit suited to the wealthy and leisured, but because their pretensions are signified chiefly by the clothes they wear, we suspect superficiality. The pretensions of Mr. Pickwick himself, however, receive most attention. We detect irony in such phrases as "the gigantic brain of Pickwick." Excitement at his "Theory of Tittlebats" (sticklebacks) warns us things are being got out of proportion. And logic-chopping is required to reward him with the deference he demands. A jealous haberdasher accuses Mr. Pickwick of being a "humbug." The quarrel is resolved by agreement that Mr. Blotton had used the word only "in its Pickwickian sense."

Mr. Pickwick does profess philanthropy, to be sure: "if ever the fire of self-importance broke out in his bosom," he is reported to have announced, "the desire to benefit the human race in preference effectually quenched it." Humanity in the abstract is the object of his benevolence, however. He says nothing of compassion toward individuals, less likely to yield the deference he craves. At the end of the chapter, to loud applause, members of the "Corresponding Society of the Pickwick Club" resolve to travel the land and report their observations. But readers are left doubtful about whether they have the ability to take on the world.

The first episode of the novel takes Mr. Pickwick and his companions to Rochester. Mr. Pickwick begins his observations in the cab conveying him to the Golden Cross, terminus of the Rochester coach. He quizzes a suspicious cabman. "How old is this horse, my friend?" he asks. "'Forty-two,' replied the driver, eying him askant." More innocent questions ensue, and more preposterous answers. Mr. Pickwick notices nothing. Then, at the Golden Cross, the cabman proposes to fight Mr. Pickwick and his companions, on the grounds that they are informers – sent to check that cabmen obey regulations. Their humiliation is the greater because of the way in which it is relieved. An end is put to the mayhem by a fellow passenger, plainly much less prosperous than they are, but with a much greater command of gentlemanly authority. His clothes are shabby, his baggage consists of a single brown-paper parcel, but "an indescribable air of jaunty impudence and perfect self-possession pervaded the whole man." He resolves the quarrel imperiously: "Here, No. 924, take your fare, and take yourself off – respectable gentleman – know him well – none of your nonsense . . ." (ch. 2).

Aboard the coach, the stranger entertains the Pickwickians with a flow of talk. Mr. Pickwick is captivated by observations on life in general, Mr. Snodgrass by a story about an epic poem, Mr. Winkle by a story about a pointer, Mr. Tupman by a story about romantic conquest in Spain. In Rochester, they cultivate the stranger's company. He repays their kindness by misbehavior at a charity ball, which results in an irascible army surgeon challenging the innocent Mr. Winkle to a duel. It is aborted when Dr. Slammer realizes he is about to fight the wrong man, but the Pickwickians are humiliated (ch. 2). One officer tells Mr. Pickwick that, if he had been the one affronted, he "would have pulled your nose, sir, and the nose of every man in this company." Their humiliation is compounded by the discovery that the stranger who has duped everyone – Mr. Jingle – is a strolling actor (ch. 3).

In the first episode alone, then, for all their pretensions, the Pickwickians find themselves equipped to cope neither with the proletarian bloody-mindedness of the cabman, nor with the elaborate protocol of the officer class. They have been outshone, moreover, by someone emulating gentlemanly style, not reverentially as they do, but unscrupulously, with the professional expertise of a man scarcely entitled to middle-class status. Against the friends' overconfidence in being what they want to be, Dickens sets Jingle's conscienceless ability to be whatever suits him for the moment. By these means, Dickens problematizes the very notion of status.

But for all the Pickwickians' delusions, they are guileless and kind, and Jingle's impudence deserves retribution. By the beginning of the second monthly part (chs. 3–5), it is clear there must be repercussions. And there are. In the course of the novel, Jingle appears, disappears, reappears, and commits more outrages, until what is between him and Mr. Pickwick is resolved. Jingle, then, is functionally important. So is Sam Weller, the bootblack who becomes Mr. Pickwick's manservant. Sam knows the streets, the sufferings of the poor on them, the tricks of scoundrels on them, the vulnerability of the unwary on them. His role is to assist Mr. Pickwick in acquiring such wisdom. Like the child Dickens, Mr. Pickwick finds his innocent yearning for distinction adjusted by a worldly acuity coming out of acquaintance with boot blacking.

Sam, though, does not instantly adopt the conventional role of faithful retainer. He tests his new employer. During the episode centered on the Eatanswill election (chs. 13–15), he tells Mr. Pickwick a story about his father, a stagecoach driver once drawn into electoral malpractice:

"'It's a wery bad road between this and London,' says the gen'l'm'n – 'Here and there it *is* a heavy road,' says my father – 'Specially near the canal, I think,' says the gen'l'm'n – 'Nasty bit that 'ere,' says my father – 'Well, Mr. Weller,' says the gen'l'm'n, 'you're a wery good whip, and can do what you like with your horses, we know. We're all wery fond o' you, Mr. Weller, so in case you *should* have an accident when you're a bringing these here woters down, and *should* tip 'em over into the canal vithout hurtin' 'em, this is for yourself,' says he – 'Gen'l'm'n, you're wery kind,' says my father, 'and I'll drink your health in another glass of wine,' says he; vich he did, and then buttons up the

money, and bows himself out. You vouldn't believe, Sir," continued Sam, with a look
of inexpressible impudence at his master, "that on the wery day as he came down with
them woters, his coach *was* upset on that 'ere wery spot, and ev'ry man on 'em was
turned into the canal."

"And got out again?" inquired Mr Pickwick, hastily. "Why," replied Sam, very
slowly, "I rather think one old gentleman was missin'; I know his hat was found, but I
a'n't quite certain whether his head was in it or not. But what I look at, is the hex-tra-
ordinary, and wonderful coincidence, that arter what that gen'l'm'n said my father's
coach should be upset in that wery place, and on that wery day!" (ch. 13)

"A very extraordinary circumstance indeed," is all Mr. Pickwick can find to say. He
cannot fathom the mischief. But if Sam is unimpressed by his master's practical
understanding, perhaps he notes the kindness of heart manifested in the concern for
immersed voters. Up to no good, Mr. Jingle materializes again at Eatanswill. Pursuing
him aboard a coach to Bury St. Edmunds, Sam begins to disclose to his master what
he has learned from his vagabond experiences. He tells Mr. Pickwick about "Sights,
sir . . . as 'ud penetrate your benevolent heart, and come out on the other side"
(ch. 16). With Sam at his side, Mr. Pickwick jostles his way toward wisdom and
dignity through a throng of those who share his longing for status, of those who
compete with him for it, and of those who would deny it to him. The name alone of
one status-seeker says it all. Its owner, Peter Magnus, complacently observes: "It's
rather a good name, I think, sir?" (ch. 22).

A central theme of the novel is disparity between style and substance. The Pickwickians adopt styles they are not up to. And the very narrative voice enacts this
theme. Elsewhere, I have used the term "archness" to indicate what is achieved (Parker
1971). Readers are exposed to a modification of mock-heroic. In place of the sonorities
of the epic style, we find the pomposities of early nineteenth-century journalese. This
emphasizes both the absurdity of the subject matter and the unreliable nature of the
narrative voice.

Dickens's use of this technique diminishes as Mr. Pickwick becomes wiser. The
narrator, so to speak, becomes wiser with him. As the novel unfolds, more room is
given to dialogue, less to description. But throughout most of the novel, moments of
arch narrative remind us what Mr. Pickwick and the narrator need to learn. Jailed in
the Fleet Prison, Mr. Pickwick observes a fellow prisoner calling to an imprisoned
butcher. The call is taken up by others crying "'Butcher!' in imitation of the tone in
which that useful class of society are wont, diurnally, to make their presence known
at area railings" (ch. 42). Dickens contrives to suggest an unspoken conspiracy here,
between Mr. Pickwick and the narrator. They are fending off squalor with comfortable
philanthropic sanctimony. By such means, readers are made to feel that they are perceiving reality despite the narrative, rather than because of it.

The stylistic complexity of this makes the straightforward affirmation found at the
end of the book all the more affecting. In the final chapter, Mr. Pickwick dissolves
the club, but defends his and his friends' escapades:

"I shall never regret having devoted the greater part of two years to mixing with different varieties and shades of human character: frivolous as my pursuit of novelty may have appeared to many. Nearly the whole of my previous life having been devoted to business and the pursuit of wealth, numerous scenes of which I had no previous conception have dawned upon me – I hope to the enlargement of my mind, and the improvement of my understanding. If I have done but little good, I trust I have done less harm, and that none of my adventures will be other than a source of amusing and pleasant recollection to me in the decline of life. God bless you all!"

Style and substance now match. Resolution has been achieved.

Mr. Pickwick has realized that his infatuation with learning is no sure foundation for the good life. Moments of ignominy for the Pickwickians – often contrived to accord with illustrations – punctuate the earlier pages of the novel. Mr. Pickwick is found lurking at night in the grounds of a girls' school (ch. 16), or deposited in an animal pound less than sober (ch. 19). His characteristic response in such predicaments is rage at forfeiting the deference he believes his due. He gradually learns to extricate himself with dignity, however, both by controlling his rage, and by learning from other emotions. In Ipswich, he and Mr. Tupman find themselves before the local mayor and magistrate, whose pretensions rival Mr. Pickwick's own. "As grand a personage" as may be found, on flimsy evidence Mr. Nupkins decides that the friends are "two cut-throats from London, who have come down here to destroy his Majesty's population." But instead of raging, Mr. Pickwick is firm: "I shall take the liberty, sir, of claiming my right to be heard, until I am removed by force" (ch. 24). His firmness, and Sam's exposure of villainy plotted by Jingle against the Nupkins family, lead to all charges being dropped.

Brevity and silence mark Mr. Pickwick's progress even more distinctly than firmness. In Bath, he is exposed to galling class distinction. The weekly balls, he is told, are "Paradise" – "rendered bewitching . . . above all, by the absence of tradespeople, who are quite inconsistent with Paradise." Forced to endure an evening in the assembly rooms, losing at cards to merciless dowagers, he does not share his friends' delight in the fine company. Stoically, he returns to his inn, soothes his feelings with "something hot," and goes to bed (ch. 35).

But it is in the Fleet Prison that he learns most. He is jailed thanks to a breach of promise action brought against him by his landlady, Mrs. Bardell. His intentions had been mistaken, and he is outraged by the court's decision for the plaintiff. "Not one farthing of costs or damages do you ever get from me," he tells her lawyers, Dodson and Fogg, "if I spend the rest of my existence in a debtor's prison" (ch. 34). In the jail, however, he becomes ever more silent and subdued. What he sees and hears refines his sympathies and enlarges his self-knowledge. He sees a "young woman, with a child in her arms, who seemed scarcely able to crawl, from emaciation and misery," and who "burst into such a passion of grief, that she was compelled to lean against the wall for support" (ch. 41). He hears the story of the Chancery prisoner (chs. 41 and

44). Mr. Pickwick eventually chooses closer voluntary confinement, exclaiming, "I have seen enough . . . My head aches with these scenes, and my heart too. Henceforth I will be a prisoner in my own room" (ch. 45).

And he discovers a capacity for compassion, too, unrelated to theory or principle. It comes to him first when, within the prison walls, he encounters Mr. Jingle and his wily accomplice Job Trotter, impoverished and near to starvation. Mr. Pickwick summons Job:

> "Come here, sir," said Mr. Pickwick, trying to look stern, with four large tears running down his waistcoat.
> "Take that, sir."
> Take what? In the ordinary acceptation of such language, it should have been a blow. As the world runs, it ought to have been a sound, hearty cuff; for Mr. Pickwick had been duped, deceived and wronged, by the destitute outcast who was now in his power.
> Must we tell the truth? It was something from Mr. Pickwick's waistcoat pocket, which chinked as it was given into Job's hand, and the giving of which, somehow or other imparted a sparkle to the eye, and a swelling to the heart, of our excellent old friend, as he hurried away. (ch. 42)

The oversold "immortal Pickwick" has now become our justly admired "excellent old friend."

Sam helps in his master's education by joining him as a prisoner. He will not pay a debt he owes, Sam declares. He will not give the creditor (secretly his father) the satisfaction: "I takes my determination on principle, sir." He follows this with the story of a man who, against medical advice, ate three shillings' worth of crumpets, and blew his brains out, "in support of his great principle that crumpets wos wholesome, and to show that he wouldn't be put out of his way for nobody!" (ch. 44). Mr. Pickwick experiences some "uneasiness" at Sam's obstinacy.

Mr. Perker, Mr. Pickwick's lawyer, tips the balance. To his dismay, Mr. Pickwick also encounters Mrs. Bardell in the Fleet. She has been committed, for not paying fees, by the rascally Dodson and Fogg. Payment of damages and costs will benefit the lawyers, Mr. Perker agrees, but it will also release the hapless Mrs. Bardell. Mr. Pickwick's remaining in prison to defend a principle, he slyly adds, "would only be imputed, by people who didn't know you, to sheer dogged, wrongheaded, brutal obstinacy" (ch. 47). Mr. Pickwick is persuaded. He pays the money and leaves the Fleet.

By the end of the novel, Mr. Pickwick has overcome his infatuation with learning, and has abandoned his claim to deference. Now he dwells, not upon what is due to him, but upon what is due to others. He retires to a villa in Dulwich on the outskirts of London, where he is "known by all the poor people about, who never fail to take their hats off, as he passes, with great respect. The children idolize him, and so indeed does the whole neighbourhood." When Mr. Pickwick had demanded deference, it had not always been forthcoming. Now he has learned behavior that yields it without his asking.

His new values belong, not with reputation, but with friendship and affection. He remains celibate. So indeed does Mr. Tupman, although he still enjoys "the admiration of the numerous elderly ladies of single condition" who frequent Richmond where he lives. Mr. Winkle and Mr. Snodgrass, however, abandon their posturings and marry. Sam Weller marries Mr. Nupkins's servant, Mary. And, celibacy notwithstanding, Mr. Pickwick becomes a sponsor of family life. After initial reluctance, he reconciles himself to "the numerous applications made to him . . . to act as godfather." And he presides over a household where a new generation is being raised: "From the circumstance of two sturdy little boys having been repeatedly seen at the gate of the back garden, there is reason to suppose that Sam has some family" (ch. 57). Mr. Pickwick has learned from his follies. His eagerness for the new opportunities opening to men of his class has been replaced by an understanding of unchanging duties.

Despite its accidental birth, then, despite its episodic structure, *The Pickwick Papers* is organized as a novel. Some elements are unintegrated, it has to be said. There are interpolated tales included for the sake of variety. But more is integrated than twenty-first-century readers often suppose. The episodes featuring medical students Bob Sawyer and Benjamin Allen, for instance, are not just gratuitous comic interludes. Until the Medical Act of 1858, university degrees qualified physicians to practice but, often rising from much humbler backgrounds, surgeons learned their profession through practical hospital training alone. Mr. Pickwick supposes Bob and Ben will be "very fine fellows; with judgments matured by observation and reflection; tastes refined by reading and study" (ch. 30). He is taken aback to find them short on ceremony, deficient in linen, and redolent of cigar smoke. He is dismayed by their indifference to convention. "Have some regard to appearances," he begs Bob (ch. 50). When they qualify, they promote their practice with tricks. He always has himself called out of church, Bob explains: "'Bless my soul,' everybody says, 'somebody taken suddenly ill! Sawyer, late Nockemorf, sent for. What a business that young man has!'" (ch. 38). Bob and Ben are upwardly mobile Cockneys. Their cavalier attitude to status is comparable to Jingle's, and contrasts as tellingly with Mr. Pickwick's. Contemporary readers of *The Pickwick Papers* were exhilarated by issues such as these, and what Dickens did with them. Little of that exhilaration is lost on modern readers.

ACKNOWLEDGMENTS

Parts of this chapter have been developed from work already published. I am happy to acknowledge the recycling of material from two papers in *The Dickensian*, "Dickens's Archness" (1971) and "Mr. Pickwick and the Horses" (1989). I am indebted to AMS Press for permission to use material from chapters 1 and 3 of my book *The Doughty Street Novels* (2002).

References and Further Reading

Bevis, Matthew (2001). Temporizing Dickens. *Review of English Studies*, 52, 171–91.

Cotsell, Michael (1986). *The Pickwick Papers* and travel: a critical diversion. *Dickens Quarterly*, 3, 5–17.

Dart, Gregory (2003). The cockney moment. *Cambridge Quarterly*, 32, 203–23.

Easson, Angus (2002). Don Pickwick: Dickens and the transformation of Cervantes. In Alice Jenkins and Juliet John (Eds.), *Rereading Victorian Fiction* (pp. 173–88). Basingstoke: Palgrave.

Feltes, N. N. (1984). The moment of *Pickwick*, or the production of a commodity text. *Literature and History*, 27, 203–17.

Goetsch, Paul (2005). Charles Dickens's *The Pickwick Papers* and *Don Quixote*. In Darío Fernández-Morera and Michael Hanke (Eds.), *Cervantes in the English-speaking World: New Essays* (pp. 143–57). Kassel, Germany: Reichenberger.

Johnson, Edgar (1952). *Charles Dickens: His Tragedy and Triumph*, 2 vols. New York: Simon and Schuster.

McCarthy, Patrick (2000). The language of "Boz": does it survive? In Rossana Bonadei, Clotilde de Stasio, Carlo Pagetti, and Alessandro Vescovi (Eds.), *Dickens: The Craft of Fiction and the Challenges of Reading* (pp. 282–91). Milan: Unicopli.

Parker, David (1971). Dickens's archness. *The Dickensian*, 67, 149–58.

— (1989). Mr Pickwick and the horses. *The Dickensian*, 85, 81–98.

— (2002). *The Doughty Street Novels: Pickwick Papers, Oliver Twist, Nicholas Nickleby, Barnaby Rudge*. New York: AMS Press.

Tillotson, Kathleen (1954). *Novels of the Eighteen-forties*. Oxford: Clarendon Press.

Welcome, John (1982). *The Sporting World of R. S. Surtees*. Oxford: Oxford University Press.

20

Oliver Twist

Brian Cheadle

When Dickens signed a contract with Richard Bentley on November 4, 1836, he agreed to supply "an original article" of his own writing as well as edit each issue of the publisher's new illustrated monthly magazine. Dickens contributed one farcical tale for the first number (January 1, 1837), but soon found continuous prose fiction easier to write than a series of separate contributions. *Oliver Twist* appeared in the second number and ran in monthly installments until April 1839. The serial publication was interrupted three times: in June 1837, following the death of Mary Hogarth, and in October 1837 and September 1838 as a result of tense negotiations with his publisher. The novel appeared in three volumes in November 1838, five months ahead of its completion in *Bentley's Miscellany*. Philip Horne (2002) provides the text as it originally appeared in the periodical; equally available is the "critical text" Kathleen Tillotson (1966) established as the Clarendon Dickens edition. That version is based on the text Dickens revised and corrected for publication in 1846. Quotations in this chapter are from the Clarendon text.

The first seven chapters of *Oliver Twist* are remarkably innovative, not only in making a child the central character but also in using the victimization of the workhouse orphan as the occasion for a fictional attack on contemporary attitudes and abuses, thus initiating the novel of serious social concern. Oliver's "Please, sir, I want some more" (ch. 2) gives a voice to the voiceless, and stands as an icon of social injustice even for those now unaware that Dickens's satire was topically ridiculing the more dubious features of the New Poor Law of 1834. This new dispensation aimed to make a pauper's life less appealing than that of the least well-off laborers. Notoriously, it prescribed a meager workhouse diet as a deterrent to supposed shirkers, the report of the Poor Law Commission having claimed that half to two-thirds of all able-bodied workers seeking relief were "cases of indolence or imposture" (quoted in Hadley 1995: 85). It also separated married couples in the workhouse and, as Dickens rightly intuited, it impacted hardest on the children.

But Dickens's concern was not simply with the new provisions, which in many ways perpetuated old abuses. He is casual about some of the detail, conveniently merging the Central Board of Commissioners and the local Board of Guardians as a single body of unfeeling "philosophers;" and he highlights the petty tyranny of Bumble the beadle, though this office, like baby-farming and parish apprenticing, was a relic of the old system which was being unevenly replaced (within the novel's chronology around the time Oliver leaves the baby-farm). Moreover, Dickens broadens his indictment to the church and the law, epitomized by the clergyman at the pauper funeral and the magistrate set on apprenticing Oliver. For Dickens, all the institutions of Oliver's society constitute a "systematic course" in inhumanity (ch. 2).

The word "systematic" and the running sarcasm directed at "philosophers" make it clear that Dickens's real target was the social thinking that lay *behind* the new procedures, the Benthamite doctrines of political economy that he saw as contributing to a profound shift in social relationships. Previously, the parish decided which individuals would be admitted to the workhouse, or given outdoor relief, and though there was much corruption and a vested interest in keeping down the poor rates, there was still some sense of the local community as paternalistically committed to helping its own. In the new system, invested with Malthusian fears of the breeding masses no less than with well-meaning reformist intentions, paupers were impersonally categorized, stigmatized, and treated as a national problem. Nassau Senior, one of the architects of the New Poor Law, epitomized its impersonal spirit in saying: "man is seen to be an enigma only as an individual, in mass he is a mathematical equation" (quoted Hadley 1995: 87). What Dickens felt and deplored was that this new social engineering was helping to entrench the ranks as strangers to one another.

Dickens knew that some might find both his subject matter and his social critique offensive, though *The Times* was spearheading a similar outcry. In the event, Lord Melbourne notoriously complained that he offered a debasing view of mankind. Dickens, however, cared enough even to risk antagonizing his publisher, Richard Bentley, who was known to be opposed to anything with a radical tone. As editor of the new *Bentley's Miscellany*, Dickens was contracted to provide 16 pages of his own material monthly; and he had difficulty in getting Bentley, who had doubtless expected contributions of a Pickwickian geniality, to accept *Oliver Twist* as a new novel satisfying that requirement.

Anticipated resistance perhaps accounts for the stylistic uncertainty in the opening chapter, though this might also relate to the piece having been initially conceived as one of a set of satirical sketches in the tradition of the *Mudfog Papers*. Whatever the reason, Dickens tries to ease the reader into his serious purpose by adopting an exaggerated offhandedness. At the same time, barbed terms in the opening paragraph, such as "item of mortality," "office of respiration," and "a new burden . . . imposed upon the parish," mock the tendency of public discourses to address the problem of the poor in language whose self-important generality obfuscates the suffering at issue; and not "*prudent*" to name (emphasis added) in the first sentence suggests an imprudent anger barely restrained from shaking the reader out of the complacent detachment parodied by the style. The anger and facetiousness are so much at odds, however, that the effect is overwrought, particularly in contrast with the brisk narrative that begins to take over even before the end of the paragraph.

Dickens's tendency to force his effects upon the reader is often held to have a distancing effect. Comparably, his kind of comedy lays him open to the charge of remaining untouched. "One boy . . . hinted darkly to his companions that unless he had
another basin of gruel *per diem*, he was afraid he might some night happen to eat the
boy who slept next him" (ch. 2) is characteristic in its droll petting of verbal effects:
for the comic play between the mock solemnity of "*per diem*" (a phrase the boy would
never have used) and the apologetic lugubriousness of "might happen to eat" makes
the desperation sadly endearing rather than shocking. The point is worth dwelling
on both because Dickens's comedy is at the heart of his greatness and because it opens
a large critical divide. John Carey claims that in the workhouse sequence "the pity or
anger we would normally feel at the sufferings of the little victims is extinguished in
laughter" (Carey 1973: 71). Humor can be heartless and distancing, but consider the
spectacularly gruesome passage in which Gamfield the sweep butters up the Board
by proffering his trade secrets: "Boys is wery obstinit, and wery lazy, gen'lmen, and
there's nothink like a good hot blaze to make 'em come down vith a run. It's humane
too, gen'lmen, acause, even if they've stuck in the chimbley, roastin' their feet makes
'em struggle to hextricate theirselves" (ch. 3).

For Carey, Gamfield seems less funny when we consider that boy sweeps were liable
to develop deformity of the spine and cancer of the scrotum. But Dickens's passage
is not realism, to be judged by how comprehensively it attends to the suffering. His
mode here is the comic preposterous which finds pleasure in contemplating the sheer
monstrosity of the sweep, much as Shakespeare, according to Keats, takes equal
delight in imagining an Iago and an Imogen. But Dickens is far from indulging an
appetite for human lunacy. If there is a lack of feeling for the victim's pain, this is
because the focus is on the sweep's vicious indifference. Dickens precisely defines
Gamfield's callous mix of sadism and ingratiation, while making it clear that his boast
of being humane implies a deep contempt for the "gen'lmen" of the Board, so easily
appeased by specious gestures. Gamfield's contempt becomes a conduit for Dickens's
own contemptuous anger toward those for whom humanitarian cant obfuscates cruelty.
Moreover, the justification for the comic mode becomes clear when Gamfield goes on
to give "an arch look at the faces round the table . . . observing a smile on all of them."
To smile is to be aligned with the Board; and because it is impossible not to smile,
the reader is disconcertingly implicated. Far from encouraging indifference, the
comedy, under the pressure of Dickens's anger, forces the recognition that Gamfield
can inflict pain only because of the connivance of the Board, and ultimately of all who
should know better than to be indifferent.

Dickens saw other things in the spirit of the times as helping to breed indifference.
The Board and Gamfield haggle over the price to be paid for taking on Oliver; Mrs.
Mann appropriates most of the stipend paid for feeding the children at the baby-farm.
When, with Oliver's move to London, the novel shifts focus to the band of thieves,
their greedy materialism is consistently foregrounded. Charley Bates assures Oliver
that Fagin won't allow him to be "unprofitable" (ch. 18), the Dodger schools him in
the material "advantages of the trade" (ch. 18), and Fagin keeps insisting that the

gang are "in the way of business" (ch. 42), anticipating modern works such as *The Godfather* and *The Sopranos* in which the worlds of the mafia and of business shade into one another. Fagin consistently parodies respectable attitudes, and in doing so highlights the extent to which these have become suffused with the money ethic: he prudently proposes after Oliver's recapture to give him another suit "for fear you should spoil that Sunday one" (ch. 16); he berates him for escaping and putting the gang to the "trouble and expense" of recovery (ch. 18).

The gang's greedy ethos, and its much-breached agreement that none will betray the others, virtually stand in for the development of England into a market economy held together only by the cash nexus, self-interest, and contractual obligations which dissolve when no longer convenient. Oliver is twice abandoned. In leaving him after the aborted robbery, Toby Crackit says it was a case of "every man for himself" (ch. 25), and after the botched attempt on Mr. Brownlow, Charley and the Dodger demonstrate "the beautiful axiom that self-preservation is the first law of nature" (ch. 10), picking up the Malthusian allusion in the opening pages to the proficiency of the lower classes in surviving. Dickens saw Malthusianism, the market culture, and political economy as working together to entrench a distressing indifference to anything but the happiness and needs of what Fagin pointedly calls "number one" (ch. 43).

Dickens also submits Oliver to the newly central experience of the age, the *estranging* effect of the labyrinthine city. The novel documents many of London's alienating aspects, from Smithfield market, which "confounds the senses" (ch. 21), to Jacob's Island (ch. 50), whose dehumanized desolation repudiates all notions of picturesque decay. Equally disconcerting is Dickens's determination to controvert the comfortable tradition stretching from *The Beggars' Opera* to the Newgate novels which glamorized delinquency, and to show instead, as the 1841 Preface insists, "criminals in all the misery of their lives," moving homelessly, despite their brittle bonhomie, from den to den among "the cold, wet, shelterless midnight streets of London." (The Newgate tradition is well described by Stephen Gill [1999] in Appendix 2.)

Oliver comes most alive in his lonely isolation in London, particularly when, after his recapture, he is shut away daily for well over a week in Fagin's house. His nightmarish fears in an enclosure peopled only by mice and strange shadows, as he pitifully crouches by the street door to be as near human contact as possible, vividly evoke a child's sense of having been totally abandoned – as Dickens felt himself to be at the blacking warehouse when not much older than Oliver. But when Oliver looks out through a chink onto the "confused and crowded mass of house-tops, blackened chimneys, and gable ends" (ch. 18), and occasionally glimpses a head that peers out and abruptly disappears among the labyrinthine alien shapes, the detail is not specific to the consciousness of a child. The effect is to evoke the oppressiveness of urban experience, the anguish and estrangement endemic to modernity.

More broadly, the defining feature of *Oliver Twist* is the brutal antagonism of the world that Dickens presents. What ultimately tells is not so much the almost formulaic administering of beatings that Oliver suffers or has wished on him, as when the Board expresses the cheerful hope that if he were sent away to sea the captain might "knock his brains out with an iron bar" (ch. 4); nor the spectacle of him tearing the bits left by Sowerberry's dog "with all the ferocity of famine" (ch. 4); nor even the later threat that Fagin's ill-usage will reduce him "to a state of brutal stupidity and sullenness" (ch. 4). Rather, it is the almost casually gratuitous hostility of society at large. When the exhausted Oliver trudging to London meets a stagecoach, the outside passengers encourage him to keep up to the top of the hill, promising a halfpenny if he will then show them how fast he can run, and pocketing the money abusively when he falls behind (ch. 8); when another stagecoach passes a laboring country wagon, its driver bestows "an admonitory lash upon the heavy waggoner" who has "endangered his arriving at the office a quarter of a minute after his time" (ch. 21). Brutality seems taken for granted as the condition of life in this world. The tone is set at the outset when the maudlin Mrs. Thingummy, made "misty" by her allowance of beer, says over Oliver's dying mother (whom she will shortly proceed to rob): "When she has lived as long as I have, sir, and had thirteen children of her own, and all on 'em dead except two, and them in the workus with me, she'll know better than to take on in that way" (ch. 1).

Dickens's perceptions work in a broad and intuitive rather than systematic or analytic way, but to bring these varied features of the novel together is to recognize its overriding and admonitory sense of a society in which everything seems to work toward the alienation of individuals one from another. Within this context, what are rightly deemed the novel's weaknesses seem more understandable. Brownlow's benevolence seems less a sentimental reflex and more an index of a need which barely survives disappointment; Henry Maylie's pious determination to eschew money and status gains greater point; and Dickens's central complaint that in exalting self-interest his society was "putting entirely out of sight any considerations of heart, or generous impulse and feeling" (ch. 12) seems less a rather naïve idealism than the mainspring on which humane survival precariously depends. Nothing in the novel is more heartfelt than Dickens's admonition, "Men who look on nature, and their fellow-men, and cry that all is dark and gloomy, are in the right: but the sombre colours are reflections from their own jaundiced eyes and hearts. The real hues are delicate, and need a clearer vision" (ch. 34) – but nothing is more of its age in protesting too much to sound confident.

To an extent, the novel splits apart at its midpoint, the end of chapter 22, when the wounded Oliver faints after the robbery, to be reborn into a new life. From this point, and there are still 31 chapters, overt social critique is virtually left behind. Moreover, the focus ceases to be the fate of Oliver as an isolated and threatened victim (though the scene in which Monks and Fagin regard him through the window suggests Dickens might have contemplated a further assault). The issue is now simply whether Monks will manage to keep Oliver's real identity from being revealed. A proliferation of improvisations (the courtship of Bumble and Mrs. Corney, the illness of Rose and her initial refusal of Henry Maylie, the movement of Noah Claypole and Charlotte to London) confirms that Dickens is to an extent making up pages, albeit with some sublime touches when Bumble is onstage. Nevertheless, Dickens achieves a thrust of continuity by balancing the crimes against the child in the first half by a movement, centered on Nancy, toward restitution and retribution in the second.

Restitution, for Oliver, is not to be achieved within the confident providential frame suggested by the allusion to Bunyan in the subtitle, "The Parish Boy's Progress," for Oliver with his inviolate innocence does not progress, just as there is no real likelihood of him regressing, as do the characters in Hogarth's print series *The Harlot's Progress* (1732) and *The Rake's Progress* (1678–84), toward the "brutal stupidity and sullenness" (ch. 4) demanded by realism. Nor, like Little Nell and Paul Dombey who are too good for this world, does restitution take the form of Oliver's being "summoned into another world" (ch. 2) – though, in the wake of his sister-in-law, Mary Hogarth's death in May 1837 which upset Dickens so much that he missed an installment, there is a pull toward "that calm and peaceful rest which it is pain to wake from" (ch. 12). Rather, within a rhapsodically rendered rural serenity, the opposite of the "noise and brawling" (ch. 32) of the criminal world, Oliver is restored to his middle-class station, and made secure within a caring family.

The question of class affiliation, however, is not that straightforward. Throughout the workhouse sequence, the middle classes are presented as immoral and unfeeling: they sit on the Board or are myopic magistrates. With Oliver in Fagin's hands, there is a bifurcation between Brownlow's unselfish virtue and the power-corrupted malignancy of the magistrate Fang, while the more materialistic bourgeois values are downwardly displaced onto the gang. Proper middle-class virtue is presented as something quite apart from the institutional authority and commercial preoccupations of the public world. Its justification is simply compassionate goodness of heart. But if Oliver's new home is "a *little* society, whose condition approached *as nearly* to one of perfect happiness *as can ever be known* in this *changing* world" (ch. 53, emphasis added), the highlighted phrases suggest the problem Dickens has in reconciling his moral fable of Edenic restitution with the commitment to truth-telling he avowed in his 1841 Preface. The socially disengaged "little society" is not just fragile and pre-sexual: it has a class and monetary valence at odds with the moral fable.

This becomes clearer with the entrance of Oliver's half-brother Monks, an uneasy acknowledgment of the power of money to corrupt the middle-class family. Monks is a villain from stage melodrama, with intimations of the Gothic in the allusion to "Monk" Lewis, and Dickens would seem content to say with sweeping vagueness that in him "all evil passions, vice, and profligacy, fester" (ch. 49). But when Dickens's truth-telling intuitions approach these passions more closely, he teeters on the unspeakable. After destroying the evidence of Oliver's ancestry, Monks sends an unnamed boy before him to the room in which he seemingly sleeps and finds solace, a detail much more disturbing than Sikes's salacious reference to Fagin's "in-sa-ti-a-ble" (ch. 13) relish for his boys. Yet, as the verb "fester" suggests, Monks's villainy is coded in terms of disease rather than criminality; and despite his being morally "a party" (ch. 49) to the murder of Nancy, he is given a second chance and sent off with his sole inheritance from his father, "a prior claim upon his purse" (ch. 51).

By contrast, the second half of the novel shows a powerful impulse toward punishing the lower-class members of the gang who victimized Oliver. Fagin is dispatched on the gallows; Sikes dispatches himself in a gruesome parody, as though the momentum toward the noose were irresistible; and the chief remaining members of the gang die "far from home" (ch. 53). Unsurprisingly, given the way that the institutions of social control are discredited, this ideological disciplining is effected with some strain, as is clear in the Dodger's defiant challenge, "this ain't the shop for justice" (ch. 43), and by the fact that the mob's pursuit of Sikes releases all the latent antagonism of the city and of class in feeding the same lust for "hunting something" (ch. 10) as the earlier pursuit of the innocent Oliver. Moreover, the final vigilantism is spurred by the furious Harry Maylie on horseback and by Brownlow, whose only authority is the monetary rewards they offer for the capture of Sikes.

The break-up of the gang is precipitated by the murder of Nancy who replaces Oliver both as victim and as exemplification of "the principle of Good" surviving, which Dickens claims in the 1841 Preface to be the novel's central concern. Nancy shows a capacity for compassion in reflecting imaginatively on the fate of the wretches about to be hanged, and then decisively confirms what the amazed Sikes calls her "humane and gen-teel side" (ch. 16) when with hysterical fury she struggles to save the recaptured Oliver from being torn apart by Sikes's dog and beaten by Fagin. In this protectiveness, she figures as a surrogate for Oliver's lost mother. Later, she even more determinedly champions his cause, eavesdropping on Fagin and Monks, and providing Rose and Brownlow with the crucial information about Monks that establishes who Oliver is.

Nancy's compassion erodes the previously clear-cut distinction between villains and victims. In recompense for putting her life at risk, she will accept only Rose's white handkerchief, a reminder of what unsullied womanhood might have been and an absolute contrast to the harlot's "red gown, green boots, and yellow curl-papers" (ch. 13) which she initially flaunts. Before she is murdered, she pleads with Sikes for pity and flourishes Rose's gift as though its whiteness were a talisman of grace. Roland Barthes says the motif of "the Madonna with Raised Eyes" sacralizes the victim whose eyes, raised to the heavens, say "see what I will not see, do as you like with my body" (Barthes 1974: 169), but Sikes's furious whipping of Nancy's upturned face is a terrifying repudiation of the power of humane feeling, the more awful in that he has sufficient self-awareness in his "headlong course" (ch. 47) to realize that firing his pistol would invite immediate detection. His willed implacability would seem to repudiate the idea that the moral universe can be sustained on the basis of kindness of heart.

Dickens does his best in the remainder of the novel to restore a sense of moral authority by investing Nancy's eyes with panoptical power. When Sikes wakes after the murder it is to find her eyes "glaring upward, as if watching the reflection of the pool of gore that quivered and danced in the sunlight on the ceiling" (ch. 48), but this energetic dance of death is less horrifying to Sikes than to *imagine* the eyes "moving towards him" after he has covered the body with a rug. The sequence that follows, economically punctuated with the recurrence of the eyes, is the most powerfully realized in the whole novel, with the reader for the first time inhabiting an individual consciousness in sustained intensity. Oliver reads, when he is at Fagin's, about murderers who "yelled for the gibbet to end their agony" (ch. 20), but there is nothing of the conventionally homiletic about the last days of Sikes and Fagin.

The fear and desperation of Oliver and Nancy is punitively displaced onto Sikes as he feels himself hunted down, and the outcast spends the day frenziedly putting distance between himself and the corpse. He cannot, however, evade the sense of being pursued any more than he can eradicate the bloodstains. When he at last tries to sleep in a dark hut, the "eyes were as he saw them when he stole away" (ch. 48). The following night when he comes to Jacob's Island, he is chased out onto the roof, and as he is about to lower himself to safety by a rope, he looks up and thinks he sees the eyes continuing to haunt him. This horror makes him stagger and draw the noose tight around his neck as he falls. The eyes are thus given the full force of retributive justice, and its power is further internalized when Dickens ironically intimates that what Sikes saw was his staring dog that had followed him onto the roof. Later, Fagin in the trial scene also becomes an outcast. He registers with blank clarity an artist casually sharpening his pencil and other trivial goings-on around him, and the implication of his detachment, though it lacks the self-awareness, is what the desolate Macbeth defines in saying "[Such things] I must not look to have" (*Macbeth* V. iii. 28). Even more starkly, Fagin, like Sikes, finds himself confronted in the court by "a firmament" of "gleaming eyes" (ch. 52), the cosmic image suggesting a more than human implacability in its juridical power.

Dickens returned obsessively to Nancy and Sikes in the readings he gave until the end of his life. Arguably, the murder has this compulsive quality because it taps deeply conflicted impulses and opens fault-lines which cut across attempted moral demarcations. At an obvious level, the brutality of Sikes engages anxieties about the aggressive lower classes. The descriptive headlines inserted into the 1867 edition for the second part of chapter 50 are "The Wild Beast Hemmed In / The Wild Beast Laid Low." Forster's review of the novel, in referring to these events as "fearful delineations of Terror and its Retribution" (quoted in Tillotson 1982: xii), suggests the specter of social anarchy underlying the image of the beast. But the murder has the power to fascinate as well as to appall, because it engages with more than class anxieties. Nancy's masochistic submission to Sikes is extremely unsettling in part because a powerful loyalty and devotion to one's lover is a prime attribute of *good* women. It is, however, the *ecstatic* intensity in the motif of the "Madonna of the Raised Eyes," as of sexual climax, that Bernini brings out in his famous sculpture of St. Theresa. Nancy flourishes her handkerchief in a denial of sexuality, as though its whiteness could purify her body, but the scene is equally a representation of sexuality, with the male beating down on the body of the half-dressed woman lying on the bed where, when they were last together, she had kissed his lips.

A contemporary comment that Nancy's murder "teaches us . . . to pity the guilty while we hate the guilt" (quoted in Paroissien 1986: 127) makes it clear that for the Victorian audience Nancy could be seen as punished for her sexual guilt. Sikes, however, is punishing her for betraying him in daring to champion Oliver – for showing the strong protective capacity that unites her with Oliver's mother and her sister Rose. Nancy's masochistic streak is, however, equally related to the preparedness to sacrifice the self shown by Rose in initially rejecting Harry, and by Oliver's mother in dying to deliver Oliver. Moreover, there is a further continuity between Nancy's sexuality, Rose Maylie's upbringing as one stained by illegitimacy, and Oliver's mother's sexual transgression (which is remembered down to the novel's last breath). Dickens's ethic assumes the ultimately generous and moral orientation of "impulse and feeling" (ch. 12), but Nancy's body becomes a site of violence precisely because it brings together the licit and illicit potentialities of female passion. In both shrinking from and abandoning herself to Sikes, she suggests the radical instability in the Victorian construction of feminine identity, no less than of moral virtue, on the basis of a capacity for feeling.

Oliver Twist can still touch us on the raw, in large part because it engages so powerfully with what it would expunge – which is why the last word must be on Fagin. He tempts Nancy to poison Sikes; he prods Sikes to murder Nancy; he seemingly lusts for Oliver's very soul. He is a repulsive demon who must be butchered to make available the uncomplicated moral reading of the universe that melodrama purveys. But in compounding criminality and devilry, he is also archetypally seductive, proffering warmth, sausages, and fun to the young orphan in a beguiling parody of home. Dickens was grappling with a very personal demon in Fagin for, as John Bayley says, "Dickens himself had been at Fagin's school" (1962: 53). His boyhood experience at the blacking factory was traumatic because he knew that the fall from class and the sense of having been abandoned could easily have turned him into "a little robber or a little vagabond" (Forster bk. 1, ch. 2). Yet the experience was deeply ambivalent. Dickens took the name Fagin from the boy at the blacking warehouse who had been particularly kind to him, and the most telling comment in his account of that time is "No words can express the secret agony of my soul as I sunk into this *companionship*" (emphasis added). The temptation to accommodate with the socially base had to be strenuously repudiated, but the survivor was proudly aware that the experience had confirmed his independent selfhood and fed his creativity. As Dickens puts it, "all these things . . . worked together to make me what I am." It is thus peculiarly apt that at the climax of *Oliver Twist* it should be Fagin who gives Oliver the papers that prove his identity.

REFERENCES AND FURTHER READING

Barthes, Roland (1974). *S/Z*. (Richard Miller, Trans.). New York: Hill and Wang (original work published 1970).

Bayley, John (1962). *Oliver Twist*. In John Gross and Gabriel Pearson (Eds.), *Dickens and the Twentieth Century* (pp. 49–64). London: Routledge and Kegan Paul.

Carey, John (1973). *The Violent Effigy*. London: Faber and Faber.

Connor, Steven (1989). They're all in one story. *The Dickensian*, 85, 3–16.

Gill, Stephen (Ed.) (1999). *Oliver Twist*. Oxford: Oxford University Press.

Hadley, Elaine (1995). *Oliver Twist* and melodramatic resistance to the New Poor Law of 1834. In *Melodramatic Tactics: Theatrical Dissent in the English Market Place, 1800–1885* (pp. 77–132). Stanford: Stanford University Press.

Horne, Philip (Ed.) (2002). *Oliver Twist, or, The Parish Boy's Progress*. Penguin Classics. London: Penguin.

House, Humphry (1941). *The Dickens World* (esp. pp. 92–105). Oxford: Oxford University Press.

Jordan, John O. (1989). The purloined handkerchief. *Dickens Studies Annual*, 18, 1–17.

Larson, Janet (1985). *Dickens and the Broken Scripture*. Athens: University of Georgia Press.

Marcus, Steven (1965). The wise child, and Who is Fagin? In *Dickens: From Pickwick to Dombey* (pp. 54–91, 358–78). London: Chatto and Windus.

Newey, Vincent (2004). *Oliver Twist*: hegemony and the transgressive imagination. In *The Scriptures of Charles Dickens* (pp. 61–108). Aldershot: Ashgate.

Paroissien, David (1986). *Oliver Twist: An Annotated Bibliography*. New York: Garland.

— (1992). *The Companion to Oliver Twist*. Edinburgh: Edinburgh University Press.

Tillotson, Kathleen (Ed.) (1966). *Oliver Twist*. The Clarendon Edition. Oxford: Clarendon Press.

— (1982). Introduction to *Oliver Twist*. Oxford: Clarendon Press.

Tracy, Robert (1988) "The old story" and inside stories: modish fiction and fictional modes in *Oliver Twist*. *Dickens Studies Annual*, 17, 1–33.

Wheeler, Burton M. (1984). The text and plan of *Oliver Twist*. *Dickens Studies Annual*, 12, 41–61.

21
Nicholas Nickleby

Stanley Friedman

The Life and Adventures of Nicholas Nickleby, Containing a Faithful Account of the Fortunes, Misfortunes, Uprisings, Downfallings and Complete Career of the Nickleby Family, edited by "Boz," appeared in 20 monthly parts (19 with the last as a double number) between March 31, 1838 and September 30, 1839. The work grew out of a contract with Chapman and Hall, who were eager to extend the success they had achieved with *Pickwick*. Accordingly, Dickens agreed on November 18, 1837 to supply a work "of similar character and of the same extent and contents in point of quantity" as *Pickwick* (*Letters* 1: 659). The descriptive title of the monthly parts was reduced to *The Life and Adventures of Nicholas Nickleby* and Dickens named as the author when the novel was published as a single volume in October 1839.

In many ways, *Nicholas Nickleby* is a paradoxical work. The title used during the original serialization – *The Life and Adventures of Nicholas Nickleby, Containing a Faithful Account of the Fortunes, Misfortunes, Uprisings, Downfallings, and Complete Career of the Nickleby Family* – initially seems misleading. This ponderous, 24-word description suggests that we can expect a full-scale biography and also a family saga. But the narrator focuses on only a brief period of approximately one year in the life of Nicholas himself and appears somewhat indifferent to the entire family history. Yet on further reflection, we may decide that the original title is not inappropriate. Nineteen-year-old Nicholas's experiences during the single year depicted evidently determine the course of his future life. He develops his identity by becoming the protector not only of his sister, Kate, but also of Smike and then of Madeline Bray; he finds remarkably generous benefactors who give him employment that will lead to a partnership in a profitable business; and he gains an ideal mate. Moreover, the second promise of the original title also appears to be fulfilled, since the scope of the narrative extends beyond Nicholas to include consideration of his sister, their mother, their uncle, their only first cousin, and their children.

Indeed, the book's initial chapter presents the backgrounds of Nicholas and Kate's mother and father, as well as their paternal uncle, paternal grandparents, and paternal great-granduncle. For all of these members of the Nickleby family, economic concerns become dominant: Nicholas's paternal grandfather moves quickly from suicidal despair over poverty to inherited financial comfort, and then Nicholas's father falls precipitously from sufficient means to life-defeating scarcity as the result of following his wife's disastrous advice to speculate. Meanwhile, Nicholas Sr.'s older sibling, Ralph, having shown a talent for exorbitant usury at an early age, has gone to London, where "he quite forgot his brother" (ch. 1).

During the course of the novel, Nicholas, Kate, and their mother go from economic hardship to affluence, while the wealthy, cruel Ralph finds that his malicious schemes go awry. He loses vast sums of money, faces severe legal penalties, and learns that his only son has died. In despair, Ralph takes his own life, thereby wiping out his branch of the Nickleby family. Young Nicholas is to be viewed both as an individual and as a part of a family in which some members are driven by need and others by greed. Need results in temporary suffering for Nicholas Sr.'s widow and children, but greed causes the extinction of Ralph's line.

If this novel is both the story of its protagonist and at the same time a family history, it is also paradoxical in various other ways. It is certainly melodramatic in presenting extremes of behavior, language, and situation, and in including features such as confrontations of defiant adversaries, highly emotional requests, a stolen child, a purloined will, crucial instances of eavesdropping, and extraordinary coincidences that imply supernatural intervention. Yet in the Preface to the one-volume edition of the novel in 1839, Dickens strongly defends its credibility. He insists that the descriptions of Squeers and Dotheboys Hall are not exaggerations but "faint and feeble pictures of an existing reality," and that the benevolent Cheeryble brothers are "drawn from life." Moreover, a later Preface, written for the Cheap Edition in 1848, concludes with the assertion that Nicholas is "a young man of an impetuous temper and of little or no experience," a "hero" who is accurately drawn, since he has not been "lifted out of nature."

One explanation for the seeming conflict between the many elements of melodrama and these claims to realism is suggested in the Preface to the Charles Dickens Edition of a later novel, *Martin Chuzzlewit*. Here Dickens, again concerned with credibility, affirms in his opening sentence: "What is exaggeration to one class of minds and perceptions, is plain truth to another." In depicting Dotheboys Hall, Dickens sought to expose the horrifying abuses actually found in a number of Yorkshire schools, many of which served as a dumping ground for unwanted children. Similarly, when Kate is placed by her uncle in Madame Mantalini's millinery establishment, Dickens reveals the hardships facing young women employed in such work: long hours, low pay, and the danger of sexual exploitation, as well as "dullness, unhealthy confinement, and bodily fatigue" (ch. 18).

Realistic features also appear elsewhere in *Nicholas Nickleby*: for example, in the depictions of actual problems in speculative investments (Ralph's fraudulent scheme involving a muffin and crumpet company) and parliamentary politics (Nicholas's disillusioning employment interview with Mr. Gregsbury, MP). This novel also includes a motif that may be regarded as either realistic or melodramatic: the difficulties caused by parental interference in marital choice, evident in Walter Bray's domination of his daughter, Madeline, and in the control given to the brother (who serves as the dead father's surrogate) of the woman who secretly married Ralph. In both instances, economic considerations are placed ahead of romantic factors, and the consequences involve, in one case, Madeline's nearly fatal illness following Bray's death, and, in the other, the disharmony in Ralph's furtive marriage, as well as the need for the destructive concealment of Smike.

Although most of *Nicholas Nickleby* seems melodramatic, Dickens could still regard his story as true to human experience. Not even a year before starting to write this novel, he published, in the March 1837 issue of *Bentley's Miscellany*, an essay that refers to pantomime as "a mirror of life" (Eigner 1983: 118). Dickens may also have considered melodrama (which is derived from pantomime, as well as from romance and fairytale) to be a reflection of the actual world. In fact, Nicholas frequently appears to consider himself a protagonist in a melodrama.

The narrator refers to Nicholas's "sanguine imagination" (ch. 4) and his "elasticity of spirit" (ch. 22), and we are told that Nicholas would "interpose to redress a wrong offered to another, as boldly and as freely as any knight that ever set lance in rest" (ch. 16). Moreover, Nicholas's sense of himself as a chivalric figure is confirmed by his extravagant exclamation to Madeline Bray — "'You have but to hint a wish,' returned Nicholas fervently, 'and I would hazard my life to gratify it'" (ch. 46) — as well as by his subsequent willingness to sacrifice his own feelings for Madeline in deference to what he thinks are the Cheeryble brothers' plans for her to marry Frank.

Nicholas's self-image as a chivalric protagonist is reinforced by encounters that appear providential. After leaving Dotheboys Hall and confronting Ralph, Nicholas departs from London, and on the road he benefits from a chance meeting with Vincent Crummles, the manager of a theatrical company then in Portsmouth, who persuades him, with Smike, to join the players. His experiences with this troupe reinforce his sense of self. He becomes a leading actor in the melodramas the company performs, and achieves additional success as both a writer and translator of plays in which happy endings prevail and heroes overcome trials and tribulations.

After returning to London, Nicholas finds benefactors whose altruism makes them seem, in the words of one commentator, "fairy godfathers" (Stone 1979: 84). Providential care is suggested by the extreme benevolence of the Cheeryble brothers, humbly born men, and also by the numerous coincidences associated with their involvement with Nicholas. The latter first sees and starts conversing with Charles Cheeryble outside the General Register Office, the place in which he first noticed and was attracted to the young woman later revealed to be Madeline Bray. Madeline reappears at the Cheerybles' office, and we discover that she is the daughter of a woman whom Charles Cheeyble once wooed unsuccessfully. Her mother's sister was engaged to Charles's twin brother, Edwin Cheeryble, but died before the wedding. When Nicholas intervenes in the dispute caused by Frank Cheeryble's anger that a woman has been spoken of in a disrespectful way, the lady is subsequently identified as

Madeline. Charles Cheeryble tells Nicholas: "it was she in whose behalf he [Frank] made that turmoil which led to your first acquaintance" (ch. 46).

There is a hint of destiny, too, in later coincidences: Arthur Gride has dishonestly acquired a deed leaving a bequest to, of all young women, Madeline Bray, and he then seeks help from Ralph Nickleby. Moreover, when the plot to get Madeline to agree to marry Gride, a repulsive figure more than a half-century older than Madeline, reaches its climax, both Cheeryble brothers happen to be out of England "on urgent business" (ch. 52), thereby providing for Nicholas both a test and an opportunity.

As the hero of a tale of wonder, Nicholas also is aided by other benefactors. Newman Noggs, although impoverished, offers assistance as vital to Nicholas as the help given by the affluent Cheeryble twins. While the Cheerybles' benevolent acts can be attributed solely to their generosity and to their belief that Nicholas is a worthy young man, Noggs remembers the kindness shown him years ago by Nicholas's father. Coincidentally, Newman has later become involved with Nicholas's uncle, first as the usurer Ralph's victim, then as his underpaid employee. Noggs, besides sending Nicholas timely warnings, gives him and Smike shelter after they have come to London and later, through eavesdropping and the furtive perusal of a letter, discovers the plot of Ralph and Arthur Gride against Madeline. When Noggs realizes that this is the young woman to whom Nicholas has become attracted, he warns him and then encourages him not to abandon hope of saving Madeline, "the very advice Nicholas needs" (Horne 1989: 174).

After hearing from Brooker, the man who gave the child Smike to Squeers, that Snawley's claim to be Smike's father is false, Noggs conveys this news to the Cheeryble brothers and arranges for Brooker to tell his story to them, thereby revealing the identity of Smike, who by this time has died. Finally, Newman, with the help of Frank Cheeryble, recovers the stolen deed from Squeers, who has just received it from Peg Sliderskew, Gride's housekeeper. In assisting Nicholas by helping to thwart Ralph's schemes, Noggs himself "finds a way to become a new man," as his given name hints (Horne 1989: 169). Nicholas also receives valuable assistance from John Browdie, who rescues Smike from Squeers in London and joins Nicholas in aiding Frank Cheeryble. Additional help comes from an unlikely source: Lord Frederick Verisopht dies in a duel because of his opposition to Sir Mulberry Hawk's plan to obtain revenge on Nicholas. This death, by forcing Hawk to flee the country, removes a real danger.

Although the opportune arrival in London of John Browdie and his wife is another fortunate coincidence, the occurrence that most clearly seems providential is the sudden death of Bray just before Madeline is to be given to Gride. Bray's death could perhaps be attributed to the emotional strain caused by a conflict between his desire for the liberating power of wealth and his guilt over sacrificing his devoted child, but Nicholas sees Bray's demise as an example of divine intervention, for he tells Ralph and Gride: "your schemes are known to man, and overthrown by Heaven" (ch. 54).

Dickens's defense of extreme benevolence in the Preface on the grounds of realism relates to his belief in astounding coincidences. John Forster refers to Dickens's "favourite theory as to the smallness of the world, and how things and persons apparently the most unlikely to meet were continually knocking up against each other" (Forster bk. 1, ch. 5). Other major coincidences occur in addition to those already mentioned. Ralph, who does not realize that his only son has survived and is at Dotheboys Hall, happens to know Squeers because of other business and sees the advertisement for an assistant just when Nicholas arrives in London. Nicholas, on his return to London from Portsmouth, is "strongly attracted" to "a handsome hotel," and in the hotel's coffee-room he overhears Hawk's insulting reference to Kate and confronts the rake (ch. 32). Then, the return of Brooker to London, after he has served his sentence as a transported criminal, coincides with the efforts of Ralph to harm Nicholas by separating him from Smike.

Like the stage melodramas that Dickens enjoyed, *Nicholas Nickleby* includes both tragic and comic events. The positive elements are dominant, since Nicholas, besides gaining a spouse and a partnership in the Cheerybles' business, manages to reunite his family and regain his father's old home. Just as Madeline in her self-renunciation and other virtues resembles Kate, so the latter's eventual mate, Frank Cheeryble (evidently the son of an unmentioned and presumably deceased brother of the Cheeryble twins), is very like Nicholas. Nicholas, who is treated by the Cheeryble twins as a surrogate son, marries a young woman whom they also regard as a surrogate child, and Nicholas's sister, Kate, is matched with the twins' nephew, another surrogate son. The "virtual interchangeability" of the young people (Friedman 2003: 38) gives Dickens a way to allow the Nickleby siblings to follow their desires but to avoid incest. As the novel ends, other admirable characters also are rewarded: Newman Noggs regains his genteel status, Tim Linkinwater and Miss La Creevy marry, and the Cheeryble twins find pleasure in contemplating the happiness that their generosity has brought to others.

The novel is clearly a comedy in both senses of the word: a story that ends happily and one that includes farcical events, absurd speeches, and various characters who bear ludicrous names like Cheeryble, Wackford Squeers, Sir Mulberry Hawk, and Lord Frederick Verisopht. When the narrative describes anxiety-inducing threats, these are usually soon followed by reassuring events. For example, when Smike is about to be severely beaten by Squeers, Nicholas quickly intervenes. When Squeers captures Smike on a London street, John Browdie appears in the next chapter as his liberator. When Ralph, Squeers, and Snawley seek to claim Smike, Charles Cheeryble, also in the very next chapter, insists that he will not allow the youngster to be harmed. Just when Madeline is about to be given to Gride, Bray suddenly dies.

Tragic or pathetic features, however, remain important. Unlike the stolen children in Shakespeare's romance, *Cymbeline*, who receive good care, grow to healthy adulthood, and are restored to their father, Smike has been damaged too much in his early years to recover, and his death is foreshadowed by his own anticipations. When Nicholas is about to introduce him to Kate and Mrs. Nickleby, Smike asserts, "I shall never be an old man," and then adds, "In the churchyard we are all alike, but here there are none like me" (ch. 35). For him, a "surrogate for his more fortunate cousin [Nicholas]" (Herst 1988: 131), only death can bring full relief from pain. For Smike, being attracted to Kate merely deepens his torment, since he knows that he can never win her. Nicholas, however, gains Madeline despite her father's wish that she marry Arthur Gride.

Despite the villainy of Ralph, his suicide, in the same room in which Smike was kept hidden as a very young child, is distressing. He is not without some tenderness, evidence of which we see when he wonders if bringing his niece to live with him might soften him (ch. 31). The Cheeryble brothers and Tim Linkinwater all show him compassion; and just before he kills himself, Ralph speculates about his misspent life. Had he not lost his son, he thinks, Smike "might have been a comfort to him and they two happy together" (ch. 62). But Ralph is destroyed by his "two passions" (ch. 44), for the hatred that is second only to his avarice begins to consume him. In an earlier chapter, he recalls with bitterness being compared to his younger brother – "always in my disfavour" (ch. 34) – and suggests that this recollection evoked his hostility to Nicholas, an antipathy that eventually leads Ralph to self-destruction. Just before his death, we are told that Ralph's hatred of his nephew "attained a height which was sheer wild lunacy" (ch. 62).

The hilarious features in *Nicholas Nickleby* often serve a satiric purpose, so that at times the humor in this novel is bitter in its implications. Chapter 2, which presents the meeting to promote the United Metropolitan Improved Hot Muffin and Crumpet Baking and Punctual Delivery Company, depicts Ralph and his associates trying to persuade the audience at the gathering that "there was no [other] speculation so promising, or at the same time so praiseworthy." The pompous overstatements, the claims of social benevolence, and the preposterous title of the company all seem ludicrous, but we should remember that the financial ruin and subsequent death of Nicholas Nickleby Sr. were possibly attributable to a fraudulent speculation like this one, resembling many actual cases in early nineteenth-century England. Soon after, Squeers's ignorance and hypocrisy are absurdly funny, but we are not allowed to forget that the schoolmaster is a sadistic bully who inflicts suffering on young children, that his incompetence and negligence have evidently caused death. Mrs. Nickleby's vanity and her indulgence in garrulous, disconnected, irrelevant anecdotes make her a comic figure, but she nevertheless causes great pain by offering heedless advice to her husband, and her ridiculous misjudgments of Ralph and Hawk expose her children to discomfort and danger.

Nicholas Nickleby has often been categorized as episodic and loosely structured. Nicholas travels from Devonshire to London, then to Yorkshire, back to London, to Portsmouth, back to London, and then between Devonshire and London. Nevertheless, readers have cogently argued for the novel's thematic unity, pointing to various motifs that recur with frequency: prudence, love and money, selfishness and altruism, optimism and pessimism, acting, speculation, and melodrama. The inclusion of so many motifs may be attributed to the fact that they are interrelated, for all seem subsumed by the idea of melodrama.

This artistic form demands risk-taking, or imprudence. Its hero is often motivated by idealistic romantic love, while the villains manifest lust and a greedy appetite for money. Egoism competes with generosity, and the mixture of tragic and comic events evokes both hope and anxiety – optimism and pessimism. Since the villains in melodrama are usually hypocritical and duplicitous, they must be skilled actors. In *Nicholas Nickleby*, both Ralph and Squeers are noticeably histrionic, playing roles that disguise their evil intentions. Besides Vincent Crummles's professional actors, whose melodramas include incidents that at times anticipate or echo those in the novel, other characters also perform roles. Mantalini acts as the devoted lover ready to commit suicide to expiate any offense; Hawk pretends to be a true friend to Lord Frederick; Snawley poses as Smike's caring father; and the Kenwigses all play devoted relatives when Mr. Lillyvick, Mrs. Kenwigs's uncle, pays a visit. Indeed, acting has been called the "central metaphor" of this novel (Gold 1972: 67). Specu-lation, however, noticeably dominates the first chapter. The bequest given by the uncle of Nicholas's grandfather, Godfrey Nickleby, is evidently a response to Godfrey's "desperate speculation" in naming his first son after this relative, and the death of Nicholas's father, the initiating event of the main narrative, results from following disastrous advice to engage in financial speculation. Moreover, both basic meanings of "speculate" – to gamble and to guess – assume significance throughout the rest of the novel.

As we previously observed, the second chapter depicts Ralph Nickleby's involve-ment in an investment scheme, and although this venture is not mentioned again, we find numerous examples of speculation. When Nicholas gains popularity as an actor, Vincent Crummles decides that arranging a benefit performance for the young man would be "a very promising speculation" (ch. 29). Arthur Gride seeks to be married to Madeline Bray as a speculation, since she does not know that he has in his keeping a stolen will naming her as the beneficiary. Ralph's willingness to pay Squeers to obtain the stolen deed from Peg Sliderskew also constitutes an investment, even though its goal is to deprive Nicholas of the bequest rather than to gain money for Ralph.

Interwoven with speculation in the sense of risk-taking is the theme of speculation as conjecturing, imagining, predicting, and fantasizing, although the two meanings often coalesce, since a risk-taker usually tries to anticipate results. At various times, Mrs. Nickleby indulges in speculation or daydreams in which Kate is taken by Madame Mantalini into partnership in the millinery business or in which Kate becomes the wife of Sir Mulberry Hawk or marries Mr. Wititterly after he is widowed. Nicholas, as he walks in London, begins "speculating on the situation and prospects of the people who surrounded him" (ch. 16).

The card game of speculation, played during the tea arranged by Fanny Squeers and also at the Kenwigses' anniversary celebration, directs our attention to this motif: Fanny is imagining that Nicholas finds her attractive, and the Kenwigses have devoted much attention to Mr. Lillyvick in anticipation of his showing generosity to their family in his will. Near the end of the novel, Brooker confesses to kidnapping Smike and admits that it was a speculation, since he originally had a "design of opening up the secret one day, and making it a means of getting money" (ch. 60). We learn, too, that Ralph's marriage was a speculation as his wife's inheritance could only be gained through the consent or death of her brother. At the end, when Ralph commits suicide after his schemes fail, we realize that he and his younger brother, two men very different in temperament, both die as a result of failed speculations.

The theme of multiple or diverse perspectives is often vital in Dickens's works and is embedded in various ways in *Nicholas Nickleby*. The opening chapter, with its exploration of family origins, notices that Ralph and his young brother, Nicholas Sr., reacted in antithetical ways to their mother's oft-repeated "accounts of their father's sufferings in his days of poverty, and of their deceased uncle's importance in his days of affluence," with the younger son deciding to seek security in "the quiet routine of a country life" and his brother, Ralph, determining to devote himself to an obsessive quest for riches.

Subjective responses also figure in the interpolated tales in chapter 6, "The Five Sisters of York" and "The Baron of Grogzwig." These stories seem highly relevant to Nicholas at this stage of his life, when he is first setting forth on his own, for, as one commentator observes, this novel "persistently raises the question of outlook . . . of joy and gloom as postures towards the world," and "Dickens suggests that one's response to the world is really a matter of decision" (Gold 1972: 77).

While the "merry-faced gentleman" calls the story of the five sisters "a melancholy tale" (ch. 6), he and the story's teller ultimately agree that "all good pictures" contain both "shades" and "lights" and that "the good in this state of existence preponderates over the bad" (ch. 6). Moreover, the account of Alice and her four siblings is not wholly sad. The memory of the dead young woman's personality and love strengthens the surviving sisters in their determination to reject the monk's advice that they abandon the world for a cloister, while their tapestries eventually endure in the stained glass windows, works that celebrate beauty and devotion. The subsequent tale told by the "merry-faced gentleman" about the baron is introduced as "a story of another kind" (ch. 6), but it too is mixed in its import. Although the name of the baron, "Grogzwig," and the maiden name of his austere spouse, "Swillenhausen," facetiously suggest indulgence in liquor, the story itself deals with the serious subject of suicidal depression. The baron eventually overcomes the distress caused by his wife's restrictions, but he must first confront the personification of his own despair. Each tale presents characters who face temptations to withdraw from life – the convent and suicide – but manage to resist.

We realize, too, that *Nicholas Nickleby* is replete with ironies. Mrs. Nickleby, after creating a multitude of preposterous fantasies, indulges in two daydreams which come to fruition: the Cheeryble brothers make Nicholas a partner in their business, and their nephew Frank proposes marriage to Kate. Other ironies, however, seem to reflect a severe poetic justice. For example, Ralph, in trying to take Smike from Nicholas, invents the story that Smike's father was misled into believing that the boy was dead, but Ralph subsequently learns that his fabrication, except for the identity of the deceiver, is true. Later, when Squeers is transported and Dotheboys Hall comes to an end, the schoolmaster's downfall is caused not by his cruel, criminal mistreatment of young children. He is caught with a stolen deed that he has, at Ralph's behest, obtained from Peg Sliderskew. Perhaps the greatest irony, however, involves the money left by Ralph. Since he dies intestate, the relatives whom he had so mistreated "would have become in legal course his heirs," but because of their aversion to the means by which Ralph had acquired his wealth, they "made no claim" to it, and it went to the state, a government that had not restrained the greed and cruelty of men like Ralph and Squeers (ch. 65).

Despite the rewards and retribution at the conclusion, and despite the novel's pleasing energy and entertaining humor, the tone is often elegiac. The book's opening chapter closes with Nicholas Nickleby Sr.'s death, while the final chapter, which describes Nicholas's regaining of his father's home, concludes with a reference to Smike, a person deprived of both childhood and adulthood, denied both his given name and his surname, unaware of his identity as a Nickleby. The children of Nicholas and Kate play sadly near the grave of Smike and talk of "their poor dead cousin," whom they never knew, their parents' contemporary.

Paradoxically, Nicholas, the young hero who sets out seeking maturity and independence, remains, despite his success in finding a livelihood and a worthy spouse, bound emotionally to the past. Just as Smike longs for the release of death, Nicholas apparently desires to regain the joys of childhood. At critical times – when he takes the dying Smike to Devonshire, and when he and Kate, in a spirit of self-sacrifice, resolve to relinquish their desires for Madeline and Frank – Nicholas thinks of his childhood, "the happiest years of his life" (ch. 58), the days when Kate and he were "playfellows" (ch. 61). After Nicholas reacquires the old family home, he must enlarge it to accommodate his children, but he avoids destroying any of "the old rooms" or removing any "old tree": "nothing with which there was any association of bygone times was ever removed or changed" (ch. 65).

But his goal of restoring and preserving the past is not entirely possible to achieve. Much earlier in the novel, when Nicholas, Kate, and their mother rent the cottage at Bow from the Cheerybles, we are told that there they found "all the peace and cheerfulness of home restored" (ch. 35). Subsequently, however, Kate reminds us of a crucial contradiction. She finds no difference between the cottage and her old home "except that the kindest and gentlest heart that ever ached on earth [her father's] has passed in peace to heaven" (ch. 43). Even the return to the old farm in Devonshire cannot restore Nicholas Sr.

At the end of *Nicholas Nickleby*, goodness has prevailed, but poetic justice has not always been achieved, and recovery from pain remains incomplete. One of Dickens's very early books, this novel displays in both its narrative artistry and its moral vision, a complexity and a subtlety that may not be initially apparent.

References and Further Reading

Bowen, J. (2000). *Other Dickens: Pickwick to Chuzzlewit*. New York: Oxford University Press.

Eigner, E. M. (1983). The absent clown in *Great Expectations*. *Dickens Studies Annual*, 11, 115–33.

— (1989). *The Dickens Pantomime*. Berkeley, CA: University of California Press.

Friedman, S. (2003). *Dickens's Fiction: Tapestries of Conscience*. New York: AMS Press.

Ganz, M. (1976). *Nicholas Nickleby*: the victories of humor. *Mosaic*, 9, 131–48.

Gold, J. (1972). *Charles Dickens: Radical Moralist*. Minneapolis, MN: University of Minnesota Press.

Herst, B. F. (1988). *Nicholas Nickleby* and the idea of the hero. *Dickens Quarterly*, 5, 128–36.

Holway, T. M. (1992). The game of speculation. *Dickens Quarterly*, 9, 103–14.

Horne, L. (1989). Covenant and power in *Nicholas Nickleby*; or, the guidance of Newman Noggs. *Papers on Language and Literature*, 25, 165–77.

MacKay, C. H. (1988). The melodramatic impulse in *Nicholas Nickleby*. *Dickens Quarterly*, 5, 152–63.

Manning, S. (1994). *Nicholas Nickleby*: parody on the plains of Syria. *Dickens Studies Annual*, 23, 73–92.

Marcus, S. (1965). *Dickens: From Pickwick to Dombey*. New York: Basic Books.

Meckier, J. (1970). The faint image of Eden: the many worlds of *Nicholas Nickleby*. *Dickens Studies Annual*, 1, 129–46, 287–8.

Monod, S. (1968). *Dickens the Novelist*. Norman: University of Oklahoma Press.

Parker, D. (2002). *The Doughty Street Novels: Pickwick Papers, Oliver Twist, Nicholas Nickleby, Barnaby Rudge*. New York: AMS Press.

Reed, J. R. (1967). Some indefinable resemblance: moral form in Dickens' *Nicholas Nickleby*. *Papers on Language and Literature*, 3, 134–47.

Rem, T. (1996). Playing around with melodrama: the Crummles episodes in *Nicholas Nickleby*. *Dickens Studies Annual*, 25, 267–85.

Russell, N. (1981). *Nicholas Nickleby* and the commercial crisis of 1825. *The Dickensian*, 77, 144–50.

Slater, M. (1982). The composition and monthly publication of *Nicholas Nickleby*. In Charles Dickens, *The Life and Adventures of Nicholas Nickleby*, vol. 1 (pp. vii–lxxii). Philadelphia: University of Pennsylvania Press.

Stone, H. (1979). *Dickens and the Invisible World: Fairy Tales, Fantasy, and Novel-making*. Bloomington, IN: Indiana University Press.

Thompson, L. M. (1969). Mrs. Nickleby's monologue: the dichotomy of pessimism and optimism in *Nicholas Nickleby*. *Studies in the Novel*, 1, 222–9.

22

The Old Curiosity Shop

Gill Ballinger

Dickens's fourth novel grew out of a contract he signed with Chapman and Hall on March 31, 1840 to "compose and write" a new work called *Master Humphrey's Clock* (*Letters* 2: 464). This work, published weekly in parts, was to consist of 16 pages, 12 of which were to be "original Literary Matter" supplied by Dickens. The first issue of this weekly miscellany appeared on April 4, 1840, but the original plan for a collection of stories and sketches faltered after three more installments. The design called for Master Humphrey and a circle of friends to meet once a week and read from papers they had written and stored at the base of the clock. To halt declining sales, Dickens altered the format. He turned the single episode of Humphrey's night-time encounter with a young girl lost in the streets of London into an extended story and discarded Master Humphrey as the narrator (see the end of ch. 3). What became *The Old Curiosity Shop* then ran continuously from the fourth number (April 25, 1840) until its conclusion in 40 parts on February 6, 1841. Later that year, the first edition of *The Old Curiosity Shop* appeared, published independently of the framework from which the story grew.

Dickens conceived and completed *The Old Curiosity Shop* during a busy period: it was the fourth of five novels published between 1836 and 1841. The work proved a resounding success as sales of the weekly serial reached 100,000 copies in England; unconfirmed stories tell of quayside crowds in the United States awaiting the ship carrying the latest installment, desperate to know if Little Nell was still alive (*Oxford Dickens* 426). The critical fortunes of *The Old Curiosity Shop* have been more mixed. Contemporaries such as William Charles Macready, Lord Frances Jeffrey, and Thomas Hood followed the serial with "passionate interest" (Gissing 1924: 119). Later critics, however, were less enthusiastic, despite their admiration for Dickens as a great writer. Oscar Wilde declared "One must have a heart of stone to read the death of Nell without laughing" (Ellman 1987: 441); Swinburne said that Nell was "a monster as inhuman as a baby with two heads" (1913: 21); Aldous Huxley argued that the "history of Little Nell . . . is distressing in its ineptitude and vulgar sentimentality" (1930: 57).[1] Undoubtedly, the novel is flawed, uneven, and possibly unsuited to current tastes, yet it offers many compensatory pleasures. Prominent among them are the comic exuberance of Dick Swiveller and the grotesque dark humor of the malignant dwarf Quilp.

The Old Curiosity Shop was not a novel Dickens intended to write. Although he insisted that he "never had the design and purpose of a story so distinctly marked" in his mind from its commencement, this assertion belies Forster's verdict that the novel took "gradual form, with less direct consciousness of design on his own part" than at any other time in Dickens's career (*Letters* 2: 233; Forster bk. 2, ch. 7). The original plan he revealed to Forster by letter in July 1839 had been quite different. Fearing that readers might tire of the monthly format of his three previous novels, Dickens proposed a new weekly miscellany in the style of eighteenth-century periodicals like "*The Tatler, The Spectator*, and Oliver Goldsmith's *Bee*." Issues would include topical essays, descriptions of London as it had been in former times, as well as "tales, adventures, letters from imaginary correspondents and so forth." Dickens added that he would seek further variety by introducing a "little club or knot of characters" whose "personal histories" would inform the work, as well as reintroduce Pickwick and Sam Weller (*Letters* 1: 563–4). Initially, he planned to enlist contributors as well, although the project was to be under his overall management. The venture appealed because it offered Dickens the prospect of a stable income, editorial control, and a hiatus from the demands of writing a long novel in monthly installments.

The first number published on April 4, 1840 sold well, but public interest fell rapidly when readers discovered the absence of a continuous story. Looking at the early numbers, we can see why. The first introduces Master Humphrey as "a mis-shapen, deformed old man," who gathers three friends around him once a week to read papers they have written and placed in the bottom of the clock "where the steady pendulum throbs and beats with healthy action" ("Master Humphrey's Clock"). The first three issues contain disparate tales set in the past, of giants telling a story about a broken-hearted apprentice who eventually kills his loved one's aristocratic seducer ("Introduction to the Giant Chronicles"), of a murderer confessing on the eve of his death ("A Confession found in a Prison in the Time of Charles the Second"), and the first of Master Humphrey's "Personal Adventures." Comic correspondence to the editor relieves the stories, and the whole endeavor has, as Dickens remarked in the 1848 Preface to the first Cheap Edition of *The Old Curiosity Shop*, a "desultory" character. It was soon clear that he needed to provide a continuous narrative if he wanted to halt the decline in weekly sales; hence the introduction of Nell in Number 4. Miscellaneous material, however, continued to feature for another three numbers until "the little-child story" stood alone on June 12 and continued without interruption until its completion on February 6, 1841.

The novel bears the scars of this improvised beginning. At the end of chapter 3, Master Humphrey bows out "for the convenience of the narrative." Dickens found that he needed a third-person narrator to carry the story of Nell through varied settings, all of which were clearly at odds with the periodical's original machinery. (Over half of the 73 chapters take place in London; the remaining chapters are set on the road.) The opening of chapter 42 illustrates the often clumsy transitions that these frequent changes of scene necessitated, as the action alternates between London and Nell on her travels: "It behoves us to leave Kit for a while, thoughtful and expectant, and to follow the fortunes of little Nell; resuming the thread of the narrative at the point where it was left some chapters back." Directing the action to a new set of characters on another occasion, Dickens has to adopt the guise of "the historian" in order to take "the friendly reader by the hand," and perform like an intrepid aeronaut in order "to alight before a small dark house, once the residence of Mr. Sampson Brass" (ch. 33).

Coincidences serve a similar purpose and add to the sense of improvisation and overall episodic structure apparent in these awkward transitions. Nell faints at the feet of the schoolmaster in chapter 45 whom she first met in chapter 24; on other occasions, remarkable meetings reveal unsuspected family connections. It transpires that the old bachelor is the brother of Mr. Garland; Master Humphrey is the single gentleman at the end of the tale. In this instance, as Dickens attempts to wrap up the narrative, he sows confusion since Master Humphrey narrated the first few chapters, notwithstanding his declaration when he introduced Nell in the original machinery that his night-walking adventure "was fictitious."

Evidence of second thoughts between earlier episodes and their sequel months later add further to the novel's improvisatory and episodic nature. For example, Dickens omits his original intention to reveal Sally Brass as the mother of the Marchioness (ch. 66), but retains Quilp's jokes about the "Virgin of Bevis" (ch. 33) and the dwarf's covert and narrow inspection of the small servant, the result of which "secret survey" hints discreetly that he may be her father (ch. 51). The machinations and appearance of Fred Trent early in the narrative suggest he will be a significant character, yet he rapidly fades from view once the central focus on Nell is established, only to be dealt with summarily in the novel's conclusion. Conversely, Dick Swiveller, initially an apparently minor character, becomes an increasingly important one as the story of Nell and her trials progresses.

Frequent shifts in the scene necessitate abrupt changes, as Dickens resorts to the "streaky bacon" principle he had invoked to justify similar narrative features in *Oliver Twist* (ch. 17). In a variation of the practice "sanctioned in books by long usage" and considered by many as "the great art of authorship," the narrator in *The Old Curiosity Shop* extends the rational he had offered in the earlier novel to emphasize the effectiveness of rapid changes. "Everything in our lives," he writes, "whether of good or evil, affects us most by contrast." Thus, "If the peace of the simple village had moved the child more strongly, because of the dark and troubled ways that lay beyond and through which she had journeyed . . . what was the deep impression of finding herself alone in that solemn building" (ch. 53). The resultant infusion of interest generated by a change in one scene is therefore juxtaposed with that of another one as, for example, variety and movement in one installment give away to a melancholy and pensive tone in the next. For example, chapter 8 recounts Dick Swiveller's antics at the dance at the Ladies' Seminary, as he impresses the audience with his "feats of agility." This spirited scene contrasts with Nell's "sadness and sorrow" at home, and the "dark shadows on its hearth" in chapter 9. More sustained oppositions and dualities feature in the novel: death and sorrow are pervasive, yet the comedy is strongly realized; romance and allegory work alongside topical social commentary.

Rapid and abrupt changes occur in the novel's prose, as different episodes reflect corresponding changes in the emotional register. When good children die, Dickens loses no opportunity to wring a heightened response from his readers, lapsing unconsciously into blank verse at the demise of Little Nell: "She was dead. No sleep so beautiful and calm, so free from trace of pain, so fair to look upon. She seemed a creature fresh from the hand of God, and waiting for the breath of life; not one who had lived and suffered death" (ch. 71). Many of Dickens's contemporaries responded to the prevailing sentiment, finding it, like R. H. Horne, "profoundly beautiful" (1907: 46), an appropriate form of language in which to express grief at the loss of young life. Huxley, however, railed against such writing: this "atrocious blank verse . . . is meant to be poetical . . . and succeeds in being the worst kind of fustian" (1930: 56). "Oh! it is hard to take to heart the lesson that such deaths will teach, but let no man reject it, for it is one that all must learn . . . When Death strikes down the innocent and young . . . a hundred virtues rise, in shapes of mercy, charity, and love," the narrator apostrophizes on another occasion (ch. 72). Strained prose like this makes little headway among contemporary readers, who tend to deplore such obvious pathos.

Yet turgid and preacherly writing hardly typifies all the chapters in which Nell appears. The provincial scenes possess an imaginative vitality, particularly those featuring the itinerant show people, such as Thomas Codlin and Harris Short and Mrs. Jarley. The beginning of chapter 18, for instance, introduces a gathering of the traveling showmen in the Jolly Sandboys, who irreverently discuss the fate of old giants. "How's the Giant?" asks Short, as the company sit around the fire smoking, only to learn from his manager that he is "rather weak upon his legs" and that "he's going at the knees." "Once get a giant shaky on his legs," continues Mr. Vuffin, the showman who also exhibits a limbless lady, "and the public care no more about him than they do for a dead cabbage-stalk" (ch. 19).

These alternations in both manner and subject matter seem to have worked for Dickens's original readers, who responded favorably to the mixture of romance, folk tale, and allegory that Dickens employs. Nell appears as the beautiful princess, pursued by a relentless enemy. Kit features as a domestic version of the heroic knight who follows in her steps, hoping to rescue her. Dickens's technique in such scenes is to concentrate on the extraordinary by taking characters who owe something to romance and then placing them in incongruous settings. Kit imagines stock features of the genre drawn from fairytales as he rings the bell at "a beautiful little cottage with a thatched roof," while his head fills with images of "giants' castles, and princesses tied up to pegs by the hair of their heads, and dragons bursting out from behind gates," only to face a modest and demure "little servant-girl" as the door "was gently opened" (ch. 22).

Quilp is a malevolent, superhuman dwarf; Mrs. Quilp lives in a "bower," the victim of a cruel and demanding husband (ch. 4); the many strolling players Nell and her grandfather meet on their travels appear to be out of the ordinary, such as "Grinder's lot" on stilts, whose elevated gaunt figures cast monstrous shadows that strike terror in Nell's heart when she encounters them (ch. 17). The rescue team eventually locates Nell, the fair maiden, whose quest has been to find peace and tranquility. Unfortunately, her trials kill her, denying readers the happy ending the romance conventionally offers. The unexpected union between Dick Swiveller and the Marchioness, however, offers partial recompense.

When Nell and Grandfather Trent are on their travels, the narrator makes several allusions to *The Pilgrim's Progress*, a religious work infused with allegory and elements of the romance. In chapter 15, we learn that Nell had access to "an old copy" of *The Pilgrim's Progress* at home, "over which she had often pored whole evenings, wondering whether it was true in every word, and where those distant countries with the curious names might be." When resting on a beautiful day, she remarks to her grandfather: "I feel as if we were both Christian, and laid down on this grass all the cares and troubles we brought with us; never to take them up again." In the following chapter, they reach, like Christian, a "wicket-gate," beyond which further trials lie. These include Nell's ordeal at the racecourse and the theft of her money by her grandfather, who, driven by his mania to continue gambling, steals her savings.

The idea of "the lonely figure of the child" "existing in a kind of allegory" (Dickens added the phrase to chapter 1 of the first book edition in order to emphasize the symbolic nature of the story) is reinforced throughout the narrative. Accompanied by Hopeful, Christian meets simplified characters (Evangelist, Piety, Faithful, Giant Despair, Atheist, and Ignorance) who help or hinder his progress. Although Dickens avoids completely suggestive names, Nell is clearly an embodiment of goodness, and the figures she meets are representatives of various foibles and attitudes.

The landscape through which Nell and her grandfather pass shares this allegorical element. In chapter 28, the two travelers enter a "pretty large town," whose streets are described as "very clean, very sunny, very empty, and very dull." The same could be said of prose so singularly devoid of specificity and hardly the kind of descriptive writing we associate with the observing eye praised by Walter Bagehot in 1858, describing what he termed Dickens's "special excellences" (Collins 1971: 393). "There are scarcely anywhere such pictures of London as he draws," wrote Bagehot, a complement he could not extend to descriptive passages like the following from chapter 45: "In all their journeying, they had never longed so ardently . . . for the freedom of pure air and open country." Abandoned to "the mercies of a strange world," Nell wonders how many more days she and her grandfather can carry on, without food, without resources, and prompted only by "some vague design of travelling to a great distance among streams and mountains, where only the very poor and simple people lived."

Hints of the writer who described London "like a special correspondent for posterity," however, are not entirely absent from *The Old Curiosity Shop*. Dickens spent a whole morning looking for a house in Bevis Marks, determined to find the appropriate local color to suit the novel's rascally attorney. The effort caused him to miss calling on Forster, as he had intended, but yielded the splendid description of "a small dark house, once the residence of Mr. Sampson Brass" (*Letters* 2: 118; ch. 33). Scenes depicting Quilp's waterside bolt-hole on the Surrey side of the Thames are similarly evocative, a tumble-down wooden dwelling amidst coils of ropes and marine supplies, reached only by crossing the river thick with "long black tiers of colliers" (ch. 5).

Equally compelling and cast in a different register is the nightmarish sequence that occurs when Nell and her grandfather pass through a riot-torn industrial town. Determined to proceed, they advance slowly past tall chimneys pouring out "their plague of smoke" and obscuring the light falling "on bands of unemployed labourers" who paraded in the roads, or clustered by torchlight round their leaders:

> who told them in stern language of their wrongs, and urged them on to frightful cries and threats; [and] maddened men, armed with sword and fire-brand, spurning the tears and prayers of women who would restrain them, rushed forth on errands of terror and destruction, to work no ruin half so surely as their own . . . (ch. 45)

Moving beyond the allegorical mode, Dickens sounds in these episodes a clear warning of the dangers of contemporary social unrest, the result of trade recession, bad harvests, and protests by Chartists eager to exploit class tensions. The implications of the torchlight parade of unemployed workers for readers in the 1840s would have been plain. Grandfather Trent's gambling carried a similar topical resonance, as does the novel's persistent emphasis on Nell as representative of children at risk. Childhood should be nurtured as a special state, as a time when adults cared for and protected children rather than allowed their roles to be reversed. Nell may, like Christian, reach her heavenly reward, but Dickens emphasizes the injustice of forcing children into the workplace and assuming adult responsibilities. The view that sanctions industrial work for children is exposed in the scene with Miss Monflathers, who lectures Nell stridently:

> "Don't you feel how naughty it is of you . . . to be a wax-work child, when you might have the proud consciousness of assisting, to the extent of your infant powers, the manufactures of your country; of improving your mind by the constant contemplation of the steam-engine; and of earning a comfortable and independent subsistence of from two-and-nine-pence to three shillings per week? Don't you know that the harder you are at work, the happier you are?" (ch. 31)

In denial of the harmful consequences of child labor, Miss Monflathers champions industrial development at the expense of the young. Nell's initiation into work and adult responsibility to support herself and her grandfather leads to her death. In killing Nell, Dickens played on the sentimental propensity of an age that witnessed a shocking level of infant mortality. Her death, remarked Gissing, came across to readers in 1840 not only as pathetic but "fresh and original." Remember, he observed, "that Dickens spoke with a new voice on behalf of children; at a time when children were horribly neglected, and often horribly ill-used, he found a way of calling attention to their unregarded lives" (1924: 122).

The novel, however, does more than offer pathos. Comedy relieves the sentimental scenes, and, as James Kincaid notes, "for all its celebration of the grave, *The Old Curiosity Shop* is rooted in a comic impulse" (1971: 79). This "comic impulse" takes various forms, including the *joie de vivre* of the Nubbles' family night out to celebrate Kit's first pay-day at Astley's theater followed by a meal at an oyster shop. Accommodated in a private box fitted out with red curtains, Kit and his guests consume "the newest loaves, and the freshest butter, and the largest oysters, ever seen" (ch. 39). Other instances include the good-natured theatrical exuberance of Dick Swiveller and the dark humor of Daniel Quilp.

This latter figure is a vibrantly grotesque and paradoxical creation, a dwarf with the strength of a lion, a hideous hunchback who appears irresistible to the opposite sex. If she were to die tomorrow, boasts his pretty young wife, "Quilp could marry anybody he pleased" (ch. 4). Even Nell finds herself "much inclined to laugh" at Quilp's "uncouth appearance and grotesque attitude" (ch. 6). Though comic, he is clearly menacing in his behavior, lolling in Nell's bed when he takes possession of her grandfather's shop and voicing his predatory appreciation of her young flesh. "Such a fresh, blooming, modest little bud," he remarks to her grandfather, "such a chubby, rosy, cosy, little Nell!" (ch. 9). On another occasion, when he arrives at an inn, he answers the chambermaid's query if he wanted a bed by making faces at her before saying he wants to kiss her (ch. 48).

Quilp's other appetites are manifest in wonderfully bizarre and unusual ways. Mealtimes at his house invariably prove memorable. Sitting down at the breakfast table with his wife and mother-in-law, he eats "hard eggs, shell and all, devoured gigantic prawns with the heads and tails on, chewed tobacco and water-cresses at the same time and with extraordinary greediness, drank boiling tea without winking, bit his fork and spoon till they bent again" (ch. 5). Quilp accompanies this display with so many other "horrifying and uncommon acts" that he almost frightens his wife and mother-in-law out of their wits. Can he really be "a human creature," they wonder. In scenes like these, the novel resonates with Quilp's vibrant ubiquity. This "conjuror" defies time by traveling from London to an inn 60 miles away, where Nell was last sighted, more quickly than the single gentleman and Mrs. Nubbles, who had set off hours before him. Returning home by herself, Kit's mother is constantly tormented as Quilp defies gravity by hanging off the top of the coach in order to peer in at the window "with his great goggle eyes." "I really don't believe he's human," she explains to her son at the conclusion of the journey. He has been "a terrifying of me out of my seven senses all this blessed day" (ch. 48).

Quilp's excessive energy manifests itself in other extreme behaviors. He punishes his wife for listening to her friends by threatening to bite her, and makes her stay up with him as he "blaze[s] away all night" in a "smoking humour" (ch. 4), hostage to the end of his cigar, "a deep fiery red." Outsmarted by Kit, whom he frames on false charges of stealing, he takes further revenge by attacking his effigy, screwing gimlets into him, sticking forks in his eyes, and cutting his name on him with the intention of burning him (ch. 62). This insane figure meets an appropriately theatrical end. Nothing short of a threefold demise will take him out of the plot. After panicking and falling into the Thames one foggy night, he drowns, only to have his body bruised against slimy piles, dragged over rough stones and gravel, and then dumped onto a dismal swamp where in former times pirates "had swung in chains." At the inquest held near the spot where his corpse had been washed ashore, the jurors supposed that he had committed suicide and so he was left "to be buried with a stake through his heart in the centre of four lonely cross roads" (ch. 73). Clearly for Quilp, Mr. Peggotty's "drowned dead" would not have sufficed.

Imaginative exuberance of a different sort defines Richard Swiveller, whose cheerful outlook and good humor counter the novel's dark episodes. Whereas the reader sees a gloomy curiosity shop, Dick perceives a "gay and festive scene, and halls of dazzling light" (ch. 3). He transports the world from its grim reality to another realm through his "figurative and poetical" mind (ch. 7). Indeed, "[t]o be a friend of Swiveller you must reject all circumstantial evidence, all reason, observation, and experience, and repose . . . a blind belief" in his vision of the world (ch. 7). Eclectic quotations drawn from a range of sources fuel Dick's fertile imagination, the effect of which is to keep alive his fancy, much in the way fiction helped David Copperfield maintain his spirits when faced with "the gloomy theology of the Murdstones" (ch. 4). *Hamlet*, William Mee's ballad "Alice Gray," Milton's "L'Allegro," Goldsmith's "Edwin and Angelina," Gay's *The Beggar's Opera*, Burns's "A Red, Red Rose," and Byron's "To Thomas Moore" are among the literary allusions he makes all within two chapters (chs. 7–8). Thus, Dick renders life livable by elevating his impecunious circumstances, buttressed by a flow of literary allusions. His "single chamber" for a gentleman in Drury Lane "was always mentioned in the plural number," when he spoke, conveying to his hearers "a notion of indefinite space," leaving their minds to wander "through long suites of lofty halls, at pleasure." Deceptive flights of fancy supply the furniture and improve his beverages, turning the bedstead into a bookcase and a glass of "cold gin-and-water" shared by two into a more appealing bottle of "rosy wine." "Implicit faith in the deception was the first article" of Swiveller's creed, comments the narrator (ch. 7).

Dickens's initial conception of this figure as a careless rake ready to connive with Nell's brother underwent a serious change in the course of the novel's composition. Later redeemed by illness and aided by the fantasy world he inhabits, Dick discards his theatrical role as the unrequited suitor of Sophy Wackles in favor of a touching and genuine relationship with the oppressed little servant girl cruelly exploited by the Brasses. Their friendship develops during a series of games of cribbage, as Dick introduces levity into her life for the first time. His kindness pays important dividends. When he falls seriously ill, the little servant, nicknamed the Marchioness by Dick, runs away to nurse him in his lodgings. "I strongly suspect I should have died, Marchioness," Dick declares, "but for you" (ch. 64).

With help from the Marchioness, who overhears the Brasses plotting against Kit, Dick discloses their false accusations and so frees Kit. A modest inheritance Dick receives from his aunt makes possible the small servant's final metamorphosis. He uses the money to pay for the little drudge to be educated and renames her Sophronia Sphynx, "as being euphonious and genteel, and furthermore indicative of a mystery." She blossoms and they marry, settling down to life in a small cottage in Hampstead and "many hundred thousand games of cribbage" (ch. 73). This character, whom Dickens said he meant "to make much of" (*Letters* 2: 70), fulfills Dickens's expectations and so does much to relieve at the close the weight of Nell's death.

The Old Curiosity Shop contains both faults and glories. Loosely constructed and episodic, the novel's form suffered from the hasty adjustments Dickens was forced to adopt when readers reacted negatively to the lack of a continuous story. Comedy, pathos, and the lively but malignant behavior of Daniel Quilp offset the improvisation, as did the design imparted by Nell's "progress" through a world full of both wicked and good folk. The weekly installments also opened a new and more intense level of engagement between Dickens and his readers. As he noted in his Preface to volume 1 of *Master Humphrey's Clock*, by shortening "the intervals of communication between himself and his readers," he was able "to knit more closely the pleasant relations they held" (September 1840). This close relationship was to continue for the rest of Dickens's career and redouble with the public readings, which were such a strain on his life. Forster also acknowledged that the novel "increase[d] the sense" of Dickens's ability to write with pathos and humor (bk. 2, ch. 7). If the pathos of some chapters fails to engage some modern readers, the novel's rich vein of comedy retains its power to delight, as does the vitality of Quilp and the linguistic inventiveness of Dick Swiveller.

NOTE

1 It is worth noting that Swinburne declared that Dickens was "a genius of such inexhaustible force and such indisputable originality" (1913: 71) and Huxley acknowledged that Dickens was a "great writer" (1930: 43), but neither could abide Nell.

REFERENCES AND FURTHER READING

Collins, Philip (Ed.) (1971). *Dickens: The Critical Heritage*. London: Routledge and Kegan Paul.

Ellman, Richard (1987). *Oscar Wilde*. London: Hamish Hamilton.

Gissing, George (1924). *Critical Studies of the Works of Charles Dickens*. New York: Greenberg.

Horne, Richard Henry (1907). *A New Spirit of the Age*. London: Oxford University Press (original work published 1844).

Huxley, Aldous (1930). *Vulgarity in Literature*. London: Chatto and Windus.

Kincaid, James (1971). *Dickens and the Rhetoric of Laughter*. Oxford: Clarendon Press.

Pope, Norris (1996). *The Old Curiosity Shop* and the new: Dickens and the age of machinery. *Dickens Quarterly*, 13, 3–18.

Schlicke, Paul (1988). *Dickens and Popular Entertainment*. London: Unwin Hyman.

— (2002). Embracing the new spirit of the age: Dickens and the evolution of *The Old Curiosity Shop*. *Dickens Studies Annual*, 32, 1–35.

Sroka, Kenneth (2000). The death of spirit and the failure of art in Charles Dickens's *The Old Curiosity Shop*. *Religion and the Arts*, 4, 184–216.

Swinburne, Algernon Charles (1913). *Charles Dickens*. London: Chatto and Windus.

Winters, Sarah (2000). Curiosity as didacticism in *The Old Curiosity Shop*. *Novel*, 34, 28–55.

23

Barnaby Rudge

Jon Mee

Despite its appearance as a weekly serial in 42 parts (February 13 to November 27, 1841), immediately following *The Old Curiosity Shop* in *Master Humphrey's Clock*, *Barnaby Rudge* was the first novel Dickens planned to write. Its origin dates back to May 1836 when he accepted an offer from John Macrone to write a three-volume historical novel tentatively called "*Gabriel Vardon, the Locksmith of London*" (*Letters* 1: 150). Troublesome and complicated negotiations with Macrone and then Richard Bentley led to its delay. Several thwarted efforts to begin followed. Finally, under a new title – *Barnaby Rudge* – and with four novels behind him, Dickens set to in earnest in January 1841. He found the short, weekly installments cramping, but he worked rapidly and confidently to finish in November when the novel also appeared as a single volume published by Chapman and Hall.

For a young writer in the 1830s, setting out to write an historical novel was a sign of pursuing a serious literary vocation. Following the success of *Sketches by Boz*, Dickens had decided he should follow the example of Sir Walter Scott and announce his arrival as a novelist by taking on the genre. Dickens chose for his subject an episode from the eighteenth century still known to Victorian readers as the most terrifying example of public disorder and violence in the previous hundred years of British history. The Gordon Riots of 1780 had witnessed an outpouring of religious hatred and popular violence unrivaled in the eighteenth century. They had originated in the opposition of the Protestant Association, led by the unstable Scottish aristocrat Lord George Gordon, to government plans to improve the rights of Catholics in Britain. Provoked by the Association's propaganda, but also expressing a range of social and political resentments, the London mob rampaged through the capital, causing fear that the social order was about to collapse.

The destruction of the recently rebuilt Newgate prison stood out as the great symbol of the havoc wrought by the rioters and also provides the centerpiece of Dickens's novel. His treatment of the riots sees them – as modern historians still see them – not simply as an expression of religious intolerance, but also as the articulation of a deep resentment felt by the populace against the political and social order of the day (see chapter 10 of this volume). The spectacle of the mob in full flow supplies *Barnaby Rudge* with much of its ambivalent energy. Dickens condemns the effects of the riots, acknowledges their origins in social conditions, but also wonders at and sometimes even thrills with their violent fury.

The novel, however, begins not with this larger historical canvas, but by detailing an altogether smaller domestic sphere, albeit one with darkness and violence of its own. Barnaby Rudge opens in 1775, five years before the riots, and over several chapters builds up the plot of a murder mystery. It begins at the Maypole Inn, outside London, where the keeper, John Willet, and his cronies are telling the murder story to an unknown customer. The tale centers on the Haredale family, Sir Geoffrey Haredale, the local Catholic landowner, and his niece Emma. Emma's father was murdered two decades before the story begins. Another body found at the time was taken to be his steward Rudge, survived by his wife, Martha, and their son, Barnaby, whose mental instability is ascribed to the effects of his father's bloody murder. The cast at the Maypole also includes the stable-boy Hugh, wild like Barnaby, but also possessing a threatening cunning.

Around this murder mystery, a series of other conflicts revolves. Emma Haredale is in love with Edward Chester, son of Sir Geoffrey's enemy, the smooth politician Sir John. Willet's son Joe is in love with Dolly Varden, daughter of the other major figure introduced in the opening chapters, the kindly locksmith Gabriel Varden. For all his benevolence, however, even Varden's world is not peaceable. His wife is a bigoted Protestant, in league against him with her bitter maidservant Miggs. His apprentice Simon Tappertit, the object of Miggs's desires, has sexual and social ambitions of his own centered on the unfortunate Dolly. Only in chapter 35, after a break of five years, does Dickens provide this murder mystery with the larger historical context of the Gordon Riots. Lord George Gordon is introduced for the first time in the company of his villainous secretary Gashford. Barnaby and Hugh become involved in the machinations of the Protestant Association, throwing their lot in with the unhinged public hangman Ned Dennis. The vortex of violence created by the rioters threatens to destroy completely the familiar domestic world that Dickens has painstakingly constructed over the first half of the novel.

Many critics have seen *Barnaby Rudge* as a displaced commentary on conflicts facing Dickens and his contemporaries in their own society (Rice 1983). Intolerance toward Catholics was a feature of the British political landscape in the 1830s; again, as in 1780, partly because of government attempts to improve their lot. The Catholic Relief Act of 1829 had allowed Catholics for the first time to take up seats in both houses of parliament: the result in England was that the Protestant Association was brought to life again amid a tide of anti-Catholic feeling (Walder 1981: ch. 4). But more often invoked now as a context for the novel are Victorian fears about popular revolt, associated mainly with the Chartist movement (see, for instance, Marcus 1965: 173–5; House 1971: 180). Dickens had read Thomas Carlyle's "Chartism" (1839) by the time he started on the novel properly in 1841. Carlyle defined Chartism as a manifestation of an inner fury latent in popular consciousness. *Barnaby Rudge* seems interested in exploring Carlyle's idea of a deep-seated conflict between unconscious forces of order and anarchy. Dickens would have already come across such ideas in Carlyle's *History of the French Revolution* (1837), a book that directly influenced *A Tale of Two Cities* (see chapter 30). From Carlyle, an idea of the mob as a manifestation of an elemental force figured in terms of volcanic flows or oceanic convulsions seems to have made its way into *Barnaby Rudge*:

> A mob is usually a creature of very mysterious existence, particularly in a large city. Where it comes from or whither it goes, few men can tell. Assembling and dispersing with equal suddenness, it is as difficult to follow to its various sources as the sea itself; nor does the parallel stop here, for the ocean is not more fickle and uncertain, more terrible when roused, more unreasonable, or more cruel. (ch. 52)

Both Carlyle and Dickens often write with a relish about the energy of the mob, even though they revile its mindless destruction elsewhere in their books. Most readers still find the descriptions of the mob in action the most compelling parts of *Barnaby*. In September 1841, Dickens himself wrote to Forster of his enthusiasm for these sections of the novel: "I have let all the prisoners out of Newgate, burnt down Lord Mansfield's, and played the very devil . . . I feel quite smoky when I am at work" (*Letters* 2: 385). Seething with energy at his desk, Dickens seems to go beyond any simple rational understanding of the social causes of popular unrest and deeper into a desire to participate in the destructive energy of the crowd itself. Carlyle conceived of the French Revolution as a self-destructive force, but one whose immolation revealed a new order of things in nineteenth-century modernity. In his descriptions of the riots, Dickens also returns again and again to the spectacle of the rioters "sucked and drawn into the burning gulf" (ch. 55). Individual characters, too, often seem overwhelmed by forces within themselves that they may have roused but cannot control: "I struggled against the impulse," says Barnaby's father, "but I was drawn back, through every difficult and adverse circumstance, as by a mighty engine" (ch. 62). Where Dickens would seem to differ from Carlyle is by searching for a secure private and domestic space beyond these dramatic conflicts (Sanders 1978: 74). Nor does Dickens offer any clear sense of a new order emerging from his conflagration. Carlyle was attracted to the crowd's energy because of its role in this historical drama. For all his explicit admiration of Carlyle's writing, this overarching idea of history seems absent from *Barnaby Rudge*.

Untangling the novel's attitude to social order and rebellion is complicated by the fact that the novel is an historical fiction looking back to a period 60 years before (in a conscious echo of Scott's *Waverley*). Dickens seems to be urging his readers to learn the lessons of the past and apply them to their situation in the 1840s. One lesson proposed by the Preface seems to be that the eighteenth century's bloody legal code and unreformed political system had produced an equal and opposite reaction. "Bad criminal laws, bad prison regulations, and the worst conceivable police" (ch. 49) are explicitly identified as the causes of the riots. Dickens was committed to, and campaigned for, reform on all three of these fronts during his own lifetime. Yet history in the novel does not always yield up a story of progress to encourage the reformer. Simon Tappertit's hostility "to the innovating spirit of the times" (ch. 8), like the bizarre notions of the ancient constitution he shares with Ned Dennis, may comically indicate their ignorance, but making sense of the past often seems more difficult than the novel's ostensible didactic aspects would suggest. Indeed, Dickens raises questions about the authority of historical narratives in the very first chapter of *Barnaby Rudge*. "Matter-of-fact and doubtful folks" (ch. 1) question the traditional story of Queen Elizabeth's visit to the Maypole. Should Dickens himself be numbered among these matter-of-fact, doubtful folks?

The novel does not always provide its readers with a single, comfortable vantage point from which to view the past, even if sometimes it does affirm the superiority of Victorian England. Carlyle's idea of the sterility of the eighteenth century is affirmed in some respects by the description of the stolid presence of the inn in the first chapter, reflected in owner John Willet's "profound obstinacy and slowness of apprehension" (ch. 1). Willet refuses to have anything to do with newfangled stage coaches (the eighteenth-century equivalent of the railways that were starting to define the age of Dickens) or to allow his son any independence. When Joe Willet runs away from his father and the inn, it seems an entirely natural development; a new generation is breaking with the complacency and intolerance of the old. Dickens sometimes represents the Gordon Riots too as the regrettable, but inevitable outcome of the failings of a social order based on denial, but he does not offer obvious routes to a new order for society. On the personal level, Joe may finally manage to attain domestic bliss, but it is less clear what progress is available for society at large.

Dickens opens up the possibility that progress is itself a phantasm. While far from abandoning the idea of reform, the return of the repressed and other kinds of repetition are integral to the Gothic aspects of the novel. "Blood will have blood" is a principle announced early on in the novel. The circumstances of his birth seem to have marked Barnaby out with "a smear of blood but half washed out" (ch. 5). The sins of the fathers are also visited on the Chesters and even the Willets. The reconciliation of Catholic and Protestant in the marriage of Emma Haredale and Edward Chester may suggest a message of national reconciliation of the kind often found in Scott, but the sense of lurking violence and inexplicable terror that permeates the novel is not completely absorbed by the wedding. Hugh's curse, for instance, leaves something hanging over the novel that Barnaby's pardon does not entirely eclipse. Hugh repeats his mother's fate on the scaffold and may also pass on a malediction to the society that punishes him. Indeed, the novel seems ambivalent about whether Hugh is victim or villain. His animality is sometimes sublime, like the crowd he orchestrates.

Although Gabriel Varden was displaced from the original title of the novel, his shop still provides one of its central motifs: "a great wooden emblem of a key, painted in vivid yellow to resemble gold, which dangled from the house-front, and swung to and fro with a mournful creaking noise, as if complaining that it had nothing to unlock" (ch. 4). Even before we encounter Varden's "emblem" itself, the very first chapter of the novel makes a distinction between signs and things with regard to the inn run by the Willets. Dickens tells his readers that by the Maypole "from henceforth is meant the house, and not its sign" (ch. 1), but how to understand signs in relation to the things that they signify is a thorny issue in the novel. "The old practice of hanging out a sign" (ch. 16) does not seem to help anyone navigate his or her way through the city. When, in chapter 27, Haredale looks up at the Golden Key "as in the hope that of its own accord it would unlock the mystery," the mute emblem offers him no guidance. The obscure significance of the Golden Key takes us to the heart of the novel's fascination with the relationship between repression and liberation. Despite the open, good nature of its master, darker energies simmer away under the sign of the Golden Key. Varden's apprentice, Sim Tappertit, even has a grotesque key of his own, which lets him in and out under cover of night.

The darkness of Newgate, where Sim ends up, towers over the novel as much as the Golden Key offers to illuminate it. Dickens sometimes treats it with all the visceral bitterness of the mob. Elsewhere in the novel, it seems a necessary guarantee of the safety of the social order. Good-hearted Gabriel Varden himself, who fitted the lock to its gates in the first place, refuses to open the prison up to the crowd that finally tears it down. Haredale hugs its walls with gratitude and relief when he finally has the murderer Rudge Senior locked away inside. For them, the prison may offer an affirmation of civil and domestic harmony, but Dickens also points out to us among the mob two sons animated by the filial desire to release a father condemned by the Bloody Code, and one woman, "disguised in man's attire," bent upon "the rescue of a child or brother" (ch. 62). The prison is both a bastion of the natural order and cruelly insensitive to the feelings of nature. Like many men of liberal opinions in his time, Dickens seems torn between the desperate cries of the crowd and a fear of a descent into social chaos.

Even in the eighteenth century, the Protestant zeal of the Gordon Rioters was regarded as an anachronistic manifestation of the Puritan enthusiasm of the seventeenth century. The eighteenth century's own idea of itself as a time of Enlightenment was usually predicated on the assumption that such phenomena had passed away. Thomas Holcroft's *Plain and Succinct Narrative of the Late Riots* (1780), one of Dickens's principal sources, represented the riots as an anachronism in a philosophic age. Of course, Dickens was less concerned than Holcroft to defend the idea of the eighteenth century as an age of Enlightenment. Like Carlyle, he often represents the century as one of stasis and hypocrisy. Irony and satire complicate the picture further. Attitudes to religious enthusiasm found in eighteenth-century novels such as Fielding's *Tom Jones* and Smollett's *Humphry Clinker*, influence the comic representation of the religiosity of Miggs and her mistress, but Dickens's ideas on religious "enthusiasm" are more ambivalent than theirs. He can see something potentially glorious in enthusiasm for an idea beyond the self, and perhaps even a necessity for such feelings in an age of cant and hypocrisy. The "pure enthusiasm" (ch. 77) exhibited by Barnaby in the face of the gallows, for instance, is presented as moving rather than foolish (a perception reinforced by Hugh's curse).

The problem Dickens explores is the relation between enthusiasm as a form of popular fanaticism and the higher kind of sympathy. Enthusiasm is a force that may lift us beyond self-interest, and potentially into heroic action, but also one that may lead to the loss of all rational control and even of proper subjectivity itself. Simon's enthusiasm for his legs points to a deeper and more troubling personality trait that helps explain his participation in the Protestant Association. His "soul" continually threatens to get "into his head" (ch. 4) and overwhelm such power of rational judgment as Dickens grants him. Enthusiasm was always regarded as operating by a kind of sympathy – turning red embers into white heat – that required no rational articulation to transmit itself. Dickens himself, as we have seen, was capable of letting go of his more considered attitude to the riots when he smoked in sympathy with the rioters. These powerful forces of sympathy and liberation seem to have both fascinated and repelled Dickens when writing *Barnaby Rudge*.

Describing Rudge Senior's dash to London through a storm, Dickens comments that "those who are bent on daring enterprises, or agitated by great thoughts, whether of good or evil, feel a mysterious sympathy with the tumult of nature, and are roused into corresponding violence" (ch. 2). Dickens suggests that such sympathetic powers – "whether of good or evil" – are attracted to whatever is most vivid. Dickens might almost be describing his own situation in writing of the riots in his description of the rider merging his identity with his environment. Sympathy has an important role in the novel's sense of what is "natural." The calculations of Stagg and the desperation of her husband threaten the domestic idyll based on "natural" affections that Mary Rudge creates in the countryside. What is usually thought of as the sentimental side of Dickens operates in *Barnaby Rudge* to contrast this domestic haven with the ferocity of Hugh and the cruel veneer of Sir John Chester. Yet distinctions between natural and unnatural sympathies are not very stable in the novel. Dickens writes of Gordon possessing "something wild and ungovernable which broke through all restraint" (ch. 35), but only a few pages later admits him to be "sincere in his violence and in his wavering" (ch. 36). When castigated by Forster for being too sympathetic toward Gordon, Dickens countered that he "must have been at heart a kind man, and a lover of the despised and rejected, after his own fashion" (*Letters* 2: 294). Sympathy in the novel weaves a tangled skein of human affections. The "strange promptings of nature" (ch. 68) that unite Barnaby and his father seem ineluctable, moving, and, at the same time, dangerously destructive.

Ought the Golden Key to liberate such energies or lock them away? Although the novel encourages its readers to believe in some more sincere mode of relation than the hypocrisies Chester has imbibed from Lord Chesterfield's axioms of aristocratic comportment, what lies under the surface of things is often resistant to divination. The problem is that looking beneath the appearances, discerning the substance from the surface, continually proves to be a problem. Eyes do not always have the power to see into the heart of things to which they regularly pretend in the novel. Simon Tappertit has great faith in the magnetic "power of his eye" (ch. 4) over those he wants to control, but the results are more laughable than dangerous. Hugh exercises an animal magnetism through his eyes more successfully, able even to bend Sir John Chester to its power: "There was a kind of fascination in meeting his steady gaze so suddenly, which took from the other the presence of mind to withdraw his eyes, and forced him, as it were, to meet his look" (ch. 28). So the possibility of the kinds of powers Tappertit imagines himself to have is not discounted in the novel, but their operations are mysterious and unpredictable.

Eyes, indeed, are everywhere, looking people over and trying to control them, but often unable to make sense of what they see. Varden calls on his own eyes as his witness, but quickly wishes himself "half blind if I could but have the pleasure of mistrusting 'em" (ch. 26). Stagg, the blind man who feels faces to understand their owners, is more successful than those who can see. Physiognomy may offer uncanny clues to character in the novel, but understanding those clues is another matter (Hollington 1991). Those with eyes to see more often find themselves in something like the situation of Willet, surrounded by the ruins of his inn: "John saw this desolation, and yet saw it not" (ch. 55). Not only Barnaby suffers from "blindness of the intellect" (ch. 45). With its "various degrees and kinds of blindness" (ch. 45), *Barnaby Rudge* offers its readers no art really sufficient to find the mind's construction in the face.

As an historical novelist, Dickens follows Scott in attempting to explain the relevance of the past to the present, but he also develops from his predecessor an interest in the uncanny that gives *Barnaby Rudge* strong tinges of Gothic coloring. *Barnaby Rudge* too is not so much concerned with the supernatural aspect of the Gothic tradition as the idea that the human psyche is governed by powerful unconscious drives that escape rational control and even explanation. There are always energies beneath the surface, working away at confident rational judgments about the truth in *Barnaby Rudge*. Society cannot see through Sir John Chester's smiling knavery, for instance, but if his case seems a clear-cut one of villainy lurking beneath a smooth exterior, others are more opaque. Behind the face of Mary Rudge, which Varden thinks he knows so well, there lies "the faintest, palest shadow of some look, to which an instant of intense and most unutterable horror only could have given birth" (ch. 5). For Varden, this look is "the very one he seemed to know so well and yet had never seen before" (ch. 5). Varden recognizes in Mary Rudge's face the horror of a past event and its consequences that he has repressed and told himself to forget.

Certainly, as if anticipating Freud's idea of the *unheimlich*, in Dickens such fears seem to disrupt even the safe haven of home. The return of Barnaby's father ironically spells the destruction of the fragile home his mother has built in their rural retreat. What was once known and familiar – the father of the family – haunts the present in strange and threatening forms. Victorian readers thinking about the crowds around them in the modern metropolis may have found the past depicted in the novel a comfortably different place, but its tentacles reached out uncannily into the present. The character upon whom Dickens probably based Gashford, Gordon's sometime secretary Robert Watson, lived on into Victorian times, if only to commit suicide

(McCalman 1991). Discovered after Dickens had decided to write on the riots of 1780, but during his novel's long gestation, Watson's body was found to be covered with 19 wounds at the inquest reported in *The Times*. These wounds may have suggested the name Gashford to Dickens once he got to work, but they may also have provided him with a sign of the uncanny ways in which the past could scar the present.

Barnaby Rudge is an historical novel, but one that defies neat lessons about the relationship between past and future. Similarly, its concern with human sympathy and toleration is not made into the stuff of easy didacticism. Hugh is a centaur: his affections shift between animal fury and humane fellow feeling. His violent enthusiasm translates into an almost heroic sympathy for Barnaby as he waits to be taken to the scaffold:

> "If this was not faith, and strong belief!", cried Hugh, raising his right arm aloft, and looking upward like a savage prophet whom the near approach of Death had filled with inspiration, "where are they! What else could teach me – me, born as I was born, and reared as I have been reared – to hope for any mercy in this hardened, cruel, and unrelenting place!" (ch. 77)

The rough enthusiasm of the crowd seems to be sublimated in an altogether higher kind of energy here: like a biblical prophet, Hugh is granted a vision of a deeper sense of justice unknown to the legal codes of his society. The fact that Barnaby is reprieved may seem a potential vindication of the possibility of public authorities coordinating the interests of both order and mercy, but even here we are made aware of other possibilities haunting the novel's happy resolution. "The general enthusiasm" of the crowd in its joy at Barnaby's homecoming puts Varden "in a fair way to be torn to pieces" (ch. 79). These phrases may be appearing in a comic context here, but they remind the reader of other sorts of enthusiasm that sustained the violent crowd scenes earlier in the novel. Later still, in another scene that marks the novel's resistance to neat closure, Edward Chester stands by Hugh's grave and makes his comment about "monsters of affection" (ch. 79). Dickens may differ from Carlyle in proposing "the bright household world" (ch. 80) as a redemptive space beyond the patterns of historical conflict, but this space is not without shadows of its own. Dickens may not approve Sir John's view that we must "be content to take froth for substance, the surface for the depth, the counterfeit for the real coin" (ch. 12), but telling them apart in the novel proves no easy matter. "So do the shadows of our own desires," as the narrator tells us at one point, "stand between us and our better angels, and thus their brightness is eclipsed" (ch. 29).

Barnaby Rudge has not been the most popular of Dickens's novels. Forster thought there were serious structural problems with the book: "The interest with which the tale begins, has ceased to be its interest before the close" (Forster bk. 2, ch. 9). Many readers have thought that the murder mystery made an uneven fit with the historical aspects, but others find the interlacing of these two features a great achievement (Marcus 1965: ch. 5). Perhaps now we can see that the excitement of reading Barnaby Rudge lies in the way in which Dickens keeps questions about the relation between repression and liberation open for the reader. If there is a kind of resolution in the marriages of the coming generation, it is tenuously private and domestic rather than historical. Outside these fragile domestic spaces, others are left facing a less comfortable future. For the past has not simply created the present, it continues to haunt it in dangerous ways. "Bygone bugbears which had lain quietly in their graves for centuries" may have been raised again by Gordon "to haunt the ignorant and credulous" (ch. 37), but few characters, be they ever so wise or good-natured, seem to be able to escape this fate entirely in the novel. "I have no peace or quiet," Haredale tells Varden, "I am haunted" (ch. 42). Surface and depth, past and present, sympathy and violence remain entangled in each other in profoundly disturbing ways throughout Barnaby Rudge.

The pattern was to be a recurrent one in the later, even darker fiction of Dickens. Betsey Trotwood tells David Copperfield that "It's in vain, Trot, to recall the past, unless it works some influence upon the present" (ch. 23). Yet, like so many characters in *Barnaby Rudge*, David finds himself constantly besieged by vague memories and inarticulate sympathies. No less than Barnaby's father riding through the storm, David finds "something within me, faintly answering to the storm without, tossed up the depths of my memory, and made a tumult in them" (ch. 55). *Barnaby Rudge* represents a compelling staging post in Dickens's understanding of the disruptive persistence of the past in the life of both the individual and of society.

References and Further Reading

Bowen, John (2000). *Other Dickens: Pickwick to Chuzzlewit*. Oxford: Oxford University Press.

Brantlinger, Patrick (2001). Did Dickens have a philosophy of history? The case of *Barnaby Rudge*. *Dickens Studies Annual*, 30, 59–74.

Case, Alison (1990). Against Scott: the antihistory of Dickens's *Barnaby Rudge*. *Clio*, 19, 127–45.

Chittick, Kathryn (1990). *Dickens and the 1830s*. Cambridge: Cambridge University Press.

Craig, David (1983). The crowd in Dickens. In Robert Giddings (Ed.), *The Changing World of Charles Dickens* (pp. 75–90). London: Vision.

Duncan, Ian (1992). *Modern Romance and Transformations of the Novel: The Gothic, Scott, Dickens*. Cambridge: Cambridge University Press.

Glavin, John (2001). Politics and *Barnaby Rudge*: surrogation, restoration and revival. *Dickens Studies Annual*, 30, 95–112.

Hollington, Michael (1991). Monstrous faces: physiognomy in *Barnaby Rudge*. *Dickens Quarterly*, 8, 6–14.

House, Humphry (1971). *The Dickens World*, 2nd edn. Oxford: Oxford University Press.

McCalman, Iain (1991). Controlling the riots: Dickens, *Barnaby Rudge* and romantic revolution. *History*, 84, 458–76.

McGowan, John (1981). Mystery and history in *Barnaby Rudge*. *Dickens Studies Annual*, 9, 33–52.

Magnet, Myron (1985). *Dickens and the Social Order*. Philadelphia: University of Pennsylvania Press.

Marcus, Steven (1965). *Dickens: From Pickwick to Dombey*. London: Chatto and Windus.

Newman, S. J. (1976). *Barnaby Rudge*: Dickens and Scott. In R. T. Davies and B. G. Beatty (Eds.), *Literature of the Romantic Period, 1750–1850* (pp. 171–88). Liverpool: Liverpool University Press.

O'Brien, Anthony (1969). Benevolence and insurrection: the conflicts of form and purpose in *Barnaby Rudge*. *Dickens Studies Annual*, 5, 26–44.

Oddie, William (1972). *Dickens and Carlyle: The Question of Influence.* London: Centenary Press.

Palmer, William J. (1977). Dickens and the eighteenth century. *Dickens Studies Annual*, 6, 15–39.

Rice, Thomas J. (1983). The politics of *Barnaby Rudge.* In Robert Giddings (Ed.), *The Changing World of Charles Dickens* (pp. 51–73). London: Vision.

Sanders, Andrew (1978). *The Victorian Historical Novel 1840–1880.* London: Macmillan.

Scheckner, Peter (1987). Chartism, class and social struggle: a study of Charles Dickens. *Midwest Quarterly*, 29, 93–112.

Stignant, Paul and Widdowson, Peter (1975). *Barnaby Rudge*: a historical novel? *Literature and History*, 2, 2–42.

Stuart, Barbara L. (1991). The centaur in *Barnaby Rudge. Dickens Quarterly*, 8, 29–37.

Walder, Dennis (1981). *Dickens and Religion.* London: Allen and Unwin.

24
Martin Chuzzlewit

Goldie Morgentaler

Dickens's sixth novel is familiarly known by the hero's name or perhaps more formally as *The Life and Adventures of Martin Chuzzlewit*. Throughout its serial appearance, running continuously in 19 monthly parts from January 1843 to July 1844, it had a more cumbersome title: "The Life and Adventures of Martin Chuzzlewit, His Relatives, Friends and Enemies. Comprising all his Wills and his Ways; with an Historical Record of What he Did, and What he Didn't: showing, moreover, Who inherited the Family Plate, Who came in for the Silver Spoons, and Who for the Wooden Ladles. The Whole forming a Complete Key to the House of Chuzzlewit. Edited by 'Boz.' With Illustrations by 'Phiz.'" The story's publication on July 16, 1844 as a one-volume novel brought to conclusion a period of intense literary activity broken only by the interval between the completion of *Barnaby Rudge* (November 1841) and the publication of *American Notes* (1842), the travel book based on the many long letters Dickens wrote from North America during his trip to the United States and Canada that year. Upon finishing *Chuzzlewit* in mid-June 1844, Dickens acted on a resolution formed some months before: to remove himself from the pubic eye, rest from serial fiction, and take his family abroad for a year.

The Life and Adventures of Martin Chuzzlewit is a triumph of character over structure, a demonstration of how a great writer can overcome the limitations of a weak plot by infusing his characters with so much life that the weaknesses of the plot become secondary. Not all of Dickens's characters in *Martin Chuzzlewit* are transcendent in this way, certainly not young Martin Chuzzlewit himself, the novel's eponymous hero. But Dickens's less-heroic creations, Mr. Pecksniff and Mrs. Gamp, are inspired examples of the comedic imagination at work and amply demonstrate how easily Dickens's creativity was ignited by the negative aspects of personality – and how easily it could be dampened by the positive ones.

Dickens began work on *Martin Chuzzlewit,* his sixth novel, in November 1842. Serialization in monthly parts began in January 1843 and ended in July 1844. Characteristically, Dickens was full of enthusiasm when he began writing, telling his friend and adviser, John Forster, "I think *Chuzzlewit* in a hundred points immeasurably the best of my stories" (*Letters* 3: 590). The public, unfortunately, did not agree with this assessment, and sales of the monthly numbers were disappointing (20,000 copies sold, far fewer than the 40,000 to 100,000 copies of his other serials). The lack of sales has sometimes been attributed to a recession in the book industry in the early 1840s (*Oxford Dickens* 370), although it is difficult to judge the extent to which this and not the quality of the text itself played a role. What is clear is that the looming loss of readership forced Dickens to improvise a change of plot and send his protagonist to America in the hope of improving sales. The stratagem did not work and Dickens then turned to the shorter format of the Christmas books – beginning with the iconic *A Christmas Carol* – in order to recoup some of his lost popularity.

Martin Chuzzlewit has remained one of the most problematic of Dickens's novels with readers and critics ever since. Forster thought the story defective in "construction and conduct" (Forster bk. 4, ch. 2). R. H. Horne wrote in *A New Spirit of the Age* (1844), a book that was generally favorable to Dickens, that "Dickens evidently works upon no plan; he has a leading idea, but no design at all" (quoted in Ackroyd 1990: 424). Nor has the more modern view of this novel completely improved its reputation, despite suggestions by such influential critics as Steven Marcus that *Martin Chuzzlewit* is one of the most comically successful of Dickens's novels, the most "Joycean, for language itself is one of its subjects" (Marcus 1985: 217) and "the first novel of Dickens's maturity" (1985: 213). Not everyone agrees: in her introduction to the most recent Penguin edition of *Martin Chuzzlewit,* Patricia Ingham complains that what we have in this novel is "a text at odds with itself" (2004: xi).

Certainly, in its great inventiveness, especially its linguistic inventiveness, and in the humor and energy that it confers on some of its characters, *Martin Chuzzlewit* is an example of Dickens at his best. But the plot creaks and mystifies, characters are poorly motivated, and sentimentality too often threatens to smother the reader, especially in the sections dealing with Tom and Ruth Pinch. Nevertheless, *Martin Chuzzlewit* was perhaps a necessary novel for the 30-year-old novelist to write because the poor sales and lack of public response taught him to be more careful in the future, especially with the construction of his plots. *Martin Chuzzlewit* thus paves the way for the great multilayered novels of Dickens's middle and later period. In fact, the stronger control and more coherent focus on theme and structure are already evident in *Dombey and Son, Chuzzlewit's* immediate successor.

Martin Chuzzlewit tells the story of the Chuzzlewit family, beginning with an involved genealogical spoof that signals the novel's satirical intentions by suggesting that "no lady or gentleman, with any claims to polite breeding, can possibly sympathize with the Chuzzlewit Family without being first assured of the extreme antiquity of the race" (ch. 1). The sarcasm in this chapter is laid on quite thickly. Nancy Metz has suggested that Dickens had a personal reason for bitterness because during his tour of the United States and Canada (from January to June 1842) he had been attacked in an American newspaper for having no established pedigree (Metz 2001: 29–30). If Metz is correct about the motivation behind this chapter, then the urge somehow to get even with America seems not to have been very far from Dickens's consciousness, even before he decided to send young Martin across the Atlantic.

The first chapter's genealogy introduces the theme of family and inherited traits within a family, which the novel that follows will illustrate. It also introduces the theme of selfishness, which was the starting-point of the novel. As Dickens wrote in his Preface to the Cheap Edition of 1850, "My main object in this story was, to exhibit in a variety of aspects the commonest of all vices; to show how Selfishness propagates itself; and to what a grim giant it may grow from small beginnings."

In its use of the theme of selfishness, *Martin Chuzzlewit* taps into the black-and-white morality usually associated with fairytales. The characters are one-dimensional, since they are intended to embody one specific characteristic; the plot is picaresque and peripatetic, moving restlessly from one location to another. When Martin goes to America, the chapters move back and forth between the two continents. *Martin Chuzzlewit* betrays its adherence not only to Dickens's early reading of fairytales, but also to his reading of such eighteenth-century classics as *Tom Jones* and the novels of Tobias Smollett, as can be seen by the long, descriptive chapter titles.

While *Martin Chuzzlewit* deals with the theme of hereditary transmission, Dickens's portrayal of this motif owes more to popular psychology than to biology. Specifically, he was intrigued by how easily vice could be handed down as a hereditary trait within a family, and so he has the young Martin Chuzzlewit "inherit" his selfishness from his grandfather, old Martin Chuzzlewit, the rich, eccentric patriarch of the Chuzzlewit clan. Old Martin and young Martin have the same name in order to emphasize the fact that this is a family chronicle, a family chronicle in which one characteristic – selfishness – is passed like a bad seed from grandparent to grandson. And the transmission works laterally as well. Old Martin has a brother, Anthony, who is just as selfish as he is, and if young Martin takes after old Martin, then Anthony's son, Jonas, takes after Anthony:

> From his early habits of considering everything as a question of property, [Jonas] had gradually come to look, with impatience, on his parent as a certain amount of personal estate, which had no right whatever to be going at large, but ought to be secured in that particular description of iron safe which is commonly called a coffin, and banked in the grave. (ch. 8)

In a nice irony at the expense of family, old Anthony's funeral is described by the undertaker Mr. Mould as the most "filial" he has ever seen.

Whether inherited or learned – Dickens seems never entirely sure which it is – selfishness is also the defining characteristic of young Martin, since he was brought up in his grandfather's home. But the emphasis on this one characteristic in young Martin's make-up means that there is no psychological or moral complexity to the way in which this protagonist is presented in the novel that bears his name. In Patrick McCarthy's memorable phrase, young Martin is "the very model of the English gentleman as cardboard hero" (1980: 645). This problem relates to a weakness that Dickens seems never entirely to have overcome in his fiction, namely, the anemic presentation of the central male character. From *Oliver Twist* to *Barnaby*

Rudge to *Little Dorrit* to *A Tale of Two Cities*, Dickens seems to have had a difficult time endowing his male protagonists with enough personality to carry the plots in which they are centrally concerned. And while this is a less obvious flaw in the two "autobiographical" novels, *David Copperfield* and *Great Expectations*, where the main character is also the narrator, it is the case that when both David and Pip grow up, all the interest evoked by their childhood selves seems to leach out of them. In the case of *Martin Chuzzlewit*, the focus on young Martin, who is intended as the central representative of the plot of selfishness and who is redeemed from selfishness by his experiences in America, weakens the very heart of the novel.

And that is not the only weakness in this novel: Dickens's loyalty to his beloved fairytales can result in some very strange plot twists. For instance, one of the main premises of the plot is that young Martin has been disinherited by his grandfather because he has fallen in love with Mary Graham, a beautiful young orphan who has come under old Martin's guardianship. But old Martin had originally intended just such an outcome when he made Mary his ward, so why would he disinherit his grand-son for doing something that he intended him to do in the first place? We are meant to understand that Old Martin is miffed that his grandson fell in love without his permission, but it is difficult to believe that this is a strong enough motive for disin-heritance, especially since, as we learn later, old Martin has never stopped loving his grandson and has been a kind of *éminence grise*, watching over him on his various adventures. Disinheritance is a strange way to show love!

Strange, that is, unless one is familiar with fairytale devices. What is at work here is Dickens's favorite trick of having a benevolent character – usually a parental figure – masquerade as evil in order to test the protagonist. Dickens used this topsy-turvy kind of reversal in several novels, notably in *David Copperfield* where Betsey Trotwood pretends to have lost her fortune in order to test young David's mettle, in *Great Expectations* where Magwitch is first a terrifying convict and then a benevolent father-figure, and in *Our Mutual Friend,* where the kind-hearted Noddy Boffin turns into a mean-spirited miser in order to test Bella Wilfer's essential good-heartedness. But it is too magical a notion to be totally convincing within the psychological framework of a realistic novel. And it does not work in *Martin Chuzzlewit.* In truth, both old and young Martins eventually prove themselves to be kind at heart rather than selfish. Old Martin is the secret benefactor of the Pinches, while young Martin is described as having a "frank and generous nature" (ch. 33), which has been corrupted by his grandfather's example. Selfishness is the Martin Chuzzlewits' veneer, good-heartedness is their essence.

And this fact, in turn, seems to undermine the major thematic thread of the novel, since if both old and young Martins are essentially good, then their selfishness cannot be a very serious character flaw, as indeed it is not. In fact, young Martin's selfishness seems to consist of nothing more serious than patronizing both Tom Pinch and Mark Tapley, thinking a little too well of himself, sitting between the fire and Tom Pinch, and taking Mary Graham's love for granted. It is all rather insignificant. It is as if

Dickens could not really bring himself to imagine truly negative characteristics in characters whom he has conceived of as essentially "good."

There is a similar problem associated with young Martin's trip to America, since it is in the United States that he sees the error of his ways and is reformed. This suggests that America functions – again in fairytale fashion – as a land of trial for Martin, the place where he must go in order to be cleansed of his faults. The result of this purgation is to turn America into a land of symbolic possibility and hope since, after all, it represents the place where young Martin finds his true self.

As noted earlier, Dickens sent Martin to the United States in an effort to pick up the lagging sales of the early numbers of his novel. He also had some scores to settle with the Americans, and, in the heavy-handed satire that informs the American sections, he seems determined to settle them. Dickens had returned from his trip to the United States and Canada just six months before he began writing *Martin Chuzzlewit*. He had first written of his impressions in *American Notes*. Forster suggests that the American sections of *Martin Chuzzlewit* are an answer to those American readers who were outraged or disappointed by *American Notes* (Forster bk. 4, ch. 2, quoted in *Oxford Dickens* 367).

It is no surprise, then, that some of the same incidents that appeared in *American Notes* recur in *Martin Chuzzlewit,* but in much darker form. As *American Notes* makes clear, not all of Dickens's impressions of his US trip had been negative. He had, for instance, been quite favorably impressed with Boston, the city where he began his tour and which he described in *American Notes* as handsome and elegant. But he conspicuously leaves the positives out of young Martin's experience of the country. So, instead of first landing in Boston, as Dickens himself had done, young Martin sails directly into New York harbor. As Metz notes, Dickens disliked New York. It was the city where his enthusiasm for the New World had first cooled (Metz 2001: 206), so by making New York Martin's first stop in America, Dickens signals that the portrait of the United States that follows will not be particularly positive.

Like Dickens, young Martin sets off for the New World with high hopes, expecting to make his fortune. Instead, like Dickens again, he is disappointed in the new country, put off by the bad manners of its inhabitants who spit, ask impertinent questions of strangers, boast endlessly about the merits of their country, and think nothing of cheating a young man out of his last cent. The novel depicts America as a vast wilderness both geographically and culturally, peopled by boastful, violent, narrow-minded, dishonest chauvinists, addicted to cant, inflated rhetoric, and hyperbole. To use Ingham's phrase, America is "Pecksniff writ large" (2004: xxi). And America is selfishness and deceit writ large. Martin is conned into buying a piece of land in what he believes to be the thriving city of Eden where he could work as an architect. Instead, the symbolically named Eden turns out to be a fever-infested swamp where both Martin and Mark fall ill.

This American swindle finds its counterpart in Montague Tigg's Anglo-Bengalee Disinterested Loan and Life Assurance Company, a British version of the same kind of double-dealing that can trap the credulous and greedy on both sides of the Atlantic.

Thus, in *Martin Chuzzlewit,* fraud, deception, and treachery are not depicted as the defining characteristics of only the Americans or only the British. Human perfidy seems to be alive and well in both countries. Nevertheless, it is hard to avoid the suspicion that Dickens finds these failings much more contemptible when they occur among the Americans. What saves England from the satirist's barbs is the fact that there are good people in it, in addition to the humbugs. However, with the exception of one or two individuals, Dickens allows no such saving dispensation to America. Which begs the question that Dickens never really addresses: if Britain was really so much better than America, then why did Martin and other emigrants like him try to leave it?

Dickens's novel may be called *The Life and Adventures of Martin Chuzzlewit,* but its most vivid character is named Pecksniff. Mr. Seth Pecksniff, to be exact, the Old Testament name being a frequent marker of authorial disapproval. Pecksniff is an architect, another sign of authorial disdain. Architecture, as a profession, had acquired a negative reputation during the early 1840s when Dickens was writing *Martin Chuzzlewit.* The rebuilding of the House of Commons after a fire seven years earlier, the construction of new railway stations, and the expansion of London had all ensured that architects and architecture would have been very much on the public's mind. But the lack of regulation and a host of unscrupulous practices had brought the integrity of architects into question. Pecksniff, we are told, has never designed or built anything himself; instead, he has passed off his students' work as his own, while charging those students exorbitantly high premiums (Metz 1994: 63).

Seth Pecksniff is one of the great comic achievements of *Martin Chuzzlewit.* He is a prig and a moralist, a libertine and a hypocrite. He is introduced in chapter 2, and when we first meet him he has just been knocked down the stairs by a great gust of wind. This pratfall signals that we are in the realm of farce and that Pecksniff is a character for whom we need not feel sorry because it is quickly revealed that he is a self-satisfied hypocrite and manipulator. Dickens takes great delight in skewering Pecksniff's pretensions and high-minded pomposity, turning him into a man whom it is a genuine pleasure to despise, if only because of the verve with which Dickens invites us to do so. There is nothing subtle in this presentation. We are not intended to make up our minds about Pecksniff for ourselves; Dickens tells us what to think: "If ever man combined within himself all the mild qualities of the lamb with a considerable touch of the dove, and not a dash of the crocodile, or the least possible suggestion of the very mildest seasoning of the serpent, that man was he" (ch. 4).

And here is a taste of what the man himself sounds like when he speaks – here addressing old Martin Chuzzlewit who has just surprised Pecksniff in his garden:

> "Mr Chuzzlewit! Can I believe my eyes! My dear sir; my good sir! A joyful hour; a happy hour indeed . . . You find me in my garden-dress. You will excuse it, I know. It is an ancient pursuit, gardening. Primitive, my dear sir; for, if I am not mistaken, Adam was the first of our calling. *My* Eve, I grieve to say, is no more, sir; but" – here he pointed

to his spade, and shook his head, as if he were not cheerful without an effort – "but I do a little bit of Adam still." (ch. 24)

This is only one example of many in which Dickens limns the psychological outlines of his character through speech. One can hear here the unctuousness, the pomposity, the false sentiment, the verbal dexterity, and the extraordinary flight of rhetoric that seem to twist reality into the shape of humbug. In Pecksniff one can see the forerunner of such great Dickensian windbags as Wilkins Micawber in *David Copperfield* and William Dorrit in *Little Dorrit.* Like them, Pecksniff uses his facility with language to keep his listeners from examining too closely the underlying motives behind his speech, or from suspecting that what he says does not necessarily correspond to what he means. He is an example of verbosity as screen, and he demonstrates beautifully not only the inherent instability and hence malleability of language, but the fact that we human beings are constructs of speech, that our personalities are both revealed and hidden in language.

Yet, despite Dickens's clear intention that we hold Pecksniff in contempt, that we abhor him for the pretentious hypocrite and manipulator that he is, he is almost impossible to dislike. The novel sparkles whenever he appears, largely because of the sheer inventiveness of speech that Dickens puts in his mouth. Pecksniff is never at a loss for words. In the climactic scene in chapter 52, where he is denounced and beaten by old Martin Chuzzlewit, he still has the temerity to "forgive" those who have "wronged" him: "If you wish to have anything inscribed upon your silent tomb, Sir, let it be that I – the humble individual who has now the honour of reproaching you: forgave you. That I forgave you when my injuries were fresh, and when my bosom was newly wrung." Pecksniff's disgrace is thus not a disgrace, if only because he refuses to acknowledge that it is. The ability of words to turn reality into anything one wishes it to be is the Pecksniffian modus vivendi – and one of the delights of the novel.

Dickens's other great comic creation in *Martin Chuzzlewit*, Sarah Gamp, is also defined by her speech, but not in quite the same way as Mr. Pecksniff is, although she too uses language in order to fictionalize reality. But in Mrs. Gamp's case, the fictionalization has to do with her own creation of a certain Mrs. Harris, whom the narrator describes as a "phantom of Mrs. Gamp's brain . . . created for the express purpose of holding visionary dialogues with her on all manner of subject" (ch. 25). Mrs. Harris, in other words, is a creature of Mrs. Gamp's own self-serving imagination, which exists to bolster whatever argument or point of view Mrs. Gamp wants bolstering, including her predilection for liquor. Not surprisingly, most of Mrs. Harris's conversation with Mrs. Gamp (as reported by Mrs. Gamp) ends with a compliment to Mrs. Gamp. Mrs. Harris exists to make Mrs. Gamp feel good, but she also exists to let the world know what Mrs. Gamp is thinking and that Mrs. Gamp is not the only one thinking it. In this way, Mrs. Gamp manages to create her own consensus of opinion, solely through the act of imaginative assertion. By inventing this alter ego for Mrs. Gamp, Dickens seems to suggest that the power of imaginative creation need not belong only to (male) novelists, but may be tapped into by the proletarian female population as well, although in an obviously more debased and self-serving form.

Because of her powers of imaginative creation, Mrs. Gamp may be seen, as Harry Stone suggests, as "a grotesque monster-goddess, presiding over life and death" (1979: 93). And, in truth, there is a metaphysical dimension to her, so much so, in fact, that her clothes retain their shape even when she is out of them and "the very fetch and ghost of Mrs. Gamp, bonnet and all, might be seen hanging up, any hour of the day, in at least a dozen of the second-hand stores about Holborn" (ch. 19). Her supernatural potential is also enhanced by the fact that she ministers to the two extremes of life, birth and death. Oddly, Dickens suggests that there is something unfeminine in her presence at these events: "Like most persons who have attained to great eminence in their profession, she took to hers very kindly; insomuch, that setting aside her natural predilections as a woman, she went to a lying-in or a laying out with equal zest and relish" (ch. 19). One wonders where Mrs. Gamp's "natural predilections as a woman" might better be displayed, given that lyings-in and layings-out were traditional female functions. But perhaps it is Mrs. Gamp's "zest and relish" that is unfeminine. An example of this enthusiasm for her work occurs in chapter 25, where Mrs. Gamp has been called upon to nurse a man who is in a state of delirium. Ghoulishly, "a horrible remembrance of one branch of her calling" takes hold of her, so that she cannot resist pinning her patient's wandering arms to his side to see what he would look like in his coffin. "He'd make a lovely corpse," she concludes, as she studies the effect (ch. 25).

Much of the humor associated with Mrs. Gamp is of this gallows kind, as befits a woman in her walk of life. She remembers seeing her husband lying on his deathbed with his wooden leg under his left arm – and the narrator helpfully informs us that she then sold his body "for the benefit of science" (ch. 19). She wishes her fellow nurse, Betsey Prig, "lots of sickness . . . and may our next meetin' be at a large family's, where they all takes it reg'lar, one from another, turn and turn about, and has it business-like" (ch. 29). She mangles words and sayings continually, especially biblical sayings: "Rich folks may ride on camels, but it ain't so easy for 'em to see out of a needle's eye" (ch. 25). And she is given to assertions that imply more than they say: "Gamp is my name, and Gamp my nater" (ch. 26).

The humor of Mrs. Gamp extends to her actions as well. The character was inspired by the nurse of a friend of Angela Burdett Coutts, who had a habit of running her nose along the fender. Dickens confers the same habit on Mrs. Gamp (see ch. 25). At a time when home nursing was the rule, Dickens's portrayal of the snuff-taking, cucumber-loving, gin-swilling, money-grubbing, callous Sarah Gamp gave home nurses a bad name, and, Anne Summers suggests, contributed to the masculinization of the medical profession (1989: 374–6). Summers also points out that Dickens vilified Mrs. Gamp for expecting to be paid for her work, but it never occurred to him to vilify the doctors for exactly the same pecuniary interest (1989: 385). The fact that nurses must live off the misfortune of their patients, that they make a living from disease and death, seems to have been part of what Dickens objected to in Mrs. Gamp.

The fact that she is a woman earning an independent living in this way is perhaps what he means by her lack of femininity. After all, Mrs. Gamp is truly independent; she relies on no husband, she is her own boss, and has her own rules:

> "It is not an easy matter, gentlemen, to live when you are left a widder woman; particular when your feelings works upon you to that extent that you often find yourself a-going out on terms which is a certain loss, and never can repay. But in whatever way you earns your bread, you may have rules and regulations of your own, which cannot be broke through." (ch. 19)

The portrayal of Mrs. Gamp is one strand of a misogynistic strain that runs through *Martin Chuzzlewit,* and which is most evident in the treatment of the two Pecksniff daughters. It has become a commonplace of Dickens criticism to point to his weakness in creating believable female characters, especially young heroines. While Dickens's attitude toward older women often strays into caricature, as it does so memorably with Mrs. Gamp, his depiction of younger women is either overly reverential, as is the case with Mary Graham, or overly physical, as, for instance, in the following synecdoche from chapter 5, which seems to distill women down to their body parts: "Sparkling eyes and snowy breasts came hurriedly to many an upper casement as [Tom] clattered by"; or, in the following reduction of Ruth Pinch to "the best sauce for chops ever invented," a metaphor that Dickens likes so much, he expands on it: "The potatoes seemed to take a pleasure in sending up their grateful steam before her; the froth upon the pint of porter pouted to attract her notice" (ch. 37).

While the language surrounding Mary Graham, the novel's nominal heroine, is less cloying, it is nevertheless drained of color, and Mary is presented as having about as much personality as the usual Dickens heroine – which is to say almost none. Pure, gentle, loving, perfect, Mary is significantly 17 years old when we first meet her, the same age as Mary Hogarth when she collapsed and died in Dickens's arms. The fact that Dickens confers on Mary Graham the same first name as his idealized sister-in-law suggests one reason why she seems never to acquire any personality of her own.

But it is in the relish with which Dickens humiliates the two Pecksniff sisters that one can best discern the negative thrust of his feelings toward women. Stone has suggested that these two sisters get their come-uppance because they are modeled on the two stepsisters in Cinderella (Stone 1979: 94). Maybe so, but Dickens's pleasure in punishing both sisters – Mercy by marrying a brute who beats her and Charity by being jilted on her wedding day and thus being for a second time disappointed in her marital hopes – is hard to justify, since neither sister sins more grievously than young Martin Chuzzlewit himself. Both sisters are selfish, pretentious, and hypocritical, but Martin ultimately suffers no ill consequences from his character flaws, while the sisters' lives are ruined forever.

Mercy is flighty and flirtatiously cruel to Jonas Chuzzlewit when he is courting her. She calls him "monster" and "griffin" and teases him. But no sooner are they married than Jonas turns the tables, telling Mercy that he has only married her in order to punish her. Of course, Jonas signals his duplicity early in the courtship by deliberately leading Charity to think that she is his choice before proposing to Mercy. Jonas is a villain and eventually a murderer, but it is hard to escape the suspicion that Dickens takes a certain pleasure in the fact that Mercy becomes an abused wife and so is repaid for her teasing and taunting with blows.

Dickens depicts Mercy as suffering meekly under Jonas's harsh treatment when he beats her: "Even her weeping and her sobs were stifled by her clinging around him" (ch. 28). We are invited to be outraged at the brutality of Jonas's behavior by the narrator's apostrophe to womankind that closes the chapter: "Oh woman, God-beloved in old Jerusalem! The best among us need deal lightly with thy faults, if only for the punishment thy nature will endure, in bearing heavy evidence against us, on the Day of Judgment!" (ch. 28). Mr. Pecksniff could not have said it any better! Sanctimonious, outrageous, brilliant, hilarious, and infuriating, the Dickens of *Martin Chuzzlewit* already embodies all the strengths and weaknesses that will make him one the greatest novelists of all time.

References and Further Reading

Ackroyd, Peter (1990). *Dickens*. London: HarperCollins.

Dickens, Charles (1850) Preface to the Cheap Edition of *Martin Chuzzlewit*. London: Penguin, 1999.

Edgecombe. R. S. (1993). Locution and authority in *Martin Chuzzlewit*. *English Studies*, 2, 143–53.

Ingham, Patricia (2004). Introduction to *Martin Chuzzlewit*. London: Penguin.

Lougy, Robert E. (2000). Nationalism and violence: America in Charles Dickens's *Martin Chuzzlewit*. In Wendy J. Jacobson (Ed.), *Dickens and the Children of Empire* (pp. 105–16). Houndmills: Palgrave.

McCarthy, Patrick J. (1980). The language of *Martin Chuzzlewit*. *Studies in English Literature*, 20, 637–49.

Marcus, Steven (1985). *Dickens from Pickwick to Dombey*. New York: Norton.

Metz, Nancy Aycock (1994). Dickens and the "quack architectural." *Dickens Quarterly*, 11, 59–69.

— (2001). *The Companion to Martin Chuzzlewit*. Mountfield, East Sussex: Helm Information.

Stone, Harry (1979). *Dickens and the Invisible World*. Bloomington, IN: Indiana University Press.

Summers, Anne (1989). The mysterious demise of Sarah Gamp: the domiciliary nurse and her detractors, c.1830–1860. *Victorian Studies*, 32, 365–86.

25

Dombey and Son

Brigid Lowe

Dickens achieved the break he sought from writing serial fiction after he completed *Martin Chuzzlewit* in June 1844. But the interval between that date and the publication of the first installment of *Dombey and Son* on October 1, 1846 requires qualification. Although he expressed a wish to "fade away from the public eye" (*Letters* 3: 587), he maintained a steady presence among readers. The series of Christmas Books Dickens inaugurated with *A Christmas Carol* the year before was followed by another two, *The Chimes* in December 1844 and *A Cricket on the Hearth* a year later. He also published a second travel book (*Pictures from Italy*) in May 1846, a portion of which had appeared as a series of eight "Travelling Letters" in the *Daily News* between January 21 and March 11, 1846. The newspaper itself further extended Dickens's contact with the public. This new daily, pledged to promote liberal causes, began on January 21 with Dickens as its editor, a position from which he withdrew on February 9, finding the responsibilities of editorship incompatible with his career as a novelist. Shortly before making that decision, Dickens confided to Forster that he had been revolving plans in his mind "for quitting the paper and going abroad again to write a new book in shilling numbers" (*Letters* 4: 485). On May 31, Dickens left for Switzerland with his family, announcing soon after settling there that he had begun *Dombey* (*Letters* 4: 573). About a month later, he sent the first number to Forster, together with a detailed outline of the story. Number 1 was published on October 1 and ran continuously until April 1848. The novel also appeared in one volume the same year.

From *Dombey and Son* onward, it became Dickens's practice to pre-plan each of the monthly numbers in which his novels were issued well before he started writing. This forward thinking gave him new opportunities to orchestrate the details, themes, narrative strands, and emotional registers he intended to contribute to the book's core idea. In the case of *Dombey,* as Dickens explained to John Forster, his main creative impulse was "to do with Pride what its predecessor [*Martin Chuzzlewit*] had done with Selfishness" (Forster bk. 6, ch. 2). Thanks to his altered compositional method, however, in *Dombey* Dickens achieved a newly intense and complex novelistic unity.

Pride, in any case, is of quite another order to selfishness. In the Christian tradition, it is a sin of spiritual, cosmic gravity, the source of all other sins, the most serious of all the ways of sinning against love. It means something more than overvaluing your own position in the world, or being vain about the figure you cut in it. It is the primal sin of Adam – a belief in one's own abilities and efforts so overweening that it is in defiance of due recognition of the grace of God. "Thou sayest, I am rich, and increased with goods, and have need of nothing; and knowest not that thou art wretched, and miserable, and poor, and blind, and naked," reads Revelations (3: 17). Dombey's conception of himself as the invincible center of the universe is the essence of Pride:

> The earth was made for Dombey and Son to trade in, and the sun and moon were made
> to give them light. Rivers and seas were formed to float their ships; rainbows gave them
> promise of fair weather; winds blew for or against their enterprises; stars and planets
> circled in their orbits, to preserve inviolate a system of which they were the centre . . .
> A.D. . . . stood for anno Dombei – and Son. (ch. 1)

Throughout *Dombey*, Dickens makes a newly sophisticated use of changes in narrative mode and voicing to enforce this central theme. Here, by presenting Dombey's thoughts in the free indirect style, unmarked by grammatical signs to show that it is Dombey's perspective, he demonstrates graphically that for Dombey, the story of "Dombey and Son" is not just one story among many others, but *the* story: Dombey apprehends his own perspective not as a perspective at all, but as objective truth.

The novel has been criticized for failing in its portrayal of individual psychology,[1] but Dombey is characterized quite purposefully as a rather thin, insubstantial character: "Dombey and Son" are the "three words [that] conveyed the one idea of Mr. Dombey's life" (ch. 1); he is the unreflecting, walking embodiment of the pride of a whole age. The true target of this famous passage, as it is of the novel as a whole, is the rising mid-Victorian confidence in the all-conquering power of science, of empire, of progress and, most of all, of money. It is Dickens's first attack against the spirit of the age, conceived as more than the sum of its social ills and personal vices. In *Dombey's* first chapter, as throughout, Dombey's pride, which has all the precariousness of illusion, is seen to arm itself against the revelation of human frailty, the hard, non-sycophantic and unbribable facts of nature, most absolutely embodied in death. The legitimacy that seems to be given to the triumphant commercial narrative of "Dombey and Son" by the fact that father and son are initially referred to as "Dombey" and "Son" is quickly and disconcertingly undermined by a change of register away from the colloquial business-speak of the city into that of allegory:

> On the brow of Dombey, Time and his brother Care had set some marks, as on a tree
> that was to come down in good time – remorseless twins they are for striding through
> their human forests, notching as they go – while the countenance of Son was crossed
> with a thousand little creases, which the same deceitful Time would take delight in
> smoothing out and wearing away with the flat part of his scythe, as a preparation of the
> surface for his deeper operations. (ch. 1)

Dombey and Son are from the outset marked men. Against the seeming certainty of the success of the business, and the power of wealth, are set the real certainties of

Time and Care. Dombey's repeated jingling of his "heavy gold watch chain" is a visualization of his hubristic trifling with the grim brothers.

Dombey's world habitually believes, as Dombey tells his son, that anything can be achieved with money, or with what produces it – effort. Paul, first in his wonderings, and later in his death, is a forceful reminder to his father that this is not the case. His son's death not only shakes Dombey's plans for the firm, but is a reminder of his vigorously repressed sense of "the impotence of his will, the instability of his hopes, the feebleness of wealth" (ch. 20).

Dickens's plan for issue number 5 specifies that Paul's illness should be "only expressed in the child's own feelings – Not otherwise described." This narrative focalization, as also in passages such as those describing the deathly train journeys of Dombey and Carker, is widely regarded as the precursor to the full-blown, first-person narration of *David Copperfield*, *Great Expectations*, and *Bleak House*. And so it is. But the self-introducing, personal accounts of David, Pip, and Esther all convey a confidence in the solidity and centeredness of the self, and of its power to tell a coherent story; the grammar of their first-person narratives and their acts of recollection serve as guarantees that, as protagonists/narrators, they are sure to come through with us, alive and ultimately undamaged, to the end of the story.

The narrative focalized through Paul, on the other hand, emerging as it does only in the course of chapter 14, as his illness really sets in, and he begins to drift away from the world, serves primarily to emphasize the fragility and transience of human subjectivity and its hold on the world: "there seemed to be something the matter with the floor, for he couldn't stand upon it steadily; and with the walls too, for they were inclined to turn round and round, and could only be stopped by being looked at very hard indeed." The free indirect style leads us seamlessly into Paul's phantasmagorical world, and we feel that Son is already losing the definiteness and objective centrality suggested by the novel's title. His tenuous subjectivity swamped by the things outside it, he wonders poignantly whether his existence, subjectively no more than a stream of passing and confused impressions, is ever likely to be given a more substantial reality by another sharing a like experience, or by anybody remembering him:

> He had to peep into those rooms up-stairs . . . and wonder through how many silent days, weeks, months, and years, they would continue just as grave and undisturbed. He had to think – would any other child (old-fashioned, like himself) stray there at any time, to whom the same grotesque distortions of pattern and furniture would manifest themselves; and would anybody tell that boy of little Dombey, who had been there once. (ch. 14)

The import of this passage of free indirect speech is precisely the opposite of the passage adumbrating, in chapter 1, the extent of Dombey's pride. Whereas Dombey imagined the very sun itself coming up for Dombey and Son, Son, on the other hand, is only too vividly conscious that the smallest details of inanimate furnishing will remain undisturbed when he is gone. Dombey sees time itself as revolving around his firm – AD standing for anno Dombei – while Son imagines a relentless rolling on of "silent days, weeks, months, and years" that pitifully marginalizes his own small life. His perspective is a sand bar encroached upon by rising water. Indeed, Dickens's plan for the number following Paul's death underlines the ironic, tragic sense of the ephemerality of human life hidden in the novel's title; he heads it "throw the interest off Paul, *at once on Florence.*"

Pride entails, first and foremost, a repression of the facts of human frailty. The skeletal Mrs. Skewton hides from nature and mortality behind makeup and false curls; the Major, "staring through his apoplectic eyes at Mrs. Skewton's face with the disinterested composure of an immortal being," expostulates unbelievingly that "some people will die. They will do it . . . They're obstinate" (ch. 40). The collision between illusions of power and the reality of weakness is the organizing principle of the novel. The first chapter sets up the opposition: Dombey, "exulting" at the birth of his son and heir, is presented with coat buttons that "sparkled phosphorescently in the feeble ray of the distant fire. Son with his little fists curled up and clenched, seemed in his feeble way, to be squaring at existence." The death at the end of the chapter drives home the point. Confronted with death, those personifications of human "effort" – Dombey the wealthy businessman, Doctor Parker Peps the court physician, and Mrs. Chick the "experienced and bustling matron" – stand by, helpless. It is a ghost-like Florence alone who has comfort-giving powers:

> "Mama!" said the child.
>
> The little voice . . . awakened some show of consciousness, even at that ebb. For a moment, the closed eyelids trembled, and the nostril quivered, and the faintest shadow of a smile was seen.
>
> "Mama!" cried the child sobbing aloud. "Oh dear Mama! oh dear Mama!"
>
> The Doctor gently brushed the scattered ringlets of the child, aside from the face and mouth of the mother. Alas how calm they lay there; how little breath there was to stir them!
>
> Thus, clinging fast to that slight spar within her arms, the mother drifted out upon the dark and unknown sea that rolls round all the world. (ch. 1)

The delicately worded death-scene points up the vainglorious delusions of the proud. Human fragility, the transience of flesh, lie fully exposed, undisguised by any of the trappings of progressive civilization. The details of the description of dying mother and living child – eyelids, nostril, scattered ringlets, ebbing breath – rivet us on naked humanity, infinitely slight and emotionally and physically susceptible. The close focus on breath and its expiration sounds the first of the novel's persistent echoes of *King Lear*. And, as in the last scene of that play, here vulnerability finds its reflex in tenderness – qualities subtly coupled in Florence's repeated cries of "Mama," in the word "little," repeated, and in the mother's dying embrace.

Just as Florence somehow creeps from the darkened margins to the core of this scene, later, when Paul dies, she again moves into a position of indispensability that signals to Dombey the possibility of his own unimportance. Herein lies the root of his growing dislike of her. She demonstrates that, at root, it is not power but love, not the denial of human frailty but the accepting embrace of it, that are needed to deal with life *in extremis*.

The contrast between Florence and her father is part of another grand opposition structuring the book: between what we might call the "masculine" world of money and power and the "feminine" world of human need, connection, and love, which, unsurprisingly, has provoked a degree of feminist critique.[2] Fuel is added to the flame by the fact that, in chapter 2, the narrator presents Polly as "a good plain sample of a nature that is ever, in the mass, better, truer, higher, nobler, quicker to feel, and much more constant to retain, all tenderness and pity, self-denial and devotion, than the nature of man" (ch. 3) – a formulation of the innate difference between the sexes that might almost be read as an alibi for Dombey's hardness.

However, if Dickens does suggest an innate difference between the sexes, he grants femininity genuine superiority, not only morally but also practically, over masculinity. *Dombey* goes a long way toward presenting nurturing "feminine virtues" as the most essential of all human attributes, far more than ameliorative supplements to the true business of life. Though Dombey may disdain to deal "in hearts," preferring to leave "that fancy ware to boys and girls," his Son's need for a wet-nurse is richly expressive of the family firm's dependency upon what Dombey most disparages: "That the life and progress on which he built such hopes, should be endangered in the outset by so mean a want; that Dombey and Son should be tottering for a nurse, was a sore humiliation . . . the thought of being dependent for the very first step towards the accomplishment of his soul's desire, on a hired serving-woman" (ch. 2). At the time of the novel's publication, in spite of new efforts to perfect and patent baby formula, the chances of a baby surviving being brought up, like Pip in *Great Expectations*, "by hand" were still terrible. The firm of "Dombey and Son" is thus totally reliant on Polly for its very continuance, a fact scarcely concealed even by Dombey's strenuous efforts to present it as just another "question of wages" in which all the dependency, all the favor-giving, flows the other way: "I understand you are poor, and wish to earn money by nursing the little boy, my son . . . I have no objection to your adding to the comforts of your family by that means" (ch. 2).

For Paul to thrive, of course, his nurse must needs love him as well as feed him. The symbolic linkage of breast milk with the milk of human kindness is emphatic and clear. Love is a law, Dickens suggests, as inexorable as those other, more cruel, laws of nature, and acts as a necessary balance to them. It is in vain that Dombey insists that:

> "It is not at all in this bargain that you need become attached to my child, or that my child need become attached to you . . . When you go away from here, you will have concluded what is a mere matter of bargain and sale, hiring and letting: and will stay away. The child will cease to remember you; and you will cease, if you please, to remember the child." (ch. 2)

Love is no more to be bargained with than Time and Care; its bonds are not easily bought, or easily severed, and they radically undermine Dombey's absurd fantasies as to the scope of money's power. "Paul and myself will be able, when the time comes, to hold our own – the House, in other words, will be able to hold its own, and maintain its own, and hand down its own of itself", he urges (ch. 5). Pride clings to the abiding myth of capitalism – individual self-sufficiency.

Throughout the novel, breast-feeding recurs as a symbol of the enduring *necessity*, as well as the virtue and desirability, of loving human connection in the face of the apparently triumphant progress of commerce and technology beyond such primitive things. Mrs. Skewton's death is raised closer to tragedy when she forces some pity from Edith with the reminder, "I nursed you" (ch. 41), though what it highlights more than anything is the terrible lack of natural caring relations between them since that time. In her illness she herself is rendered childlike: timid, unable to articulate clearly, helpless. A similar reversal occurs when Florence and Dombey come together at the end of the novel, in a scene that has echoes of the famous tableau of "Roman Charity," in which a daughter breast-feeds her own starving father in prison: "Upon the breast that he had bruised . . . she laid his face . . . 'Papa, love, I am a mother . . .'" (ch. 59).[3] No human being, the image suggests, is beyond being reduced again to the utter dependence of childhood. We are all children; we are all in mortal need of the sustenance of unconditional love.

Of course, regardless of the narrator's early comment on the loving nature of Polly and other women like her, the novel as a whole provides a thoroughgoing deconstruction of any practical division of the world along gendered lines; love is too important to be so contained. Polly, Fanny Dombey, and Florence aside, *Dombey* teems with bad, even deadly, mothers and surrogate mothers: Miss Tox and Louisa Chick, Mrs. Wickam and Mrs. Pipchin, Edith, and, of course, Good Mrs. Brown and Mrs. Skewton. For the last two especially, the world of money and power has fatally infected the world of love and nurture. In this novel, the world of women is all too often just as inhuman as the world of business. The best mothering, in fact, is done by men, within the novel's paradigm of a perfect domestic space: "the little midshipman."

Dombey is Dickens's first truly "domestic" novel, and like the rest of the genre to which it belongs, it explores the domestic as the ambit of a range of human values increasingly marginalized in the industrialized world of capital. In an ironic inversion of the genre's usual conventions, however, the "home" sheltering the "family" about whom the novel is ostensibly chiefly concerned, is presented "on the shady side of a tall, dark, dreadfully genteel street," "as blank a house inside as outside" (ch. 3), while the true domestic heart of the novel is *a shop* "within the liberties of the City" (ch. 4).

The contrast between the chill of a proud household and the warmth of a true loving home is most graphically worked out in *Dombey*'s series of parallel meal scenes. Chilliest of all is Paul's christening breakfast:

> There they found Mr. Pitt turning up his nose at a cold collation, set forth in a cold pomp of glass and silver, and looking more like a dead dinner lying in state than a social refreshment . . .

"I have got a cold fillet of veal here . . . What have you got there, Sir?"

"This," returned Mr. Dombey, "is some cold preparation of calf's head, I think. I see cold fowls – ham – patties – salad – lobster. Miss Tox will do me the honour of taking some wine? Champagne to Miss Tox."

There was a toothache in everything. The wine was so bitter cold that it forced a little scream from Miss Tox . . . The veal had come from such an airy pantry, that the first taste of it had struck a sensation as of cold lead to Mr. Chick's extremities. (ch. 5)

The marble bust of William Pitt, former prime minister and enthusiastic supporter of Adam Smith's doctrine of *laissez-faire*, conveys the uncomfortable continuity between the cold, public world and the frigid formality and icy food of this private breakfast. Details suggest the intimate connection of pomp with death: there is "a dead dinner lying in state," a "sensation . . . of cold lead" imparted by veal. "Refreshment" in this passage, besides hinting at yet further cooling, which is the last thing the company needs, also suggests, in line with Pride's rejection of the humble necessities of nature, a downgrading of the act of consumption from necessity to indulgence. Wealth – embodied in glass and silver and expensive foodstuffs – is what casts the chill. Possession blights enjoyment. The awkward phraseology emphasizes a strained detachment between people and things: "I *have got* a cold fillet," "Champagne *to* Miss Tox," "*This . . . is some* cold preparation of calf's head, I think" (emphasis added). Dombey, high priest of this rite of Mammon, surveys, as it were from afar, a fare of strangely austere luxuries served up by an invisible and unknown staff: "I see cold fowls – ham – patties – salad – lobster," each dash suggesting the cold blank of disconnection (ch. 5).

Dickens artfully contrasts this "chill" meal on an "iron-grey" morning near the start of the novel with a "warm" one prepared on a "rosy," "bright" evening near the end. This time, the energetic cook/host, the painstaking preparation of the meal, the appetizing sensuality of the fare, and the mode of its presentation before a "cherished guest," are all elements indispensable to a glorious ceremony of heartfelt human hospitality, though the person so dexterous in these "feminine" arts is not the pretty lady one might presuppose:

The Captain had spread the cloth with great care, and was making some egg-sauce in a little saucepan: basting the fowl from time to time during the process with a strong interest, as it turned and browned . . . the Captain pursued his cooking with extraordinary skill, making hot gravy in a second little saucepan, boiling a handful of potatoes in a third, never forgetting the egg-sauce in the first, and making an impartial round of basting and stirring with the most useful of spoons every minute . . . the Captain had to keep his eye on a diminutive frying-pan, in which some sausages were hissing and bubbling in a most musical manner; and there was never such a radiant cook as the Captain looked, in the height and heat of these functions: it being impossible to say whether his face or his glazed hat shone the brighter.

The dinner . . . quite ready, Captain Cuttle dished and served it up, with no less dexterity than he had cooked it. He then dressed for dinner, by taking off his glazed hat and putting on his coat . . . unscrewed his hook, screwed his fork into its place, and did the honours of the table.

"My lady lass," said the Captain, "cheer up, and try to eat a deal. Stand by, my deary! Liver wing it is. Sarse it is. Sassage it is. And potato!" all which the Captain ranged symmetrically on a plate, and pouring hot gravy on the whole with the useful spoon, set before his cherished guest. (ch. 49)

The Captain's "strong interest" in the cooking of his dinner implicates him thoroughly in the "cheer" of nurturing, life-sustaining, human reality. Dombey's frozen stillness before his banquet of vanities has its riposte in the humming engagement of the Captain's turning, "boiling," "basting," "stirring," of humble food so comprehensive in its appeal to the senses that even the ear, thanks to the "hissing and bubbling" of sausages, can be pleased. The "impartial round" of the Captain's culinary attention, his symmetrical arrangement on the plate of "all" the delicacies, the thorough dousing of this "whole" in "hot gravy," suggests the warm-hearted companionship of a "family" of equals quite unlike the Dombey household where even blood relations must know their place. Humanity infuses all, from the "handful" of potatoes to the musical sausages. The humor of this representation of human warmth only adds to its affecting intensity, as the radiant old Captain, face and hat aglow, becomes a Dickensian symbol of transcendent love every bit as resonant as a Florence or an Agnes.

That Dickens, in all his novels, uses meals and cooking as invocations of human warmth and camaraderie is highly suggestive of his particular vein of humanism. If he insists upon the limited nature of man, it is because he traces the sources of virtue back to the most fundamental and humble springs of human need and desire. His humane, physical Christianity, far from being darkly flesh hating, demands embodiments of the world to come in this life, now. It is no bad reflection on Captain Cuttle that he confounds religious and secular texts in his continual misquotation. Dickens has no dualist conviction that the things and relationships of the world come between man and true spiritual reality. In some ways, Dombey is not too much, but too little of a materialist. Like most of Dickens's rich men, he inhabits a house furnished without the least regard for homely comfort. Indeed, his possessions, like his food, defy it:

Ugh! They were black, cold rooms; and seemed to be in mourning, like the inmates of the house. The books precisely matched as to size, and drawn up in line, like soldiers, looked in their cold, hard, slippery uniforms, as if they had but one idea among them, and that was a freezer. The bookcase, glazed and locked, repudiated all familiarities. (ch. 5)

Unlike Cuttle's spoon, which is, in the truest sense, "useful," Dombey's emblems of wealth, his showy books, locked away behind cold glass and with all their individual particularities of content negated, can serve no possible human need. His possessions are no more than embodiments of abstract cash value to him, just as his daughter is "a piece of base coin that couldn't be invested" (ch. 1). Cuttle, on the other hand, who has not even the merest conception of the value of money – "It an't o' no use to *me* . . . I wonder I haven't chucked it away afore now" (ch. 49) – has a most intimate, loving engagement with things, just as he does with his friends:

> the Captain being an orderly man, and accustomed to make things ship-shape, converted the bed into a couch, by covering it all over with a clean white drapery . . . [he] converted the little dressing-table into a species of altar, on which he set forth two silver teaspoons, a flower-pot, a telescope, his celebrated watch, a pocket-comb, and a song-book, as a small collection of rarities, that made a choice appearance. Having darkened the window, and straightened the pieces of carpet on the floor, the Captain surveyed these preparations with great delight, and descended to the little parlour again, to bring Florence to her bower. (ch. 48)

Things, it seems, are what we humans make of them, and if Dombey can transform a book into a frozen soldier, Cuttle can turn a dressing-table into an altar. The materiality of his domestic life converts into a spirituality far more authentic than that represented by the hollow religious ceremonies dotted through the narrative. The spoons may be made to stand for the need of human nature for sustenance, the flowerpot for the miracle of growth, the telescope and the watch for the space and time that make up the wide range of small human lives, and the comb and song-book for the human power to make life beautiful. By placing these objects lovingly on his altar, the Captain brings back comfort and meaning to life on earth.

For Dombey's pride, and the pride of his world, is not just a sin, but also, perhaps primarily, a tragedy. He is the creature of the money and station he craves, "the slave," as Carker puts it, "of his own greatness . . . yoked to his own triumphal car like a beast of burden, with no idea on earth but that it is behind him and is to be drawn on, over everything and through everything" (ch. 45). Though *Dombey* may be open to criticism as a study of individual psychology, it is startlingly acute as an analysis of "alienation" – the socio-psychological phenomenon that so exercised Marx. The proud are not just bad, they are mistaken: pride blinds them to their own good and their true needs, and their bad faith detaches them from their own free will. *Dombey*, a fable of pride, illustrates how natural it is to be unnatural, how human to be inhuman. "One don't see anything, one don't hear anything, one don't know anything; that's the fact. We go on taking everything for granted, and so we go on, until whatever we do, good, bad, or indifferent, we do from habit" (ch. 33).

The interior of Solomon Gills's little shop is designedly resistant to the tossing seas of a fluid world in which humans are subject to continual and far-flung dislodgements and displacements:

> Everything was jammed into the tightest cases, fitted into the narrowest corners, fenced up behind the most impertinent cushions, and screwed into the acutest angles . . . Such extraordinary precautions were taken in every instance to save room, and keep the thing

compact; and so much practical navigation was fitted, and cushioned, and screwed into every box . . . that the shop itself, partaking of the general infection, seemed almost to become a snug, sea-going, ship-shape concern, wanting only good sea-room, in the event of an unexpected launch, to work its way securely to any desert island in the world. (ch. 4)

Snugness is secure against alienation; it fixes and concentrates human values in a world in which we might otherwise drown.

Dickens uses symbolism in this novel with unprecedented consistency and resonance, and no symbol recurs more often than that of water. Though we are never told "what the waves are saying," watery imagery reminds us again and again of the inexorable flow of human life, and how infinitely wider and more awe-inspiring is our world than pride will allow. Water seems at once threatening and wonderful; Paul is alternately lulled and threatened by the stream rushing onward. All that is clear is that the mysteries of the universal waves are best navigated in a vessel secure and snug in human values. In the face of the infinite, we need the loving support of our fellow-beings, just as Paul and Mrs. Dombey need to cling to that "slight spar," Florence.

Dombey's other awe-inspiring symbol of superhuman power – the train – is, like the water, ambiguous in its resonances. It precipitates both chaos and prosperity by turns. What then, some critics wonder, is Dickens's attitude to what the railway surely symbolizes – progress, the march of history, the rise of capital (see chapter 13 of this volume). The novel provides a radically oblique answer. Economic progress is neither beneficent *nor* evil; it is only projections like Dombey's nightmarish imaginings on the way to Leamington that bestow on it such human characteristics. History is a "power that forced itself upon its iron way – its own – defiant of all paths and roads" (ch. 20), no more subject to human will or value, good or bad, than the earthquakes and volcanic eruptions to which the advent of the railway is compared in chapter 6. Progress, the triumph of capital and of technology, these things may sometimes be destructive and sometimes useful, but they are not *human*. Investing too much confidence in the possibilities of their shifting, titanic powers, to the neglect of our own enduring, physical and emotional needs and potentials as human beings, is to sleepwalk like Dombey into nightmare. If our pride prevents us from acknowledging what it means to be human – that we are limited creatures, terribly dependent on love – history, Dickens suggests, will quite simply submerge us.

NOTES

1 This was a repeated criticism from the earliest reviews until the declaration of John Lucas (1966) that the theme of pride is "unimportant" in comparison with money marked a shift away from "psychological" readings in the late twentieth century.

2 The most interesting examples have been attempts to read the novel "against the grain." See, for example, Julian Moynahan (1962) and Nina Auerbach (1976).

3 Dickens alluded to this tableau more explicitly in *Little Dorrit* (bk. 1, ch. 19). It suggests further echoes of *King Lear*.

References and Further Reading

Auerbach, Nina (1976). *Dombey and Son*: a daughter after all. *Dickens Studies Annual*, 5, 95–105.

Butt, John and Tillotson, Kathleen (1957). *Dickens at Work*. London: Methuen.

Lucas, John (1966). Dickens and *Dombey and Son*: past and present perfect. In D. Howard, J. Lucas, and J. Goode (Eds.), *Tradition and Tolerance in Nineteenth Century Fiction* (pp. 99–140). London: Routledge and Kegan Paul.

Marcus, Steven (1965). *Dickens: From Pickwick to Dombey*. London: Chatto and Windus.

Moynahan, Julian (1962). Dealings with the firm of Dombey and Son: firmness *versus* wetness. In J. Gross and G. Pearson (Eds.), *Dickens and the Twentieth Century* (pp. 121–31). London: Routledge and Kegan Paul.

Sanders, Andrew (1982). *Charles Dickens, Resurrectionist*. London: Macmillan.

Walder, Dennis (1981). *Dickens and Religion*. London: Allen and Unwin.

26

David Copperfield

Gareth Cordery

Dickens's eighth novel had its origins in an autobiography he began perhaps during the period he worked on *Dombey and Son* (1845–8). Recalling early memories, however, proved rather too painful so Dickens put the project aside, but not before entrusting its contents to Forster. He responded by suggesting that Dickens might attempt to write a novel in the first person, a proposal Dickens took "very gravely" and which led ultimately to *David Copperfield* (Forster bk. 6, ch. 6). In serial form, the novel appeared in 20 monthly parts (issued as 19) between May 1, 1849 and November 1, 1850 as *The Personal History, Adventures, Experience, & Observation of David Copperfield the Younger of Blunderstone Rookery (Which He never meant to be Published on any Account)*. A one-volume edition of the novel followed in 1850 with the abbreviated title, *The Personal History of David Copperfield*, and a brief Preface dated October 1850. In it, Dickens expressed pleasure in his achievement but regret that finishing separated him from interests "so recent and strong" that he felt in danger of wearying readers "with personal confidences, and private emotions," the full import of which was restricted to Forster.

After 17 attempts to find a suitable title for his eighth novel, Dickens finally settled on what appeared on the cover of each monthly number: *The Personal History, Adventures, Experience, & Observation of David Copperfield the Younger of Blunderstone Rookery (Which He never meant to be Published on any Account)*. All but one of the trial titles included "personal history," and the first part of this chapter explores the implications of this phrase, while the second part extends the discussion beyond David to include an examination of the fiction as a creation of its author and a product of its times, a site where the fractured ideologies of mid-Victorian England are played out. The fundamental assumption informing both parts is that the surface narratives of David's personal and Dickens's cultural histories disguise the tensions underneath and that the interplay between text and subtext suggests the complexities that inhabit novel, author, and age.

David Copperfield's Personal History

David Copperfield is for many a classic *Bildungsroman* that traces the life of the eponymous hero from birth to, eventually, a happy marriage with "the real heroine" (Tambling 2004: 914), Agnes Wickfield. The plot charts David's progress from the
romantic idealism of his childhood and the youthful illusions of his courtship and
first marriage to his child-wife Dora Spenlow, to a gradual understanding of the realities of human relationships and existence. Like other *Bildungsroman* protagonists, he
must confront obstacles to his progress in the form of Murdstone, Heep, and others,
and he must learn to recognize and rectify his weaknesses, especially his undisciplined
heart which initially leads him to marry the wrong woman. But his triumphant position at the end, as successful novelist, happily married man, and mature individual,
is as inevitable as the genre demands that it be.

At the end of 1848, Dickens "very gravely" embraced the suggestion "thrown out"
by Forster that he should write his next novel "in the first person." Despite struggling
initially, he soon wrote with the confidence (and trepidation) of someone who was
revisiting his own past. "The story," remarked Forster, "bore him irresistibly along"
(bk. 6, ch. 6). There is the masterly interweaving of the three main plot-lines – David's
own trials and tribulations, the Steerforth–Emily affair, and Heep's schemes against
the Wickfields – while the several subplots to do with the Micawbers, the Strongs,
Aunt Betsey's financial difficulties, and even Traddles's romancing of Sophy Crewler,
all contribute to the making of David's character. Dickens "constructed the whole
with immense pains" and had "so woven it up and blended it together" that he could
not "separate the parts" (*Letters* 7: 515) for his public reading version of 1861.

Yet Dickens had no grand design for *David Copperfield* as he had for its predecessor.
Perhaps because of its autobiographical nature, he did not need one. The monthly
number plans are little more than Dickens thinking aloud: "No Steerforth this time.
Keep him out" (Tambling 2004: 920). Part way through the third number he wrote
to Forster: "Copperfield half done . . . I feel, thank God, quite confident in the story.
I have a move in it ready for this month; and another for the next; and another for
the next" (bk. 6, ch. 6). These three moves were the death of David's mother, his time
at Murdstone and Grinby's, and his flight to his aunt's cottage at Dover. And some
four months later he could write: "I have carefully planned out the story, for some
time past, to the end, and am making out my purposes with great care" (*Letters*
6: 131).

Several of the major events were clear in his mind from the start for David "flags"
them, as he does Emily's "fall" at the hands of Steerforth when the little girl at Yarmouth beach runs along the jagged timber as if "springing forward to her destruction
(as it appeared to me) with a look I have never forgotten directed out to sea. This may
be premature. I have set it down too soon perhaps. But let it stand" (ch. 3). Since the
passage was added after the draft of this chapter, we can see in the penultimate sentence Dickens the author ruminating on the appropriateness of such foreshadowing

and in the "stet" of the final phrase is Dickens the proofreader. The adult David is also present ("I have never forgotten") as is the younger David's reaction ("as it appeared to me") to the original event. We shall see in the second part of this chapter that these three narrative voices have a bearing on how the reader assesses those to whom they belong.

Local hesitancies aside ("Dora to die in *this* No.? Yes, at the end"; Tambling 2004: 932), confidence and control are the hallmark of much of Dickens's writing of *David Copperfield*. Yet this authorial assurance disguises some deep-seated uncertainties and anxieties at the personal level, something I will also address later, but something that is true for David's own narrative as well. When David asks the reader in the opening sentence to consider "[w]hether I shall turn out to be the hero of my own life, or whether that station will be held by anybody else," the 592 original pages of his personal history do indeed seem to show that it is he – for who else is there? The reader is initially sympathetic to the lonely child, early victim of brutal assaults by Murdstone and Creakle, of the degradation at the bottling warehouse, and of several nightmarish experiences on the Dover road. We are thus predisposed to embrace the narrative of David's heroic progress. We are also seduced into accepting his engaging character at face value because it combines apparent honesty, friendliness, naivety, loyalty, self-reliance, and industriousness, and because the adult David looks back on his own innocence and on the mistakes committed by his younger self with touching forbearance. Thus, in chapter 3, along with the adult David, we can see why the child is literally carted off to Yarmouth by Barkis, for then Murdstone is left free to woo his mother.

Dickens's strategy for exposing the younger David's limitations is clear enough. Take the case of Dora, for example: he creates subplots, such as the Strongs' marriage, that bear directly on David's own situation; he allows characters such as his aunt to comment directly: "Ah, Trot! . . . blind, blind, blind!" (ch. 35); and the older David retrospectively criticizes, though with tender regret, his earlier propensity for romantic illusion: "What an unsubstantial, happy, foolish time it was!" (ch. 33).

Yet the adult David does not subject his precious childhood to the same clear-headed scrutiny. The marvelous evocation of childhood in those first 14 chapters is universally recognized as one of Dickens's greatest achievements, but how well do his early experiences and memories of them serve David's growth to adulthood? The older David describes himself as "an innocent romantic boy, making his imaginative world out of such strange experiences and sordid things!" (ch. 11), a successful survival tactic for a child. When he is locked in his bedroom after biting Murdstone's hand, the books he reads "as if for life" "kept alive my fancy" so that the barns, church, and churchyard he sees from his window become "some locality" from the novels of Smollett (ch. 4). This imaginative transformation of the real world, a necessary defense mechanism for the victimized boy David, is a barrier to the adult's maturation. Thus, instead of admitting the possibility that Clara in marrying Murdstone abandoned him, he remembers only "the young mother of my earliest impressions, who had been used to wind her bright curls round and round her finger, and to dance with me at twilight in the parlor" (ch. 9). Similarly, the image of his hero Steerforth, "with his head upon his arm, as I had often seen him lie at school" (ch. 55), is so burned into his brain that it extinguishes the seducer of his childhood sweetheart.

So the question is: does David grow up or is his a case of arrested development? Professionally, there can be no doubting his artistic achievements, which he not infrequently alludes to with a reluctance born of false modesty: "I laboured hard at my book . . . and it came out and was very successful." All the time, his "growing reputation" (ch. 48) is remarked by characters as various as Mrs. Steerforth, Mr. Omer, Tommy Traddles, Mr. Chillip, Agnes, and Creakle. But this success in the public domain is not matched in David's private life. In marrying Dora, he is, as has often been noted, also marrying a version of his mother since they are both childish, pretty, petulant, and incompetent housekeepers. But if Dora is a kind of Clara Copperfield, then David is another Murdstone, attempting to form his child-wife's mind as his stepfather had his mother's. He is released from the unpleasant consequences of that identification by Dora's fortuitous demise but not, to be fair to David, before he gives up his Murdstonian efforts "to adapt Dora to myself." During his marriage he realizes "there was always something wanting" that stemmed from the "first mistaken impulse of an undisciplined heart" (ch. 48). That something is a suitability of "mind and purpose" (ch. 45), lacking in Dora but present in Agnes. Presumably, then, David learns from his past and is appropriately rewarded with a woman who not only is an omnicompetent "little housekeeper" (ch. 15) but who, instead of merely sharpening pens and copying the odd page of manuscript as Dora does, is David's creative inspiration, beside him at the end as he writes his final words.

The reward, though, comes at a cost. "Dora has that delightful 'shape' and pretty hair, Agnes merely has sides against which her keys hang" (Collins 1977: 48). In exchanging Dora for "the real legless angel of Victorian romance" (Orwell 1954: 109), David seems to be abandoning sexual passion for boring domesticity, even if, as Carey laughingly suggests, Agnes is "pointing not upwards but towards the bedroom" (1973: 171). But if we take this hint half seriously, we can detect that David is "blind" to Agnes in more than her love for him. Taking her for granted, he seems totally unaware that his insensitivity must cause his "sister" considerable anguish. Her silent suffering remains unacknowledged even by the adult David, blinded by his egocentricity. So "David does not grow up; he marries a mother-sister-angel named Agnes . . . [whose] presence indicates the need not to change" (Westburg 1977: 89–90). Even Dickens told Forster that David found "dangerous comfort in a perpetual escape from the disappointment of heart" (bk. 8, ch. 2), but he escapes from more than this. He avoids his moral and social responsibilities as well, and the instrument of that evasion is memory.

If *David Copperfield* is the paradigmatic *Bildungsroman*, it is also the quintessential novel of memory, "quite the artistic equal of *A la Recherche du Temps Perdu*" (Wilson 1972: 214). David's hypersensitivity triggers memories so intensely that past becomes present: "How well I recollect the kind of day it was! I smell the fog that hung about the place; I see the hoar frost, ghostly, through it; I feel my rimy hair fall clammy on my cheek" (ch. 9). In passages such as these and in the four retrospective chapters (18, 43, 53, and 64), the historic present registers the collapse of the original experience and David's memory of it into an instantaneous now, even to the point of the latter overcoming the former: Traddles's face "impresses me more in the remembrance than it did in the reality" (ch. 41). And through those sacred moments that David preserves from destruction in the formaldehyde of his memory sounds the music of time: "I am reminded of a certain Sunday morning on the beach, the bells ringing for church, little Em'ly leaning on my shoulder, Ham lazily dropping stones into the water, and the sun, away at sea, just breaking through the heavy mist, and showing us the ships, like their own shadows" (ch. 3). This is "Dickens's secret prose, that sense of a mind speaking to itself with no one there to listen" (Greene 1951: 53).

But there is someone there to listen to the adult David: the reader, who hears what he does not or does not want to hear. "Even though this manuscript is intended for no eyes but mine" (ch. 42), it is a published novel, its parenthetical subtitle notwithstanding. It is this simultaneous urge to conceal and confess ("confessions" frequently turned up in the trial titles) that leads to some evasive fictionalizing of spectacular proportions. As father confessor, the reader seriously doubts at times David's emotional honesty. For example, his grief at Dora's death is perfunctory to say the least: "this is not the time at which I am to enter on the state of my mind beneath its load of sorrow" (ch. 54), for he has more urgent matters to relate before returning four chapters later to indulge his own desolation.

Even clearer is his "own unconscious part" in Steerforth's "pollution of an honest home." This fleeting insight is as quickly dismissed as it is reluctantly given: "I believe that if I had been brought face to face with him, I could not have uttered one reproach" (ch. 32). He never does, and for the rest of his life continues to think of Steerforth at his best. As for Emily, once she is "fallen" he never meets her face to face. His final glimpse of her aboard the emigrants' ship bound for Australia is "a masterpiece of narrative duplicity" whereby he turns her "into a sentimental religious icon" thus avoiding "addressing her as a woman" (Jordan 1985: 85–6). In this way, he distances himself from the guilt he feels in betraying her. In fact, he feels *she* has betrayed *him*. The fallen Emily, destroyer of his boyhood's "etherealised" vision of her as "a very angel" (ch. 3), must be punished. Hence David remains typically uninvolved as he secretly watches Rosa Dartle's tongue-lashing of his childhood sweetheart (ch. 50). His spectatorship of the encounter is silent endorsement of Rosa's vitriol, the instrument of his own rage toward his betrayer.

Together with memory, this unconscious displacement of unrecognized feelings screens David from what he finds unpalatable, thus rendering him incapable of moral growth. To put this in psychological terms, his unacknowledged and socially unacceptable impulses are projected onto other characters who then act out his forbidden desires. Thus, Steerforth and Heep are David's doubles who give expression to his repressed sexual fantasies for Emily and Agnes respectively. The introduction of David's hero to the Peggottys at Salem House coincides with Daniel's revelation that Emily "was getting on to be a woman," something David thinks about "a good deal and in an uneasy sort of way" (ch. 7). These ambivalent feelings re-emerge when he returns as a young man to Yarmouth with Steerforth for he does not know if he "was still to love little Emily" (ch. 21). His friend subsequently "lives out David's desire for aggressive adult sex and pays for it, leaving David with clean hands and innocent memories" (Westburg 1977: 88). David's hatred for Heep is intensified to the point of delusion when Uriah, in the privacy of David's chambers, confesses his love for Agnes. David's erotically charged fantasy of "seizing the red-hot poker out of the fire, and running him through with it," and his phallic vision of Uriah seeming "to swell and grow before my eyes" (ch. 25), are symptoms of his own unadmitted desire for Agnes and the self-loathing it engenders. (Nicola Bradbury in chapter 2, pp. 29–30, also discusses this scene.) His detestation of Heep is matched only by his hero-worship of Steerforth, yet both function to reveal a disturbing undercurrent in David's psychology that his own surface narrative attempts to disguise.

David Copperfield: The History of Mid-Victorian England

So far, we have examined the novel as David's personal history and seen that it is nothing like the uncomplicated *Bildungsroman* it supposedly is. In resisting the invitation to take David's story at face value and accept him as the hero of his own narrative, another story has emerged. A similar strategy reveals the novel to be not a transparent expression of some dearly held and deeply revered Victorian values and beliefs, but a site where they are interrogated, tested, and even subverted. The novel may lack the extreme topicality of *Bleak House*, but it is as much a history of mid-Victorian England as it is David's personal history, as much a dialogic, dynamic work that records and addresses personal and social instabilities (without necessarily solving them), as it is an expression of a unique voice. In participating in and contributing to wider cultural discourses about class, gender, marriage, childhood, work, and so on, *David Copperfield* shows, as it were, the very age and body of the time.

According to Forster, "Dickens never stood so high in reputation as at the completion of *Copperfield*." Here is his apology for mid-Victorian, middle-class ideologies: "By the course of events we learn the value of self-denial and patience, quiet endurance of unavoidable ills, strenuous efforts against ills remediable; and everything in the fortunes of the actors warns us, to strengthen our generous emotions and to guard the purities of home. It is easy thus to account for the supreme popularity of *Copperfield*" (bk. 6, ch. 7). Forster and his fellow readers shared David's rather complacent view of the world expressed from his comfortable position at the end as successful public figure and happily married man, and they subscribed to the means by which he achieved it.

How, then, does the text undermine what it overtly endorses? In order to try to answer that question, it will be useful to address those issues that are at the heart of the novel: class and gender. Crucial to the first are David's relationships with the aristocratic Steerforth and the humble Heep. From the start, David considers himself and is considered by others to be a cut above the rest. The Peggottys treat the child "as a visitor of distinction" (ch. 3). At Murdstone and Grinby's, his "conduct and manner" differentiate him from Mealy Potatoes and his ilk who call him "the little gent" (ch. 11). As an adult, he passes off Steerforth's contempt for the "chuckle-headed" Ham as a "joke about the poor" that supposedly disguises his sympathy for "that sort of people" (ch. 21). His class consciousness predisposes him to fall under the "spell" of his friend's "inborn power of attraction" (ch. 7), peculiarly thought by those below to belong exclusively to those above. His persistent misrepresentation of Steerforth to himself has as much to do with his aspirations for social status as with his repressed feelings for Emily. Not that the two are unrelated: they are linked by the *droit de seigneur* for working-class girls. In David's admiration for Steerforth is there not the middle-class envy of a lifestyle no longer possible in mid-Victorian England?

At the same time, there is the middle-class distaste for the parvenu. David's loathing for Heep is, like his envy of Steerforth, a disturbing combination of sexual and social anxieties. As Orwell put it, "It is the thought of the 'pure' Agnes in bed with a man who drops his aitches that really revolts Dickens" (1954: 85). Or rather David. The 'umble Heep's rise from articled clerk to partner in Wickfield's firm, his aspiration for the hand of his employer's daughter Agnes, his dedication and hard work in studying law in Tidd's *Practice* – all have their equivalents in David's rise from articled clerk to successful novelist, marriage to Spenlow's Dora, and his perseverance with Gurney's handbook on shorthand. David's determined refusal to acknowledge Uriah as his social double is countered by Heep's equal determination to remind him of it through the alternation of his form of address from "Master" to "Mister" Copperfield and back again.

Heep's repeated insinuations that David is no better than he is are fueled by his resentment of David's righteous superiority. Once Micawber exposes his hypocrisy, Uriah drops his mask of humbleness and vents his repressed feelings: "Copperfield, I have always hated you. You've always been an upstart, and you've always been against me" (ch. 52). It is an honesty that David is incapable of, for by his own admission Uriah "knew me better than I knew myself" (ch. 42). This honesty also exposes the double standards of a system that sustains David, thus providing a perspective that David does not share: "They used to teach at school . . . from nine o'clock to eleven, that labor was a curse; and from eleven o'clock to one, that it was a blessing and a cheerfulness, and a dignity . . . You preach, about as consistent as they did" (ch. 52). But this genie of devastating social criticism cannot be allowed to spread his subversive doctrine, so he is put back in the bottle of his solitary cell at Pentonville prison where he can continue to exploit but not destroy the system he so well understands.

Understood in this way, the controversial prison episode of chapter 61, far from being a "purely journalistic intrusion" (Wilson 1972: 212), is a topic of contemporary interest relevant to Dickens's vision of his own society. In the same way, two other issues of current concern, prostitution and emigration, not only expose the limitations of David's moral universe but also illuminate Dickens's own uncertainties. For sure, Dickens was more willing to confront the "great social evil" than his protagonist. He decided "in the history of Little Em'ly (who *must* fall – there is no hope for her) to put it before the thoughts of the people, in a new and pathetic way, and perhaps to do some good" (*Letters* 5: 682). The novel carries out this laudable aim by having Martha and Emily emigrate to Australia where the former marries a bushman and the latter finds peace in the burly bosom of Dan Peggotty and doing good to others. For once, the fiction seems commensurate with historical fact, for, like Martha, several of the inmates of Urania Cottage, the refuge for the rehabilitation of prostitutes that Dickens was helping to run at the time, found husbands and led productive lives down under. Yet many who did not emigrate remained to walk the streets of London, and if the "sheer absurdity" of having Mrs. Gummidge receive a proposal of marriage and the constitutionally impecunious Micawber become a magistrate is, as Grace Moore suggests, "ironic" (2004: 12), then this hints at Dickens's reservations about a utopian Australia as a solution to England's social problems.

The novel also interrogates the institution of marriage and the wife's disadvantaged position within it. The Wickfield household, the Strongs' marriage, and the Peggotty boat home, are all under threat from male intruders like Heep, Jack Maldon, and Steerforth. The eventual success of traditional marriages like the Strongs, the Traddleses, and the Copperfields is to be seen alongside Dora's to David, Edward Murdstone's iron-fisted control of his two wives, the Micawbers' loving but chaotically unstable relationship, and the blackmailing of Betsey Trotwood by her mysterious husband. Through this last, Dickens attacks the unfairness of laws that allow the inequalities that women suffer within marriage to continue after the separation of husband and wife.

Because of the role assigned to them in mid-Victorian society, middle-class women were denied the outspokenness allowed to men like Heep, so the novel's critique of their disadvantaged position is conveyed in more subtle ways. Dickens's women have generally received a bad press, Dora and Agnes in particular stereotyped as the ornamental doll and angel in the house, respectively. Yet the dying Dora voices, however mutedly – "I was not fit to be a wife" (ch. 53) – her resistance to David's campaign to mold her into the "little housekeeper" that Agnes always is and he (and his fellow Victorians) expected their spouses to be. It was, of course, Agnes whom reviewers had in mind when they praised Dickens for "his deep reverence of the household sanctities, his enthusiastic worship of the household gods" (Collins 1977: 244). David, from his privileged position as male narrator and husband, constructs her as an icon of domestic sainthood that guarantees his role as paternal protector and provider for his family. But the fragility of this gender-based fabrication is clear if we recall that David is a novelist who works at home, writing his final words with Agnes beside him. The ideology of separate spheres, in which the husband works in the office or factory to return home to be soothed and uplifted by his domestic angel ever pointing upwards, collapses in *David Copperfield* since David's is true domestic labor and without his wife's "dear presence" he would be "nothing" (ch. 64), personally or professionally. It is the silent Agnes who at the end claims authority in both spheres. Is David eventually emasculated and does the novel's hero turn out to be a heroine?

Finally to Dickens. "There was a suspicion," wrote Forster, "that underneath the fiction lay something of the author's life" (bk. 6, ch. 7), not least because Dickens had made his protagonist an author who "laboured hard . . . and was very successful" (ch. 48). David's not infrequent references to his "progress" are Dickens's reminders to his readers of the respectability and profitability of authorship, "a worthy calling, and my sole fortune" (*Letters* 5: 341). David calculates (as Dickens was wont to do) his income from magazine contributions alone to be £350 (ch. 43). In this sense, the novel may be seen as propaganda for the professional writer.

There was, of course, another aspect to the autobiographical nature of the novel that no one except Forster knew about. David's time at the bottling warehouse draws directly upon Dickens's own experience as a 12-year-old at Warren's Blacking factory: "what I know so well" (Tambling 2004: 912) as he writes in the plan for number 4. Dickens recorded this in the "autobiographical fragment" (see chapter 2 of this volume), and it appears almost verbatim in chapter 11. In addition, the novel reworks much else from his own life: David and Dickens work in Doctor's Commons, learn shorthand, and become parliamentary reporters; Salem House is based on Wellington House Academy; Micawber's imprisonment for debt mirrors John Dickens's, and David's infatuation for Dora, Dickens's for Maria Beadnell. And so on. There can be little doubt that Dickens was somehow reliving his past life while writing the novel. "It had such possession of me when I wrote it" (*Letters* 7: 515), and when he put down his pen it was "as if he were dismissing some portion of himself into the shadowy world" (1850 Preface).

Although the author expressed surprise when Forster pointed out that his protagonist's initials were a reversal of his own, it would appear that CD identified to some degree with DC and the temptation is to read the novel as if it were a transmutation and continuation of the abandoned autobiographical fragment with a few names and places changed here and there. It is, of course, nothing of the sort, but if it is not Dickens's fictional autobiography is it David's unsullied autobiographical fiction? The dichotomy is false for it is neither, but in Dickens's own words "a very complicated interweaving of truth and fiction" (*Letters* 5: 569) which nevertheless raises the question of his relation and attitude to the person who is his supposed stand-in.

Of the three narrative voices – the young David's, his "mature" reflections, and Dickens's – the last is the most difficult to pin down since it is present only by implication. I have argued that we should not take the second voice at face value: thus Dickens exposes David's continued blindness to Steerforth's immorality, but whether the author acknowledges David's culpability in Emily's fall is less certain. Still, in this particular instance, we can turn to a fourth voice – that of Phiz. Browne provides another point of view through his illustration "We Arrive Unexpectedly at Mr. Peggotty's Fireside" (ch. 21; figure 26.1). It is the crucial moment when David introduces Steerforth just as Emily's engagement to Ham is revealed. Their entrance stops Emily "in the very act of springing from Ham to nestle in Mr. Peggotty's

We arrive unexpectedly at Mr. Peggotty's fireside.

Figure 26.1 Phiz, *David Copperfield.*

embrace" – her engagement is as much to the uncle as to the nephew – a reversal of
her "springing forward to her destruction" at Yarmouth beach. "If I were a draughts-
man," wrote David on that occasion, "I could draw its form here" (ch. 3). Phiz may
have missed his first cue but not the second. All eyes are turned on Emily, her bonnet,
emblem of her social aspirations and forthcoming travels with Steerforth, ready to be
picked up. David, in his gentleman's clothes, stands hesitantly in the doorway, pointing with his right hand to Steerforth and with his left to the space between Ham and
Dan Peggotty, as if he were offering Emily to his friend, a gesture that reciprocates
Steerforth's invitation to David in the previous chapter to "help himself" to Rosa
Dartle. Phiz visualizes Steerforth's literal intervention and David's culpability in the
whole affair, something, given Dickens's close supervision of Browne, we must assume
that the former endorses. The illustration provides a perspective on David that the
written text does not.

Dickens, then, distances himself from his adult fictional hero and undermines his
authority as a narrator by deploying various rhetorical strategies: the disclosure of
David's own imperceptions and narrative duplicities; illustrations that point up these
textual evasions; character doubles that reveal his social and sexual anxieties; hints or

direct comments by other characters that uncover his desire for control and social status; and a subtext that suggests David's success at the end to be less triumphant than he thinks it is. Dickens could not push his skepticism too hard for fear of pursuing its radical implications, alienating his readership, and abandoning his favorite child. Yet is he, with 20 prolific years still to live, not suspicious of a writer who so resoundingly closes his life story with an exclamation mark as if there is nothing more to be said? And is he not suspicious of a writer who can find no room for the greatest comic character in English fiction? Micawber, exiled to Australia, passage paid for by that spokesperson for mid-Victorian values Aunt Betsey, is, along with his punch-making, magnificent grandiloquence, and those flights of fancy so dear to Dickens's heart, excluded from the sober earnestness and cozy domesticity of David's world. If this is Dickens's indictment of England in 1850, it is every bit as devastating as the overt criticisms of its social institutions and structures in the novels that follow *David Copperfield*.

REFERENCES AND FURTHER READING

Bloom, H. (Ed.) (1987). *Charles Dickens's David Copperfield*. New York: Chelsea House.

Bomarito, J. and Whitaker, R. (Eds.) (2006). *David Copperfield*. In *Nineteenth-century Literature Criticism*, vol. 161 (pp. 1–142). Detroit: Gale.

Carey, J. (1973). *The Violent Effigy: A Study of Dickens's Imagination*. London: Faber.

Collins, P. (Ed.) (1971). *Dickens: The Critical Heritage*. London: Routledge and Kegan Paul.

— (1977). *Charles Dickens: David Copperfield*. London: Edward Arnold.

Dunn, R. J. (1981). *David Copperfield: An Annotated Bibliography*. New York: Garland.

— (Ed.) (2004). *Charles Dickens's David Copperfield: A Sourcebook*. London: Routledge.

— and Tandy, J. (2000). *David Copperfield: An Annotated Bibliography, Supplement I, 1981–1998*. New York: AMS Press.

Greene, G. (1951). *The Lost Childhood and Other Essays*. London: Eyre and Spottiswode.

Hornback, B. G. (1981). *"The Hero of my Life": Essays on Dickens*. Athens, Ohio: Ohio University Press.

Jordan, J. O. (1985). The social sub-text of *David Copperfield*. *Dickens Studies Annual*, 14, 61–92.

Lankford, W. T. (1979). "The deep of time": narrative order in *David Copperfield*. *English Literary History*, 46, 452–67.

Moore, G. (2004). *Dickens and Empire: Discourses of Class, Race and Colonialism in the Works of Charles Dickens*. Aldershot: Ashgate.

Needham, G. (1954). The undisciplined heart of David Copperfield. *Nineteenth-century Fiction*, 9, 81–104.

Orwell, G. (1954). *A Collection of Essays*. New York: Doubleday.

Peck. J. (Ed.) (1995). *David Copperfield and Hard Times: New Casebooks*. London: Macmillan.

Poovey, M. (1988). The man-of-letters hero: *David Copperfield* and the professional writer. In *Uneven Developments: The Ideological Work of Gender in Mid-Victorian Britain* (pp. 89–125). Chicago: Chicago University Press.

Storey, G. (1991). *David Copperfield: Interweaving Truth and Fiction*. Boston: Twayne.

Tambling, Jeremy (Ed.) (2004). *David Copperfield*. London: Penguin.

Welsh, A. (1987). *Dickens from Copyright to Copperfield: The Identity of Dickens*. Cambridge, MA: Harvard University Press.

Westburg, B. (1977). *The Confessional Fictions of Charles Dickens*. De Kalb: Northern Illinois University Press.

Wilson, A. (1972). *The World of Charles Dickens*. Harmondsworth: Penguin.

27

Bleak House

Robert Tracy

The interval between the completion of *David Copperfield* in November 1850 and the beginning of *Bleak House* the following year saw Dickens busy with several projects. Routine editorial work on *Household Words*, which he had launched while writing *Copperfield*, continued to occupy him. To the journal, he also contributed numerous essays, including *A Child's History of England* (see chapter 16), weekly installments of which began in January 1851. Amateur theatricals and philanthropic work on behalf of Angela Burdett Coutts (see chapter 10) further crowded his agenda as ideas for his ninth novel hovered "in a ghostly way" about him during the same period (*Letters* 6: 298). By early October, those ideas "whirling" in his mind had precipitated him into a state whereby pre-writing and planning had become a "wild necessity," leaving him "a prisoner all day" at his writing desk (*Letters* 6: 510, 544–5). By early December, Dickens had almost finished the first number of *Bleak House*, which commenced its serial run in 20 monthly parts (issued as 19) in March 1852 and ran continuously until September 1853. The novel was also issued in one volume in the same year.

Dickens began writing *Bleak House* late in November 1851, and the novel opens in "Implacable November weather" (ch. 1). He wrote following the careful plan for its serial development he had already drawn up. *Bleak House* was Dickens's most successful novel to date, outselling even *David Copperfield* as serialization proceeded. "I believe I have never had so many readers as in this book," Dickens announced in the Preface to the volume edition, with an understandable touch of pride. This increase in readers suggests that his public was ready to accept the darker atmosphere and savage indignation of the later novels.

"It is desirable that a story-teller and a story-reader should establish a mutual understanding as soon as possible," Dickens declared in the opening sentence of *The Chimes* (1844). He ran some risk of jeopardizing that mutual understanding by his technical innovations in *Bleak House*. This novel has not one but three opening chapters. Chapter 1, "In Chancery," begins a story about a lawsuit, Jarndyce and Jarndyce, caught in the lethargic procedures of the Court of Chancery, in Dickens's day a frequent target of reformers. Chapter 2 refers to Jarndyce and Jarndyce again, but seems to be about fashionable life. The third chapter is a first-person autobiographical narrative by a young woman, but brings her into touch with Jarndyce and Jarndyce.

Dickens further risked puzzling or alienating readers, who could abandon a serial publication at any time, by inventing two narrators, "a difficult enterprise," according to his skeptical friend and literary adviser, John Forster, "full of hazard in any case, not worth success, and certainly not successful" (Forster bk. 7, ch. 1). One narrator is invisible but apparently masculine. In chapter 1, he can look in on "the Court of Chancery, which has its decaying houses and its blighted lands in every shire," and warn: "Suffer any wrong that can be done you, rather than come here!" In chapter 2, he brings us into Sir Leicester and Lady Dedlock's London town-house. They represent "the world of fashion," the class who rule England, "not so unlike the Court of Chancery" in resisting change, "a world too much wrapped up in jeweller's cotton" that "cannot hear the rushing of the larger worlds." This narrator is supplemented by the young woman who introduces herself in chapter 3, Esther Summerson, who begins by telling us about her childhood and education. John Jarndyce has recently invited her to live at Bleak House as companion to a young lady who is a party to the Jarndyce lawsuit.

Narrator A, let us call him, observes events that are necessarily outside Esther's ambit. Like the Spirits in *A Christmas Carol* (1843), he can take us everywhere. He can show us the Dedlocks on a road in France, the private life of a law-stationer or a bassoon-player, bring us to the squalid slum of Tom-all-Alone's, an inquest at the Sol's Arms, a law-office, the House of Commons, a factory in the Black North. He is emotional but not sentimental, excitable, sometimes outraged at evidence of England's failure to deal with conspicuous problems – Chancery, slums, illiteracy – and at the "Telescopic Philanthropy" that would evangelize Africa but neglects London.

The charity burial of Nemo, an impoverished copier of legal documents who is eventually revealed as Esther's father, moves Narrator A to a characteristic outburst. When the body of "our dear brother here departed" is taken to "a hemmed-in churchyard, pestiferous and obscene, whence malignant diseases are communicated to the bodies of our dear brothers and sisters who have not departed," he excoriates a society that could so disregard the dignity of the dead and the health of the living:

> while our dear brothers and sisters who hang about official backstairs – would to Heaven they *had* departed! – are very complacent and agreeable. Into a beastly scrap of ground which a Turk would reject as a savage abomination . . . they bring our dear brother to receive Christian burial . . . sow him in corruption, to be raised in corruption . . . a shameful testimony to future ages, how civilization and barbarism walked this boastful island together. (ch. 11)

The passage is one in a persistent series of references to infection that extends Dickens's images of Chancery as a source of decay and infection, responsible for the fetid squalor of Tom-all Alone's, property tied up in the Jarndyce case, for the death of Gridley and the madness of Miss Flite, and later for the death of Richard Carstone, another party to Jarndyce who puts his hopes in the lawsuit despite John Jarndyce's warning to avoid it. By associating disease, madness, and abject poverty with Chancery and with Sir Leicester, a member of parliament opposed to change, Dickens makes his case for reform, for recognition that England as she is governed no longer functions responsibly. It is Narrator A who imagines, on the first page of *Bleak House*, "a Megalosaurus, forty feet long or so, waddling like an elephantine lizard," a metaphor for Chancery, and for parliament as then constituted, a clumsy antediluvian monster that ought not still to encumber the earth.

"I had always rather a noticing way," Esther tells us, establishing *her* credentials as narrator, "not a quick way, O no! – a silent way of noticing what passed before me, and thinking I should like to understand it better" (ch. 3). Esther writes 33 of the novel's 67 chapters, and the mystery of her parentage is a major preoccupation of the plot. Her adventures at Bleak House allow her to witness the destructive effects of a Chancery suit, as Richard Carstone dreams of a fortune when the suit is settled in his favor. Chancery, and the lawyers who live off its mismanagement, provide the most conspicuous public failure which Dickens attacks; at the same time, Chancery is a symptom of other ways in which "The system!" (ch. 15) is both indifferent and cruel. The mystery about Esther's parentage drives the novel's private or domestic plot, and she becomes the heroine of the love story that a Victorian novel must have.

Put off by Esther's constant references to her own industry, we can at first fail to appreciate the narrative and descriptive skills that Dickens has lavished on her, along with his own gift for spotting the significant detail. Spending a night with the slovenly Mrs. Jellyby, who is busy planning the resettlement of England's "superabundant home population" in Africa, Esther notes the unpolished name plate on the door, the dirty children, "the lame invalid of a sofa," Mrs. Jellyby's unbrushed hair and badly laced dress. Her workroom is "not only very untidy, but very dirty." Doors will not shut, the chimney smokes, dinner is late and inedible, the servants quarrel, the cook clearly drinks. Mrs. Jellyby's eyes have "a curious habit of seeming to look a long way off. As if . . . they could see nothing nearer than Africa!" (ch. 4). Like Chancery, like parliament, she is guilty of the self-satisfied indifference toward England's problems – toward keeping her own and England's house in order – that Dickens condemns.

That word *house*, variously *The Ruined House* or *The Solitary House*, almost always associated with Tom-all-Alone's, recurs in Dickens's preliminary list of possible titles for this novel before he settled on *Bleak House* (Stone 1987: 186–205). For Dickens, it represents the need for order, good housekeeping, in public life as well as private. In October 1851, he even linked his own new house and the novel he was about to begin as "the tangible house and the less substantial Edifice" (*Letters* 6: 513).

Esther writes a clear, direct prose, often sentimental, sometimes sardonic when she narrates her many encounters with hypocrisy. Her collaborator has a wider range, and a greater passion. It is he who opens the novel by evoking a cold, wet, November day in London, with pedestrians hardly able to progress in the muddy streets, hardly able to see their way forward with the all-pervading fog. Their inability to go forward and their confusion prepare us for the delays and obscurities of the Court of Chancery, where Chancellor, lawyers, clerks, ushers, and attendants in the courtroom can hardly see each other in that same fog as they muddle through another hearing about Jarndyce and Jarndyce, "tripping one another up on slippery precedents, groping knee-deep in technicalities" (ch. 1).

As soon as Esther arrives at Bleak House, to take up her duties as companion/chaperone to Ada Clare, she is surprised to find herself appointed housekeeper, with a basket of keys to every cellar and storeroom and cupboard. Her role as housekeeper is a metaphor both for the part she plays in narrating the novel and for the need for a responsible national housekeeper to clear away the literal and figurative dirt and cobwebs that Dickens finds everywhere in the neglected household of England. "When I see you . . . intent upon the perfect working of the whole little orderly system of which you are the centre," declares Mr. Skimpole, "I feel inclined to say to myself – in fact, I do say to myself, very often – *that's* responsibility" (ch. 37).

The house that Esther controls is another metaphor. She describes Bleak House as "delightfully irregular," full of odd nooks and sudden little staircases and "steps that branched off in an unexpected manner from the stairs," passages where "you lost yourself" and doors that took you back to where you had started, "wondering how you got back there, or had ever got out of it" (ch. 6). Mr. Jarndyce calls his private room at Bleak House the Growlery, the place where he comes to brood when angry, "deceived or disappointed" (ch. 8). When he describes the Jarndyce case to Esther in the Growlery, he sounds most like Narrator A, who similarly has his own places set aside in the book to exhibit and denounce what is wrong with contemporary England.

Bleak House is *Bleak House*, with its unexpected twists and turns of plot (Guppy's encounter with Mrs. Chadband, who tells him of Esther's childhood, Tulkinghorn's murder) and its odd, unexpected interludes (Mr. Chadband's evening with the Snagsbys or Mrs. Bagnet's birthday party). Narrator A can digress to examine Little Swills, the comedian who improvises a routine based on Nemo's inquest. Esther is Henry James's ideal novelist, "someone on whom nothing is lost." Setting the scene for a brief encounter, she describes W. Grubble, innkeeper of the Dedlock Arms, who appears in the novel for less than a single page. She lets us know that Grubble always wears his hat and top-boots indoors. When he escorts Esther into the parlor, he bears the hat before him with both hands "as if it were an iron vessel." Once there, she provides a detailed inventory of the curious array of knick-knacks he has on display before getting to business by narrating a conversation with Richard Carstone that advances the plot (ch. 37).

Esther successfully navigates the twists and turns that make it easy to get lost in Bleak House, and with equal success handles the intricacies of plot she must report as a narrator of *Bleak House*. In writing "my portion of these pages" (ch. 3), she exercises control over much of the novel, and once she has captured our attention she becomes, for most readers, the more memorable of the two narrators. But she knows that she has a collaborator, and as she proceeds she makes, as it were, space for him. Bleak House is not a stately home, but at Chesney Wold we learn that one of the

housekeeper's duties was to show the house to visitors. They see the rooms and portraits, including Lady Dedlock's, "considered a perfect likeness, and the best work of
the master" (ch. 7). I suggest that Esther performs a similar duty toward the chapters
written by her collaborator, positioning us to look at his descriptions of Tom-all-
Alone's (supplemented by one of Phiz's gloomiest drawings), of Chancery as a court-
room full of men doing nothing of any use, of that squalid graveyard where Nemo is
buried.

When Dickens began writing *Bleak House*, he had, like many of his countrymen,
recently experienced the Great Exhibition of 1851 (see chapter 13). Initiated by Prince
Albert, the Exhibition (May–October 1851) celebrated the technological wonders of
the new machine age in a structure of iron and glass that was itself a technological
wonder, Sir Joseph Paxton's Crystal Palace. Dickens's discomfort with the triumpha-
lism of the Great Exhibition was a major element in shaping *Bleak House* and determining both its themes and its form. In "The Last Words of the Old Year," written
for his magazine *Household Words*, Dickens imagines the departing year 1850 looking
back at his life, and describing the legacies he is leaving to 1851, "a vast inheritance
of degradation and neglect in England," including the Court of Chancery. "I have
seen a wonderful structure, reared in glass," the Old Year declares, "a great assemblage
of the peaceful glories . . . of ingenuity and industry." But "Which of my children
shall behold the Princes, Prelates, Nobles, Merchants, of England, equally united, for
another Exhibition," he wonders,

> for a great display of England's sins and negligences, to be, by steady contemplation of
> all eyes, and steady union of all hearts and hands, set right? . . . Wake, Colleges of
> Oxford, from day-dreams of ecclesiastical melodrama, and look in on these realities in
> the daylight, for the night cometh when no man can work! Listen, my Lords and Gentle-
> men, to the roar within, so deep, so real, so low down, so incessant and accumulative!
> Not all the . . . Quantities of anything but work in the right spirit, will quiet it for a
> second, or clear an inch of space in this dark Exhibition of the bad results of our doings!
> Where shall we hold it? When shall we open it? (*Journalism* 2: 313–14; *Household Words*,
> January 4, 1851)

The pages of *Bleak House* are Dickens's Great Exhibition of 1852, reminding
England that all is not well. The efficient machines in the Crystal Palace – a working
model of a coal mine, a machine that folded 2,500 envelopes an hour – are not matched
by an efficient social or legal machinery. Chancery is an obsolete and inefficient
machine, a "Monster" (ch. 35) that draws people to destruction and produces nothing
save grief, squalor, and waste, a metaphor for a corrupt and outmoded system. Government is Chancery writ larger, private theatricals for the ruling class. If Boodle and
Coodle and Doodle and the Duke of Foodle cannot agree to form a ministry, then
Buffy and Cuffy and Duffy must do so. "A People there are, no doubt," Dickens
concedes,

a certain large number of supernumeraries, who are to be occasionally addressed, and relied upon for shouts and choruses, as on the theatrical stage; but Boodle and Buffy, their followers and families, their heirs, executors, administrators, and assigns, are the born first-actors, managers, and leaders, and no other can appear upon the scene for ever and ever. (ch. 12)

Dickens will return to this recipe for misgovernment again, with the aristocratic Barnacles who idle in government offices in *Little Dorrit* (1855–7) and the indifferent French aristocrats in *A Tale of Two Cities* (1859).

In *Bleak House*, Dickens mounts that alternative Exhibition, that "great display of England's sins and negligences" that the Old Year 1850 had demanded. Led on by the romantic plot, readers are shown collapsing slums, disease-breeding graveyards, illiteracy, and that pervasive "dandyism" that mistakes style for substance, aspects of mid-Victorian England they might easily avoid in their daily rounds. "Is it possible . . . that this child works for the rest?" asks Mr. Jarndyce, face to face with two small children whose 13-year-old sister supports them by washing; "Look at this! For God's sake look at this!" (ch. 15), a phrase that might serve as Dickens's motto for the book. When Mr. Tulkinghorn mentions Nemo's squalid death in poverty, Sir Leicester protests "that to bring this sort of squalor among the upper classes is really – really – " (ch. 12). But Dickens demands that his readers look at the misery all around them. To recognize an evil, he hoped, is to move to end it.

"In Bleak House, I have purposely dwelt upon the romantic side of familiar things," Dickens tells us in his Preface, echoing his "Preliminary Word" for *Household Words*, promising to show "that in all familiar things . . . there is Romance enough, if we will find it out . . . to bring the greater and the lesser in degree, together . . . and mutually dispose them to a better acquaintance and a kinder understanding." He will unsettle the reader by merging the two antithetical categories of familiarity and romance (Newsom 1977: 3–7; *Journalism* 2: 177–9; *Household Words*, March 30, 1850), until what is sordid becomes grotesquely fascinating, and we cannot bring ourselves to turn away. The Great Exhibition is incomplete without English misery and want. The ingenuity that created the Crystal Palace and the wonderful new machines must address social and political issues as well.

The 1851 Exhibition expressly reminded the upper and middles classes of their dependence on the workers, and Dickens continually insists on the interdependence of classes in *Bleak House*. If Sir Leicester and Lady Dedlock represent high society, Jo the crossing-sweeper, ragged, dirty, illiterate, is lowest of the low. But Lady Dedlock must seek him out to find Nemo's grave, and so establish a link with him that connects her with Esther and with Tom-all-Alone's. "What connexion can there be, between the place in Lincolnshire, the house in town," and Jo the crossing-sweeper, "the outlaw with the broom?" asks Narrator A, who then goes on to describe the "tumbling tenements" of Tom-all-Alone's and the "swarm of misery" that inhabits them:

As, on the ruined human wretch, vermin parasites appear, so, these ruined shelters have bred a crowd of foul existence that crawls in and out of gaps in walls and boards; and coils itself to sleep, in maggot numbers, where the rain drips in; and comes and goes, fetching and carrying fever, and sowing more evil in its every footprint than Lord Coodle, and Sir Thomas Doodle, and the Duke of Foodle, and all the fine gentlemen in office, down to Zoodle, shall set right in five hundred years – though born expressly to do it. (ch. 16)

The diseases sown in Tom-all Alone's can overcome all social barriers. In Phiz's illustration for chapter 18, "The little church in the park," the Dedlocks worship in a box pew, above and curtained off from their servants, as the Lord Chancellor in court is "softly fenced in with crimson cloth and curtains" (ch. 1). Respectable parishioners worship from less spacious box pews, while the tenantry kneels on the stone floor – a graphic commentary on the separation of rich and poor in a place where all are supposed to be equal before God. But Dickens has earlier noted that sometimes the little church is "mouldy" and "there is a general smell and taste as of the ancient Dedlocks in their graves" (ch. 2). The past is never quite over, as Richard Carstone, Gridley, born into lawsuits, and Lady Dedlock with her secret, discover. Tom-all-Alone's and Chesney Wold are alike sources of infection. Esther's aunt tells her that her illegitimacy is a kind of infection: "Your mother, Esther, is your disgrace, and you were hers" (ch. 3).

Esther and Narrator A combine to give us their guided tour of the *Bleak House* Exhibition to enable us to recognize the connections between the apparently unrelated worlds of Chancery, Chesney Wold, Bleak House, and Tom-all-Alone's as the developing plot gradually reveals them, and so to discover the anatomy of England's flawed social structure. They show us how England operates, or fails to operate, just as the exhibits at the Crystal Palace showed visitors how the machines which already dominated their lives operated. They also show us those who manipulate the political and social machinery of England, and those who are caught and destroyed by that machinery, categories omitted from the Great Exhibition.

Light and shadow are almost characters in *Bleak House*, associated respectively with orderliness or mystery and decay. Like most novels published serially, *Bleak House* appeared each month with two illustrations by "Phiz" (Hablot K. Browne), Dickens's illustrator for most of his novels. Phiz's illustrations make light and shadow graphic, pairing dark plates with light as the novel moves toward its somber ending. As the story darkens, "Sunset in the long Drawing-room at Chesney Wold" (part 13, chs. 39–42) shows a shadow falling upon Lady Dedlock's portrait, as in Dickens's text, where "a weird shade falls" upon the picture "as if a great arm held a veil or hood, watching an opportunity to draw it over her" (ch. 40), and over the story itself, where her past liaison with Nemo threatens her with scandal and drives her out into the long, dark night to die alone. In "The Lonely Figure" (part 17, chs. 54–6), she almost disappears into the darkness of the plate, as in the plot she disappears into the darkness of a winter evening. "Light" and "Shadow" contrast in part 16 (chs. 50–3), but

"The Night" and "The Morning" in part 18 (chs. 57–9) are both dark plates, as is the final illustration, "The Mausoleum at Chesney Wold."

If *Bleak House* is an exhibition of Victorian England's social failures, it also exhibits the narrative forms available to the Victorian novelist, and lets Dickens display his virtuosity in the genre he had made his own. He introduces one type of contemporary fiction after another into his narrative, so much so that reading *Bleak House* can serve as a general introduction to Victorian fiction. In *Coningsby* (1844) and *Sybil* (1845), Disraeli introduced contemporary political and social issues into fiction, and dramatized the division of England into two nations, the rich and the poor. Poe had arguably invented the detective story in "The Murders in the Rue Morgue" (1841), where Dupin, like Inspector Bucket, works partly by logical reasoning and partly by intuition. An intelligent young woman describes and comments on her upbringing, education, life as a governess, and eventual marriage in *Jane Eyre* (1847). Lady Dedlock, with her beauty, ambition, and "insolent resolve" (ch. 2) to marry for money and rank, resembles the heroine of *Vanity Fair* (1847–8). While Henry Mayhew's interviews with the London poor in the *Morning Chronicle* (1849–50) were not fiction, Dickens adopts his device of letting his subjects describe their lives in their own words when Jo appears. *Bleak House* is by turns satiric, sentimental, and melodramatic. "O my child, my child!" cries Lady Dedlock, learning of Esther's existence; "Not dead in the first hours of her life, as my cruel sister told me . . . O my child, O my child!" (ch. 29).

Narrator A often echoes the apocalyptic cadences of Carlyle's *History of the French Revolution* (1837) and *Latter-day Pamphlets* (1850). George Rouncewell's journey to the Black North gives us a preview of *Hard Times* (1854), the industrial novel Dickens is soon to write. Dickens also draws on his own earlier work. Esther tells her story as David Copperfield had done. Chadband's hypocrisy and eloquence recall Pecksniff, Jarndyce's spontaneous generosity Mr. Brownlow and the Cheerybles. Guppy, Jobling, and Smallweed at dinner (ch. 20) are in the style of early Dickens. To this exhibit of fictional modes, we can perhaps add his portraits of such contemporaries as Leigh Hunt (Skimpole), Walter Savage Landor (Boythorn), and the philanthropist Caroline Chisholm (Mrs. Jellyby).

Dickens wrote *Bleak House*, almost a thousand pages in the Penguin edition, with a series of quill pens, over a period of 21 months. Each printed number of 32 pages required 20,000 words; the press had always to be fed. It is not surprising that accumulations of written papers and the acts of writing and reading should recur in the novel. J. Hillis Miller called *Bleak House* "a document about the interpretation of documents. Like many great works of literature, it raises questions about its own status as a text. The situation of characters within the novel corresponds to the situation of its reader or author" (Miller 1971: 11). In chapter 1, "bills, cross-bills, answers, rejoinders, injunctions, affidavits . . . mountains of costly nonsense" are piled up in court when Jarndyce and Jarndyce comes on; Lady Dedlock faints on recognizing her old lover's handwriting in a legal document about the case (ch. 2). Like Dickens beginning a new novel, Esther admits to "a great deal of difficulty in beginning to write" (ch. 3), and she feels any writer's relief when "the last words of these pages" are "not so very far before me" (ch. 61). Mrs. Jellyby dictates letters to her ink-spattered daughter "in a room strewn with papers" at a "great writing-table covered with similar litter" when we meet her in chapter 4.

In the next chapter, Esther visits Krook's waste paper shop, nicknamed "the Court of Chancery," with its heaps of discarded legal documents and ink bottles, and idly reads a written notice that Nemo – who lives upstairs – does legal copying. Krook is illiterate, but chalks "JARNDYCE" and "BLEAK HOUSE" on the wall, one letter at a time, erasing each before writing the next. Tulkinghorn looks for specimens of Nemo's handwriting and Lady Dedlock's old letters to him. Later, she writes a confessional autobiography for Esther. Mr. Jarndyce proposes to Esther by letter, and Sir Leicester, after a stroke, scrawls his forgiveness of Lady Dedlock on a slate. Journalists report Krook's inquest with "ravenous little pens" (ch. 33). At the end of the novel, after a valid will has been found, "all in the Testator's handwriting," and the Jarndyce fortune turns out to have been consumed in legal costs, "great bundles of papers" are carried out of court: "bundles in bags, bundles too large to be got into any bags, immense masses of papers . . . which the bearers staggered under, and threw down for the time being . . . while they went back to bring out more" (ch. 65).

All this writing provokes reading. *Bleak House* is about reading: reading texts, reading character, reading situations, and reading Phiz's illustrations. The pointing allegorical figure on Mr. Tulkinghorn's ceiling and Guppy's reading of Lady Dedlock's portrait remind us how pictures supplement text. Esther teaches Charley to read, and is herself a shrewd reader of character and situations. Tulkinghorn and Guppy seek clues to read the concealed narrative that will connect Nemo with Lady Dedlock, Lady Dedlock with Esther; as they do so, they give us access to the plot. Bucket reads Sir Leicester's glances to understand he is to find Lady Dedlock, then reads the clue she has left behind – a handkerchief marked with Esther's name – which suggests her destination, then finally guesses the trick by which she has thrown him off her track. Mrs. Snagsby's imagination, perhaps fed by melodramas and novels like *Oliver Twist*, believes she is solving another mystery of concealed parentage, in which Jo will turn out to be Snagsby's illegitimate child. Bucket points out that her misreadings of characters and events, and her frantic determination to find and solve a mystery "has done a deal more harm in bringing odds and ends together than if she had meant it" (ch. 54). She has helped to reveal the "connexion . . . between the place in Lincoln-shire" and "Jo, the outlaw with a broom" and sensed Dickens's organizing principle: "What connexion can there have been between many people in the innumerable his-tories of this world, who, from opposite sides of great gulfs, have, nevertheless, been very curiously brought together!" (ch. 16). Such "connexions" pervade *Bleak House*, repeatedly raising Dickens's implicit question: what is my relationship to my fellow human beings?

Finally, there are the readers of *Bleak House*, we who read our way into a recogni-tion of wrongs that are still with us: litigation that only benefits lawyers, ignorance and prejudice, ecological neglect, poverty, diseases that a little effort could eradicate. When she goes out alone into the dark, cold night, like Lear, Lady Dedlock has been affected by reading her own story. She abandons the icy aloofness that has character- ized her and goes on her penitential journey into the world invisible from the House of Commons or the house at Chesney Wold. Dickens hoped that his readers would also be reached by what they had seen and feel some responsibility for trying to set things right.

REFERENCES AND FURTHER READING

Butt, John and Tillotson, Kathleen (1971). *Dickens at Work*. London: Methuen.

Johnson, Edgar (1952). *Charles Dickens: His Tragedy and Triumph*, 2 vols. New York: Simon and Schuster.

Miller, D. A. (1988). *The Novel and the Police*. Berkeley, CA: University of California Press.

Miller, J. Hillis (1971). Introduction to *Bleak House*. Harmondsworth: Penguin. Reprinted in *Victorian Subjects* (pp. 179–88). Durham, NC: Duke University Press, 1991.

Newsom, Robert (1977). *Dickens on the Romantic Side of Familiar Things: Bleak House and the Novel Tradition*. New York: Columbia University Press.

Shatto, Susan (1988). *The Companion to Bleak House*. London: Unwin Hyman.

Stone, Harry (1987). *Dickens's Working Notes for his Novels*. Chicago: University of Chicago Press.

Tracy, Robert (2003a). Lighthousekeeping: *Bleak House* and the Crystal Palace. *Dickens Studies Annual*, 33, 25–53.

— (2003b). Reading and misreading *Bleak House*. *Dickens Quarterly*, 20, 166–71.

— (2004). Time in *Bleak House*. *Dickens Quarterly*, 21, 225–34.

Welsh, Alexander (2000). *Dickens Redressed: The Art of Bleak House and Hard Times*. New Haven, CT: Yale University Press.

28

Hard Times

Anne Humpherys

The completion of *Bleak House* in August 1853 opened up a space from writing that Dickens had perhaps intended to enjoy (*Letters* 7: 157, 453). Events, however, dictated otherwise. A fall in the profits from *Household Words* reported for the six months up to September 30, 1853 prompted the publishers, Bradbury and Evans, to propose that Dickens write a novel to run serially in the journal. This was such "a fixed idea" on their part, Dickens later reported to Angela Burdett Coutts, that he complied, and by January 23 he had "fallen to work again." It will be as long as "five Nos. of Bleak House," he explained, "and will be five months in progress" (*Letters* 7: 256). The requirements of the weekly format, however, proved troublesome. Dickens found himself without the room of the ample monthly installment and compelled to work within limitations that left him "perpetually rushing at" the novel and "addled" and "stunned with work" (*Letters* 7: 369, 365, 368). The first of 20 weekly installments began in *Household Words* on April 1, 1854 and ran continuously until August 12. Dickens's tenth and shortest novel was also published, by Bradbury and Evans, in the same year. This novel and *Great Expectations* were the only two to appear without illustrations when they were first published.

> Utilitarian economists, skeletons of schoolmasters, Commissioners of Fact, genteel and used-up infidels, gabblers of many little dog's-eared creeds, the poor you will have always with you. Cultivate in them, while there is yet time, the utmost graces of the fancies and affections to adorn their lives so much in need of ornament.
>
> (*Hard Times* bk. 2, ch. 6)

Hard Times, Dickens's tenth novel, has generated the most varied response of all of his fictions. From the beginning, critics and general readers have charged the novel with oversimplification or sheer inaccuracy in its critique of industrialization and attack on the utilitarian preference for "facts" and statistics over "fancy" or imaginative play. Harriet Martineau complained that:

> its characters, conversations, and incidents, are so unlike life, – so unlike Lancashire or English life, – that the novel is deprived of its influence. Master and man are as unlike

life in England, at present, as Ogre and Tom Thumb: and the result of the choice of subject is simply, that the charm of an ideal creation is foregone, while nothing is gained in its stead. (1855: 36)

Others saw the depiction of "fancy," represented by Sleary's horse-riding circus, and Sleary's insistence that people must be "amuthed," a woefully inadequate alternative to the "hard facts" complex of industrialization and utilitarianism.

F. R. Leavis in 1947 rescued the novel from nearly a hundred years of such criticism in an influential essay that asserted that *Hard Times* was a "moral fable" and the only Dickens novel "possessed by a comprehensive vision" (1947: 227–8), thus making its putative weaknesses (its method of character typing and its universalizing social critique) its greatest strength. Though some post-Leavis critics have continued to see the novel as the least successful of Dickens's fictions because of what is perceived as thin characters and reductive critiques, others have turned from the debate about the inaccuracy of Dickens's representation of industrialism in Bounderby, utilitarianism in Gradgrind, union organizers in Slackbridge, or the working class in Blackpool, to the rich patterns of theme and language and to the complexity and paradox in the novel.

Still the question of the novel's artistic success remains, for *Hard Times* tends to register low in lists of favorite Dickens novels. Given that all of his fictions contain flat characters, both as central and minor figures, and that he tends to criticize social institutions in a more or less simplistic way – the Poor Law in *Oliver Twist*, Yorkshire boarding schools in *Nicholas Nickleby*, the legal system in *David Copperfield* and *Bleak House* – why should *Hard Times* bear the brunt of complaints about Dickens's tendency to simplify, to allegorize, to sentimentalize?

Several factors account for this. Perhaps the most significant is the constraints to which Dickens submitted in order to publish the novel in weekly installments in *Household Words*. Lacking the room provided by the expansive monthly format of 32 pages he had grown used to, he found the requirements of the much shorter weekly form irksome. A letter to Forster written during the composition of *Hard Times* leaves no uncertainty about Dickens's ordeal: "The difficulty of the space is CRUSHING," he wrote. "Nobody can have an idea of it who has not had an experience of patient fiction-writing with some elbow-room always, and open places in perspective. In this form, with any kind of regard to the current number, there is absolutely no such thing" (*Letters* 7: 282). To Mrs. Richard Watson he complained: "the compression and close condensation necessary for that disjointed form of publication [weekly parts], gave me perpetual trouble" (*Letters* 7: 453).

The need for this sustained compression went against one of Dickens's principal narrative inclinations. Though he could show complex development within a single character, he mainly achieved scope and profundity through a multiplication of characters, all embedded in an expansive variety of settings. If Dickens's social critiques were sometimes a little simplistic, his representation of them in most of his novels was not. He complicated his fictions through the multiplication of plots which commented on and sometimes critiqued the main plot. For example, several of the abused and abandoned children in *Bleak House* come to sadder ends than does Esther Summerson, the central representative of this trope. Thus Dickens can give Esther a happy ending but still represent the permanently devastating impact of child mistreatment in characters like Jo, who dies either of pneumonia or pulmonary tuberculosis, and Caddy, who is oppressed first by her mother and then by her father-in-law and finally has a deformed baby. It is this expansive narrative quality of Dickens's work that gives us a sense of the plentitude of life and hence of realism in his novels.

Not only did the compressed format of *Hard Times* require Dickens to reduce the number of characters and plot strands that he usually introduced, it also demanded a simplification of the large philosophical system that structures the whole novel, a system usually labeled "utilitarianism," though Dickens never uses the word in *Hard Times* (it was first used in print by John Stuart Mill in 1863), or "Benthamism" after Jeremy Bentham who is most associated with the philosophy. Dickens's effort to expose the limitations of this philosophical system inevitably suffers from the strategy of condensation.

Utilitarian theory had many aspects, but, as represented in *Hard Times*, five are most in force. First is a general tendency to draw conclusions based on the characteristics of groups of people rather than to recognize individual differences – as when the hard facts men think of the workers in *Hard Times* only as "hands." In terms of human behavior, this system of thought asserted that all actions were motivated by the desire to avoid pain and seek pleasure, and hence all people acted only in self-interest. In economics, it gave as the best system "buying in the cheapest market and selling in the dearest." Utilitarianism also argued for *laissez-faire* ("let it alone") in government, based on the belief that the economic system was naturally balanced and any intervention by government to address perceived ills would result in greater harm by throwing that equilibrium off balance. In education and the production of knowledge, utilitarianism favored the practical, sometimes "fact"-based type (increasingly representing qualitative aspects of life quantitatively), sometimes with the unintended consequence of marginalizing, if not denigrating, emotion, particularly as connected to art. As Bentham notoriously wrote, "prejudice apart, the game of push-pin is of equal value with the arts and sciences of music and poetry." What disappoints some readers is that, in order to attack this system, Dickens seems to reduce his characters to types, both limiting the human interest and oversimplifying utilitarianism at the same time.

There are, however, more positive consequences of the need to compress, one of which is a less-obtrusive narrative voice. The narrator's moral commentary usually comes in short bursts – "It was very strange that a young gentleman who had never been left to his own guidance for five consecutive minutes, should be incapable at last of governing himself; but so it was with Tom" (bk. 2, ch. 3) – or in resonant metaphors like the following: "Although Mr. Gradgrind did not take after Blue Beard, his room was quite a blue chamber in its abundance of blue books" (bk. 1, ch. 11). In the latter example, the fused metaphor of Bluebeard/blue books is packed by the linking of wife-murder with the general tendency of utilitarianism to reduce human beings to objects or statistics, thus compressing into one figure several of the themes of the novel.

Because Dickens did not have the space to introduce into *Hard Times* a variety of characters or a number of different plots, the action is relatively abstract. It takes place in one industrial town among about a dozen representative people who do not change, with the single exception of Gradgrind, whom the narrator insists has a good heart, demonstrated by his taking the abandoned Sissy into his home against Bounderby's strong objections, and who is thus able to be educated by experience. There are two uncomplicated good angels in the novel: Sleary, the owner of a horse-riding circus, and the circus girl Sissy Jupe, whose moral stature is indicated by her speech, which resembles that of a lady rather than that of the daughter of a stroller. One melodramatic "villain," the bored, aristocratic dandy James Harthouse, generates several of the plot conflicts. Two characters, Stephen and Rachael, whose realism is enhanced by Dickens's representation of their northern, working-class accent, typify the whole workforce of Coketown, and though we know Stephen is a loom weaver in Bounderby's factory, Dickens does not reveal what Rachael does or show where she works. One factory owner in a town of many factories also doubles as the town's banker (Bounderby), though we never see him at work in either place. The central philosophy of the system under attack is represented by Thomas Gradgrind, retired "from the wholesale hardware trade" (bk. 1, ch. 3), who has set up a school for the children of the town and has entered parliament as a member of the "hard facts" party (paralleling the "hardware trade"), thus combining in himself the industrial, educational, and governmental forces under the sway of utilitarianism.

Dickens portrays Gradgrind's home life on a similarly compact scale. Though Gradgrind has five children, the family is reduced to four, who seldom interact: Gradgrind, his wife, and Louisa and Tom. Two of his other children appear once under symbolic names (Adam Smith and Malthus), while Jane, the third child, plays a small role in demonstrating Sissy's good influence.

Dickens provides the reader, however, with one additional emotionally deformed child, Bitzer, and in his juxtaposition with Louisa and Tom, we can see Dickens's method of narrative multiplication at work even within the compressed scheme of *Hard Times*. Louisa, Tom, and Bitzer share the same education and all are damaged emotionally by it, but they develop differently. Tom and Bitzer show in simple terms the corrosive effect of the Gradgrind system of education by becoming complete egotists. But the form of this egotism is instructively different: Tom, untutored in ethics and morals, becomes a slave to instant gratification, while Bitzer, the school's star pupil, puts his learning to use only in the service of his future advancement. In this way, Dickens both keeps the coherence of his thematic structure and suggests variations and complexity.

Louisa demonstrates a further modification, even a contradiction, to the scheme. Like Oliver Twist, despite everything that has happened to her, she has an incorruptible core of generosity and love, "a starved imagination keeping life in itself somewhat, which brightened [her face's] expression" (bk. 1, ch. 3). Of course, she is more intelligent than Tom and Bitzer, and she is also her father's favorite child, which might suggest to us – post-Freud – a reason for this outcome. This core of goodness, however, by being untouched by anything in her education or environment, partially qualifies the novel's attack on the industrial/utilitarian complex, even as Oliver's innate and unchanging goodness undermines the attack on the workhouse system. These incorruptible characters – and many other people in Dickens's novels – may be in miserable circumstances, but their essential goodness is never impacted by the conditions around them. As Raymond Williams said, there are in *Hard Times* two "incompatible ideological positions": one "that environment influences and in some sense determines character" and, second, that "some virtues and vices are original and both triumph over and in some cases can change any environment" (1983: 169). Thus, through the narrative process of multiplication, Dickens implies that the issue of social forces is not as simple as the rest of the novel suggests.

For readers who have lost their ability to respond to allegory or "moral fable," *Hard Times* remains thin, thesis-driven, and didactic. Yet compression has its advantages as well as its limitations in *Hard Times*. For one thing, it gives the novel a thematic and narrative coherence that is powerful. As Leavis put it, "the intention is peculiarly insistent, so that the representative significance of everything in the fable – character, episode, and so on – is immediately apparent as we read" (1947: 227). Rather than diffusing the emotional and thematic effects as can happen in more expansive novels, what Henry James later called "loose baggy monsters" (1909: 84), the thematic critique of the industrial/utilitarian complex in *Hard Times* is unremitting and the cumulative effect clear and uncomplicated. The only ambiguity in the novel is a moral one that sees Tom Gradgrind escape legal punishment for his robbery and incrimination of Stephen. Since this is achieved through Sleary's artistic sleights of hand, and Gradgrind is humiliated by having Bitzer parrot back to him his utilitarian ideas about self-interest, the message about the power of "fancy" is allegorically clear and simple. But Tom's escape is morally confusing; there is never any doubt on the part of the moral and ethical spokesman Sissy or anyone else that Tom should, as Gradgrind says, "be saved from justice" (bk. 3, ch. 7). And Dickens conveniently ignores the likely punishment of Sleary by Bitzer and Bounderby for his help in getting Tom away.

Dickens's need to compress had another positive effect, at least from our perspective, if not from that of his contemporaries. The near-allegorical nature of nearly all the characters and the simplification of the plot can be seen as enabling the dark ending of *Hard Times*, unique in Dickens's novels if we accept the second "happy" ending of *Great Expectations*. For, despite the wonderfully antic scenes involving Bounderby and Mrs. Sparsit, the entertaining Sleary with his brandy-soaked, asthmatic lisp (a tick that is difficult for some readers to follow but which is also intended for comic purposes), and the sentimentality of Stephen's death, where everybody behaves bravely and selflessly, *Hard Times* is much darker than even the late dark novels *Great Expectations* and *Our Mutual Friend*. For example, one scene that readers might have expected to end sentimentally, Louisa's confrontation with her father at the end of book 2, fails to lighten the emotional devastation. The reconciliation of father and daughter was a frequently sentimentalized scene in melodrama which conventionally ended with an embrace between the two. But in *Hard Times* the scene contains no forgiveness, only Louisa's recriminations; her father is helpless in the face of her misery, and finally, as she collapses, she violently rejects his support. This reaction is later softened but neither Gradgrind nor Louisa ever recovers fully from it.

With the reader's emotions and attention primarily focused by the narrative structure on the allegorical thematic developments rather than engaged with characters as rounded human beings, *Hard Times* can betray the Victorian expectations of a "happy ending" for the central "good" characters, and let some of the "bad" characters go unpunished (Bitzer, for example). The more allegorical we experience Louisa to be, the more willing we are for her not to be rewarded and to accept her lonely end — husbandless, childless, a looker-on at life – as appropriate. Louisa, Tom, Stephen, Mrs. Sparsit, Bounderby, and even Gradgrind end badly or sadly. What passes for a love plot (a standard, almost mandatory element in the Victorian novel) – Louisa and Harthouse – is frustrated. Only those outside the system, the circus people Sleary and Sissy, are free of the sadness, and Sissy's "happy" ending in marriage and mother-hood actually has no effect on the dark coloring of the novel's closure because it is unrealized. We don't know whom she marries or how.

The novel's single-minded treatment of its theme does not swerve at the end, implying instead that mistakes, however well intentioned, cannot always be rectified and human misery is not always remediable. Ironically, this dark ending makes *Hard Times* more realistic, precisely because of the novel's "fanciful" form of allegorical fiction. Despite Stephen Blackpool's unlikely but impassioned speech before his death in which he exhorts employers and employees to know each other better (a common Victorian, middle-class "cure" for industrial unrest, and what Dickens himself calls for in the article "On Strike" on the Preston weavers, out of which some of *Hard Times* grew), the novel does not end with any evidence that industrialists and workers might be brought together as Elizabeth Gaskell suggested at the end of her two industrial novels *Mary Barton* (1848) and *North and South* (which followed *Hard Times* in *Household Words* in 1854). Bounderby remains the self-satisfied and hard man he always was, despite the unmasking of his false self-myth of having been "born in a ditch," abandoned by his mother, and abused by his grandmother. (Bounderby, one of the hard fact men, is really the great fiction-maker in the novel, not just about himself but also about Mrs. Sparsit's class superiority and about the "hands" only wanting gold spoons and turtle soup.) Stephen's sad fate can seem gratuitously punishing partly due to an under-motivated private promise he made to Rachael to avoid trouble. Stephen oddly interprets this promise as a prohibition against joining his fellow-workers in supporting a union, but then he essentially breaks his promise by arguing with Bounderby and getting fired. This part of the novel is perhaps more confused than Dickens intended, for in a deleted passage Stephen's rage at the maiming of

Rachael's little sister in an industrial accident frightens Rachael and causes her to ask for the promise (bk. 1, ch. 13).

The contemporary sense that this dark ending was unusual – another reason perhaps for the lack of enthusiasm for the novel among Dickens's initial readers – is evidenced in a dramatic version of *Hard Times* by Fox Cooper in 1854. In the final act of this three-act play, Tom is saved by Louisa paying back the money he stole, Stephen does not die, and Bounderby has a complete change of heart, arranging Stephen and Rachael's marriage, giving his workers a week's paid holiday, and more money to Louisa to distribute to his workers. Louisa happily returns to him as his wife. As was frequently the case, the contemporary popular dramatization of the novel tried to repair places in the original that went against conventional and popular expectations. In this case, comparing the novel and the play points up exactly how dark the closure of the novel is.

A third way that compression has a positive effect on *Hard Times*, and one that several late twentieth-century critics have chosen to address, is the way in which figures of speech are deployed. Of course, all of Dickens's novels are rhetorically rich, but in *Hard Times* metaphors, through repetition, are compacted into symbols that can express emotion and comment in a single figure, a technique Dickens calls in *Hard Times* striking "the keynote" (bk. 1, chs. 5, 8). In 1959, Monroe Engel argued that "the brief, largely figurative renderings of experience in this novel . . . most effectively accomplish the destruction of the 'hard facts' point of view . . . Imagination makes its own best case for itself" (1959: 175). Efraim Sicher (2003) goes further and proposes metaphor as a theme in the novel, saying it establishes a critique of utilitarian language.

For example, the keynote in the description of the factories is both a synecdoche and a metaphor and, through repetition, a symbol: the movement of the piston of the steam engine is referred to several times as that of "melancholy mad elephants" and the smoke from the chimneys as "monstrous serpents" (bk. 2, ch. 11). The metaphor of "fire" is then developed symbolically in reference to Louisa who looks into the fires at home in an effort to understand her emotional devastation and culminates when, in her discussion of Bounderby's marriage proposal with her father, she warns, speaking figuratively about herself, though her literal-minded father cannot understand the figure: "There seems to be nothing there, but languid and monotonous smoke. Yet when the night comes, Fire bursts out, father!" (bk. 1, ch. 15). Through this compressed symbolic pattern, Dickens achieves an almost lyrically poetic style.

Other types of figures are similarly rich through compression. The narrator's comments are heavily inflected with biblical references which introduce a moral and ethical commentary on the philosophy of Coketown. Other webs of figures are drawn from natural processes and also from fairytales and nursery rhymes, the very literature that the little Gradgrinds have been denied by their father's system of education, both of which symbolically oppose the mechanistic and fact-based system of Coketown. For example, the names of the three major divisions of the novel that Dickens introduced in the book version, "Sowing," "Reaping," and "Garnering," come from an alternative system to that which dominates the novel: the natural cycle of nature as opposed to the artificial clock time that governs factory work. Further, the figures of agrarian fertility are unusually coherent and comprehensive in *Hard Times*. As Philip Collins (1963) noted, a flower motif begins in the opening scene where Sissy Jupe is humiliated by Mr. M'Choakumchild for preferring carpets with flowers on them when "in fact" we do not walk on flowers; this is picked up later when we learn that Josephine Sleary does a "Tyrolean flower-act" in the circus (bk. 1, ch. 3), and then again in the scene of Tom's tearing apart roses, while discussing Louisa with Harthouse (bk. 2, ch. 7). In the confrontation with her father at the end of book 2, Louisa cries out "What have you done . . . with the garden that should have bloomed once, in this great wilderness here!" (bk. 2, ch. 12).

Another set of references from the natural world that turns into a symbol begins with Sissy's inability to provide the required definition of a horse supplied by Bitzer: "Quadruped. Graminivorous. Forty teeth, namely twenty-four grinders, four eye-teeth, and twelve incisive" (bk. 1, ch. 1). The public house where the circus folk stay in Coketown is called the Pegasus Arms, and Mr. E. W. B. Childers is described as a Centaur. At the end of the novel, the initial scene between Sissy and Bitzer is neatly reversed when Bitzer's effort to capture Tom is frustrated by Sleary's ability to maneuver a trained dancing horse. In all these cases, the symbolic references tighten the narrative at the same time as they expand the thematic meaning in a minimum number of words.

Perhaps the most remarkable metaphor — what the narrator calls "an allegorical fancy" (bk. 2, ch. 10) — is Mrs. Sparsit's staircase, the elaborate metaphoric structure she builds in her mind to represent Louisa's slow movement toward adultery with Harthouse. Through this metaphor, Dickens is able to condense his narrative impressively because he does not have to detail the scenes by which Harthouse's attempted seduction takes place. Instead, Louisa's descent, though punctuated by a few scenes between Harthouse and Tom and a couple between Harthouse and Louisa, is mainly seen — and misread by Mrs. Sparsit — through her references to the staircase.

The compression of the novel has encouraged a focus on the novel's industrial and utilitarian themes. Dickens himself prompted this concentration by dedicating the first book edition of *Hard Times* to Thomas Carlyle, author of the social critiques, *Chartism* (1839) and *Past and Present* (1843). Writing to Carlyle, he explained: "I know it contains nothing in which you do not think with me, for no man knows your books better than I" (*Letters* 7: 367). There is, however, a third theme in the novel, what I have called, in another context (Humpherys 1996), "the marriage and divorce theme," which is also woven into the text through two characters who also carry the industrial/utilitarian and education themes.

When the theme of divorce is mentioned at all, it is usually with reference to Dickens's marriage and the concurrent debates in parliament about a proposed reform of the divorce laws, which was subsequently passed in 1857. But matrimonial issues are an integral thread in the novel, and linked in their symbolic reference to procreation with its three major parts: Sowing, Reaping, and Garnering. More importantly, the structure of these three parts points directly to Louisa's marriage story – "Sowing" ends with Bounderby's proposal, Louisa's painful interview with her father about the proposal, and then her marriage. "Reaping" ends with her running away from her near seduction by James Harthouse and her flight from her husband's house to return to her father's, which she never again leaves, and at the end of "Garnering" the narrator summarizes briefly the rest of her solitary life. Thus, it is Louisa's marriage story that partially shapes the narrative.

Just as all institutional relations have been corrupted by the industrial/utilitarian complex in Coketown, so have all personal connections, as figured in *Hard Times* by the institution of marriage, which Tony Tanner has called "The structure that maintains the Structure" (1979: 15). All the Coketown marriages are bad, most abusively so (Sissy's notwithstanding), and none of them is repaired. All are corrupted by the lack of imagination and human compassion that has warped the lives of the children of Coketown. Mrs. Sparsit was forced into a marriage with a young wastrel who left her without a penny when he died; Mrs. Gradgrind has been driven into semi-imbecility by always being repressed by her husband (as she puts it, "whenever I have said anything, on any subject, I have never heard the last of it" [bk. 2, ch. 9]), and dies without even a right to her own pain ("there's a pain somewhere in the room . . . but I couldn't positively say that I have got it" [bk. 2, ch. 9]). Louisa, not unlike Mrs. Sparsit, has been handed over to her father's best friend and manipulated into accepting the transfer by her selfish brother. Though the details of her married life are omitted, and we never in fact know what she really feels for her would-be seducer Harthouse, nor even what she thinks about her marriage, the reader knows without question, as with nearly all events in the novel, that this marriage is an abomination.

The keynote of bad marriages, however, is that of Stephen Blackpool, whose marriage to a drunken and seemingly criminal wife introduces the discussion of the need for affordable divorce, though none of the marriages, except perhaps Stephen's, actually would have qualified for a divorce that would have allowed remarriage. (Bounderby is quite within his legal rights to demand that Louisa be home by noon the next day or he will no longer support her.) Divorce at the time Dickens was writing *Hard Times* was difficult to achieve (there had been only just under a hundred full divorces since 1801 and only four by a woman). The only grounds for divorce was adultery, and for women the husband's adultery had to be compounded by some other offense – incest, rape, sodomy, bestiality, or extreme cruelty. It took three separate court actions to complete, the last one the passing of a private bill in the House of Lords.

But Stephen's need for a divorce stands in for Louisa's, another efficient compression in the novel, for the narrative links the two characters through Tom's betrayal of them both, and in terms of plot through Louisa's unconscious role in raising the suspicion that Stephen robbed the bank. Both are victims of the industrial/utilitarian complex and the marriage laws. Louisa's descent down Mrs. Sparsit's staircase to a "dark pit of shame" (bk. 2, ch. 10) is figuratively completed when Stephen falls into the Old Hell Shaft.

Thus, marriage and divorce are linked to the industrial and education themes in *Hard Times* through both Stephen and Louisa, even as the industrial and education themes are linked symbolically by the friendship of Gradgrind and Bounderby. Gradgrind's daughter Louisa's marriage to Bounderby solidifies the connections between the men – and between the themes – even as Stephen's relationship to Bounderby as his employee links, through his seeking help from Bounderby for his bad marital situation, these themes to marriage and divorce. The novel as a result is balanced with Gradgrind/Bounderby (and Bitzer) on one side against Louisa/Stephen (and Sissy) on the other. Tom and Harthouse are the opponents to Louisa and Stephen's search for happiness, and Sleary is a symbolic but actually somewhat impotent helper.

This schematic structure in its simplicity may seem a weakness to twenty-first-century readers. But the issues that it articulates so efficiently, coherently, and powerfully are still very much a part of our lives: repression and abuse of children, the unintended consequences of abstract theories of child-rearing, the persistence of unsafe and unrewarding work, education made dull and useless by rote and drill, social and political decisions based on general ideological principles rather than on individual human needs, mistaken and mercenary marriages and their consequences, and the healing power of love and pleasure and art. The clarity and intensity of these persistent human issues continue to resonate in *Hard Times*. For while we must be amused, we must also be reminded again and again of the universal human needs for art and play, for moral virtues and compassion not only in personal relations, but also in the work-place and in government, and, above all, for the imaginative power to understand and sympathize with the lives of others, a power that literature like *Hard Times* always gives us.

REFERENCES AND FURTHER READING

Bentham, Jeremy (1825). *The Rational of Reward*, book III, chapter 1 (available at www.ucl.ac.uk/Bentham-Project/Faqs/f_pushpin.htm; accessed June 10, 2006).

Collins, Philip (1963). *Dickens and Education*. New York: St. Martin's Press.

Cooper, Fox (1854). *Hard Times: A Domestic Drama in Three Acts*. London: Dicks Standard Plays.

Dickens, Charles (1854). On strike. *Household Words* (February 11), 8, 553–9.

Engel, Monroe (1959). *The Maturity of Dickens*. Cambridge, MA: Harvard University Press.

Humpherys, Anne (1996). Louisa Gradgrind's secret: marriage and divorce in *Hard Times*. *Dickens Studies Annual*, 25, 177–96.

James, Henry (1909). Preface to *The Tragic Muse*. In R. P. Blackmur (Ed.), *The Art of the Novel* (pp. 79–97). New York: Scribner's.

Leavis, F. R. (1947). The novel as dramatic poem (1): *Hard Times*. *Scrutiny*, 14, 185–203. Reprinted as "*Hard Times*: an analytic note" in *The Great Tradition* (pp. 227–48). London: Chatto and Windus, 1948.

Martineau, Harriet (1855). *The Factory Legislation: A Warning against Meddling Legislation*. Manchester: A. Ireland.

Sicher, Efraim (2003). The factory: fact and fancy in *Hard Times*. In *Rereading the City, Rereading Dickens: Representation, the Novel, and Urban Realism* (pp. 220–61). New York: AMS Press.

Tambling, Jeremy (2006). Sameness and otherness: versions of authority in *Hard Times*. *Textus*, 19 (2), 439–60.

Tanner, Tony (1979). *Adultery and the Novel: Contract and Transgression*. Baltimore, MD: The Johns Hopkins University Press.

Williams, Raymond (1983). The reader in *Hard Times*. In *Writing in Society* (pp. 166–74). London: Verso.

29

Little Dorrit

Philip Davis

The compulsion behind Dickens's eleventh novel originated clearly from within. Entries in a notebook he began in January 1855, in which he jotted down ideas for future works, provide teasing glimpses into his creative process. "The unwieldy ship taken in tow by the snorting little steam Tug," "A series of little-closets squeezed up into the corner of a dark street . . . The whole house just large enough to hold a vile smell. The air breathed in it at the best of times, a kind of Distillation of Mews." Such pregnant sentences, together with longer paragraphs and lists of names – amongst which are "Chivery," "Mrs: Flinks-<Fil> Flinx," "Plornish," "Nandy," "Meagles," and "Merdle" – are among the few that readers of the novel will instantly recognize (Kaplan 1–12). Earlier in the same year as these were duly recorded, Dickens had written to Angela Burdett Coutts: "motes of new stories [are] floating before my eyes in the dirty air," traces of which he set down on "little bits of paper" (*Letters* 7: 525, 555). By spring, the afflatus had taken hold to the point that the story, he told Forster, was "breaking out all round me." In May, Dickens instructed Bradbury and Evans, his publishers, to advertise a new novel for November publication (*Letters* 7: 608, 625–6n.). *Little Dorrit* commenced in December 1855 and ran in 20 parts (published as 19) continuously till June 1857. Browne provided the illustrations and Bradbury and Evans published the novel in one volume the same year.

Amidst the uncertainties he felt at the commencement of this novel, Dickens asked himself three times, in his working notes for the monthly parts, whether he should introduce "The Theatre" where Fanny Dorrit works as a dancer. "Not yet," he writes before beginning number 3, then "No," and again "No" in the months following, until finally he gives it his "Yes" for part 6, chapter 20, which appeared in May 1856. Directed to "a furtive sort of door," Amy makes her way to the theater – "Indistinctly seen" – as Dickens reminds himself in another of his notes, until "they came into a maze of dust, where a quantity of people were tumbling over one another, and where there was such a confusion of unaccountable shapes of beams, bulkheads, brick walls, ropes, and rollers, and such a mixing of gaslight and daylight, that they seemed to have got on the wrong side of the pattern of the universe" (bk. 1, ch. 20). It is a stunning formulation – "on the wrong side of the pattern of the universe" – so explosive in the sudden enlargement of meaning. But this is how Dickens does his thinking:

it is not just a way of illustrating the "theme" of disorientation; what is experienced as a discovery here are the very laws of *Little Dorrit*'s composition, the language of what turns out to be the book's cosmology.

For one thing, it is characteristic of the novel's whole viewpoint – *as* novel rather than play – that any given scene is rarely registered by the audience as from out front; rather it is witnessed, as here, from the other side, backstage, from behind the heads of the acting protagonists. It is a viewpoint that often wincingly removes the illusion from the performance. So it is with one of the novel's worst actors, the Father of the Marshalsea, seeking to co-opt all those around him to sustain his play. Take "the gentleman from Camberwell," whom Mr. Dorrit met but whose name he has forgotten. "Frederick," he says, "do *you* remember his name? . . . the gentleman who did that handsome action with so much delicacy." "Ha! Tush!" Mr. Dorrit continues. "The name has quite escaped me. Mr. Clennam, as I have happened to mention handsome and delicate action, you may like, perhaps, to know what it was." "Very much," replies Arthur, withdrawing his eyes from Little Dorrit, whose "delicate head" began to droop as "a new solicitude" stole over her pale face:

> "It is so generous, and shows so much fine feeling, that it is almost a duty to mention it. I said at the time that I always would mention it on every suitable occasion, without regard to personal sensitiveness. A – well – a – it's of no use to disguise the fact – you must know, Mr. Clennam, that it does sometimes occur that people who come here desire to offer some little – Testimonial – to the Father of the place."
> To see her hand upon his arm in mute entreaty half-repressed, and her timid little shrinking figure turning away, was to see a sad, sad sight. (bk. 1, ch. 8)

Consider those two painfully "mute" places between the acts and between the speeches: Arthur averting his eyes from seeing the effect upon Little Dorrit; Little Dorrit half trying to stop, half trying not to see, her father's habitual exhibition of himself; both of them unsuccessfully seeking to avoid being the audience that readers are forced to be, as though, by an infection in the book, the shame were also theirs. It is in those places of reluctant and suppressed judgment that the silent meaning of real "delicacy" is painfully felt. For amidst the hollowness of tone ("Frederick, do *you* remember his name?"), these true meanings – hidden in the father's "it's of no use to disguise" or displaced in the daughter's pale face with something "stealing over it" – most usually go unrecognized or are distorted.

"So unspoilt, so simple, such a good soul!" says Gowan with such indirect slyness, in speaking to Clennam of Daniel Doyce (bk. 1, ch. 26). Too often in *Little Dorrit* such tone betrays meaning, when in a more straightforward and sincere world, it should be committed to it (see Godwin 1976: bk. 4, ch. 6, "Of Sincerity"). That is why moral intelligence, squeezed out of this world, is passed on to the reader by tacit inference, by a language very close to a sub-vocal silence: " 'By Jove, he is the finest creature!', said Gowan. 'So fresh, so green, trusts in such wonderful things!' Here was one of the many little rough points that had a tendency to jar on Clennam's hearing.

He put it aside by merely repeating that he had a high regard for Mr. Doyce" (bk. 1, ch. 26). That is what praise can be like here: that while Gowan "seemed to be scrupulously finding good in most men, he did in reality lower it where it was and set it up where it was not" (bk. 1, ch. 17). When Clennam tries to overcome his misplaced love for young Pet Meagles and to behave well toward this same unworthy Gowan who has won her instead, he for once makes explicit, to himself at least, the ironic costs involved in being "generous to a man who was more fortunate than I, though he should never know it or repay me with a gracious word" (bk. 2, ch. 27). On the wrong side of the universe, goodness feels like impotence.

This, then, is the back-to-front world in which a prisoner gets so used to his prison as to declare, in twisted reality, "It's freedom, sir, it's freedom." It is like living in a squalid realist version of Plato's cave: "Crushed at first by his imprisonment, he had soon found a dull relief in it. He was under lock and key; but the lock and key that kept him in, kept numbers of his troubles out" (bk. 1, ch. 6). Had he been a strong man made for straight and direct ways, the prisoner might have tried to face his troubles – and, says Dickens, either have broken the net that held him, or broken his heart in the attempt. As it is, what he does instead, in the name of a middling survival, is to make of the wonderful human capacity for adaptation something also terrifying, in order to achieve that equivocally good–bad thing in this novel: keeping life going. It is what in *Dombey and Son* Dickens had called a paradoxically natural unnaturalness (ch. 47): living things will seek to grow or at least somehow to persist in the shapes and spaces left them. William Dorrit clings to a feeble status in his little world. What should be human strengths and life forces – and imaginably would be in some other world – are here turned into stubborn failures, felt weaknesses, or sapping pains.

That is to say, *Little Dorrit* itself results from "the pattern of the universe" turned round upon itself and gone wrong. That is why it is symptomatically so full of those orientational features of language technically known as "deixis" – the little words of space and time and relation such as "here" or "there," "now" or "then," "this" or "it," "his" or "hers." As signifiers in search of extra-linguistic referents, they should help identify and clarify the true setting, yet in *Little Dorrit* too often they only add to the profound unsettlingness of life in an untrue and unreal world. As thus, amongst so many instances (with emphasis added): "Arthur Clennam stood in the street, waiting to ask some passer-by *what* place *that* was" (bk. 1, ch. 8); "*Something* Wrong *Somewhere*" followed by "*Something* Right *Somewhere*" (the titles of bk. 2, chs. 5 and 6 respectively); "She is *somebody's* child – *anybody's* – *nobody's*" (bk. 2, ch. 9); "In short, *all* the business of the country went *through* the Circumlocution Office, *except* the business that *never* came *out* of *it*; and *its* name was Legion" (bk. 1, ch. 10); "*This somebody* pretended to do *his something* and made a reality of walking out again as soon as he *hadn't* done it" (bk. 1, ch. 6). No wonder Dickens's original and ironically equivocal title for the book was "Nobody's Fault."

But the best of these deictic formulations come out of the struggle to locate *something* in the midst of such a world which holds good, even without a recognized name or place for itself in the system. "What" Little Dorrit's pitiful look actually saw in her father and the rest of her family, "how much, or how little" of the wretched it pleased God to make visible to her, says Dickens, "lies hidden" – like so much else in this novel. But "it" is "enough," he says in this careful Braille-like language in the dark "that she was inspired to be something which was not what the rest were, and to be that something, different and laborious, for the sake of the rest" (bk. 1, ch. 8). "Something . . . *not what* the rest were," yet *"that something" "for* the sake of the rest": it is a code as subtle as Dickens's writing of that look of hers toward her father, "half admiring him and proud of him, half ashamed for him, all devoted and loving" and specifically, amidst the halves and wholes, *not* saying "half ashamed *of* him" (bk. 1, ch. 8). A minute change of relation, the equivalent "for" not "of" in the interstices of an otherwise unchangeable life: that is the vital scope available when, as Henri Bergson was to put it in *Creative Evolution*, sometimes life can only succeed by making itself very small, even humble.[1] So too with Clennam, whose one achievement it is to retain "a belief in all the gentle and good things his life had been *without*," for "*this*," says Dickens repeatedly – as if "this" were the only name for a desperate hand-hold – "had rescued him" from the meanness and coldness of his upbringing, not to be mean and to be warm:

> And this saved him still from the whimpering weakness and cruel selfishness of holding that because such a happiness or such a virtue had not come into his little path, or worked well for him, therefore it was not in the great scheme, but was reducible, when found in appearance, to the basest elements. A disappointed mind he had, but a mind too firm and healthy for such unwholesome air. Leaving himself in the dark, it could rise into the light, seeing it shine on others and hailing it. (bk. 1, ch. 13)

In this almost lost language, pointing at what others cannot see, "this" is not "himself" but is also what is called "it" – where "it" in that last sentence refers to both the mental belief despite self's experience and the light it gives way to against the dark. As Doyce says, on the thought that gave him his invention: "he must follow it where it leads him . . . It's not put into his head to be buried. It is put into his head to be made useful. You hold your life on the condition that to the last you shall struggle hard for it" (bk. 1, ch. 16). "It," "he," and "you" are the beyond-personal terms of what he also calls "the thing." It is like being trapped on the wrong side of the pattern whilst trying to hold in mind what it means on the other side, beyond you, whence the thought first came.

In *Little Dorrit*, as in Arnold's "Stanzas from the Grande Chartreuse" (1855), the best are well-nigh silent now. A simple man of defiant empirical belief such as William Cobbett could *see* the primary physical facts of much land and fine harvests: if people were going hungry, he could loudly and angrily proclaim, then there must be something wrong with the secondary system. He knew the key detail and trusted it as an organizing moral indicator, whatever the surrounding and distorting context. But if at times people in *Little Dorrit* can just about recognize the muffled realities in this noisy world, they are mostly, like Affery, hearing sounds in the house but giving them a supernatural origin: "right in her facts . . . wrong in the theories she deduced from them" (bk. 2, ch. 31).

Part of what silences the best, denying them a straightforward simplicity of indignant response, is the spectacle of human beings such as Little Dorrit's brother Tip. The best thing about him is that he respected and admired his sister:

> The feeling had never induced him to spare her a moment's uneasiness, or to put himself to any restraint or inconvenience on her account; but, with that Marshalsea taint upon his love, he loved her. The same rank Marshalsea flavour was to be recognised in his distinctly perceiving that she sacrificed her life to her father, and in his having no idea that she had done anything for himself. (bk. 1, ch. 20)

In the face of a spreading taint, it is hard to know whether what we are seeing here is more the Good to be found even within the bad, or the Bad still there in the good. In an age of faith, Lancelot Andrewes could say of Mary Magdalene, in her weeping for the loss of her Lord, that there was error in her love but there was love in her error too (Andrewes 1967: Sermon 14, "Of The Resurrection: Easter 1620"). But this is fallen much further, the larger terms of redemption or condemnation too big and too distinct for a case that remains hopelessly just itself, not two things but one that is a denial of both separately. It is a life that exists in an impassive syntax characterized by that ordinary, little, unused connective placed between Tip's "distinctly perceiving" her sacrifice for her father *and* his "having no idea" that she had done likewise for him. "What can you *do* with people like this?" the novel keeps tacitly asking, too coarsely for explicitness but with a frustration and a savagery born of desperation. One moment something of the truth may get through, and Fanny will say in contrition to her sister, "I beg your pardon, Amy," "Forgive me, Amy," but within moments of recovery, Fanny resumes the defense of her old habitual character, "gradually beginning to patronize" again (bk. 1, ch. 20). Only for such moments can she bear to see what she feels she must continue being. It makes for intense worry as to how far what the novel also wants to say can indeed be true: "half a grain of reality, like the smallest portion of some other scarce natural productions, will flavour an enormous quantity of diluent" (bk. 2, ch. 24).

Dickens calls Flora, the canceled love of Clennam's early life, "a moral mermaid," losing in her jumbled syntax the very insights she can still painfully glimpse: "which her once boy-lover contemplated with feelings wherein his sense of the sorrowful and his sense of the comical were curiously blended" (bk. 1, ch. 13). These new amalgams of sentiment had been with Dickens from the start of his career. But in *Little Dorrit*, the inextricable pattern of reciprocally opposing pulls demands an intelligence that baffles clear responses and drains straightforward energy, as again with Clennam even in his fairness:

> He had come to attach to Little Dorrit an interest so peculiar – an interest that removed her from, while it grew out of, the common and coarse things surrounding her – that

he found it disappointing, disagreeable, almost painful, to suppose her in love with young Mr. Chivery in the back yard, or any such person. On the other hand, he reasoned with himself that she was just as good and just as true, in love with him, as not in love with him; and that to make a kind of domesticated fairy of her, on the penalty of isolation of heart from the only people she knew, would be but a weakness of his own fancy, and not a kind one. (bk. 1, ch. 22)

George Henry Lewes complained of Dickens's want of formal intelligence – his was an animal intelligence, said Lewes – but the syntax here is as complex as anything in Henry James or George Eliot. Yet complexity is not what Dickens wanted, nor was it for him a good sign: he is driven into it, compromised, by the almost spatial feel of the predicament given in the act of writing. There are very hard, not entirely just, and almost unthinkable single thoughts half-hidden here – that, morally, Little Dorrit's corrupted family are not worth all her sacrifice; that what is admirable in John Chivery is compensatory upon his also being a lower-class buffoon; that Clennam's is an unacknowledged jealousy for which he has not until much later the simplification of courage. They are what John Stuart Mill in his *Autobiography* actually called "half thoughts," split-off thoughts without a framework in which to bring themselves together to one conclusion. In seeking not to think these harsh things, for a variety of reasons both good *and* bad, Clennam is trying to get it right, to be fair and scrupulous – and, even so, is still getting it wrong within his continuing limitations.

In the world of this book, though it may sound simple just to say so, you cannot expect a single character to be right and absolute and ideal. The characters are that, partial characters, persons with their own histories and problems, just parts of the social whole and not answers to it. That is why, in his Preface to the publication of the novel as one volume rather than as a periodic series, Dickens insists more than usually on the importance of the book being now read as a whole. It is terrible for Dickens that the characters cannot do all that is necessary *directly* for themselves, for he wants the parts to transcend the whole or to be able to personalize it, but as Mr. Ruggs says of such partiality when Clennam has brought financial ruin upon Doyce and is desperate to alleviate the situation: "He takes too strong and direct an interest in the case. His feelings are worked upon. There is no getting on, in our profession, with feelings worked upon, sir" (bk. 2, ch. 26). It is, then, the novel's overall *form* that has to do the thinking, in competition with the social structures that repress it. That form exists in a complex syntax at the local level: "an interest that removed her from, while it grew out of, the common and coarse things surrounding her." And it also exists at higher levels in the division of the whole novel, for example, into two books called "Poverty" and "Riches." For in the silenced thinking of *Little Dorrit*, the form is now implicitly saying the unpalatable: if Little Dorrit is really so selfless when the family is in trouble, then let us test that selflessness, see what lack of self or selfish neediness lies twisted beneath it, by taking the family out of trouble and marginalizing her capacity to help.

Talking about his writing, Dickens offered one of the easier examples of this sort of thinking when he wrote to John Forster, while at work on the sixth number, that "Society, the Circumlocution Office, and Mr. Gowan, are of course three parts of one idea and design" – the idea of a world without energy, without emotion, without values, in which averting the threat of humans doing anything more real becomes the major institutional priority (*Letters* 8: 79). But in the writing itself, Dickens is even subtler when he has Fanny say, in her own way, of her sister, that her virtues are "of that still character" which "require a contrast – require life and movement around them, to bring them out in their right colours" (bk. 2, ch. 24). Characters are "required" by those spaces between themselves and others that they fill or they create. It is Clennam who senses all that is going on in the area of thought and feeling that exists so painfully between father and daughter in the Marshalsea. It needs Little Dorrit and her uncle to come together for William Dorrit, the father and brother, to see, momentarily from outside the life he is usually trapped within, all he has missed of true connectedness since the acquirement of his riches (bk. 2, ch. 19). It takes John Chivery for Clennam to begin to see what Little Dorrit might really mean to him. In Dickens, as in a sort of subdued allegory, the spaces between the characters are more important and more animate with thought than even the characters themselves. Thus, suddenly, Physician bursts in like reality itself, in the form of something inescapably physical, whatever the mind tries to think:

> The guests said to themselves, whether they were conscious of it or no, "Here was a man who really has an acquaintance with us as we really are, who is admitted to some of us every day with our wigs and paint off, who hears the wanderings of our minds, and sees the undisguised expression of our faces, when both are past our control; we may as well make an approach to reality with him . . ." (bk. 2, ch. 25)

"Where he was, something real was." And something real can sometimes only now enter through the language of death, as it does for that hollow actor, the great Merdle, evading Physician in his suicide.

This is why *Little Dorrit* began to find direction for Dickens only when he thought of the characters as "travellers meeting and parting," leaving open the future connection, in what he calls in his working notes an initial "non-putting of them together." It is by this loosening means, in the deployment of time and space, that the characters can then truly come to "act and react on one another" thereafter (bk. 1, chs. 2, 15), forming a whole system of silent cross-references and transferred thoughts. Thus: Little Dorrit has to have for him the thoughts her father will not; what is good in Flora is magnanimously drawn toward Little Dorrit for reasons deeper than just liking; you cannot quite "place" Tattycoram without thinking not just about Pet, her obvious rival, but also about the case of Miss Wade on one side of her and that of Little Dorrit on the other. This thought process works not only on the page and between the characters but also in the mind of the tacitly summoned reader, as the novel continually and cumulatively composes and recomposes itself. F. R. Leavis described this well:

"About Dickens's art there is nothing of the rigidly or insistently schematic . . . If in our diagrammatic notation we have been representing groupings by lines linking names, the lines run across one another in an untidy and undiagrammatic mess. The diagrammatic suggestion is soon transcended as the growing complexity of lines thickens". (Leavis and Leavis 1972: 287–8)

If there is no language that can quite deal with Tip on his own, if the separate *thoughts* about him are still that – all too separate, while somehow he holds himself together as one thing – then a different language has to be found by dint of comparing him with a separate but related *person* instead: Tip compared with his father, in terms of how they each respond to Little Dorrit, with the likenesses and differences pitched very closely together. This is the thinking of a novelist going on not through abstraction or conceptualization but in precisely human terms, steering between human characters for direction toward a subtler orientation. He cannot otherwise think it out. A moral language is almost forced out of the world. And in the world's very tissue the little good is too intricately intervolved with the much that is bad for major surgery. This is the best at ground level that a mortal can achieve in this cosmology, for want of a higher intelligence:

> So does a whole world, with all its greatnesses and littlenesses, lie in a twinkling star. And as mere human knowledge can split a ray of light and analyse the manner of its composition, so, sublimer intelligences may read in the feeble shining of this earth of ours, every thought and act, every vice and virtue, of every responsible creature on it. (*A Tale of Two Cities*, bk. 2, ch. 16)

Only sporadically and momentarily can *Little Dorrit* find its lost center from the right side of the universe – as here, for once, in feeble Frederick's stunning defense of the despised and neglected good in Little Dorrit at a family breakfast in Venice when he rises out of his chair and strikes his hand upon the table, saying "Brother! I protest against it!" Comments the narrator: "If he had made a proclamation in an unknown tongue, and given up the ghost immediately afterwards, he could not have astounded his audience more." For if not entirely "unknown," this is a language on behalf of Little Dorrit that has been long silenced and forgotten:

> It was extraordinary to see of what a burst of earnestness such a decrepit man was capable. His eyes became bright, his grey hair rose on his head, markings of purpose on his brow and face which had faded from them for five-and-twenty-years, started out again, and there was an energy in his hand that made its action nervous once more.
> "My dear Frederick!" exclaimed Mr. Dorrit, faintly, "What is wrong? What is the matter?"
> "How dare you," said the old man, turning round on Fanny, "how dare you do it? Have you no memory? Have you no heart? (bk. 2, ch. 5)

Energy, memory, and heart go together here as they seldom otherwise do in this book. Twenty-five years are suddenly reversed for a moment until Fanny and her father can desperately normalize their situation again by talking of something gone wrong somewhere in poor Frederick. Time has not been like this in the *Little Dorrit* universe. For those who come from the right side of the universe but have to live on the wrong, it is more as it was for Clennam meeting his childhood sweetheart again and finding in Flora, undeservedly but also incontrovertibly, not only a parody of the past but a sign to him of his own life's misdirection. "Most men will be found sufficiently true to themselves to be true to an old idea," but through the looking glass of *Little Dorrit* being true means being dislocated:

> It is no proof of an inconstant mind, but exactly the opposite, when the idea will not bear close comparison with the reality, and the contrast is a fatal shock to it . . . For while all that was hard and stern in his recollection, remained Reality on being proved – was obdurate to the sight and touch, and relaxed nothing of its old indomitable grimness – the one tender recollection of his experience would not bear the same test, and melted away. (bk. 1, ch. 13)

The particular nature of this Reality, the double negatives necessary to deal with it ("*no* proof of an *in*constant mind"): these are characteristic of the pattern.

Or, again, it is characteristic of how it is with time in the *Little Dorrit* universe that when Pet Meagles is at her closest to Clennam – so close that in some parallel universe she might have married him – all too late, at that very moment she informs him she is to marry Gowan: "and as he came near her, it entered his mind all at once that she was there of a set purpose to speak to him . . . her wonderful eyes raised to his for a moment with a look in which regard for him and trustfulness in him were strikingly blended with a kind of timid sorrow for him" (bk. 1, ch. 28). That *that* would be the silent moment of almost complete, mutual telepathy between them, a moment nearer to death than life! From this time, he becomes in his own eyes a much older man. And it is this agedness that for so long stops him truly finding Little Dorrit, caught in her own form of arrested development.

It is a world that does not make sense, as Little Dorrit herself sees more and more in the book's second half when the rest of her family think they must have got themselves on the right side of the pattern. But in respect of her father, "she was not strong enough to keep off the fear that no space in the life of man could overcome that quarter of a century behind the prison bars" (bk. 2, ch. 5); and later, as she writes of her response to "the famous leaning tower at Pisa," she confides to Clennam:

> I could not at first think how beautiful it was, or how curious, but I thought, "O how many times when the shadow of the wall was falling in our room, and when that weary tread of feet was going up and down the yard – O how many times this place was just as quiet and as lovely as it is to-day!" (bk. 2, ch. 11)

This strange relativism amidst change is, as it is said in *Dombey and Son*, "a metaphysical sort of thing" (ch. 33), causing time to turn back on itself and space to dissolve, forcing imagination to baffle itself, and making the idea of a home something larger and more intangible than a local given.

That sort of structural metaphysics in the novel is why Forster gets the order of things wrong when he sees *Little Dorrit* biographically as the point of tired decline, from which Dickens could no longer find "against whatever might befall . . . a set-off in his imaginative resources, a compensation derived from his art that never failed him, because there he was supreme. It was the world he could bend to his will, and make subserve to all his desires" (Forster bk. 8, ch. 2). *Little Dorrit* is not a sign of declining powers – precisely because it involved Dickens in *not* making a world that he could bend to his will and desire. Rather, in a wholly paradoxical use of his creative powers, he made a world on the wrong side of the ideal pattern, in which creativity itself was then faced with terrible odds. It is the cosmological and metaphysical sort of thing that Dickens glanced at in *A Tale of Two Cities* – only now in *Little Dorrit* the question asked of the traumatized prisoner released from the Bastille is asked of a whole world:

> Beneath that arch of unmoved and eternal lights; some, so remote from this little earth that the learned tell us it is doubtful whether their rays have even yet discovered it, as a point in space where anything is suffered or done: the shadows of the night were broad and black. All through the cold and restless interval, until dawn, they once more whispered in the ears of Mr. Jarvis Lorry – sitting opposite the buried man who had been dug out, and wondering what subtle powers were for ever lost to him, and what were capable of restoration – the old inquiry:
> "I hope you care to be recalled to life?"
> And the old answer:
> "I can't say." (*A Tale of Two Cities* bk. 1, ch. 6)

Little Dorrit is a hard-fought attempt to "say" – through silence and despite negation, through and despite its own structures; as Clennam and Little Dorrit once more at the close go down into the still fallen world, quietly together.

NOTE

1 "Life seems to have succeeded in this by dint of humility, by making itself very small and very insinuating, bending to physical and chemical forces, continuing even to go a part of the way with them, like the switch that adopts for a while the direction of the rail it is endeavouring to leave" (Bergson 1914: 103–4).

REFERENCES AND FURTHER READING

Andrewes, Lancelot (1967). *Sermons 1605–1623*. Oxford: Oxford University Press.

Bergson, Henri (1914). *Creative Evolution.* (Arthur Mitchell, Trans.). London: Macmillan.

Cobbett, William (1980). *Rural Rides*. Harmondsworth: Penguin (original work published 1830).

Davis, Philip (2002). *The Victorians*. Oxford: Oxford University Press.

Godwin, William (1976). *Enquiry Concerning Political Justice*. (Isaac Kramnick, Ed.). Harmondsworth: Penguin (original work published 1793).

Leavis, F. R. and Leavis, Q. D. (1972). *Dickens the Novelist*. Harmondsworth: Penguin (original work published 1970).

Lewes, G. H. (1872). Dickens in relation to criticism. *Fortnightly Review*, 17, 143–51.

Mason, Mary (1982). Deixis: a point of entry for *Little Dorrit*. In Ronald Carter (Ed.), *Language and Literature: An Introductory Reader in Stylistics* (pp. 29–38). London: Allen and Unwin.

Mill, John Stuart (1969). *Autobiography*. (Jack Stillinger, Ed.). Oxford: Oxford University Press (original work published 1873).

Myers, William (1998). *The Presence of Persons*. Aldershot: Ashgate.

Trilling, Lionel (1955). *The Opposing Self*. New York: Harcourt Brace.

30

A Tale of Two Cities

Paul Davis

Dickens wrote and completed his twelfth novel amidst distractions. Shadowy thoughts about a new book can be traced back to 1857. In September, he made reference to "new ideas" coming into his head (*Letters* 8: 432) as he acted in *The Frozen Deep*, an amateur drama written by Wilkie Collins, with assistance from Dickens. An entry in his *Book of Memoranda* roughly contemporaneous gives a little more detail, indicating that he was thinking of "Representing London – or Paris, or any other great place" (Kaplan 14), the earliest surviving hint of a story set in both capitals. Further gestation occurred during the spring of 1858, only to be usurped by personal problems. In May, Dickens separated from his wife in a glare of publicity of his own making. He insisted on publishing a "Personal" statement in *Household Words* about his "domestic troubles" on June 12, 1858. He then quarreled with the journal's publishers when they refused to allow him space to defend himself in the pages of *Punch*, which Bradbury and Evans also owned. Dickens retaliated by dissolving his partnership in *Household Words* and resolving to launch a rival publication with a lead story of his own. By February of the next year, he had put in place the arrangements for the new journal, *All the Year Round*, but remained unhappy with the opening of his new story and incapable of settling "at it" or taking "to it" (*Letters* 9: 30). Two weeks later, he reported to Forster that he had "got exactly the name for the story that is wanted," one that would "fit the opening to a T" (*Letters* 9: 35). *A Tale of Two Cities* inaugurated the first issue of *All the Year Round*, running in the journal from April 30 to November 26, 1859. The 31 weekly portions were followed by monthly parts with two illustrations, thus giving the story double exposure, in addition to its nearly simultaneous appearance in the United States in *Harper's Weekly* (May 7 to December 3). The novel was also published as a single volume in December 1859.

On the Rochester coach, Mr. Jingle, in a style that comically prefigures that of the mob scenes in *A Tale of Two Cities*, tells Pickwick that he has written an:

> Epic poem, – ten thousand lines – revolution of July – composed it on the spot – Mars by day, Apollo by night, – bang the field-piece, twang the lyre . . . fired a musket, – fired with an idea, – rushed into wine shop – wrote it down – back again – whiz, bang – another idea – wine shop again – pen and ink – back again – cut and slash – noble time, sir. (ch. 2)

There are times in Dickens's later novel, as it alternates between the frenzy in Paris and the tranquility of Soho, that recall Jingle's epic, for Dickens too would be inspired to a kind of poetry when writing about the Revolution of 1789, an event that cast its magnified shadow over all of Europe during the succeeding century. Dickens, inspired by the revolutionary events in Paris in February 1848, wrote to Forster in French and signed himself "Citoyen Charles Dickens" (*Letters* 5: 256–7). The desire for reform that prompted this temporary enthusiasm would soon be overcome by a fear of anarchy, for Dickens, like many of his fellow countrymen, saw in France a warning of the dangers of radicalism and mob rule, and by the mid-1850s, he worried about a "sullen, smouldering discontent" in England that reminded him of "the general mind of France before the breaking out of the first Revolution" (*Letters* 7: 587).

The story of that first revolution was well known, for it was the subject of numerous histories, especially Thomas Carlyle's best-selling *History of the French Revolution* (1837) which Dickens, with characteristic hyperbole, claimed to have read five hundred times (*Letters* 6: 452). So in choosing the revolution as his subject, Dickens was not proposing to illuminate an obscure corner of history, but rather to retell a familiar story. The "popular and picturesque" elements that he proposed to add to Carlyle's history were also derived from familiar sources (Preface). The story of the lover who gives his life to save that of his rival was inspired by Wilkie Collins's play, *The Frozen Deep*, in which Dickens had acted the hero; several novels and plays about the revolution had already employed the story of a substitute dying on the guillotine. Relying on such familiar material, the task Dickens set himself was closer to that of the epic poet than that of the historian.

Although he does not list Dickens's novel among those he includes in "the epic strain in the English novel," E. M. W. Tillyard's catalogue of the characteristics of such works is particularly applicable to *A Tale of Two Cities*. Such a work has "a communal or choric quality," expressing "the feelings of a large group of people," and a "width of emotions . . . embracing the simplest sensualities at one end and a sense of the numinous at the other." It also has a hero with "something heroic about him," and expresses a "faith in the system of beliefs or way of life that it bears witness to." The epic novelist will also "densify his language" in ways uncommon in "the easy and fluid medium of prose fiction" (Tillyard 1958: 15–17).

These epic elements may account for the novel's popularity. Many Dickensians dismiss it as "uncharacteristic" and fault it for lacking humor, overusing coincidences, relying on incident rather than dialogue, descending into melodrama, and self-indulgently repeating tired metaphors and imagery, but the popular consensus is closer to the view of Peter Ackroyd who describes it as "one of Dickens's most powerful and interesting novels, not at all inferior in theme or execution to the larger and more imposing novels which surround it" (Ackroyd 1991: 149). Although the work of an English novelist, it is probably the best-known literary treatment of the French Revolution. Even those who know it only by reputation are likely to recognize the oratorical opening sentence, the character of Madame Defarge, and the oft-quoted closing sentence. The only other work by Dickens similarly lodged in the collective memory is *A Christmas Carol*. These three familiar elements can serve as touchstones to open a wider discussion of the book.

The novel's opening sentence calls attention to itself by its sheer length (120 words) and its rhetorical structure. Its bald and antithetical assertions invite oration, but the longer it goes on, the less it seems to be about the eighteenth century ("The Period" of the chapter title) and the more it seems to be about itself as a sentence (a period). As the antitheses cancel each other out, the sentence reaches a Micawberish turning point ("in short"), and then concludes that there was nothing so special about the time, that it was just like the present. The repetition, contradiction, and reflexivity in this sentence establish in microcosm the dialectical principles of division suggested by the *Two* in the novel's title. Reading *A Tale of Two Cities* calls for double vision, for England is implicit in the images of France, characters divide within themselves or mirror others, the present lingers as a palimpsest in the annals of the past. The novel's self-conscious narrative is marked by instability, its surface figures shadowed, displaced, or deflected by their opposites. Echoing ambiguities in character, language, and structure turn each episode into a vacillating figure in the larger field of the novel. The chapter "The Night Shadows" (bk. 1, ch. 3) provides a good illustration of this density in Dickens's narrative technique.

The chapter builds on physical images from the chapter that precedes it, which established the familiar metaphor of the journey of life in its account of a coach traveling from London to Dover with three passengers. Fearing highwaymen and suspicious of each other, the three seek anonymity by isolating themselves in their cloaks and hiding in the shadows of the dark and misty night. This emblematic scene is interrupted by Jerry's message and Lorry's puzzling reply, "recalled to life," which, in the first chapter seemed to refer to the process of bringing history to life in the novel, but now assumes an enigmatic presence within the story itself.

"The Night Shadows" presents three meditations: the narrator's meditation on the "profound secret" of individuality, Jerry Cruncher's ruminations on the message he carries, and Lorry's night thoughts about his mission. The "mist" of chapter 2 becomes the "mystery" of chapter 3, the physical analogue to the secret of individuality hidden within each person. Repeated six times in the narrator's meditation, "secret" is in turn linked to death and mortality. This meditation, reminiscent of the popular eighteenth-century poetic genre of "night thoughts," introduces an important theme of the novel, the secret self hidden in the depths of the individual, central to the stories of Doctor Manette and Sydney Carton. Two metaphors extend its significance: unfathomable water, a comparison that will take on symbolic importance, and the unfinished book, reflexively connecting this meditation to the novel itself as, perhaps, another work in the night-thoughts tradition.

Jerry Cruncher's ruminations are less philosophical. Muffled like the travelers in the coach, he is only briefly glimpsed "when he stopped for a drink . . . moved this muffler with his left hand, only while he poured his liquor in with his right; as soon as that was done, he muffled again." Yet even this comic parody contains a mystery about just why Jerry concludes that the message "recalled to life" he is charged to deliver "wouldn't suit *your* line of business!"

Finally, Lorry's night thoughts, three semi-conscious meditations on his "recalled to life" mission, seek to unmuffle a face that has been buried for 18 years. Resembling a recurrent dream, each of his three meditations repeats the act of digging into the unconscious, encountering a ghostly face, and recovering the same dialogue:

> "Buried how long?" . . .
> "Almost eighteen years."
> "You had abandoned all hope of being dug out?"
> "Long ago." . . .
> "I hope you care to live?"
> "I can't say."

This obsessive process ceases only with the rising of the sun, "bright, placid, beautiful," a moment foreshadowing the sunrise on the day of Carton's execution.

Closer to poetry than prose fiction, the repetitive words, images, and structural elements in this chapter call attention to the artistry in the telling. Word play, the structure using threes (three meditations, three repetitions of Lorry's inner dialogue), and repeated words and images give density to its style. Layering with the preceding chapter and symbolic foreshadowing further concentrate its effect. Even the introduction of Jerry Cruncher, the most novelistic passage, is germane to the symbolic purposes of the chapter, comically parodying the secretiveness and mystery that each person is to every other. We do not have Dickens's working notes for this novel, but such structural and stylistic density justifies Monod's conclusion that "every detail has been conceived and presented with a view to the whole, and there has been an amount of premeditation never before achieved by Dickens" (Monod 1967: 466).

Described the next morning (bk. 1, ch. 4) as if he is sitting for his portrait, Lorry is the first character to appear unmuffled. The face in the portrait – "suppressed and quieted . . . though lined, bore few traces of anxiety" – hides the worries of the restless traveler and is distinctly different from the ghostly faces in his night thoughts that vacillate between "pride, contempt, defiance, stubbornness, submission, lamentation." When he first meets Lucie at the hotel in Dover, her face is similarly elusive, her "forehead with a singular capacity (remembering how young and smooth it was) of lifting and knitting itself into an expression that was not quite one of perplexity, or wonder, or alarm, or merely of a bright fixed attention, though it included all the four expressions." Lorry – and Dickens – has only this single scene to transform this unformed adolescent into the ministering angel who will recall her father from the grave. When Lucie realizes that she will no longer be "free," but will be haunted by her father's ghost, she is cast into a kind of paralysis, an imprisonment in the symbolic role demanded by her father's return, that recognition "looking as if it were carved or branded into her forehead." By the end of this initial interview, Lucy is fixed into the symbolic figure that she will repeat through the rest of the novel. The freedom that she gives up to occupy this almost totally passive and reactive role, turns her into "a golden-haired doll," another of Dickens's impossible virgin heroines. Wendy

Jacobson, in a spirited defense of Lucie, has argued that she was intended only as a mythological, symbolic figure, an angel of light who restores the *anima* to her father and Sydney Carton. The language describing her and her own speech is poetic, appropriate to her role as a visiting angel charged with translating "into visible reality *the world within*" and countering her symbolic opposite, Madame Defarge (Jacobson 1997: 101).

In the broken light of the Parisian garret where he is working, Manette's "spectral face" displays "vacancy" and reveals only momentary flashes of recognition "through the black mist that had fallen on him" (bk. 1, ch. 6). When his gaze meets Lucie's, "so exactly was the expression repeated (though in stronger characters) on her fair young face, that it looked as though it had passed, like a moving light, from him to her," beginning a healing process written, for the reader's scrutiny, into the "characters" on their faces. Viewed as realistic prose narrative, this scene is impossibly melodramatic, especially Lucie's incantation: "If you hear in my voice – I don't know that it is so, but I hope it is – if you hear in my voice any resemblance to a voice that once was sweet music in your ears, weep for it, weep for it!" The pattern of the conditional clause and its "weep for it" refrain is repeated ritualistically. The public reading from this scene that Dickens prepared, but never performed, ends just after this incantation. Dickens may have imagined this scene – and many others in the novel as well – not as staged melodrama but rather as oral narrative. As in oral epic poetry, the repetitions heighten the emotional effect and facilitate comprehension by an audience listening to rather than reading the story.

Unlike Lucie, Madame Defarge grows into her symbolic role over the course of the novel. She first appears (bk. 1, ch. 5) as a typical French shopkeeper's wife, whose "watchful eye" is focused on the till, so that "she did not often make mistakes against herself in any of the reckonings over which she presided." She turns ominous later as she stands beside her husband at the fountain where Gaspard's child has been killed, remaining there after the others have left, a "stout dark" silent presence, knitting "with the steadfastness of Fate" (bk. 2, ch. 7). In only two sentences here Dickens extends her significance, and evokes both the fear and the sympathy that accompany her through the novel.

After she is identified as the "memory" of the Jacquerie, her knitting a "register" of crimes against the people, she speaks for the first time on the visit to Versailles, telling a stranger in the crowd that she is knitting "shrouds" (bk. 2, ch. 15). Her words further unsettle the road mender, who has been "constantly haunted" by a "mysterious dread of madame." Her ensuing dialogue with him on how he would destroy the "richest and gayest" in a "great heap of dolls" and "strip . . . the birds of the finest feathers" sustains the surrealism of her initial remark. She acts out the sadism implicit in her catechizing of the road mender as she knots the wine shop's money in her handkerchief into a "chain" of coins, pulling tight each added knot as if she is throttling a foe (bk. 2, ch. 16). As she performs this wifely task, she answers her husband's doubts about whether the revolution will ever come with the assurance that "vengeance and retribution require a long time."

"It does not take a long time to strike a man with Lightning," said Defarge.

"How long," demanded madame, composedly, "does it take to make and store the lightning? Tell me?"

Defarge raised his head thoughtfully, as if there were something in that, too.

"It does not take a long time," said madame, "for an earthquake to swallow a town. Eh well! Tell me how long it takes to prepare the earthquake."

Such ritualized dialogue, reinforced by the incantatory repetitions in the prose, enlarges the growing symbolic importance of Madame Defarge, now shown to be the power behind her husband, justifying Monod's judgment, who compares her to Lady Macbeth, as "the most Shakespearean character in the novel" (Monod 1970: 167). Yet even as her symbolic role expands, Madame Defarge remains the Parisian shopkeeper who began the novel, a role she plays admirably in her cat-and-mouse interview with Barsad (bk. 2, ch. 16) by responding to his prying questions with: "All we think, here, is how to live. That is the subject *we* think of, and it gives us, from morning to night, enough to think about."

At the turning point in the novel (bk. 2, ch. 21), the only chapter in which England and France have equal treatment, the symbolic roles of Lucie and Madame Defarge are juxtaposed. Lucie occupies the first half of the chapter as the angel in the house on Soho Square; Madame Defarge looms over the tumultuous storming of the Bastille as an "immovable" presence until, "suddenly animated, she put her foot on his [the prison warden's] neck, and with her cruel knife – long ready – hewed off his head." This eruption from immobility into murder magnifies her earlier eruption into speech and aptly illustrates the violent method of characterization that Dickens described as "a story of incident . . . pounding the characters out in its own mortar, and beating their interests out of them" (*Letters* 9: 113).

By the scene of the taunting, torture, and murder of Foulon (bk. 2, ch. 22), Madame Defarge has taken over active leadership of the mob of knitting women, the vanguard of the revolution. Described "like all the forty Furies," their attack, recounted in incantatory style, reads like a scene from *The Bacchae*. One from this sisterhood, The Vengeance, a grocer's wife turned allegorical, surfaces as Madame Defarge's double. When Lucie kneels with her child before these two women and pleads as a "sister woman" and a "wife and mother" for aid (bk. 3, ch. 3), Madame Defarge, childless and bitter, responds with a litany from another sisterhood of women who "suffer, in themselves and in their children, poverty, nakedness, hunger, thirst, sickness, misery, oppression, and neglect of all kinds."

By the time that Madame Defarge's personal interest in the events that led to Manette's imprisonment is revealed (bk. 3, ch. 12), she is linked to the guillotine itself. She tells her confederates: " 'Let me but lift a finger – !' She seemed to raise it . . . and let it fall with a rattle on the ledge before her, as if the axe had dropped." And she reveals:

that peasant family so injured by the two Evrémonde brothers . . . is my family . . . That sister of the mortally wounded boy upon the ground was my sister, that husband was my sister's husband, that unborn child was their child, that brother was my brother, that father was my father, those dead are my dead, and that summons to answer for those things descends to me!

Her wrath rises to a crescendo with the repeated refrain: "Tell the Wind and the Fire where to stop; not me." Assured that she will make a "celestial witness" against Lucie, Madame Defarge, in her final appearance (bk. 3, ch. 14), assumes the full stature of a dark angel, "the wife of Lucifer," as Pross describes her. As she prepares to arrest the Manettes, her qualities are cataloged in the fullest description of her in the novel:

> strong and fearless . . . shrewd sense and readiness . . . great determination . . . that kind of beauty which not only seems to impart to its possessor firmness and animosity, but to strike into others an instinctive recognition of those qualities . . . But, imbued from her childhood with a brooding sense of wrong, and an inveterate hatred of class, opportunity had developed her into a tigress. She was absolutely without pity.

So the wine merchant's wife, the memory of the Jacquerie, the registrar of the revolution, the missionary to the Furies, the murderess, the tigress, the angel of death, the wife of Lucifer, La Guillotine, she sets out across the streets of Paris, like Satan striding across Hell, to bring Lucie to her doom.

To bring Madame Defarge to this ultimate and full expression of her character and symbolism, Dickens reversed his usual method of characterization. Instead of beginning with a full description of the character and repeating it with variations, he developed Madame Defarge incrementally until, in her final appearance, she draws together the complex and contradictory elements in her character. As she sets out to arrest Lucie, Dickens describes her with the surprising sentence: "walking with the confident tread of such a character [an armed revolutionary], and with the supple freedom of a woman who had originally walked in her girlhood, bare-foot and bare-legged, on the brown sea-sand, Madame Defarge took her way along the streets." That "freedom" is the measure of her completeness, of the self-defining energy in her character that melds girl and woman, revolutionary and shopkeeper, dark angel and tigress, evoking both sympathy and revulsion. Lucie is no match for this richly symbolic figure.

Some commentators have seen the outcome of this journey as one of the weaknesses in the novel, for it ends not with a confrontation between the two contending angels, Madame Defarge and Lucie, but in the struggle with Miss Pross, ending in Madame Defarge's accidental death by her own gun. Dickens's defense of this outcome reveals a good deal about his conception of Madame Defarge and her role:

> Where the accident is inseparable from the passion and action of the character; where it is strictly consistent with the entire design, and arises out of some culminating proceeding on the part of the individual which the whole story has led up to; it seems to

me to become, as it were, an act of divine justice. And when I use Miss Pross . . . to bring about such a catastrophe, I have the positive intention of making that half-comic invention a part of the desperate woman's failure; and of opposing that mean death, instead of a desperate one in the streets which she wouldn't have minded, to the dignity of Carton's. (Forster bk. 9, ch. 2)

Lacking the vocabulary of existentialism, Dickens describes the absurdity in the "freedom" of her resolution as "half-comic." As she fulfills her chosen destiny, Dickens displaces the symbolic confrontation at the heart of his story from one between Madame Defarge and Lucie to one between two better-matched antagonists, Madame Defarge and Sydney Carton.

In spite of its textual presence in the novel, the document from the Bastille wall that condemns Darnay does not establish historical fact (bk. 3, ch. 10). It exemplifies instead the instability of the written word. Doctor Manette has so repressed his prison experience that the story he told in the document has, like the story buried in the Tower of London (bk. 2, ch. 6), turned to dust in his mind. The closest he seems to be able to come to recalling the document to life is in his more generalized memory of "a time in my imprisonment, when my desire for vengeance was unbearable" (bk. 2, ch. 17). He has, in fact, recast his prison experience as "the story of the Bastille Captive" (bk. 3, ch. 4), a tale of heroic suffering that gives him entrée into the prisons. Both Lorry and Lucie suppress the doctor's prison suffering to concentrate on his recovery in versions of the tale that might be entitled "Recalled to Life." Madame Defarge also largely ignores Manette's suffering, reading the story as one about the virtual genocide of nearly her entire family at the hands of the Evrémondes. Although he does not know of her personal involvement, Darnay hears the story as an Evrémonde and sees for himself no escape from the "line of the narrative." Among the English characters, only Sydney Carton, who eavesdrops on Madame Defarge's confession to her confederates, knows the depth of her personal enmity and understands the danger she poses to Lucie.

Things that have been forgotten, lost, repressed, or never known destabilize the many versions of the story. Darnay seems to recognize the impossibility of ever coming to a single account when, in his last letter to Lucie, he instructs her not to press her father about whether he knew of the existence of the document or whether it had been recalled to him when he heard "the story of the Tower" (bk. 3, ch. 13). A repressed element in every version of the story is the fact that the events described in the document took place in Christmas week 1757. By leaving this recognition subliminal, Dickens maintains the multiple possibilities of his text and makes problematic a strictly allegorical reading of the ending.

As he exchanges identities with Darnay in the prison, Carton has Darnay begin writing yet another version of the story. Here the doubling between the two men achieves its fullest ambiguity, for the scene shows Darnay writing Carton's story or, perhaps, Carton dictating Darnay's story, and it recalls a scene of similar confusion in the tavern after the trial in London. There the physical similarity between the two men that has saved Darnay, so befuddles Carton that he asserts "You hate the fellow," while observing his own face in the mirror, an assertion that clearly applies both to himself and Darnay (bk. 2, ch. 4). The instability in these scenes is magnified in the larger novel with its cast of twins, look-alikes, doubles, multiple characters who repeat each other, and characters who are split within themselves.

Amid all this replication and confusion, it is difficult to decide just who is the hero of the story. As an historical novel in the manner of Scott, *A Tale of Two Cities* casts Darnay as its Waverley figure. Caught between two cultures, he is condemned in France as an émigré and tried in England as a French spy, but his attempt to lose this bifurcated identity in domestic anonymity cannot resolve the intractable contradictions of his situation to make him an heroic representative of historical change. In the *Tale* as psychological novel, Doctor Manette, as A. E. Dyson suggests, is "the central figure . . . one of the most masterly fusions of psychological insight and symbolism in Dickens's work" (Dyson 1970: 223). A more engaging character than his son-in-law, he proves less than heroic, however, as his belief in his power to release Darnay from prison fails and he exits the novel in a state of semi-comatose regression. In the *Tale* as heroic poem, Sydney Carton seems to offer a hope of transcending the determinism of the historical situation. For those who read the novel as Christian allegory, his death, repeating Christ's passion, becomes the blood sacrifice necessary to redeem the time. Carton's heroic decision, his triumphant final words, and his hopeful vision of the future make his sacrifice compelling, even if he is not left standing at the final curtain. The audience listening to a recitation of this spectacle or watching the cathartic demise of the tragic hero on the stage can keep a safe communal distance. Muffled in the isolation of their individual night thoughts, novel readers must identify more closely with their heroes, reading themselves into the conventionality of Darnay, the denial of Manette, and the dangerous heroism of Carton.

Dickens said that, in writing the novel, "I have so far verified what is done and suffered in these pages, as that I have certainly done and suffered it all myself" (Preface). Written in the year after he separated from his wife and began his secret relationship with Ellen Ternan, Dickens may have projected himself into his tripartite hero: into Manette, the older man recalled to life by the love of a young woman after 18 years of (marital?) imprisonment; into Darnay, who shared his initials and escaped prison to achieve domestic happiness; into Sydney Carton, the noble and martyred epic hero, who entered the manuscript as Dick Carton, bearing Dickens's initials in reverse. Whatever the psychological dynamics of the tangled relationships between the three heroes and their creator, they are harrowing to the narrator, who surfaces within the action only when the Darnays, Doctor Manette, and Lorry are escaping from France, leaving Carton to his doom. The narrator describes the journey as one of the party in the carriage, speaking of "our impatience" to get on, and of looking out of the carriage to "see if we are pursued." Like the three heroes who have been drawn to Paris by the loadstone rock of revolution, the narrator has been drawn to this story, perhaps, because "in seasons of pestilence, some of us will have a secret attraction for the disease – a terrible passing inclination to die of it" (bk. 3, ch. 6).

The attraction of Carton's heroism, the magnet that drew Dickens, still draws the reader to the story.

As the antagonist to Madame Defarge, Carton must be more than simply a symbolic counter to her embodiment of the revolution. He too must be "free." Although there are allegorical elements in his ending, Dickens chose to keep many of them subliminal. He does not indicate, for example, that Carton's death provides an Easter ending to Manette's Christmas story. Carton's sacrifice may re-enact the crucifixion, but he is dimly aware of the connection, recalling the words "I am the Resurrection and the Life" only as something said at his father's funeral. He does not consider his action as countering revolution, redeeming history, or saving mankind. He simply chooses to save one life for the love of one woman. A bachelor with no family ties, Carton is not defined by his family or his history; he is an outsider to the domestic world of Darnay and Lucie; an idler who rejects Stryver's social gospel of getting ahead, he does not seek to save himself through shoe-making or tutoring. Lacking definition from family, work, or history, he acknowledges the absurdity in his situation, that he can only give meaning to his life by choosing to die.

In choosing to become Darnay, he also becomes Evrémonde, an everyman affirming the absurd contradiction in the human situation, that mortality is the secret buried within each individual. Since the narrator has left Paris with the Darnays, the account of Carton's death must be based on hearsay, speculation, or divine intelligence, the uncertainty leaving the reader to wonder whether Carton's final vision is prophetic inspiration or wishful thinking. Though his death is dignified, it is also, like Madame Defarge's "half-comic." Whether it is sacrifice or suicide becomes the final haunting uncertainty in the novel's hall of mirrors.

References and Further Reading

Ackroyd, Peter (1991). *Introduction to Dickens*. New York: Ballantine.

Brooks, Chris (1984) *Signs for the Times: Symbolic Realism in the Mid-Victorian World*. London: George Allen and Unwin.

Dyson, A. E. (1970). *The Inimitable Dickens*. London: Macmillan.

Glancy, Ruth (1991). *A Tale of Two Cities: Dickens's Revolutionary Novel*. Boston: Twayne.

Jacobson, Wendy S. (1997). "The world within us": Jung and Dr. Manette's daughter. *The Dickensian*, 93: 95–108.

Monod, Sylvère (1967). *Dickens the Novelist*. Norman: University of Oklahoma Press.

— (1970). Some stylistic devices in *A Tale of Two Cities*. In Robert B. Partlow Jr. (Ed.), *Dickens the Craftsman: Strategies of Presentation* (pp. 165–86). Carbondale, IL: Southern Illinois University Press.

Sanders, Andrew (1988). *The Companion to A Tale of Two Cities*. London: Unwin Hyman.

Stoehr, Taylor (1965). *Dickens: The Dreamer's Stance*. Ithaca, NY: Cornell University Press.

Tillyard, E. M. W. (1958). *The Epic Strain in the English Novel*. London: Chatto and Windus.

31

Great Expectations

Andrew Sanders

External events brought Dickens's thirteenth novel unexpectedly to life, accelerating its composition and altering its original design. Meditating another tale "in the old twenty-number form" in September 1860 (Forster bk. 9, ch. 3), Dickens was compelled to revise this plan when it became clear that Charles Lever's serialized novel in *All the Year Round* had failed to take hold of readers. The introspective ruminations of Lever's hero proved "too detached and discursive," Dickens thought, and threatened what had been a healthy circulation. The one remedy was for Dickens "to strike in" and to act quickly (*Letters* 9: 321, 319). "The property of *All the Year Round*," Dickens explained to Forster, "is far too valuable, in every way, to be much endangered." Consequently, he abandoned his initial plan and changed the format of the story he contemplated by writing one "of the length of the *Tale of Two Cities*," which would take pole position in the journal and push Lever's *A Day's Ride* aside (*Letters* 9: 319–20). This emergency intervention, however, took no toll on the novel that resulted. Dickens quickly decided on a title, making rapid progress with a novel many consider his most nearly perfect artistic achievement. *Great Expectations* began on December 1, 1860 and ran continuously for 36 installments, concluding on August 3, 1861. It also appeared serially in *Harper's Weekly*, one week ahead of the British installments, and was published in three volumes in London in 1861. No illustrations accompanied this edition or the text in *All the Year Round*.

In early October 1860, Dickens gave Forster this account of the novel he was writing: "The book will be written in the first person throughout, and during these first three weekly numbers you will find the hero to be a boy-child, like David [Copperfield]. Then he will be an apprentice. You will not have to complain of the want of humour as in *The Tale of Two Cities*" (*Letters* 9: 325). The essence of *Great Expectations* was therefore already distilled in Dickens's mind. It was to be an autobiography like *David Copperfield*, but published in weekly parts rather than in monthly numbers. Unlike the central character of *David Copperfield*, the new boy-hero was to be born into the social class where becoming apprenticed to a trade was normative. David, the "young gentleman" to his workmates at Murdstone and Grinby's, had been obliged to experience being *déclassé* and had found the process agonizing. Pip, by contrast, would follow the artisan norms of his class. The new novel would also be essentially *humorous* unlike its predecessor in *All the Year Round*. Forster must have privately expressed his disquiet at the "want of humour" in *A Tale of Two Cities*, and he was to reassert this criticism when he later wrote that "there was probably never a book by a great humourist . . . with so little humour and so few rememberable characters" (Forster bk. 9, ch. 2). *Great Expectations* was therefore to revert to an established Dickens type: the humorous, first-person narrative, but with a distinctively working-class central character.

In the same letter of October 1860, Dickens expanded on his conception of the nub of the plot and the essential narrative mode of *Great Expectations:*

> I have made the opening . . . in its general effect exceedingly droll. I have put a child and a good-natured foolish man, in relations that seem to me very funny. Of course I have got in the pivot on which the story will turn too – and which indeed, as you will remember, was the grotesque tragi-comic conception that first encouraged me. To be sure I had fallen into no unconscious repetitions, I read *David Copperfield* again the other day, and was affected by it to a degree you would hardly believe. (*Letters* 9: 325)

Weeks earlier, Dickens had outlined this "very fine, new and grotesque idea" to Forster and had evidently shown him the manuscript in order to give substance to the themes that the novelist enthusiastically described as "opening up" before him. His serial, he declared, would revolve around what he called his "grotesque" idea "in a most singular and comic manner" (*Letters* 9: 310). Writing later to Mary Boyle on December 28, 1860, Dickens repeated his emphasis on the comic and the droll elements. The first chapters, he reported, were "universally liked" probably because the novel "opens funnily and with an interest too" (*Letters* 9: 354). It seems to me, in view of a tendency to ignore this emphasis on the comic, worth pursuing two issues. First, just how "droll" is the "grotesque" side of *Great Expectations?* Secondly, what significance lies in the effort Dickens made to distinguish his new novel from the earlier, and ostensibly sunnier, *David Copperfield?*

Forster seems to have remained persuaded that *Great Expectations* was essentially *comic* both in its conception and its achievement. Comparing it with *A Tale of Two Cities*, he insisted in his anonymous review of the novel in the *Examiner* in July 1861 that "its contrivance allows scope for a fuller display of the author's comic power" (Forster 1861: 452). A decade later, after offering a complimentary account of the characterization of Joe and Magwitch, Forster went on to comment on other aspects of the dramatis personae of *Great Expectations*. He was particularly delighted by Jaggers and by Wemmick ("both excellent, and the last one of the oddities that live in everybody's liking for the goodheartedness of its comic surprises"); he found the Pumblechooks and Wopsles "as perfect as bits of *Nickleby* fresh from the mint"; and he considered the scene in which Pip and Herbert make up their accounts as "original and delightful as Micawber himself" (Forster bk. 9, ch. 3).

Like other nineteenth-century critics, Forster preferred the earlier, breezy, optimistic Dickens novels over the later, darker, ambiguous ones. When he reaches out for flattering parallels he finds them in *Nickleby* and *Copperfield*. The early reviews of *Great Expectations* are generally complimentary, though one dissenter, writing in the *Westminster Review* in 1862, insisted that nothing "but the talisman of Mr. Dickens's name, would induce the general public to buy and read 'Great Expectations.' " He then went on to declare that "there is not a character or a passage" in the whole novel "which can afford enjoyment to anybody twenty years hence" (Anon 1862: 286–7).

What other reviewers noted, however, was not the familiar Dickensian rehash that the partisan *Westminster* had complained about, but a happy return to an earlier, essentially comic manner. The *Saturday Review* commented that "after passing under the cloud of *Little Dorrit* and *Bleak House* . . . *Great Expectations* restores Mr. Dickens and his readers to the old level. It is . . . quite worthy to stand beside *Martin Chuzzlewit* and *David Copperfield*" (quoted in Collins 1971: 427). E. S. Dallas rejoiced that "Mr. Dickens has good-naturedly granted to his hosts of readers the desire of their hearts . . . [he] has in the present work given us more of his earlier fancies than we have had for years . . . there is that flowing humour in it which disarms criticism." Dallas concluded his review in *The Times* by stressing the restored triumph of Dickens's "rare faculty of humour" (quoted in Collins 1971: 430–1, 434). A similar expression of relief at being delivered from gloom permeates the review in the *Dublin University Magazine* of December 1861 ("Expecting little, we gained on the whole a rather agreeable surprise . . . The favourite of our youth still stands before us . . . the old humour still peeping playfully from lip and eye"). Moreover, the reviewer insisted that *Great Expectations* presented readers with "an entertainment got up by the oldest, yet still the first of our living humorists" (quoted in Collins 1971: 435–6).

Critics today tend not to share these views. Instead, they ignore Dickens's professed intentions and read the novel as an expression of pessimism occasioned by the novelist's personal estrangement from and disillusion with society. Social bankruptcy, non-communication, guilt, and confession number among the topics frequently explored in the current literature about the novel.

Certainly there is ambiguity in the comedy of *Great Expectations*. The opening chapters, for example, are recounted with a degree of "double-take." Pip's account of the threat presented by Magwitch's supposed companion ("That young man has a secret way pecooliar to himself, of getting at a boy, and at his heart, and his liver") can be read in two ways. From the perspective of a child's world it remains truly terrifying, but adult perceptions tend to diminish the menace much as adults suppress fear of the imagined dangers and perils of the night. The funny, if slightly melancholy, Christmas dinner scene in chapter 4 can be seen as serving to condition those memorably jolly earlier Dickensian Christmasses at Dingley Dell and at the Cratchits. Nevertheless, the *dénouement* of Christmas at the forge has a brilliantly contrived ambiguity as Pip runs for the door only to be stopped by the party of soldiers ("one of whom held out a pair of handcuffs to me saying, 'Here you are, look sharp, come on!' "). As readers were to learn at the opening of the next number, it is not Pip who is to be arrested, but Magwitch for whom Pip has committed the "crime" of stealing the brandy and the pork pie.

Other primarily "comic" scenes share something of this ambiguous edge. Most notable is Wopsle's chilling revelation to Pip that Compeyson has been observed seated behind him in the waterside theater to which Pip had repaired one evening for light entertainment (ch. 47). Nevertheless, what Forster and Victorian critics admired as evidence of Dickens's return to a predominantly "humorous" mode should surely be acknowledged to be as vital in determining the nature of the novel as the melancholy which has informed so many latter-day readings. One might cite here, as Forster did, the characterization of Herbert Pocket and of Wemmick, and especially the comic delicacy with which Dickens explores Wemmick's "commuter" mentality, delineates his relationship with the Aged P, and delights in his semi-clandestine marriage (an example, perhaps, of what Forster meant by "the goodheartedness of the comic surprises").

A further key to the way *Great Expectations* was originally read as predominantly *comic* may lie in the ending Dickens gave to the published version. Not till Forster printed the original last paragraphs of the novel in 1874 did Victorian readers have access to Dickens's first, bleaker, and far less ambiguous conclusion. The fact that Dickens so readily acceded to Bulwer Lytton's suggestion that he change the ending indicates that Dickens himself was never really happy with what he had first written. He was rarely so responsive to friendly criticism and never before had he reacted either so positively or so radically. His original three hundred odd words were scrapped in favor of a more extended meditation of some thousand words which, as Dickens explained to Bulwer Lytton, arose from his need to avoid "doing too much." As he went on to say: "My tendency – when I began to unwind the thread that I thought I had wound for ever – was to labour it, and get out of proportion. So I have done it in as few words as possible; and I hope you will like the alteration that is entirely due to you" (*Letters* 9: 428–9).

He had earlier told Wilkie Collins that he felt that his change was "for the better," and a week later he wrote to Forster insisting that he had "put in as pretty a piece of writing as I could, and I have no doubt the story will be more acceptable through the alteration" (*Letters* 9: 432–3). Dickens was not simply throwing a sop to his middlebrow readership by rendering the new ending more "acceptable." By having so scrupulously "unwound" the thread of his first ending, he was effectively obliged to reweave a number of threads that had run through the story from its inception. His new emphasis was not on alienation, or loneliness, or estrangement but on Pip's shaky achievement of a kind of wholeness and integrity. Estella may remain as distantly unachievable as she always was, but Pip himself seeks to aspire to a new set of "expectations" which are founded not on economic exploitation but on emotional achievement.

The new ending does not serve to resolve the Pip/Estella story (though it does not emphatically deny that there *might* be some happy resolution of it); what it properly does for readers is to suggest that Pip has moved on, and retains the potential for further growth. The revision stands as a development of, and from, what had gone before. The rising morning mists are now rising evening mists, and "the broad expanse of tranquil light" contains, as far as Pip sees it, no "shadow." He may be wrong, of course, but surely Dickens implies that Pip's experiences have matured him, and that this achievement of maturity is essentially integral to a predominantly *comic* narrative rather than a *tragic* one. Jack may, or may not, have Jill, but that is not the only issue at stake in this bitter-sweet revision. The change may not strike many readers as artistically satisfying as the original, but it must be conceded that it is quintessentially *Dickensian*.

It seems to me that the revised ending serves to move readers on from the earlier resolution of the two other key relationships in Pip's life: the "exceedingly droll" and "very funny" relationship with Joe and the "grotesque tragi-comic" one with Magwitch. As Dickens noted in his letter to Collins of June 23, 1861, he had only changed concluding matter dealing with events "after Biddy and Joe are done with" (*Letters* 9: 428). Whether or not Pip might have proposed to Biddy much earlier in the novel, and whether or not Biddy would have accepted him, is not the issue at stake. What matters is Joe's improved status – a mutually responsive marital relationship and birth of his own child – both of which had been denied him in his marriage to the first Mrs. Joe. Also made clear before this final chapter is the extent to which Pip and Joe are reconciled. As so often in the latter stages of *Great Expectations*, the process is built not simply on expressions of love and acceptance, but also of repentance (on Pip's part) and ready forgiveness (on Joe's), themes that remain firmly grounded in the novel:

> "But I must say more. Dear Joe, I hope you will have children to love, and that some little fellow will sit in this chimney corner of a winter night . . . Don't tell him, Joe, that I was thankless; don't tell him, Biddy, that I was ungenerous and unjust, only tell him that I honoured you both, because you were both so good and true . . .
>
> "I ain't a going," said Joe, from behind his sleeve, "to tell nothink o' that nature, Pip. Nor Biddy ain't. Nor yet no one ain't."
>
> "And now though I know you have already done it in your own kind hearts, pray tell me, both, that you forgive me! . . .
>
> "Oh dear old Pip, old chap," said Joe. "God knows as I forgive you, if I have anything to forgive!" "Amen! And God knows I do!" echoed Biddy. (ch. 58)

The Christian language here is hardly arbitrary. It echoes the parallel confessions and reconciliations presented in the account of Magwitch's last hours in Newgate prison and Pip's final prayer asking for forgiveness for his benefactor (ch. 56). Neither scene comes off as "humorous" or "droll." Nor is there any suggestion of the "tragi-comic." But we should surely recognize that Pip's reconciliation first with Magwitch and then with Joe suggests that he is also reconciled with his past. Such a steady movement toward that end cannot properly be described as "tragic." It may not offer the neat resolutions of *Nicholas Nickleby* or *Martin Chuzzlewit*, to which some Victorian critics sought to compare it. But the last chapters of *Great Expectations* can be seen as profoundly "comic" in the sense that they allow for a new potential in Pip and for something of a happy and unexpected resolution to his "expectations." If some critics find Pip as "disillusioned" at the end of his narrative, it seems to me that Dickens's revised ending allows us to see a man not only chastened by experience but also one reconciled both to the strengths and to the weaknesses of his character.

G. K. Chesterton scores a direct hit when he describes *Great Expectations* as a book in which "for the first time the hero disappears." Chesterton sees the narrative as a whole as possessing "a quality of serene irony and even sadness" and he accredits this to the particular nature of Dickens's development as a novelist. Early in his career, Dickens had presented readers of *Nicholas Nickleby* with an updated version of the hero of Romance whom Chesterton typifies as a "demi-god in a top hat." This figure, according to Chesterton, continues to evolve through Kit Nubbles, Walter Gay, David Copperfield, and Sydney Carton, as each becomes less heroic and more complex. "The study of Sydney Carton," writes Chesterton, "is meant to indicate that with all his vices, Sydney Carton was a hero."

> The study of Pip is meant to indicate that with all his virtues Pip was a snob. The motive of the literary explanation is different. Pip and [Thackeray's] Pendennis are meant to show how circumstances can corrupt men. Sam Weller and Hercules are meant to show how heroes can subdue circumstances. (Chesterton 1911: 198–9)

As ever, Chesterton resorts too readily to the aphoristic manner, but his central point remains valid: Dickens was attempting something new in *Great Expectations* and much of that novelty depended on the character and manner of its narrator. Pip's is the dominant consciousness in the novel, but as a describer, delineator, and analyst, both of himself and of his circumstances, he is essentially flawed and "un-heroic." This lack of "heroism" may have contributed to what critics have seen as the novel's "gloom" and to what has been interpreted as estrangement and guilt, but it can also be read as integral to Dickens's humorous "tragi-comic conception."

This leads us back to Dickens's determination to make Pip and his narrative distinct from that of David Copperfield. Pip was to be of a lower social class than David, and, ostensibly, he was almost certainly to be far less of a surrogate Dickens. The novelist's confession to Forster that he was "affected by it to a degree you would hardly believe" by re-reading his earlier work suggests not only the extent to which his own private emotions had molded the "personal experience" of David Copperfield but also the fact that he now sought to distance himself from Pip's experiences, both personally and artistically. This was not how George Bernard Shaw saw it. In comparing Pip with David in 1937, Shaw gave the distinction between the two a distinctly socio-political edge. He insists that in the ten years that separate the two novels, Dickens had developed both as an artist and as a critic of himself and the world about him. Dickens's "reappearance" in the character of a blacksmith's boy, Shaw famously asserted, "may be regarded as an apology to Mealy Potatoes," one of David's work associates at Murdstone and Grinby's. For Shaw, the shades of Warren's Blacking fall darkly over the whole novel, as Dickens re-explores an embarrassing secret with a renewed and more perceptive sense of guilt (Shaw 1958: 45–6).

To clinch his point, Shaw may have selected the peculiarly named Mealy Potatoes as the object of Dickens's "apology" rather than the more likely figure of Mick Walker. Mick's original, Bob Fagin, was the senior boy worker at Warren's, who had proved to be particularly attentive to Dickens. By contrast, Mealy's original, Poll (Paul) Green, seems to have had a vague air of romance about him because his father worked as a fireman "at one of the large theatres." No such romance is associated with Mick/Bob. As Dickens's autobiographical fragment reveals, it was Bob Fagin who had attempted to assuage the pain in the boy Dickens's side with blacking-bottles filled with hot water and who had attempted to see the boy safe home. It was of Bob Fagin too that Dickens disarmingly remarks "I took the liberty of using his name, long afterwards, in *Oliver Twist*." This admission has served to disconcert many latter-day readers (how could Bob's kindness have been rewarded with such despicable associations?). The answer seems to lie in Dickens's boyhood fear that somehow associating himself with the likes of Bob and Poll might taint him socially and trap him for ever in a working-class world in which he felt acutely ill at ease. Readers must remember how Dickens (and David) express their distress at the loss of status represented by the real Warren's and the fictional Murdstone and Grinby's. "No word can express the secret agony of my soul," Dickens wrote, describing how he sunk into the companionship of common men and boys and how he felt his hopes of growing up "to be a distinguished man" crushed in his bosom (*David Copperfield* ch. 11).

But it *was* written, twice over, both as a record of fact and as fiction, and we must surely appreciate the force of Dickens's phrasing and choice of words. This world of boyhood drudgery represents a fall from middle-class grace. Instead, a proletarian hell predominates where gestures of kindness and fellow-feeling are distorted into Mephistophelian entrapments. Shaw's assumption that what Pip's narrative represents is some kind of apology to Mealy Potatoes may indeed find justification in the reference by Joe on his visit to London that he and Mr. Wopsle have made a point of seeking out "the Blacking War'us" (though the one they visited is Warren's rival, Day and Martin's). The reference compounds Pip's embarrassment before Herbert at this point in the story, but it may also indicate something of Dickens's own uneasiness at a stirring of uncomfortable associations with the past.

Since Shaw's time, issues of social class have come to dominate the discussion of *Great Expectations*. Critics have all too often chosen to concentrate on ideas of class guilt or Marxist ideas of alienation and class betrayal, thereby distorting readings of the novel. As Dickens indicated in the outline he sent to Forster, Pip was to become an apprentice. This obviously distinguishes him both from David Copperfield and from Dickens himself. If David appears to have been born into the gentlemanly class, Dickens's own lower-middle-class origins suggest a rather more tenuous grasp on gentility. While John Dickens consistently aspired upwards, the family's fall in 1822 seems to have marked Charles all the more severely given the social and educational ambitions he took for granted. Pip wants to be a gentleman, just as Emily had wanted to be a lady, but neither was born with the assumptions instilled in the boy Dickens. Precarious as those assumptions were to prove, we must accept that Dickens seems to have been brought up to see himself as a cut above Mick Walker and Mealy Potatoes.

It does not seem to me that Dickens shaped *Great Expectations* as an apology for his earlier social aspirations, as Shaw insisted. Rather, he wanted to explore a new fictional idea. Pip is not of his own class, just as he is not of David's, but he will be given a series of false economic and social expectations that he will have to work out. Pip's promotion to the status of a gentleman by means of Magwitch's money makes an artificial and socially inadequate man of him (at least in Dickens's eyes). Everything depends on work, and Magwitch effectively, if temporarily, removes Pip from the world of work. What is required of Pip as his narrative develops is sound *professional* promotion rather than mere *status* promotion. Pip's work as a clerk, and later a partner, in Clarriker and Co., gives him a role in society; Magwitch's manipulation of him merely takes him out of the forge and, in making him a "gentleman," gives him nothing to do.

The word "gentleman" has its ambiguities even for Magwitch. It is thus that he defines his arch-enemy, Compeyson, when the pair are arrested together on the marshes. "He's a gentleman, if you please, this villain. Now, the hulks has got its gentleman again, through me." When, later in the novel, he explains to Pip what he has done for him, Magwitch claims that he has sought not only to lift his protégé above the world of work but also to possess the thing that he could never himself be: "Yes, Pip, dear boy, I've made a gentleman on you! It's me wot has done it! I swore that time, sure as ever I earned a guinea, that guinea should go to you . . . I lived rough, that you should live smooth; I worked hard, that you should be above work" (ch. 39).

It is not that Magwitch is taking revenge on all the gentlemanly Compeysons through Pip, as Miss Havisham is taking revenge on all the manly jilters though Estella. But somehow he *does* want to claim a vicarious place among the gentlemen in order to prove that their gentility is not innate but manufactured. "The blood horses of them colonists might fling up the dust over me as I was walking," he explains to Pip, and "what do you say? I says to myself, 'I'm making a better gentleman nor ever *you'll* be!'" (ch. 39). In a sense, the "gentleman" Pip is a product of the kind of "trade" that real Victorian gentlemen pretended to despise. Perhaps worse, he is a product of "speculation" by a transportee, tainted by the associations of crime, the hulks, indenture, and colonial venture.

Until Magwitch's revelations at the end of the novel's second stage, Pip has, of course, been unquestioningly happy with what he sees as his good fortune and his social advancement. Since his boyhood meeting with Estella, he had aspired to rise above the class into which he was born and his un-named benefactor has enabled him to realize richly his ambitions. He has also willingly, and to him "naturally," altered his perspectives:

"Since your change of fortune and prospects, you have changed your companions," said Estella.

"Naturally," said I.

"And necessarily," she added, in a haughty tone, "what was fit company for you once, would be quite unfit company for you now." (ch. 29)

Coldly and astutely, Estella puts her finger on Pip's new-found snobbery, and, on this particular occasion, Pip readily abandons any thought of visiting Joe at the forge. What readers have to place against these manifestations of Pip's snobbish assumptions, however, is the fact that though, by any moral and human standard, he ought to remain the intimate of a blacksmith, he can now never resort to working as a blacksmith's apprentice. His own inclinations, as much as his "expectations," have prepared him for something different. What he must learn is that he cannot afford to feel superior. In a telling exchange with Biddy, as he sets out to begin his new and snobbish life in London, Pip professes himself determined "to do something for Joe" in view of his own higher prospects. In the garden at the forge, Pip asks Biddy to help Joe on "a little." Asked to explain "how," Pip is forced to say that Joe's "learning and manners" lacked something and that if he were to remove Joe into "a higher sphere" when he comes fully into his property, Joe would need to be improved. "And don't you think he knows that?" Biddy asks, plucking a blackcurrant leaf and then rubbing it to pieces in her hands. "Have you never considered that he may be proud?"

> "Proud?" I repeated, with disdainful emphasis.
>
> "Oh there are many kinds of pride," said Biddy, looking full at me and shaking her head; "pride is not all of one kind – "
>
> "Well, what are you stopping for?" said I.
>
> "Not all of one kind," resumed Biddy. "He may be too proud to let anyone take him out of a place that he is competent to fill, and fills well and with respect. To tell you the truth, I think he is: though it sounds bold in me to say so, for you must know him far better than I do." (ch. 19)

This is perhaps the most crucial exchange in the whole novel. Biddy throws the responsibility for understanding back on Pip, but, at the time, Pip fails to grasp this responsibility. We know that he *will* come to understand the import of the conversation because of Dickens's introduction of the blackcurrant leaf, the smell of which will bring back the memory, freshly and involuntarily. What Pip has to learn is that Joe not only accepts his role in life: he is *proud* of it and of the respect it earns him. Joe has an integrity that, at this stage in his expectations, Pip singularly lacks. It is not a matter of Joe "knowing his place" but of Joe being happy with what he is.

It is obvious to Pip and Biddy in this scene that although Joe represents a moral standard, he does not offer either a model of professional or class aspiration. Pip has to learn the distinctions that Biddy wisely intuits, but we need to acknowledge that at no stage in the novel does Joe seek social promotion or possess expectations. Those expectations are given to Pip, and the novel is about what he does with them. Dickens knew this when he hit on the name for his story and when he announced that his hero was to be a boy-child, "then he will be an apprentice." Pip is not to *stay* an apprentice.

But, having acquired the status and manners of a gentleman, nor is he to stay the kind of "gentleman" that Magwitch wanted to make him. Pip has to learn about a different kind of status, one defined by work, rather than by a distaste for work. *Great Expectations* is not, in the end, a novel about disillusionment, or alienation, or non-communication, or estrangement, but one concerned with finding one's place in the world of work and, as so often in Dickens's novels, being defined by work. Pip is obliged to discover the middle way between the working artisan and the workless gentleman. The novel's focus on class is ultimately, and unromantically, about the process of *embourgeoisement*. This is why, to a critic like Chesterton, Pip can never emerge as "heroic," and why, to Marxists, the story seems to dwell darkly on social estrangement.

During their last encounter, Pip admits to Estella that he works "pretty hard for a sufficient living" and therefore he does "well." These words perhaps reflect Samuel Smiles's comments about the character of "The True Gentleman" in the last chapter of his popular ethical manual *Self Help* (1859): "Riches and rank have no necessary connection with genuinely gentlemanly qualities. The poor man may be a true gentleman – in spirit and in daily life. He may be honest, truthful, upright, polite, temperate, courageous, self-respecting, and self-helping – that is, be a true gentleman" (Paroissien 2000: 420). For Smiles, all work was "noble" whether it be manual labor, administration, composition, or cerebration. This was, of course, an echo of Carlyle's insistent demand that work should be seen as giving meaning both to the individual and to society.

Much as Carlyle had outlined in his 1840 lectures on *Heroes, Hero-worship and the Heroic in History*, David Copperfield was given a mission to find his own "heroism" in becoming a man of letters. David's first sentence asks whether or not he will be the "hero" of his own life, and his narrative shows him developing both independence and social standing through writing. David was also to be an example of the Dickensian self-made man, one who overcomes disadvantage in order to prove himself worthy of happiness. Pip's realization of his destiny is to be equally a matter of struggle and self-help, but his destiny lacks the glamor of literary success. To work oneself up from a clerk to a partner in Clarriker and Co. may seem to lack flamboyance and romance, but that is precisely what becomes the "unheroic" Pip. In his own eyes, he has done "well" by dint of "hard work."

Readers may baulk at the subdued nature of the novel's ending, and may see Pip's occupation as a sign of his disillusion, but that is not how Victorian readers seem to have taken it. There is certainly nothing for tears in either ending that Dickens provided, though so few latter-day critics feel stimulated to do justice to the "flowing humour" and the "entertainment" that contemporary readers rejoiced in. In some ways, *Great Expectations* is a typical Dickensian comedy of manners in which the worthy central character loses illusions in order to find his true *métier*. Pip sees mists rising at the end of his narrative and he interprets them as portending no shadow of a parting from Estella. What they may also portend is a future in which men like Pip build a world that dispenses both with class assumptions and with assumptions about class.

References and Further Reading

Anon (1862). Review of *Cloister and the Hearth*. *Westminster Review*, 77, 286–7.

Cheadle, Brian (2001). The late novels: *Great Expectations* and *Our Mutual Friend*. In John O. Jordan (Ed.), *The Cambridge Companion to Charles Dickens* (pp. 78–91). Cambridge: Cambridge University Press.

Chesterton, G. K. (1911). *Appreciations and Criticisms of the Works of Charles Dickens*. London: J. M. Dent.

Collins, Philip (Ed.) (1971). *Dickens: The Critical Heritage*. London: Routledge and Kegan Paul.

[Forster, John] (1861). Review of *Great Expectations*. *The Examiner*, July 20, 452–3.

Miller, J. Hillis (1958). *Charles Dickens: The World of his Novels*. Cambridge, MA: Harvard University Press.

Moynahan, Julian (1960). The hero's guilt: the case of *Great Expectations*. *Essays in Criticism*, 10, 60–79.

Paroissien, David (2000). *The Companion to Great Expectations*. Robertsbridge: Helm Information.

Ricks, Christopher (1962). *Great Expectations*. In John Gross and Gabriel Pearson (Eds.), *Dickens and the Twentieth Century* (pp. 199–211). London: Routledge and Kegan Paul.

Shaw, George Bernard (1958). Foreword to *Great Expectations*. In Dan H. Laurence and Martin Quin (Eds.), *Shaw on Dickens* (pp. 45–59). New York: Frederick Ungar (original work published 1937; text revised 1947).

32

Our Mutual Friend

Leon Litvack

The gestation of Dickens's fourteenth and last completed novel developed slowly against a background of major achievements. His two contributions to *All the Year Round* had secured the journal's prominence among weekly journals; his reputation as a professional reader of scenes from his works stood equally high, consolidated by successful appearances throughout the country over the past three years. In this context, a determination to return to the old monthly format seemed inevitable, particularly since that intention had been thwarted (see headnote to *Great Expectations*). The transition from weekly to monthly numbers, however, proved unexpectedly slow. Ideas began to accumulate, but a start on the new novel remained elusive. "I am always thinking of writing a long book," he wrote to Wilkie Collins on August 9, 1863, "and am never beginning to do it" (*Letters* 10: 281).

The scale required for a panoramic novel offers a partial explanation, some sense of which we can gain from Forster's reference to "three leading notions" for the novel that emerge from comments Dickens made in letters and recorded in his *Book of Memoranda* dating from 1861 (see Kaplan). Among them are threads generated during his "waterside wanderings" for *Great Expectations*, when Dickens had come across handbills describing "persons drowned in the river" and witnessed the "ghastly calling" of longshoremen engaged in dredging bodies from the Thames; there was also "the uneducated father in fustian and the educated boy in spectacles" seen on a trip to Chatham, hints of which he develops in Charley Hexam and his father (Forster bk. 9, ch. 5). A second group centered on some "perfectly New people. Everything new about them. If *they* presented a father and a mother, it seems as if THEY must be bran new, like the furniture and the Carriages, shining with Varnish, and just home from the manufacturer's" (Kaplan 101). Other figures included "a benevolent old Jew" made "the unconscious agent of a rascal," "A man –young and eccentric? – [who] feigns to be dead" and "A poor imposter of a man [who] marries a woman for her money; she marries *him* for *his* money: after marriage both find out their mistake, and enter into a league and covenant against folks in general" (Forster bk. 9, ch. 5; Kaplan 92, 93). Several names recorded earlier by Dickens in his *Book of Memoranda* also made their way into the novel.

Persevering in the face of further attempts to get the story underway, Dickens expressed characteristic resolve, reporting to Forster on August 30, 1863 how, once the Christmas number of *All the Year Round* had been organized and "cleared out of the road," he would be ready to "dash into" the new 20 monthly numbers and commence "the grander journey" (*Letters* 10: 283). Six weeks later, he wrote that he saw his opening "perfectly, with the one main line on which the story is to turn" (*Letters* 10: 300). By the following January, he had completed the first two numbers and was ready to begin a third, thus ensuring a generous cushion before the serial commenced. *Our Mutual Friend* began in May 1864 and ran until November 1865, published in 20 monthly parts (as 19) by Chapman and Hall and with illustrations by

Marcus Stone. Chapman and Hall also published the novel in two volumes (February and November) and as a single volume the same year.

Unlike most of his other works, *Our Mutual Friend* is set in the novelist's present, "In these times of ours" (bk. 1, ch. 1). Dark in its conception, and containing two of his most powerful images – the river and the dust heaps, which give the text its "distinctive poetic texture" (Daleski 1970: 271), Dickens offers a panoramic survey of society, from the river scavengers Gaffer Hexam and Rogue Riderhood (who are "allied to the bottom of the river rather than the surface", bk. 1, ch. 1) to Mr. Veneering (MP for the Borough of "Pocket-Breaches", bk. 2, ch. 3), and Lady Tippins (whose husband was knighted "in mistake for somebody else" by King George III, bk. 1, ch. 10). Dickens conceives a multiplicity of plots, in which characters and events seem initially unconnected, but as the novel progresses he unravels a "fully elaborated definition of what it means to be interlaced with the world" (Miller 1958: 280). The effect is in part achieved by the employment of the overarching symbol of the river, the ramifications of which make it a more "cogent and bearing" emblem than it had been in the novelist's previous work (Engel 1959: 139).

The Thames, which runs through the heart of London, is the physical setting for some of the key events in *Our Mutual Friend*. In the opening chapter, Gaffer Hexam and his daughter Lizzie row in a small boat "between Southwark Bridge which is of iron, and London Bridge which is of stone" (bk. 1, ch.1), earning a living by scavenging the polluted river for items of value, including corpses. Thus, from the outset, the river serves as a place of life and livelihood, but also of death; indeed, a number of characters either die or have brushes with death in the vicinity of the river: Gaffer Hexam (bk. 1, ch. 14), John Harmon (bk. 2, ch. 13), Betty Higden (bk. 3, ch. 8), Eugene Wrayburn (bk. 4, ch. 6), Bradley Headstone (bk. 4, ch. 15), and Rogue Riderhood (bk. 3, chs. 2–3; bk. 4, ch. 15).

Dickens wishes to emphasize the importance of the river to the commercial life of the city, but he believes that the obsession with money and position has a malevolent effect; ultimately, he judges metropolitan London to be, in moral terms, a "Dismal Swamp" (bk. 1, ch. 17). The wealthy and influential classes (who come in for particularly harsh criticism in this novel) have lost touch with the positive elements embodied by the river: emotional and physical vitality; natural rhythms; physical labor, with its attendant skills and strengths; and seriousness of ambition or purpose (Garis 1965: 229). Instead, they worship social aspiration and mobility (personified by the Veneerings, "bran-new people in a bran-new house in a bran-new quarter of London," bk. 1, ch. 2), financial speculation (epitomized by the belief that "traffic in Shares is the one thing to have to do in this world", bk. 1, ch. 10), and, in a sardonic twist of Darwinian ideas, survival of the fittest ("Recollect, we must scrunch or be scrunched", bk. 3, ch. 5).

Though Dickens is sparing in his overt biblical references in *Our Mutual Friend*, there are nevertheless a number of key parallels between Dickens and the Bible in the symbolic uses of the river, particularly in connection with prosperity and tragedy, life and death, baptism, resurrection, and healing. The case of John Harmon, "the novel's prime example of fluidity of human personality" (Litvack 2003: 48), provides useful evidence of how the river can serve as the agent for both death and rebirth or resurrection. At the actual and metaphorical center of the novel, Harmon reconstructs the story of his attempted murder: he recounts how, in a troubled state over the terms of his father's will, he planned to exchange identities with George Radfoot, in order to withdraw from an economically motivated marriage to Bella Wilfer, and observe her anonymously instead; but Radfoot had conspired with Rogue Riderhood to kill him. The plot fails, and Radfoot, dressed in Harmon's clothes, dies instead. In an extended monologue, Harmon forces his memory to recapture the sensations of being drugged and thrown in the river:

> I cannot possibly express it to myself without using the word I. But it was not I. There was no such thing as I, within my knowledge.
>   It was only after a downward slide through something like a tube, and then a great noise and a sparkling and crackling as of fires, that the consciousness came upon me, "This is John Harmon drowning! John Harmon, struggle for your life. John Harmon, call on Heaven and save yourself!" I think I cried it out aloud in a great agony, and then a heavy horrid unintelligible something vanished, and it was I who was struggling there alone in the water. (bk. 2, ch. 13)

The imagery in this passage is replete with the well-known psychoanalytic symbols of the trauma of birth, and firmly links the river with the creation of life. Harmon, who is assumed to be dead at the start of the novel, is "resurrected" as John Rokesmith; this transition allows him to discover and establish a new identity for himself: he is freed from the burden of being his father's son and heir. Thus he can subject his intended bride to a series of trials designed to prove her worth. Initially, the independent-minded Bella exclaims "I love money, and want money – want it dreadfully" (bk. 1, ch. 4), but by the time she accepts the offer of marriage from Harmon (in the guise of Rokesmith) it is with an "engaging shyness . . . coupled with an engaging tenderness" (bk. 3, ch. 16). Indeed, she exclaims "Oh, Mr. Rokesmith, if you could but make me poor again! O! Make me poor again" (bk. 3, ch. 15). Here Dickens's message is that the discovery of real wealth entails the loss of worldly riches. John and Bella undergo trials in order to free themselves from the love of money; only in this way can they discover the "regenerating power of human love" (Sanders 1978: 140). They are, nevertheless, rewarded at the novel's close by having the Harmon fortune restored to them (bk. 4, ch. 13).

The river also alters the fate of Eugene Wrayburn, the gloomy, indolent, unambitious barrister who lacks purpose, living in expectation of inherited wealth. He displays an interest in Lizzie Hexam, whom he first sees at her father's house, "by where the accumulated scum of humanity seemed to be washed from higher grounds, like so much moral sewage" (bk. 1, ch. 3). Yet the reason for the attraction remains unclear:

it is neither a serious romantic interest nor an attempt at casual seduction. He lacks passion, and admits that he has "no design whatever" on Lizzie. He adds, tellingly, "I am incapable of designs. If I conceived a design, I should speedily abandon it" (bk. 2, ch. 6). Like Harmon, then, he must find purpose in the course of the narrative, and "something really worth being energetic about" (bk. 1, ch. 3).

Lizzie, too, is unsure about Wrayburn's motives. She assists her father in his grisly river scavenging, and so is able to maneuver a boat expertly; thus she represents a new "passionate vitality" which in earlier novels would have seemed unwomanly, or difficult and dangerous (Garis 1965: 246). She is, however, distinguished from other Thameside characters by her wariness of the river from the outset, despite Gaffer Hexam's declaration, "As if it wasn't meat and drink to you!" (bk. 1, ch. 1). She also has integrity, defending her violent father against a false charge of murder, sacrificing everything for her selfish brother Charley, and escaping to the countryside to save her honor (Sedgwick 1987: 260); perhaps to emphasize her laudable qualities, Dickens unrealistically endows her with middle-class speech patterns. Lizzie recognizes how ridiculous a relationship with the upper-class Eugene would seem; she asks him, "How can I think of you as being on equal terms with me? If my mind could put you on equal terms with me, you could not be yourself" (bk. 4, ch. 6). Wrayburn nevertheless pursues her relentlessly, and finally discovers in her his reason for living. Late on in the novel he stumblingly expresses his love for Lizzie by the river:

> I never thought before, that there was a woman in the world who could affect me so much by saying so little. But don't be hard in your construction of me. You don't know what my state of mind towards you is. You don't know how you haunt me and bewilder me. You don't know how the cursed carelessness that is over-officious in helping me at every other turning of my life, WON'T help me here. You have struck it dead, I think, and I sometimes almost wish you had struck me dead along with it. (bk. 4, ch. 6)

Even though the prize of Lizzie's affection is here within Wrayburn's reach, Dickens does not allow the union to proceed forthwith; instead, he throws Eugene one further challenge, in the form of the vengeful schoolmaster Bradley Headstone.

This character is in part introduced to evoke the novelist's interest in the theme of education, specifically the professionalizing of teaching (Collins 1963: 159). Headstone is an example of the college-trained teacher who has risen from humble origins, and acquired some status and a decent salary: well earned rewards for hard work. Yet he is not satisfied: "There was a kind of settled trouble in the face. It was the face belonging to a normally slow or inattentive intellect that had toiled hard to get what it had won, and that had to hold it now that it was gotten" (bk. 2, ch. 1). Dickens depicts Headstone with a thoroughly vicious temperament, in order to highlight the defects of a system that took no account of the social and intellectual difficulties faced by the newly trained teachers, who wanted reassurance that they would be accepted into middle-class society (Collins 1963: 160). The novel presents a crucial exchange between Headstone and Wrayburn on this very topic:

"You think me of no more value than the dirt under your feet," said Bradley to Eugene, speaking in a carefully weighed and measured tone, or he could not have spoken at all.

"I assure you, Schoolmaster," replied Eugene, "I don't think about you." . . .

"Mr. Wrayburn, at least I know very well that it would be idle to set myself against you in insolent words or overbearing manners. [Charley Hexam] could put you to shame in half-a-dozen branches of knowledge in half an hour, but you can throw him aside like an inferior. You can do as much by me, I have no doubt . . . You reproach me with my origin . . . you cast insinuations at my bringing-up. But I tell you, sir, I have worked my way onward, out of both and in spite of both, and have a right to be considered a better man than you, with better reasons for being proud." (bk. 2, ch. 6)

This clash over respectability and position is exacerbated by Headstone's overpowering interest in Lizzie. Though she is grateful for the assistance he renders to her brother Charley, she finds him personally obnoxious. He is a tormented soul: "Suppression of so much to make room for so much, had given him a constrained manner . . . Yet there was enough of what was animal, and what was fiery (though smouldering), still visible in him" (bk. 2, ch. 1). Bradley serves as a powerful study of repression, and Dickens displays remarkable understanding of his character's sexual passion; at the point where the schoolmaster urges Lizzie to break off her relationship with Eugene, the novelist describes his tortured state:

> It seemed to him as if all that he could suppress in himself he had suppressed, as if all that he could restrain in himself he had restrained, and the time had come – in a rush, in a moment – when the power of self-command had departed from him. Love at first sight is a trite expression quite sufficiently discussed; enough that in certain smouldering natures like this man's, that passion leaps into a blaze, and makes such head as fire does in a rage of wind, when other passions, but for its mastery, could be held in chains. (bk. 2, ch. 11)

Headstone has no effective outlet for his desires; he "sheds his civilised skin and becomes a monstrous animal" once the trappings of respectability are discarded (David 1981: 79). When he proposes marriage to Lizzie, instead of speaking gently to her in an attempt to win her over, he shouts, displays "wild energy," and pounds upon stones so hard that his knuckles bleed (bk. 2, ch. 15). She naturally refuses him; he then embarks on a pursuit of Eugene that will eventually lead back to the Thames, and to attempted murder.

The near-drowning of Wrayburn (bk. 4, ch. 6) serves as his ultimate trial: in order to be worthy of Lizzie, he must experience the violence, brutality, and corruption of river life first-hand. He, like Harmon, undergoes a form of baptismal regeneration (Engel 1959: 144), though this later one occurs further upstream, near Henley-upon-Thames, a rural setting where the waters are cleaner. Dickens is, however, careful not to transform this non-metropolitan location into a natural realm of Romantic innocence: the fact that Headstone can find Wrayburn and subject him to a violent beating points to Dickens's "powerful insistence on the impossibility of escape from the human condition which is circumscribed by social realities" (Lucas 1980: 337). Nevertheless, the novelist consistently favors Eugene, who is "the Abel to Bradley Headstone's Cain" (Sanders 1978: 140) in the rivalry over Lizzie. Once his "Byronic qualities" are negated (Harvey 1969: 314; see also John 2001: 190–8), he can be rescued by the object of his affections; it is, however, ironic that in order to save him Lizzie must employ those boating skills associated with her family's unsavory profession, and she could not have acquired this nautical education if she had lived a more genteel life away from the river.

The second great motif that dominates *Our Mutual Friend* is dust – an emblem of all the negative aspects of the Victorian capitalist economy. Its visible aspect, the material waste gathered into heaps or mounds, is described early on in the novel. Old John Harmon, the "tremendous old rascal" (bk. 1, ch. 2) who prearranged the match between his son and Bella, made his living from dealing in dust; his business is described at the Veneerings' dinner party:

> He grew rich as a Dust Contractor, and lived in a hollow in a hilly country entirely composed of Dust. On his own small estate the growling old vagabond threw up his own mountain range, like an old volcano, and its geological formation was Dust. Coal-dust, vegetable-dust, bone-dust, crockery dust, rough dust and sifted dust, – all manner of Dust. (bk. 1, ch. 2)

The collection of refuse was an important aspect of the economy, especially for contractors employed by parish authorities. It was deposited in yards, such as the "Harmony Jail" of the novel (bk. 1, ch. 5), then sorted, mostly by women and children for starvation wages; much of the sifted material went to the building trade. The value of dust is emphasized in an article written by R. H. Horne for *Household Words* in 1850, which may have influenced Dickens in his conception of *Our Mutual Friend* (see Gibbon 1985). It tells the story of three cinder-sifters who bring back to life a Mr. Waterhouse, a middle-class man who attempts to drown himself in a canal; he experiences a renewal, and marries the daughter of the dust contractor, who offers Waterhouse as a dowry either the dust heap or twenty thousand pounds. He chooses the money, and the dust is subsequently sold for double that amount ("Dust; or Ugliness Redeemed," *Household Words* 1 [July 13, 1850], 379–84).

The dust heaps and their contents dominate the plot of the novel. They are the source of the Harmon fortune, some of which was initially meant to have been bestowed on John Harmon's sister, had she married a man of her father's choosing; she, however, refused to "make Dust of her heart and Dust of her life" in a loveless union, and so died penniless (bk. 1, ch. 2). Young John Harmon returns from South Africa to claim his inheritance, which (as a condition of his father's will) will only be released when he marries Bella. These situations, which are explained early on by the young solicitor Mortimer Lightwood (intimate friend of Eugene Wrayburn), set the tone for a text that continually illustrates the point that the inappropriate pursuit and use of money only produce suffering, and thus are at the root of society's ills.

Until young John Harmon (the "mutual friend" of the title) returns to claim the estate, it is placed in the care of Nicodemus or "Noddy" Boffin, also known as "the Golden Dustman" (bk. 1, ch. 11); he was a trusted servant of old Harmon and the executor of his will, and pretends to be corrupted by money in order to demonstrate its destructive force. The Boffins become prey for "all manner of crawling, creeping, fluttering, and buzzing creatures" (bk. 1, ch. 17) who are attracted by the couple's new wealth. They include not only members of high society, but also Silas Wegg, a ballad monger who is hired as reader to the illiterate Boffin, then as caretaker of the dust yard; he, however, is dissatisfied with the meager salary offered by Boffin, who adopts the role of a miser and displays such avarice that Wegg observes of him at one point "He's GROWN too FOND of MONEY for THAT, he's GROWN too FOND of MONEY" (bk. 3, ch. 7) – a critique which may be leveled at numerous characters in the novel. Wegg searches the dust mounds for items of value; with the assistance of his acquaintance, the taxidermist Mr. Venus, he finds a will written by old Harmon which is dated after the one favoring Boffin, and which leaves all of the estate to the Crown. Wegg attempts to blackmail Boffin if the Golden Dustman will not share the wealth (bk. 4, ch. 3). Unbeknown to Wegg, however, there is a third, even later, Harmon will, which leaves everything unconditionally to Boffin; it was cynically conceived by old Harmon in the hope that the Boffins' simplicity and integrity would be infected and quickly ruined by sudden access to wealth.

The dust heaps "have power to dominate the lives that are lived in their midst" (Miller 1958: 295), and serve as a "unifying symbol of economic situation" (David 1981: 95) in *Our Mutual Friend*. Wegg, with his interest in the dust heaps, is the "official expounder of mysteries" (bk. 1, ch. 5) in the text: he can penetrate economic secrets, and, by extension, the heart of the capitalist system. Ultimately, however, he becomes obsessed and deluded by his pursuits. It is significant that he undertakes to read to Boffin Edward Gibbon's *Decline and Fall of the Roman Empire* (bk. 1, ch. 5), that work which traced "the downward fortunes of those enervated and corrupted masters of the world who were . . . on their last legs" (bk. 2, ch. 7); in Dickens's view, Victorian England was re-enacting the fall of Rome. Though Wegg manages to live in Boffin's Bower, he never becomes master of the mounds; instead, he thrives on fantasies, and is in the end appropriately banished in a dust-cart (bk. 4, ch. 14).

The fact that Boffin is not corrupted by his wealth offers a ray of hope in a novel dominated by the destructive aspects of a "superficial, heartless, meaningless and self-satisfied" society (Muir 1966: 94). The appellation "the Golden Dustman" places him partly in the realm of fairytale (Cockshut 1961: 180); he becomes a surrogate father, bestowing with love and affection what old Harmon had sought to refuse, and a "philosopher's stone" in a text dedicated to the "reassertion of values" (Sadrin 1994: 144–6). The Boffins adopt Bella to compensate her for the supposed loss of John Harmon; she, however, becomes tainted by the contact with money. Harmon (in the guise of Rokesmith, who becomes Boffin's secretary) observes of her, "So insolent, so trivial, so capricious, so mercenary, so careless, so hard to touch, so hard to turn! . . . And yet so pretty, so pretty!" (bk. 1, ch. 16). Bella does redeem herself somewhat through such actions as using a gift of fifty pounds from Boffin to purchase a suit for her father, who works as an underpaid clerk for Veneering, and with whom she has a positive, fulfilling relationship; yet she confesses to him that she cannot control her urge to become a "mercenary little wretch" (bk. 2, ch. 8), which is partly a result of her early experience of not having money.

Another philanthropic gesture on the part of the Boffins (who recognize their obligation to do something positive with the money they have received) is their adoption of Johnny, the great-grandson of Betty Higden, to remind them of the young John Harmon. Mrs. Boffin makes a heartfelt proposal to Betty: "'If you trust the dear child to me,' said Mrs. Boffin, with a face inviting trust, 'he shall have the best of homes, the best of care, the best of education, the best of friends. Please God I will be a true good mother to him!'" (bk. 1, ch. 16). Though the old woman agrees, the plan is never carried into effect: Johnny falls ill, and is taken by the Boffins, Rokesmith, and Bella to the Children's Hospital. Once there, in a scene filled with pathos, the child dies (bk. 2, ch. 9). In this rather brief episode, and the subplot involving Betty Higden (who wishes to be beholden to no one, and whose greatest fear is that she will end up in the workhouse), Dickens emphasizes that genuine emancipation involves the maintenance of moral independence, with no strings attached (Kettle 1962: 218–19).

There are other extremely interesting minor characters who contribute significantly to illustrating how the moral values of mainstream society have been warped beyond recognition. For example, the diminutive and misshapen doll's dressmaker, Jenny Wren (with whom Lizzie temporarily lodges after Gaffer Hexam's death) is a "master of turning life into art" (Marks 1988: 27). In an extension of her trade, she creates alterative life-models for those around her – not only Lizzie, but also Eugene, who asks her to "stay and help nurse me" after his injury; he adds "I should like you to have the fancy, here, before I die" (bk. 4, ch. 10). There is an interesting exchange between these two earlier in the novel, which points to how fancies can be real:

> "I wonder how it happens that when I am work, work, working here, all alone in the summer-time, I smell flowers."
>
> "As a commonplace individual, I should say," Eugene suggested languidly – for he was growing weary of [Jenny] – "that you smell flowers because you DO smell flowers."
>
> "No I don't," said the little creature . . . "this is not a flowery neighbourhood. It's anything but that. And yet as I sit at work, I smell miles of flowers." (bk. 2, ch. 2)

Jenny has great power of imagination, a faculty that is vital in art, and "crucially important to the reconcilement of classes and the development of social harmony" (Slater 1999: 26). These assuaging elements are painfully absent from much of *Our Mutual Friend*; if Eugene, Bella, and others like them can learn to look beyond the pragmatic and the material, then they will have completed their journeys of self-discovery, and will find more satisfying roles in their troubled, avaricious society.

It is difficult to identify a central figure who clearly presents Dickens's own perspective on the situation he surveys: in this novel, unlike *Bleak House*, a prominent omniscient voice or perspective is absent (Jaffe 1987: 91). There is, however, a strong satirical current that runs through Dickens's "reflection" on "Society":

> The great looking-glass above the sideboard, reflects the table and the company. Reflects the new Veneering crest, in gold and eke in silver, frosted and also thawed, a camel of all work . . . Reflects Veneering; forty, wavy-haired, dark, tending to corpulence, sly, mysterious, filmy – a kind of sufficiently well-looking veiled-prophet, not prophesying. Reflects Mrs. Veneering; fair, aquiline-nosed and fingered, not so much light hair as she might have, gorgeous in raiment and jewels, enthusiastic, propitiatory, conscious that a corner of her husband's veil is over herself. Reflects Podsnap; prosperously feeding, two little light-coloured wiry wings, one on either side of his else bald head, looking as like his hairbrushes as his hair . . . Reflects Mrs. Podsnap . . . quantity of bone, neck and nostrils like a rocking-horse, hard features, majestic head-dress in which Podsnap has hung golden offerings. Reflects Twemlow; grey, dry, polite, susceptible to east wind, First-Gentleman-in-Europe collar and cravat . . . Reflects mature young lady; raven locks, and complexion that lights up well when well powdered – as it is – carrying on considerably in the captivation of mature young gentleman . . . Reflects charming old Lady Tippins . . . with an immense obtuse drab oblong face, like a face in a tablespoon, and a dyed Long Walk up the top of her head, as a convenient public approach to the bunch of false hair behind, pleased to patronise Mrs. Veneering opposite, who is pleased to be patronised. (bk. 1, ch. 2)

There is clearly narratorial disgust and contempt, as well as humor, in this passage; it is outspoken in its criticism of such inanimate specimens of humanity, who lack vibrancy or real purpose, but nevertheless occupy the corridors of power and privilege. Yet these two-dimensional, cardboard cut-outs are given the last word by Dickens, in a chapter entitled "The Voice of Society." They gather at the home of the Veneerings (who are about to flee from their creditors to the Continent) and Lady Tippins questions Mortimer Lightwood (who mediates between "Society" and the more vital aspects of the text) about the fate of the "savages." He reports on the marriage of Eugene Wrayburn and Lizzie Hexam – a union that is deemed by the assembled company to be a "*mésalliance*," ill advised, and a violation of established rules. Lightwood speaks up for his friend, calling him a "greater gentleman" (a term with great social significance in the Victorian period) for marrying Lizzie. His audience is, of course, unmoved; they live in a world of illusion, and continue to hold to the tenet that "A man may do anything lawful, for money. But for no money! – Bosh!" (bk. 4, ch. 17).

There is, then, no single, unifying point of view from which to take comfort. *Our Mutual Friend* is filled with disguises and fraudulent dealings; at times, there are insights offered into the difference between a "deceitful surface and an underlying truth" (Jaffe 1987: 95), but the pattern is difficult to discern because deception is used for both benevolent and malevolent purposes. The reader never feels comfortable with this scheme, and is always in danger of being overwhelmed by the river or the dust heaps. But Dickens does not care because he does not set out to reorganize, reform, or rescue society. Instead, he acknowledges that its citizens must, like Mortimer Lightwood, go about their daily lives "gaily" (the word with which the novel closes), albeit with an awareness of both individual and communal responsibility.

References and Further Reading

Bodenheimer, R. (2002). Dickens and the identical man: *Our Mutual Friend* doubled. *Dickens Studies Annual*, 31, 159–74.

Brattin, J. J. (2002). Constancy, change, and the dust mounds of *Our Mutual Friend*. *Dickens Quarterly*, 19, 23–30.

Cockshut, A. O. J. (1961). *The Imagination of Charles Dickens*. London: Collins.

Collins, P. (1963). *Dickens and Education*. London: Macmillan.

Daleski, H. M. (1970). *Dickens and the Art of Analogy*. London: Faber and Faber.

David, D. (1981). *Fictions of Resolution in Three Victorian Novels: North and South, Our Mutual Friend, Daniel Deronda*. London: Macmillan.

Engel, M. (1959). *The Maturity of Dickens*. Cambridge, MA: Harvard University Press.

Gallagher, C. (1991). The bioeconomics of *Our Mutual Friend*. In D. Simpson (Ed.), *Subject to History: Ideology, Class, Gender* (pp. 47–64). Ithaca, NY: Cornell University Press.

Garis, R. (1965). *The Dickens Theatre: A Reassessment of the Novels*. Oxford: Clarendon Press.

Gibbon, F. (1985). R. H. Horne and *Our Mutual Friend*. *The Dickensian*, 81, 140–3.

Ginsburg, M. P. (1996). *Economies of Change: Form and Transformation in the Nineteenth-century Novel*. Stanford: Stanford University Press.

Grossman, J. H. (1996). The absent Jew in Dickens: narrators in *Oliver Twist, Our Mutual Friend* and *A Christmas Carol*. *Dickens Studies Annual*, 24, 37–57.

Harvey, W. R. (1969). Dickens and the Byronic hero. *Nineteenth-century Fiction*, 24, 305–16.

Jaffe, A. (1987). Omniscience in *Our Mutual Friend*: on taking the reader by surprise. *Journal of Narrative Technique*, 17, 91–101.

John, J. (2001). *Dickens's Villains: Melodrama, Character, Popular Culture*. Oxford: Oxford University Press.

Kettle, A. (1962). *Our Mutual Friend*. In J. Gross and G. Pearson (Eds.), *Dickens and the Twentieth Century* (pp. 213–25). Toronto: University of Toronto Press.

Litvack, L. (2003). Images of the river in *Our Mutual Friend*. *Dickens Quarterly*, 20 (1), 34–55.

Lucas, J. (1980). *The Melancholy Man: A Study of Dickens's Novels*. Brighton: Harvester Press.

Marks, P. (1988). Storytelling as mimesis in *Our Mutual Friend*. *Dickens Quarterly*, 5, 23–30.

Metz, N. A. (1979). The artistic reclamation of waste in *Our Mutual Friend*. *Nineteenth-century Fiction*, 34, 59–72.

Miller, J. H. (1958). *Charles Dickens: The World of his Novels*. Cambridge, MA: Harvard University Press.

Morris, P. (2000). Taste for change in *Our Mutual Friend*: cultivation or education? In J. John and A. Jenkins (Eds.), *Rethinking Victorian Culture* (pp. 179–94). Basingstoke: Macmillan.

Muir, K. (1966). Image and structure in *Our Mutual Friend*. *Essays and Studies* 19, 92–105. London: John Murray.

Paroissien, D. (2004). Ideology, pedagogy, and demonology: the case against industrialized education in Dickens's fiction. *Dickens Studies Annual*, 34, 259–82.

Poovey, M. (1993). Reading history in literature: speculation and virtue in *Our Mutual Friend*. In J. E. Smarr (Ed.), *Historical Criticism and the Challenge of Theory* (pp. 42–80). Urbana, IL: University of Illinois Press.

Robson, J. M. (1991). Crime in *Our Mutual Friend*. In M. L. Friedland (Ed.), *Rough Justice: Essays on Crime in Literature* (pp. 114–40). Toronto: University of Toronto Press.

Sadrin, A. (1994). *Parentage and Inheritance in the Novels of Charles Dickens*. Cambridge: Cambridge University Press.

Sanders, A. (1978). "Come back and be alive": living and dying in *Our Mutual Friend*. *The Dickensian*, 74, 131–43.

Sedgwick, E. K. (1987). Homophobia, misogyny, and capital: the example of *Our Mutual Friend*. In H. Bloom (Ed.), *Charles Dickens*. Modern Critical Views (pp. 245–61). New York: Chelsea House.

Sicher, E. (2003). *Rereading the City, Rereading Dickens: Representation, the Novel, and Urban Realism*. New York: AMS Press.

Slater, M. (1999). *An Intelligent Person's Guide to Dickens*. London: Duckworth.

Surridge, L. (1998). John Rokesmith's secret: sensation, detection, and the policing of the feminine in *Our Mutual Friend*. *Dickens Studies Annual*, 26, 265–84.

Waters, C. (1997). *Dickens and the Politics of the Family*. Cambridge: Cambridge University Press.

33

The Mystery of Edwin Drood

Simon J. James

The proposal Dickens put to Chapman and Hall on August 20, 1869 for a shorter novel is unique. The work to follow *Our Mutual Friend* was to be published either in "12 shilling monthly Nos." or perhaps in weekly installments in *All the Year Round* (*Letters* 12: 398). Critics have read Dickens's willingness to forgo the longer format differently. Perhaps interest in a shorter novel reflected awareness of his failing health; alternatively, the proposal suggested a shrewd assessment of market forces less favorable to long serials in 20 installments. No copy of the original contract exists, but it is known that the publishers were to be compensated in the event of Dickens dying before he completed the work. Further thought during the same month produced a list of prospective titles as Dickens went through the "preliminary agonies" of beginning a new fiction. By late October, he had written the first monthly number and replaced the original illustrator, Charles Collins, who withdrew on account of ill health. Progress continued during the following months against a background intensified by preparations for Dickens's farewell series of public readings planned for the following spring and by his own deteriorating health. The serial began publication in April 1870 and ran until September, six of the projected 12 parts of an incomplete fifteenth novel whose conclusion remains hinted at and yet for ever elusive. A one-volume edition, together with the illustrations by Marcus Stone accompanying each number, was also published on August 31, 1870.

If the truths asserted by literary criticism can only ever be provisional, anything written about an unfinished text can only be more provisional still. The meaning produced by any text is always to some degree "imaginary," unique and specific to the consciousness of each individual reader; this is still more the case for the meanings of a text that one knows its author did not live to complete. Peter Brooks has written eloquently of the reader's desire to anticipate looking back on the text from the point of view of having read it to the end, a kind of satisfaction exemplified by the detective story (Brooks 1984: 22–3). A whodunit without an ending, such as *The Mystery of Edwin Drood*, can never give this kind of satisfaction, but only provoke the desire to know what can never be known. Historically, then, readers of *The Mystery of Edwin Drood* have always been tempted to hypothesize what Dickens's ending might have been, whether from a postmodern concern with fissures, absences, and gaps in the text, or, more feasibly, an old-fashioned desire to imagine how the story might have turned out.

Only Dickens's first and last novels have their own epithet: Pickwickian, Droodian. This last novel almost produces its own subset of Dickens criticism: "Droodians" enthusiastically offer their identifications of the figure in the carpet whose identity Dickens's plotting would eventually unravel. As early as 1914, Montagu Saunders wrote of "the comparatively long list of those which have been written upon the subject of Dickens's unfinished story" (Saunders 1914: vii). The 1974 Penguin edition dryly notes that "the literature on *The Mystery of Edwin Drood* is extremely extensive, though much of it is of doubtful value" (Cox 1974: 31). One might be tempted to ask, like Gerhard Joseph (1996), "who cares who killed Edwin Drood?" Joseph boldly reads Dickens's last novel as if *Edwin Drood* were a completed work of art, since in reality there is no choice but do so.

Each reader or critic sees his or her own solution in *The Mystery of Edwin Drood*. To choose to read this novel is to presuppose one's own ability to spot the ending that Dickens might have written had he lived. To "finish" this text is not merely to read it all the way through, but to "complete" it. *Edwin Drood* will always produce additionally to its actual contents a ghostly hypothetical completion imagined by each reader: a novel such as this "gives the reader more collaborative responsibility" (Connor 1993: 86). By ending where it does, the novel no longer merely represents the mystery but becomes the mystery itself, the text as riddle. It is, of course, by no means certain that the "mystery" is the one that the reader might expect. If Jasper is signposted as obviously the murderer as many believe, the novel's "mystery" must lie in something else; the notes ask: "the loss of Edwyn Drood. Dead? Or alive?" (Paroissien 2002: 281).

Edwin Drood is thus a novel whose critical history has been dominated by something that does not exist: its ending. Attention "has been directed more toward the second than toward the first half, that is, more toward what Dickens did not write than what he did" (Mitchell 1996: 228). If, as W. H. Wills suspected, anxiety over plotting this novel itself hastened Dickens's demise (Cardwell 1972: xxvii), *Edwin Drood* presents an exemplary case of the "death of the author." The meaning is no longer contained by the authority of the writer's chosen destination for the plot, but is exploded, becomes plural, rather than unitary; this text in particular refuses to "assign a 'secret,' an ultimate meaning to the text" (Barthes 1977: 147). *Edwin Drood* is a fragment whose landscape is dominated by fragments: the churchyard, the crypt, even the inn (Frank 1999). The critical history of *Edwin Drood* has also turned to the archaeology of the fragments that surround it: as well as the six completed serial parts, letters and confidences to Forster, family recollections, instructions to illustrators. Perhaps the most important of these fragments is Forster's memorializing of the novel's origin and likely destination, which, if it is veracious, is likely be the closest to the novel's intended design:

His first fancy for the tale was expressed in a letter in the middle of July. "What should you think of the idea of a story beginning in this way? — Two people, boy and girl, or very young, going apart from one another, pledged to be married after many years — at

the end of the book. The interest to arise out of the tracing of their separate ways, and
the impossibility of telling what will be done with that impending fate." This was laid
aside; but it left a marked trace on the story as afterwards designed, in the position of
Edwin Drood and his betrothed.

I first heard of the later design in a letter dated "Friday the 6th of August 1869," in
which after speaking, with the usual unstinted praise he bestowed always on what moved
him in others, of a little tale he had received for his journal, he spoke of the change that
had occurred to him for the new tale by himself. "I laid aside the fancy I told you of,
and have a very curious and new idea for my new story. Not a communicable idea (or
the interest of the book would be gone), but a very strong one, though difficult to work."
The story, I learnt immediately afterward, was to be that of the murder of a nephew by
his uncle; the originality of which was to consist in the review of the murderer's career
by himself at the close, when its temptations were to be dwelt upon as if, not he the
culprit, but some other man, were the tempted. The last chapters were to be written in
the condemned cell, to which his wickedness, all elaborately elicited from him as if told
of another, had brought him. Discovery by the murderer of the utter needlessness of the
murder for its object, was to follow hard upon commission of the deed; but all discovery
of the murderer was to be baffled till towards the close, when, by means of a gold ring
which had resisted the corrosive effects of the lime into which he had thrown the body,
not only the person murdered was to be identified but the locality of the crime and the
man who committed it. So much was told to me before any of the book was written;
and it will be recollected that the ring, taken by Drood to be given to his betrothed
only if their engagement went on, was brought away with him from their last interview.
Rosa was to marry Tartar, and Crisparkle the sister of Landless, who was himself,
I think, to have perished in assisting Tartar finally to unmask and seize the murderer.
(Forster bk. 11, ch. 2)

Dombey and Son is often taken to signal the beginning of Dickens's "mature phase";
Monroe Engel speculates about what kind of writer Dickens might have become had
he lived to complete *Drood*, this novel both a "forced retreat" from the scale of previous novels, and an "advance" in its depiction of the mind (Engel 1959: 181). Whatever
Forster's reservations, or the "permanent exhaustion" diagnosed in *Our Mutual Friend*
by Henry James in 1865 (Collins 1971: 469–73), Dickens's later prose has lost little
of his vigor, but is distinctive for the energy as potential, rather than kinetic. "What
Henry James saw as Dickens's imaginative exhaustion is a reaching out for new modes
of characterization, an attempt, perhaps, to break with the conventions of his own
novels" (Frank 1984: 240).

As in *Little Dorrit*, the slow progress of the plot produces a greater intensity of
language, even "fine writing amounting to prose poetry" (Thacker 1990: 12). *Edwin
Drood* may possess a Wilkie Collins-ish atmosphere, but shows more of a resistance
to narrativity than a lurching toward melodramatic plotting. Frequently in the later
novels, narrative threatens to come to a standstill: Clennam and Pip await, more than
earn, the ends of their plots; repeated images in *Our Mutual Friend* show not economic
progress but the threat of time standing still. In *Edwin Drood*, Dickens's prose paradoxically exerts itself in expressing a failure of movement. Not only does this novel

fail to end, but it struggles to get started. The opium vision of the opening chapter even struggles to perceive objects, as if overweighed with proto-Conradian delayed decoding. Here the most visual and the most verbally profligate of novelists begins a novel within a haze of inaccurate words and unanswered questions:

> An ancient English Cathedral town? How can the ancient English Cathedral town be here! The well-known massive grey square tower of its old Cathedral? How can that be here! There is no spike of rusty iron in the air, between the eye and it, from any point of the real prospect. What is the spike that intervenes, and who has set it up? Maybe it is set up by the Sultan's orders for the impaling of a horde of Turkish robbers, one by one. It is so, for cymbals clash, and the Sultan goes by to his palace in long procession. Ten thousand scimitars flash in the sunlight, and thrice ten thousand dancing-girls strew flowers. Then, follow white elephants caparisoned in countless gorgeous colors, and infinite in number and attendants. Still the Cathedral tower rises in the background, where it cannot be, and still no writhing figure is on the grim spike. Stay! Is the spike so low a thing as the rusty spike on the top of a post of an old bedstead that has tumbled all awry? Some vague period of drowsy laughter must be devoted to the consideration of this possibility. (ch. 1)

Jasper is far from being the only character in a dysfunctional relationship to the present in which he lives: plot and characters both struggle alike to emerge from torpor. "All things in [Cloisterham] are of the past" (ch. 3) observes the narrator; Grewgious declares the view of the crypt to be "like looking down the throat of Old Time" (ch. 9); Edwin's watch even stops in chapter 14. The Victorian metanarrative of forward progress requires the imagining of an optimistic future, but the view is blocked by an image of the past.

> "Now say, what do you see?"
> "See, Rosa?"
> "Why, I thought you Egyptian boys could look into a hand and see all sorts of phantoms. Can't you see a happy Future?"
> For certain, neither of them sees a happy Present, as the gate opens and closes, and one goes in and the other goes away. (ch. 3)

The future of Edwin and Rosa seems to be blighted by the vampiric desires of their fathers; Crisparkle is still a boy to his mother (Morgentaler 2000: 193); even London, in Rosa's eyes, has the air "of waiting for something that never came" (ch. 21). Ruskin's accusation that Dickens was "a pure modernist – a leader of the steam-whistle party *par excellence*" (Collins 1971: 443) is somewhat unjust, but Dickens does dramatize in *Edwin Drood* the attritional effect of living in an environment that dwells overmuch in its own history. As with George Eliot's *Middlemarch*, which also began publication in 1870, history will ironize those who fail to foresee the consequences of the passing of time and the onrush of modernity, but both the attenuated pace and the unfinished condition of the narrative leave Cloisterham permanently stranded in the 1840s (on the dating of the novel, see Dubberke 1992; Paroissien 2002: 307–8). "To add to all of *Edwin Drood*'s distortions of time there is one other. Because it is unfinished *The Mystery of Edwin Drood* must exist forever within the frame of cyclical time. It permanently exists in the form of process rather than completion" (Morgentaler 2000: 197).

This condition of social paralysis seems to have the effect of blurring the edges of identity: since the unfinished self cannot move forward, it moves sideways, across its own boundaries. This is particularly the case for Jasper. The "cramped monotony" (ch. 2) of Jasper's existence produces a "scattered consciousness" (ch. 1). Unlike Crisparkle and Grewgious, Jasper does not fit comfortably within his niche in the cathedral town, and his moral being is overcome by an imagination that his environment is unable to satisfy (O'Mealy 1985). Robert Tracy sees Jasper as a frustrated artist whose imaginative urges have become directed toward creating the elaborate fiction of framing Neville for Drood's murder, Jasper's mental rehearsals of the deed itself the product of Dickens's repeated rehearsals of the murder of Nancy in his final course of public readings (Tracy 2006). Torn between the different roles he has to inhabit, Jasper seeks to escape the prison of his self in externalized states of being, such as music or a drugged trance:

> Impassive, moody, solitary, resolute, so concentrated on one idea, and on its attendant fixed purpose, that he would share it with no fellow-creature, he lived apart from human life. Constantly exercising an Art which brought him into mechanical harmony with others, and which could not have been pursued unless he and they had been in the nicest mechanical relations and unison, it is curious to consider that the spirit of the man was in moral accordance or interchange with nothing around him. (ch. 23)

A part of Jasper's self is uneasily invested not only in Rosa, but also in Edwin: Jasper's diary is oddly both a diary of himself and of his nephew; the narrator uses the curious phrase, "Jasper's self-absorption in his nephew" (ch. 20); Forster records above that Jasper's confession was to be made "as if told of another." If Jasper is indeed Edwin's murderer, he must be seeking a kind of mutual self-destruction. (Dickens continued to support murder remaining a capital crime: *Letters* 12: 176–7.)

It is not only Jasper who is self-divided. "As, in some cases of drunkenness, and in others of animal magnetism, there are two states of consciousness which never clash . . . so Miss Twinkleton has two distinct and separate phases of being" (ch. 3). Like Scrooge or Wemmick, she has become subordinated by the professional role she occupies; Durdles too has killed his inner man with drink and habit and is "a walking dead man" (Mitchell 1966: 232–3); Sapsea takes pleasure in being addressed as mayor in the third person, rather than by his name in the second; Neville claims to be "engaged in a miserable struggle with myself" (ch. 14). The presence of two twins in Cloisterham, of different gender but impossibly near-identical, unsettles the security of the self still further, the Landlesses appearing impossibly to constitute more than one self but not as many as two. The borders of their identities are also permeable: Helena has even passed as a man. In Dickens's notes for the novel, the Landlesses' "Mixture of Oriental blood" or eastern nature is marked as having been "imperceptibly acquired" (Paroissien 2002: 284). It is as if even inherited racial origins can be altered by experience, like Princess Puffer appearing to opium-smoke herself "into a strange likeness of the Chinaman" (ch. 1). Neville himself confesses: "I have been brought up among abject and servile dependents, of an inferior race, and I may easily have contracted some affinity with them. Sometimes, I don't know but that it may be a drop of what is tigerish in their blood" (ch. 7).

The Landlesses are not as easily assimilated by the body of Cloisterham society as the eastern commodities (tea, opium) with which Cloisterham is awash. Rather, the orientalized nature of their identities disturbs, like Jasper's erotic and evil dream of the East (O'Kane Mara 2002). As Patricia Plummer notes, whereas in previous novels problematic or irresolvable characters are shipped off to the colonies, in *Edwin Drood* such characters travel from the colonies to Britain (Plummer 1998: 275). Here they should function as an infusion, as it were, of new blood, but the racially ambiguous nature of the Landlesses' origins makes Cloisterham's backward community view Neville as a suspect when Edwin eventually disappears (Moore 2004: 60).

Not only does *The Mystery of Edwin Drood* have a slow beginning and no ending, but there is a vacuum at its middle as well. Pre-eminently among the book's characters, the eponymous hero cheerfully admits his own lack of distinguishing characteristics. The center of the novel is a non-entity:

> "I am afraid I am but a shallow, surface kind of fellow, Jack, and that my headpiece is none of the best. But I needn't say I am young; and perhaps I shall not grow worse as I grow older. At all events, I hope I have something impressible within me, which feels – deeply feels – the disinterestedness of your painfully laying your inner self bare, as a warning to me." (ch. 2)

True to type, Drood disappears and his body is never found. This absence is made unarguably permanent by the unfinished condition of the novel; he never reappears. He may, like John Harmon, be planning to disappear in order to find himself: after all, in no fewer than eight Dickens novels, somebody believed dead turns out to be alive (Karbacz and Raven 1994). Drood, however, can only be said to have been murdered, and skepticism about the words of another is frequently dramatized in this novel. Landless refuses to accept Drood's version of the truth, Rosa Jasper's; "I wish to ask of yourself, as a lady, whether I am to consider that my words is doubted?" (ch. 22) demands Mrs. Billickin of Miss Twinkleton. It is almost as if the novel's characters suspect each other of withholding secrets – which, of course, one of them is. The knowledge that there is an unrevealed secret only seems to drive the characters further into their nervous interiority, even the virtuous muscular Christian Crisparkle:

> This fairness troubled the Minor Canon much. He felt that he was not as open in his own dealing. He charged against himself reproachfully that he had suppressed, so far,

the two points of a second strong outbreak of temper against Edwin Drood on the part
of Neville, and of the passion of jealousy having, to his own certain knowledge, flamed
up in Neville's breast against him. He was convinced of Neville's innocence of any part
in the ugly disappearance, and yet so many little circumstances combined so wofully
against him, that he dreaded to add two more to their cumulative weight. He was among
the truest of men; but he had been balancing in his mind, much to its distress, whether
his volunteering to tell these two fragments of truth, at this time, would not be tanta-
mount to a piecing together of falsehood in the place of truth. (ch. 16)

Jasper, strangely or unknowingly if he is the murderer, writes in his diary, "I nev-
ermore will discuss this mystery with any human creature until I hold the clue to it
in my hand" (ch. 16). Literally, of course, he does hold that clue, in the shape of the
pen that he is using to write with, but the reader does not see him write his secret
down. The relationship of the novel's main characters to the act of committing themselves to paper varies according to their comfort with their own self: "Writing is that
neutral, composite, oblique space where our subject slips away, the negative where
all identity is lost, starting with the very identity of the body writing" (Barthes 1977:
142). Virtuous Crisparkle keeps a diary but writes, " a line for a day; nothing more";
Neville Landless, confident even to bumptiousness in the validity of his own self,
keeps all his papers; Drood, seeking to disappear, destroys his. John Jasper, who keeps
his opium in an ink bottle, and is tormented by the state of his own self-annulling
consciousness, keeps a diary but declares an unfulfilled intention to destroy it.

Narratives, and especially detective stories, suspend their resolution by the possession of secrets which are only gradually imparted to the reader. Since Dickens did not
commit the secret of *Edwin Drood*, the "incommunicable idea" of which he wrote to
Forster, to paper, any discussion of its end can only be gossip, any accusation only
calumny. Readers of Dickens can choose to doubt the novel's words, but those words
are all that remain of the ur-*Drood*. The ironies of *The Mystery of Edwin Drood* are
many: set in a cathedral town, but drained of spirituality (Morgentaler 2000: 186);
written by the novelist most closely associated with Christmas, but in which a murder
may take place on Christmas Day; a murder mystery with no solution; a novel (or a
fragment of a novel) about someone who apparently disappears and about people with
insubstantial consciousness, whose ending disappears as the novelist's own consciousness evanesces (Parker 1996: 187). Although Edwin Drood is mourned by the novel's
other characters, he is not much missed.

There is a sense of bereavement in finishing a good novel for the first time, knowing
that one will never read it for the first time again. This sense of loss of innocence is
stronger still when one finishes all the novels of a writer whom one loves, and Dickens's unfinished novel is the last Dickens book that many of his readers will read for
the first time. If *Edwin Drood* is ruined by its premature demise, this ruin becomes a
monument, one that readers of Dickens will be compelled to revisit as long as Dickens
is read. In more than one way, the loss of Edwin Drood is one that will always be
mourned.

References and Further Reading

Aylmer, Felix (1964). *The Drood Case*. London: Hart-Davis.

Barthes, Roland (1977). The death of the author. In *Image–Music–Text* (pp. 142–8). (Stephen Heath, Trans.). London: Fontana (original work published 1968).

Beer, John (1984). *Edwin Drood* and the mystery of apartness. *Dickens Studies Annual*, 13, 143–91.

Brooks, Peter (1984). *Reading for the Plot: Design and Intention and Narrative*. Cambridge, MA: Harvard University Press.

Cardwell, Margaret (Ed.) (1972). *The Mystery of Edwin Drood*. Oxford: Clarendon Press.

Collins, Philip (Ed.) (1971) *Dickens: The Critical Heritage*. London: Routledge.

Connor, Steven (1993). Dead? Or alive? Edwin Drood and the work of mourning. *The Dickensian*, 89, 85–102.

Cox, Arthur (Ed.) (1974). *The Mystery of Edwin Drood*. Harmondsworth: Penguin.

Dubberke, Ray (1992). The murder of Edwin Drood: dating *Edwin Drood*. *The Dickensian*, 88, 19–24.

Engel, Monroe (1959). *The Maturity of Dickens*. Cambridge, MA: Harvard University Press.

Frank, Lawrence (1984). *Charles Dickens and the Romantic Self*. Lincoln: University of Nebraska Press.

— (1999). News from the dead: archaeology and detection in *The Mystery of Edwin Drood*. *Dickens Studies Annual*, 28, 65–102.

Joseph, Gerhard (1996). Who cares who killed Edwin Drood?, or I'd rather be in Philadelphia: an essay on Dickens's unfinished novel. *Nineteenth-century Literature*, 51, 161–75.

Karbacz, Elsie and Raven, Robert (1994). The many mysteries of *Edwin Drood*. *The Dickensian*, 90, 5–18.

Mitchell, Charles (1966). *The Mystery of Edwin Drood*: the interior and exterior of self. *English Literary History*, 33, 228–46.

Moore, Grace (2004) *Dickens and Empire: Discourses of Class, Race and Colonialism in the Works of Charles Dickens*. Aldershot: Ashgate.

Morgentaler, Goldie (2000). *Dickens and Heredity: When Like Begets Like*. Houndsmill: Macmillan.

O'Kane Mara, Miriam (2002). Sucking the empire dry: colonial critique in *The Mystery of Edwin Drood*. *Dickens Studies Annual*, 32, 233–46.

O'Mealy, Joseph (1985). "Some stray sort of ambition": John Jasper's great expectations. *Dickens Quarterly*, 2, 129–36.

Parker, David (1996). Drood redux: mystery and the art of fiction. *Dickens Studies Annual*, 24, 185–95.

Paroissien, David (Ed.) (2002). *The Mystery of Edwin Drood*. London: Penguin.

Plummer, Patricia (1998). From Agnes Fleming to Helena Landless: Dickens, women and (post-) colonialism. In Anny Sadrin (Ed.), *Dickens, Europe and the New Worlds* (pp. 267–80). Basingstoke: Macmillan.

Saunders, Montagu (1914). *The Mystery in the Drood Family*. Cambridge: Cambridge University Press.

Thacker, John (1990). *Edwin Drood: Antichrist in the Cathedral*. London: Vision.

Tracy, Robert (2006). Jasper's plot: inventing *The Mystery of Edwin Drood*. *Dickens Quarterly*, 23, 29–35.

Wales, Kathleen (1984). Dickens and interior monologue: the opening of *Edwin Drood* reconsidered. *Language and Style*, 17, 234–50.

Part V
Reputation and Influence

34
Dickens and the Literary Culture of the Period

Michael Hollington

Dickens was the first on the scene of a remarkable group of writers who, appearing in the early and middle years of the long reign of Queen Victoria, established the novel as the dominant literary genre, a position it has held in Britain and elsewhere ever since. "Novels are in the hands of all of us, from the Prime Minister down to the last-appointed scullery maid," wrote Anthony Trollope in 1870, the year Dickens died (David 2001: 1); and, indeed, by then, a second and even a third generation of major talents had emerged. It is thus perhaps useful to begin this survey of some of the views held of him by Dickens's contemporaries by remembering – whatever else they may have thought of him – that there was widespread acknowledgment of the major role of his own personal dedication to writers and to writing in bringing about this triumph of the novel. Here is Trollope again, testifying to Dickens's practical involvement in the promotion of the art of fiction: "He was always enthusiastic in its interests, ready to push on beginners, quick to encourage contemporaries, and greatly generous to all those who were failing." And here is the global assessment of another great novelist with decidedly ambivalent views of Dickens's artistic achievement, Henry James, looking back on the literary landscape after Victoria's death and writing simply that "no other debt in our time has been piled so high" (Hollington 1995: 451, 637).

"Ambivalent," indeed, will be the watchword of this account. Like many tall poppies, Dickens frequently provoked backbiting and envy from his commentators in the same breath as they expressed admiration and delight. It would be easy, in a more general study, to uncover a spectrum of reaction from contemporary observers and fellow writers, ranging all the way from enthusiastic approval, and even idolatry, to manifold varieties of critical caviling and even contempt. But there can be no question that at all times he was consciously and unconsciously set apart from the general herd in the minds of those who undertook to assess him. There is an amusing, symptomatic story of 1852 to illustrate his special standing, told by the war correspondent

William Howard Russell about a shooting party in Watford to which Dickens had been invited. He had to cancel at the last moment, and asked Thackeray to bear a letter of apology for him. Upon reading the note, the hostess promptly exclaimed: "Martin, don't roast the ortolans; Mr. Dickens isn't coming." Thackeray was, of course, amused and joked ruefully that, despite his own not insignificant fame, which for a time, with *Vanity Fair* above all, rivaled that of Dickens, there would be "no ortolans for Pendennis!" (Ray 1945–6: 3. 455n).

But, to repeat, Dickens had the advantage of emerging first. Perhaps the widespread perception of the particular time in which he emerged, the 1830s, in what was felt by many contemporaries to be a relatively fallow period in English literature, helped his cause. Looking through the lens of an organicist episteme which detected cyclical rising and falling patterns in history, many Victorians discerned "a season of lull," as Margaret Oliphant wrote in 1892, "such as must naturally come after the exhausting brilliance of the days just gone by," by which she meant the era of the great Romantic poets, which for many came to an end with the death of Byron in 1824 (Poston 1999: 5). Yet, nowadays, the 1830s are often seen in a more positive light, as a season of budding and stirring rather than a lull, a period of fruitful hybrid experimentation and transition toward new forms and subject matter, with Dickens of course as the major exemplar. And, indeed, this is precisely how many contemporary critics reacted at the time of the appearance of his first works: they saw in him something exciting and new. And for many that sense of excitement never rubbed off.

Thus, we must first explore the various kinds of exciting newness that contemporaries found in Dickens as they sought to account for the phenomenal success, first of *The Pickwick Papers*, which began most notably in 1837 with the eruption of Sam Weller's "low" humor in the fourth number of its publication as a serial, and later of *Oliver Twist*. George Ford provides statistics to show just how unprecedented the phenomenon was – that is to say, that whereas Sir Walter Scott (previously the most commercially successful novelist in the English language) had achieved sales that peaked at 13,000, Dickens quickly reached and sustained a level of 40,000 copies a month (Ford 1965: 6).

The most thoughtful early attempt to explain such immense appeal, perhaps, is Richard Ford's 1839 review of *Oliver Twist*. In this survey, he describes Dickens as an essentially urban writer, whose strength is that he manages to step across the threshold of class barriers to bring into the light of day some of the shadowy recesses of the great cities of nineteenth-century Britain, experiencing explosive growth and transformation as a result of the industrial revolution and the coming of the railways. "Life in London, as revealed in the pages of Boz," he writes, in phrasing that carries obvious resonance for Disraeli's later analysis of Britain's two nations, opens "a new world to thousands bred and born in the same city, whose palaces overshadow their cellars – for one half of mankind lives without knowing how the other half dies; in fact the regions about Saffron Hill are less known to our great world than the Oxford Tracts, the inhabitants are still less" (Hollington 1995: 271).

Part of what Richard Ford identifies here is how Dickens, in his early and indeed later fiction, decisively revitalizes Gothic fiction by reorienting its search for sensation and terror, seeking these not in distant places and times but in the here and now of contemporary cities. This appears as a quite conscious program in a number of passages in early Dickens. In "Criminal Courts" in *Sketches by Boz*, for instance, he comments ironically on the superiority of the Gothic terrors unveiled by Elizabeth Fry, the Quaker prison visitor and reformer, over those contained in the pages of *The Mysteries of Udolpho*: "We have great respect for Mrs. Fry, but she certainly ought to have written more romances than Mrs. Radcliffe" (*Journalism* 1: 195). But Ford goes beyond writing about the discovery of new subject matter and the transformation of a genre to talk also about the discovery of new territories of language. In an amusing oxymoronic phrase that highlights hybridity and the juxtaposition of disparate words in Dickens's writing, Richard Ford dubs him the "regius professor of slang," tapping the immense linguistic resources of urban speech to be found in "the mother-wit, the low humour of the lower classes, their Sanscrit, their hitherto unknown tongue, which, in the present phasis of society and politics, seems likely to become the idiom of England" (Hollington 1995: 272).

Other observant contemporary readers perceived other relative novelties which were also to become commonplaces of Dickens criticism in his lifetime. Mary Russell Mitford, for example, bearing witness to the first wave of *Pickwick* excitement in a frequently quoted passage from a letter of June 1837 expressing astonishment that her correspondent had not heard of Dickens, both anticipates Ford's observations about the new novel's capacity to mediate between the social classes – "Sir Benjamin Brodie takes it to read in his carriage, between patient and patient; and Lord Denman studies *Pickwick* on the bench while the jury are deliberating" – and adds emphases of her own. She is one of the first to observe the powerful moral charge in Dickens's writing, which for her goes beyond the superficial level of avoiding indelicacy – "London life – but without anything unpleasant: a lady might read it all *aloud*" – to reach deeper levels of seriousness. She searches for comparable great critical moralists of the past to convey her amazement that anyone could be so blind to what is newly afoot in the literary world: "It seems like not having heard of Hogarth, whom he resembles greatly, except that he takes a far more cheerful, a Shakespearean view of humanity" (Hollington 1995: 266).

The Hogarth comparison reverberates throughout Dickens's lifetime – in R. H. Horne's *A New Spirit of the Age* of 1844, for instance (Hollington 1995: 94), as well as in Forster's biography (bk. 6, ch. 3). It reflects, among other things, an awareness of Dickens's role in ushering in the new tone of "high seriousness" in Victorian writing. In the 1830s, he was responding to Thomas Carlyle's slogan in *Sartor Resartus* (1834), "Close your Byron and open your Goethe," a call to abandon, on the one hand, Byron's cynicism and levity and, on the other, his Romantic idealism, in favor of urgent address to the economic and social issues of the day. Carlyle was the dominant philosopher of the early Victorian period, and the most important thinker to study in relation to Dickens. As observers like Ford and Mitford noted, however, he followed

Carlyle in an idiosyncratic way, without discarding either the humorous and satiric vein of the interregnum period or the visionary power of the Romantic poetic imagination.

Despite his perceived seriousness as a moralist, Dickens's popular success was enough to damn him in some of the more high-minded reaches of novel criticism in Victorian England, for there were plenty there who thought that success meant pandering to the vulgar tastes of the masses. Still more thought that, whatever its ephemeral merits, his popularity would quickly fade. In a famous phrase, Abraham Hayward wrote condescendingly in 1837 that "Mr. Dickens writes too often and too fast, on the principle, we presume of making hay while the sun shines . . . if he persists much longer in this course, it requires no gift of prophecy to foretell his fate – he has risen like a rocket, and he will come down like the stick" (Ford 1965: 43). The phrase stuck because, as so often with tall poppies, there were many who waited rather longingly for Dickens to droop, and reported frequent sightings of the supposed downward curve, as in the amusing parodic requiem published by Albert Smith at the time of *Dombey and Son*, in which a chorus of booksellers sings:

> Thou art gone from our counter
> Thou art lost to our pocket,
> Thou has fallen, brief mounter,
> Like a stick from a rocket.
> (Ford 1965: 52)

And it was indeed at the time of *Dombey and Son*, published in monthly parts from October 1846 to April 1848, that the first serious challenges to Dickens's pre-eminence among novelists emerged, with the publication in 1847 of *Jane Eyre*, *Wuthering Heights*, and *Vanity Fair*. Thackeray's novel, in particular, running as a serial almost concurrently (between January 1847 and July 1848) offered stick-watchers an opportunity to proclaim that the Dickensian rocket had at last fallen. "[B]eats Dickens out of the world," was Jane Carlyle's cosmological verdict, and George Henry Lewes, with what, we shall see, is an obvious side glance at Dickens, declared that Thackeray stood out "in a literary age which has a tendency to mistake spasm for source." John Lockhart, likewise, thought *Jane Eyre* "Worth . . . fifty Dickenses and Bulwers." The original rocketeer, Abraham Hayward, wrote Thackeray a letter of congratulation, proclaiming: "You have completely beaten Dickens out of the inner circle already." Somewhat later, writing in 1855 on a visit to England, Nathaniel Hawthorne noted such preferences, ascribing them to the fact that Thackeray's success had come far less easily than Dickens's and so might arouse far less jealousy: "Dickens evidently is not liked nor thought well of by his literary brethren – at least, the most eminent of them, whose reputation might interfere with his. Thackeray is much more to their taste. Perhaps it is for his moral benefit to have succeeded late" (Ford 1965: 111, 119, 120). Whatever the motives that guide them, these off-the-cuff reactions have the merit of developing an important debate in the mid-century about the relative merits of Dickens and Thackeray – the Dickery-Thackins controversy, as it was dubbed (Ford 1965: 122) – that was to culminate in one of the finest contemporary assessments of both, by David Masson.

Some aspects of the comparison had to do with questions of class. From the start, there was a significant strain of opinion that held Dickens, however talented, to be a vulgar upstart. In the early Victorian period, the very profession of writer was fraught with class implications. Douglas Jerrold recalled, for instance, that in the 1830s the English aristocracy "still considered the writer as a clever kind of vagabond" (Ray 1958: 154). The fact that Dickens came to the novel through journalism made him even more suspect. To quote Ray again, fiction was in the 1830s "by and large still a precarious trade which drew its rank and file from the forlorn hacks who haunted the taverns of literary Bohemia" (Ray 1955: 195). So it is not surprising that these issues came to the fore again in many mid-century assessments of the relative merits of Dickens and Thackeray, who after the publication of *Vanity Fair* in 1847, knew that he was being tipped to outshine his eminent contemporary ("I am become a sort of great man in my way – all but at the top of the tree: indeed there if the truth were known and having a great fight up there with Dickens" (Ray 1955: 427). Many readers felt that what mattered most was that, in George Ford's words, "Thackeray wrote with the easy grace of a gentleman and Dickens with the 'factitious ornament' and 'constant straining for effect' of a journalist" (Ford 1965: 115, quoting from *The Times*, December 22, 1852).

That contrast – between the gentlemanly good taste of Thackeray and the lower-middle-class vulgarity of Dickens – had its purely personal, biographical dimensions. It was felt, for instance, by Thackeray, in the course of the regular social contact with each other, in Dickens's very appearance and manners: "how splendid Mrs. Dickens was in pink satin and Mr. Dickens in geraniums and ringlets," he writes sarcastically in a letter of 1843 about a ball they both attended (Ray 1955: 286). But it has a much more significant literary dimension. Rather more Victorians than we might suspect – conservatives, at any rate – felt uncomfortable with the impassioned moral tone of Dickens's writing, and in particular the relentlessness of his indictments of a wide range of contemporary institutions: the church, the law, parliament. For them, it was the importance of not being too earnest that mattered. Thackeray was one of the leaders of this current of opinion in his opposition to the powerful moral emphasis of Dickens's work. Dickens might be a greater moralist than himself, he declared, but "anyone can be a moralist":

> If we want instruction we prefer to take it from fact rather than from fiction . . . when suddenly . . . a comic moralist rushes forward, and takes occasion to tell us that society is diseased, the laws unjust, the rich ruthless, the poor martyrs, the world lop sided and *vice versa*, persons who wish to lead an easy life are inclined to remonstrate against this literary ambuscadoe. (Ray 1955: 327)

And although the tone here is relatively light-hearted, its influence can clearly be discerned in later, fiercer views along the same lines, such as those expressed by another contemporary, Walter Bagehot, who saw Dickens developing into an extreme radical stirring revolutionary impulses:

> He began by describing really removable evils in a style which would induce all persons, however insensible, to remove them if they could: he has ended by describing the natural evils and inevitable pains of the present state of being in such a manner as must tend to excite discontent and repining . . . Mr. Dickens has not infrequently spoken . . . in what really is . . . a tone of objection to the necessary constitution of human society. (Ray 1955: 15)

However, of all the numerous rivals in Dickens's time, Thackeray was probably the most generous in accepting and praising Dickens's superior natural gifts as a writer. Reviewing *A Christmas Carol*, he described it as "the work of the master of all English humourists now alive"; and at the very moment that *Vanity Fair* was beginning to make its impact, in February 1847, he confronted Mark Lemon with the latest number of *Dombey and Son*, exclaiming: "There! read that. There is no writing against such power as this – no one has a chance. Read the description of young Paul's death; it is unsurpassed – it is stupendous" (Ray 1955: 427). In 1840, he had already despaired of competing with him: "What is the use of my trying to run before that man, or by his side? I can't touch him"; in 1854, reacting to a review that placed Bulwer Lytton as a superior writer to himself and Dickens, he declares Dickens "the greatest *genius* of the three"; and in the 1860s he sees himself as "played out . . . but if he live to be ninety Dickens will still be creating new characters. In his art that man is marvelous" (Ford 1965: 119, 120). Elsewhere in a letter to David Masson of May 1851, he eulogizes Dickens's "divine genius," and declares his own incapacity to write in a Dickensian manner: "I should never think of trying to imitate him, only hold my tongue and admire him" (Ray 1945–6: 2. 772).

Yet in the same letter he also puts forward the negative side of his ambivalent feelings about Dickens's work, which are of interest here because of their representativeness. They show the emergence of a Victorian consensus in favor of realism as the dominant aesthetic for the novel, which was to last for the rest of the nineteenth century, and, at the *fin de siècle*, to contribute to the sharpest dip in reputation that Dickens's work has ever experienced. Thackeray writes thus to qualify his enthusiasm for the "delightful and admirable" notes in Dickens's song: "I quarrel with his Art in many respects: which I don't think represents Nature duly; for instance Micawber appears to me an exaggeration of a man; as his name is of a name. It is delightful and makes me laugh: but it is no more real than my friend Punch is" (Ray 1945–6: 2. 772). The key word here is "exaggeration," seen from the perspective of realist verisimilitude, and it echoes throughout innumerable contemporary discussions of his work, including some from critics otherwise thoroughly supportive of his art and moral criticism of Victorian society. Ruskin is an important example; where others failed to be impressed by *Hard Times*, for instance, he responded in *Unto this Last* of

1860 to the "essential value and truth" that it displays, in common with Dickens's other novels: "He is entirely right in his main drift and purpose in every book he has written." And yet here and elsewhere, Ruskin wishes "that he could think it right to limit his brilliant exaggeration to works written only for public amusement" (Hollington 1995: 379), and laments the "delight in grotesque and rich exaggeration . . . [which] . . . has made him, I think, nearly useless in the present day" (Ford 1965: 94).

Interestingly, too, Ruskin links this critique with reaction against Dickensian "theatricality." Hosts of contemporary critics point out how the writer who, early in his career, edited *Bentley's Miscellany* as its "Stage Manager," and narrated *Pickwick Papers* as "Mr. Pickwick's stage manager" (*Oxford Dickens* 374, 500) inextricably mingled in his work the art of the novel with the art of drama or, more especially, melodrama. Dickens himself acknowledged this facet of his work in a speech of March 29, 1858, in which he put forward the proposition that "every writer of fiction, though he may not adopt the dramatic form, writes in effect for the stage" (*Speeches* 262). This speech was in fact given in the presence of Thackeray as chairman, and contains numerous compliments to the "skilful showman" who had mounted the "airy booths of *Vanity Fair*." But, for Ruskin, we risk missing the power and penetration of Dickens's novels because of their habit of theatrical exaggeration, and the critic feels obliged to urge us not to "lose the use of Dickens's wit and insight, because he chooses to speak in a circle of stage fire." And really there is a large measure of agreement from Thackeray when he insists on a different kind of drama for the novel than that favored in Dickens's writing. It is the "drawing-room drama" of realism and naturalism that he prefers, in which "a coat is a coat and a poker a poker . . . not an embroidered tunic, nor a great red-hot instrument like the Pantomime weapon" (Ray 1945–6: 2. 773).

David Masson – to whose important article *"Pendennis* and *Copperfield"* (1851, later reworked in 1859 as a chapter of *British Novelists and their Styles*) Thackeray's letter is an appreciative reply – was a Scot who became Professor of English Literature at the University of London in 1853 and later at Edinburgh University. He is distinguished from most of his contemporaries by his ability to see the Thackeray/Dickens comparison from both sides, and to see the two writers as powerful exemplars of different modes of realism. In this, he foreshadows some major critical accents and discriminations of today: the now widely accepted contrasts between the idea of "classic realism," as in George Eliot or Tolstoy (as described by Colin MacCabe in his *James Joyce and the Revolution of the Word*, 2003), and the "romantic realism" of Balzac, Gogol, Dickens, and Dostoevsky (as defined by Donald Fanger in his influential book *Dostoevsky and Romantic Realism*, 1967). To think in such terms has, at the very least, the merit of short-circuiting the various dialogues of the deaf between protagonists who use the word "realism" in quite different senses, as in Dickens's own time – where George Henry Lewes, as we shall see, might accuse Dickens of not being a realist in a scientific sense, and Dickens would defend himself as a realist in quite another sense – and even beyond, into our own time.

Masson's related yet contrasting terms are "real" and "ideal." Thackeray for him is the "real realist": "he belongs to what, in painting, would be called the school of low art. All that he portrays – scenes as well as characters – is within the limits, and rigidly true to the features, of real existence." Dickens by contrast "works more in the ideal." Then, at this point in his argument, Masson takes the decisive turn of dismissing questions of whether Dickens's characters are life-like; in any "accurate sense," he insists, the answer must be "no." This applies not only to his "serious or tragic creations," who are for Masson "persons of romance"; it is also true of his "satiric portraitures." "There never was a real Mr. Pickwick, a real Sam Weller, a real Mrs. Nickleby," he asserts, and the "reality" they have as characters on the page is only that of "transcendental renderings of certain hints furnished by nature." Equally decisively, Masson refuses to accept "classic realism" as the gold standard of novelistic excellence. Indeed, he puts Dickens in the most exalted company, with Shakespeare for instance, whose creations are "grand hyperbolic beings," and quotes in support of his high estimate of such workers in "the sublime," Goethe's aesthetic dictum: "Art is called Art . . . precisely because it is *not* Nature" (quoted in Ford 1965: 116–17). And so, despite certain limitations that prevent him from wholly transcending his era (such as the sexist mapping of the binaries "masculine" and "feminine" onto the categories "real" and "ideal" so that Thackeray is a masculine writer, Dickens a feminine one), Masson looks forward to modernist criteria for the revaluation of Dickens that took place in the early twentieth century, by T. S. Eliot or Mansfield or Joyce.

Turning to Anthony Trollope's assessment of Dickens, we find even stronger adherence to realist criteria, and rather less ambivalence of attitude than is to be found in any of the colleagues and contemporaries surveyed here. Yet their personal relations, if never intimate, were certainly friendly, ran a smooth course, unlike those between Dickens and Thackeray – this, despite Trollope's awareness of Dickens's relationship with Ellen Ternan, whose sister Fanny was married to Trollope's brother – and grew toward a relative pitch of cordiality in the last years of Dickens's life.

One meeting place that became more frequent as Trollope rose to prominence and fame was the shared platform of public dinners. Speechmaking, as one might expect with such a histrionic writer, oriented toward oral performance, was a specialty that Dickens raised to a kind of minor art form, and Trollope's obituary essay records his thorough appreciation of the elder novelist's genius in this sphere: "He spoke so well, that a public dinner became a blessing instead of a curse, if he was in the chair" (Hollington 1995: 452). At the farewell dinner prior to Dickens's departure to America in November 1867, Trollope also praised Dickens as one of those who has "taught purity of life, nobility of action, and self denial," and who has "taught these lessons with allurements to both the old and the young which no other teacher of the present day can reach, and which no prophet can teach" (*Speeches* 374).

Yet these public pronouncements can be seen as primarily of the surface – Trollope, in fact, displaying a degree of reluctance even to attend this occasion: "I am not specially in that set, but having been asked I did not like to refuse," he wrote (Glendinning 2002: 367). Even in the public speeches themselves it can be felt that

Trollope measures his praise, and implies limitations, as in the case of his speech at the banquet in Dickens's honor in Liverpool of April 10, 1869, marking out the sphere in which he believes Dickens to excel: "In the ranks of light literature he is *facile princeps*" (*Speeches* 390). Though the term was widely used at that time in connection with the novel – for example, by Masson – the fact that Trollope felt obliged to go on to defend "light literature" seems to indicate his reservations. At any rate, the gloves are well and truly off in a letter to George Eliot and George Henry Lewes of 1872, expressing negative reaction to Forster's biography, describing Dickens as "no hero . . . very ignorant and thick-skinned . . . not a hero at all" (Glendinning 2002: 405).

Dickens's "ignorance" is in fact a constant theme of Trollope's essentially rather acid view of his work. The famous lampoon of "Mr. Popular Sentiment" included in chapter 15 of *The Warden* in 1855 strikes this note. Unlike earlier commentators such as R. H. Horne, Trollope contrasts Dickens's methods with those of Hogarth and the eighteenth-century satirists, who "set about their heavy task with grave decorum and laborious argument." He follows Thackeray's misgivings about morality and social criticism as these are dispensed in serial novels – "ridicule is found more convincing than argument, imaginary agonies touch more than true sorrows, and monthly novels convince, when learned quartos fail to do so" – and echoes both Thackeray and Ruskin in complaining once more about "exaggeration" ("his heroes and heroines walk upon stilts") and parodying Dickens's red-hot poker style in a physiognomic description of one of his putative villains, "who looked cruelly out of a hot, passionate, bloodshot eye . . . [and] . . . had a huge red nose with a carbuncle, thick lips, and a great double, flabby chin, which swelled out into solid substance, like a turkey cock's comb, when sudden anger inspired him." Such ambivalence as there is seems to reside in a rueful recognition that, despite the crudity of his methods, Dickens's formulae actually work, both in attracting custom and in effecting reform:

> The artist who paints for the million must use glaring colours, as no one knew better than Mr. Sentiment when he described the inhabitants of his alms-house; and the radical reform which has now swept over such establishments has owed more to the twenty numbers of Mr. Sentiment's novels than to all the true complaints which have escaped from the public for the last half century. (Hollington 1995: 159–60)

As George Ford remarks, "it is always amusing to watch the struggle between his own distaste and his sturdy respect for the public taste which idolized Dickens" (1965: 106).

Although both writers tended to envy, and desired to emulate Dickens's success as a writer, pecuniary and otherwise, Anthony Trollope's relation to Dickens has in other respects little in common with that of Wilkie Collins, and pales into insignificance beside it. Of all the major Victorian novelists, it is Collins whose career clearly owes most to Dickens. In view of the many letters of praise and encouragement that the latter sent to Collins, it is possible to concur with Eliza Lynn Linton's characterization of the relationship between the two as that of a "literary Mentor to a younger Telemachus" (see *Oxford Dickens* 110). Dickens's letter of September 1862, recording warm enthusiasm for Collins's *No Name*, is a representative example:

> I was certain from the Basil days that you were the Writer who would come ahead of all the Field – being the only one who combined invention and power, both humorous and pathetic, with that invincible determination to work, and that profound conviction that nothing of worth is to be done without work, of which foreigners and triflers can have no conception. (*Letters* 10: 128)

Collins, by no means an effusive sentimentalist, was clearly touched on this occasion, writing to his mother that "if I was the vainest man alive, I could not have written of the book or thought of the book, what he has written and thought of it" (*Letters* 10: 128n).

Be that as it may, it is impossible here to study such a rich, complex, and essentially two-sided relationship – for, indeed, after the success of *The Woman in White*, Collins was as much a rival of Dickens as Thackeray had been with *Vanity Fair*, and, according to Percy Fitzgerald, "came at last to think himself a very great writer, almost on a level with his chief" (Davis 1956: 265) – of which there is still perhaps no authoritative account. Critics have tended to veer from seeing one protagonist or another in the relationship as wholly benign to seeing him as wholly malign, and vice versa. We have, for example, on the one side, early commentators like J. W. T. Ley, who (following Forster's hostility toward the man who more or less supplanted him as Dickens's closest friend in his latter years) regarded Collins's influence on Dickens's later writing as tending toward "a prostitution of his genius" and threatening to turn him into "little more than a story-manufacturer" (Nayder 2002: 199), and, on the other, Lillian Nayder's *Unequal Partners*, which, invaluable for its scholarship as it is, tends to depict Dickens as a bigoted tyrant stifling the expression of Collins's more enlightened genius. The truth surely lies somewhere in between, but what is aimed at here – to show once more the ambivalence of Collins's views of Dickens, though with an emphasis on how perceptive and interesting a critic he can be – merely gestures in its direction.

It may be desirable in the interests of balance to pass rather lightly over Collins's various negative assessments of Dickens's works, as these are to be found in Robinson's biography – his criticism of the "helplessly bad construction" of *Oliver Twist*, for instance, or his assertion that "the latter half of *Dombey* no intelligent person can have read without astonishment at the badness of it," or his description of *Edwin Drood* as "Dickens's last laboured effort, the melancholy work of a worn out brain" (Robinson 1952: 258–9) – except, perhaps, to point out that these, unlike those of many Victorians, have always to do with questions of their literary merit and/or artistic skill, and never to do with questions of class, morality, or philosophical truth. There is surely at least as much interest to be found in his positive commentary on Dickens, and general statements of aesthetic principle. We shall here single out three of many: his views on the relation of fiction and drama, his views on the aesthetics of realism, and his views on Dickens's treatment of sexuality.

Concerning the first of these, there is near identity between Dickens's view, quoted above, that "every writer of fiction, though he may not adopt the dramatic form, writes in effect for the stage," and Collins's, in the Preface to *Basil* of 1852, where he states his belief that "the Novel and the Play are twin-sisters in the family of Fiction: that the one is a drama narrated, as the other is a drama acted" (Davis 1956: 121). Interestingly, however, these words were written not long after Collins's invaluable testimony to Dickens at work on the writing of *Bleak House* in Dover in September of that year: "You will have a glorious number of 'Bleak House,'" he wrote to his mother on September 9, referring to number 8 and chapters 23 and 24 in particular, "Dickens read us the two first chapters as soon as he had finished them speaking the dialogue of each character, as dramatically as if he was acting his own personages; and making his audience laugh and cry with equal fervour and equal sincerity" (*Letters* 6: 761n). It is difficult to believe that this first-hand experience was not also a major spur to his views on the close affinities of fiction and drama.

The same Preface goes on to elaborate what might be called the rudiments of a theory of "romantic realism," and here again, Collins's thinking appears closers to Dickens's than that of many contemporaries, including George Henry Lewes's, shortly to be discussed. The key statements are the following: "I have not thought it either polite or necessary, while adhering to realities, to adhere to common-place, everyday realities. In other words, I have not stooped so low as to assure myself of the reader's belief in the probability of my story, by never once calling on him for the exercise of his faith" (Davis 1956: 121). There is interesting ironic play with the religious connotations of the word "belief" here, with Coleridge's "suspension of disbelief" perhaps hovering somewhere in the background, and it is perhaps amusing, in the light of what many contemporaries thought of Dickens's own way with the "probabilities," in such matters as "spontaneous combustion," to find that Dickens himself, despite his admiration for *Basil*, thought that the novel went a little too far in the romantic realist direction: "I think the probabilities," he writes, "here and there require a little more respect" (*Letters* 6: 823). But an aesthetic that maintains that "those extraordinary accidents and events which happen to few men, seem to me to be as legitimate materials for fiction to work with, when there was a good object in using them, as the ordinary accidents and events which may, and do, happen to us all" (Davis 1956: 121) clearly has a good deal in common with Dickensian fictional practice.

Lastly, it is perhaps useful, in an era like our own, discovering, with some excess as well as success, that Dickens has a lot to say, through oblique representation, about sexual relationships, to remember a little known passage in Collins's writings that makes clear that at least one contemporary thoroughly realized and appreciated this. This occurs amongst the marginal comments in Collins's copy of Forster's biography of Dickens, and it records reaction to Forster's view that the purity and innocence of almost every page by Dickens is such that it can be safely given to a child to read. Collins fumes at this: "If this wretched English claptrap means anything it means that the novelist is forbidden to touch on sexual relations which literally swarm about him, and influence the lives of millions of his fellow creatures," and vigorously defends Dickens against the "charge": "if it is true, which it is not, it would imply the condemnation of Dickens's books as works of art, it would declare him to be guilty of deliberately presenting to his readers a false reflection of human life" (Robinson 1952: 259). Thus, for Collins, Dickens is again a realist in the domain of sexual behavior, though not in anything like the same way as later naturalist writers.

Turning finally to Dickens's relationships with George Eliot and George Henry Lewes, our attention is inevitably drawn to the latter's famous criticisms of Dickens in his article of 1872 in the *Fortnightly Review*, doubtless representative of the views of both partners. With the benefit of hindsight, it clearly stands as a major document in the history of the decline of Dickens's reputation in the years following his death, yet to see it only in a retrospective arrangement runs the risk of obscuring its deep ambivalence, and of radically simplifying the couple's attitudes toward Dickens. A first corrective of focus is provided if we go back to December 1837, when Lewes reviewed Dickens's early work in the *National Magazine*, and gave it fulsome praise: "no one has ever combined the nicety of observation, the fineness of tact, the exquisite humour, the wit, the heartiness, sympathy with all things good and beautiful in human nature, the perception of character, and accuracy of description, with the same force that he has done" (Ashton 2000: 24–5). And lest we are tempted simply to conclude that Lewes, like Trollope, condescendingly responded to Dickens as a master of "light literature," we must give full weight to his description in the same piece on *Oliver Twist* as "a work pregnant with philosophy and feeling, such as a metaphysician would be proud to have developed" (Hollington 1995: 249).

In fact, Lewes's 1872 essay is thoroughly conscious of ambivalence in his own attitudes, and indeed of a general climate of ambivalence in Victorian England concerning Dickens's achievement – that is to say, the paradoxical way in which so many of his contemporaries loved to hate him: "it is not long since I heard a very distinguished man express measureless contempt for Dickens, and a few minutes afterwards, in reply to some representation on the other side, admit that Dickens 'had entered into his life.'" He is writing not only to deliver pungent criticism, but equally to ensure proper recognition of a writer "whose genius was so little *appreciated* by the critics." Thus he berates those who, like Trollope, merely "admitted, because it was indisputable, that Dickens delights thousands . . . that he stirred the sympathy of the masses not easily reached through Literature, and always stirred healthy, generous emotions," and goes beyond Thackeray in placing Dickens, not as someone writing in the shadow of the great eighteenth-century humorists, but – because of his "overflowing fun" – at the very apex of the English comic tradition, "so great that Fielding and Smollett are small in comparison" (Hollington 1995: 456–7).

Similar emphases might be appropriate in the case of George Eliot. Though she too wrote trenchant criticism of Dickens in her 1856 essay, "The Natural History of German Life," her views of him, considered as a whole, are again more rounded. We must certainly take into account here her reaction to the letter of January 18, 1858 in which Dickens gives warm praise to *Scenes of Clerical Life*, following this up later with further encouragement and a firm invitation in 1859 to write for *All the Year Round* (*Letters* 8: 508; 9: 92–3) – another instance of his ability to spot rising novelistic talents and of his eagerness to promote them. Eliot writes, in a more heartfelt manner than Wilkie Collins perhaps, of being "deeply moved by the finely-felt and finely-expressed sympathy of the letter," and adds, "there can hardly be any climax of approbation for me after this." This last phrase in particular suggests that she, too, whatever reservations she may otherwise have had, acknowledged Dickens as the dominant literary figure of the age.

And, in fact, in her essay of 1856, George Eliot describes Dickens as a "great novelist." His gifts, in her view, however, are limited by the strong emphasis she places on the word "external." "We have one great novelist who is gifted with the utmost power of rendering the *external* traits of our town population," she writes (emphasis added), and subsequently regrets that he cannot probe more deeply into interior lives: "if he could give us their psychological character – their conceptions of life, and their emotions – with the same truth as their idioms and manners, his books would be the greatest contribution Art has ever made to the awakening of social sympathies." This binary internal/external later expands into "the humorous and external" versus "the emotional and tragic," with again a sharp contrast between the one and the other: he is "transcendent . . . in artistic truthfulness" in the one, and "transcendent in his unreality" in the other (Hollington 1995: 378). Yet the stress here on the word "transcendent" perhaps nudges her position a little further toward Masson's view of Dickens as an artist of "the ideal" than Lewes's, whose later, sharper, essentially materialist critique also goes further than hers in exploring and deploring the absence of reflective mind in Dickens's characters. However that may be, her criticism here seems essentially constructive: the proposition – that *if* he could add a further dimension of psychological inwardness to his work he would be something like the greatest writer that has ever lived – has the air almost of a friendly invitation for him to attempt to do so.

Yet despite the friendly feeling between Dickens and Lewes (forged in the period of Dickens's early fame), which later expanded to include George Eliot, their attitudes drifted apart as the center of Lewes's and Eliot's intellectual interest moved from metaphysics to science. The extravagant early praise of the "philosophical" and "metaphysical" dimensions of *Oliver Twist* must later have counted for little in the mind of someone who would declare in 1856 that "Metaphysics is dry biscuit – especially to a man hungry for zoology!" (Ashton 2000: 173). The gap that opens up is already apparent at the time of their spat over Krook's famous death by "spontaneous combustion," an episode contained in the January 1853 number of *Bleak House*, which appeared at a time when Lewes was at work on Goethe as a great poet who was also a notable scientist. By contrast, in Lewes's view, Dickens had given credence to an unscientific "vulgar error" by admitting "spontaneous combustion" into his novel, and despite the surface magnanimity of his tone – "As a novelist he is not to be called to the bar of science; he has doubtless picked up the idea among the curiosities of his reading from some credulous adherent to the old hypothesis, and has accepted it as not improbable" (Ashton 2000: 144) – there is clearly some half-heartedness in his defense of an author's right to be unscientific. Many of Lewes's critical pronouncements henceforth will be built on the premises that truth or truths are knowable, that science is the means whereby we may know them, and that literary authors have a "serious responsibility" to render these in imaginative form.

Nevertheless, Dickens and Lewes remained friends, and curiously enough, as the 1872 essay makes plain (Hollington 1995: 466; see also Ashton 2000: 234), the subject of their conversation was often psychology, and, in particular, the psychology of dreams, that is to say, the innermost recesses of the mind. And yet the core critique of that essay is a restatement of a familiar reproach, that his figures are "wooden, and run on wheels," like the toy horses of a child's nursery, or, in a famous analogy drawn from Lewes's own scientific experiments, like galvanized frogs "whose brains have been taken out for physiological purposes," but who continue to live for some months in a state that Lewes described as "as uniform and calculable as the movements of a machine." Lewes, in fact, simply amplifies Thackeray's critique of Micawber through this analogy: he is one of Dickens's "'catchwords' personified as characters," "always presenting himself in the same situation, moved with the same springs, and uttering the same sounds" (Hollington 1995: 461).

Yet, despite their more sustained and authoritative tone, Lewes's arguments are not necessarily more convincing than Thackeray's mild remonstrances. The essential weakness of Lewes's essay, it seems to me, is again that it relies too heavily on the aesthetic criteria of "classic realism" to evaluate Dickens's achievements, which are of a different order. It looks at all points for "verisimilitude" in his work (and delivers the general verdict that in Dickens we find "human character and ordinary events portrayed with a mingled verisimilitude and falsity altogether unexampled"), but the criteria of "verisimilitude" tend in his handling of them to belong to a known world containing prosaic, materialist, pre-existent, cause-and-effect truths (as an example we might take his rather arbitrary interpretation of a Dickens dream, after a reading, of being surrounded by people dressed in scarlet, as a reflection of the afterglow of ladies dressed in opera cloaks at the performance, when it might just as readily be linked to Dickens's own favorite dandy apparel, geranium-colored waistcoats, as mentioned by Thackeray above).

Though Lewes is an outstanding critic who transcends most of his contemporaries in brilliance of argument and scrupulous honesty and many-sidedness, it is perhaps Masson, amongst Dickens's contemporaries, who comes closest to recognizing what it is that sets Dickens's achievement apart from that of most of his British contemporaries (with the Brontës or George Eliot arguable exceptions). That is to say, he achieved, in his greatest novels, what Baudelaire called "the miracle of a poetic prose." "Which one of us," Baudelaire asked rhetorically, "in his moments of ambition, has not dreamed of the miracle of a poetic prose, musical, without rhythm and without rhyme, supple enough and rugged enough to adapt itself to the lyrical impulses of the soul, the undulations of reverie, the jibes of conscience?" (1951: ix–x). The

Dickensian might answer that we find that dream realized in great novels like *Little Dorrit* or *Our Mutual Friend*, not just in the restricted dimensions of the prose poem, but for more than eight hundred pages.

REFERENCES AND FURTHER READING

Ashton, Rosemary (2000). *G. H. Lewes: An Unconventional Victorian*. London: Pimlico Books (original work published 1991).

Baudelaire, Charles (1951). *Paris Spleen*. (Louise Varèse, Trans.). London: Peter Owen (original work published 1869).

David, Deirdre (2001). Introduction. In Deirdre David (Ed.), *The Cambridge Companion to the Victorian Novel* (pp. 1–16). Cambridge: Cambridge University Press.

Davis, Nuell Pharr (1956). *The Life of Wilkie Collins*. Urbana, IL: Illinois University Press.

Fanger, Donald (1967). *Dostoevsky and Romantic Realism: A Study of Dostoevsky in Relation to Balzac, Dickens, and Gogol*. Chicago: University of Chicago Press.

Ford, George (1965). *Dickens and his Readers: Aspects of Novel Criticism since 1836*. New York: W. W. Norton (original work published 1955).

Glendinning, Victoria (2002). *Trollope*. London: Pimlico Books (original work published 1992).

Hollington, Michael (Ed.) (1995). *Charles Dickens: Critical Assessments*, vol. 1: *Contemporary Assessments*. Robertsbridge: Helm Information.

MacCabe, Colin (2003). *James Joyce and the Revolution of the Word*. Basingstoke: Palgrave Macmillan.

[Masson, David] (1851). *Pendennis* and *Copperfield*: Dickens *and* Thackeray. *North British Review*, 15, 57–89.

Masson, David (1859). *British Novelists and their Styles: Being a Critical Sketch of the History of British Prose Fiction*. Cambridge: Macmillan.

Nayder, Lillian (2002). *Unequal Partners: Charles Dickens, Wilkie Collins, and Victorian Authorship*. Ithaca, NY: Cornell University Press.

Poston, Lawrence (1999). 1832. In Herbert F. Tucker (Ed.), *A Companion to Victorian Literature and Culture* (pp. 3–18). Oxford: Blackwell.

Ray, Gordon N. (Ed.) (1945–6). *The Letters and Private Papers of W. M. Thackeray*, 4 vols. London: Oxford University Press.

— (1955) *William Makepeace Thackeray*, vol. 1: *The Uses of Adversity (1811–1846)*. London: Oxford University Press.

— (1958). *William Makepeace Thackeray*, vol. 2: *The Age of Wisdom (1847–1863)*. London: Oxford University Press.

Robinson, Kenneth (1952). *Wilkie Collins: A Biography*. New York: Macmillan.

35

Dickens and Criticism

Lyn Pykett

Dickens has proved his power by a popularity almost unexampled, embracing all classes.
Surely it is a task for criticism to exhibit the sources of that power?

(George Henry Lewes, quoted in Ford and Lane 1966: 58)

The paradox of Dickens's power to attract and repel points up the problems that face
any historian of Dickens criticism . . . An approver of Dickens's social criticism disap-
proves his imaginative flights of fancy; an admirer of his poetic imagination dislikes his
propagandizing; a reader who delights in the comic genius of his early novels deplores
the brooding melancholy of his later ones; one who is moved by the power of his sense
of the macabre and the demonic has no taste for his irrepressible extravagances of comic
character and language.

(Ada Nisbet, quoted in Stevenson 1964: 73)

University departments of English, literary studies, and cultural studies now contribute to an international Dickens industry. Surveys of critical work on Dickens's writings, such as those to be found in *Dickens Studies Annual* or *The Year's Work in English
Studies*, regularly begin or end with a comment on its quantity and quality, both of
which are taken as evidence of the continuing vitality and relevance of Dickens's
fiction. It was not ever thus. In the last few years of his career and in the period
immediately following his death, Dickens's critical reputation suffered as literary
fashions changed and the new realism or naturalism vied with the new romance and
a new aestheticism sought to capture the novel for art's sake. According to Edmund
Wilson, writing in 1940, Dickens remained the most critically neglected of all the
"great English writers," snubbed alike by "the literary men from Oxford and Cambridge, who have lately been sifting fastidiously so much of the English literary heritage," and by a "Bloomsbury that talked about Dostoevsky" but "ignored Dostoevsky's
master" (Wilson 1961: 1). Indeed, it was not until the 1950s that Dickens could be
said to have secured his place in a critical canon that was, by then, increasingly under

the guardianship of university professors. Even then, he was excluded from F. R. Leavis's "great tradition" of English fiction on the grounds that his was the genius of "a great entertainer" which did not offer a "challenge to an unusual and sustained seriousness" to the "adult mind" (Leavis 1948: 29).

The First Hundred Years of Dickens Criticism

The lowering of Dickens's critical stock had begun with Henry James, whose conception of the novel as a personal impression of life and a tightly organized and intricately interconnected "architectonic" form was to remain a powerful influence on novel criticism until the middle of the twentieth century. James's influential review of *Our Mutual Friend* in *The Nation* in 1865 relegated Dickens to the second division of literature on the grounds that he could not "see beneath the surface of things." Dickens's fiction is both fantastical and mechanical and it adds nothing to the reader's understanding of human character, James argued. Dickens "is a master of but two alternatives: he reconciles us to what is commonplace, and he reconciles us to what is odd." He is a "great observer and . . . humorist," but he is not a philosopher: "he knows men but not man" (quoted in Ford and Lane 1966: 52–3).

James's view was echoed by George Henry Lewes, when, two years after Dickens's death, he considered how to reconcile his immense popularity with the "critical contempt" which it attracted (Lewes quoted in Ford and Lane 1966: 57). Lewes, a prominent advocate of the kind of philosophical social realism practiced by George Eliot, acknowledged the force and vitality of Dickens's fiction, but, like James, found it lacking in both realism and reflection: "one sees no indication of the past life of humanity having ever occupied him; keenly as he observes the objects before him, he never connects his observations into a general expression, never seems interested in general relations of things" (quoted in Ford and Lane 1966: 69). Clearly, Dickens was not a George Eliot. Nor was he a Tolstoy, whose moral realism, philosophical reflection, and engagement with history were admired by "highbrow" critics at the turn of the century. Nineteenth-century literary criticism had still to find a vocabulary with which to account for the distinctiveness of Dickens's work, its force and power.

Perhaps the most significant attempt to argue Dickens's case in the late nineteenth century came from George Gissing, whose writings on this author began with a volume for Blackie and Son's Victorian Era series in 1898 (*Charles Dickens: A Critical Study*). Despite the fact that his own novels were influenced by the European naturalism that was in the ascendant at the *fin de siècle*, Gissing sought to defend Dickens against the tenets of the new realism (or naturalism) and "to vindicate him against the familiar complaint that, however trustworthy his background, the figures designed upon it, in general, are mere forms of fantasy" (Gissing 1926: 9). Gissing's reconsideration of Dickens's work starts from the assumption that it

suffers from a comparison with novelists, his peers, of a newer day, even with some who
were strictly his contemporaries . . . [and] his work differs markedly from our present
conception of the art of novel-writing . . . theoretically, he had very little in common
with the school of strict veracity, of realism . . . the school which . . . has directed fiction
into a path it is likely to pursue for many a year to come. (Gissing 1926: 58)

While many of his contemporaries dismissed Dickens's characters as non-realistic
types and abstractions, Gissing argued that it was precisely their "loud peculiarities"
and "rich extravagances" that made their creator "so true a chronicler of his day and
generation" (Gissing 1926: 11). If Gissing found a way of accounting for the extravagance of Dickens's characters, he was unable to accommodate the extravagance of his
plotting: "the art of adapting simple probabilities to the ends of a narrative he never
mastered . . . Too often he prefers some far-fetched eccentricity, some piece of knavish-
ness, some unlikely occurrence, about which to weave his tale" (Gissing 1926: 40).
Gissing attributed this failure of novelistic plotting to what he saw as an unfortunate
love of the theater and of theatricality. In Gissing's account, it was only in *Bleak House*
that Dickens succeeded in producing a good theatrical plot, but even this success is
marred by excess. The novel is over-plotted: "it is a puzzle, yet ingeniously simple;
the parts fitting together very neatly indeed. So neatly, that poor untidy Life disclaims
all connection with these doings" (Gissing 1926: 50).

Criticism was not to engage fully with Dickens's multiple plots, nor with the
nature and significance of the theatricality of his art until the latter part of the twentieth century. However, another aspect of Gissing's revaluation of the author and his
work – his concern with Dickens the radical – was taken up immediately and
remained a matter of, sometimes heated, critical debate throughout the twentieth
century and into our own time. Gissing's Dickens was a radical insofar as he was
"discontented with the slow course of legislation" and with "the aristocratic ideas
underlying English life," and "desired radical changes, in the direction of giving
liberty and a voice to the majority of people." Writing in "a day of advancing Social-
ism," Gissing argued that Dickens was in most respects a Conservative, and "never
in his intention democratic" (Gissing 1926: 188). Indeed, for all his sympathy with
the poor and oppressed, Dickens "could not look with entire approval on the poor
grown articulate about their wrongs." As evidence of the failure of Dickens's radicalism, Gissing cites: the absence from his fiction of "the workman at war with capital"
(p. 193), an absence that he attributes to the author's lack of knowledge of the industrial north of England; the fact that his depiction of victims of social wrong does not
take due account of the effect of social conditions upon character ("Think of little
Oliver Twist, who has been brought up . . . amid the outcasts of the world, yet is as
remarkable for purity of mind as for accuracy of grammar" [p. 198]); and his reliance
on private benevolence in the person of the "man of heavy purse and large heart"
(p. 200) as the rectifier of social ills. This analysis of Dickens's radicalism and its
failings was to set the terms of the debate on this matter for some time (see the discussion of Orwell and others below).

Describing Gissing as "the soundest of the Dickens critics" (Chesterton 1911: 5) in his own book-length study of Dickens in 1906, G. K. Chesterton nevertheless sought to defend Dickens from what he saw as Gissing's underestimation of his strengths. Rather than being a timid radical, Chesterton's Dickens "destroyed [certain] institutions simply by writing about them" (1911: 278). For Chesterton, Dickens's genial humanitarianism had had more effect than Gissing's pessimistic social determinism: "Both agreed that the souls of the people were in a kind of prison. But Gissing said that the prison was full of dead souls. Dickens said that the prison was full of living souls" (p. 276). Chesterton's Dickens was an "optimistic reformer" who describes "how good men are under bad conditions" (p. 271). He sought to defend Dickens from what he described as "this self-conscious, analytical and descriptive age" (p. 117), and also (like Gissing) from devaluation by recent critical trends: from "the Realists with their documents," who objected that Dickens's scenes and types were "not like life," and from the "more symbolic school of criticism" which followed, for whose proponents "life is within." Even the return of romance at the end of the nineteenth century had not benefited "this great romantic" because he "exaggerates the living thing" too much for turn-of-the-century taste (Chesterton 1911: 16–17). Dickens may not have found favor in "the hour of the absinthe" (p. 286) but, for Chesterton, this "most English of our great writers" (p. 249) was not for an age but for all time; he was "the last of the great mythologists" (p. 87).

Gissing's timid radical who was really more of a conservative, or Chesterton's optimistic humane reformer who destroyed institutions simply by writing about them – these versions of Dickens's social vision and politics shaped an important aspect of the Dickens debates in the first four decades of the twentieth century from George Bernard Shaw through T. A. Jackson's *Charles Dickens: The Progress of a Radical* (1937) to George Orwell's much-quoted essay on Dickens in his 1940 collection, *Inside the Whale and Other Essays*. For Shaw, the Dickens of *Hard Times* is "Karl Marx, Carlyle, Ruskin . . . rising up against civilization itself as against a disease, and declaring that it is not our disorder but our order that is horrible; that it is not our criminals but our magnates that are robbing and murdering us" (quoted in Ford and Lane 1966: 127–8). However, Shaw's Dickens was also an "unphilosophic radical" who failed to portray convincing social prophets or to embody a convincing political vision. The Marxist, T. A. Jackson, sought to claim Dickens for the proletarian cause by exploring the "vein of rebellion" (Jackson 1937: 23) that he found throughout Dickens's works. This Dickens was a dark writer who saw the future as belonging to the illegitimate orphan rather than to the Victorian family and who (*pace* Gissing) propounded the idea that the working class must liberate itself. Despite the rigidity of its vulgar Marxism, Jackson's study does make a serious attempt to read Dickens's fiction in relation to the history of the time in which it was written; and, more particularly, it seeks to account for its changing tone by charting the movement from optimism to disillusion between early and late Dickens in relation to the changing political climate, and most notably in relation to the changing fortunes of various radical movements and causes.

George Orwell rejected Jackson's "spirited efforts to turn Dickens into a blood-thirsty revolutionary" (Orwell 1940: 9), but he conceded that this indisputably "bourgeois" writer was nevertheless a subversive, a radical, and a rebel. Orwell's 1940 essay borrows from both Gissing and Chesterton, and like them – and many more subsequent critics – he sought to solve the puzzle of the politics of Dickens's novels. More particularly, he sought to address the paradox of how a series of novels which "attacked English institutions with a ferocity that has never since been approached" should have been so popular with those that they attacked that they made their author "a national institution" (Orwell 1940: 10). Orwell's answer to these conundrums was that Dickens's criticism of society is almost exclusively moral; his target is human nature rather than society, and he fails to suggest that "the economic system is wrong *as a system*" (Orwell 1940: 13) or to attack private enterprise or private property. Like Gissing, Orwell deplores the pervasiveness in Dickens's novels of both the "good rich man," who hands out guineas and rights social wrongs, and the apparently platitudi-nous message that if only people behaved decently then the world would be decent (Orwell 1940: 15). But, in the end, he defends Dickens from the charge that he is a "humbug," concluding that a moral criticism of society may be "just as 'revolutionary' – and revolution, after all, means turning things upside down – as the politico-economic criticism which is fashionable at this moment" (Orwell 1940: 31).

Orwell's short essay succinctly summarized and contributed to a particular British critique of Dickens as social critic and reformer. Two other works from the early 1940s inaugurated important new directions for Dickens criticism. These were Edmund Wilson's "Dickens: The Two Scrooges" (first published in *Atlantic Monthly* in 1940), and Humphry House's *The Dickens World* (1941). Beginning from the premise that Dickens was often read "for his records and criticism of social abuses, as if he were a great historian or a social reformer," House sought to show the connections between Dickens's spirit of reformism and what he wanted reformed, "between the attitude to life shown in his books and the society in which he lived" (House 1941: 14). House made a persuasive case for both historicizing and contextualizing Dickens's fiction – a case which was to be taken up by scholars such as Philip Collins in his *Dickens and Crime* (1962) and *Dickens and Education* (1963). Moreover, through his later involve-ment in the Pilgrim Edition of Dickens's letters, House was to play an important part in providing the means for other scholars and critics to undertake these tasks. In *The Dickens World*, House focused on Dickens more as a journalist – "a journalist of the finest kind" (1941: 215) – than as a creative artist. Far from being a limitation, this provided a new direction for Dickens studies and new ways of addressing the issue of Dickens's radicalism, which are still being explored.

In his shorter but densely packed – and extremely influential – essay, Edmund Wilson combined a socio-historical approach with psycho-biography to produce a new psycho-social perspective on the nature and sources of Dickens's creative vitality and on the politics of his novels. Dickens's own uneasy class position and his personal childhood traumas (especially his experience at Warren's Blacking) are seen as the sources of an unstable dualism which fueled his art and led him to "create a new tradition" in fiction (Wilson 1961: 31). For "the man of spirit whose childhood has been crushed by the cruelty of organised society," Wilson argued, "one of two attitudes is natural: that of the criminal or that of the rebel" (1961: 13), and Dickens was repeatedly to play out and explore both roles in his fiction. Despite its focus on the unconscious sources of Dickens's rather manic creative energies, one of the most influential aspects of Wilson's essay is its emphasis on the way in which these energies were shaped into increasingly complex and organized works of art. Wilson's Dickens was a novelist of social inter-relationships – the creator of the novel of the social group – whose fiction was shaped by his own changing relationship with society and, in particular, his growing disillusion with "the self-important middle class who had been making such rapid progress in England and coming down like a damper . . . on the spontaneity and gaiety, the frankness and independence" which he "admired and trusted" (p. 28).

Wilson, whose essay has been described as a "watershed between the new view of Dickens and the old" (Nisbet in Stevenson 1964: 74), saw *Dombey and Son* as the watershed novel in which Dickens "sets out to trace an anatomy of . . . society," beginning to "organize his stories as wholes, to plan all the characters as symbols, and to invest all the details with significance" (Wilson 1941: 31–2). Thereafter, Dickens creates a new kind of plot in *Bleak House* – "the detective story which is also a social fable," which develops a "symbolism of a more complicated reference and a deeper implication" (1941: 34), and in *Little Dorrit*, no longer content merely to anatomize society and its oppressive institutions, he develops a focus on "imprisoning states of mind" (p. 50). Drawing on T. A. Jackson's discussion of the symbolism of the prison in this novel, Wilson offered a new way of reading the recurring motifs and figures in Dickens's work which was to be taken up by Lionel Trilling in his 1953 essay on *Little Dorrit*. More generally, by combining something of Jackson's Marxism with Freudian psychoanalysis, Wilson contributed to developing critical interest in the social construction of the writer's psyche and in his fictional representations of the complex interdependence of psychological and social organization.

Another important study of the construction of the writer's psyche was J. H. Miller's *Charles Dickens: The World of his Novels* (1958). Drawing on the phenomenology of Georges Poulet, Miller conceived of the literary text not as the "mere symptom or product of a pre-existent psychological condition" nor as the "symptom of the age" (Miller 1958: ix), but as "the very means by which a writer apprehends and, in some measure, creates himself" (p. viii), and as playing a part in "determining the 'Victorian spirit' itself" (p. ix). For Miller, Dickens's fiction was preoccupied with "the search for a viable identity," and it is this search that unifies the "swarming multiplicity" (p. viii) and "hallucinated vision" (p. 329) of the novels; the successive adventures of the isolated protagonist at the center of Dickens's novels are "essentially attempts to understand the world, to integrate . . . in it, and by that integration to find a real self" (p. 328). This view of Dickens's novels as a series of self-fashionings, in which the author and his protagonists seek to achieve selfhood through performance, was developed further by Robert Garis in *The Dickens Theatre* (1965). Although not an explicit refutation of Leavis's earlier dismissal of Dickens from the "great tradition" as, for the most part, merely a popular entertainer, Garis's book celebrates the dramatic energy which (as he sees it) derives precisely from Dickens's closeness to popular forms such as melodrama and the detective story, and which resists containment by a formalistic criticism.

The 1950s and 1960s saw the beginning of the Dickens boom in higher education in Britain and the USA, with a growing number of doctoral dissertations leading to more and more articles and books. Writing in 1970, Ada Nisbet described the mid-twentieth-century rebirth of Dickens as being as "much a phenomenon as his leap to fame with the publication of *Pickwick*" (Nisbet 1970: 380). Dickens was an early beneficiary of the growth of an interdisciplinary Victorian studies, and indeed much important work in this period came from scholars working on his relationship to his literary contemporaries and to the literary marketplace, and on the relationship between his writings and the history of his times. A flurry of new lives of the author from both inside and outside the academy led to new critical readings: for example, Jack Lindsay's Marxist–Freudian *Charles Dickens: A Biographical and Critical Study* (1950), Julian Symons' psychoanalytic volume in the Barker English Novelists series (1951), and Edgar H. Johnson's mammoth *Charles Dickens: His Tragedy and Triumph* (1952). Other scholars, such as John Butt and Kathleen Tillotson (1957), cast new light on the design and organization of Dickens's novels through a study of his manuscripts and working methods. Tillotson was also involved in the major project of collecting and editing Dickens's letters for what was to become the 12-volume Pilgrim Edition (1965–2002).

Literary critics, on the other hand, continued to explore the fiction as social critique or sought ways of defending the form of what W. J. Harvey described as the novel of episodic intensification (Harvey 1965: 90) from the tyranny of the Jamesian and New Critical focus on the verbal icon. The centenary of Dickens's death in 1970 was the occasion for a number of "reconsiderations" of his literary achievement. Perhaps the most extraordinary of these was the Leavises' *Dickens the Novelist* (1970), which sought "to enforce as unanswerably as possible the conviction that Dickens was one of the greatest of creative writers . . . [who] developed a fully conscious devotion to his art," and, at the same time, to protest "against the trend of American criticism of Dickens, from Edmund Wilson onwards, as being in general wrong-headed, ill-informed . . . and essentially ignorant and misdirecting" (Leavis and Leavis 1970: ix). By 1970, Dickens's popularity and fecundity was no longer seen by F. R. Leavis as a barrier to seriousness and profundity, and the important thing was to rescue him from "the echoes and elaborations" of Wilson's theory of his art as being "the volcanic explosions of a manic-depressive" (1970: xiii) which were being inflicted on academic audiences in the centenary year by "the bright-idea merchants" (p. 177) who were taking over literary studies.

At the heart of the Leavises' 1970 study is the approach to Dickens offered in F. R. Leavis's essay on *Hard Times*, which inaugurated a series of essays on "The Novel as Dramatic Poem" in *Scrutiny* in 1947 (reprinted as "something of an appendix" to *The Great Tradition* in 1948). The Leavises' answer to the supposedly wrong-headed criticism of the psycho-biographers was to bring together the emphasis on form and symbol found in Anglo-American New Criticism with the critique of modernity, or (to use Leavis's preferred term) technologico-Benthamism found in the nineteenth-century English writers John Ruskin, Matthew Arnold, and William Morris. The value of Dickens, in this reading, is that he is on the side of "life": what others saw as his chaotic energies and hallucinatory vision was, in fact, a "creative exuberance" which is "controlled by a profound inspiration that informs, directs and limits" (Leavis and Leavis 1970: 188), and is put in the service of "a sustained and searching inquiry into contemporary civilization" (1970: 212).

Dickens's engagement with contemporary civilization was also the subject of Raymond Williams's *The English Novel from Dickens to Lawrence* (1970), which belongs with the "Marxizing and other ideologically-slanted interpretations of Dickens's achievements" (Leavis and Leavis 1970: xiii) which the Leavises pronounced to be a "dead letter." For Raymond Williams, the significance of Dickens's novels was that they represented "a new kind of consciousness" (Williams 1970: 9), a new way of seeing, knowing, and showing the individual, the crowd, the city, modern social forms and institutions, and the power of industrialism. In his 1940 essay, Edmund Wilson had compared Dickens's vision of London to that of Marx's patron and collaborator Friedrich Engels:

> Friedrich Engels, visiting London in the early forties, had written of the people in the streets that they seemed to "crowd by one another as if they had nothing in common, nothing to do with one another, and as if their only agreement were the tacit one that each shall keep to his own side of the pavement in order not to delay the opposing streams of the crowd . . . The brutal indifference, the unfeeling isolation of each in his private interest, becomes the more repellent the more these individuals are herded together within a limited space." This is the world that Dickens is describing. (Wilson 1961: 35)

Williams argued that it was precisely in this way of seeing and representing the urban crowd that Dickens articulated a new kind of consciousness and developed a new mode of fictional representation which was "uniquely capable" of expressing the experience of living in cities, and of dramatizing the hurry and confusion of modernity: "as we stand and look back at a Dickens novel," Williams wrote, "the general movement we remember – the decisive movement – is a hurrying seemingly random passing of men and women, each heard in some fixed phrase, seen in some fixed expression" (Williams 1970: 32).

Williams sought to address what Leavis had earlier described as "the challenge of Dickens": "the challenge he presents to criticism to define the ways in which he is one of the greatest of writers" (letter to the *Spectator*, January 4, 1963, reprinted in Leavis 1974: 96). In particular, Williams was concerned with the challenge that

Dickens presented to the Jamesian and New Critical orthodoxies of the twentieth century. Judged according to these standards,

> Dickens's faults – what are seen to be his faults – are so many and so central as to produce embarrassment . . . his characters are not "rounded" and developing but "flat" and emphatic. They are not slowly revealed but directly presented. Significance is not enacted in mainly tacit and intricate ways but is often directly presented in moral address and indeed exhortation. Instead of the language of analysis and comprehension he uses, directly, the language of persuasion and display. His plots depend often on arbitrary coincidences, on sudden revelations and changes of heart. He offers not the details of psychological process but the finished articles: the social and psychological products. (Williams 1970: 31)

Instead of trying to accommodate Dickens's fiction to the standards of the great tradition (which was in part what the Leavises were trying to do), Williams read it through a humanist Marxism to produce a Dickens who did not simply offer a powerful inquiry into contemporary civilization (as the Leavises put it), but rather made a creative intervention in it by articulating an emergent form of consciousness. However, even as Williams's book appeared, the orthodoxies from which he and critics such as Robert Garis (see above) had sought to rescue Dickens, were being displaced by the challenge of "theory" (or a range of theories) imported into Anglo-American criticism from continental Europe.

Dickens in Theory

The "massive theoretical upheavals and reconstitution of the cultural landscape during the 1970s and 1980s" (Connor 1996: 16), which resulted from the explosion of "theory" from the late 1960s onward, may not have reconstituted the very landscape of Dickens's fiction but they have certainly given readers new maps for navigating it and new perspectives from which to view it. Since the 1970s, Dickens's novels have (among other things) undergone structuralist analysis and then deconstruction; they have been historicized, Marxized (or post-Marxized), and newly psychoanalysed by being read through Lacanian or Deleuzian (rather than Freudian) psychoanalysis; they have also been disposed of or appropriated by a variety of feminist approaches, and read through queer theory and post-colonial theory. One important consequence of the "theory revolution" has been the reconfiguration of the field of literature itself and the development of new ways of reading cultural history.

Dickens is one of many nineteenth-century authors whose work is now read differently as a result of attempts to relocate it in the conditions of its production, both material and imaginative. Materialist readings of the history of cultural production (for example, Feltes 1986) and the new history of publishing (for example, Jordan and Patten 1995) have offered new perspectives on this most prolific of novelists whose life and work were bound up with the professionalization of the writer and the commodification of literary production in the nineteenth century. Dickens criticism has also been reinvigorated by a renewed interest in popular genres such as melodrama (both in the theater and in fiction), the gothic novel, the sensation novel, and the literature of crime and detection, including the Newgate novel. Juliet John's *Dickens's Villains: Melodrama, Character, Popular Culture* (2001) is a good example of this re-examination of Dickens's connections with popular culture, linking both his theatricality and his interest in the "Amusements of the People" (to quote the title of his *Household Words* essay) to his "belief in the principles of communality and cultural inclusivity" (John 2001: 3; see also Vlock 1998; Glavin 1999).

Like the New Criticism which it replaced, structuralist criticism of the 1970s and 1980s was interested in *how* texts mean rather than in *what* they mean and *what kind of world they represent*. Structuralists focused on novels as both linguistic structures and as forms in a cultural system that was structured like a language. Read thus, Dickens's novels were seen as both the products and enactments of signifying systems in which meaning derives from structured oppositions and differences (see Connor 1985: 4). This approach resulted in a new attentiveness to the peculiar energies of Dickens's language, and made the traditional critical preoccupation with the formal coherence of his fiction or its conscious artistry a non-issue, since, as Stephen Connor argues, it did not "leave so much room for the author as controlling agent," but rather – as in *Pickwick Papers* – "put him in the position of his central character, seeking to explore, absorb and contain a world of signs and discourses, but finding himself always a differential product of those signs" (Connor 1985: 19).

Post-structuralist criticism and deconstructive criticism – structuralism's successors – derive in part from the perception that the effect of the system of differences and oppositions is more complex and indefinite than structuralism allowed. Taking up Jacques Derrida's concern with the mutual implications of the opposing terms in a system of difference and the tendency of language to become divided against itself, J. Hillis Miller – in one of the most influential deconstructive readings of Dickens, first published in 1971 – read *Bleak House* as a representation of interpretation; it is a text in which one thing stands for another and can only be understood in terms of another, and in which meaning is repeatedly deferred. The structure of the novel thus replicates the structure of the society it represents and explores, assimilating everything it touches "to a system of meaning . . . [and] made up of an incessant movement of reference in which each element leads to other elements in a constant displacement of meaning" (Miller 1971: 30).

Deconstructive critics read Dickens's novels against the grain, paying attention to their inconsistencies, gaps, and contradictions, and focusing on how they disrupted or "undid" themselves. Another way of accounting for and exploring these aspects of the Dickens text was provided by the work of Mikhail Bakhtin and his circle, which became more widely known and used after being translated into English in the 1980s. The Bakhtinian concepts of "dialogism" (double-voicedness), "polyphony" (multi-voicedness), and "heteroglossia" (a means of "giving bodily form" to "the co-existence of socio-ideological contradictions between the present and the past" and "between differing socio-ideological groups in the present") were particularly productive for reading Dickens (Bakhtin 1981: 291). Moreover, by locating Dickens in a long-established, subversive, popular tradition of fiction, which offers a "comic-parodic reprocessing of almost all the levels of literary language . . . that were current at the time" (p. 308), Bakhtin also presented critics with a new way of making sense of Dickens's dramatic, multi-voiced, and complexly plotted novels.

Bakhtin's view of language as a system of signs which is produced in and by a particular society at a particular time also contributed to shifting Marxizing and his-toricist criticism from an interest in the ways in which Dickens's novels *reflected* their times to a focus on their role in *constructing* and *mediating* a particular socio-historic perspective or form of consciousness. Given the history of the vexed question of Dickens's radicalism and its relationship to his realism, it was, perhaps, inevitable that some later twentieth-century critics were more inclined to see the dissident, carnivalesque, many-voicedness of his early novels as being suppressed by what they saw as the inherent conservatism of "classic realism" which came to be the dominant mode of the Victorian novel. On the other hand, Terry Eagleton, in his Althusserian Marxist (or post-Marxist) *Criticism and Ideology* (1976), sees the "impurity" of Dickens's later realism as its saving grace: "dispersed, conflictual discourses . . . cease-lessly offer to displace the securely 'over-viewing' eye of classical realism" (Eagleton 1976: 103).

Discourses and their dispersal are at the center of the work of Michel Foucault, who has been a key point of reference for a wide range of Dickens critics since the 1980s. Particularly influential has been Foucault's insistence that discourse is not merely a way of representing the world, but rather that it is a form of action in and on the world. From D. A. Miller's *The Novel and the Police* (1988) through Mary Poovey's *Uneven Developments* (1989) to her *Making a Social Body* (1995), Dickens's work has been used to demonstrate the ways in which literature is not only produced in and by discourse, but is itself a discourse which does its own ideological work in the world.

Foucault's later work on discipline and punishment, and on prisons and the nine-teenth-century development of what he variously describes as the surveillance society and the "carceral society," provided a new direction for the interest in Dickens's prison imagery which had come to the fore in the 1940s and 1950s. For example, using Foucault's concept of a "technology of subjection," Jeremy Tambling re-read *Great Expectations* not as a *Bildungsroman* which charts the growth of its hero to maturity, but rather as a narrative which both explores and enacts the ways in which language functions to imprison a person in an internalized sense of identity which is neverthe-less imposed from outside the self (Tambling 1986). D. A. Miller's widely cited *The Novel and the Police* (1988) also read Dickens's fiction as both a symptom and critique of disciplinary society, and sought to demonstrate that both the form and the content of the long Victorian novel were evidence of the way in which it "systematically participate[d] in a general economy of policing power" (Miller 1988: ix) by simultaneously taking social discipline as its subject and constructing the disciplined subject (through developing a particular form of reading practice).

Foucault's earlier work on the history of sexuality and his theorization of the social and discursive construction of gender, sexuality, and desire have produced a multiplicity of studies both of sex-gender identity in Dickens's fiction and of the complex inter-relationships between the processes involved in the construction of these identities and issues of class, culture, economics, and empire. For example, Nancy Armstrong's *Desire and Domestic Fiction* (1987), a Foucauldian account of the way in which the rise of the domestic novel in the nineteenth century coincided with and contributed to the construction and disciplining of the gendered subject, draws briefly on *Oliver Twist* and *Hard Times* to demonstrate how "respectable fiction . . . presented political conflict in terms of sexual differences" and "charted new domains of aberrance requiring domestication" (Armstrong 1987: 41, 163).

Similarly, Mary Poovey explored what she described as "the ideological work" performed by Dickens's novels in constructing and representing gender and sexuality, by reading them in relation to the wider field of cultural meanings in which they were produced and read and subsequently reproduced and re-read. Thus, in *Uneven Developments* (1989) she reads *David Copperfield* in connection with the gendering of novel writing, the professionalization of the role of the writer, and the construction of masculinity in relation to normative concepts of both femininity and domesticity. Poovey returns to the mutually constitutive relationship between masculinity and domestic femininity in *Making a Social Body* (1995), in which she reads *Our Mutual Friend* as a narrative about the conversion of material wealth into human value (a metaphoric wealth) – a conversion narrative which is also the narrative of male power in the domestic sphere, where "men are able to exercise precisely the kind of control that is not available in the unpredictable world of financial speculation" (Poovey 1995: 166).

Poovey's focus on the interconnections of class, economics, race, and colonial expansion in Dickens's last completed novel, and her interest in its engagement with the assumption "that the identities that we call gender and race contributed natural bases for making moral discriminations about business and everything" (Poovey 1995: 157) was developed further in Deidre David's investigation of the "textual construction of empire" in *Rule Britannia* (1995). David is interested in what Poovey describes as the "uneven" and often contradictory ideological work performed by Dickens's fiction, and seeks to demonstrate how it contributes to both the construction and critique of the imperial imagination. Her particular interest is in how (as she reads them) novels such as *The Old Curiosity Shop* and *Dombey and Son* linked gender and race, the home and the colony, in ways which served both to keep women in the private domestic sphere and to subordinate "millions of indigenous peoples to Britannic rule," and, in the process, "worked to create, explain and negotiate the difficulties attendant upon the possession of an immense and always changing empire" (David 1995: 8). This is just one example of the way in which Dickens has been re-read in the light of a post-colonialist criticism that focuses on the role of the nineteenth-century novel in consolidating imperial authority through constructing particular versions of Englishness, Britishness, the metropole, and the imperial subject in relation to the oriental "other," the colony, and the subaltern subject of imperialism.

Both Poovey and David contribute to a broadly feminist re-reading of Dickens's fiction. Feminist criticism has also made a significant impact on the study of Dickens's women. While earlier critics bemoaned Dickens's failure to represent any other kind of woman than the eccentric, the imbecile, and the shrew (Gissing), or the "legless angel" (Orwell 1940: 83), or were repelled by the sickly sentimentality of his heroines, several late twentieth-century feminists turned their attention to re-reading those dark, brooding, troubling women – such as Nancy, Lady Dedlock, and Miss Wade – who seem to transgress or challenge the gender order. Others, such as Monica Cohen (1998) and Hilary Schor (1999), have revisited the daughters and mothers of the house of Dickens.

Hilary Schor has addressed Dickens's woman problem by looking again at the stories that he tells about the daughter and the stories that the daughters in his novels tell, arguing that both kinds of story are part of the larger story that nineteenth-century culture told about the daughter – as a legal entity, as a chain in patterns of exchange and inheritance, and as a transmitter of "ideology, memory, and faith" (Schor 1999: 4). Schor has traced Dickens's obsession with female narrative power from the "uncanny daughter" (Nancy, Nell, and Kate Nickleby) of (as she sees it) his messy early novels, through to the stories of the orphaned daughter's reclaiming of the "weapons of writing" (1999: 101) as the means of reclaiming her property and inheritance from her mother (in *Bleak House*), and Amy Dorrit's role in providing "a kind of narrative last testament" to secure collective memory (p. 129). Estella's story is read as yet another retelling of the story of "inheritance, guilt and masochism" (p. 154), but one that lacks the consolations of romance offered by the stories of Florence, Esther, and Amy; it also acts as a critique of Pip's autobiographical story of masculine development. The "bitter end" of these stories is reached in *Our Mutual Friend*, in which "the attempt to free the novel from the darkest toils of the inheritance plot . . . notoriously come to dust" (p. 178) in its story of turning daughters (Lizzie and Bella) into the wives and property of men who return from deaths by drowning. Dickens's stories of wives and mothers are more positively evaluated in Monica Cohen's *Professional Domesticity in the Victorian Novel* (1998) which discusses *Great Expectations* and *Little Dorrit* in its attempt to revise recent understandings of the domestic ideology by showing how domestic work gained social credibility and moral authority by positioning itself in relation to the vocabulary of nineteenth-century professionalism.

Like many Victorian writers, Dickens has long been held to be a writer who was squeamish about representing sex and sexuality and eager to spare the blush on the cheek of the young person (or the young person's mother). However in the past 25 years the whole question of Dickens and sex has been rethought in the light of Foucault's questioning of the image of the Victorian "'imperial prude' [which] is emblazoned on our restrained, mute and hypocritical sexuality" (Foucault 1979: 3) and his rethinking of "the repressive hypothesis." In volume 1 of his *History of Sexuality*, Foucault argued that the rise of repression, which is assumed to have reached its height with the Victorians, resulted not in silence (as is generally supposed), but in a veritable explosion of discourse, "an institutional incitement to speak about" sex and "to cause *it* to speak through explicit articulation and endlessly accumulated detail" (Foucault 1979: 18). This endless speaking of sex was also the means by which sexuality was constructed; sexuality and desire were neither natural nor universal, but historically produced in and by discourse.

Developing Foucault's ideas, in *Between Men* (1985) Eve Kosofsky Sedgwick used *Our Mutual Friend* and *The Mystery of Edwin Drood* to demonstrate her hypothesis that Victorian culture was built on networks of "homosociality," a range of asexual bonds between men (friendship, apprenticeship, professional camaraderie, and so on) which depended on strong prohibitions against homosexual bonds. Sedgwick argued that these homosocial bonds included those that were made through women – through marriage or birth, for example – and could be seen at work in the triangular relationships which she found in Dickens's novels. Thus Sedgwick sees Lizzie Hexam as being placed in a series of overlapping triangles – linking her father and her self-improving brother Charley, Charley and his self-improved teacher Bradley Headstone, Bradley and the upper middle-class professional Eugene Wrayburn – which map class and gender and the ways in which each is defined in terms of the other.

Taking a different route out of Foucault, William A. Cohen, in *Sex Scandal: The Private Parts of Victorian Fiction* (1996), uses (or abuses, depending on one's point of view) *Great Expectations* to demonstrate the interconnections between novel-reading practices and the discourse on the novel, on the one hand, and the discourse on masturbation on the other: "the novel . . . so perilously implicated in encouraging . . . forms of imaginative self-abuse," he claims, "had to find ways of managing the erotic reveries it was accused of arousing in its readers" (Cohen 1996: 27). With a preternatural alertness to the possibility of a sexual pun, Cohen finds Dickens's novel to be brimming with covert or displaced references to the male body, especially to hands, as it "relegates sexual sensations to parts of the body different from those in which they are usually imagined to originate," and thus contrives "to anatomize whole species of erotic dispositions without ever mentioning sex" (1996: 29). No doubt unspoken and displaced sexuality will continue to prove fertile ground for post-millennium Dickens critics. Indeed, the call for papers for a recent conference on "Dickens and Sex" at the University of London's Institute of English Studies (2004) invited papers on "Dickens and" – Fetishism, Homoeroticism, Incest, Masturbation, Paedophilia, Pornography, Prostitution, Racialized Sexualities, and Sadomasochism, as well as on "Dirty" language in Dickens.

From the end of the nineteenth century to the beginning of the twenty-first century Dickens's work has been subjected to a bewildering array of readings and re-readings as literary and critical fashions have come and gone. The energetic quirkiness of Dickens's writings has been derided, exalted, or shaped into significant form by one means or another. The Dickens text has been playfully deconstructed or forensically dissected by apologists and antagonists alike. Whatever the critical methodology employed, the main issues for the Dickens critics have retained a surprising consistency. Whether they have found for or against him, twentieth-century – and now twenty-first-century – critics, like some of their Victorian predecessors, have been concerned to explore such issues as: the relative status of early and late Dickens; Dickens's relationship to the past, the modern, and modernity; his artistry (conscious, unconscious, or merely lacking?); his "truth to life," realism, lack of realism, surrealism, or anti-realism; his use of and his relationship to the forms of popular culture; the theatricality of his plots and characterization; caricature versus character; the aesthetics and ideology of his narrative forms; the uses and abuses of coincidence and the complex multiple plot; the politics of the novels (there is a renewed interest in Dickens's radicalism and its links to both popular radicalism and popular cultural forms); Dickens's own class position and his representation of social class in his novels; his representation of gender and the gender of his writings; issues of sex and sexuality. The debate continues, as Dickens's novels continue to exert their force and to issue their challenge to literary and cultural criticism.

REFERENCES AND FURTHER READING

Armstrong, Nancy (1987). *Desire and Domestic Fiction*. New York: Oxford University Press.

Bakhtin, Mikhail (1981). Discourse in the novel. In *The Dialogic Imagination* (pp. 259–422). (Caryl Emerson and Michael Holquist, Trans.). Austin: University of Texas Press.

Butt, John and Tillotson, Kathleen (1957). *Dickens at Work*. London: Methuen.

Chesterton, G. K. (1911). *Charles Dickens*. London: Methuen (original work published 1906).

Cohen, Monica (1998). *Professional Domesticity in the Victorian Novel*. Oxford: Oxford University Press.

Cohen, William A. (1996). *Sex Scandal: The Private Parts of Victorian Fiction*. Durham, NC: Duke University Press.

Collins, Philip (1962). *Dickens and Crime*. London: Macmillan.

— (1963). *Dickens and Education*. London: Macmillan.

Connor, Steven (1985). *Charles Dickens* (Re-reading Literature Series). Oxford: Blackwell.

— (1996). *Charles Dickens* (Longman Critical Reader Series). London: Longman.

David, Deirdre (1995). *Rule Britannia: Women, Empire and Victorian Writing*. Ithaca, NY: Cornell University Press.

Eagleton, T. (1976). *Criticism and Ideology: A Study in Marxist Literary Theory*. London: Verso.

Feltes, N. N. (1986). *Modes of Production of Victorian Novels*. Chicago: University of Chicago Press.

Ford, George H. and Lane, Lauriat, Jr. (Eds.) (1966). *The Dickens Critics*. Ithaca, NY: Cornell University Press (original work published 1961).

Foucault, Michel (1979). *The History of Sexuality*, vol. 1. (Robert Hurley, Trans). London: Penguin.

Garis, Robert (1965). *The Dickens Theatre: A Reassessment of the Novels*. Oxford: Clarendon Press.

Gissing, George (1926). *Charles Dickens: A Critical Study*. London: Blackie and Sons (original work published 1898).

Glavin, John (1999). *After Dickens: Reading Adaptation and Performance*. Cambridge: Cambridge University Press.

Harvey, W. J. (1965). *Character and the Novel*. London: Chatto and Windus.

House, Humphry (1941). *The Dickens World*. London: Oxford University Press.

Jackson, T. A. (1937). *Charles Dickens: The Progress of a Radical*. London: Lawrence and Wishart.

John, Juliet (2001). *Dickens's Villains: Melodrama, Character, Popular Culture*. Oxford: Oxford University Press.

Johnson, Edgar H. (1952). *Charles Dickens: His Tragedy and Triumph*, 2 vols. New York: Simon and Shuster.

Jordan, John O. and Patten, Robert L. (Eds.) (1995). *Literature in the Market Place: Nineteenth-century British Publishing and Reading Practices*. Cambridge: Cambridge University Press.

Leavis, F. R. (1948). *The Great Tradition*. London: Chatto and Windus.

— (1974) *Letters in Criticism*. (John Tasker, Ed.). London: Chatto and Windus.

— and Leavis, Q. D. (1970). *Dickens the Novelist*. London: Chatto and Windus.

Lindsay, Jack (1950). *Charles Dickens: A Biographical and Critical Study*. London: Andrew Dakers.

Miller, D. A. (1988). *The Novel and the Police*. Berkeley, CA: University of California Press.

Miller, J. H. (1958). *Charles Dickens: The World of his Novels*. Cambridge, MA: Harvard University Press.

— (1971). Introduction to *Bleak House*. Harmondsworth: Penguin.

Nisbet, Ada (1970). Foreword to the Dickens Centennial Edition of *Nineteenth-century Fiction*, 24, 379–82.

Orwell, George (1940). *Inside the Whale and Other Essays*. London: Gollancz.

Poovey, Mary (1989). *Uneven Developments: The Ideological Work of Gender in Mid-Victorian England*. Chicago: University of Chicago Press.

— (1995). *Making a Social Body: British Cultural Formation, 1830–1864*. Chicago: University of Chicago Press.

Schor, Hilary (1999). *Dickens and the Daughter of the House*. Cambridge: Cambridge University Press.

Sedgwick, Eve Kosofsky (1985). *Between Men: English Literature and Male Homosocial Desire*. Ithaca, NY: Cornell University Press.

Stevenson, Lionel (1964). *Victorian Fiction: A Guide to Research*. Cambridge, MA: Harvard University Press.

Symons, Julian (1951). *Charles Dickens*. London: Barker.

Tambling, Jeremy (1986). Prison-bound: Dickens and Foucault. *Essays in Criticism*, 36, 11–31. Reprinted in Dickens, Violence and the Modern State: *Dreams of the Scaffold* (pp. 17–47). London: Macmillan, 1995.

Trilling, Lionel (1953). *Little Dorrit. Kenyon Review*, 15, 577–90. Reprinted as Introduction to *Little Dorrit* (pp. vi–xvi). London: Oxford University Press, 1953.

Vlock, Deborah (1998). *Dickens, Novel Reading and the Victorian Popular Theatre*. Cambridge: Cambridge University Press.

Williams, Raymond (1970). *The English Novel from Dickens to Lawrence*. London: Hogarth Press.

Wilson, Edmund (1961). Dickens: the two Scrooges. In *The Wound and the Bow: Seven Studies in Literature* (pp. 1–93). London: Methuen (original work published 1940).

36

Postcolonial Dickens

John O. Jordan

When I was a child I *devoured* Dickens. I think there is hardly any volume of Dickens'
work that I have not read. There was something that fascinated me about the kind of
life he depicted and I remember that in school I read literally all Dickens' novels.

(Soyinka 2001: 158)

In the early 1970s, I recall reading one or two children's editions of books by Charles
Dickens. The memory holds because I also remember a drawing in the book, of a boy
asking a man for some more soup. The books were full of suffering, and the suffering
involved children. The stories made me fearful. They discouraged me from reading. But
it was in Dickens that I would have first come across the city named London.

(Kumar 2002: 105)

In primary school I now read simplified Dickens and Stevenson alongside Rider Haggard.
Jim Hawkins, Oliver Twist, Tom Brown . . . were now my daily companions in the
world of imagination (Ngugi 1986: 12) . . . [L]ines like "Yo ho and a bottle of rum/
Sixteen men on a dead man's chest . . ." or "Please sir can I have some more" kept
intruding in my mind like one's favorite tunes.

(Ngugi 1993: 136)

I was too young for newspapers. I was old enough only for stories . . . the early chapters
of *Oliver Twist*; Mr. Murdstone from *David Copperfield*; Mr. Squeers. All this my father
introduced me to . . . It was the richest and most serene time of my childhood.

(Naipaul 1984: 25–6)

Early exposure to Dickens often figures prominently in narratives of youthful initiation into the pleasures (and pains) of reading imaginative literature. In correspondence, memoirs, interviews, and essays, as well as in poetry and fiction, many
twentieth-century writers have recorded the story of their first encounter with novels
by Dickens and the vivid imaginative world that opened to them as a result. George

Orwell's account of reading *David Copperfield* as a boy and believing that the novel's early chapters were actually written by a child is one well-known version of this story. What is unusual, therefore, about the excerpts quoted above is not so much any originality in the experience they describe as the locations in which that experience took place: Nigeria, India, Kenya, and Trinidad.

That Dickens should have a global reach and impact is hardly surprising. His stature as one of the giants of world literature has long been recognized, and the list of writers and filmmakers who have been deeply affected by his work is both extensive and international. Dostoevsky, Galdós, Joyce, Kafka, Faulkner, Nabokov, and Beckett, Eisenstein, Griffith, Chaplin, Lean, and Polanski – these are only a few of the artists who have drawn on Dickens for inspiration or who have acknowledged a debt to him and an admiration for his work.

Dickens has, of course, never been the property only of a cultural or artistic elite. From the moment of *Pickwick* onward, his appeal has always been to a wider audience, and to a great extent this remains true today. His presence as an enduring force in popular culture is evidenced by the steadily growing number of TV mini-series and film adaptations of his novels, as well as by the appearance of his iconic features on postage stamps, British £10 notes, and a toy action figure with detachable top hat and quill pen. Stage versions of *A Christmas Carol* regularly flood community theaters across North America during the holiday season, and children who have never read a word of the story know what it means to call someone a "Scrooge." The *Carol* has transcended its original, printed form and become what Paul Davis (2000) calls a "culture text," something between a folktale and a modern myth. More recently, Jay Clayton's *Charles Dickens in Cyberspace* (2003) has wittily directed attention to the postmodern afterlife of a writer who belongs as much to the twenty-first century as to the nineteenth.

Until lately, however, and despite the general recognition of his international fame, studies of Dickens's reputation and cultural impact have focused chiefly on Britain, the United States, and Europe and on writers and filmmakers from these areas of the world.[1] Relatively little attention has been devoted to the efforts of postcolonial artists to come to terms with the legacy of Dickens and the consequences of their (often early) engagement with his work. What does it mean to read Dickens in the colony or post-colony? How have Dickens's novels been adapted, appropriated, and transformed by postcolonial writers and film directors, and how has Dickens himself been figured in these works? These are some of the questions that this chapter seeks to address, drawing on examples from literature and film produced in the former British colonies since the end of World War II.

At the beginning of his influential essay, "Signs Taken for Wonders," Homi Bhabha outlines a model of intertextual ambivalence that is useful in theorizing the postcolonial afterlife of Dickens.

> There is a scene in the cultural writings of English colonialism which repeats so insistently after the early nineteenth century – and, through that repetition, so triumphantly

inaugurates a literature of empire – that I am bound to repeat it once more. It is the scenario, played out in the wild and wordless wastes of colonial India, Africa, the Caribbean, of the sudden, fortuitous discovery of the English book. It is, like all myths of origin, memorable for its balance between epiphany and enunciation. The discovery of the book is, at once, a moment of originality and authority. It is, as well, a process of displacement that, paradoxically, makes the presence of the book wondrous to the extent to which it is repeated, translated, misread, displaced. It is with the emblem of the English book – "signs taken for wonders" – as an insignia of colonial authority, and a signifier of colonial desire and discipline, that I want to begin. (Bhabha 1994: 102)

According to Bhabha, the discovery of the "English book" in the colonies produces a curiously paradoxical effect. In the first instance, the book functions as an instrument of colonial authority, a sign of imperial power and discipline. At the same time, however, because the sign of power has been removed from its original context, its authority is to that extent weakened, called into question. Colonial discourse, Bhabha argues, finds itself transformed and sometimes undermined through the very process of dissemination and repetition that it elicits. Imitation leads to mimicry, to misreading and interpretation, and in this way opens new paths of exploration for the post-colonial artist.

Dickens – understood here as a complex cultural sign as well as a set of specific literary texts – may be taken as exemplary of what Bhabha means by the "English book," and the quotations from Soyinka, Kumar, Ngugi, and Naipaul may likewise be seen as instances of the transcultural encounter that he posits as inaugural of a certain literature of empire. Indeed, unexpected encounters with "Dickens" in a colonial or postcolonial context have yielded a rich body of work that has largely gone unnoticed by mainstream Dickens criticism and that deserves wider recognition and appreciation.

It is perhaps more than coincidental that three of the four writers whose encounters with Dickens I have used to launch this investigation refer to the early chapters of *Oliver Twist*, and that two of them specifically mention the scene where Oliver asks for "more" as having a special impact on them as young readers. (Even Soyinka, when he speaks of having "*devoured*" Dickens as a boy, suggests something of Oliver's hunger for life.) If there is any scene in all of Dickens that epitomizes the paradoxical combination of deference and rebellious desire that so often characterizes the colonized subject in its encounter with authority, surely this is it. Bill Ashcroft has perceptively analyzed the trope of the child within colonial discourse – at once "amenable to education and improvement," but also "a site of difference and anti-colonial possibility" (Ashcroft 2000: 199). Oliver's famous demand captures both aspects of this relation. It is therefore little wonder that *Oliver Twist* should be a favorite text for postcolonial revision, or that versions of Oliver's memorable scene reappear under different guises in colonial and postcolonial contexts.

"Fagin & Me," a short poem by the Indo-Guyanese Canadian writer, Cyril Dabydeen (1998), is one such example. The poem begins:

I encountered Fagin in a far place,
and asked, "You, what can you tell me?"

Imagining being Oliver Twist, and the book
I'd borrowed at the plantation library and

Read a dozen times over, and feared not returning
because of what the penalty might be.

So I talked to Mr. Bumble, the beadle,
and Bill Sykes [*sic*], Nancy, and Mr. Bronlow [*sic*];

But it was Fagin who remained with me
day after day, as voices kept calling out —

"Stop thief! Stop thief!" — still coming at me
in my sleep with sugar-cane smells and molasses,

Amidst the factory's louder hum everywhere;
and I continued running along, sweltering —

Heaving in, or trying to withstand
the Artful Dodger somewhere far from England . . .

(ll. 1–16)

The poem is cast in the form of a childhood memory and recounts the speaker's experience of reading *Oliver Twist* in a copy borrowed from the plantation library in his
native land, the "far place" of the poem's first line. For Dabydeen, reading Dickens is
a disturbing experience, an "encounter," he calls it, with the scary and seductive figure
of Fagin. "You," he demands of Fagin (and of Dickens and of himself) "what can you
tell me?" — tell him, that is, about himself, his history, and his relation to books. It
is a challenge as much as a question, and the answer requires him to look more deeply
into the past.

Dabydeen's colonial child reads *Oliver Twist* with a mixture of guilty pleasure and
painful identification. Remembering his early encounter with Dickens takes the poet
back to a time of frightening vulnerability that is also closely connected to his love
of literature and the awakening of his desire to be a writer. The specific memory that
he recalls is of identifying with the Oliver who is accused of being a thief. Here, the
poem conflates two different scenes from the novel. One is the scene in which an angry
crowd chases Oliver through the streets, crying "Stop thief!" because they think he
has stolen a handkerchief. The other is when he fails to return Mr. Brownlow's books
to the bookseller because he has been seized by Bill Sikes and handed back to
Fagin.

For Dabydeen's speaker, these two scenes merge into a single image that mirrors
his own ambivalent relation to the library book and all that it represents. On the one
hand, he fears being punished if he is late in returning the book; on the other hand,
he would like to keep it permanently for himself in order to preserve his access to the
rich imaginative world it contains. He has already read the novel "a dozen times over,"

and his desire for it (his hunger for "more") is not yet exhausted. The poem locates the initial stirrings of creativity, the wish to become a writer, in this small fantasy of Promethean theft. The postcolonial poet imagines himself stealing the master's book and turning it to his own use. This is also, I believe, what draws him back to Fagin. Although he talks to Bumble, "Sykes," Nancy, and "Bronlow" [I take the misspelling of the names as deliberate], it is the Jew, a fellow outsider, and not these more conventionally "English" characters, who remains with him and to whom he looks for answers.

The poem concludes with a guilty nightmare of flight and pursuit, punctuated by the remembered smells and sounds of the speaker's tropical childhood. In his dreams, the poet is still "trying to withstand / the Artful Dodger somewhere far from England." In the local context of *Oliver Twist*, to "withstand" the Artful Dodger means to resist the temptation to become a thief. But by becoming a poet and appropriating Dickens's language and characters to describe his own awakening to literature, Dabydeen has in effect already yielded to that temptation. The Artful Dodger may also be a reference to Dickens. To withstand the Artful Dodger could thus equally suggest the postcolonial writer's continuing struggle to come to terms with the anxiety of influence – to resist as well as to repeat and transform the most Artful of Dodgers, Dickens himself.

A very different transformation of *Oliver Twist*, one that appropriates the entire story and locates it in a contemporary South African context, is Tim Greene's full-length feature film, *A Boy Called Twist* (2004).[2] Set largely in modern-day Cape Town, the film follows its protagonist's career from rural orphanage and employment by various harsh masters, including a somewhat sympathetic undertaker, to his escape and journey to the city, where he is recruited into a gang of glue-sniffing young thieves led by a dreadlocked Rastafarian Fagin. Greene's adaptation stays remarkably close to Dickens's plot and even includes a sinister Monks, here Twist's great uncle, who lurks on the margins of the story and instigates the plot to disinherit him.

One of the more interesting features of Greene's adaptation is his handling of the Mr. Brownlow figure from the novel. Rather than give the role of benevolent middle-class gentleman to someone white, as he might easily have done, Greene assigns it to a Cape Malay Muslim, a Mr. Bassedien, who turns out to be Twist's grandfather and who comes to represent the principles of community and reconciliation that the film endorses as its core values. Although the film depicts a wide range of ethnic and racial differences, racial politics as such seldom figure in the story, and there are only a few traces of the old apartheid system. White characters appear mostly in the film's early scenes, set in the country: the orphanage matron, the landowner who hires orphans to harvest his crops, the undertaker and his wife. The closest that the film comes to making a political statement is in the scenes of child labor, when the white matron hires out her young wards as contract workers to harvest crops for a local white farmer whose black overseer subjects the children to savage whippings. The scene in which Twist asks for more occurs on the farm, not at the orphanage, as we might have expected, and thus stands as an explicit protest against this residue of apartheid's exploitative labor practices. When Twist asks the overseer for more pap and gruel, the other children bang their cups and chant "more" in unison, an expression of solidarity with his act of resistance and a glance back perhaps at the mass-movement politics of the 1980s. For the most part, however, the film avoids any show of "liberal" politics, preferring instead to move beyond protest and participate in what South African cultural critic Njabulo Ndebele (1994) has called the "rediscovery of the ordinary."[3]

When the story shifts to Cape Town, these traces of political protest largely disappear, and the film focuses more on contemporary social problems – homelessness, street children, AIDS – and on working out the "Sykes"–Nancy plot and the reunion of Twist with his grandfather. Fagin recedes in importance (we never learn what happens to him), and the story reaches a climax with Sykes's failed effort to escape. One nice detail in the film's final sequence involves Twist's fall from the rooftop where he has been forced to accompany the fleeing Sykes. The "good" characters on the ground spot a large white blanket wrapped around the shoulders of a black woman carrying a baby on her back and stretch it out to catch Twist's falling body. Linked by association to maternity and thus to Twist's mother, whose tenderness toward him before she dies we witness in the film's opening scenes, as well as to Nancy, who also tries to protect him (and who at one point takes cover under a blanket), the safety blanket stands as a symbol of the love that Twist has been seeking from the film's beginning. Its whiteness not only figures purity and innocence but also recalls an important image from the novel: Rose Maylie's white handkerchief, which Nancy holds up to ward off the blows from Sikes's club. Film and novel thus unexpectedly converge around a common visual image.

A second Dickens novel that has proved particularly generative for postcolonial writers is *Great Expectations*. Not surprisingly, the most sustained efforts to re-imagine the story of Pip and Magwitch have come from Australian writers and filmmakers, who have not hesitated to fill the narrative gap produced by the convict's lengthy absence in New South Wales. Dickens took a keen interest in Australia. Two of his sons emigrated there. He collaborated with Caroline Chisholm during the 1850s on her project of providing loans to families seeking to emigrate. He even briefly considered an invitation to do a reading tour in Australia during the 1860s. As early as *Pickwick*, he had shown an interest in the story of a returned convict; later, there are the Peggottys and the Micawbers, who emigrate at the end of *David Copperfield*.

The earliest attempt at revision of *Great Expectations* by an Australian writer is Michael Noonan's 1982 novel, *Magwitch*. In it, Pip narrates the story of his adventures in and around Sydney, where he has traveled from Cairo years after the end of the events recounted in Dickens's novel. Ostensibly there for business reasons, Pip is in fact motivated more by the wish to discover what happened to Magwitch during the convict's 15-year absence from England. Upon his arrival in Sydney, however, Pip is swept up in a series of mysterious events. Magwitch, it appears, left behind him in Australia a huge undiscovered fortune for which many people have been searching, the clues to whose location Pip, unbeknown to himself, still possesses. The search for hidden treasure and the quest for information about Magwitch's past form two strands in what develops as a mystery/detective plot that takes Pip back over much of the ground covered in *Great Expectations*. He meets a series of characters who uncannily recall people from his earlier life, among them a Miss Havisham figure who dies in a fire and an Estella look-alike named Charlotte – a beautiful, part-Aboriginal young woman, perhaps Magwitch's daughter, with whom he falls in love. Jaggers, now living in Australia, even makes a brief appearance.

Despite its promising point of departure and its attractive group of non-traditional female characters, Noonan's *Magwitch* never deeply engages or contests the cultural model on which it is based. Essentially a colonial adventure story, *Magwitch* offers few new perspectives on its title character. Likewise, its Pip remains a relatively colorless figure, who lacks the psychological complexity and ironic perspective on himself that distinguish Dickens's narrator. It is perhaps no wonder that Charlotte spurns him in the end, preferring the romantic bushranger, Spikey Simmins, to the better mannered, but less interesting English gentleman. Fortunately for Pip, her rejection leaves him free to return to Egypt and eventually to England, where he meets and marries Estella, thereby bringing about the novel's conventional happy ending. The colonial gold winds up back in England, where the book's main characters all happily join the metropolitan middle class. The last we see of Pip, he is headed toward his club to have a drink with Spikey Simmins, while Estella and Charlotte go off shopping. Noonan's novel breaks little new ground; it neither extends Dickens's analysis of class relations to the colony, nor provides any new insight into the convict experience, the dispossession of Aboriginal peoples, or its own relation to Dickens's text. Dialogical only to a limited degree, it remains a colonial sequel to *Great Expectations* rather than a postcolonial revision.

A more ambitious and, in many respects, more successful attempt to rewrite Dickens's novel from an antipodean perspective is the six-hour television series, *Great Expectations: The Untold Story*, produced for nationwide broadcast in 1987 by the Australian Broadcasting Corporation. Written and directed by Tim Burstall, one of the country's leading producer/directors and an important figure in the Australian film industry since the 1970s, *Great Expectations: The Untold Story* is at once an adaptation of Dickens's novel and an imaginative expansion of it. As its subtitle indicates, it undertakes to recover the "untold" portions of the novel – essentially, the story of Magwitch's years in New South Wales. In this effort, it resembles Noonan's *Magwitch*, although it takes a very different approach to its subject. Unlike *Magwitch*, it is not a sequel, but a full-scale re-telling that moves back and forth between the narrative of Pip's growing up and events that occur simultaneously to Magwitch in the colony.

As I have discussed elsewhere at greater length (Jordan 2003), Burstall's script retains the basic framework of Dickens's novel, but inserts new material – roughly five out of the six hours' total running time – focused on Magwitch. Magwitch, not Pip, becomes the film's protagonist in what develops as a foundational narrative of Australian nationhood, one designed to appear on the eve of the 1988 bicentenary of the arrival of the First Fleet in Sydney harbor. After opening with the scene of his original trial and sentencing, the film follows Magwitch from his escape from the hulks and subsequent transportation to New South Wales, through his experiences in the convict camp, his release and probationary "assignment" to a wealthy free settler named Tankerton, and his ultimate establishment as a rich landowner in his own right. In the course of these experiences, Magwitch emerges as a version of the ideal national type: the frontiersman who combines rugged independence and defiance of authority with a strong sense of loyalty or "mateship."[4] From the beginning, he is presented as a "natural gentleman," in contrast to the artificial English gentleman, Compeyson, whose reappearance in Australia and periodic conflicts with Magwitch provide a narrative thread for much of the film's middle sections. Although he remains loyal to Pip and faithful to Molly, Magwitch ceases altogether to be English; his clipped Australian accent contrasts sharply with the English voices in every speaking context.

With Magwitch's return to England, the film rejoins the plot of Dickens's novel, but in the end gives it a bold, revisionary twist. Recaptured after the failed escape attempt, Magwitch falls ill and apparently dies; we see a coffin being removed from the prison hospital. The death is a fake, however, cleverly staged by Jaggers and Wemmick in order to allow Magwitch to go free and join Pip, Estella, and Molly on a ship sailing for Australia. The film thus ends with a trick on the authorities, but also with a joke at the expense of the viewer/reader who already "knows" how the story ends. The characters we most enjoy head off for their new home in the colony, perhaps to be joined by Jaggers and Wemmick. Nor do they leave penniless. Whereas in Noonan's *Magwitch* the colonial gold ends up back in England, Burstall's film makes sure that Pip carries off with him to Australia a strongbox stuffed with banknotes and other portable property.

Generically as well as culturally, *Great Expectations: The Untold Story* is a hybrid production. It draws on Dickens in order to tell the story of Australian nationhood in a form that at many points resembles a Hollywood western. As a postcolonial revision of *Great Expectations*, the film makes a stronger intervention than Noonan's *Magwitch*. It writes back against the "English book" both by virtue of the changes it makes in Dickens's plot, especially the ending, and by its affirmation of distinctively Australian qualities as opposed to those of the dominant, English-identified group. The film pays homage to Dickens through its faithful adaptation of many scenes from the novel, as well as through its use in a new medium of Dickens's characteristic formal mode: serial presentation. At the same time, however, it departs productively from its source, resituating Dickens's novel in a global context and forcing it to speak, along with its most memorable character, in a different accent.

The most recent and best-known Australian version of *Great Expectations* is Peter Carey's novel, *Jack Maggs*.[5] Neither a sequel like Noonan's *Magwitch* nor a parallel expansion like Burstall's film, *Jack Maggs* is by far the most radical of the three in its reworking of Dickens's text. Its revisionary strategy is to strip away from its source every detail but one and then to focus intensely on the possibilities remaining in that single charged moment, the moment of the transported convict's return. Gone from Carey's version are the defining features of Pip's life: his childhood, the forge, Joe and Mrs. Joe, Miss Havisham, Estella, and, above all, the privilege of narration. Instead, Carey's novel is told largely from the perspective of the convict, here rechristened Jack Maggs. Even the famous opening sequence on the marshes is all but elided. It remains only in the convict's memory, transformed into a desperate fantasy that has sustained him through the long ordeal of the penal colony and now brings him back to London, at the risk of his life, to see the object of his benevolent generosity.

Without relinquishing the intensity of this moment of return or the ferocious longing that motivates it, Carey turns Dickens's familiar story in several startling new directions. The Pip character, here named Henry Phipps, is not at home when his benefactor calls. Forewarned of his arrival, Phipps goes into hiding in order to avoid being exposed as the corrupt and deceitful parasite he has become while living grandly at his benefactor's expense. Frustrated in his immediate objective, Maggs falls almost by accident into employment as a footman in the adjacent household of Mr. Percy Buckle, hoping by this means to keep watch on the house next door until his darling "son" returns. The story takes another dramatic turn when, on the first night of his employment in Percy Buckle's service, Maggs waits upon the popularly acclaimed young novelist, Tobias Oates, whom Buckle has succeeded in claiming as a dinner guest. Oates is a version of the young Dickens, just as Phipps and Maggs are versions of Pip and Magwitch. The similarities are unmistakable, and part of Carey's metafictional game is to keep the resemblances constantly before us while at the same time introducing discrepancies, beginning with their names, that force us to recognize that these are *not* Pip, Magwitch, or Dickens.

In the course of the evening, Maggs and Oates each discover that the other has something he powerfully desires. Maggs overhears Oates mention a "thiefcatcher" who can supposedly find any man in England. Maggs, of course, wants Oates to put him in contact with this man in order to locate the missing Phipps. While waiting on table, Maggs falls victim to a fit of *tic douloureux*, from which Oates helps him to find relief by employing the new science of mesmerism, which Dickens is also known to have practiced. If Maggs wants help in finding his lost son, what Oates wants is material he can use for his novels. His ambition is to become a "cartographer" of the criminal mind, and he sees in Maggs and mesmerism a way to achieve this goal.

The two strike a desperate bargain. Maggs agrees to sit for two weeks of mesmeric sessions in exchange for an agreement to provide him with access to the "thieftaker." Maggs has no idea that the young novelist is plundering his closely guarded secrets; indeed, the last thing he wants is for his criminal past to become a public spectacle. Oates concocts an elaborate cover story about what transpires during the mesmeric sittings and even goes so far as to keep a set of false notebooks for the convict's benefit, crammed with conventional gothic nightmares. As the sessions proceed, Oates begins to draft scenes for a new novel to be called *The Death of Maggs*, sections of which appear in the text.

A protracted struggle of wills ensues between the two men. The issue of who will control the story of Jack Maggs turns literally into a question of life and death. As Maggs begins to realize what the writer has stolen from him, he becomes uncooperative and violent. Pressured by mounting financial and domestic problems of his own, Oates is forced to take increasingly drastic measures to restrain his informant and keep their agreement intact. Finally, as the action reaches its feverish climax, it is Maggs who triumphs over the young novelist, forcing him to throw away his manuscript and burn all the notes he has taken.

It is important to recognize the extent to which Carey's novel focuses on, and at the same time revises, what I have been calling, after Bhabha, the scenario of the "English book." More than either of the two earlier versions of *Great Expectations* that I have considered, *Jack Maggs* is centrally concerned to dramatize the struggle for cultural authority and enunciative power that Bhabha links to this generative scene. Rather than locate the English book in a colonial context, however, Carey brilliantly shifts the site of cultural struggle from the colonies to the metropolis and from the book as completed artifact to the process of its construction. The book in question is *The Death of Maggs*, which Oates will eventually complete and publish, but which he is at least temporarily compelled to abandon.

The struggle for enunciatory power in *Jack Maggs* operates simultaneously on two distinct levels. At the level of content, it is thematized in the conflict between Oates and Maggs over the control of Jack's story. At the level of form, it emerges in the language of Carey's fiction, in his efforts to imitate the look and feel of a Victorian novel – and of a Dickens novel in particular. In his effort to recreate the atmosphere of a Dickens novel, Carey is remarkably successful. The novel is thick with vivid detail, pungent description of persons and places, and a wealth of late eighteenth- and early nineteenth-century criminal slang, derived from Carey's study of various dictionaries and compilations of thieves' cant.

The conclusion to *Jack Maggs* combines high melodrama with a touch of sweet romantic comedy. For purposes of comparison with the other texts I have considered, the most interesting feature of Carey's novel is the resolution it gives to the convict's story. A central component of Maggs's character throughout most of the book is his fierce, misguided devotion to the fantasy of an English "son." In order to escape from this imprisoning illusion, a prison more damaging in its way than the penal colony he has managed to survive, Maggs must undergo a dramatic disillusionment with Henry Phipps. Only then can he give up his misguided quest and begin a life of his own. The disillusionment does occur, and with it Maggs is granted a merciful release. Mercy comes to him literally in the person of Mercy Larkin, Percy Buckle's housemaid, who realizes at last that she loves the convict, not her nouveau riche master, and is loved by him in turn. Together, they escape to Australia, where they found a large dynastic family and settle into a prosperous colonial existence. As in *Great Expectations: The Untold Story*, an underlying narrative of nationhood emerges, with the transported convict, now reconciled to his Australian identity, as its foundational figure. Unlike Burstall's film, however, Carey's novel does not require either reconciliation with the English "son" or the sanitizing of its protagonist into a virtuous ideal type.

Of the three versions of *Great Expectations* that I have considered, *Jack Maggs* departs most radically from its Dickensian source. Yet of the three, it is the one that engages most deeply with "Dickens" as a sign of English cultural authority and power. It does so through its formal mimicry of Dickens's style and through its aggressive, often hostile treatment of Tobias Oates, whose life bears many uncanny resemblances to Dickens's biography. *Jack Maggs* is a violent book, and much of its violence, both circumstantial and personally motivated, takes Oates as a target. In interviews, Carey has acknowledged that he was initially very angry with Oates and that it took him a long time while writing the novel to find anything to like in the ambitious young Englishman.

In the end, however, the novel extends some sympathy toward the young writer. There are scenes where Oates, even as he fears deeply for his life, finds himself clasped tenderly against the convict's body. "With that [Maggs] hugged him, wrapping his arm tight around his shoulders and pulling Toby's face into his breast, thus forcing him to inhale what would always thereafter be *the prisoner's smell* – the odour of cold sour sweat" (Carey 1997: 265). In this moment of intimacy and repugnance, the text offers us a counter-emblem to its scenes of violence. Perhaps there is some reconciliation with the English "son" after all, though in displaced form. By analogy, I think it is fair to say that Carey's novel displays sympathy, perhaps even love, toward its predecessor text. Despite the postcolonial violence it enacts symbolically on his life and books, *Jack Maggs* holds Dickens in a rough but affectionate embrace.

Other Australian writers who engage with Dickens, though not directly with *Great Expectations*, include playwright David Allen and novelist Carmel Bird. Allen's 1990 play, *Modest Expectations*, entertains the fantasy that Dickens actually came to Australia on a reading tour near the end of his life, accompanied by Ellen Ternan. Set in Melbourne in 1868, the play not only reunites Dickens with his son Plorn (Edward Bulwer Lytton Dickens), who was living in Australia at the time of the supposed visit, but also brings him into contact with a brash theatrical impresario, George Coppin, owner of the "Iron Pot" theater where Dickens is to perform. The Dickens of the play is a tired, egotistical, jealous old man – an Old World figure who compares poorly to the crass, outspoken, but vigorously optimistic Coppin, who offers hope for the future and who persuades Ellen to remain in Melbourne to pursue her acting career. Despite its somewhat schematic opposition of generations and national temperaments, the play acknowledges Dickens as a source of imaginative vitality. "If Australia hadn't existed," Coppin exclaims near the end of the play, "you would have invented us!" (Allen 1990: 57)

Bird's 1990 novel, *The Bluebird Café*, is a more puzzling and intriguing text. A postmodern gothic romance (and cookbook) set in Tasmania, it is studded with references to Dickens. The story takes place largely in the village of Copperfield (so named for the adjacent copper mines) and features an anorexic teenage heroine who aspires to become a novelist and writes letters to the long-deceased Dickens. The original village of Copperfield has been torn down and reproduced in facsimile, under a gigantic glass dome, as a theme park, "the Disneyland of the Antarctic." In it are the Abel Magwitch Hotel and the replica of a Charles Dickens Library that dates from the early twentieth century and contains copies of all of Dickens's works. Dickens figures both as an aspect of colonial discourse (early colonists give Aboriginal people the names of characters from his books) and as a source of inspiration to the aspiring writer. She quotes admiringly from *The Mystery of Edwin Drood*, but also regards Dickens, along with her father and uncle, as her "gaolers" – that is, as benevolent but oppressive patriarchs. Anorexia here is the female mirror image of Oliver's hunger, a form of resistance to authorities like her family who would make her eat; interestingly, as soon as she begins writing to Dickens, her eating disorder disappears. Playfully self-conscious to the end, the novel combines plucky feminist irreverence with a plangent lament for lost children and environmental degradation.

No survey of postcolonial responses to Dickens would be complete without some consideration of two major writers, V. S. Naipaul and Salman Rushdie, who, though different in many ways, share a longstanding admiration for Dickens and his work. Both Naipaul and Rushdie have written at length about the impact of Dickens on their early work. Here, for example, is Naipaul in his autobiographical novel, *The Enigma of Arrival* (1988):

> The London I knew or imaginatively possessed was the London I had got from Dickens. It was Dickens – and his illustrators – who gave me the illusion of knowing the city . . .
>   Years later, looking at Dickens during a time when I was writing hard myself, I felt I understood a little more about Dickens's unique power as a describer of London and his difference from all other writers as a describer of London. I felt that when as a child far away I read the early Dickens and was able with him to enter the dark city of London, it was partly because I was taking my own simplicity to his, fitting my own fantasies to his. (Naipaul 1988: 133)

Later, the narrator recalls some of his earliest imaginative efforts:

> As a child in Trinidad I had projected everything I read onto the Trinidad landscape, the Trinidad countryside, the Port of Spain streets. (Even Dickens and London I incorporated into the streets of Port of Spain. Were the characters English, white people, or were they transformed into people I knew? A question like that is a little like asking whether one dreams in color or in black and white. But I think I transferred the Dickens characters to people I knew. Though with a half or a quarter of my mind I knew that Dickens was all English, yet my Dickens cast, the cast in my head, was multiracial.) . . . Very few [writers] had the universal child's eye of Dickens. (Naipaul 1988: 169–70)

And here is Rushdie in a somewhat similar vein, describing the process of fitting Dickens's vision of the city to his own imaginative needs:

> Charles Dickens . . . struck me from the first as a quintessentially Indian novelist. Dickensian London, that stenchy, rotting city full of sly, conniving shysters, that city in which goodness was under constant assault by duplicity, malice, and greed, seemed to me to hold up the mirror to the pullulating cities of India, with their preening elites living the high life in gleaming skyscrapers while the great majority of their compatriots battled to survive in the hurly-burly of the streets below. In my earlier novels I tried to draw on the genius of Dickens. I was particularly taken with what stuck me as his real innovation: namely, his unique combination of naturalistic backgrounds and surreal foregrounds. In Dickens, the details of place and social mores are skewered by a pitiless realism, a naturalistic exactitude that has never been bettered. Upon this realistic canvas he places his outsize characters, in whom we have no choice but to believe because we cannot fail to believe in the world they live in. (Rushdie 2002: 64)

For Rushdie, as for Naipaul, Dickens has been particularly well suited to portraying the fantastic incongruities of colonial and postcolonial life.

It is not surprising, then, that both Naipaul and Rushdie should incorporate bits of Dickens into their own fiction, though neither has attempted, or is likely to attempt, a full-scale appropriation. Naipaul's most Dickensian novel is *A House for Mr. Biswas* (1961). Toward the end of the novel, Biswas (who is modeled on Naipaul's father) finds solace from the humiliations of daily life in colonial Trinidad by reading Dickens and sharing his favorite novels with his son Anand. At one point, Anand (a version of Naipaul himself) gloomily records in his diary, "I feel like Oliver Twist in the workhouse" (Naipaul 1961: 355). However, like Oliver, he hungers for "more," and the novel concludes with his departure for England, the land of Dickens, where he will pursue in exile the literary career that his father imagined for himself, but was never able to achieve.

Rushdie's most sustained fictional homage to Dickens is a brilliant piece of pastiche in *The Satanic Verses* (1989). In this riotously comical scene (nicely analyzed by Martine Hennard Dutheil de la Rochère in her 1999 study of Rushdie), the novel's protagonist, Saladin Chamcha, attends a fashionable London party on the stage set where a film version of a musical comedy adaptation of *Our Mutual Friend* is being made. Playfully mangling Dickens's language and mixing his own characters with actors from the film dressed in Victorian costume, Rushdie at once satirizes and celebrates the popularization of Dickens, a practice in which his own novel clearly participates. Unlike *Jack Maggs*, however, where admiration for the predecessor text is mixed with hostility, *The Satanic Verses* betrays little ambivalence. Rushdie's is a loving revision, a joyous embrace of Dickensian profusion and heterogeneity. As his example shows, although the postcolonial writer may sometimes begin as a hungry child, anxiously asking for "more," he and she just as often grow to be mature artists, nourished by Dickens and capable of producing their own versions of the "English book."

NOTES

1 A notable exception is volume 36 of *Dickens Studies Annual* (2005), which contains a series of essays on Dickens in Latin America.

2 Dickens occupies an honorable place in the anti-apartheid movement in South Africa. As early as the 1950s, Ezekiel (now Es'kia) Mphahlele staged scenes from *A Tale of Two Cities* in the townships, a daring step in view of the novel's revolutionary content (Mngoma 1989: 32; Taylor 1989: 26). During the 1970s, when the government attempted to impose Afrikaans as the official language of instruction for certain subjects in the schools, *Oliver Twist*, and the scene of Oliver asking for "more" in particular, were an inspiration to young anti-apartheid activists. In one notable example, after reading the novel, students at historically black Lovedale College formed a committee to ask for more lessons, more food, and more and better books. As a result, 152 students were charged with public violence and expelled from the college, and some were jailed (Lee 2006).

3 Ndebele has been an outspoken advocate of the need for South African literature to move beyond the oversimplified binaries of protest writing (see Ndebele 1994). For Greene's own comments on his reasons for choosing to adapt *Oliver Twist* and his effort to "distance myself from my own liberal urges to be helpful," see the *Boy Called Twist* website.

4 The canonical description of this national character type is by Russel Ward in *The Australian Legend* (1958). Ward's thesis has often been contested as (among other things) essentialist, masculinist, and too narrowly focused on Anglo-Celtic culture.

5 Here, and in the following paragraphs, I have drawn on my earlier essay, "Dickens Re-visioned" (Jordan 2000).

REFERENCES AND FURTHER READING

Allen, David (1990). *Modest Expectations: An Entertainment*. Sydney: Currency Press.

Ashcroft, Bill (2000). Primitive and wingless: the colonial subject as child. In Wendy S. Jacobson (Ed.), *Dickens and the Children of Empire* (pp. 184–202). Basingstoke: Palgrave.

Bhabha, Homi (1994). Signs taken for wonders. In *The Location of Culture* (pp. 102–22). London: Routledge.

Bird, Carmel (1990). *The Bluebird Café*. New York: New Directions.

Carey, Peter (1997). *Jack Maggs*. London: Faber and Faber.

Clayton, Jay (2003). *Charles Dickens in Cyberspace: The Afterlife of the Nineteenth Century in Postmodern Culture*. New York: Oxford University Press.

Dabydeen, Cyril (1998). Fagin and me. *Ariel: A Journal of International Literature*, 29, 65–6.

Davis, Paul (2000). *The Lives and Times of Ebenezer Scrooge*. New Haven, CT: Yale University Press.

Dutheil de la Rochère, Martine Hennard (1999). *Origin and Originality in Rushdie's Fiction*. Bern: Peter Lang.

Jordan, John O. (2000). Dickens re-visioned: *Jack Maggs* and the "English book." In Rossana Bonadei, Clotilde de Stasio, Carlo Pagetti, and Alessandro Vescovi (Eds.), *Dickens: The Craft of Fiction and the Challenges of Reading* (pp. 292–300). Milan: Unicopli.

— (2003). *Great Expectations* on Australian television. In John Glavin (Ed.), *Dickens on Screen* (pp. 45–52). Cambridge: Cambridge University Press.

Kumar, Amitava (2002). *Bombay; London; New York*. New York: Routledge.

Lee, Carol (2006). Why Dickens was the hero of Soweto. *Times on Line*, June 21, 2006 (www.timesonline.co.uk/article/0, 923–2217234,00. html).

Mngoma, Kahbi (1989). Criss-crossing cultural lines with the syndicate of African artists: a conversation with Bhekizizwe Peterson. In

Peter N. Thuynsma (Ed.), *Footprints along the Way: A Tribute to Es'kia Mphahlele* (pp. 28–34) Braamfontein: Justified Press.

Naipaul, V. S. (1961). *A House for Mr. Biswas*. New York: McGraw-Hill.

— (1984). Prologue to an autobiography. In *Finding the Center* (pp. 1–72). New York: Knopf.

— (1988). *The Enigma of Arrival*. New York: Vintage.

Ndebele, Njabulo (1994). *South African Literature and Culture: Rediscovery of the Ordinary*. Manchester: Manchester University Press.

Ngugi wa Thiong'o (1986). The language of African literature. In *Decolonizing the Mind: The Politics of Language in African Literature* (pp. 4–33). London: Heinemann.

— (1993). Biggles, Mau Mau and I. In *Moving the Centre: The Struggle for Cultural Freedoms* (pp. 136–41). London: Heinemann.

Noonan, Michael (1982). *Magwitch*. London: Hodder and Stoughton.

Rushdie, Salman (1989). *The Satanic Verses*. New York: Viking.

— (2002). Influence. In *Step across this Line: Collected Nonfiction 1992–2002* (pp. 62–9). New York: Random House.

Soyinka, Wole (2001). *Conversations with Wole Soyinka*. Jackson: University Press of Mississippi.

Taylor, Norah (1989). Going back to Tagore: a conversation with Peter Esterhuizen. In Peter N. Thuynsma (Ed.), *Footprints along the Way: A Tribute to Es'kia Mphahlele* (pp. 25–7). Braamfontein: Justified Press.

Thuynsma, Peter N. (Ed.) (1989). *Footprints along the Way: A Tribute to Es'kia Mphahlele*. Braamfontein: Justified Press.

Ward, Russel (1958). *The Australian Legend*. Melbourne: Oxford University Press.

Index

Index

Printed and bound by CPI Group (UK) Ltd, Croydon, CR0 4YY
03/03/2022
03115748-0001

"It is difficult to overstate the importance of *A Companion to Charles Dickens*. The whole provides a rich seam of knowledge, placing Charles Dickens' writings in their literary and historical contexts, a serious work of scholarship. A copy should be placed in every library, whether public, college or academic. Not only is it an invaluable and multi-faceted resource for students, teachers and scholars of Dickens, it is a cornucopia of delight for everyone who loves to read Dickens for pleasure alone."
Reference Reviews

"This is an excellent book, to read with intellectual profit, stimulation, and pleasure. Distinctive in its own right in permitting long essays on a wide range of Dickensian topics. Volumes with a particular outwards-facing intention and stylistic accessibility such as this one, with their imagined audiences that include undergraduates and general readers as well as scholars, show it with clarity. A welcome and valuable book, an engaging collection to read, and a volume worthy of its subject."
Dickens Quarterly

"Students of Dickens will find this handbook useful. In particular, the entries on the individual novels take the reader to the most important issues. Recommended."
Choice

"A handy reference book for a graduate course on Dickens or more advanced studies, this Companion is indeed companionable. Organized both logically and comprehensively, the book is divided into five categories. In short, this Companion inspires one to go back and read all of Dickens's novels again."
English Literature in Transition

Blackwell Companions to Literature and Culture

This series offers comprehensive, newly written surveys of key periods and movements and certain major authors, in English literary culture and history. Extensive volumes provide new perspectives and positions on contexts and on canonical and post-canonical texts, orientating the beginning student in new fields of study and providing the experienced undergraduate and new graduate with current and new directions, as pioneered and developed by leading scholars in the field.

Published Recently